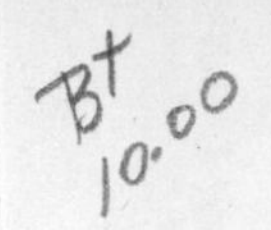
Bt
10.00

P9-CLP-957

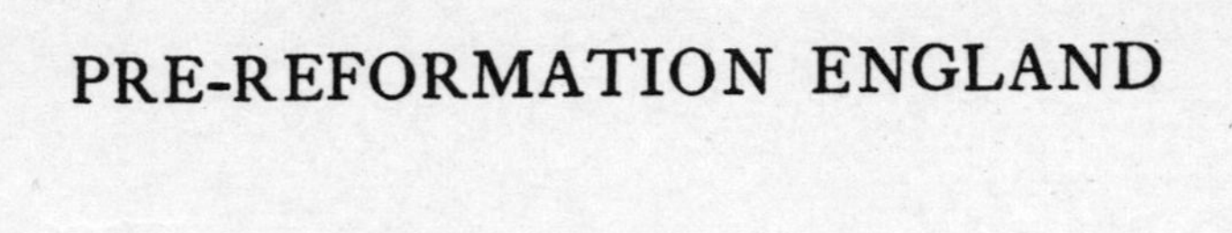

PRE-REFORMATION ENGLAND

By the same author

*

HENRY VIII AND THE REFORMATION

PRE-REFORMATION ENGLAND

BY

H. MAYNARD SMITH, D.D.Oxon

SOMETIME CANON OF GLOUCESTER

NEW YORK

RUSSELL & RUSSELL, INC.

1963

First Published in 1938
Reissued by Russell & Russell, Inc.,
by arrangement with Macmillan & Co. Ltd.
L.C. Catalog Card No. 63-15182

PRINTED IN GREAT BRITAIN

THIS BOOK

IS DEDICATED

WITH HIS PERMISSION

TO

ARTHUR CAYLEY

LORD BISHOP OF GLOUCESTER

BY

HIS SON AND SERVANT

THE AUTHOR

AS A TOKEN OF

AFFECTIONATE

REGARD

PREFACE

ROMAN CATHOLICS often write as if the Reformation in England would not have taken place if it had not been for the desire of Henry VIII for a divorce. Protestants, on the other hand, assert that it was due to the corruption of the clergy and the superstitions of the people. Economic writers emphasise the fact that the Church was excessively wealthy and politically powerless, so that the temptation to plunder her was irresistible. Political theorists maintain that the rampant nationalism of the English in the XVI century was incompatible with England's belonging to an international church. In this book the truth of these theories is tested ; but the object of the author is first of all to describe what Pre-Reformation England was like and the opinions of Englishmen at the time. He does not believe that any one theory will account for the Reformation ; and he does not believe that it is possible to understand how the Reformation came about, unless we are alive to the many aspects of life in the preceding period.

The book opens with the death of Henry VII in 1509, and closes with a review of the *Assertio Septem Sacramentorum*, which was published in 1521 ; but the author looks before and after in his endeavour to understand, so that his book is not so much a history as the survey of an historical situation. All men in 1509 were not of the same age. The man who was then seventy had been fifteen when the Wars of the Roses broke out ; and his grandson aged twenty-one did not reach seventy until the accession of Queen Elizabeth. To understand any period it is necessary to take into account what was within the experience of men then living, while the memories and reflections of men fifty years later are often of great value.

The first half of the book is devoted to an enquiry into the condition of the Church and the repute of the clergy ; into the nature of the popular religion and the prevalent superstitions ; into the social and economic causes of the changes that were taking place ; and into the uneasy and still undetermined relations of Church and State.

The second half of the book has been written to account for the mental, moral and spiritual outlook of the men of the early XVI century. They had all inherited a tradition, but it was not the same tradition ; so that there was no common culture derived from the past, and no living prophet to whom all bowed. In consequence the author has traced to their source many tributary streams to the Reformation torrent.

The majority did not read even when they could, but were dependent for enlightenment on the priest in the pulpit, on the ballad-singer in the street, on proclamations at the market cross, and on gossip retailed by topers in the ale-house. There were, however, poor men reading in secret the prohibited books of the Lollards, and ready to support any attack on the Church. There were devout people who bought up edition after edition of XIV century mystics, who, cultivating the interior life, became indifferent to the claims of institutional religion. There were up-to-date and go-ahead young people who read romances which justified the satisfaction of their lusts ; and there were worldly men who quoted the latest satire on the clergy as a proof of their intellectual freedom. There were schoolmen, who styled themselves Thomists, Scotists and Ockhamists, who took their common faith for granted, and spent their time in scoring points against each other ; and there were the humanists who hated the schoolmen, and thought that the world could be regenerated by classical learning. To understand the background of such men it has been necessary to trace the history of Lollardy, scholasticism, mysticism and humanism, and to give some account of the vernacular literature. Each chapter has been brought down to the period of the Reformation—a coming event which casts its shadow over all.

The book may be regarded as an introduction to the history of the Reformation in England, and should it meet with approval, the author hopes to write another volume covering the period from the divorce of Henry VIII to the death of Elizabeth. In it he will deal at length with some subjects which are inadequately treated in the present book.

The author has not undertaken original research, but he has read a multitude of books—good, bad and indifferent. He has acknowledged his indebtedness to the writers, and has exercised his own judgment in interpreting the facts with which they have supplied him. While emphasising all that is good in his period, he has not wittingly suppressed the evidence for much that was bad, although he has put the best construction possible upon it, because he believes that by so doing he is more likely to approximate to the truth.

The Rev. Dr. Blakiston, President of Trinity College, Oxford, has read each chapter as it was first written, and, thanks to his criticism, the author has been preserved from many a slip and made to reconsider many doubtful points. The Bishop of Gloucester has read three of the chapters, with the result that one of them has been entirely rewritten. The Rev. Dr. Watson, Professor of Ecclesiastical History at Oxford, read as much of this book as was written at the time of his death, and the author owes much to his encouragement and advice. Miss Jeffries Davies has saved the author from three errors concerning the case of Richard Hunne, and Professor Jourdan of Trinity College, Dublin, has cleared up a difficulty arising out of his essay on Erasmus. Dr. G. G. Coulton and Dom Benedict Stewart have lent him books which were not in the London Library. As none of these distinguished people is likely to be in complete sympathy with his point of view, he is the more grateful for the generosity which they have shown to an adventurer into a province where they have established their reputations. His thanks are also due to the Reader of Messrs. Macmillan, whose name is unknown to him, for pertinent criticisms ; to Mr. Lennox Morison and the Rev. G. W. O. Addleshaw for their great kindness in helping him to correct the proofs, and to the Reader of Messrs. R. & R. Clark who, when they had done their work, discovered errors that they had overlooked ; to Mr. William Liversidge for verifying references; and to the Rev. Philip Usher for allowing him to make use of three articles which had appeared in the *Church Quarterly Review*.

H. M. S.

College Green
Gloucester, 1938

CONTENTS

CHAPTER VI

PART II

THE TENDENCIES OF THE TIME ACCOUNTED FOR

CHAPTER I

CHAPTER II

CHAPTER III

CHAPTER IV

CHAPTER V

CHAPTER VI

CHAPTER VII

SOME ABBREVIATIONS

Used in the Notes

A. & M.	=*Acts and Monuments*, by John Foxe.
B.C.P.	=Book of Common Prayer.
C.S.P.	=*Calendar of State Papers.*
D.N.B.	=*Dictionary of National Biography.*
E.E.T.S.	=Early English Text Society
E.H.R.	=*English Historical Review.*
E.R.E.	=*Encyclopaedia of Religion and Ethics.*
H.M.C.	=Historical Manuscripts Commission.
L. & P.	=*Letters and Papers of Henry VIII.*
N.E.D.	=New English Dictionary.
O.H.S.	=Oxford Historical Society.
R.H.S.P.	=*Royal Historical Society's Proceedings.*
R.S.	=Rolls Series.
V.C.H.	=*Victoria County Histories.*

PART I

THE CONDITION OF PRE-REFORMATION ENGLAND

Chapter I

HENRY VII: HIS FUNERAL AND WILL

Modern history may be said to begin with the accession of Henry VII—politically speaking, it was the beginning of a new age. Both Edward IV and Richard III had been inspired with the new ideas of kingship and government,[1] but they had been hampered by men who had grown old in faction fights. After Bosworth the field was clear for the new sovereign and he was supported by the new generation mightily resolved that the bad old days should not come again.

Never safe on his throne, and never personally popular, Henry VII had triumphed over all obstacles, and his blind poet, Bernard André, compared his achievements with the twelve labours of Hercules.[2] He was, as Barclay says, " The patron of peace and primate of prudence ",[3] and well deserved those alliterative titles. He ever preferred the chicanery of diplomacy to the brutality of arms ; and he restored order to his kingdom, prudently dealing with those who might disturb it—a few he executed, more he imprisoned, and many were ruined by fines and exactions which rendered them powerless. He put down livery and maintenance ; he saw that all artillery was in his own hands ; he fostered trade, patronised learning, and accumulated £1,800,000 in gold, besides vast quantities of plate and jewels. Bacon calls him one of the *Tres Magi*,[4] the others being Louis XI and Ferdinand of Aragon—but the wisdom of these kings was subterranean and not heavenly. They did not hitch their wagon to any star ; but crept stealthily along byways, and preferred darkness rather than light.

The days were past when men believed in Rights, and the

[1] Green, *Hist. of the English People*, vol. ii., begins his book on *The Monarchy*, 1461. Hallam, *Const. Hist.* i. 10, Busch, *England under the Tudors*, 8, dispute the constitutional importance of the reign of Edward IV.

[2] *Memorials of King Henry VII*, R.S. 131-153. For an account of Bernard André see Gairdner's *Introduction*, viii. ff. Bishop Stubbs, *Lectures*, 337, 338, worked out the same parallel in a fashion of his own.

[3] Barclay, *Eclogues*, i. 691.

[4] Bacon, *Henry VII*, 222.

days were far distant when men should come to believe in the sanctity of Contracts. No one any longer trembled before the moral judgments of the Holy See, and there was no public opinion for any king to fear. In State affairs craft was expected and respected. When Louis XII complained that he had once been cheated by Ferdinand of Aragon, that monarch indignantly exclaimed, " He lied, the drunkard ! I cheated him three times." [1] Politics knew nothing of morality, and there was no power on earth to judge a sovereign, save a victor with a sword : criticism was only possible beyond a frontier, and even then it was dangerous. The kings of the new age recognised no limitations on their will to power.

It was because of this complete divorce between public and private morality, that it was possible for a king to be unscrupulous in his king-craft and exceedingly devout in his private life. Louis XI was curiously superstitious. Ferdinand of Aragon had earned his title of the Catholic King, and three Popes sent symbolic gifts to Henry VII expressing their approbation. Moreover, it appears that Henry was a really religious man, much influenced by his pious mother.[2] When he came to die, his will epitomised and revealed the practice and devotion of the later Middle Ages.

His death took place at Richmond on April 21st, 1509 ; and if it be correct to say that politically a new age began with the accession of Henry VII, it is equally correct to say that socially and religiously mediaevalism died and was buried in his grave. He had instructed his executors about his funeral, " Wherein we wol that they have sp'ial respect and consideration to the laude and praising of God, the welthe of our Soule, and somewhat to our dignitie roial, eviting alwaies dampnable pompe and other otterageous superfluities ".[3]

How far his executors faithfully interpreted his wishes is unknown. On May 9th the funeral started from Richmond.[4] The coffin, surmounted by an effigy, clad in royal robes with crown, sceptre and orb, was placed on a chariot surrounded with banners, and drawn by seven horses, covered with black velvet. Prelates prayed as they went, and 600 servants in black liveries followed

[1] Gairdner, *Henry VII*, 199.
[2] Cooper, *Margaret Beaufort*, *passim*.
[3] Astle, *Will of Henry VII* (1775), 8.
[4] Leland, *Collectanea* IV. 303. Cp. Hall, 506, and the extracts from the Harleian MSS. in *L. & P.* i. 20.

with torches. The Lord Mayor and Corporation of London met the body in Southwark and accompanied it to St. Paul's where it was censed and placed in the choir under a stately hearse of wax.[1]

Next morning the Bishop of London, assisted by the abbots of Reading and St. Albans, celebrated a solemn Mass; and Fisher, Bishop of Rochester, preached the funeral sermon. He dwelt on the late king's merits and achievements very briefly in a series of compact clauses, but he emphasised in no uncertain manner that the king had died repentant. He told how Henry had wished to live that he might show himself a new and changed man, and how he wished to issue a general pardon to those who had been entrapped "in the daungers and jeopardyes of his lawes".[2]

The funeral train then proceeded to Charing Cross where the body was again censed by the abbots of St. Albans, Reading and Winchcombe, and so to Westminster, where it was censed once more by the Archbishops of Canterbury and York. Six peers carried the coffin into the Abbey, and placed it in a hearse blazing with lights. Garter King-of-Arms then cried aloud for the soul of the noble prince, Henry VII, king of this realm, and *placebo* and *dirige* were duly sung.

Next morning there were three Masses, and at the last the king's courser, banner, coat-of-arms, sword, shield and helmet were offered, while the nobility spread on the coffin rich palls of cloth of gold and baudekin.[3] Then the body was interred in the newly erected chapel, and *libera me* was sung. The great officers of State broke their staves and cast them into the vault. The herald proclaimed Henry VIII, and the whole company went to a sumptuous entertainment in the palace.

So, as Fisher said, Henry had to leave "all his goodly houses, so richly dekte and apparayled, his walles and galleries of grete pleasure, his gardyns large and wyde, with knottes curiously wrought".[4] It was natural for a mediaeval prelate to emphasise

[1] A hearse was a metal framework holding a multitude of candles. 1557 pounds of wax was used for the hearse at St. Paul's, and 3606 for the hearse at Westminster. *L. & P.* i. 20.

[2] Fisher's *Works*, E.E.T.S., 271. While Fisher preached, the mourners refreshed themselves in the Bishop's palace. *L. & P.* i. 20.

[3] Baudequin = an embroidered stuff with warp of gold thread and woof of silk. N.E.D.

[4] Fisher's *Works*, 278.

the transitoriness of worldly riches. A generation later the Protestant chronicler Hall writes : " He undoubted is assended into the celestial mansion, where he hath the sure fruicion of the Godhead, and the joy that is prepared for such as sit on the right hand of our Savyour, ever worlde without ende ".[1] A century later the half-pagan philosopher, Francis Bacon, thinking only of the immortality of fame, concludes : " He lieth at Westminster in one of the stateliest and daintiest monuments of Europe, both for the chapel and sepulchre. So he lieth more nobly, dead in the monument of his tombe, than he did alive in Richmond or any of his palaces." [2]

Henry VII had not built the chapel for himself, but as a shrine for the murdered Henry VI, and as a monument to the divine approval of the Lancastrian cause. There was already an unauthorised cult of Henry VI; hymns had been written in his honour, a collect and prayers had been composed.[3] Blackman, his chaplain, had collected evidence of his miracles,[4] but Alexander VI, Pius III and Julius II had failed to canonise him. The Abbot of Westminster had paid £500 for leave to translate his body from Windsor, no doubt hoping to recoup himself out of the profits of the shrine ; [5] but as the king was not raised to the altar he was probably allowed to remain in his second grave.[6] The chapel that had been designed for the centre of a cult became the monument of Henry VII and a witness to his conspicuous piety.

Who drew *the plat* from which it was built cannot certainly be known. Old writers ascribed it to Sir Reginald Bray or Bishop Alcock, but they were both dead before the work was well begun. It is much more probable that the design is due to Robert Vertue, the king's mason, perhaps with the assistance of Jenyns who was employed at Windsor and on the Divinity School at Oxford. Richard Bolton, Prior of St. Bartholomew's, was clerk

[1] Hall, 505.
[2] Bacon, *Henry VII* (Lumby's ed.), 221.
[3] *Trevelyan Papers*, Pt. I. 53 ff. The Office was printed by Wynkyn de Worde in the *Horae*, 1502, and has been reprinted by Maskell, *Monumenta Ritualia*, iii. 367-371.
[4] *York Fabric Rolls*, 36. For further reference see Hutton, *English Saints*, 162-165, and Knox and Leslie, *Miracles of Henry VI* (C.U.P., 1923).
[5] Westlake, *Story of Westminster Abbey*, 36. The petition to move the body is in Wilkins, *Concilia*, iii. 635. The Indenture is printed by Stanley, *Memorials of Westminster Abbey*, 568. The receipt for the £500 still exists.
[6] He had been first buried at Chertsey.

of the works.[1] The chapel is, with the exception of Bath Abbey, the last great ecclesiastical work of the Middle Ages in England. With it the long evolution of Gothic architecture ends. The inspiration was exhausted and no further progress could be expected. The new world in time was to be inspired by classic models, and to express itself in new forms, neither so complex nor so ornate, in order to serve the needs of a less mystical and more rationalised religion.

It was very fitting that this last and most daring adventure in Gothic construction should have been just ready to receive the body of the king who devoutly believed in all that it stood for. Much indeed remained to be done.[2] Ten years later the tomb by Torrigiano was not finished, nor the screen by Thomas Dutchman which enclosed it. The glass of the windows perhaps came " in sheafs " from Normandy or the Rhineland to be used by English glaziers.[3] We know what these windows were like, for some of those at King's College, Cambridge, were copied from them, at sixteen pence the foot.[4] The vestments of silk and velvet, embroidered with Tudor badges, were made in Florence, and if the gold and silver plate was English, it was because Benvenuto Cellini had refused to come here with such an uncomfortable companion as Torrigiano.[5] Lastly, there were the relics—a piece of the True Cross set in gold and adorned with pearls and jewels,[6] and " oon of the leggs of St. George set in silver parcell gilte ". A college of priests was endowed to serve the chapel. Poor men were to pray there continually for the repose of the king's soul, and alms on set days were to be distributed at the tomb. The whole round of prayer, praise, petition and almsgiving had been elaborated by the king himself; and by his sovereign might he decreed that all should so go on as long as the world endured.

[1] Alcock died in 1500, Bray in 1503. In 1503 the foundation stone of the chapel was laid by Abbot Islip; but before the work could begin the Lady Chapel of Henry III had to be pulled down, and also a tavern adjoining it with the unfashionable sign of " The White Rose ". Stow, *Survey* (1603), 461. The arguments for attributing the design to Vertue may be seen in Lethaby, *Westminster Abbey Re-examined*, 161 ff.

[2] Westlake, 47. Cf. Loftie, *Westminster Abbey*, 44.

[3] Coulton, *Art and the Reformation*, 462 and 473.

[4] Lethaby, *Westminster Abbey Re-examined*, 174 ff. cp. Clark and Willis, i. 498 ff.

[5] Benvenuto Cellini's *Memoirs*, 22 (Everyman).

[6] Hook, *Archbishops*, vi. 187, states that this relic was given to Henry by the Cardinal Amboise on St. George's Day, 1505; but Rosmital claims to have seen it in the Abbey in 1477. *Vide* quotation in Stanley's *Memorials*, 606.

With equal care and with the same mastery of detail he had thought out the other provisions of his will. In the month after his decease ten thousand Masses were to be said for him in London and its neighbourhood. The Masses for each day of the week are particularised, and for each Mass the priest saying it was to receive sixpence, which was twopence more than the ordinary rate.[1] Nineteen great churches had agreed to keep his obit in perpetuity. The money for this had been already paid and legal indentures duly sealed. Two thousand pounds were to be distributed at his burial, half to those who came to his tomb and half to the sick and halt in their own homes. He also provided money to pay the fees of those who were kept in prison from inability to do so. And with each bequest comes the desire for prayers. It is on the prayers of the poor that he relied, and on the prayers of the more austere religious orders. He left money to the Charterhouses of London and Sheen; and, because the Friars Observant of Greenwich could receive nothing, he arranged for the building of a brick wall to protect their orchard and left money to trustees on their behalf, knowing that they had " divers and many tymes been in manifest perill of ruyne, and danger of perdicion for lake of fode ".

Also he spoke in his will of the Hospital of the Savoy and of how meritorious such a work of mercy is, but he had lived long enough to complete that benefaction. He left £5000 for the completion of King's College, Cambridge, out of zeal for learning and reverence for Henry VI. He left money for a new road from Windsor to Canterbury—a pilgrim's way. He ordered that silver statues of himself in an attitude of prayer should be set up, facing the three English Shrines of Edward the Confessor,

[1] A groat = 4d. was, I believe, the normal fee. Coulton, *Life in the Middle Ages*, iii. 158, prints the will of a farmer in 1473, who left 5 marks for Masses for half a year. Cutts, *Parish Priests and their People*, 181, records that Sir Thomas Newys, Vicar of Tillingdon in 1491, left £6 : 8 : 4 for Masses for a year. Palmer, *Bad Abbot of Evesham*, 141, tells of a Somersetshire squire who ordered that 3000 Masses should be sung for his soul at 4d. a-piece. Bishop Fox, *Letters*, 168, left 12d. to the priest who should sing his Requiem. On the other hand, they might be much cheaper. Jack Upland (Wright, *Pol. Poems, Etc.*, ii. 21, 23) states that the prices of a trental (30 Masses) varied from 5s. to 10s., and that the friars would sing a Mass for a penny. Gregory, *Collections of a London Citizen*, xliii., left only £8 : 13 : 4 for 2000 Masses. Tyndale, *Practice of Prelates*, 286, says that for 40s. a man might have a Mass said for him daily for a year. Marti, *Economic Causes of the Reformation*, 144, says that Henry VII contracted for 10,000 Masses to be sung for the dead Garter Knights at 1d. a-piece.

St. Thomas of Canterbury, and Our Lady of Walsingham. Lastly, because in " many Churches of oure Realm, the holie Sacrament of the Aulter (is) kept in ful simple and inhonest Pixes [1] of copre and tymbre " he orders for each church, that is unprovided, a pyx of silver to the value of £4, " garnished with oure armes, and rede Roses and Portcolis crowned ". The gift was to be for " the wele of our Soule, and for a perpetual memorie of us ".

It is easy to criticise this will and to emphasise its self-regarding nature, to exclaim against its magical conception of the Mass and its mechanical conception of prayer—to sum it all up by saying it was an attempt to buy heaven at the expense of his heirs ; but those who say such things betray their lack of understanding.

In this will the king tells us that he had prayed from childhood, " Domine Jesu Christe, qui me a nichilo creasti fecisti redemisti et predestinasti ; ad hoc quod sum, tu scis quid de me facere vis, fac de me secundum voluntatem tuam, cum misericordia " ; [2] and then he goes on to confess his sinfulness " knowing perfitely that of my merits I cannot attaign to the life everlasting, but only by the merits of thy blessed passion and of thi infinite mercy and grace ". He never imagined that he would ascend at once to the right hand of the Saviour ; he did not, like the Protestant Hall, lay that flattering unction to his soul : Henry had a nobler conception of God's holiness, and real consciousness of his own demerits ; but on the other hand he never thought of himself as standing alone. He was a member of the Church, and on the Church he relied for help in his hour of need. That Church is in heaven and on earth. So he calls on " the Sweetest Lady of Mercy, very Moder and Virgin, welle of pitie ", on angels and saints, especially upon his " accustomed Avowers ", on priests and religious, on poor men and prisoners—on all men to succour and defend him against " the auncient and gosteley enemye ner none other evill or dampnable Esprite ". He feels that it is only as a member of the mystical body of Our Lord that he can be saved.

[1] It was the English practice to reserve the Blessed Sacrament in a hanging pyx. Lyndwood, *Provinciale*, 248 (cum clausura), preferred the Dutch and Portuguese practice of reserving in a tabernacle, because there was less danger of sacrilege. At the same time he admits that the Sacrament in a pyx is more easily seen.

[2] " As late as 1540 a little book was printed in Paris to demonstrate that *michi* and *nichil* were incorrect " (Allen, *Age of Erasmus*, 52).

When making all these provisions Henry never doubted that the religious system in which he had been brought up would last as long as the world endured. He never dreamed that *his* world was passing rapidly away, and that in less than thirty years his magnificent foundation would be overthrown, his plate and jewels confiscated and his precious relics lost. Still less did he dream that his granddaughter would sit in that chapel under a canopy made out of his Florentine copes,[1] or that later still a "Captain Walter Lee of the Yellow Regiment,[2] haberdasher" would break the windows of painted glass, or that the Puritan, Sir Robert Harley, would cast down the altar and hack in pieces its reredos—that miracle of Torrigiano's art.[3] Yet his chapel remains, his tomb is inviolate, and the altar has been set up on its old bases. The ornaments have been lost, but the fabric is secure. The breaks in continuity were spectacular, but the changes were more apparent than real. The chapel may be regarded as a parable in stone, illustrating the fact that while the Church may change her clothes and adornments from time to time, she is herself indestructible because she belongs to God.

[1] Westlake, *Story of Westminster Abbey*, 110.

[2] For Walter Lee see *Archaeologia*, lii. 136.

[3] H.M.C., *Portland Papers*, iii. 132, 134; Ryves, *Mercurius Rusticus*, ii. 155, speaks of Robert Harlow, and Loftie, *Westminster Abbey*, 42, follows him. Stanley, *Memorials*, 483, has the name right.

CHAPTER II

THE STATE OF THE CHURCH

I. *Its Apparent Strength*

NEVER did the Church appear more powerful than when Henry VII died. The *Ecclesia Anglicana*—I use the words in their mediaeval significance as denoting the clerical estate—was dominant in the land. It was part of an international body ; it had sanctions and support outside the country ; it had within privileges and immunities recognised by law and consecrated by custom. Its leading bishops were the counsellors of the king, whose Civil Service was largely staffed by ecclesiastics.[1] The Church was enormously wealthy ; it owned at least a fifth part of the land of England ; its buildings were treasure houses, and every art was the handmaid of religion. Its services were necessary on all important occasions in life—at christenings, marriages and funerals. Its courts alone decided all matrimonial cases, and ratified or did not ratify all wills. Its courts, too, took cognisance of all transgressions of the moral law—the fornicator and the village scold might alike be summoned for punishment. The clergy almost entirely controlled education and hospitals, besides administering all charitable funds. Merchant guilds and craft guilds had their chapels and their chaplains, and the parish churches were the centres of social life. Priests abounded ; and the bells were always jangling in the steeples, calling men to prayer and devotion. The holy days of the Church were the holidays of the people, and those who wished for adventure and a change of air went on pilgrimages ; while those who loved dramatic shows were satisfied with miracle plays and moralities. In fact the Church was everywhere apparent and everywhere dominant. She seemed to have captured the world and to be capable of controlling it. Yet when attacked she showed no power of organised resistance. She was bereft of her privileges and

[1] Empson and Dudley, both laymen, were the forerunners of the lay officials who were so powerful under the Tudors.

despoiled almost without a struggle. Is it true to say that the Church had become so identified with the national life that she had no separate existence ? Is it true to say that she was so corrupt that only the purging fires of the Reformation could save her ? Where did her weakness lie, or if she was not weak, how did it come about that the nation acquiesced in changes it had never desired ?

II. *The Papacy : Its Repute and its Exactions*

There had been a time when the strength of the Church in England had depended on the support of Rome. With that support she had been able to defy despots and maintain a moral code, which was an inspiration and an ideal even when disobeyed. The only law then current throughout Western Christendom was that to which the leaden seal of the fisherman was attached ; and men at least expected that an appeal to the Lateran would be answered by an impartial award. But those days had gone by. The Popes had proved unequal to the strain of universal sovereignty, and the machinery for administering so wide and intimate an empire had proved inadequate. The Hildebrandine ideal of a Kingdom of God on earth was not realised when the powers, which had been grasped so boldly, were administered by a prosaic and corrupt bureaucracy.

From the tragedy of Anagni onwards papal prestige had declined. First there was the Babylonian captivity at Avignon, then the Great Schism, and thirdly the conciliar movement for the reform of the Church. That movement had failed because of internal dissensions, because its leaders were animated by too academic a spirit, and because they were not themselves convinced of the claims which they advanced. But if the Popes had triumphed over conciliar opposition, the works of Marsiglio of Padua, Ockham and Gerson were still being read, and the most orthodox of princes could still threaten an appeal to a free General Council.[1] Such princes fought against the Pope with an undisturbed conscience, while their citizens told one another salacious tales about the papal court. None the less the papacy was so bound up with the structure of society that politicians

[1] Janelle, *Angleterre catholique à la veille du schisme*, 108-111.

were for long united in maintaining its existence. It is often maintained that the renaissance Popes were no worse and even better than the Italian despots who surrounded them; but the despots did not claim to be Vicars of Christ. It is also argued that the scandals at Rome have been grossly exaggerated, but the fact remains that they were generally believed and determined men's attitude towards the Papacy. The Borgias certainly cannot have poisoned so many people in the ways supposed, for no one at the time had the requisite toxicological knowledge.[1] But people were credulous—including the Borgias—and charlatans abounded who professed to sell love philtres or poisons that were efficacious and potent, secret and sure. Richard Pace, not yet a seasoned diplomat whom nothing could surprise, was horrified by the wickedness and profligacy of the Eternal City.[2] Capello and other Venetian envoys forwarded to their senate not only news of a political nature, but gossip to tickle their ears. The grave Burchard kept his diary unashamed: scandal for him was of less importance than the details of ceremonial. He takes the scandal for granted, but is careful to relate how Alexander VI performed his religious functions with exactitude.

Ambassadors were in a position to know, and they wrote for people well informed. It is possible that they were careless about the truth, but they had to be careful about verisimilitude. Merchants and pilgrims knew no such restraint, and the stories heard by the Flaminian Gate lost nothing in the telling when repeated north of the Alps, while stories that in Italy were regarded as merry tales, excited indignation in England and Germany.

This is seen in *Julius Exclusus* [3] which was probably written by Erasmus in Cambridge in 1514, for Lupset lent his copy to More long before its publication in 1517. The Italians rather

[1] Creighton, *Papacy*, iv. 263-265.

[2] Pace in *L. & P.* ii. 5523. Pace (1482 ?–1536) was in Rome, 1509–1515. The letter referred to was not written until 1517 and records his impressions as a young man.

[3] For Erasmus' authorship of *Julius Exclusus*, see P. S. Allen's edition of his *Letters*, ii. 419, the same author's *Age of Erasmus*, 184 ff., and Gee, *Life and Works of Thomas Lupset*, 53 ff. Erasmus never acknowledged his authorship. He fenced with Bucer, and assured Wolsey and Campeggio that he had nothing to do with its publication. Lupset had shown Sir T. More the MS. more than a year before it was printed (*Ep.* 502). It was one of the MSS. that More recovered from the indiscreet Lupset and sent to Erasmus. In *Epistle*, 783, Erasmus makes it clear that the book is not to be known as his.

admired their Ligurian Pope, who had some virtues in the English sense, and was liberally endowed with those qualities which went to make up the Machiavellian concept of *virtu*. But for Erasmus he was only an ill-tempered braggart, smirking over filthy sins and boasting of unprovoked crimes. Northern Europe took the crimes for granted, savoured the wit with which they were exposed, and endorsed the author's unmitigated scorn.

When a Pope could be so regarded religion was bound to suffer even though the Pope maintained the rights of the Church by arms or diplomacy. All renaissance Popes did not do that, but allowed kings to fleece their clergy in return for political support.

Such being the repute of the Papacy, men, always unwilling to pay taxes, began to think that there was some merit in their reluctance, and even to ask themselves whether the demands were not " unreasonable and uncharitable usurpations ".[1] Protests against papal taxation had been made both by parliaments and churchmen from the days of Henry III onwards ; and, if all was quiet when the XVI century dawned, a few years later voices were strident enough. In 1529 Simon Fish, barrister of Gray's Inn, published his famous *Supplication for Beggars*.[2] In it he praises that noble prince, King John, and represents him as the victim of papal aggression. Addressing Henry VIII, he tells him that in consequence " your most noble realm wrongfully (alas for shame !) hath stood tributary (not unto any kind temporal prince but unto a cruel devilish bloodsupper drunken in the blood of the saints and martyrs of Christ) ever since ".[3] Simon Fish was a reckless anti-clerical, who understood the temper of his time, and how to appeal to the people's prejudice and the king's avarice. Foxe says that Henry, although he was still posing as the most orthodox prince in Christendom, kept the little pamphlet for days in his bosom ;[4] and he must have connived at its very wide circulation.[5]

A sensible man reads a political agitator not with a view to ascertain the facts, but as evidence of what the agitator thought

[1] 25 Henry VIII, cap. 21 in Gee and Hardy, *Documents*.

[2] *Vide* Arber's introduction to his reprint in which he shows that Foxe, *A. & M.* iv. 657, is wrong in dating it 1525.

[3] *Supplication for Beggars*, 6.

[4] Foxe, *A. & M.* iv. 657, tells two stories about Henry's reception of the tract. They are not necessarily contradictory.

[5] Creighton, " Simon Fish ", in *D.N.B.*

would be believed. Very few of Simon Fish's facts can be substantiated, but he provides good evidence as to the popular opinion that papal taxation was excessive, and like the Tudor parliamentary draughtsmen he does not distinguish between direct levies and the fees paid by those who had business at Rome.

The papal collector who lived in London like a duke might be the most unpopular man in England,[1] but he had it in his power to be very useful to the king, and on returning to Rome was frequently his agent.

Hadrian di Castello was rewarded with the bishopric of Hereford and afterwards translated to Bath and Wells. John de Giglis also managed to feather his own nest. He was Dean of Wells, Archdeacon of Gloucester and London, held two prebends in cathedrals and also three livings. In addition, on returning to Rome as the king's agent, he was consecrated Bishop of Worcester and secured the reversion of that see for his nephew, Sylvester.[2] Even the sub-collectors were important. Ammonius became Latin secretary to Henry VIII and a pluralist, while Polydore Vergil, Archdeacon of Wells, might have been more fortunate if he had not offended Wolsey. He had his revenge, for, after Wolsey's fall, he wrote the life of the great Cardinal and successfully blackened his character for three centuries.

When we turn from the eminence of the collectors to view the amounts of the collections, we find that the money paid in direct taxation has been exaggerated. Peter's Pence was described by the subservient Commons of England in 1534 as an "intolerable exaction",[3] but as a contribution to the central work of a Catholic Church it was almost negligible; and it was the only papal tax which was paid by the laity. Its origin in Saxon times is obscure, for different chronicles give different accounts of how it arose, what it was for, and when it was first paid. It was supposed to be a tax of one penny on every hearth, but in the time of Ethelwulf it came to 300 marks a year, and the Popes never got any more.[4] Innocent III complained that the English bishops

[1] Stubbs, *Const. Hist.* iii. 362. "They say," says Trevisan, "that this office is worth from 800 to a 1000 crowns per annum" (*Italian Relation*, 95). What "they say" is often an exaggeration.

[2] Smith and Onslow, *Diocese of Worcester*, 123.

[3] Gee and Hardy, *Documents*, 210.

[4] *R.H.S.P.*, New Series, xv. 171-183.

collected a great deal and retained most of it for their own use, but his protest made no difference.[1] The amounts derived from each diocese varied. Of those contributing, Lincoln paid most, £47; and Ely least, £5. Carlisle and Durham do not appear to have contributed anything. The Archbishop of York, nine bishops and eight archdeacons were responsible for the collection in 1509, and Peter Gryphius'[2] return in the Vatican archives shows that he received £197 : 0 : 8.[3] In 1355 the collector had done a little better, receiving £199 : 8 : 8.[4] £200 or 300 marks was the sum aimed at, or £4000 a year in modern money.[5]

The demand of tenths from the clergy was first made by Nicholas IV on the ground that the High Priest of the Jews had received from the Levites a tenth of their tithes.[6] This must have been in 1500 far and away the most productive tax, but it was based on a valuation made in 1292 when the gross revenue of the Church was in round figures £220,000. From this amount we must deduct £80,000, which were temporalities, though collectors sometimes claimed that they were liable to the tax. There were many abatements and exemptions, there were the commissions of collectors and sub-collectors, and there were the demands of the king, which had to be satisfied or the collector was impeded in his work.[7] Professor Lunt writes: "From the late years of the

[1] *R.H.S.P.*, New Series, xv. 203. The letter there printed is from the Vatican Archives. Innocent III was quite right. John XXII also tried to secure for the Papacy the full sum collected as Peter's Pence. He also failed (Lunt, *Papal Revenues*, ii. 66). The diocese assessed the parishes. Many paid nothing. Those that did brought their quota, or considerably less, to the cathedral in procession with banners on Whitsunday. Now the assessment of St. Edmund's Salisbury was 5s. 0½d., but the tax on the whole diocese was £7. When Peter's Pence was abolished, the cathedrals went on with the collections, called officially "Pentecostals", but vulgarly "smoke farthings". So in the Churchwardens' accounts of Minchinhampton, Gloucestershire, we note in 1576, "For Pentecost money, otherwise Peterpence, sometyme payed to the Antichryst of Rome—xvid." See Cox, *Churchwardens' Accounts*, 73 and 313.

[2] Peter Gryphius was Papal Collector from 1509 to 1511. He was a year in England before he was allowed to exercise his office. He then received permission "in the Public Assembly which they call Parliament". He wrote a history of Peter's Pence. *L. & P.* i. 1235.

[3] *R.H.S.P.*, New Series, xv. 206.

[4] *Ibid.* 222.

[5] I accept the conclusion of Prof. Marti, *Economic Causes of the Reformation*, 23 ff., about the value of money, but we must always remember that many things which we now consider necessary were then luxuries, and that luxuries were disproportionally dear. Coulton, *Hist. Assoc. Leaflet*, 95 (1934), would multiply by 25 or 30.

[6] Phillimore, *Eccles. Law*, 1355.

[7] Lunt, *Papal Revenues*, i. 257.

XIII century to the close of the Middle Ages, the income taxes levied from the clergy by the *plenitudo potestatis* were probably more profitable to others than they were to the Popes, though the Camera did not fail to obtain large sums therefrom ".[1] The tax was naturally unpopular with the clergy and in 1532 Convocation protested against it on the ground that their wealth was not derived from the Pope, but from the king's progenitors and the nobles of the realm.[2] A sympathetic monarch noted the point and in 1534 tenths were transferred to the king.[3] A new valuation was also made—the *Valor Ecclesiasticus*—whereby an increase of 50 per cent was added to the taxes of the clergy.

Annates were only paid by archbishops and bishops—England alone of all the countries of Europe having repudiated successfully the papal claims to first-fruits on inferior benefices.[4] Like modern death duties this was a very bad tax, for a poor man on succeeding to a bishopric had to find a much larger sum than he was likely to have by him. Winchester, for instance, was assessed at 12,000 ducats[5] (£2100 = £42,000 of our money).[6] This sum had to be borrowed at very high interest from Italian bankers, and was only lent on the security of the see.[7] The bishop was in consequence crippled for years ; and if he died before the debt was fully paid, his successor was responsible for the arrears. But bishops did not die every day, and if we may trust the Act of Parliament, the average of such payments from England worked out at £3333 a year.[8]

Servitia were exacted for the confirmation and institution of exempt abbots. They were free from episcopal jurisdiction and the privilege was much prized. The monks of St. Augustine's,

[1] *Ibid.* i. 77.

[2] Strype, *Eccles. Memorials*, I. ii. 158. Gairdner, *L. & P.* v. 344, calls this document " A Petition of Parliament ", but Dixon, *Church History*, i. 144, has shown good reason for supposing that Strype's attribution to be correct.

[3] 26 Henry VIII, cap. 3. It is printed at length in Gibson, *Codex* 872.

[4] Platina, *Lives of the Popes* (English trans.) ii. 150. Gibson, *Codex*, 122, also quoted Polydore Vergil to the same effect.

[5] The ducat was at this time worth 3s. 6d. (*N.E.D.*). When Wey, *Itineraries*, visited Venice in 1462 it was worth 3s. 2d. Fuller, *Ch. Hist.* Bk. iii. ch. 3, is wrong in saying 8s.

[6] This immense sum was not altogether due to Annates, but included Services, *i.e.* fees for confirmation, institution, etc. Annates and Services are confused in Henry VIII Statute for the restraint of Appeals. Lunt, *Papal Revenues*, i. 44.

[7] Coulton, *Five Centuries of Religion*, iii. 504 ; Marti, *Economic Causes of Reformation*, 31 ff. ; Lunt, *Papal Revenues*, i. 91.

[8] Gee and Hardy, *Documents*, 25 Henry VIII, cap. 21.

Canterbury, for example, were only bound to open their doors to a *Legatus a latere*, and even then claimed that he could not visit them unless they were expressly named in his commission.[1] An Abbot of Malmesbury wrote :

> Poor and wretched are the abbots who do not utterly abolish the power of bishops, when for an ounce of gold they can obtain from the Roman See complete freedom.[2]

As the price of freedom, an ounce of gold proved a very inadequate estimate. Simon, Abbot of Bury St. Edmunds in 1257, was the first of the exempt abbots of England who went to the Roman see for confirmation, and it cost him 2000 marks.[3] This was a small amount compared with what the Abbot of St. Albans had to pay in 1302. An abbey saved money by obtaining a licence for the elected abbot to be blessed in England, but such a licence cost St. Augustine's, Canterbury, £183 : 2 : 6. In the XV century the greater abbeys compounded with the Camera offering an annual tribute. St. Albans, for instance, paid £13 : 3 : 4.[4]

It will be noted that practically the whole of this taxation was imposed on the clergy ; and the real grievance felt by the laity was not the tax, but that the money went out of the country. It was also impossible to prove that the nation derived any benefit in return. " Is it not unreasonable ", asks Starkey, " the first fruits to run to Rome, to maintain the pomp and pride of the Pope, yea, and war also, and discord among Christian princes, as we have seen by long experience ? " [5]

Besides these taxes, there were fees by which papal officials profited, if not the Pope. In the first Act for the restraint of Annates we read of " bulls for confirmation, elections, admissions, postulations, provisions, collections, dispositions, institutions, installations, investitures, orders, holy benedictions, palls, and other things requisite and necessary to the attaining of these their functions " [6]—and we note that the draughtsman is using every word he knew, and that some of them are alternatives

[1] Watson in *Cam. Med. Hist.* vi. 556.

[2] Quoted Lunt, *Papal Revenues*, i. 64.

[3] Document in Lunt, ii. 238. It, of course, includes the expense of the journey.

[4] Lunt, ii. 244. Cp. another account in Coulton, *Five Centuries of Religion*, iii. 499, 500.

[5] Starkey, *England*, Pt. II. 126.

[6] Gee and Hardy, *Documents*, 179, 23 Henry VIII, cap. 20.

for others. Some of the fees were very heavy. The Archbishop of Canterbury had to pay £1000 (£20,000) for his pall. We can sympathise with the English clergy in the amounts exacted for the writing of Bulls. " For so should parchment and lead be very dear merchandize at Rome, and in some cases a hundred times more worth, than the weight of a counterpoize of fine gold." [1]

The fact was that at Rome the bureaucracy was far too numerous, and the bureaucrats were compelled to multiply business in order to maintain themselves. They had, moreover, this excuse—they had bought their positions. Boniface IX had begun the practice of selling places to the highest bidder. Sixtus IV had appointed eighteen new secretaries and received 2600 florins from each of them. Alexander VI had created eighty new offices, any of which might be bought for 760 ducats. Julius II established a new College of Scriveners and received from them 74,000 ducats, while Leo X received 202,000 ducats for the new posts he created.[2] So it came to pass that in every process documents had to pass through many hands, and every hand was stretched out for a fee. When Adrian VI attempted a reform he found himself faced by vested interests with equitable claims to compensation.

The Tudor draughtsman in 1534 in describing papal exactions had an even larger list than he had two years earlier. He speaks of " pensions, censes, Peter's pence, procurations, fruits, suits for provisions and expedition of Bulls for archbishoprics and bishoprics, and for delegacies and rescripts in causes of contentions and appeals, jurisdictions legative, and also for dispensations, licences, faculties, grants, relaxations, writs called *perinde valore*, rehabilitations, abolitions and other infinite sorts of bulls, briefs and instruments ". [3]

It is impossible to estimate the amount that went to Rome for licences or dispensations.[4] The *Corpus Juris Canonici* was badly

[1] Address of the Clergy. Strype, *Eccles. Mem.* I. ii. 159.

[2] Lindsay, *Hist. of the Reformation*, i. 15, 16. Not only were the offices bought, but they were often bought with borrowed money. Insurance Companies advanced the price of the office and took 12 per cent of the profits. Flick, *Decline of the Mediaeval Church*, i. 134, 135. Lunt, *Papal Revenues*, i. 135.

[3] Gee and Hardy, *Documents*, 210, for 25 Henry VIII, cap. 21.

[4] Dispensations : St. Thomas Aquinas, *Summa*, II. i. Q. xcvii., A. 4, vindicates the right of rulers to dispense with human laws, provided that such dispensations were not prejudicial to the common good. The limitation was not regarded, as may be seen in the *De Emendanda Ecclesia* of the Cardinals appointed by Paul III. Cardinal Contarini followed this up by his *De Potestate Pontificis in Compositionibus*,

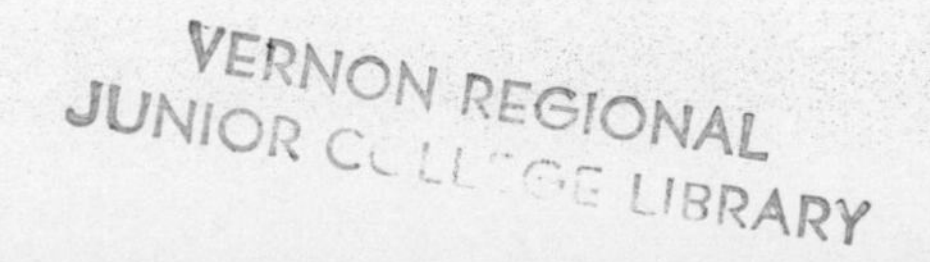

in need of simplification and revision. It had grown up in an age with a passion for legislation, and this legislation had been rendered obscure by the interpretations and glosses of able jurists, until, to escape from the inconveniences of a well-nigh impossible obedience, a dispensation became necessary on any number of occasions. It was clear that all human laws could be dispensed by the power that imposed them, and the Popes were most accommodating at a price. Agents at Rome spent busy lives in expediting such licences and dispensations to their clients.[1]

Lastly, pardoners infested the land with their wallets "bret full of pardon come from Rome all hot";[2] and here we must remember that Penitentials had been barbarous in their rigour and sometimes grotesque in their punishments.[3] They had been designed for and were applicable to men in a primitive condition, but they had become inappropriate or impossible. Was it not better, men argued, a penitent should do some act of mercy or perform some social service, than that he should pass his days in fasting and flagellation or go a long journey to Rome or Jerusalem? The indulgence was only valid for a penitent who had received absolution, and it only remitted the ecclesiastical penance which was due. But theory is one thing, and practice another. Priests accepted money for indulgences and were reproved by bishops; bishops yielded to the same temptation until the Pope reserved to himself the regulation of the system; and

a work which was ultimately placed on the Index. After the Reformation the Jesuit Suarez is definite and careful. *De Legibus VI*, ch. 18. The Dispensator is not an absolute Lord who can act in an arbitrary manner. A dispensation given without due cause is a mortal sin. A just cause is considered under the headings of *Necessitas*, *Utilitas*, and *Pietas*. A dispensation given without due cause by one who has authority to dispense is valid though illicit.

[1] The Letter Book of William Swan, a papal notary of the XV century, is in the Bodleian. He did a great deal of the English business at the Court of Rome, and was capable of giving disinterested advice. For instance, Thomas of Towton was presented by the King to the Prebend of Stillington, to which the Dean and Chapter of York presented John Francis. Swan advised Thomas not to persevere in his appeal to Rome, which would not regard the royal title, but to bring his case into the King's Court where he was sure to win, and then to obtain a writ summoning Francis to return home and answer for his contempt of the royal regalia. Thomas took his advice and won his case. Francis pursued his appeal to Rome and was served with a writ of *Praemunire* on his return. E. F. Jacob, *Bulletin of the John Ryland's Library*, xiv. No. 2.

[2] Chaucer, *Canterbury Tales*, Prologue.

[3] *The Catholic Encyclopaedia* has a good article on Indulgences. See also H. C. Lea, *Auricular Confession and Indulgences*. For a summary see Creighton, *Papacy*, v. 58-64; or better still, Symonds, *The Council of Trent and Anglican Formularies*, ch. xvii.

then papal indulgences became the greatest of all scandals. Sin had been commercialised at Rome, and made to yield a profit.

The theological theory was maintained. Bulls still declared that money given for indulgences rendered them null and void; but a shameless traffic went on; and indulgences were boomed with vulgar loquacity.[1] Councils protested against the abuses, satirists held up the pardoners to scorn, but they throve in spite of contempt and derision, often protected by princes who received a percentage of the profits. Practical men bought indulgences to escape from an unpleasant penance; superstitious people bought them as some sort of insurance against the flames of purgatory; and casual people bought them because they were cheap. At times a pardoner was ready to sell one for twopence or even a penny, but the usual price was fourpence—" The stake ", says Gascoigne, " of a game of ball ".

Here it may be argued—as the purchase of an indulgence or the procuring of a dispensation was optional, those who paid for either had no grievance. But those who did neither were still indignant because the money went abroad to the impoverishment of the realm. There were plenty of people ready to maintain that the distress of the poor might be relieved if money were more plentiful and retained in the country.[2] Bluff King Hall might squander as much as he chose in senseless extravagance, but he was English, the money was spent in England, and English eyes were dazzled by his splendour. It was different and men were filled with rage when they thought of Italian eyes delighting in the pomp of the papal court.

In fact, Rome had come to stand for an alien power and had ceased to be the focus of Christendom. Men were becoming more and more conscious of their nationality. The nation was something which they understood, whereas Christendom was

[1] Gascoigne, *Loci e Libro Veritatum*, 123. Cp. Erasmus, *Militis Confessio: Colloquia*, i. 31. It was popularly supposed that a jubilee indulgence provided pardon of the guilt as well as remission of the penance. Lunt, *Papal Revenues*, i. 125.

[2] The Laws were very strict in forbidding the export of gold and silver, as Erasmus discovered when he arrived at Dover with £20 and had all but £2 confiscated (*Ep.* i. Allen's ed., i. 16). It is therefore probable that the bulk of papal money went no further than the cellars of Lombard Street bankers who sent the Pope credits on their Italian houses. *Vide* Lunt, *Papal Revenues*, i. 53. Such money would only slowly return into circulation, for everyone who could hoarded as they do in the East to-day, because the precious metal contained the greatest value in the smallest compass, and its possession was of the first importance in political and civil emergencies. *Vide* Cunningham, *English Industry and Commerce*, pp. 150, 151.

becoming an abstract idea, a literary word or a legal fiction. Wise statesmen might shake their heads at the peril of Islam; they heard that Rhodes was in danger, that Turkish horsemen were sweeping across the Hungarian plain, and that Turkish corsairs were raiding the towns of the Adriatic—they heard, and did nothing but talk.[1] It was evident to them that the Pope or Emperor ought to do something, and were to be blamed for their lethargy. It was not so evident to them that they ought to contribute something besides criticism. Wise statesmen knew that the unity of Europe no longer existed, and that the day for a crusade had gone by.[2]

On the other hand, the Popes knew quite well that though they could no longer call armies into existence, there was still money to be obtained by proposing a crusade. There were plenty of simple folk who would loosen their purse strings, and there were even young men who would enlist for adventure.[3] When in 1500 Alexander VI called for a crusade and produced a complete plan of how it should be conducted, £12,000 was subscribed by the Province of Canterbury, and Margaret Beaufort declared: "If the Christian princes would have warred upon the enemies of the faith, she would be glad to go follow the host, and help to wash their clothes for the love of Jesus".[4] Elizabeth of York,

[1] Sir Thomas More, *Dialogue of Comfort*, 129: "If the princes of Christendom everywhere about would where as need was, have set to their hands in time, the Turk had never taken any one place of all those places. But partly dissensions fallen among ourselves; partly that no man careth what harm other folk feel; but each part suffereth other to shift for itself; the Turk is in few years wonderfully increased, and Christendom on the other side very sore decayed; and all this worketh our wickedness, with which God is not content."

[2] Aeneas Sylvius had seen this as early as 1454. He was then only a secretary, but he argued against the possibility of a new Crusade, saying, "Christendom is a body without a head; a republic without laws or magistrates. The Pope and the Emperor may shine as lofty titles, as splendid images; but they are unable to command, and none are willing to obey: every state has a separate prince, and every prince has a separate interest . . . what mortal could reconcile the English and the French, Genoa with Arragon, the Germans with the natives of Hungary and Bohemia? If a small number enlisted in the holy war, they must be overthrown by the infidels; if many, by their own weight and confusion." Quoted Gibbon, *Decline and Fall*, xii. 253. Twenty years later Aeneas Sylvius, who had become Pius II, died while attempting to lead a crusade which he had once known to be impossible. Creighton, *Papacy*, ii. 473-475.

[3] In 1481 there had been also an appeal for a crusade. To further it Caxton translated *Godefroy of Bologne* "to the end that every Christian man may be the better encouraged to enterprise war for the defense of Christendom" (Caxton, *Prologues*, 48).

[4] Fisher's *Mourninges Remembrance*, ed. Baker, 34.

Henry's Queen, commended to Ferdinand of Aragon young Henry Still who was eager to fight the infidels,[1] and Robert Curzon joined Maximilian's expedition and came back a Baron of the Holy Roman Empire—but he seems to have had reasons of his own for being out of England at the time.[2]

Such projects met with little support from kings and princes. Henry VII wrote an admirable letter commending the papal plans,[3] and explaining why at that particular time he could do nothing—" He was rather solemn than serious " is Bacon's comment.[4] However, he allowed the collection to be made and handed the money over to the papal legate who was in England about the jubilee indulgences. He did so, although he had been advised by Ferdinand and Isabella to pay the money to Genoese bankers or direct to the knights of Rhodes, and by no means to the Pope who would certainly misappropriate it.[5] Other princes also allowed collections to be made and then shared the proceeds with the Papacy. The money which reached Rome was ridiculously inadequate for a war against the Turks, but it enabled Caesar Borgia to conquer Romagna.[6] In 1507 Henry himself proposed a crusade to Julius II, stating that " he had always been inclined to shed the blood of the enemies of the Christian Faith . . . and to reconquer the Holy Sepulchre ". Julius II replied how he had rejoiced in his letter, had read it ten times, and how all the Cardinals praised the king's virtue and piety.[7] Julius, however, had no intention of attacking the Turks : he was much more anxious about humbling Venice, and retaining Bologna. Afterwards he made use of Bainbridge, Cardinal Archbishop of York. It was not however for a crusade, but to

[1] Gairdner's *Memorials of Henry VII*, S. ii. 111. Queens' College, Cambridge, still possesses an absolution which was priced at a golden florin—the money to go to the Crusade. Searle, *Queens' College, Cambridge*, i. 129.

[2] Gairdner, *Henry VII* (XII English Statesmen), 186. Cf. Busch, *England under the Tudors*, 168, 364, with Gairdner's comments in the same volume, 441 ff.

[3] Collier, *Eccles. Hist.* i. 700.

[4] Bacon, *Henry VII*, 184 ; Busch, *op. cit.* 232. Malvezzi, papal envoy, wrote to Innocent VIII, 1489 (*C.S.P. Venice*, i. 553) about a collection made at Court for the Crusade : " We have opened the money-box which the King was pleased to have at his Court ; we found in it £11 : 11s. 0d., which result made our hearts sink within us, for there were present the King, the Queen, the mother of the King, the mother of the Queen, besides Dukes, Earls and Marquises, and other Lords and Ambassadors, so that we had expected to have had much more ".

[5] Bergenroth, *C.S.P. Spanish*, i. 260.

[6] Gregorovius, *Rome in the Middle Ages*, vii. 439.

[7] Collier, *Eccles. Hist.* i. 702. The king's reply is printed i. 735.

conquer Ferrara.[1] No one understood papal policy better than Henry VII, so we need not take his proposals too seriously. His letter was a move for position in the diplomatic game.

The unity of Christendom was about to be shattered : and it was shattered because of weakness at the centre. The Papacy had for the time ceased to be religious, and no well-informed man trusted the Pope, while the scandals at the Roman Court were a byword. That is why so many men, undoubtedly catholic in faith and practice, regarded the repudiation of the Papacy with approval or unconcern. Perhaps they thought that the separation would be temporary. Many nations had been out of communion with Rome for a time. Only a few foresaw the consequences which would follow the disruption, or anticipated the wars, revolutions, spoliations and persecutions which would ensue. No one probably at the beginning of the XVI century held that religious faith in the see of Peter which characterises Roman Catholics to-day. Even Sir Thomas More felt it his duty to warn his master against too great a subservience to the Pope.[2]

III. *The Early Tudor Bishops*

The chief officers of the State were bishops, and from this we might conclude that the Church was politically powerful, but it was the reason why the Church was politically weak.[3] The king made his principal servants bishops, and too often they remained his servants, enjoying the revenues of a Church they did not serve. In consequence the Church was deprived of her natural leaders, or was led by men with a bias in favour of the royal autocracy. This must be borne in mind if we would understand the history of the English Reformation.

When Magna Carta provided that the Church of England

[1] Bacon, *Henry VII*, 216.

[2] Roper, *Life of Sir T. More* (Chiswick ed., 1903), 189. See also More's letter to Cromwell in Strype, *Memorials*, I. ii. 200. He there confesses that he was convinced of the Pope's primacy, but on p. 201 concludes, " Yet never thought I the Pope above a General Council ". Janelle, *Angleterre catholique à la veille du schisme*, 85, says that a Catholic before the Council of Trent did not regard the Papacy as a Catholic after the Council of the Vatican.

[3] Innocent III in 1215 forbade the clergy to take offices in the State or to be clerks in the royal household ; but in England his decree remained a dead letter. *Vide* Gibbs and Lang, *Bishops and Reform*. When Henry VIII ascended the throne, there were 17 diocesan bishops in England : 15 had been busy in State affairs, one was the step-brother of Henry VII, and one, Fisher, the confessor of his mother.

should be free, it was freedom of the clerical estate from royal interference that was intended.[1] The chapters, for instance, wished to be free to elect their own bishops, but in spite of the charter this was rarely allowed, except for a few years under Henry V. The usual practice was, then as now, for the king to issue a *congé d'élire*, and with it a nomination of the man to be chosen. The Pope, however, claimed the right to decide in all cases of dispute, and to appoint a successor if a bishop died in Rome. Then, he made further claims—first to "provide" a bishop in all cases of translation, and finally to "provide" whenever he chose. When the king was weak like Henry VI, the Pope did much as he liked; but in most cases a compromise was effected. The king nominated, the chapter elected, and then the Pope was petitioned "to provide". [2] In 1345, when Edward III was king, Clement VI remarked, "If the king of England were to petition for his ass to be made a bishop, we could not say him Nay".[3] In 1500, when Henry VII was king, no one disputed that monarch's right to appoint whom he chose, and Dudley in his *Tree of Commonwealth*, attempted to justify the right, arguing that as the love of God is the root of a true commonwealth, so the prince is the ground in which that root grows. He appoints bishops and provides them with necessary force, and so "assisteth his Maker and Redeemer, of Whom he hath all his power and authority".[4]

But the bishop elect could not be consecrated until he had taken an oath that he would be "faithful and obedient to St. Peter and the Holy Church of Rome"; that he would "cause to be conserved, defended, augmented and promoted" the regality of the Holy See; that he would keep and cause to be kept "all the decrees, ordinances, sentences, dispositions, reservations,

[1] In the reign of Henry III out of 78 elections only 15 were free: Gibbs and Lang, *Bishops and Reform*.

[2] The subject is well discussed in Puller, *Orders and Jurisdiction*, 155-182. For the forms connected with election see Jenkins on the Mediaeval Bishop in *Episcopacy, Ancient and Modern*, 78, 79.

[3] Stubbs, *Const. Hist.* iii. 338. Fuller, *Ch. Hist.* Bk. iv. 30, states that the jest was made when Thomas of Hatfield was nominated for the bishopric of Durham in 1345. Four years later when Bradwardine was consecrated for the see of Canterbury at Avignon, Hugo Cardinal of Tudela introduced an ass at the banquet with a placard petitioning for his consecration. *D.N.B.*: Bradwardine.

[4] Dudley, *Tree of Commonwealth*. The author wrote this book in the Tower after the death of Henry VII. I am indebted to Pickthorn, *Henry VII*, 177, for the quotation

provisions and commandments apostolic ". Having sworn to all this and much more to the same effect, he had to sue the king for the restitution of the temporalities of his see. Before receiving them he had to assert on oath, "I utterly renounce and clearly forsake all such clauses, words, sentences and grants, which I have or shall hereafter have of the Pope's Holiness . . . that in any wise hath been, is, or hereafter may be prejudicial to your highness', your heirs' and successors' dignity, privilege or state royal ".[1]

In taking these two oaths the mediaeval prelate must have had a lively faith that King and Pope would always be at one; and in the case of conflicting loyalties he was pretty sure to exercise his discretion in observing the oath most convenient for himself. The proclamation of the Royal Supremacy relieved the consciences of subsequent bishops.

The bishops appointed by Henry VII were as a rule men of high character who had deserved well of the nation. We may except James Stanley—a loose-living man—but he was the king's step-brother. We may also except the Italians. Hadrian di Castello enjoyed great fame as the reputed poisoner of Alexander VI, and was certainly involved in a plot to murder Leo X. John di Giglis was a humanist and an adroit man of business; his nephew Sylvester di Giglis was subsequently accused, not without reason, of instigating the murder of Cardinal Bainbridge. The other bishops were excellent laymen who had been obliged to take holy orders in order to qualify for receiving episcopal revenues. Their vocations for the priesthood were dubious and their pastoral experience was nil. Warham with an honourable career behind him, as an ambassador, lawyer and civil servant, was ordained a sub-deacon at the age of forty-three, and proceeded to the priesthood ten years later in order to be consecrated Bishop of London. Others had enjoyed benefices for years without receiving any but minor orders. The one great exception was the learned and pious Fisher, confessor to Margaret Beaufort, and when in 1504 he was appointed to Rochester, Henry wrote to his mother, " I have in my days promoted many a man unadvisedly, and I would now make some recompense to promote some good and virtuous man, which I doubt not should best please God ".[2]

[1] Hall, *Chronicle*, 788.

[2] Quoted by Baker in his edition of Fisher's *Mourninges Remembrance*, 41.

It was inevitable that bishops concerned with State affairs should not be resident in their dioceses. From the time of his appointment to the see of York Bainbridge resided at the papal court. So did the Italians, except Sylvester di Giglis, who was for some years in London. There is no evidence, however, that he ever visited Worcester, and his Register contains no record that he ever performed any of the duties of his see.[1] Smyth, Bishop of Lincoln, was for years President of the Welsh Marches, Warham was Lord Chancellor. Fox was Lord Privy Seal, Sherbourne was continually on embassies, and Ruthall, Bishop of Durham, was the typical bureaucrat—he was to be Wolsey's factotum and " to sing treble to the Cardinal's bass ".[2]

It is therefore interesting to note how conscience could assert itself. After Fox had been superseded by Wolsey, he spent the last twelve years of his life in the active administration of the Diocese of Winchester, and was not to be lured back to the court. In 1517 he wrote to the Cardinal:

> Since the King's Grace licensed me to remain in my Church and thereabouts upon my cure—wherein I have been almost by the space of thirty years so negligent, that of four several Cathedral Churches that I have successively had, there be two, *scilicet* Exeter and Wells that I never saw, and innumerable souls whereof I never saw the bodies —and specially since by this licence I left the keeping of the Privy Seal, and more especially since my last departing from your good Lordship and the Council: I have determined and, betwixt God and me, utterly renounced the meddling in worldly matters, especially concerning the War or anything to it appertaining. Whereof, of the many intolerable enormities that I have seen ensue by the said War in time past, I have no little remorse in my conscience: thinking that if I did continual penance for it all the days of my life, though I should live twenty years longer than I may do, I could not make sufficient recompense thereof.[3]

Nor was Fox alone in retiring to his diocese in his old age. Smyth did the same and left the Cathedral Church of Lincoln not only a House of God but a House of Smyths—so many of his relations had he beneficed therein.[4] Sherborne retired to Chichester to live

[1] Creighton, *Hist. Essays*, 213.

[2] Giustiniani, *Relazione*, July 1516. Quoted Gurney-Salter, *Tudor England through Venetian Eyes*, 93.

[3] *Letters of Richard Fox*, 93. However in his very next letter to Wolsey (p. 97) he confesses that he is always thinking of State affairs, " as if I were daily attending on you in the King's Council ".

[4] Churton, *Lives of Smyth and Sutton.*

magnificently and quarrel with his old colleague Fox. Nix found Norwich a suitable place for his pugnacity. He fought with Wolsey for the rights of his see, he fought with heretics and burnt "little" Bilney. He suspended Skelton, Oxford's Laureate and Henry's tutor. He contended with the king over his rights at Thetford, and was fined 4000 marks. At the age of eighty he built a new chamber to his palace on the ground floor in which he might live twenty years later when he expected to be somewhat feeble.[1] At eighty-eight, Cromwell's commissioners still found him "a devilish man" to deal with,[2] and he died protesting against the new age.

More pathetic is the case of Wolsey, who, after being for sixteen years Archbishop of York, came for the first time to the confines of his vast diocese as a disgraced man. There he reconciled men who were at variance, gave great alms to the poor and confirmed hundreds of children. He made great preparations for his enthronement, but was arrested and died without seeing his minster.[3]

It must not be supposed that the dioceses were in a state of chaos because their bishops were absentees. The bishops were admirable men of business, and knew how to delegate their work without compromising their ultimate authority.[4] Episcopal functions such as ordaining, confirming and consecrating were performed by men in episcopal orders and with titles *in partibus infidelium*, or by Irish bishops who preferred to live in comfortable English benefices away from their distressful country. Such men were often assistants to more than one bishop.[5] They had no jurisdiction and only acted by the request of the Vicar-General. That official attended to institutions, issued licences, held visitations and exercised discipline ; but his authority terminated as

[1] Strype, *Memorials*, V. ii. 84, says that Gardiner told this to Clement VII as "a merry tale".

[2] Nix in *D.N.B.*

[3] Cavendish, *Wolsey* (Singer's ed., 327-337).

[4] Creighton, *Hist. Essays*, 227 ff.

[5] Stubbs, *Registrum Sacrum Anglicanum*, 194-209, has a list of suffragans. Twemlow's *Cal. of Papal Registers* contains much about Irish bishops : xi. 309. a Bishop of Mayo was allowed to assist the Bishop of Worms, because his diocese was *in partibus infidelium* ; p. 323. the Bishop of Dromore was allowed to assist the Archbishop of York and hold two benefices ; xii. 407. another Bishop of Dromore was to assist the Archbishop of York ; 192. the Bishop of Down and Connor to be Rector of St. Bartholomew Without, Bishopgate ; 420. the Bishop of Ardfort to be Rector of Kingham and Daylesford.

soon as the bishop arrived at his diocese. The third person of importance was the Receiver-General who collected the episcopal revenues, saw to the upkeep of the bishop's residences and presided at his manorial courts. He was expected to keep detailed accounts; and in consequence we know that ten prisoners in the palace at Worcester cost for their maintenance a farthing a day apiece.[1]

The machinery no doubt worked smoothly enough, but the Church is not a machine, and how could a bishop care "for souls whose bodies he never saw"? Visitations were regularly held, for otherwise no procurations were paid; but synods were rarely summoned, and so the bishop was out of touch with his clergy; while to the pious laity he was just a splendid personage who lived somewhere in the Strand. When the struggle came there was little enthusiasm for the Church as an institution. Neither clergy nor pious laity could rally to their natural leader the bishop, and the bishop was impotent, knowing himself to be a creature of the king.

How far the bishops were unpopular it is impossible to say. We must not over-estimate the evidence of rhetorical reformers or the obvious gibes of satirists. The exaggerations of Simon Fish may be disregarded. Erasmus tells us that Colet had a particular dislike for all bishops and spoke of them as wolves in sheep's clothing;[2] but Colet was so consciously a superior person, and like many deans before and since, not on good terms with his bishop, Fitzjames, who was too learned for Colet to despise and too conservative to merit his approval. Erasmus himself in his *Moriae Encomium* speaks of bishops' simoniacal contracts and asserts that they were only *episcopi*, because such careful overseers of their gains and income.[3] Bishops had been very kind to Erasmus, especially English bishops; but he no doubt explained to them that he had assumed in the *Encomium* the character of a fool and claimed the privileges of the cap and bells. Barclay[4] in his eclogues is severe enough on the bishops,

1 Pearce, *Hartlebury Castle*, 9.
2 Erasmus, *Ep.* 1211.
3 Erasmus, *Encomium Moriae*, ii. 377 (*Colloquia et Encomium*, Leipsic, 1893).
4 Barclay, *Eclogues*, i. 484:

> "Upon the hye chaire and seat of Moyses
> Sitte the olde Scribes and sect of Pharisees.
> Live as they teach, but live not as they do."

but he immediately excepts Morton and Alcock, and it turns out that they were the only bishops with whom he had been in personal contact. It is perhaps safe to conclude that *the* bishops were unpopular, but that *a* bishop was often respected. Neither were *the* bishops so unpopular as in Scotland or Germany, or at the Reformation they would have been swept away. It was not their fault that painstaking services to the State were rewarded with spiritual appointments. It was hardly their fault that preoccupation with secular affairs disqualified them for spiritual leadership. It was natural that their studies and their habits led them to over-emphasise in the Church the claims of the Temporal Prince.

In looking through the list of early Tudor bishops, we note that few of them were skilled in theology. Fisher had indeed a great reputation and Fitzjames was also a learned divine. They were the two preaching bishops—Fisher being the more popular since Fitzjames read his sermons.[1] In the early years of Henry VIII another theologian, Standish, a Friar Observant of Greenwich, was promoted to the See of St. Asaph, a poor diocese and therefore fit for a friar.[2] Apart from these three, nearly all the bishops had graduated in Civil Law—Tunstall was a Doctor of Padua, Clerk and Nix were Doctors of Bologna, and most of the others had legal degrees and legal experience which was not always confined to the ecclesiastical courts. All the bishops were orthodox in belief, but the study of theology was at a discount, while skill in civil law was at a premium, and ensured rapid promotion. All the bishops bowed their heads in assent to the supremacy of the *Corpus Juris Canonici*, but they found the civil law more useful during embassies, and in the Chancery Court, and in the conduct of State affairs.[3] They were more familiar with the Digest and Institutes of Justinian than with Gratian's Decretum, the Decretals, the Sext, Clementines and

[1] Seebohm, *Oxford Reformers*, 251.

[2] The Welsh bishoprics were usually accepted as a stepping stone. When Richard III nominated Langton to St. David's, he remarked that he hoped soon to be an Englishman again and no more Welsh. *Ch. Ch. Letters*, Camden Soc., xxx.

[3] The Bull of Honorius III in 1219 forbidding the study of Civil Law at Paris was published out of respect for the theological school. The Bull of Innocent IV, 1253, with wider prohibitions, is not supposed to be genuine. Rashdall, *Universities*, i. 323, ii. 740, maintains that the hostility of the Church to the Civil Law has not been proved. Maitland, *Canon Law*, 92-94, shows that there was reason for such hostility.

Extravagants.[1] Quite unconsciously their minds became attuned to Byzantium rather than to Rome ; and so when Gardiner wrote *De Vera Obedientia* and Bonner contributed a preface [2] they were not improvising original arguments for the Royal Supremacy, but applying ideas with which they had been long familiar to a new political situation.

When Henry VII died, the bishops had no premonition of the changes that were so close at hand, but they did much unwittingly to precipitate the Reformation by the colleges and schools which they founded. Smyth, indeed, after being a liberal benefactor to Lincoln College, Oxford, founded Brasenose in conjunction with Sir Richard Sutton to be a stronghold of the Old Learning, where youths might be instructed in the scholastic theology and philosophy. Fitzjames, also strenuous for the Old Learning, had been so munificent to Merton, that he may almost be regarded as a second founder.[3] But Alcock, in founding Jesus College, Cambridge, distinctly laid it down that he did so in order that scholars might be instructed in grammar, that is, in the classical authors.[4] Fox in founding Corpus Christi College, Oxford, lays most stress on the Latin and Greek lectures that were to be given therein ; Fisher also was a patron of the New Learning. He was largely responsible for Margaret Beaufort's two colleges—Christ's and St. John's at Cambridge ; he also persuaded the lady to endow at both universities the professorships which go by her name. Some bishops kept schools in their houses. Sir Thomas More, for instance, was for a short time in the household of Cardinal Morton, and Richard Pace was brought up in that

[1] Gardiner, *De Vera Obedientia*, 116 (Janelle's ed.), draws out the parallel between Justinian and Henry VIII, " Who did ever disallow Justinian's fact that made laws concerning the glorious Trinity and the Catholic faith, of bishops, of men of the clergy, of heretics, and other such like ? "

[2] S. R. Maitland, *Reformation*, 345-395, doubted the authenticity of Bonner's preface which occurs in the Hamburg edition of 1536. He did not believe, (1) that there was any printing press in Hamburg in 1536, or (2) that Franciscus Rhodes the printer ever existed, (3) or that Bonner, who was not on good terms with Gardiner, would have praised his book. He guesses the book was a fabrication by Marian exiles to bring Bonner into discredit. But Bonner was in Hamburg in 1536, a royal envoy commissioned to defend the king's cause. Franciscus Rhodes was printing in Hamburg 1536–1539. The date and the printer are correct, and the format of the volume suggests a book intended for presentation to notabilities : see Janelle's edition of *De Vera Obedientia*, pp. xxxii-xxxv.

[3] Wood, *Athenae Oxonienses*, ii. 722, concludes his notice of Fitzjames by writing : " After good deeds had trod on his heels even to Heavengate, he gave way to fate in a good old age in the beginning of fifteen hundred twenty and two ".

[4] Cooper, *Memorials of Cambridge*, i. 365.

of Langton, Bishop of Winchester. Of the latter Pace writes how "he was vastly delighted to hear the scholars repeat to him at night the lessons dictated by their teacher during the day, and of his commendations because he was always insisting that 'merit grows with praise'".[1]

The bishops likewise founded schools. Smyth founded two, one at Leicester and another at Farnworth, and Fuller says, "Wherever he went, he may be followed by the perfume of charity he left behind him".[2] Rotherham founded a grammar school in his native place in connexion with his Jesus College there. He appointed a married layman as the master, and left to the school a selection of his books, including three copies of the *Art of Love* by Ovid.[3] Sherbourne founded a school at Rolleston, Fitzjames one at Bruton, and Hugh Oldham the Manchester Grammar School. By the deed of 1525 the master of this last school had to be a "syngilman",[4] priest or no priest, "so that he be no religiouse man". Oldham had his private reasons for disliking monks, due to his disputes with the Abbot of Tavistock, and he wrote to dissuade Fox from connecting Corpus at Oxford with the monastery of St. Swithin at Winchester. "What, my lord, shall we build houses and provide livelihood for a company of bussing monks, whose end and fall we may live to see; no no, it is more mete a great deal that we should have care to provide for the increase of learning, and for such as who by their learning, shall do good in the church and commonwealth."[5]

No one need be surprised that the bishops were none too favourable to monks and friars. The exemption of abbeys and the papal privileges of the mendicant orders were grievances of long standing. Neither is it surprising that these bishops, so essentially men of the world, should be antagonistic to that "other worldliness" which inspired all that was best in monastic life. They stood for the betterment of the world, for common sense, and practical piety. They were enthusiastic for classical culture, and believed that progress in every direction would result from the diffusion of humane learning; but they did not

[1] *De Fructu*, 27.
[2] Fuller, *Worthies: Lancs*, 119. Cp. Stow, *Chronicle*, 495.
[3] Leach, *Mediaeval Schools*, 276. Cp. Green, *Town Life in XV Cent.* ii. 13.
[4] *Ibid.* 297.
[5] Quoted by Fowler in article on Corpus, in Andrew Clark's *Oxford Colleges*, 274.

anticipate a revolution. They stood rather in the dawn waiting for the light to brighten on a glorious day. When Alcock died in 1500, Cranmer was eleven years of age, and the most notable *alumnus* of Jesus would hardly have been approved by its founder. Twenty-six years later Fox died. The sky was still serene in England, although clouds were on the horizon, and the storm had burst in Germany. Fox did not foresee John Jewel, then only six, or Richard Hooker who was born some seventeen years later. And yet Cranmer, Jewel and Hooker are all in that succession of sound learning which Alcock and Fox promoted with such munificence.

IV. *Appropriations and Pluralities*

If the king paid his principal officers of State by the bestowal of bishoprics, lesser officials were paid by receiving inferior benefices, and the wealth, for which the Church was envied, was quietly appropriated for maintaining the Civil Service. The holding of pluralities was contrary to canon law, it was condemned by the Constitutions of Otto and Ottobon, and had been denounced by Archbishop Peckham.[1] But in England advowsons were private property and came within the purview of common law.[2] Nothing could in consequence prevent a patron doing what he liked with his own, and if he presented someone incapable of holding the benefice the Pope was always ready to dispense. There was a fixed tariff at Rome for such dispensations, and men paid according to the aggregate value of the benefices they wished to hold. Gibson prints a list of pluralists in the reign of Edward I.[3] One of them, Adam de Stratton, a clerk in the exchequer and a particularly disreputable person, held twenty-three livings in six different dioceses.[4] Two hundred years later things were not much better, but in 1529[5] a Bill was passed in Parliament forbidding anyone for the future to hold two livings if one was worth £8 or more *per annum*, and also forbidding

[1] Gibson, *Codex*, 941-945.
[2] Maitland, *Canon Law*, 62, 63 etc.
[3] Gibson, 946.
[4] Adam de Stratton, *D.N.B.*
[5] 21 Henry VIII, cap. 13. Tyndale, *Practice of Prelates*, 256, misrepresents this Act which he would have us believe was passed in order that the chaplains might have an excuse for being non-resident. "They must abide in the Court still, else they may not have plurality of benefices."

any application to the Court of Rome for a dispensation to do so. But then follows a list of exceptions. Royal chaplains might hold any number of benefices to which the king presented them. The chaplains of the nobility might hold two benefices, so might the brothers and sons of peers and knights, bachelors and doctors either of divinity or of law. Deaneries, archdeaconries, canonries and strangely enough vicarages were not to be reckoned as benefices within the meaning of the Act. Such a measure did very little to abate the scandal. Its object was rather to prevent money being spent at Rome for dispensations than to interfere with the privileges of the king and his nobles who were still able to provide handsomely for their friends. Another 300 years had to pass away before the scandal of pluralities ceased.

The great nobles imitated the king in their ecclesiastical establishments. The Earl of Northumberland[1] had a dean and ten priests in his chapel. When he dined, while the trumpets sounded and the guests marshalled themselves, the choristers were led by the precentor into the hall to sing grace. But these chaplains had more mundane duties. The surveyor of the lord's lands, his private secretary and clerk of his signet, the secretaries of his privy council and board of works, and those who dealt with home and foreign affairs were all of them priests and enjoyed benefices in which they rarely resided.

It was the custom also for bishops to reward scholars with livings and excuse them the obligation of residence. Fox presented Claymond, the President of Corpus, with the rich living of Cleeve in Gloucestershire, valued in the king's book at £84 : 6 : 8, or at £1680 of our money.[2] Warham presented Erasmus with the living of Aldington in Kent, valued at £38 : 6 : 8, and worth £760 of our money.[3] Erasmus, it is true, after six months, resigned the living for conscientious reasons, alleging that he could not preach in English, but he accepted a pension of £20 per annum, and Warham charged the pension on the tithes of Aldington. Linacre[4] in 1509 was made Rector of Mersham and a Prebendary of Wells, and a year later Rector of Hawkhurst. In 1517 he was a Canon of St. Stephen's, West-

[1] *Northumberland Household Book*, 323.

[2] *Letters of Fox*, 106, 107.

[3] Froude, *Letters of Erasmus*, 101, says the living was valued at £66. It is, however, £38 : 6 : 8 in Bacon's *Liber Regis* and in Ecton's *Thesaurus*.

[4] Linacre, *D.N.B.*

minster. In 1518 he became Prebendary of York and Rector of Holsworthy in Devon; in 1519 Precentor of York and in 1520 Rector of Wigan. *It was in* 1520 *that he was ordained priest.* There is no evidence that he resided on any of these benefices. As physician to the king it was probably impossible for him to do so. He vacated several of them after a short tenure, probably being bought out by the man who had the promise of the next presentation. In the language of the day he was "a Choppe Church".[1]

A still worse scandal was the way in which benefices were heaped upon favoured minors. Colet denounced this abuse, saying, "Nowe adayes boys for olde men . . . do reigne and rule". Perhaps he remembered that he had received the livings of Dennington and Thurning when nineteen, and shortly after Prebends in York, Salisbury and St. Martin's le Grand, the free chapel of Hilberworth in Norwich and the valuable living of Stepney. Thus amply endowed he had gone to Italy, and was not ordained a deacon until he was thirty years of age.[2] When Reginald Pole went to Oxford at the age of thirteen the Prior of St. Frideswide's was commanded to provide him with a pension for his education at Magdalen.[3] He was made Dean of the Collegiate Church of Wimborne when eighteen, and received in addition two Prebends in Salisbury Cathedral. At twenty-seven he became Dean of Exeter, and a little later Rector of Piddletown in Dorset. He was thirty-eight when he received the diaconate and a Cardinal's hat. He was only ordained a priest after being elected to the Archbishopric of Canterbury. With such a record it is odd that Starkey puts into his mouth such a condemnation of non-resident clergy, concluding, "They gather the wool diligently without regard to the profit of their sheep".[4]

But Colet's and Pole's preferments are insignificant when compared with those of Thomas Wynter, Wolsey's natural son. While still a schoolboy he was Dean of Wells; Provost of

[1] Floyer, *English Church Endowments*, 91.

[2] Lupton, *Life of Colet*, 116 ff. The Convocation sermon was preached in 1512. In 1508 he is supposed to have procured the chapel of St. Margaret, Hilberworth, which he had himself resigned, for Thomas Lupset, a boy of thirteen, resident in his house. This was not even necessary for Lupset's education, as he was the son of a wealthy goldsmith. The chapelry was worth £30 a year, or £600 of our money; *vide* J. A. Gee, *Life and Works of Thomas Lupset*, 35.

[3] Pole, *D.N.B.*

[4] Starkey, *England*, ii. 133.

Beverley; Prebendary of St. Peter's, Beverley; Archdeacon of both York and Richmond; Chancellor of Salisbury; Prebendary of Lutton (Wells); Strenshall (York); Bedwin (Salisbury); Milton (Lincoln); and Norvell (Southwell); Rector of Rudley (Yorkshire); and St. Matthew's, Ipswich. As he grew up further preferments were provided, until his revenues from the Church came to £2700 a year or £54,000 of our money. It is true that his prudent father received and retained this income and only allowed him £200 a year to live on, or £4000 of our money.[1]

Such scandals—though there were too many of them—had only a temporary and occasional importance; but absenteeism was very common, and the number of appropriated livings was very large. Rather more than a generation before the time we are considering, Gascoigne, the Chancellor of Oxford, had written:

> Some never or rarely reside in their cures, and either he to whom the church is appropriated, or he who does not reside in it, comes once a year to the cure, or sends to the church at the end of autumn, and having filled his purse with money and sold the tithes, goes away from his cure into the Court, where he idles in gain and luxury. Whence are made true the words written by Solomon in the seventh chapter of Proverbs, "For the goodman is not at home. He is gone on a long journey. He hath taken a bag of money with him, and will come again at the day of the full moon", *i.e.* in autumn when there is fulness of fruits.[2]

Gascoigne harps on this subject. He thought that souls perished through appropriated churches, and later maintained that, "to the parsons are the tithes and oblations due by reason and law".[3] Later still he tells of a rector, having his full rights, who kept twenty young men at school and university and made them priests;[4] but we fear he must have been a very exceptional parson.

Appropriations became a terrible abuse, but like most abuses they had in the beginning some justification. When monasteries were undoubtedly making the greatest contribution to religion in

[1] Pollard, *Wolsey*, 309. Considering the household he was expected to keep in Paris, Lupset, his tutor, thought his allowance insufficient. J. A. Gee, *Thomas Lupset*, 127-129. See also *L. & P.* iv. 2806.

[2] Gascoigne, *Loci e Libro Veritatum* (ed. Rogers), 3.

[3] *Ibid.* 21.

[4] *Ibid.* 112.

the country, it was natural for patrons to put their livings into the hands of monks and leave it for them to appoint suitable vicars. Ultimately monasteries became greedy for this kind of property, because wealthy and devout laymen, who were ever ready to build, were very unwilling to pay for the upkeep of what others had built, and still more unwilling to provide a permanent endowment for those who were inmates of the buildings. The appropriated living was the easiest solution, because the donor was not actually out of pocket. The patron had to obtain a licence from the king, the ordinary and the incumbent, for the first two had rights in case of lapses, and the last had to see that his vested interest was respected.[1] After the Statute of Mortmain appropriations were only allowed when a monastery pleaded poverty ; and when the plea was allowed the result was that instead of a well-to-do rector spending his income in the parish, the parishioners paid tithes to a distant abbey and were served by a poorly paid vicar. The parishioners had no rights in the matter for the common law had decided that advowsons were private property.[2]

Popes and councils decreed that the vicars should have a competence, and Parliament also legislated on the subject ; but there was no fixed scale.[3] In some places a vicar received as much as £10 : in Buckinghamshire it was only £5 and a house, in Exeter diocese it was proportionate to the value of the rectory, and in Lincoln it was one-third of the total income.[4] Bishops had the power to compel the appropriators to increase the vicar's stipend ; but the monks countered this by requiring anyone they appointed to take an oath before institution that he would not plead for an augmentation.[5]

An abbey with the right to tithes from many parishes found it hard to collect them, as they were paid in kind. In consequence it became necessary to farm out the tithe to some layman on the spot. Peterborough had six rectories, Tewkesbury sixteen, but they both farmed out all but one.[6] Cirencester had eleven livings, and farmed out all of them. There is a petition to John XXIII in 1412 from Norwich complaining that these laymen took the

[1] Phillimore, *Eccles. Law*, 220.
[2] Maitland, *Canon Law*, 63.
[3] 15 Richard II, cap. 6 ; 4 Henry IV, cap 4.
[4] Offer, *The Bishop's Register*, 14.
[5] Hartridge, *Vicarages*, 193.
[6] *Ibid.* 203.

obventions of the altar, lorded it over the clerks and other persons deputed for the sacred functions, dilapidated the rectories and committed many excesses.[1] The dissolution of the abbeys therefore made very little change in appropriated parishes. The people had always been accustomed to pay their tithes to laymen, and the transition to lay rectors did not disturb them.

No doubt the abbeys often abused their patronage and treated their vicars badly. Kings, bishops and nobles did the same. Patronage was property and not a trust. At the same time the evils can be over-stated. Parochial life was very strong at this time, and religion was an active force in the lives of men. The scandals were real, and they are on record ; but it is only by accident that we hear of the poor parsons and of their quiet self-sacrificing lives—and yet England was a Christian nation because of them.[2]

V. *The Clergy and Their Learning*

When we turn to consider the conditions of the inferior clergy we are first of all impressed by their numbers. There were 29,161 entered on the Poll Tax returns in 1381, exclusive of friars, and there were probably more and not less a hundred years later. It has been reckoned, says Capes, that " one in fifty-two Englishmen above fourteen years of age was nominally a cleric ".[3] It is true that a very large proportion of them were only in minor orders, and engaged in secular pursuits. They had received the tonsure in order to obtain benefit of clergy without any intention of proceeding to the priesthood. It is also clear from episcopal registers that bishops ordained a hundred or two hundred priests at a time, and there was very little enquiry into their spiritual qualifications. " All who offer themselves," said Colet, " are forthwith admitted without hindrance. Hence proceed and

[1] Hartridge, *Vicarages*, 203.

[2] Caxton, in his Epilogue to *Aesop's Fables*, tells the story of two priests—one ambitious and a pluralist, the other pastorally-minded. The story is delightfully told and would not have been appreciated unless both types had been well known. *Prologues and Epilogues*, 88.

[3] Capes, *Ch. Hist.* 255. Coulton, *Ten Mediaeval Studies*, 142, says : " The clergy formed perhaps only one-fiftieth and at most one twenty-fifth of the total adult population ". According to Raine, *Hist. Towns, York*, 182, 184, 202, York had a population of 10,800, 41 parish churches and 500 clergy. Over 100 were attached to the Minster, but they would not all have been in residence.

emanate those hosts of both unlearned and wicked priests which are in the Church." [1]

Sir Thomas More agreed with him, and in planning his *Utopia*, says, "They have priests of exceeding holiness, and therefore very few ".[2] In his *Dialogue*, he says of the clergy: "I wot well there be therein many very lewd and naught. And surely wheresoever there is a multitude it is not without miracle possible to be otherwise. But now if the bishops would once take into priesthood better laymen and fewer (for of us be they made) all the matter were more than half amended." [3] And again: "For the number, I would surely see such a way therein, that we should not have such a rabble, that every man must have a priest in his house to wait upon his wife, which no man almost lacketh now, to the contempt of priesthood, in as vile office as his horsekeeper ".[4]

Sir Thomas More thought all would be well if the law of the Church was kept, and no one was ordained unless to some cure or on his patrimony. Unfortunately the church law allowed too many loopholes. The bishop was responsible for providing for clerics he ordained, unless they had some cure or patrimony. So he insisted on a title; but he was easily satisfied if the cleric professed to have a pension, or even if some reputable person promised

[1] Colet, *Convocation Sermon*; quoted Seebohm, *Oxford Reformers*, 241. In 1510–1511 there were ordained in York:

Acolytes .	. 298	of whom 17	were regulars
Subdeacons	. 296	" 51	"
Deacons .	. 248	" 41	"
Priests .	. 265	" 173	"
	1107	282	

Cutts' *Parish Priests, &c.* 146. For the numbers ordained in the Worcester diocese at an earlier date, see Stubbs, *Const. Hist.* iii. 395. Smyth was consecrated Bishop of Lichfield in 1496. At his first ordination at Tutbury he ordained 200 acolytes, subdeacons, deacons and priests. He held two other ordinations in the same year with similar numbers: Churton, *Lives of Smyth and Sutton*, 47, 48.

[2] *Utopia*, 282.

[3] *Dialogue*, Bk. III. ch. xi. Barclay's version of *The Ship of Fools*, ii. 63, agreed with More:

"The cause so many prestes lacketh wyt
Is in you bysshops, if I durst trouth expresse,
Which not consyder what men that ye admyt
Of lyvinge cunninge person and godlynes,
But whosoever hymself thereto wyll dresse,
If an angel to his broker to the scibe
He is admyttyd, howebeit he be wytles—
Thus solde is presthode for an unhappy bribe."

[4] *Dialogue*, Bk. III. ch. xii. To illustrate More's statement, Nicholas Blackburn, Lord Mayor of York, in 1432 left a special bequest to his wife to find her a gentlewoman, a priest and a servant. (Will quoted by Cutts, *Parish Priests, &c.* 430.)

to provide for him.[1] The canon law laid it down that the patrimony must not be sold or alienated, but as Christopher Saint German pointed out, this was only binding in conscience as the common law refused to allow an ecclesiastical court to limit a man's right to dispose of his property.[2] The patrimony was sometimes a fictitious conveyance, reconveyed as soon as orders were obtained, or the candidate arrived with a presentation to a living, which he was secretly pledged to resign. So, as Sir Thomas More says, " The law is deluded, and the order (of priesthood) is rebuked by the priests' begging and lewd living, which either is fain to walk at rovers and live upon trentalls or worse ".[3]

The evil was greater because a number of young people were thrust by parents and guardians into religion while still children. Oblates, as they were called, had long been a scandal, though Hannah's dedication of Samuel provided a biblical precedent. Starkey makes Pole declare that youths should not be admitted to monasteries, but only mature men. " I dare well say," he goes on, " their number would not be over-great. We should have fewer in number religious men, but better in life."[4] As it is, he says in another place, " You shall see some friars whom you would judge to be born in the habit, they are so little and young admitted thereto ".[5] Margaret Paston was a wise woman when, though she desired that her fourth son, Walter, should become a priest, wrote to Sir John Gloys at Oxford : " Bid him that he should not be too hasty in taking of Orders that shall bind him, till that he be of 24 years of age or more, though he be counselled the contrary, for often rape reweth. I will love him better to be a good secular man than to be a lewd priest."[6]

It is usual to represent the priests of this period as illiterate. We hear much about the lack of learning from men like Erasmus, Colet, Lupset and Starkey, but these humanists had a very high standard of classical attainments, and had a fine contempt for old-fashioned scholars trained in logic and the scholastic philo-

[1] Gibson, *Codex*, 161, 162. [2] *Doctor and Student*, ch. xliv.

[3] *Dialogue*, Bk. III. ch. 12.

[4] Starkey, *England*, Pt. II. 156. So, Erasmus in *Coll. Militis et Carthusiani*, i. 185, lays stress on the point that the Carthusian was not professed until he was 28.

[5] *Ibid.* 127. In 1535 Thomas Solmes, Canon of St. Osyths', petitioned for licence to leave his Order, and stated that he had joined the Abbey at the age of 13 owing to the threats of his schoolmaster, had been professed at the age of 14, and had never willingly submitted " to the yoke of Religion ". *V.C.H. Essex*, ii. 161.

[6] *Paston Letters*, No. 176. Should not *rape* be *rathe* ?

sophy. Oxford and Cambridge, however, at this time turned out many brilliant scholars : and it is only reasonable to suppose that ten times their number, men of moderate abilities, derived some benefit from the instruction they shared with their betters. It is true that many boys went to Oxford and Cambridge insufficiently grounded and at too early an age to follow the lectures which were given in Latin. But it was Latin they were required to speak, in and out of the schools : and Vulgarisantes were fined a farthing for failing to do so, or were publicly whipped by the Principal of their Hall on Saturday night.[1] Many indeed never proceeded to a degree, and it may be that Bachelors of Arts sometimes only knew enough to construe their Breviary or master an episcopal mandate.[2] Most no doubt spoke no better Latin than the imaginary authors of the *Epistolae Obscurorum Virorum*. They were in fact ignorant men from a professional standpoint, but they were not illiterate in the common acceptance of that term.

It may be argued that the majority of the priests had never been to a university ; but there were a multitude of grammar schools—they all taught Latin, and some knowledge of the language must have been very widely diffused. We suspect Starkey of exaggerating when he wrote, " For commonly you shall find that they can nothing do but patter up their matins and mass, mumbling up a certain number of words, nothing understood ".[3] The same suspicion is aroused by Skelton's verses :

Yet take they care of souls
And wotteth never what they read,
Paternoster, Ave, nor Creed,
Construe not unto a whistle
Neither Gospel nor Pistle,
Their matins madly said,
Nothing devoutly prayed :
Their learning is so small,
Their Primes and Hourés fall
And leap out of their lips
Like sawdust on dry chips.
I speak not now of all
But the most part in general.[4]

Skelton is not the only scholar, accustomed to courts and polite

[1] Rashdall, *Universities*, ii. 626. Cf. Emden, *An Oxford Hall*, 209.
[2] Rashdall, ii. 700.
[3] Starkey, *England*, 132.
[4] Skelton, *Poems* : " Colin Clout ".

society, who has found the country clergy stupid and unlettered. "Some can scarcely read", he says in his disdain; but we must not take him too literally. Neither need we believe Tyndale when he wrote, "I daresay that there are 20,000 priests, curates this day in England, and not so few, that cannot give the right English unto this text in the Paternoster, *Fiat voluntas tua, sicut in coelo et in terra*, and the answer thereto".[1] This would imply that two-thirds of the priests in England were illiterate at a time when grammar schools abounded.

As a matter of fact, the general education of the clergy at the beginning of the XVI century was probably higher than it was fifty years later, and for this we can appeal to the *Complaint of Roderick Mors*, and the works of Bishops Hooper and Latimer.[2] We must not exaggerate in either direction. When Mr. Kingsford tells us that Walter Crome, Rector of St. Benet's Shorehog, left ninety-three books to the University of Cambridge,[3] and Mr. Froude tells us that the Parson of Aldington had a hundred and thirteen books,[4] we must not argue from them to the library of the ordinary cleric. Neither must we be misled by tales of ignorance. When Richard Pace in 1517 tells of an old parish priest who was corrected for reading in the Mass, *Quod in ore mumpsimus*, and replied, "I will not change my old *mumpsimus* for your new *sumpsimus*",[5] we ask, what does it prove? Only that Pace had a merry tale which he was sure would amuse his readers. It did, and humanists used the word *mumpsimus* as a term of contempt for the Old Learning. Erasmus also tells us a story in his *Encomium Moriae*. He says that he was present at a meeting where the punishment of heretics was discussed. An old divine arose and quoted the text *Haereticum hominem post unam et alteram correptinam, devita*, reiterating *devita, devita* to the amazement of his audience, until he explained it meant *de vita tollendum hereticum*.[6] Erasmus says that some laughed but

[1] Tyndale, *Works*, iii. 75.

[2] Brinklow, *Complaint of Roderick Mors*; Hooper, *Later Writings*, 151; Latimer, *Works*, i. 102, 269.

[3] Kingsford, *Prejudice and Promise in the XV Century*, 41.

[4] Froude, *Hist. of England*, i. 40. The Inventory runs, "Item Greek Books covered with boards, 42. Item, small books covered with boards, 33. Item, books covered with leather or parchment, 32." It is evident that *Greek* is a misprint for *Great*.

[5] Pace, *De Fructu*, 80.

[6] *Encomium Moriae*, ii. 391. Seebohm, *Oxford Reformers*, 248, in telling the story has improved on Erasmus.

many were convinced. Perhaps they were, but Erasmus was not there to see, and in the third edition of his *Annotations* [1] he admits that he had the story from Colet and wrote it up for his own purposes. It is another merry tale, and when it comes to jokes scholars like most to hear of the howlers made by the unlearned.

It is sometimes said that the monks as a class were the most ignorant of the clergy, but if so it is strange, as Jessopp remarks, that "the Regulars monopolised all the preferment in the Church, and a great deal of preferment in the State that was worth having. It is also strange that in the last years of Henry VIII's reign so many of the new bishops should have been old monks."[2] The monks as a class may have been solid for the Old Learning; [3] but the Benedictines at any rate maintained their "nurseries" at the universities, and those who were sent to them subsequently filled the more important offices in their monasteries.

Some writers would have us believe that the monasteries alone cared for the education of the poor: this is not true, but they did do something for poor children. Most of the greater abbeys maintained an almonry school where little choristers were taught to sing, and were also taught the rudiments of grammar. If, however, there was a local grammar school they were generally sent there for instruction; and it was only when there was no grammar school that poor boys were admitted to share in the education of the choristers. When the monasteries were suppressed some 1500 almonry boys were deprived of a free education.[4] That is the outside number. It may have been only a thousand.[5]

On the other hand, many of the monasteries kept boarding schools, and the boys who went to them belonged to the abbot's family—their parents paying handsomely for their entertainment. Generally they were instructed by a paid usher, but they were under the abbot's supervision; and the Abbot of Reading at least could take a personal interest in a very small pupil. He wrote to Lord Lisle:

[1] *Annotations*, 558.
[2] Jessopp, *Norwich Visitations*, xxxviii.
[3] *Ibid.* xxxix. Cp. Pantin, *Black Monks*, iii.
[4] Leach, *Mediaeval Schools*, ch. xi.
[5] Baskerville, *English Monks, &c.*, 38, says 1500, but Leach, *op. cit.* 230, says 1000.

I have set your young gentleman with William Edwards, my under-Steward, that he be well seen to by a woman for his dressing, for he is too young to shift for himself. He is the most towardly child in learning that I have known.[1]

Bromhele, Abbot of Hyde (*fl.* 1450) always kept eight young gentlemen in his house and educated them. William Selling, Prior of Canterbury 1472–1489, was in Italy more than once between 1462 and 1469.[2] He established a school of his own and taught Linacre whom he afterwards took to Florence to pursue his studies.[3] Bere, Abbot of Glastonbury, also studied in Italy, was known to Erasmus and befriended Pace.[4] His abbey became " a well-disciplined court ", where young noblemen and gentlemen received " a virtuous education ". Whiting, the last abbot, is said to have educated 300 boys. John Holt, Abbot of Wymondham, the titular Bishop of Lydda, was the author of the first Latin Grammar printed in England by Wynkin de Worde in 1497.[5] Robert Whitgift, Abbot of Wellhow in Lincolnshire, also kept a school at which his nephew, the future Archbishop of Canterbury, received his education.[6] Considering these facts, we need not unduly stress the importance of the fictitious abbot in the Colloquies of Erasmus who had no book in his house, and discouraged learning in his sixty-two monks for fear that they might question his authority.[7]

We may conclude that the monks, though they were adverse to the New Learning, were not the most ignorant of the clergy. We can go further and say that the secular clergy in the richer and better populated parts of the country were not illiterate.

[1] Baskerville, 37.

[2] Furnivall, Introd. to *Manners and Meals*, xix.

[3] Gasquet, *Eve of the Reformation*, 23, says Selling was the pupil of Politian at Bologna in 1464, but Politian was not born before 1454. It is possible that Selling may have met Politian when passing through Florence on an embassy to Rome in 1487 : *Cam. Med. Hist.* viii. 800. Gasquet was misled by Leland : Sandys, *Classical Scholarship*, ii. 225.

[4] Gasquet, *op. cit.* 37, says, " It was through Abbot Bere's generosity that Richard Pace was enabled to pursue his studies in Italy ". He gives as his reference " Erasmus, *opera* : *Ep.* 700 ". The letter to Bere (1490 in Allen's ed.) makes no reference to Italy. Pace himself (*De Fructu*, 27) distinctly states that he was sent to Italy by Langton, Bishop of Winchester.

[5] Jessopp, *op. cit.* xv., is wrong in stating that John Holt, the grammarian, taught Sir Thomas More. It was Nicholas Holt who was master of St. Anthony's School. R. W. Chambers, *Sir T. More*, 56.

[6] Strype, *Whitgift*, i. 3.

[7] *Coll. Abbatis et Eruditae*. There is a similar story in *Epistolae Obscurorum Virorum*, ii. 63.

There was a low level of learning in Wales and the adjacent counties, but Tyndale, who was born in the Vale of Berkeley, had received a good education, probably at the Grammar School of Wotton-under-Edge, before matriculating at Magdalen Hall, Oxford.[1] In Yorkshire poverty and ignorance were allied. Archbishop Lee wrote in 1535 that his livings were so "exile" no learned man would take them, so that he had to be content with such as could read and administer the sacraments. He says that there were not twelve secular priests in his diocese qualified to preach; and he excuses them for not receiving at once the doctrine of the Royal Supremacy. "Many of them", he says, "can scant perceive it."[2]

VI. *The Morals of the Clergy*

Much has been written about the sexual immorality of the Pre-Reformation clergy; but the evidence is far from conclusive. In England most of the higher clergy lived decorous lives, though Bishop Stanley had a bad reputation. Protestants have defamed Bishop Nix on very insufficient evidence;[3] and Bishop Wordsworth of Salisbury has credited Warham with a wife and family, because Le Clerc labelled a letter of Erasmus "to Warham" instead of "to Mountjoy".[4] Wolsey indeed had two children by Rose Dark; and Cranmer, a widower when he

[1] Demaus thinks Tyndale was born in 1484, Mozley in 1494; but 1490 is more probable. He graduated as B.A. from Magdalen Hall in 1512 and proceeded M.A. in 1515. Shortly afterwards he migrated to Cambridge. As Colet left Oxford 1504, Tyndale cannot have attended his lectures as Seebohm, *Oxford Reformers*, 157, suggests. As Erasmus left Cambridge in 1513, he cannot have taught Tyndale Greek.

[2] Strype, *Eccles. Mem.* i. 291, 292. Nearly a century before, Robert Rypon, sub-prior of Durham, had given an equally poor account of the secular clergy in the Northern Province. "Many knew not how to expound a single article of the Faith, nor one precept of the Decalogue": quoted Owst, *Preaching in Med. England*, 29, 30. In other parts of the country there was an unlearned clergy. For instance, Bishop Storey founded a prebendal school at Chichester "on account of the ignorance of the priests and scarcity of ministers in our diocese". Stephens, *Chichester*, 182.

[3] Godwin, *Catalogue*, 431, gives no authority for saying, "he hath the report of a vicious and dissolute liver". The only evidence known to me is the reply of the Prior of Wymondham when threatened with delation to his bishop, "Tell my Lord and my Lady, for I care not". See Jessopp, *Norwich Visitations*, 99.

[4] *The Ministry of Grace*, 238. Erasmus (*Ep.* 783) began a letter *Mæcenas Optimus*, and Le Clerc guessed Warham, but in *Ep.* 829 Erasmus writes, *Mæcenas vetustimus Montiolus*, and again refers to his wife and child. *Ep.* 301 to Mountjoy begins, *Salve, Maecenas optime*. In consequence Allen concludes that *Ep.* 783 was addressed to Mountjoy.

was ordained, had a lady whom he regarded as his wife. Wolsey and Cranmer alike broke the rule of the Church to which they belonged.

The marriage of the clergy is not forbidden by the divine law, and Rome recognises the marriage of priests in the Uniat Churches ; it is not forbidden by the civil law, and in England it was not forbidden by the common law before the Act of the Six Articles. Secular priests took no vow of chastity ; but they were subject to the canons of the Western Church ; and those who disobeyed them could point to many other canons more honoured in the breach than the observance. At the Council of Basle, the Bishop of Lubeck made an eloquent appeal for the relaxation of the rule ; [1] and Aeneas Sylvius, not yet Pope, declared that " for weighty reasons marriage was taken from priests, and for weightier it ought to be restored ".[2] In the XVI century Charles V in Germany and the Cardinal of Lorraine in France wished that clerical marriages might be tolerated ; and it is even said that Paul III contemplated the possibility of granting dispensations to particular people.[3] In England, Starkey attributes to Pole, not yet a Cardinal, an academic approval of clerical marriage ; but we must remember that, when Starkey wrote, he was trying to commend his illustrious friend to Cromwell and Cranmer.[4]

It is undeniable that many of the clergy kept concubines but those who were faithful to one woman, although not canonically wedded to her, ought not to be placed in the same class with vicious men given to promiscuity. During Warham's visitation in 1504, eighty priests from the dioceses of Bangor and St. David's were presented for incontinence, and commanded to put away their mistresses.[5] Half a century before there had been a religious revival in Wales, and many priests had intended to separate from their concubines, but Bishop de la Bere forbade them to do so, because he received an annual revenue of 400 marks a year from them in fines.[6] Sir Thomas More admits about Wales that " incontinence is there in some places little looked unto " [7] but conditions were no better in the neighbouring

[1] Creighton, *Papacy*, ii. 118.
[2] Quoted in Bruce, *Age of Schism*, 208.
[3] Compare articles on " Celibacy " in *E.R.E.* and *Cath. Encycl.*
[4] Starkey, *England*, ii. 150.
[5] Gibson, *Codex*, 438.
[6] Gascoigne, 35, 36.
[7] *Dialogue*, Bk. iii. ch. 18.

diocese of Hereford, if we may judge from the Visitation Returns in 1397. In them we have defamed, the Prior of Hereford, the Abbot of Flaxley, and six of his monks (one of them apparently living out of community) ; one canon, four rectors, sixteen vicars, and thirty-two chaplains. The returns are from 281 parishes ;[1] but the number of the clergy is unknown.

Passing from Herefordshire to Yorkshire we have been told that the *Ripon Act Book* shows that there were twenty-eight clergy in the Liberties and that twenty-four of them were convented for incontinence.[2] This entirely misrepresents the facts. The Act Book records proceedings from 1452 to 1506, a period of fifty-four years, and during that time there must have been 100 and probably 150 priests in Ripon.[3] Thirty-one accusations of incontinence are recorded. One man was out of the jurisdiction, one was cited five times, and one three times. This reduces the number of persons incriminated to twenty-four. Of these, eight were acquitted on their purgation and eight were never tried. The notices of them begin with the word *Dicunt*, and no further action is taken. Eight were condemned to do penance, for which seven of them compounded. Of the eight convicted, two were deacons, and five were chaplains. In consequence, all that the *Ripon Act Book* proves, is that in fifty-four years six priests were convicted of incontinence. Here some one may interject : " We know that compurgation was a farce,[4] so you may safely add the eight acquitted to the guilty ; we know that where there is smoke there is fire, so probably the eight victims of scandal were no better than they should be ; and then you should add another twenty-four for those who were not found out ". Guess-work of this sort is incapable of proof or refutation ; but I am willing to admit that I should be sorry to argue that there were only six incontinent priests in Ripon, because of the imperfect records of its Act Book. It was probably not without reason that Wolsey as Archbishop of York republished the canons of his predecessors in 1518, and among them is one forbidding priests to have housekeepers who might give rise to

[1] *E.H.R.* vols. xliv., xlv.

[2] Published by Surtees Society.

[3] Nine clergy are attached to the Cathedral Church of Gloucester ; and twenty-five have served there during the last seventeen years.

[4] For *compurgation*, *vide* pp. 77-81. With regard to the accusations beginning *Dicunt* it is well to note that no priest was bound to go to his purgation unless accused by men of repute and standing : Lyndwood, 312.

sinister suspicions.[1] In 1522, Henry VIII felt it necessary to issue a proclamation against the "attempted marriages" of the clergy.[2] In it he states that such "attempts" are few, but the date of the proclamation is significant, for it was long before he assumed authority for the discipline of the Church.

We may conclude that concubinage, though by no means general was far from uncommon, that public opinion was on the whole tolerant, and that the peccant clerks were often unashamed. There is a tale that when Skelton was delated by his parishioners to the bishop as the father of a child, the poet on the following Sunday held up his naked son in the pulpit and asked, "What is wrong, for is he not as fair as the best of yours?"[3]

When a priest had a child born in his house, he was almost certainly convented in an ecclesiastical court, and condemned to an ignominious penance. He usually compounded, paying a fine, which came to be regarded as a licence, and was known in the picturesque language of the day as "a cradle crown".[4] It was not as much as "the sin rent"[5] paid by laymen who lived in mortal sin, for whereas the cleric escaped for five shillings, the layman might be mulcted in two pounds.[6]

The money was supposed to go to charity, but the satirist did not believe this, and Roy in an untruthful libel on Standish, Bishop of St. Asaph, writes:

> For whoredom and fornicacions
> He maketh many visitacions,
> His diocese to pill and polle,
> Though he be a stowte devigne,
> Yett a prest to keep a concubyne
> He then admitteth wittingly:
> So they pay their yearly tributes,
> Unto his devylishe substitutes,
> Official or Commisary.[7]

In 1529, the custom of compounding was referred to in the

[1] Wilkins, *Concilia*, iii. 696. [2] *Ibid.*

[3] Skelton, *Works*, ed. by Dyce, i. App. i. p. lxi.

[4] Cranmer, *Letters and Papers*, 37.

[5] In the Wyclifite version of the *Lay Folks' Catechism*, we read, "Froward Ordinaries and Confessors that nurse men in their sin (adultery) for annual rent . . . break cursedly this text (the vii Commandment)".

[6] Coulton, *Ten Med. Studies*, 146.

[7] "Rede me and be not wroth" in *Harl. Misc.* ix. 79.

so-called *Complaint of the Commons*,[1] and it is well to note the reply of the Ordinaries.

> We disallow the judge's doing, who taketh money for penance, for lucre or advantage, not regarding the reformation of sin as he ought to do ; but when open penance may sometimes work in certain persons more harm than good, it is commendable and allowable in that case to punish by the purse, and preserve the fame of the party ; foreseeing always the money be converted *in pios usus et eleemosynam*.[2]

The bishops might well argue that an incontinent priest who was condemned to receive six whippings in the cathedral church had much better pay a fine. The infliction of the penalty would cause scandal ; and the fustigated priest would return to his parish as an object of derision. It was the parson's freehold that made discipline difficult. An incumbent could only be deprived by a long and costly process. It was not until the reign of Henry VII that bishops obtained the right to imprison incontinent priests.[3]

No one imagines that the standard of sexual morality among the clergy was as high as it is to-day ; but it is possible to believe that the immorality has been much exaggerated. We may, for instance, pass over the dirty scurrility of Simon Fish, for he was at once contradicted by Sir Thomas More, a man of better credit and better acquainted with the clergy. We need not take too literally the declamations of friars,[4] those *clamitores in pulpitis*, as Pecock called them, for they did not love the secular clergy, and were never tired of defaming them. It is better to examine the testimony of Colet, Erasmus and More, who were all alive to the necessity of reform.

Colet was a great rhetorician, and in lecturing on the *Hierarchies of Dionysius*, cries out :

[1] Gee and Hardy, *Documents*, 145. The *Complaint* was concocted at court. Four drafts of it exist corrected in Cromwell's handwriting.

[2] *Ibid*. 163.

[3] 1 Henry VII. cap. 4.

[4] Babington, Introd. to Pecock's *Repressor*, I. xxxv. The evidence of the Friars may best be found in Owst, *Literature and Pulpit in Mediaeval Life*, Pt. II. In 1486, Convocation took alarm at the continued attacks on the secular clergy made by Friars at Paul's Cross and elsewhere ; and in consequence the Prior of St. John's and two senior members of each of the mendicant orders were summoned to St. Paul's and warned that in future clerical sinners were to be delated to the ordinary, and not gibbeted for the pleasure of merchants and apprentices (Fisher, *Hist. of England*, 133). Dr. Brewer, *Henry VIII*, i. 60, is very sceptical about the evidence supplied by poets and preachers, but I have more to say on this subject, pp. 374, 375.

O Priests ! O Priesthood ! O the detestable boldness of wicked men in this our generation ! O the abominable impiety of these miserable men, of whom this age of ours contains a great multitude, who fear not to rush from the bosom of some foul harlot into the temple of the Christ, to the altar of Christ, to the mysteries of God.[1]

No doubt Colet knew of such men, and no doubt his audience had heard of them ; but the ardent reformer was so obsessed with the wickedness of his day that he could sometimes see nothing else. He reminds one of the old-fashioned temperance advocate, who was quite sure that drink was the sole cause of all the crime, misery, disease and poverty in England, and that total abstinence would ensure a kingdom of saints. After listening to his terrifying statistics one went out into the street expecting to find every third man reeling on the verge of *delirium tremens*, and was agreeably disappointed. Drink was no doubt the curse of early Victorian England, and the immorality of some clergy was no doubt the curse of the Church in the early XVI century ; but we suspect that Colet, like the temperance advocate, was somewhat prone to exaggeration.

If Colet was hot-headed, Erasmus was cold-blooded and he took an almost malicious pleasure in exposing the sins of the clergy. Turning to his *Colloquies* we find that there is scandal about monks in *Μισόγαμος*, and about friars in *Adolescentis et Scorti*, and about monks and nuns in *Ἰχθυοφαγία*. In *Senile* there is a reference to prebendaries and their concubines, and in *Franciscani* we are told of a parson who was a sot. On the other hand in *Militis et Carthusiani* there is a good Carthusian, in *Senile* a good prebendary, while the friars in *Franciscani* are worthy of St. Francis, though they have an infusion of Erasmian common sense.

The *Colloquies* are fictitious, and so are the speakers who are made to talk according to their characters, but I imagine that the stories reflect pretty accurately the stories that might be retailed in taverns all over Europe ; and then we must remember that the standard was higher in England than elsewhere. At least Sir Thomas More thought so, when he wrote :

I wot well that the world is so wretched, that spiritual and temporal everywhere all be bad enough. God make us all better ! . . . yet as we say by our temporalty that we be as good and honest as anywhere else,

[1] Quoted Seebohm, *Oxford Reformers*, 76.

so dare I boldly say that the spiritualty of England, and especially that part in which we find most fault, that is to wit that part which we commonly call the secular clergy, is in learning and honest living well able to match number for number the spiritualty of any nation Christian.[1]

We can approach the enquiry from still another point of view. Bishop Fisher preaching on the *Penitential Psalms*, says :

All fear of God, also the contempt of God, cometh and is grounded of the clergy, for if the clergy be well and rightfully ordered, giving good example to others of virtuous living, without doubt the people by that shall have more fear of Almighty God. But contrary-wise, if the clergy live dissolutely in manner, as if they should give no account of their life past and done before, will not the lay people do the same ?[2]

This seems to be common sense, and was especially true when all belonged to the Church, and none could escape from her influence. We conclude in consequence that the bad examples of many clergy account for the low standard of moral rectitude which is evident at the beginning of the XVI century ; and also that the devotion and good examples of many priests may be assumed to account for the personal piety and parochial enthusiasm, which was also so much in evidence. During the XV century many new churches had been built, and most ancient churches had been enlarged and transformed. Charitable and devotional guilds abounded. There are known to have been 160 in London alone.[3] Books of devotion were in great demand, many laymen possessed a prymer, and " Instructions " for parish priests abounded. The wills, especially those of the moderately well-to-do, shew the interest that testators took in their parish churches, beyond a desire for the welfare of their own souls. Supported by Fisher's common sense, we may reject the paradox of Froude[4] that there was a pious and orthodox laity outraged by a dissolute and corrupt priesthood.

Sir Thomas More was probably right when he wrote that it

[1] *Dialogue*, iii. ch. 11.

[2] Fisher's *Works*, 279. Here Tyndale is at one with Fisher, and in his *Obedience of a Christian Man*, 230, uses the same argument as a reason for clerical marriage, " Chastity is an exceeding seldom gift, and unchastity perilous for that degree (Priesthood), inasmuch as the people look as well unto the living as unto the preaching, and are hurt at once if the living disagree, and fall from the faith and believe not the Word ".

[3] Kingsford, *Prejudice and Promise*, 141.

[4] Froude, *History of England*, i. 91 ff.

was easy to match the worst priest with an equally vicious layman, but impossible to find laymen who could compare with holy and righteous priests.[1] Everyone would not have agreed with More, for in the early XVI century as in our own day, there was not only a great deal of religion and religious activity, but there was a great deal of irreligion, and in London a great deal of anti-clericalism.[2] We cannot, on the other hand agree with Cardinal Gasquet, that the unpopularity of the clergy only arose four or five years before 1532, when Saint German published his *Articles on the Division of Spiritualty and Temporalty*.[3]

Saint German's book is valuable to the historian because it tells us what the laity were saying. It was mischievous at the time, because it gave currency and importance to the irresponsible chatter of agitators and lampooners in city taverns. Saint German was an old man and a very distinguished lawyer. He wrote with the gravity of a judge, and masked his prejudice by assuming the rôle of a pacifier. His book synchronised with the *Complaint of the Commons*, prepared by Cromwell and the king. More did not dare to attack the *Complaint*, but he could make fun of Saint German, and did so.

There is no reason to question Saint German's sincerity. He was one of those Englishmen who are intensely interested in ecclesiastical affairs and have a marked dislike for the clergy; who proclaim themselves loyal sons of the Church, and show their broadmindedness by patronising heretics; who think they serve their Church best by continually dwelling on her defects.

[1] *Apologye*, 92.

[2] Cardinal Gasquet's method of controversy should be noted. In his *Eve of the Reformation*, 88, he quotes two passages, one from Saint German and the other from More and concludes: " Putting one book against the other it would appear thus tolerably certain that the rise of the anticlerical spirit in England must be dated only just before the dawn of the Reformation, when the popular mind was being stirred up by the new teaching against the clergy ". This may be tolerably certain to those who do not consult the context of his quotations. Saint German only tells us, " in time past there reigned charity, meekness, concord and peace ", but assigns no date to that golden age. Sir Thomas More does not say in 1533 that anti-clericalism had only arisen in the last four or five years, but that it was only in the last four or five years that the disendowment of the clergy had been seriously considered.

[3] Saint German's *Division* has been reprinted by Taft with More's *Apologye*. It was published in 1532 and the *Apologye* a year later. Saint German replied in *Salem and Bizance*, and More wound up the controversy with his *Debellation*. The last work has a lengthy title and contains a defiance, " If the Pacifier come hither again and ten such other towns with them, embattled in such dialogues, Sir Thomas More hath undertaken to put himself in adventure, alone against them all ". Harpsfield, *Life of Sir Thomas More*, 38.

There is no need to think that he was infected by Lutheranism. He was over seventy and by nature a conservative, a *laudator temporis acti*—but Cromwell found him useful, the poor rebels of Lincolnshire denounced him, and Bale assumed that he was " an elect vessel of God ".[1] In reality, he was a common lawyer with a common lawyer's natural sympathy for those who had the misfortune to be tried in an ecclesiastical court. He wrote also with a common lawyer's caution, never asserting more than he could prove, but insinuating a great deal by his favourite formula, " Some say ". More answers tartly, " All his some says be of his own saying ".[2] He poses not as the enemy of the clergy but their friend ; and thinks it piteous that the things *some say* should get abroad ; but the retort was obvious, " If you think so, why do you print them?"[3] More had plenty of wit and was the better dialectician ; but Saint German could set out a strong case with considerable ability. If we want to know the truth about the clergy, Sir Thomas is the better guide ; but if we want to know what people in London were saying about them we must go to Saint German. He will help us to understand how so great a change as the Reformation came to pass.

VII. *The Worldliness of the Clergy*

Since the conversion of Constantine the Great there has never been a time when the Church, or at any rate many churchmen, might not be justly accused of worldliness. For the Church to be unworldly it must be persecuted, and it is after the Reformation in the reign of Elizabeth that we shall find unworldliness among persecuted Papists and despised Puritans. Regarding, therefore, worldliness as an endemic evil in the Church, any particular age must be judged by the vigorous protests it excites. In the early

[1] Christopher Saint German, 1460–1541. From Bale's *Index Britanniae Scriptorum*, 53, 54, we gather that he knew very little about him. He states, as does Fuller, *Worthies, London*, 212, that he was a bachelor, whereas he was twice married (*L. & P.* xiv. Pt. I. 1349). He says that he left nothing behind him but his books, whereas from his Will proved in 1541 he was well-to-do. He ante-dated his death by a year, while Fuller says that he died in 1593 !

[2] *Apologye*, 65.

[3] *Division*, 206 : " And verily it is a great pity that such a noise should spring and go abroad ".

Apologye, 75 : " For he, to remedy that matter with all, and to put back the noise thereof, and to stop up clearly the spring, because all should be hushed and never no words made thereof, has as ye see put it out abroad in print ".

XVI century we have the denunciations of Colet and Fisher, and in the next generation those of Latimer and Pole.

In 1486 Cardinal Morton in a Charge had condemned priests addicted to field sports, priests who wore secular clothes, who let their hair growlong, who loitered in taverns.[1] Saint German adds to this list those who played at Tables and other illicit games.[2] Under Morton there was a vigorous campaign to ensure clerical decorum ; the worst offenders were summoned before the Synod and gravely admonished, and the Archbishop published his Charge for the whole province. More,[3] who had been brought up in Morton's household, looking back on his experience, notes signs of amendment, but the incentives to worldliness were strong ; and the laity were to blame.

The higher clergy were almost bound to be men of this world rather than of another, because of the way in which the Crown exercised its patronage. The poor clergy were driven to be ladies' priests in the houses of citizens, and to supplement meagre stipends by secular business. But, according to Saint German, the squires were most to blame. They chose men for chaplains because they were " good companions " ; they insisted on their hunting and hawking ; they let them lie with their other servants, so that " they could use neither prayer nor contemplation " ; they supplied them with liveries, " not convenient in colour for a priest to wear " ; and they made them bailiffs, receivers and stewards. Then when a priest's heart " had grown cold in devotion ", his patron promoted him to a benefice, and was the first to sneer at the worldliness he had fostered and encouraged.[4]

[1] Wilkins, *Concilia*, iii. 618-620. Cp. Jenkins, " Morton's Register " in *Tudor Studies*, pp. 36 ff.

[2] *Division*, 211.

[3] *Apologye*, 77, 110.

[4] Saint German, *Division*, 218. Dudley, *Tree of Commonwealth*, addressing landowners, says, " benefices are given not to the virtuous or learned, but to such as can be good and justifiable stewards of houses and clerks of your kitchen, or to such as with good policy can survey your lands and can well increase your fines and casualties ". Barclay in his version of the *Ship of Fools*, i. 22, writes :

" That greatest foles, and fullest of lewdnesse,
Havinge least wyt and simplest science,
Are fyrst promoted : and have greatest reverence.
For if one can flatter and bere a hawk in his fyst
He shal be made Person of Honyngton or Clyst."

Honiton was then worth £40 : 4 : 2 per annum ; Clyst, £26. Bacon, *Liber Regis*, 242, 264. They were the two best livings known to Barclay while at Ottery St. Mary.

These chaplains were probably too servile, but criticism at the time was more concerned with the arrogance of the clerical estate. And here it should be noted that it is right for a priest to magnify his office ; secondly that in doing so he is tempted to magnify himself ; and whether he does the one or the other, he is likely to be condemned for insufferable pride. In the early XVI century Wolsey dominated the scene. In his arrogance he treated even the emperor as an equal, expected dukes to hold the ewer and towel while he washed, and earls to tie the latchet of his shoes.[1] His truthful servant George Cavendish had to admit that he was " the haughtiest man in all his proceedings that then lived ",[2] and Falier wrote to Venice that he desired, " not so much to be honoured as a prince as to be adored like God ".[3] In denouncing the pride of the clergy Wolsey offered a conspicuous target for the shafts of satirists. The shafts went home and the satirists went abroad. Fish and Roy escaped out of the country and Skelton took sanctuary in Westminster where he died. In popular imagination Wolsey represented the clerical estate ; and, though the clergy groaned beneath his yoke, they were bound to share his unpopularity.

This does not mean that the self-same arrogance was not to be found among the inferior clergy. Foxe, whose writing has that dramatic quality so characteristic of the time, begins one of his stories in an overcrowded Gravesend barge.

> " Dost thou know," said the priest, " who I am ? Thou sittest too near me, thou sittest on my clothes."—" No, sir," said Browne, " I know not what you are,"—" I tell thee I am a priest."—" What, sir ! Are you a parson or vicar, or a lady's chaplain ? "—" No," quoth he again, " I am a soul priest, I sing for a soul."—" Do you so, sir," quoth the other, " that is well done. I pray you sir," quoth he, " where find you the soul when you go to Mass ? "—" I cannot tell thee," said the priest.—" I pray you, where do you leave it, sir, when the Mass is done ? "—" I cannot tell thee," said the priest.—" Neither can you tell where you find it when you go to Mass, nor where you leave it when the Mass is done ; how can you then have the soul ? " said he.—" Go thy ways," said the priest, " thou art a heretic and I will be even with thee." [4]

This ridiculous dialogue is represented as the prelude to a

[1] Pollard, *Wolsey*, 318.
[2] Cavendish, *Wolsey*, 394.
[3] Quoted Gurney-Salter, *Tudor England through Venetian Eyes*, 93.
[4] Foxe, *A. & M.*, iv. 181.

tragedy in 1513. Foxe no doubt invented the conversation, but it brings vividly before us the pomposity of a stupid priest and the pertness of an ill-mannered heretic.

If arrogance provokes resentment, avarice excites contempt, but we should not be surprised if some of the clergy were justly charged with this vice. Deprived of natural relationships they turned from persons to lavish their affection upon things, or gloat over the inventory of their increasing wealth. We are told that Ruthall, Bishop of Durham, carried such an inventory about with him, and one day by mistake handed it to Henry VIII instead of a State Paper.[1] He is said to have died of chagrin, and in consequence the large benefaction which he had promised to the parish church of his native town, Cirencester, was never paid.[2]

In 1512 Colet preached his famous sermon to Convocation and denounced Covetousness as a prevailing temptation.

> O Covetousness; Paul rightly called this "the root of all evil!" For from thee comes all this piling up of benefices one on the top of the other; from *thee* come the great pensions, assigned out of many benefices resigned, from thee quarrels about tithes, about offerings; about mortuaries, about dilapidation, about ecclesiastical right and title, for which we fight as though for our very lives! O Covetousness! from *thee* come burdensome visitations of bishops: from *thee* corruptions of law courts, and those daily fresh inventions by which the poor people are harrassed; from *thee* the sauciness and insolence of officials! O Covetousness! Mother of all iniquity! from *thee* comes that eager desire on the part of ordinaries to enlarge their jurisdiction; from *thee* their foolish and mad contention to get hold of the probate of wills; from thee undue sequestrations of priests: from *thee* that superstitious observance of all those laws which are lucrative, and disregard and neglect of those who point to the correction of morals.[3]

That is an eloquent denunciation of a sin. It was addressed by a cleric to clerics, and quite naturally he insisted on clerical temptations. Colet would have been equally emphatic on the evils of covetousness had his audience been composed of courtiers, lawyers, citizens—only the instances would have been different. Covetousness was not then, any more than now, re-

[1] Ruthall, *D.N.B.*
[2] Leland, *Itinerary*, i. 129.
[3] Quoted Seebohm, *Oxford Reformers*, 235.

stricted to the clergy; and when the lawyer, Simon Fish, referred to the same points, animated by a different spirit, he was appealing as throughout his tract to those who envied the clergy and were desirous of the spoils. He writes :

> They have the tenth part of all the corn, meadow, pasture, grass, wool, colts, calves, lambs, pigs, geese and chickens. Over and besides the tenth part of every servant's wages, the tenth part of the wool, milk, honey, wax, cheese and butter. Yea, and they look so narrowly upon these profits that the poor wives must be countable to them for every tenth egg, else she getteth not her rights at Easter and shall be taken for a heretic. Hereto have they their four offering days. What money pull they in by probates of testaments, privy tithes, and by men's offerings of their pilgrimages, and at their first masses ? Every man and child that is buried must pay somewhat for masses and dirges to be sung for him, or else they will accuse the dead's friends and executors of heresy. What money get they by mortuaries, by hearing of confessions (and yet they will keep thereof no counsell), by hallowing of churches, altars, superaltars, chapels and bells, by cursing of men and absolving them again for money.[1]

This mixing up of tithes and voluntary offerings, payments for sacraments and fees paid to ecclesiastical lawyers is manifestly unfair. No doubt then as now there were clergy who insisted on their rights, but Sir Thomas More tells us that many were content to be defrauded rather than to press their claims.[2] What, however, we have especially to remember is that the majority of the clergy were miserably poor. The Church might be enormously wealthy, but the wealth was ill-distributed. It did not belong to the Church, but to a vast number of corporations within the Church. After all, the problem has not yet been solved—How ought the clergy to be paid ?

VIII. *Endowments*

Wyclif and the early Lollards had denounced all endowments and contended for the voluntary principle. Wyclif believed that all the evil in the Church could be traced back to the donation of Constantine. He quotes the tale of how an angel from heaven protested when that donation was made : " The angel said full sothe when the church was dowed, that this day is venyme shed

[1] Fish, *Supplication for Beggars*, 3.
[2] *Apologye*, 80.

into the church ".[1] Bishop Pecock replied, first, that the Church had endowments before the time of Constantine; secondly, that his donation was a fable; and thirdly, that Wyclif had his story wrong. Giraldus Cambrensis, with whom the story originated in England, said that the Devil and not an angel spoke in the air; and " Why should we believe the Father of Lesing? "[2] asks the truculent bishop.

The Lollards were not alone in denouncing endowments. Their adversaries the friars agreed with them on this point. In Gregory's *Chronicle* we read the history of the controversy that began in 1465. Henry Parker, the Carmelite, at Paul's Cross, denounced the beneficed clergy and affirmed that " Christ was a beggar and had nought but by way of alms ".[3] On the next Sunday, Dr. Ive[4] denied this and was supported by Story, afterwards Bishop of Carlisle. Then " the friars set up bills at every Church door " and the controversy waxed warm—Dr. Ive giving " full noble lessons to prove that Christ was lord of all and no beggar; and he did it after the form of the schools, for he had his habit and his pelyon, and a verger with a silver rod waiting upon him ". Alcock, doctor of law, then commissary to the Dean of St. Martin's-le-Grand, intervened and cited the Provincial of the friars to appear before the Archbishop at Lambeth, but the Prior refused to obey, claiming that his Order was exempt from episcopal jurisdiction, except for heresy. So for heresy Alcock cited him, and the Provincial, being still contumacious, was excommunicated. Then the Provincial set out

[1] Wyclif, *Dialogue*, iv. 18. Cp. Langland, *Piers Plowman*, xviii. 220, C Text:

> Whenne Constantyn of hus cortesye holykirke dowede
> With londes and leedes lordshepes and rentes,
> An angel men hurde an hih at Rome crye—
> " *Dos ecclesie* this day hath ydronke venym,
> And tho that han Petres power aren poysoned alle ".

Cp. Dante, *Inferno*, xix. 115.

> Ahi, Constantin, di quanto mal fu matre,
> non la tua conversion, ma quella dote
> che da te prese il primo ricco patre!

[2] Pecock, *Repressor*, ii. 351.

[3] Henry Parker, Carmelite, died 1470.

[4] William Ive was a doctor of Oxford and a Prebendary of St. Paul's. He wrote on scholastic themes and on the Minor Prophets. He published his dissertations on the Provincial, whose name was John Milverton—*Contra haeresim de mendicitate Christi* and *De dominio Christi*. See Bale, *Index. Brit. Script.* 129. Gairdner in *Three XV Century Chronicles*, 180, thinks that the Provincial was Dr. Thomas Halden.

for Rome, bragging of what he would do, and " men laid great wagers the Provincial would come home and do many things " ; but they lost their money, for the Pope did not support him. On the contrary, he ordered his cardinals to examine the friar, " and by his answering they found nine new points that he erred on ". So he was clapt into the Castle of St. Angelo, " for he had bound himself unto the Pope by an iron obligation, fast ysealed about his two heels ". " When he should come home " says Gregory, " I wot not, but forsooth his articles be damned. Whether he be or not, I do not know. I trust ye shall know after in time coming, by God's grace, Who have us all in His blessed keeping, Amen for charity." [1]

Gregory, who was evidently on the other side in the argument, is none the less sorry for the friar, and we may echo that " Amen for charity ". The point is worth noting, however, that the controversy was evidently a battle of texts. It took Pecock to see the practical disadvantages of a voluntary system :

> Which peril and evil would be this, that else if such stable and fixed endowing were not made to the curate, his parishioners might and would him trouble with quarrels and therein withdraw his finding, as often as he would by doing of his due cure, offend them.[2]

The voluntary principle is inconsistent with the independence of the clergy and leaves them at the mercy of the man with the purse.

Land may be the best form of endowment, but the vast estates possessed by bishops, abbeys and colleges rendered the Church most vulnerable to the attacks of her enemies. Andrea Trevisan states :

> It is computed that there are at present 96,230 of these (knights) fees ; but the English Church is in possession of 28,015 of them.[3]

This means that the Church controlled more than a fourth of the land of England, but the word " controlled " should be marked.

[1] *Collection of a London citizen* : Gregory's Chronicle, 228-232. St. Bonaventura would have agreed with Henry Parker and his Provincial. Nicholas III in 1279 issued his Bull *Exit qui seminat*, and pronounced in favour of such an opinion. John XXII, however, in 1323, by his Bull *Cum inter non nullos*, decided the question of the Poverty of Christ in a contrary way. Since then John XXII and not Nicholas III must be esteemed infallible. See Coulton, *Five Centuries of Religion*, ii. 177, 178.

[2] Pecock, *Repressor*, ii. 392.

[3] *Italian Relation of England*, 38, trans. by Miss Sneyd. Miss Sneyd attributed the *Relation* to Capello, but it is now generally attributed to Trevisan, who was in England in 1498. *Vide* Gurney-Salter, *Tudor England through Venetian Eyes*, 17.

The lord of the manor was not the same as a landlord. Before the Act of Mortmain in 1279 it had been common for lesser landowners to convey their property to some ecclesiastical body in order to escape from the incidents of feudal tenure, or to secure protection against powerful neighbours. By such arrangements the Church greatly increased its political power, without greatly increasing its revenues. These broad lands, however, provided the Reformers with a subject for denunciation, and provoked the cupidity of needy courtiers. Reformers and courtiers alike suggested to a spendthrift king that by confiscating church property he would have the means for rewarding his friends and escaping from his embarrassments.

But while the whole Church incurred the opprobrium of vast clerical estates, the ordinary rector had to be content with his glebe—usually two yardlands in the common field, from forty to sixty acres. He ploughed and reaped with his neighbours, and if he owed no service to the lord of the manor, he did owe a service to his parishioners for they depended on him to keep a bull and a boar.[1] This form of endowment may have worked well in Saxon times, but the parson had twice as much land to cultivate as the other copy-holders, and was without a family to assist him. A small farmer, over-worked, over-anxious, and over-taxed was unlikely to prove a learned or useful priest.

At the time we are considering the glebe was often let, and there were many country priests in small parishes who had very little to complain of. The memorandum of Margaret Paston [2] in 1478 when the Living of Oxnede was vacant is instructive, though we should remember that patrons are apt to overestimate the value and amenities of their advowsons. She states that the situation was convenient by a fresh river side, within two miles from Aylsham, a market town, and only six from Norwich, and ten from the sea. The church is but little though "reasonable pleasant" and in good repair. The adjoining parsonage has its "hall, chambers, barn, dove-house and all houses of office." She also says it is in good repair though we hear later that the creditors of the late incumbent had taken away the doors and windows—they were tenants' fixtures. The

[1] E. W. Watson, "The Parish" in *Dict. of Eng. Church History*, and *Camb. Med. Hist.* vi. 531, 532. The duty was sometimes disputed. See Visitations in *York Fabric Rolls*, 261.

[2] *Paston Letters*, No. 819.

dove-cote was worth 13s. 4d. a year. There are two large gardens with fruit trees worth 26s. 8d. a year. There are twenty-two acres of glebe worth 2s. an acre which she thinks might be let for £3 : 0 : 4 a year. There are tithes and altarage—making in all £10 or £200 of our money.[1]

Once when a new lord had come to the manor he had paid £23 for the corn stored in the parson's barn, but that was hardly likely to happen again. Fourteen marks would be due to the Bishop of Norwich on institution; but "iff the new parson be wytty and have favour a bowt the Bischops officers" he could arrange to spread the payment over fourteen years. It was an easy cure to kepe," for "ther are natt past XXti persons to be yerly houselyd." We may conclude that this celibate priest was well paid for the little that he had to do.

It will be seen that more than half the income was derived from tithes, for altarage must have been negligible in so small a parish: and much might be said for this form of endowment, apart from the fact that everyone in the Middle Ages supposed that tithes had scriptural authority.[2] It is true that tithes were originally only of moral obligation and could not be enforced by law. Even when they became compulsory, the tithe-payer was free to choose the cleric to whom they should be paid. However, it was natural that the landowner should pay them to the priest in the place where he lived, and by the XII century this had become so general a custom, that it came to be regarded as a right and was recognised by law. Paid by tithes, the parson shared in the prosperity of his parish and suffered like everyone else in bad years. Sometimes the farmer would try to best the priest, sometimes the priest pressed his claims unduly. Friction then ensued. There might be "a cursing for tithes" and the parish was unhappy. But it does not seem that there was any opposition to the principle involved, and we have to remember that most farmers had an uncle or a brother or a son who was a priest.[3]

[1] That is Margaret Paston's estimate. Half a century later it was valued at £9 : 1 : 5. Bacon, *Liber Regis* (690). This parish is now united with Baxton.

[2] For the origin of Tithe see E. W. Watson, *Cam. Med. Hist.* vi. 533 ff., 552. Cp. Selborne, *Ancient Facts and Fictions concerning Churches and Tithes*; Floyer, *English Church endowments*.

[3] Chaucer, Prologue—*The Plowman*:

His tythes payed he ful fair and wel,
Both of his propre swink and his catel.

Irritation only arose over the lesser tithes. A man surrendered willingly his tenth stook of corn, but lost his temper when asked for his tenth egg. Animals were generally redeemed ; and a halfpenny was accepted instead of a lamb.

Theoretically tithes should have been levied on chattels and the profits of trade, but apart from windmills and watermills this was found impracticable. Craftsmen generally compounded for a sum fixed by custom : servants and hired labourers were not in most places subject to tithes, though they were expected to pay a halfpenny to the Church four times a year.[1] At Dunstable, and probably in many towns, tradesmen were expected to make regular oblations and it was laid down that anyone who was remiss " shall offer on the eve of Easter and discharge himself thereof, as he would that the sacrament or the penance enjoined may profit him, and as he would avoid damnation at the last judgment ".[2]

If the possession of land roused envy, and the payment of tithes caused irritation, there was a perennial grumble about the payment of fees. Yet the vast number of unbeneficed priests had nothing to live on but what they received from obits, trentals and altarage. All the sacraments were sold and the whole Church in consequence could be and was accused of simony.[3] Besides there were the recognised oblations, which had begun as voluntary offerings, then hardened into customs, and finally been claimed by the clergy as rights, which could be sued for in the consistory

[1] Saint German, *Division*, 230, tells us that " in some places is claimed tithe of servants wages without deductions, and it is but in fewe places that any servanntes shall go without some tythe paying". Does this refer to the oblation of $\frac{1}{2}$d. a quarter? Myrc, *Instructions to Parish Priests*, E.E.T.S., 11, lays stress on the *custom* of different places :

After the custome of that contraye
Every man hys teythynge shale paye
Teythe of huyre and of honde
Goth by costome of the londe.

[2] Floyer, *English Church Endowments*, 99.

[3] The very orthodox *Everyman* (line 751 ff.) is clear on this abuse :

When Jesus hanged on the Cross with great smart
Then He gave, out of His blessed heart
The same sacrament in great torment :
He sold them not unto us, that Lord omnipotent.
Therefore St. Peter the apostle doth say
That Jesu's curse hath all they
Which God, their Saviour, do long and sell,
Or they for any money do take or tell.

courts. They began at birth when the parents were to find a chrisom cloth and a candle or to pay a halfpenny at the christening. Other fees varied considerably in different places, as may be seen by comparing Torksey with Bicester.

Churchings: Torksey, 2½d.—a penny from the mother and a halfpenny each from three friends.
Bicester, 1s. 0½d. to 1s. 10d.

Weddings: Torksey, 6d.—4d. for the clerk and at Mass a penny each from bride and bridegroom.
Bicester—from 2s. to 5s.

Burials: Torksey—a Mass penny and a farthing for two candles.
Bicester—¾d.[1]

Bicester seems to have been a place where you were better dead, but there were other places where the fees were much too high. In a petition of the citizens of London to Parliament in 1515 complaint is made of "two pence demanded for the two tapers at Mass; exorbitant fees for marriages, burials, month's minds; for burial in the choir; for churchings, for friends prayed for in the bede roll, for housel at Easter, for devotions on divers days; for brotherhoods kept in church, and for leases of Church lands.[2] But beyond all these the outcry against excessive mortuaries was loudest and most persistent.

Mortuaries had a long history. Originally they were a clerical "heriot", and as the lord claimed from the heirs of his vassal his best horse, so the priest claimed one of his better horses. As the lord claimed the armour which he had probably provided, so the priest claimed the bedding of the man to whom he had ministered. Even as early as Innocent III this is said to have been of immemorial custom.[3] But as feudalism declined the theory changed, the mortuary became "a corpse present" made in atonement for tithes or fees that had been withheld during life.[4] In towns the priest claimed the last garment of the deceased and the central candle upon his herse, but greedy priests claimed all the candles and did a good trade in waste wax. In London some claimed "the charette" in which the body was brought

[1] Floyer, *ut supra*, 104 ff.
[2] *L. & P.*, i. 3602. Quoted by Pollard, *Wolsey*, 41.
[3] Coulton, *Five Centuries of Religion*, ii. 79.
[4] Marti, *Economic Causes of the Reformation*, 155.

to church and the coat armour that adorned the coffin.[1] Trouble sometimes arose when a man died in one parish and belonged to another, for both priests might claim the mortuary.[2] Custom varied in different places, and the scandal caused by a few made more noise than the common practice, and so we may conclude with Saint German's admission :

> And though these abuses be not used universally (God forbid they should) for there be many good curates and other spiritual men that would not use them for the winning or losing of no earthly thing : yet when people of divers countries (counties) meet together, and one of them telleth another of some such extremities in some curates in his country and the other likewise to him : anon they esteem such covetous and extreme dealing to be in all curates.[3]

IX. *Benefit of Clergy : Sanctuaries*

It was then as now—everyone wanted the clergy to have a decent maintenance, but nobody wanted to be responsible for paying them. Objections were found to glebe, tithes, oblations and fees ; but none of them caused so much lay resentment as certain clerical privileges and immunities. Chief among them were Benefit of Clergy, Sanctuaries, the Probate of Wills, and the interference of consistory courts with the private lives of citizens. All these contributed to make the Reformation possible, although none of them came to an end with the Reformation.

The principle of clerical immunity was recognised in the laws of Cnut,[4] but it was William the Conqueror who separated the ecclesiastical from the secular courts, and warned lay judges not to meddle with bishops and clerics. From his time onwards the Canon Law was observed which decreed that :

> A clerk is not to be brought before the public courts either in a civil or criminal case, unless perhaps the bishop should not wish to decide a civil case, or unless he should in a criminal case degrade the clerk.[5]

The reason alleged is " sacerdotes a regibus honorandi sunt non judicandi ".[6]

[1] Saint German, *Salem and Bizance*, f. 2.
[2] *Ibid. Division*, 228.
[3] *Ibid. Division*, 231.
[4] H. C. Lea, *Studies in Church Hist.*, 157.
[5] *Decretum*, Pt. II. causa ix. Q. i. C. 47.
[6] *Ibid.* Pt. II. causa xi. Q. i. C. 41.

These courts were more merciful than those of the king, and in the XII century conducted on more intelligent principles. In consequence, Beket became a popular hero in championing the rights of church courts, and ensured their continuance by his martyrdom. He did not, however, obtain all that he had contended for, because criminous clerks were still indicted in the king's courts and only handed over to the bishops on proving their clergy. The rights so established were frequently violated. For instance the Council of Lambeth in 1261, complained that clerks were often seized and imprisoned by royal officials, and that secular judges outlawed clerks that refused to appear before them.[1]

Bishops could not impose the death penalty. They could only degrade from Orders and hand over the criminal to the secular power. This they were always loath to do except in cases of heresy. It was also generally impracticable because the ceremony of degradation required the presence of several bishops, and could only be performed at the place where the crime was committed. The criminous clerk was, in consequence, usually imprisoned, and it became notorious that from episcopal prisons it was not hard to escape.[2]

The time came when injured persons were unsatisfied with the justice to be obtained in ecclesiastical courts, especially as the number of people with the status of clerks increased. A clerk came to be synonymous with one who could read at any rate his " Neck Verse ", *i.e.* the first verse of the 51st psalm. As a matter of course, all schoolboys were tonsured and able to plead their clergy ; but what was to be done for schoolgirls, who could read but were debarred by sex from claiming the same privilege ? To remedy this injustice an Act was passed in the reign of Henry IV[3] whereby no woman was to suffer death for matters wherein a man might plead his clergy, while a blind man was to escape the halter if he could speak Latin " congruously ".[4] By an Act of Edward III there seem to be no limitations to the right except in the case of high treason, and even then the limitation is one of inference.[5] By a charter of Edward IV the clergy were not only secured against arrest in criminal matters, but even against

[1] H. C. Lea, *op. cit.* 187.
[2] *Ibid.* 189.
[3] 2 Henry IV, cap. 2.
[4] Lea, *ut supra,* 188.
[5] 25 Edward III, cap. 4.

civil cases under the Statute of Praemunire.[1] What had been right in a rude age had become a grievous abuse when Henry VII was king. Bacon says:

> He began, as well in wisdom as in justice, to pare the privilege of the clergy, ordaining that clerks convict should be burned in the hand: both because they might taste some corporal punishment, and that they might carry a brand of infamy. But for this good Act's sake, the King was after branded by Perkin's proclamation, for an execrable breaker of the rights of Holy Church.[2]

The Act only applied to those in minor orders; but anyone claiming to be deacon or priest was required to prove his titles. The preamble of the Act explains its necessity.

> Upon trust of privilege of the Church divers persons lettered had been the more bold to commit murder, rape, robbery, theft, and all other mischievous deeds, because they had been continually admitted to the Benefit of Clergy as oft as they did offend in any of the premises.[3]

A further limitation was made in the second year of Henry VIII when all persons in minor orders who were guilty of murder, or robbed churches or houses or on highways were deprived for the future of their privilege.[4] This was only a temporary measure and expired in 1515, just when London was excited over the alleged murder of Hunne in the Lollard's Tower of St. Paul's. In consequence of Wolsey's report on the feeling aroused on that occasion Leo X in 1516 issued a Bull in which he deplored the fact that in England so many entered into minor orders not in order that they might proceed to the priesthood, but so that they might commit infamous crimes—*ex quo improborum delicta remanent impunita, clericorum status decoloratur, ipsaque justicia non modicum impeditur.*[5] For the next five years ordination in England was only to be conferred on those who would take the five minor orders simultaneously. This was an attempt to deal with the scandal. A little later Wolsey obtained a Bull from Clement VII to allow one bishop with two abbots or dignitaries to degrade a clerk.[6] This was an attempt to simplify

[1] Collier, *Eccles. Hist.* I. 731. By this charter Miss Gabel (*Benefit of Clergy in England*, 177) thinks that Edward IV gave up all that the secular courts had gained since the time of Bracton; but that it had little effect in practice.

[2] Bacon, *Henry VII*, 64.

[3] 4 Henry VII, cap. 13.

[4] 2 Henry VIII, cap. 2.

[5] Rymer, *Foedera*, xiii. 533. Quoted Pollard, *Wolsey*, 31.

[6] Lea, *Studies in Church Hist.*, 189.

procedure. Benefit of clergy was further curtailed at the Reformation, but did not disappear altogether until 1827.[1]

When we are astonished that any State should tolerate such immunities, or that any Church should dare to justify them, we have to remember "the strayt and rygorous justice" of the criminal courts, when it was not unusual to see twenty men hanging together from one gallows, though probably most of them had only committed minor offences. When laws became too severe, evasions were connived at or even welcomed. Muddle-headed men were afraid to relax the laws lest felons should multiply; and when they multiplied they shrank from wholesale executions, and were glad to think how many escaped through benefit of clergy. In vain Sir Thomas More tried to persuade them that if stealing and murder were alike punished with death, "whiles we goe about with such cruelties to make theeves afeard, we provoke them to kil good men". In vain he insisted that the disorders of society would be better remedied by prevention than punishment.

> For great and horrible punishments be appointed for thieves, whereas such rather provision should have been made, that there were some meanes, whereby they myght get their lyving, so that no man should be dryven to this extreme necessitie, first to steale and then to dye.[2]

It was because of muddle-headedness that men acquiesced in the escape of a great number of criminals by benefit of clergy, and then attacked the Church when one of these criminals happened to be a person they wished to punish. Erasmus tells the story of the pretended alchemist who defrauded a credulous patron of large sums, but was not prosecuted because he was certain to plead his "unction", and because the injured person might be called on to support him in prison.[3]

If many escaped the gallows by pleading benefit of clergy, many also escaped by taking sanctuary. The clergy were insistent on maintaining their sanctuaries inviolate,[4] although in London they were so great a scandal that Sir Thomas More says,

[1] 7 & 8 George IV, cap. xxxviii. 6.

[2] *Utopia*, 43, 44.

[3] *Colloquia*, i. 296.

[4] In 1528 a prisoner escaped from Newgate into the neighbouring Church of the Grey Friars. The sheriff a week later "with great violence carried him back to prison". But protest was at once made, and though "they sought all ways they could to hang him", he had to be set at liberty. Palmer, *Bad Abbot of Evesham*, etc., 113.

" In good faith if they were now to begin I would not be he that should be about to make them ".[1]

There is something appealing and Christian in the thought of consecrated ground being a refuge for sinners—of salvation being granted to the worst of men who cling to the Cross.[2] The XI century story of Gualberto and the founding of Vallombrosa is well known, and in the XII century there is a somewhat similar story of a Hampshire knight told by Matthew Paris.[3] In the XV century we are told how Strensham, Abbot of Tewkesbury, came to the door of the church bearing the Host aloft, and forbade Edward IV to enter until he had promised to spare the lives of the fugitives cowering within.[4] He was not actually in time, for many had already been slain within the Church, so that it had to be ceremonially cleansed and reconsecrated three weeks later by the Bishop of Down and Connor. Neither did Edward IV keep his promise, for next day many were taken out of sanctuary and executed beyond the precincts.[5] It was not always reverence for the Cross and holy ground which prevented a sanctuary being violated, but the powers and privileges of the community who guarded it. Though all churches and churchyards were sanctuaries by consecration, Tewkesbury was not a sanctuary by royal charter or papal endorsement.[6]

It was never safe to take refuge in a parish church because it could be easily surrounded by enemies or officers of the law,[7] and they could prevent food being taken in, and did so, even though Peckham declared them excommunicate.[8] Some sanctuaries covered a wide area. At Hexham, Beverley and Ripon, they extended a mile in all directions from the churches.[9] In some sanctuaries food was provided, in some not. Ebesham, who

[1] More, *Richard III*, 28. Cp. Starkey, *England*, 140.

[2] Hallam, *Middle Ages*, iii. 302. " In the rapine and tumult of the Middle Ages the right of sanctuary might as often be a shield to innocence as an impunity to crime. We can hardly regret, in reflecting on the desolating violence which prevailed, that there should have been some green spots in the wilderness where the feeble and the persecuted could find refuge."

[3] Quoted Coulton, *Life in the Middle Ages*, i. 75.

[4] Blunt, *Tewkesbury Abbey*, 90.

[5] Leland, *Itinerary*, iv. 162.

[6] Pegge in *Archaeologia*, vol. viii.

[7] *Ibid.* See case of Hubert de Burgh.

[8] Lyndwood, *Provinciale*, 354. When Humphrey Stafford was taken from the Sanctuary of Abingdon, he pleaded before the King's Bench that the Abbey had been granted rights of asylum by a Mercian king. The judges, however, disputed the validity of the grant; and Humphrey Stafford suffered a traitor's death. Busch, *England under the Tudors*, 31.

[9] Pegge, *ut supra*.

transcribed books for Sir John Paston, wrote from Westminster, " I lie in sanctuary at great cost, and among right unreasonable askers ".[1] In taking sanctuary it was better to be a layman than a cleric, for according to Lyndwood, a bishop might withdraw a man for ecclesiastical punishment—to put him to penance or to seclude him in a monastery ; but it was very unlikely that he would do so unless the man was a clerk.[2] In the *Customall of the Cinque Ports* a clerk flying to these churches for felony was not to abjure the realm, but was to be delivered to the Ordinary and kept in the convict prison.[3] It is noteworthy, however, that in the acts dealing with sanctuary scandals there are no references to criminous clerks.[4]

In some places sanctuary could only be claimed on confessing a felony. So Walter Beket, flying from his armed enemies, entered St. John's, Cirencester, but was only received into sanctuary on confessing to the murder of a man who was in reality alive. When it became safe for him to leave the church, he had a royal pardon for the murder he had not committed.[5] The same rule apparently prevailed at Durham, for there is the case of a man who was received on confessing that he had killed a man in Shoreditch twenty-six years before.[6] He was probably more in need of free lodgings than of protection from his enemies.

We may imagine a hunted fugitive rapping the Durham knocker just in time. The door would be opened immediately by one of the monks who waited day and night in the little chamber above. Another monk would run to ring the Galilee bell which announced to the pursuers that their victim had escaped. The prior then heard the confession of his crime, and clothed him in a black cape, bearing the yellow cross of St. Cuthbert on the shoulder. For thirty-seven days he would receive food and housing at the expense of the monastery in an atmosphere of peace and prayer.[7] Afterwards he would abjure the realm, and being furnished with a crucifix, would walk by the king's highway to the port assigned to him, where he was not to tarry but one ebb

[1] *Paston Letters*, No. 596.
[2] Lyndwood, *Provinciale*, 257.
[3] *Gentlemen's Mag. Lib.: Manners and Customs*, 199.
[4] Dixon, *Ch. Hist.* i. 72.
[5] St. Clair-Baddeley, *Hist. of Cirencester*, 179.
[6] Wall, *Durham Cathedral*, 106.
[7] *Durham Rites*, ed. by Raine (1844), 36, 37 ; ed. by Fowler, 1903, 41, 42.

and flow if he might have passage. If no boat was sailing, he was to go every day into the sea up to his knees and cry, " Passage for the love of God and the king his sake ".[1] " It is not unamusing ", says Trevisan, " to hear how the women and children lament over the misfortunes of these exiles . . . saying, ' they had better have died than go out of the world ', as if England were the whole world ".[2]

Such sanctuaries caused but little scandal. At Durham between 1464 and 1534 only 331 men entered the sanctuary, or on an average less than six a year.[3] At Oxford in 1463 a tailor called John Harry took sanctuary at Broadgates Hall, which was so little used that the proctors knew nothing of its privilege.[4]

But some sanctuaries were especially privileged and could offer a permanent home to felons and debtors. Beverley and Ripon were always having trouble with their " gyrth-men ", but these were luckily not numerous.[5] St. Martin-le-Grand and Westminster, on the other hand, were vast caves of Adullam for rogues of every description. In 1457 in St. Martin-le-Grand there were :

> Misruled Persons coming and abiding in the said place, under umbre and colour of the sanctuary, the which have at divers times, issued out of the sanctuary, and committed many ryots, robberies, manslaughters and other mischiefs where through the said sanctuary hath been greatly disslandered.

These words occur in the preamble to an Ordinance of Reformation. In it it is provided :

(1) That a register shall be kept.
(2) That sanctuary men should be deprived of arms.
(3) That they shall be asked to find sureties against future misdoings.
(4) That the gates shall be shut at night.

[1] *Gentlemen's Mag. Lib.: Manners and Customs*, 199.

[2] *Italian Relation of England*, 35.

[3] Wall, *Durham*, 105.

[4] Palmer, *Bad Abbot of Evesham, etc.*, 114. For site of the Broadgates Hall on the north side of " The High ", see Maclean, *Hist. of Pembroke College, Oxford*, 29.

[5] *Ripon Act Book*, 72, 134, 151, 314. Gyrth is a variant of Grith : *N.E.D.* In Rye, 1483, the mayor, jurats and whole community tried to abolish sanctuary by the following ingenious declaration : " As holiness becometh the Lord's house, in future to the honour of God and of the glorious Virgin Mary, the parish Church of the said town, with the Churchyard and Manse of the Vicarage thereof, shall be of the same freedom, and with as much liberty as the other houses of the freemen, especially as to arrests and other matters " (*H.M.C.* v. 496. Quoted Mrs. Green, *Town Life in the XV Century*, i. 338.)

(5) That stolen goods may not be brought into the sanctuary.
(6) That those who go out to commit felony shall on their return be kept in ward.
(7) That women of ill-fame shall not be fed and clothed.
(8) That gambling be forbidden.
(9) That craftsmen and barbers being in sanctuary shall not ply their trade on Sundays.
(10) That everyone on admittance shall swear to these articles.[1]

For a few religious to maintain such a discipline among gangs of rogues was probably impossible, and we may gather that the reforms did not work from the speech which Sir Thomas More puts into the mouth of the Duke of Buckingham :

Now, unthrifts riot and run in debt ; yea, and rich men run thither with poor men's goods, there they build and there they spend and bid their creditors go whistle them. Men's wives run thither with their husbands' plate, and say that they dare not abide with their husbands for beating. Thieves bring thither their stolen goods, and then live thereon. There devise they new robberies, nightly they steal, they rob, they rive, and kill, and come again as though these places gave them not only a safeguard for the harm they have done, but a license also to do more.[2]

Henry VII obtained from Innocent VIII what Bacon calls " a very just and honourable Bull ". In future, sanctuary men who went out at night to commit mischief were to lose the right of sanctuary for ever. Secondly, the sanctuary man was only to be protected in his person ; but the property which he left outside should not be protected against his creditors. Thirdly, the king might appoint keepers to look after sanctuary men accused of high treason.[3]

His son Henry VIII went a little further, and decreed that felons and murderers who took sanctuary should be branded with an " A " on their thumb and made to abjure the realm. It was explained that abjurers might choose between foreign exile and living permanently in the sanctuary.[4]

[1] *Strype's edition of Stow*, Bk. III, 102. For the long disputes between the City of London and the Dean and Canons of St. Martin's *vide* Miss Thornley, *Tudor Studies*, 187-197.

[2] More, *Richard III*, 29. Cp. Starkey, *England*, 140. It was no new complaint as may be seen from what Langland had written long before. *Piers Plowman*, xxiii. 284, C Text.

[3] Bacon, *Henry VII*, 41. Cf. Busch, *England under the Tudors*, 272.

[4] 22 Henry VIII, cap. 14. This was probably implementing another Bull of Julius II in 1504, mentioned by Lord Herbert, *Henry VIII*, 81.

With the dissolution of the monasteries the greater number of the sanctuaries disappeared, and further legislation curtailed the immunities of those that remained ; but Whitefriars, afterwards known as Alsatia, was not finally abolished until 1697.

It may seem strange that any clergy should defend such sanctuaries as those of Westminster and St. Martin-le-Grand, but there were probably always good priests who could testify that they had known really penitent sinners within the precincts, or tradesmen who were bankrupt through no fault of their own. Others could point to a long list of political fugitives who were temporarily out of royal favour or the enemies of men in power. Even then the sanctuary of Westminster was not merely a rogues' castle. Besides, no corporate body is ever willing to surrender privileges even when they entail expense, are a cause of scandal, and impose responsibilities which it is not competent to discharge.

X. *Probate and Consistory Courts*

The probate courts also added to the unpopularity of the Church, though only lawyers derived a profit from them. That did not matter ; they were bishops' courts, and the bishops had to bear the blame for any delays or exactions. To trace the anomaly of this procedure we have to go very far back in history. Originally Saxon laws regarded the family as the unit, and did not in consequence recognise the right of the individual to dispose of his possessions by will after death. That right was derived from Roman law when ecclesiastics were the only civilians.[1] In a rude age, a testator would have had a poor chance of having his wishes observed if the Church had not taught that a will involved a sacred obligation. The Church was no doubt all the more emphatic on this as most of her own endowments were due to testamentary bequests. But in very few countries did the Church obtain the powers of probate and administration. Lyndwood admits that it was an English custom and that he did not know how it arose. Ottobon says it was granted by the approbation of the king and his barons, but he does not give the date.[2]

[1] Maine, *Ancient Law*, 173.

[2] Lyndwood, *Provinciale* (ed. 1679), 170. He refers to Ottobon's *Constitutions*, Tit. 14, but it throws no light on the matter, nor does John de Athon's Gloss : *Constitutio*, 107. Cp. Gibson, *Codex*, 572.

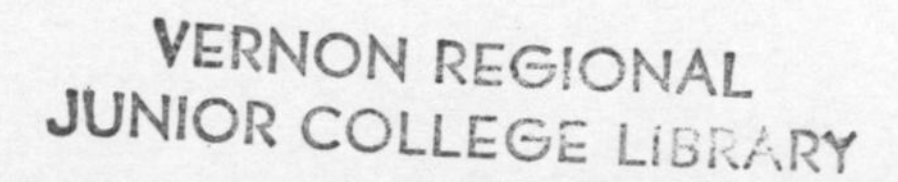

William the Conqueror, by introducing the canon law into the country, at any rate acknowledged that the bishop might compel by ecclesiastical censure the performance of a bequest *in pios usus*; and this would bring most wills within the purview of an ecclesiastical court.[1] Henry I by his coronation charter allowed the Church to distribute the goods of an intestate for the good of his soul, and this would compel an executor to prove in the bishop's court that there was a will. By the time of Henry II Glanvil could write, " If any man question a will, the plea is to be heard and determined in a Court Christian ".[2]

Difficulties, abuses and hardships almost necessarily arose. For nuncupative wills seven witnesses were necessary, and they sometimes had to travel long distances, to their great inconvenience, in order to prove the will. When the deceased had goods in more than one diocese, the will had to be proved in the Prerogative Court of Canterbury, and distances again caused inevitable delay. Inventories of the dead man's goods had to be made, exhibited and appraised. Fees had to be paid for probate, registration and letters of administration. Proctors did not plead for nothing when wills were disputed, or their interpretation was not clear. There were necessarily many officials of such courts —registrars, scribes, praisers, sumners and apparitors, who, like all bureaucrats, multiplied the forms of procedure, increasing both their work and their profits. Privy gifts also were tendered and received to expedite probate and overcome the law's delays. So we have the *Complaint of the Ploughman*:

> For who so woll prove a testament
> He shall payment make for the parchment
> The third of the money all round.[3]

This no doubt is an exaggeration, and a real ploughman, knowing that he would die with under a hundred shillings, would also know that he would be reckoned a pauper and pay nothing.[4] Legislation was passed in the reign of Edward III and Henry V to mitigate the popular grievances, but it had no effect.[5] In fact men were sometimes charged 40s. or 60s. in the reign of Henry VIII for what cost from 2s. 6d. to 5s. in the reign of Edward III.

[1] *Decretals*, c. 17. x. 3. 26. [2] Blackstone, *Commentaries*, iii. 96, 97.
[3] Wright, *Political Poems and Songs*, i. 333.
[4] Lyndwood, *Provinciale*, 170.
[5] 31 Edward III, cap. 4; 3 Henry V, cap. 8. Quoted in Gibson, *Codex*, i. 580.

In 1529 an Act was passed that sixpence should be paid on an estate under £5 and 3s. 6d. only on estates under £40. The man with £5 was no longer a pauper, but his richer brother was much relieved.[1]

It was in 1532, three years after the passing of this Act, after the *Complaint of the Commons*, and after the fall of Wolsey, that Sir Henry Guildford declared " in open Parliament and on his fidelity ", that for the probate of Sir William Compton's will he had paid to Cardinal Wolsey and Archbishop Warham a thousand marks sterling.[2] Sir William Compton, who died in 1528, had been enormously wealthy, owning estates in eighteen counties, so that the cost of probate must in any case have been heavy.[3] But the process had become more complicated because the Cardinal, as legate, had set up a testamentary court which failed to work with the Prerogative Court of Canterbury, and so sometimes executors had to pay double fees.[4] In this case Compton had nominated Warham as supervisor of his will, and Wolsey had secured the wardship of his heir. The two were at loggerheads and the lawyers had a fine time. Historians have treated the case as typical of clerical avarice, though Warham in defending the rights of his proctors stated that he himself did not benefit by a penny.[5] The costs were a record, the circumstances unprecedented. This accounts for the fact that chronicles repeat them, but the only conclusion to be drawn is that such costs were exceptional, though they might be incurred under the system of probate.

If wills were proved in ecclesiastical courts, it is also true that they were nearly always made by clerics. It was the duty of the parish priest, then as now, to admonish the sick to make their wills.[6] It was their duty, then as now, to exhort them to charitable bequests ;[7] and it is natural for a certain class of writers to suppose that they exerted undue influence for their own and the Church's benefit. Many wills were, however, nuncupative; and for their validity seven witnesses were necessary;

[1] 21 Henry VIII, cap. 5 (in Gibson).
[2] *D.N.B.* Guildford.
[3] *D.N.B.* Compton.
[4] Strype, *Memorials*, I. i. 112, explains: "The Cardinal had so disordered Wills and Testaments ". *Vide* Hook, *Archbishops*, vi. 256 ; Pollard, *Wolsey*, 193.
[5] Gee and Hardy, *Documents*, 166.
[6] B.C.P. Rubric for Visitation of the Sick.
[7] Canons of 1604, No. LXXXIV.

but it was not necessary that a priest should be one of them.[1] Many written wills have survived, and especially the wills of the moderately well-to-do.[2] They as a rule begin with the testator's profession of faith and go on to make provision for his funeral and for the Masses to be said for his soul. Before proceeding to the disposal of the bulk of his property, he often remembers the poor, those in prison, and the needs of his parish church. He is generally very specific in details, *e.g.* which image is to have a candle and for how long. Such bequests may be differently regarded. One will see in them the natural piety of the testator, and another will see the undue influence of the priest prating of purgatory.

But some will remember a colloquy of Erasmus.[3] In it is described the death of a soldier, and about his bed is the parish priest and a representative of each of the five mendicant orders. At first the friars wrangle with the priest, and then among themselves, and finally there is the will, which is replete with a ludicrous injustice such as the malign wit of Erasmus alone could devise. He also in the same colloquy describes a man who made his will when in good health ; and, when he came to die, received the rites of the Church quite quietly from his parish priest. The first story is purely farcical, but unedifying scenes faintly like it may have occurred. The second story, which is dull, relates what happened every day.

Another danger has to be noted. A testator who drew up his own will had to remember that it would be proved in an ecclesiastical court. He had in consequence to beware of rousing a suspicion of heresy. A squire named William Tracy of Toddington in Gloucestershire made his own will in 1531 and it was in due course brought to the Prerogative Court of Canterbury. It was shown to Warham, who consulted Convocation concerning its orthodoxy. After some delay the dead man was pronounced a heretic and orders were sent to Dr. Parker, Chancellor of Worcester, to cast the corpse out of consecrated ground. This

[1] Lyndwood, *Provinciale*, 179, says that in England the presence of the parish priest was not necessary as in most countries.

[2] One of the most accessible collections is the *Wills of Bury St. Edmunds*, edited by Tymms for the Camden Society. The testators are of both sexes and all classes. They all leave something *in pios usus*, and sometimes one shilling to some priest, asking for his prayers.

[3] Erasmus, *Colloquia*, ii. 54 ff. *Funus*. It should be remembered in reading this colloquy that the " religious " could not be executors. *Vide* Lyndwood, *Provinciale*, 167.

was in accordance with the law, but the Chancellor went beyond his mandate. He not only exhumed the body, but burnt it. Now, according to law, only the secular power could burn a heretic, dead or alive. In consequence the over-zealous Parker was arrested and had to pay £300, or £6000 of our money, before he could obtain a pardon from the king. The incident shows the jealousy with which the secular courts guarded their rights, however odious. It also indicates the popular hatred there was for ecclesiastical officials.[1]

Why did the ecclesiastical courts, once so popular, excite so much hatred at this time? Agitators denounced their foreign origin, but for four and a half centuries they had been naturalised. Common lawyers were jealous of them, but the development of common law was largely due to their influence. They were often notoriously corrupt; but so were the secular courts. The main reason for their unpopularity was that men resented their inquisitorial methods and interference with manners and morals.[2] The middle-class Englishman, who acknowledged that his priest had the cure of his soul, declined to admit the inference that he was himself a proper subject for discipline and correction. Again, the laity complained that in all disputes concerning tithes and mortuaries the clergy were judges in their own cause.

The ecclesiastical courts dealt with a man as a sinner to be corrected. They were not concerned with the vindication of public justice and order. If a man slandered his neighbour, they could punish the slanderer but could offer no recompense to the person slandered. Only a secular court could assess damages. The secular judge, again, could take no cognizance of perjury unless the offence was committed in his own court; the ecclesiastical court could correct anyone for false swearing anywhere with one exception—the State forbade men convicted in a secular court to sue the witnesses in a court Christian for defamation of character.[3] Again, an ecclesiastical court was only concerned with the person of the offender but not with his property,

[1] Hall, *Chronicle*, 797. Burnet, *Reformation*, i. 272, gives an inaccurate account of the incident, and does not make it better by contradictory footnotes.

[2] Stubbs, *Lectures on Med. Mod. Hist.* 315: "By its jurisdiction for correction of life, *pro salute animae*, it entered into every man's house: attempted to regulate his servants, to secure his attendance at church, to make him pay his debts, to make him observe his oaths, to make him . . . keep all the weightier matters of the law, not only judgment, mercy and truth, but faith, hope and charity also".

[3] Lyndwood, 315.

which was the concern of the State. They could only condemn him to a corporal punishment, but no royal prohibition issued, if he of his own will offered to compound for a money payment *in pios usus*. He generally did so; and, as we have seen, compounding became a scandal.[1] The greatest punishment was excommunication, and as this did not much disturb wicked and profane people, the State undertook to see that the excommunicated suffered practical inconvenience.[2] The bishop signed a *Significavit* that the man was excommunicate; and the sheriff put him in prison until the next gaol delivery. An excommunicate man could not serve on a jury or be a witness in any court; he could not sue for the recovery of lands or debt; and if he died his will could not be proved. This was logical on the mediaeval theory that Church and State were one, so that anyone cut off from the Church ceased to be within the protection of the State. The ecclesiastical judge, however, could only curse if the offence were within his legal cognizance. Otherwise an action was possible at common law, or he might be indicted at the suit of the Crown.[3]

The procedure of the court Christian had long ceased to be that of the common law. The judge was permitted to put the accused on his oath of purgation, so that if guilty he had the choice of condemning himself or of committing perjury.[4] At common law, on the other hand, a man was assumed to be innocent until he was proved guilty; and the accused could challenge the prosecution to prove its case. This had not always been so. Purgation and compurgation were of Germanic origin, and had originally been the method of procedure in both secular and ecclesiastical courts.[5] Compurgators were not jurymen, and the verdict rested with the judge. It was not until the end of the XIII century that the victory of the jury system was complete in the royal courts, and even after that compurgation held its ground in the boroughs.[6]

[1] *Vide supra*, 48.

[2] Men were excommunicated sometimes for small offences. For instance in 1521, John Redmayn and Leonard Cotten were absolved from the excommunication they had incurred by attending a synod in the Ely diocese without surplices. Wilkins, *Concilia*, iii. 693.

[3] Blackstone, *Commentaries*, iii. 102-103.

[4] *Ibid*. iii. 110. The *ex-officio* oath or oath of purgation was abolished by 13 Charles II, cap. 12.

[5] Pollock and Maitland, *Hist. of Law in England*, i. 116.

[6] Holdsworth, *Hist. of English Law*, ii. 195 and 386.

According to law, no one was allowed to go to his purgation unless he was reputed to be a credible person, and the trial had to be in the deanery where the alleged offence was committed.[1] The compurgators had to be men of the same social class as the accused,[2] so he could not produce a great man of whom the judge was afraid, or his own dependants who might be afraid of him. The ordinary might demand any number of compurgators up to twelve, according to the gravity of the offence,[3] and had the right to reject anyone whom he considered insufficiently acquainted with the accused. Something may be said for the system, for in a court of morals testimony as to character is often of the first importance, especially when there is little or no evidence beyond the assertion of the accuser and the denial of the accused. Besides, though a sinner might easily escape punishment in this world, if not in the next, by perjuring himself, it can never have been easy to persuade twelve disinterested men to perjure themselves for his sake. They lived in small communities where everything and everyone was known, and their own reputation was at stake if they supported by their oaths a notorious offender.[4]

On the other hand, there is plenty of evidence that the law was badly administered both in secular and ecclesiastical courts. In secular courts we read of corrupt judges, packed juries, and of great barons and their retainers intimidating the bench. In ecclesiastical courts there was also much that was unsatisfactory. The judge might be corrupt, and more often he was easy-going ; sometimes he was only ignorant and stupid. It is obvious that he might tender the oath in such terms that a man who was really guilty might take it without perjury ; and there was always a tendency to give the accused the benefit of the doubt. People were naturally unwilling to believe in the guilt of a popular man and ready to testify in his favour, while a plausible rogue could often persuade simple-minded people that he was innocent. I expect there were then, as to-day, amiable gentlemen who, without making many enquiries, were ready to give testimonials to those who asked for them. Anyhow, Archbishop Peckham had

[1] Lyndwood, *Provinciale*, 313.
[2] John de Athon, 57.
[3] Lyndwood, 313, 314 (*Sextae manus*).
[4] Pollock and Maitland, ii. 636, state this argument in defence of compurgation in secular courts. It is only in ecclesiastical courts that they believe the procedure to have been a farce.

to issue a solemn warning against perfunctory purgations,[1] and had to reprove the Bishop of Norwich for breaking the canon and holding trials thirty miles away from the deanery concerned with the offence.[2]

Granting all this, I do not believe that purgation in ecclesiastical courts was quite such a farce as it is represented to have been in the great work of Pollock and Maitland.[3] There is, after all, evidence that can be quoted on the other side. There is, for instance, the pitiful story of Denise Lovelich, prioress of Markyate in 1431, who was only asked to find five compurgators and failed to do so, though she went from nun to nun beseeching them to forswear themselves for her sake.[4] At any rate in that nunnery perjury was not lightly regarded.

Secondly, it would be a mistake to suppose that ordinaries were always corrupt or always fools. Bishop Hobhouse tells us of men who failed at their first purgation, but subsequently succeeded with other compurgators. He guesses that they were men of "easier conscience";[5] I guess that they were men of better repute: but, apart from guessing, it is obvious that there were ordinaries who refused to restore a man to good fame until they were satisfied with the evidence in his favour.

The real difficulty that the consistory courts had to contend with was the impossibility of getting evidence about the facts. It is probable that very few people were intentionally false witnesses; and very few regarded it as a duty to witness in a

[1] Lyndwood, 313.

[2] Coulton, *Five Centuries of Religion*, ii. 287. He also reproved him for repelling a compurgator who was poorly clad, as "though the marriage garment were needed for purgation".

[3] Pollock and Maitland, i. 145 and 445. To prove purgation a farce they quote an interesting case, ii. 395: A woman left her husband with his consent and went to live with another man, whom she married after her husband's death, and claimed her dower as a widow. The secular court refused her claim as being an adulteress, the ecclesiastical court cleared her fame on purgation. Assuming both decisions to be honest they illustrate the different mentality of men accustomed to the forum and men experienced in the confessional. From the facts disclosed any man-of-the-world would say that the presumption in favour of the secular court was overwhelming. The clerical court was more concerned with personalities. They had listened to an unlikely tale, and heard the solemn oath of the man and woman. They had examined seventeen of their friends, one of them a prioress, who knew the parties and their characters. Their decision may or may not have been a right one, but we have no evidence that the proceedings were a farce. After all, many lady housekeepers look after a widower to-day without incurring any reproach.

[4] Dr. Eileen Power, *Med. Eng. Nunneries*, 458, 459.

[5] Bishop Hobhouse, *Register of Drockensford* (Somerset Rec. Soc.), xxix.

matter with which they were not concerned.[1] Archbishop Romanus tried to obviate this by giving long notice of any trial and by inviting those who knew anything of the facts to appear; but such appeals were usually in vain.[2] This may be illustrated from the *Sede Vacante* register of Worcester.[3] One John Botiler, a clerk, was accused of many crimes and asked to be admitted to his purgation; but the court adjourned the case until proclamation had been made in the church and other places calling for witnesses. It was only because none appeared that they admitted the man to his purgation. There was a second case of Henry Waldyeve, and the same method was adopted. In his case a man appeared to swear that he believed the accused guilty of murder, and that the fact was notorious. He was, however, unable to prove notoriety; and no court could condemn anyone for murder because one man believed him guilty on hearsay evidence, and could not even produce his informer.

Miss Gabel[4] has called attention to the "overwhelming proportion of successful purgations in church courts", but this is what we should expect. Everyone was not admitted to purgation; and many who were convented found it easiest to confess, to accept penance and to compound. Those who went to their purgation either had a strong case in their favour or a reasonable hope of being restored to good fame.

In one place the system of compurgation seems to have completely broken down, and that was in the university court presided over by Gascoigne as chancellor.[5] This does not surprise me, as I have been told by more than one youthful casuist, "It can't be wrong to tell a lie, if by telling the truth you would get another boy into trouble". When the relations are those of boys and masters, of workmen and employers, or of privates and officers, it will always be a point of honour that you must not

[1] The same difficulty remains to-day. Most bishops have known of scandalous priests. Everyone in the parish says, "the Bishop ought to do something"; but not one of them will consent to give evidence against him in the consistory court.

[2] Coulton, *Five Centuries of Religion*, ii. 49. Of the 29 inquests recorded in the Register of Romanus, 16 ended in the degradation of clerics, but 10 of them were convicted on their own confessions. Miss Gabel, *Benefits of Clergy*, 105.

[3] *Worcs. Hist. Soc.: Sede Vacante Register*, Pt. II. The reader may find the facts as stated on pp. 94, 95; and what may be read into them by a prejudiced person in Mr. Willis-Bund's Introduction, p. xxviii.

[4] Miss Gabel, *Benefit of Clergy in England*, 98.

[5] *Munimenta Academica*, 536.

give your fellow away. But the university court was not an ecclesiastical court, and we ought not to condemn ecclesiastical courts because their methods were inappropriate when dealing with those *in statu pupillari*.

The ecclesiastical courts had to deal with many cases other than those involving a possible purgation. When anyone was cited to appear, by law it was necessary that the reason should be specified ; but the law was not always complied with. Then the *Actor* produced his libel and the *Reus* his defence. Both sides could call witnesses, and both could employ proctors to argue their case. There was no jury, but the judge's decision was subject to an appeal. In pronouncing sentence the judge was allowed to take into account extenuating circumstances, the notoriety of the offence, and the effect it was likely to have on the morals of the neighbourhood. Common lawyers were always ready to speak evil of the ecclesiastical lawyers, but we must allow for the rivalry between them ; and we should remember that the reputation of lawyers practising in either court did not stand very high.

Anyone who was so unfortunate as to be convented in the Court of Arches had the doubtful satisfaction of listening to much good law. He found some official principal, like Lyndwood, steeped in legal theory, knowing the decretals by heart, and having glosses without end at the tip of his tongue ; and he had to pay heavily for so much learning. In the consistory court of a diocese he would find competent canonists eager for their own promotion and equally eager for fees. In the inferior courts justice was administered more or less according to custom. Lyndwood confesses that rural deans were usually ignorant, and the officials of archdeacons only moderately learned.[1] But these gentlemen were often exceedingly active and acquired a bad reputation for avarice.

Scandals arose because judges were insufficiently paid. In the secular courts they had a miserable pittance, and had to make what they could in indirect ways. In the ecclesiastical courts they had no salaries at all and had to rely entirely on fees and presents. It was usual for both sides in a dispute to offer money to the judge, not for the perversion of justice, but only

[1] Lyndwood, *Provinciale*. For Officials of Archdeacons, 81, and for Rural Deans, 79.

for the expediting of the case. In consequence, a poor man might be compelled to hang about the court for an indefinite period, knowing that anyone with money would be heard first. Then, supposing an accused person was acquitted, he was unable to obtain his discharge until all the court fees were paid. It was an absurd injustice first to be cited by a court for an offence which you had not committed, and then to be compelled to pay the court for admitting its mistake.

The proctors in the higher ecclesiastical courts were at least on a level with the barristers practising at common law, and perhaps more often their superiors. But in the archdeacon's court they were usually chantry priests who claimed that they had read civil and canon law for three years. These men, having no clerical obligations but to say Mass once a day, were often pests in the parishes where they settled. They fomented quarrels, encouraged litigation and saw that no scandal was ever hushed up. Some of them indeed kept schools or acted as assistant curates, but too many played the part of pettifogging attorneys in the archdeacon's court.

Still more unpopular were the summoners or apparitors; attempts were made to limit their number, an archdeacon being allowed one riding apparitor and a rural dean a walking one, but Lyndwood questions if the penalties imposed for the infraction of this rule were legal.[1] They were inspectors who delated men for lechery, blasphemy, swearing and drunkenness, and it is difficult to imagine how a court dealing with morals could have gone on without them. They were currently supposed to live by blackmailing sinners, and by haling respectable people into court on trumped-up charges. The Friar of the *Canterbury Tales* says:

> that of a somnour may no good be sayd;[2]

and he was probably right, though that does not prove that they all deserved the opprobrium cast on them. Men with such duties to perform could scarcely be popular: men with an evil reputation are apt to live up to it, and the temptations to venality must have been strong. But summoners were probably as a class not so black as they were painted. The bishops and archdeacons who

[1] Archbishop Stratford in Lyndwood, 225. Note his Gloss, *Perpetuo* 226.

[2] Chaucer, Prologue to *Friar's Tale*.

licensed them were not all fools or even bad men ; and they were naturally jealous for the credit of their courts. In the *Complaint of the Commons* apparitors are said to be often "light and indiscreet persons". The ordinaries in their reply say,

> He that calleth a man *ex officio* doeth well. He that calleth one for pleasure and vexation doeth evil. Summoners should be honest men. If they offend in their office they should be punished.[1]

So they justify the office and are non-committal about the persons.

Warham had begun life by practising in the Court of Arches and knew the need of reform. When he became Archbishop of Canterbury he set about the work.[2] He limited the number of proctors and revised their fees. He appointed proctors to plead the cause of the poor gratuitously. He tried, apparently in vain, to expedite procedure. He stretched his powers as Metropolitan to draw all business to his reformed court. He stretched his powers as *Legatus Natus* to make appeals to Rome wellnigh impossible. He had all the bishops in arms against him for infringing their jurisdictions.

Twenty years later Wolsey was equally impressed with the need of reform in the ecclesiastical courts, but he insisted on undertaking it himself. He established his legatine court at Westminster in an attempt to supersede the existing courts. To begin with, he made an agreement with Warham much in his own favour ; but he did not abide by it, and the *Legatus Natus* and the *Legatus a Latere* were soon at variance, with the result that there was confusion worse confounded.

After the fall of Wolsey, and in Warham's extreme old age, the diocesan courts awoke to a really mischievous activity. The irritation they occasioned finds expression in the *Complaint of the Commons* ; but the Reformation that was then beginning did very little to restrict their powers ; because the courts, notwithstanding their abuses, ministered to real needs, and safeguarded such morals as society on the whole approved.

XI. *The Case of Richard Hunne*

It will be evident from what has been written that the ecclesiastical machinery was not working smoothly and that there were

[1] Gee and Hardy, *Documents*, 147, 161.

[2] Wilkins, *Concilia*, iii. 650.

people who believed that it might be scrapped. The Hunne case in 1515 reveals by a lightning-flash the dangers that threatened the old order, and how inflammable was the structure of the Church.[1]

Richard Hunne was a well-to-do merchant tailor, and a freeman of the City of London. Sir Thomas More commends his " worldly conversation ", and admits that he was " a fayre dealer among hys neighbours ". He had already been in trouble for heresy, hated priests, and was of a litigious disposition. More says he was " highe mynded and set on the glorie of victorie ". He hoped that long after his days men would speak of the Hunne case, and that hope has been more than fulfilled.

In 1514 his baby died and was buried by Thomas Dryfield, priest of St. Mary Matfellon, Whitechapel, who claimed the bearing-cloth as a mortuary. This Hunne refused on the ground that the infant had no property in the cloth. Dryfield sued him in the consistory court and won his case : Hunne sued Dryfield in the King's Bench as guilty of a *praemunire* in haling him before " a foreign tribunal ". The ecclesiastical authorities then arrested Hunne for heresy. His house was searched, forbidden books with marginal notes were discovered : he was examined by Fitzjames, Bishop of London, at Fulham and committed to the Lollard's Tower at St. Paul's. On Monday, December 4th, he was found dead, hanging from the wall of his prison, and the question immediately arose, Was it murder or suicide ? The populace had no doubt about the correct answer.

On December 5th the Coroner, William Barnwell, impanelled a jury who were " ryght honest men " according to Sir Thomas More, but " perjured caitiffs " according to Fitzjames. We may agree with More and yet remember that they were not insensitive to the popular excitement. After sitting for two days[2]

[1] Miss Jeffries Davis has discovered the tract which Hall largely incorporated in his Chronicle, 573-576, and from which Foxe, iv. 183-198, drew up his account which reads as an indictment. It cannot be earlier than 1536 because it mentions Tyndale's death, and was probably compiled more than twenty years after Hunne's death. More's *Dialogue*, Bk. III. ch. xv., and Tyndale in his *Reply*, discuss the case and there are comments on it in Fish, *Supplication of Beggars*. Burnet, *Reformation*, i. 38, derived some details from Keilway's Reports; but a fresh discussion began with Gairdner. *Ch. Hist*. ch. 3, who contributed an acute criticism of Hall. Miss Jeffries Davis published some fresh facts in *V.C.H. London*, i. 236, 318, and many more in E.H.R., July 1915. Lastly Professor Pollard, *Wolsey*, 31 ff., has to some extent criticised the critics.

[2] The inquest lasted two days, Dec. 5th and 6th, and the finding is dated the

they found that Hunne had been murdered and brought in a true bill against Dr. Horsey, Chancellor of the Diocese,[1] and two of his servants, Charles Joseph and John Spalding the bell-ringer.

On the following Sunday, December 10th, the Church took action and the heresies of Hunne were published at Paul's Cross. This was followed on December 16th by a court presided over by Fitzjames, with the bishops of Durham and Lincoln and twenty-five canonists as assessors. They pronounced Hunne a heretic and handed his body over to the secular power, who in accordance with law burnt it in Smithfield on December 20th. Sir Thomas More, then under-sheriff, was present at the trial and convinced of Hunne's heresies, but the man-in-the-street only said that the heresies would never have been heard of but for his action under the Praemunire Act.[2]

The excitement grew, the scandal was magnified, and fresh witnesses were found. Some of them had something material to say, but some of them only remembered what somebody else had said. At length Charles Joseph, who had hidden himself at Good Easter, was brought to the Tower and there confessed that he and Spalding had murdered Hunne by the orders of Horsey. This confession was extorted " by payne and durance ", wrote Fitzjames. It was made of his own free will, said the Constable of the Tower, and we may accept the latter statement as literally true if it means that torture was not applied, while sympathising with Fitzjames, who knew how the interrogation of prisoners was usually conducted.

Fitzjames then wrote to Wolsey asking him to intervene for " if my Chancellor be tryed by any XII men in London, they be

6th day : Hall, 579. Fresh evidence was subsequently obtained through the intervention of the Council, a body growing in importance with undefined powers. The suggestion of Professor Pollard, *Wolsey*, 38, that the inquest lasted two months is contrary to the evidence.

[1] According to Le Neve, *Fasti*, 187, Horsey was Archdeacon of London 1513–1514, and p. 200 Precentor of St. Paul's, 1514, void on the promotion of Wolsey. He was presented by the king. " The word Chancellor, though mentioned in the Statutes of Elizabeth, in the Canons of 1603, and in several modern statutes, is not mentioned, as Bishop Gibson observes, in the Commission, and but rarely in our ancient records ; but seems to have grown into use in imitation of the like title in the state, inasmuch as the proper office of a chancellor, as such, was to be keeper of the seals of the archbishop or bishop, as appears from divers entries in the registry of the Archbishop of Canterbury ". Phillimore, *Eccles. Law*, 928.

[2] So Wriothesley, *Chronicle*, 9, says : " He was made a heretic for suing a Praemunire ".

so maliciously set *in favorem heretice pravitatis*, that they will cast and condempne any clerk, though he were as innocent as Abell ".[1] This letter somehow got abroad and was much resented by the City Corporation, who sent their recorder, common clerk and four aldermen to " speke wt. the Bishop of London for certyn perillous and haynous wordes as bene surmised by hym to be spoken of the hole body of the citie touchying heresy specified in a copy of a letter supposed to be wreten by the seyd Bysshope ".[2]

Fitzjames had completely lost his temper, and behaved in a most injudicious manner. On Sunday, February 4th, 1514–1515, the day before the opening of Parliament, he appointed Richard Kidderminster, Abbot of Winchcombe, to preach at Paul's Cross, and the abbot delivered an impassioned harangue on the immunity of clerks from secular tribunals. He had recently returned from Rome bringing with him a Bull of Leo X which declared that both by human and by divine law laymen had no power over ecclesiastics. Such a sermon at such a time provoked an uproar in the city, and was severely censured by Parliament during the following week. Representations were made to the king, who consented to a debate in his presence at Blackfriars on March 10th. Before that took place, on March 3rd, a Bill was introduced into Parliament for the restitution of Hunne's property to his children.[3] Fitzjames opposed it furiously as a Bill intended to whitewash the coroner's jury and cast discredit on his own court. He declared that heresy was so rife that " I dare not kepe myne owne house for heretiques ". This was an exaggeration, but Polydore Vergil wrote to Cardinal Hadrian di Castello that " the people were exclaiming and would be raging against the Clergy were not the king appeasing their fury ".[4]

On March 10th the debate took place at Blackfriars on the

[1] Miss Jeffries Davis in E.H.R. points out that the Tract itself reads " my clerk ", and that Hall substituted " any clerk ".

[2] E.H.R., July 1915, p. 475.

[3] Pollard, *Wolsey*, 39, points out that a heretic's property passed to the king's Almoner. As the Crown was interested in the money no Bill concerning it could be introduced into Parliament without the royal consent. Hence the king's signature and Foxe's misrepresentation of its significance, *A. & M.* iv. 196.

[4] *L. & P.* ii. 215. The summary is unsatisfactory. Miss Jeffries Davis quotes the original words, E.H.R. 478 : " Nunc propter unum hereticum nuper a londiniense episcopo poena mortis affectum populo passim in clerum reclamante, et jam jam saeviente, nisi Majestas Regia furorem compesceret ".

privilegium fori claimed by the clergy. Henry Standish, a friar-observant of Greenwich, conducted the case for the Crown and argued that for 300 years clerics had been tried in the king's courts. Kidderminster replied, "there was a decree of the Church expressly to the contrary, to which all ought to pay obedience under pain of mortal sin ; and that therefore the trying of clerks in the civil courts was a sin in itself". To this Standish replied, "God forbid that all decrees of the Church should bind. It seems the Bishops think not so, for there is a decree that they should abide in their Cathedrals all the festivals of the year, yet the greater part of them do it not." He then developed his argument that no decree of the Church could have any force in England until it had been received there. To this there was no reply ; but an ignorant supporter of Kidderminster fell back on his text, *Nolite tangere meos christos*, and attributed the words to our Saviour—so laying himself open to a crushing rejoinder.

The result was that Standish became the most popular man in London. The City Fathers showed their gratitude to him by repaving the church of the Greyfriars,[1] and Parliament became so troublesome that it was prorogued until November.[2] Standish utilised the interval by delivering lectures in which he maintained his theses, and Warham in summoning convocation referred to certain matters *in grave damnum et praejudicium ecclesiae universalis*.[3] After that we are not surprised that when Convocation met, Standish was summoned to answer four questions :

(1) Can a secular court convent clergy before it ?
(2) Are minor orders holy or not ?
(3) Does a constitution ordained by Pope and clergy bind a country whose use is to the contrary ?
(4) Can a temporal ruler restrain a bishop ? [4]

Such questions contained dangerous pitfalls in whichever sense they were determined, and Standish was well advised in seeking the king's protection, for " what can one poor friar do against all the bishops and clergy ? "

This led to a second debate at Blackfriars to which bishops,

[1] Miss Jeffries Davis, *V.C.H. London*, i. 238.
[2] *L. & P.* ii. 1312.
[3] Wilkin's *Concilia*, iii. 658.
[4] Pollard, *Wolsey*, 47.

judges and the learned were invited. Here Standish denied that he had ever taught that

> of the whole body of the *Decretum*, only so much as a man could hold in his fist, and no more, did oblige Christians.

On the other hand he maintained his two theses—

> (1) That the exemption of clerks was not of divine right, and
> (2) That no positive ecclesiastical law binds any but those who receive it.

He was supported by Dr. Veysey, afterwards Bishop of Exeter, who illustrated the second point by referring to clerical marriage. Secular priests at one time could marry. That they could not do so now was due to a decree that had been received in England. The Greeks had not received that decree and no one condemned them for not being celibates. Therefore the conventing of clerks could be justified, notwithstanding a decree to the contrary, because that decree had never been received in England. Then the judges declared that Convocation in citing Standish was in their opinion guilty of *praemunire*. After which ominous suggestion the conference broke up.

A fuller assembly of notables shortly afterwards took place at Baynards Castle when Wolsey, kneeling before the king, disclaimed on behalf of the clergy any intention to derogate from his prerogative, but implored him to remember his coronation oath and defend the rights of the Church. Archbishop Warham, mindful of his predecessor St. Thomas, said that saints had suffered martyrdom in this quarrel; and Fineux, Lord Chief Justice, replied that many holy kings and holy fathers had submitted to this law which they would not have done had it been contrary to the law of God. A suggestion was then made that the question should be referred to the Pope, but it was not even entertained. It rested with the king to give judgment, and he is reported to have done so in these words: [1]

> By the permission and ordinance of God we are King of England, and the kings of England in times past had never any superior, but God only. Therefore know you that we will maintain the rights of our

[1] Burnet, *Hist. of Ref.*, i. 46. In a slightly shortened form in Gairdner, *Lollardy and the Reformation*, *i.* 281. Stubbs, *Lectures Med. and Mod. Hist.*, 318, has some hesitation. He writes: "Whether that was really said or put into his mouth afterwards, I cannot say, but certainly no scheme of change in the relation between Church and State was set on foot for nearly seventeen years".

crown, and of our temporal jurisdiction as well in this, as in all other points, in as ample a manner as any of our progenitors have done before our time, and as for your decrees, we are well assured that you of our spirituality go expressly against the words of divers of them, as hath been shown by some of our Council: and you interpret your decrees at your pleasure, but we will not agree to them more than our progenitors have done in former times.

The unfortunate Horsey had almost been forgotten through the controversies which had arisen in attempting to save him. He had been living all these months in the Archbishop's house, nominally a prisoner, knowing that if he were brought to trial no jury would dare to pronounce him "Not guilty". Henry, however, knew that the clergy were united in his favour, and, notwithstanding his great swelling words, it was not yet his policy to provoke their opposition. So yet another conference was held at Baynards Castle to review the evidence and examine the witnesses concerned in the case. Sir Thomas More, who was present, tells us that he knew the whole business "from top to toe", and he gives an amusing account of some of the witnesses and of how they broke down under cross-examination. Tyndale,[1] who was not there and had no first-hand knowledge of the matter, is content to criticise the spirit of More's pleasantries. More, however, never grapples with the evidence reported by Hall. Perhaps to have done so would have been unprofessional conduct; but he knew what the evidence was, and his judgment is all the more valuable because he had no prejudice in favour of Fitzjames and his *entourage*. We may not be so sure as More was that Hunne committed suicide, and yet there is no real evidence against Horsey on record, apart from the confession of Charles Joseph in the Tower; and he had before told two tales which cannot be reconciled. Nor was there any conceivable reason for Horsey to murder the man when he had already sufficient evidence to send him to the stake.

Apart from More's anecdotes we do not know what took place at this last meeting at Baynards Castle, but Parliament still continued to be active against the clergy, and Convocation was fully alive to the terror of the king's words. Convocation was dissolved on December 21st, and Parliament on the following day. Nothing could be done while either body was sitting.

[1] Tyndale, *Answer to More*, 166, 167.

Convocation, however, tendered to the king an apology for its attitude, and withdrew from its attack on Standish. Then Horsey was brought to trial in the king's court and pleaded "Not guilty". On that the Attorney-General declared that there was no case to go to the jury. Horsey was saved after all, and so was the royal prerogative. But it cost Horsey £300 (£12,000 of our money) and he resigned most of his positions in the London diocese,[1] but was partly compensated for these losses by preferment elsewhere, which enabled Fish to insinuate that he had secured the rewards of iniquity.[2]

So the Hunne case came to an end, and what had begun with a dispute about a mortuary worth at the most 2s. 6d. led to a declaration of the royal supremacy. Mortuaries were in consequence abolished and benefit of clergy curtailed. What Maitland [3] calls "the border warfare" which had been going on for centuries between the ecclesiastical and civil courts almost developed into a decisive campaign. An appeal to the Pope was disregarded and the obligation of the canon law as decreed by the Pope was called in question. Clerical celibacy was shown to depend on positive law alone, and there were grim mutterings about the possibilities of *praemunire*. Hunne had wished his case to be famous, and it was. We learn from it the spirit of the time, and find in it a fitting prelude for the study of the Reformation.

[1] According to Le Neve, *Fasti*, 200, he did not resign the Precentorship of St. Paul's until 1531.

[2] *Supplication for Beggars*.

[3] Maitland, *Const. Hist.*, 506.

CHAPTER III

THE POPULAR RELIGION

I. *The Devout English*

MANY years ago a contributor to the *Dublin Review* wrote about the XV century : " This epoch was an eclipse—a very Egyptian darkness ; worse than Chaos or Erebus—black as the thick preternatural night under which Our Lord was crucified ".[1] Had this statement been true it would have been easy to account for the Reformation. It is false, and the Reformation has still to be explained. In the last chapter it became clear that there were many scandals in the clerical estate, but that the clergy were by no means so black as they have sometimes been painted. In this chapter it should become clear how, in spite of wickedness and superstition, there was a popular religion—real, sincere and active. There have never been any good old times ; but in reviewing the past it is possible to overestimate our superior enlightenment.

Foreigners regarded the English as a very devout nation. A Venetian[2] in 1513 wrote that the English army had gone to France not to rob but to gain honour, that they had no women camp followers, were not profane swearers, and for the most part recited the daily office and rosary. This perhaps somewhat overtaxes our credulity, and we may suspect that the writer obtained his information from some young archer's pious and patriotic maiden aunt. On the other hand, Trevisan, another

[1] *Dublin Review*, xliv. 49. So Hardwick, *Hist. of the Articles*, 1, quotes from Bellarmine (Opera vi. 206) : " According to the testimony of those who were then alive, there was almost an entire abandonment of equity in the ecclesiastical judgments ; in morals no discipline, in sacred literature no erudition, in divine things no reverence : religion was almost extinct ". This rhetorical statement applies only to Italy and may be compared with similar statements about the Church of England in 1820. Machiavelli, *Discorsi*, I. xii., wrote : " We Italians are more irreligious and corrupt than others . . . because the Church and her representatives set us the worst examples ".

[2] Gurney Salter, *Tudor England through Venetian Eyes*, 114. Compare this statement with Hall's account of the Adventurers, 646, 686.

Venetian who wrote in 1497, was evidently an acute observer and retails his first-hand impressions. He was unprejudiced and much amused by English manners and self-sufficiency. This is what he reports about English religion : [1]

> They all attend Mass every day and say many Paternosters in public—the women carrying long rosaries in their hands, and any who can read taking the Office of Our Lady with them, and with some companion reciting it in church, verse by verse, in a low voice after the manner of churchmen. They always hear Mass every Sunday in their parish church, and give liberal alms, because they may not offer less than a piece of money, of which fourteen are equivalent to a golden ducat ; [2] nor do they omit any form incumbent on good Christians ; there are, however, many who have various opinions concerning religion.

The last clause suggests the first comment. Englishmen, so orthodox in practice, were nevertheless ready to discuss their beliefs in the presence of a foreigner ; and when the time came it was not difficult for Reformers to obtain a hearing. Religion in England had never been thought of as a subject on which priests spoke while laymen bowed their heads in unquestioning acquiescence. Trevisan, moreover, unconsciously points to the dominating ideals which were to determine the history of English religion for four centuries—the ideal of a uniform worship and the ideal of freedom of thought.

Coming from a land where some were priest-ridden and many in scornful revolt, it puzzled him to find men, so careful in religious observances, discussing religious questions with freedom. Attached as he was to an embassy, the people he was most likely to meet belonged to the upper classes. They were men of the world and not altogether unlike their descendants ; that is, they were always careful to do the right thing and punctiliously conventional, while reserving the right to grumble, to question the necessity of the duties they performed, and to express opinions at variance with their conduct. They were like the church-going Englishmen of the mid-Victorian age, who did

[1] *Italian Relation*, 23.

[2] Ducat = 3s. 6d. Therefore the coin intended would be a threepenny piece. This is an exaggeration. Trevisan was anticipating the XX century. The XV-century Englishman infrequently offered a Mass penny. From the *Northumberland Household Book*, 303, we find that the Earl offered 1s. or 3d., according to the occasion ; his eldest son 4d. or 2d. ; his younger children 2d. or 1d.

not profess to be religious and yet believed that there was a God and that they had a duty towards Him. So when Sunday came, reluctantly they put on their best clothes and went to Church. They did not perhaps enter into the meaning of the prayers, and they sat out the sermon in a spirit of resignation. They certainly did not offer up their service with joy and thanksgiving, but their service had this merit—it was an act of homage to the Majesty of God.

Passing from the formalists to the superstitious, Erasmus tells us, " There are some who cannot believe themselves to be Christians unless they hear Mass every day " : and the boy to whom he is talking replies, " It is only because they think it unlucky not to do so ".[1] Little prigs have made similar remarks since the world was young, and elderly prigs have applauded their penetration ; but it is not so easy to determine where the fear of the Lord ceases to be the beginning of wisdom and becomes the superstition of the servile. Cranmer scoffed at those who " run from altar to altar, and from sacring, as they call it, to sacring, peeping, tooting and gazing at that thing which the priest held up in his hand . . . and saying, ' This day have I seen my Maker ', and ' I can not be quiet except I see my Maker once a day ' ".[2] Some men, no doubt, talked like this and Cranmer heard them ; but it is well to remember that controversialists are apt to attribute to all their opponents what has been said by the silliest of them. Many, we may be sure, came to Mass seeking for Jesus and found peace in His Presence. Many, we are told, believed that by assisting at Mass they were insured against accidents and sudden death that day.[3] A Protestant pastor may murmur " magic " ; but the same pastor has quite rightly told his son that unless he says his prayers in the morning he cannot expect God's protection during the day ; and the boy may have said his prayers with a like " magical " intent. We then ask the further question : Is magic in either case the right word ?

All great men kept chaplains in their houses. Henry VIII, wrote Guistiniani,[4] " hears three Masses daily when he hunts, and sometimes five on other days, he hears the Office every day

[1] Erasmus, *Colloquia : Pietas Puerilis*.
[2] Cranmer, *On the Supper*, Parker Society, 219.
[3] Myrc, *Instructions to Parish Priests*, 10.
[4] Guistiniani, *Relazione*, quoted by Brewer, *Henry VIII*, 9.

in the Queen's chamber ; that is to say vespers and compline ". His devout grandmother heard six Masses every day.[1] The chaplains had sometimes to wait on their lord's convenience. Cavendish tells us how on one occasion Wolsey " rose early, about four of the clock, sitting down to write letters into England commanding one of his chaplains to prepare him to Mass ", which Mass he did not hear until four in the afternoon : after which he said his office, walked in the garden, and had dinner and supper together.[2] This was due to the pressure of State business during an embassy, but the Knight of La Tour Landry found it necessary to tell two stories of tardy worshippers—one of a knight and his lady who lay so long in bed that the parish were deprived of their Mass as the priest did not dare to begin without them—another of a great lady who took so long in arraying herself that the waiting congregation called down a curse upon her head.[3] In both cases suitable retribution followed, for the Middle Ages loved cautionary tales.

With regard to behaviour in church it would be wrong to expect that XV century people conformed to the present standard, of English decorum.[4] It would be equally wrong to suppose that the satire and denunciation of foreign preachers were applicable to England. Even to-day there is a different standard of religious behaviour in London and in Naples. In the XV century congregational worship was exceptional. While Mass was being celebrated men might be in church who were not assisting at it, and they were probably not very considerate for those who were, but behaved as tourists often do to-day in a foreign cathedral. In the XV century we are told of people who remained in the churchyard until the sanctus bell rang, and then rushed to the windows or jostled in at the door that they might see the elevation of the Host.[5] The clergy condemned them as they condemn now the village boys in their Sunday clothes, who worship on

[1] Cooper, *Margaret Beaufort*, 75, 76.

[2] Cavendish, *Wolsey* (Singers' ed.), 175.

[3] *The Book of La Tour Landry*, 68, 71. The early translation of this book, which was edited by Wright for E.E.T.S., is preferable to the version of Caxton, 1484. Robert of Brunne, *Handlynge Synne*, 135, also tells of a rich man lying in bed when the bell rang to church, enjoying " the merry morning sleep ".

[4] For a description of bad behaviour in church, see Barclay's version of Brandt's *Narrenschiff*, i. 221.

[5] *Vertue of the Mass*, stanza 4. Quoted by Simmons, *Lay Folks' Mass Book*, 163. Lydgate insists that those attending Mass should be there at the beginning, and not leave until after the last Gospel.

the churchyard wall for the greater part of the service. In the XV century those assisting at Mass were told to kneel except at the Gospel and the Creed, and the custom has continued after the Reformation. No other Church in Christendom asks worshippers to be so long upon their knees. John Myrc says : [1]

> No one in church standé shall,
> Nor lean to pillar nor to wall,
> But fair on knees they shall them set
> Kneeling down upon the flette (floor).
> And pray to God with heart so meek,
> To give them grace and mercy eke.

The *Lay Folks' Mass Book* [2] instructs

> That thou shalt good tent take
> At the Mass no jangling make.

While in *The Manner and Mede of the Mass* we are told the story of how St. Augustine saw the Devil writing down all the gossip told by certain jangling wives at Mass, and the moral comes :

> Till a Mass was said to end
> No man should talk with foe or friend
> But hold him as a stone.
> That house was made for prayer
> To Jesu and His Mother dear,
> To thank them all alone.[3]

It would be absurd to suppose that everyone at all times observed these pious precepts. It is also absurd to suppose that they were generally disregarded. When everyone went to Church, sinners as well as saints, it was perhaps more necessary than it is to-day for preachers to denounce irreverent behaviour.

In the XV century everyone assisted at Mass, but it was an age of infrequent communions. The lay brothers of the Order of Sempringham communicated eight times in the year and the third Order of St. Dominic three times ; [4] but most men were never houselled except at Easter ; and Margaret Beaufort, who

[1] Myrc, *Instructions to Parish Priests*, 9.
[2] *Lay Folks' Mass Book*, 5.
[3] *Ibid.* 138. Quoted from Vernon MS. The *Book of La Tour Landry* tells the same story of St. Martin.
[4] Dalgairns, *Holy Communion*, 222.

received the Blessed Sacrament once a month, excited wonder.[1] This infrequency was not due to the theologians. St. Thomas Aquinas had concluded, " Though it be not useful for all men to approach this sacrament daily, a man may come as often as he finds himself prepared for it " ;[2] and St. Bonaventura had written of frequent communion with a balanced judgment backed by considerable historical knowledge.[3] Law and custom are, however, more potent in determining practice than the arguments of theologians. When the Fourth Lateran Council in 1215 decreed that no one should approach the altar unless he had been shriven, they were acting no doubt out of reverence for the Blessed Sacrament, and with fear for the souls of unworthy communicants. When they decreed that everyone should partake at Easter, they only intended to fix the barest minimum ; but the world largely nullified the rules proposed for its betterment by accepting the minimum requirements as the normal practice, and went to confession and communion only once a year. Then, since they were usually communicated outside the service, the intention of our Lord was in danger of being obscured and forgotten. The culmination of the service was the communion of the priest, and the people thought of the Mass as something offered for them, rather than as an offering in which they shared.

Churchmen, however, remained fully alive to the social significance of the Sacrament, and failing to secure it in the appointed way by the communion of the faithful, emphasised customs like the kissing of the pax and the distribution of the holy loaf.

Originally the faithful kissed one another before communicating, but when this was thought unseemly a tablet of wood, metal, ivory or glass was substituted and passed round to be kissed while the priest made his communion.[4] The ceremony originated in England in the first half of the XIII century and spread to the Continent.[5] Its intention was obvious, " for ", as the *Myrour of Our Lady* says, " the sacrament cannot worthily

[1] Fisher, *Mourninges Remembrance*, Baker's edition, 13.

[2] Aquinas, *Summa*, III. q. lxxxi., a. 10.

[3] St. Bonaventura on the Sentences, IV. i. 2. See the quotations in Darwell Stone, *Hist. of the Eucharist*, i. 336.

[4] Scudamore, *Notitia Eucharistica*, 496-504.

[5] Dearmer, *Booklet of the Mass* (Alcuin Club), 115. Cp. Scudamore, *op. cit.* 890. The earliest mention of it is in 1236 when St. Edmund Rich orders that the kiss of peace and bread blessed in the Church must be refused to the concubines of priests.

be received but in peace and charity, for His dwelling is peace "[1] while Lydgate in his *Vertue of the Masse* says:

> The people of low and high degree
> Kiss the Pax, a token of unity.[2]

Becon sneered at the practice and misrepresented its intention:[3] but the Visitors of Henry VIII in issuing injunctions for the deanery of Doncaster, recognised the ceremony and charged the clerk presenting the pax to say: "This is a token of joyful peace, which is betwixt God and men's conscience: Christ alone is the Peacemaker, which straightly commands peace between brother and brother".[4]

The ceremony was beautiful and appropriate, but by the malice of the Devil this emblem of peace became a source of discord, and the kiss of charity an assertion of pre-eminence. Even in Chaucer's day the proud man wished "to kiss the pax and be censed "[5] before his neighbour. Sir Thomas More tells us "how men fall at variance for kissing of the pax".[6] In 1496 a woman was presented to the Archdeacon of Middlesex for throwing the pax on the floor because another woman had been allowed to kiss it first.[7] In England at the Reformation the custom was abolished.[8]

It has been suggested that in the Holy Loaf we have a survival of the Agape, but this is unlikely. Its intention, however, was that of the Agape—it was to emphasise the social character of the religious community. The Holy Loaf[9] was censed and blessed before it was cut up and distributed to the people after Mass. Some took it home to sick friends. It was not a sacrament,

[1] *Myrour of Our Lady*, 331.

[2] Lydgate, *Vertue of the Mass*, fol. 185.

[3] Becon, *Works*, ii. 279.

[4] Burnet, *Reformation*, v. 186. I think Burnet is right in ii. 123, in attributing these injunctions to the later years of Henry VIII. Collier, *Ch. Hist.* ii. 242, and Cardwell, *Documentary Annals*, i. 56, date them 1548, being misled by the place in which Burnet inserted the document. Burnet found it in the Johnstone Collections. It is now lost.

[5] Chaucer, *Personne's Tale*, Pt. iii.

[6] More, *Works*, *Novissima*, p. 88.

[7] Hale, *Precedents*, 192.

[8] For Flemish customs as regards the pax see Huizinga, *Waning of the Middle Ages*, 37. Le Brun, *Explication de la Messe*, 610, writing at the beginning of the XVIII century, says that the ceremony had been discontinued in most places in France, because of the quarrels to which it gave rise.

[9] For the history of the Holy Loaf see Scudamore, *op. cit.*, 887-893.

but it had a sacramental character, and in 1540 was commended by the *Rationale of Ceremonial* "as a godly ceremony and to be continued in the Church . . . to put us in mind that all Christian men be one mystical body of Christ, as the bread is made of many grains and yet but one loaf".[1] St. Paul, however, in I Corinthians x. 17 was speaking of the Holy Communion, and the Holy Loaf was a poor substitute for the ordained sacrament of unity.

It is sometimes supposed that the people did not in the least understand the Mass, but thought of it as something which the priests did on their behalf—a magical incantation which protected them in this life and rescued them from purgatory in the life to come. Of some people this may be true, for irreligion and ignorance are the parents of much superstition, and no one pretends that everyone was religious and well instructed. This was not true of devout people even when they were illiterate. Such people might have found it difficult to put into words exactly what they believed about the Holy Sacrifice, a doctrine on which the Schoolmen did not agree, but they were all convinced about the reality of our Lord's Presence. It was His Presence which focused their worship. To Him they directed their praise and prayer. They came to church, wanting to be with Him their Saviour; they came not daring to absent themselves for He was their judge. Nicholas Love, John Myrc, Langford [2] and others who wrote popular manuals never tire of insisting on the Presence. It was the overwhelming and supreme fact of life, so that Berthold of Ratisbon, the preacher, says:

> Grant now that our Lady St. Mary, Mother of God, stood here on this fair meadow, while all the Saints and all the Angels found room about her, and I were found worthy to see this sight. . . . I would rather turn, and bow the knee before a Priest bearing the Lord's Body to the sick, than before Our Lady St. Mary and all the saints of the whole host of Heaven.[3]

It is surprising how many explanations of the Mass have survived. Lydgate, the Monk of Bury, begins his with a prayer:

[1] *Rationale of Ceremonial*, edited by Cobbe, 41.

[2] John Myrc, *Festival*; Nicholas Love, *The Blessed Sacrament*, reprinted with *The Mirror of the Blessed Jesus* (Orchard Books); Langford, *Meditations of Ghostly Exercises in Time of Mass*.

[3] Quoted by Coulton, *Ten Mediaeval Studies*, 33.

God of Heaven that shook earth and hell
Give me grace some word to tell
To the lewd who cannot read
But Paternoster and the Creed.[1]

Lydgate evidently intended his explanation to be taught and had reason to believe that it would be taught ; and that it might easily be memorised, he wrote it in verse. Here are his directions for prayer at the Elevation of the Host :

And when he [the priest] resteth Him in height
Kneel adown with all thy might.
And if thou ask anything,
Speak dreadfully as to a King ;
And look thou ask no thing of right,
But of His grace and of His might.[2]

Much better known was *The Lay Folks' Mass Book.* It was written by one Dan Jeremy, Canon of Rouen and Archdeacon of Cleveland, who may have been of French or English origin, but wrote in French towards the close of the XII century. In English there are no less than six different versions written in different dialects, the latest dating from the middle of the XV century. It was evidently a classic for instruction and the different versions prove its wide distribution. It paraphrased in verse the Confiteor, the Gloria in Excelsis and the Lord's Prayer. It simplified the language of the Nicene Creed, and suggests that the worshipper should say the Apostles' Creed to himself. When it comes to the Canon of the Mass it expands and particularises. When the priest prays for pope and bishop, priest and clerk are added : when for the king, the lord of the land is not forgotten : when he prays for all the faithful, verse succeeds verse—for those " sib and well-willing " (relations and well-wishers), for friends, tenants, servants, old men, children, women, mendicants craftsmen, tilmen (ploughmen), rich and poor,

That they be keeped specially
In good health and life holy.

Then the prayer goes on for the wicked, for those slandered and those in strife, for the sick, for prisoners, for sailors on the sea and for exiles from this land.

[1] Appendix V in *Lay Folks' Mass Book*, edited by Simmons, 1879, E.E.T.S., 148. Lydgate's *Merita Missae* must not be confused with his *Vertue of the Mass.*
[2] *Ibid.* 150.

To all them Thou send succour
To Thy worship and Thine honour.

Two quotations may be added—the prayer that was to be said at the Sanctus and the prayer at the Elevation of the Host :

At the Sanctus :

Sweet Jesu, grant me now this
That I may come unto Thy bliss,
There unto angels for to sing
This sweet song of Thy loving,
Sanctus, Sanctus, Sanctus,
Jesu grant that it be thus.

At the Elevation :

Praisèd be Thou, King,
And blessed be Thou, King,
Of all Thy giftés good
And thanked be Thou, King :
Jesu, all my joying,
That for me spilt Thy Blood ;
And died upon the Rood ;
Thou give me grace to sing
The song of Thy praising.

This joyous simplicity is maintained throughout. It has the spontaneity of childhood, while so many of our modern manuals of devotion suggest a morbid middle age. So, in the XV century the Church tried to teach her children to praise and pray, and to some extent she succeeded.

Trevisan does not only say Englishmen habitually heard Mass, but also that they said many paternosters in public. In those days it was easier to say prayers in church than at home, although Whitford in his *Work for Householders* urges the latter practice and anticipates the objection :

We lie two or three sometimes together, and even in one chamber divers beds, and so many in company, that if we should use these things in presence of our fellows some would laugh us to scorn and mock at us.[1]

Fashions change. Nowadays a man feels himself conspicuous if he kneels down in a church to say his private prayers. In those

[1] Whitford, *Werke for Householders*, quoted by Gasquet, *Eve of the Reformation*, 275.

days it was conspicuous to pray at home, and the churches were the recognised places for private devotion. There was then a popular religion, a religion common to all, with practices so well understood that they occasioned no remark. Privacy did not exist in the Middle Ages. Not only did men share the same bed, but boys learned their lessons in a schoolroom where masters of other classes bawled at or flogged their pupils. It must have been very difficult "to mind your book". Craftsmen plied their trades in booths open to the street, where intending customers could note their skill. Princes dined in public without losing their appetite, while their subjects gaped at them. So men could pray before an altar undisturbed though children were playing hide-and-seek about the pillars; but could not pray at home, because custom decreed that it was unusual.

The women who came with their office books and rosaries to church also tell us of a popular religion. They needed no priest to conduct their devotions. The book they brought with them was *The Prymer*,[1] which contained the Hours of our Lady, the Penitential Psalms, the Psalms of Degrees, the Commendation of a Passing Soul and sundry prayers for special occasions. Many have survived. Some are in Latin; some have Latin and English on opposite pages, and these were recommended by directors to nuns. Some are in English only and were the lay folks' prayer books. In XV-century wills we find references to "My best prymer . . .", "my myddell prymmere . . .", "my grete Prymer . . .", a "Prymer to serve God with . . ."[2] A London grocer left "my Prymer with gilt claspes whereuppon I am wont to say my service",[3] while a certain Sir Thomas had "a littel Portose" which he took with him always when he rode. In this last instance portose must mean a prymer and not a breviary.[4] The prymer of Henry VIII is now in the British Museum, and also one that belonged to an unknown lady of his court who collected autographs. It has inscriptions by Henry VII and his wife, by Henry VIII and Katherine of Aragon, by Margaret Queen of Scotland and the Princess Mary and by Yolande, Princess of Savoy. Katherine of Aragon wrote:

[1] Littlehales has edited *The Prymer* for the E.E.T.S. Pt. II has a valuable introduction by Edmund Bishop.

[2] Wordsworth and Littlehales, *Old English Service Books*, 248.

[3] *Ibid.* 249.

[4] Littlehales, *The Prymer*, ii., xliv.

I think the prayers of a friend be most acceptable unto God; and because I take you for one of mine assured, I pray you to remember me in yours— Katherine the Queen.[1]

The Prymer was in constant use among all classes that could read. Between 1478 and 1534, 116 editions of the Sarum Prymer in Latin were printed, and many of them contain additional devotions in English. Between 1534 and 1547, 28 editions were printed entirely in English, and 18 in Latin.[2]

The question remains, how many people at the end of the XV century were able to read?[3] Sir Thomas More says, "far more than four parts of all the whole [people] divided into ten could never read English yet",[4] which is rather a clumsy way of admitting that more than half of the population could read. This is what we should expect. Illiteracy was, no doubt, very general in the Northern Counties and also in the West, while in many remote villages there could have been few opportunities for book-learning. But in towns and the better populated countryside, the great majority of the people must have been able to read. "Unless", writes Mr. Kingsford, "the capacity to read had been fairly general, the common practice of posting up bills in public places or distributing them by hand, would be inexplicable".[5] It is also noteworthy that the pews erected in churches about this time were all provided with book-rests.[6] But the best evidence is from the number of grammar-schools.[7] In them the teaching no doubt was bad, but they can scarcely have failed in teaching children to read. There were a multitude of chantry

[1] Littlehales, ii. 45.

[2] Cobbe, *Rationale of Ceremonial*, 54.

[3] Maskell, *Monumenta Ritualia*, iii. 51, says: "Taking the relative population . . . there were more people who could read two hundred years before the Reformation than two hundred years afterwards". Another Roman Catholic writer, W. E. Campbell, *Sir Thomas More's Works*, ii. 94: "Printing was then a new thing, and apart from the Clergy a very small proportion of the people were able to read what was printed". In making these contradictory assertions both were intent on scoring a controversial point in favour of their Church. Gairdner (Introd. to *Paston Letters*, ccclxiii.), a better authority than either of them, says, "No person of any rank or station in society above mere labouring men seems to have been wholly illiterate". Kingsford, Introd. to *Stonor Letters*, xlvi., agrees with him. Miss Gabel, *Benefit of Clergy*, 81, calls attention to the fact that many labourers were able to claim benefit of clergy, because they could read.

[4] More, *Apologye*, 13.

[5] Kingsford, *Prejudice and Promise*, 39.

[6] Littlehales, *The Prymer*, Pt. II. xliv.

[7] Leach, *Schools of Mediaeval England*, 330, 331, reckons that there were at least ten grammar schools in every shire, and that the number of schools in proportion to the population was greater than in 1864.

schools suppressed at the Reformation, so that it may be true that there were more illiterates in England when Elizabeth died in 1603 than a hundred years before, notwithstanding the immense improvement in teaching that had then taken place.

That many of the poor could read is proved by the wide distribution of Wyclifite tracts, written especially for them in homely language, while that better-to-do citizens could read may be proved from XV-century wills. Wallyngton, a London draper, in 1403 mentions ten books in his will, all of a religious character. John Clifford, a mason of Southwark, in 1411 had several books, including the Gospels in English, which he left to St. Olave's Church. Stephen Preston, who died in 1274, had books of grammar, sophistry, logic and law, besides a work of St. Bonaventura, Boethius and the *Prick of Conscience.*[1] Apart from private possessions it was possible to read in some churches which had often other books than those necessary for conducting services. St. Margaret Southwark had 29 volumes and St. Margaret Fish Street 59.[2] At St. Christopher le Stocks we are told that " on the south side of the vestiarie standeth a grete library with ii lecturnalles whereon to lay the Bokes ".[3] These must have been double-faced bookcases, like those at Merton College and Hereford Cathedral, with reading-desks on the top for the chained books.[4] What, however, concerns us here is to know what the people read. Men of the upper classes no doubt like John Paston collected romances, poetry and books on heraldry.[5] Sober aldermen paid large sums to have chronicles copied out, but the majority wanted books of devotion.[6] Many more MSS. of Richard Rolle and Walter Hilton have survived than MSS. of Chaucer and Gower. When the printing press began, many more editions of religious works were published than of secular. It was not merely for the clergy and devout women that such books were provided. They were bought by busy citizens and craftsmen. Prior to the printing press Robert Holland, a barber well known to the hustings, left a work of Walter Hilton which he had had made for " the common profit ". The colophon asks that the person who should inherit the work should pray for Holland's soul. The reader was to see

[1] Kingsford, *Prejudice and Promise*, 40.
[2] *V.C.H.* London, i. 241.
[3] Micklethwaite, *Ornaments Rubric*, 45.
[4] Streeter, *The Chained Library*.
[5] *Paston Letters*, No. 869.
[6] Kingsford, *op. cit.*, 41.

that it was in due course passed on with the same request. " And so be it delivered from person to person, man or woman, as long as the book endureth." Beneath the colophon is a later inscription :

James Palmer owneth this book, yet without the least intent to pray for the soul of Robert Holland, being a wicked and simple custom of sottishly ignorant Papists. J. Palmer, Junior.

We cannot help being sorry for Robert Holland, whose pious wish was frustrated. We are still more sorry for James Palmer, Junior and his lack of charity. But we are grateful to them both —to Robert Holland who had the book made, and to James Palmer who preserved it.[1]

II. *The Churches*

When we approach a modern city we see great factory chimneys belching black smoke. We pass through dingy suburbs into a town with broad streets with high and sometimes splendid buildings, with great shop windows wondrously decorated, and with advertisements artfully displayed. There are churches in the modern city—fine churches very often, but they do not immediately attract attention, and the city life goes on independent of their appeal.[2]

In the Middle Ages, on the other hand, the churches were most conspicuous, and you could not escape from the sound of their bells. As you came through meadows to the grim walls of the city, not yet picturesque through decay, you saw nothing above or behind them but towers and spires. Within the gates there was a tangle of crooked and narrow streets with dark and noisome passages opening into them. There were fine timber houses projecting story above story, miserable hovels often adjoining them. Open sewers, dirt and abominable smells were

[1] R. W. Chambers, *Continuity of English Prose*, cviii, cxxxiii, in Harpsfield, *Life of More*, E.E.T.S. Robert Holland died intestate in 1441. A similar colophon to Walter Hilton's works is to be found in Lambeth MS. 472, with John Killum's name instead of Robert Holland's. He was a grocer who died in 1416. *Vide* Dorothy Jones, Introd. to *The Minor Works of Walter Hilton* (Orchard Books), xi. ff.

[2] A. W. Pugin in his *Contrasts* has two plates, one showing a mediaeval town as he thought it was and the other as he saw it at the time of writing. The plates are not uninstructive, though his views were selected with malice.

taken for granted by the inhabitants. The churches, however, were glorious within and without—they were the real homes of the people. In them the rich man prayed, the poor man begged, and women told their beads and whispered gossip.

England was then " the ringing isle " and the citizens were attuned to the continual tintinnabulation of the bells. They called men to service, they witnessed to the consecration in the Mass, they announced the curfew ; they pealed for christenings and weddings, and tolled for the passing soul.[1] They clanged the alarm for fire and tumult, and defied the storms.[2] They rocked the steeples in the day of victory, and knelled with muffled tones disaster and defeat. They welcomed distinguished visitors, and as in duty bound rang in the archdeacon on his visitation,[3] the bishop and the king.[4]

The wealth stored in the churches astonished Trevisan. He wrote :

Above all are their riches displayed in the church treasuries ; for there is not a parish church in the kingdom so mean, as not to possess

[1] The Soul bell or Forthfarre bell was a custom peculiar to England : *vide* Cox, *Archdeacon's Accounts*, 212. The Angelus bell, on the other hand, was not introduced into England until the beginning of the XVI century. There were, however, the Ave and Gabriel bells : Rock, *Church of Our Fathers*, iii. 276-280.

[2] Durandus, *Symbolism of Churches*, trans. by Neale and West, p. 80, says : " This is the reason why the Church, when she seeth a tempest to arise, doth ring the bells, that the Devil hearing the trumpets of the Eternal King, which be the bells, may flee away through fear and cease from raising the storm ; and that the faithful also may be admonished at the ringing of the bells, and be provoked to be instant in prayer for the instant danger ". *Vide* also Latimer on holy bells, i. 498. Barnabe Googe, *Popish Kingdom*, fol. 41, writes :

> " If that the thunder chance to roar, and stormy tempest shake,
> A wonder is it for to see the wretches how they quake.
> Now that no faith at all they have, nor trust in anything,
> The clerk doth all the bells forthwith at once in steeples ring :
> With wondrous sound and deeper far, than he was wont before,
> Till in the lofty heavens dark the thunder bray no more.
> For in these Christened bells, they think, doth lie more power and might
> As able in the tempests great and storms to vanquish quite."

Bacon thought, on scientific grounds, that bells might dispel a tempest.

[3] The Archdeacon's right to this honour was sometimes contested, but he could make himself very unpleasant when it was denied him. Bells were rung for the bishop in order that the people might come out of their houses to receive his blessing. Maskell, *Monumenta Ritualia*, II. clvi.

[4] If this civility was omitted the almoner sealed the church door until a fine was paid. This custom was troublesome at Westminster, Windsor, Richmond and Greenwich, because the entrances and exits of kings were sometimes unexpected. Cox, *Churchwardens' Accounts*, 214 ff.

crucifixes, candlesticks, censers, patens and cups of silver ; nor is there a convent of mendicant friars so poor not to have all the same articles of silver, besides many other articles worthy of a cathedral church in the same metal. Your Magnificence may therefore imagine what the decorations of those enormously rich Benedictine, Carthusian and Cistercian monasteries must be . . . and I have been informed that amongst other things many of these monasteries possess unicorn's horns of an enormous size.[1]

The eyes of the Italian had evidently been dazzled. As a foreigner he had been taken to see what was notable, and he generalises a little too freely ; but we know from the inventories that have survived how great was the wealth of the Church in silver, silver gilt and even gold. It is equally true that many of the ornaments were of pewter or laten. The monasteries which possessed unicorns' horns cannot now be identified. They disappeared in the general spoliation—the largest of them no doubt being appropriated by the Crown. Hentzner [2] in 1598 saw one at Windsor, valued at £10,000, and somewhat later Peter Mundy saw another in the Tower of London and rightly guessed that it was the horn of some fish.[3] In the Middle Ages curiosities of all sorts decorated the churches. So Durandus writes : " In some churches are suspended the eggs of ostriches and other things which cause admiration because rarely seen, that by this means people may be drawn to church, and have their minds the more affected ".[4]

Up to the eve of the Reformation the work of building and decoration went on. Bath Abbey was in process of rebuilding when the monastery was dissolved.[5] Bell Harry Tower at Canterbury had only a few years before been finished. The Tower and Lady Chapel at Gloucester were not a hundred years old. The windows at King's College, Cambridge, St. Neots, Fairford and Malvern were modern. The rood loft at St. Mary's, Cambridge, was erected in 1522 and cost £92 : 6 : 8.[6] The screens at York and Ripon date from 1490,[7] while it was the " wicked Abbot "

[1] *An Italian Relation of England*, 29.
[2] Paul Hentzner, *Travels* (ed. 1797), 54.
[3] Mundy's *Travels*, iii. 1-3, New Hakluyt Society.
[4] Durandus, *Symbolism in Churches*, 67.
[5] Leland, *Itinerary*, i. 144, writes : " Oliver King, Bishop of Bath, began of late days a right goodly new church ". It was not completed until the days of Elizabeth.
[6] Cox, *Churchwardens' Accounts*, 83.
[7] Bond, *Screens and Galleries*, 156.

Wallingford of St. Albans who provided his church with a magnificent high altar and screen.[1]

It is reasonable to suppose that when the resources of art were lavished on the churches, great care would be taken for their preservation. This, in spite of exceptions to the contrary, may be admitted, although it is well to remember that our forefathers did not altogether share our views about dust and dirt.

The monastic churches were probably the best kept, for the monks were there to look after them ; and even monks, who were not overmuch given to prayer and devotion, regarded their church as the outward and visible glory of the community to which they belonged. They were, moreover, by no means eager that the rude public should frequent them, and so ran less risk of damage and dilapidation. The monks of Bury St. Edmunds built two splendid churches on either side of their abbey gateway to accommodate the townsmen and pilgrims. The monks of Evesham also built two churches, not quite so splendid, for the same reason. St. Margaret's, Westminster, was built for " the ease of the monks " and to save them from " the annoyance " of having their south aisle used as a parish church.[2] At Pershore the homely parish church shelters itself at the east end of the abbey choir which soars above it. The people were as far as possible shut out from the abbeys ; and when these exclusive corporations were dissolved there were few that loved these glorious buildings. The two churches at Bury remain, but the abbey has been destroyed ; the same is true of Evesham, while the parish church of Glastonbury survives and the abbey is a ruin. At Romsey, at Tewkesbury and Malvern on the other hand the parish churches have disappeared, because the parishioners bought the derelict monastic churches for their own use. Malvern acquired its priory church for £20,[3] while Tewkesbury had to pay £453[4] for its abbey and St. Alban's £400.[5]

When Erasmus visited Canterbury he was much impressed by the great nave, spacious and empty. He only found in it some

[1] Gairdner, *Lollardy and the Reformation*, ii. 69. Gasquet, *Abbot Wallingford*, 2, argues that the gift of the screen proves that he was not wicked ; Coulton, *Ten Mediaeval Studies*, 254, comments on this.

[2] Stow, *Survey of London*, 1603 ed.

[3] Deane, *Malvern Priory*, 24.

[4] Blunt, *Tewkesbury*, 99.

[5] The sum paid is a matter of dispute. *V.C.H. Herts*, ii. 511.

books chained to pillars and among them the Gospel of Nicodemus.[1] It was a monastic church, and the monks loved its emptiness. It was such a fitting approach to the crowded glories within the screen. Erasmus has not left us a description of St. Paul's, then and after the Reformation one of the most desecrated churches in Christendom. At each pillar in the nave a sergeant-at-law might have been found ready to interview his clients.[2] Merchants came there to discuss business and settle the rate of exchange. Groups of priests hovered about the doors hoping for chantries and chaplaincies, but idle all the day long because no one had hired them. Bullies ruffled in the aisles, prostitutes and pickpockets plied their unlicensed trades, countrymen were cozened by cheats and smallwares were sold by Autolycus.[3] Its condition was a disgrace, and the only excuse that can be offered for its condition is that it was the one place of public resort in the city which was under cover. Buying and selling went on also in the Minster of York in 1409, but it was then declared to be a scandal and contrary to evangelical discipline.[4] At Exeter booths were erected in the cathedral nave during fair-time, and there was a lengthy dispute on the subject between the town and the chapter, but it really turned on the point of who should receive the fees.[5] At Ramsey the rector had to pay the town council not to hold meetings during church time.[6] At Winchester William of Wykeham forbade boys to play games of ball within the chapel because they broke the windows.[7]

Secular cathedrals were at a great disadvantage because deans and prebendaries were so often non-resident, and in the absence of effective authority abuses became established which were difficult to reform. The people also thought that such cathedrals belonged to them, and were the natural centres of their civic life. They had a different standard of reverence to that which is now prevalent. They had no sense of separation from the

[1] Erasmus, *Peregrinatio religionis ergo :* Coll. i. 361.

[2] Capes, *Church History*, 271.

[3] W. Sparrow Simpson, *Old St. Paul's*, 236. As early as 1385 Bishop Braybrook had issued a pastoral condemning the shameful traffic in the Cathedral church.

[4] *York Fabric Rolls*, 246.

[5] Mrs. Green, *Town Life in the XV Century*, i. 362-364.

[6] In the corporation accounts of Ramsey, 1407–1408, there is a receipt for "three shillings and fourpence, a free gift of John Hacche, Vicar of Ramset, that the jurats in future shall not hold their sessions in his church, while divine service is being celebrated". *V.C.H. Kent*, ii. 61.

[7] Capes, *Ch. Hist.*, 271.

world on entering a church, and did not expect to find a solemn hush within. They expressed themselves more loudly and spontaneously than we do. They were more natural in church than we are, and many people who are quite natural are at the same time exceedingly ill-mannered and unpleasant.

The difficulties in the way of administration were also very great. There were too many people on the foundation. Everyone had a freehold, everyone was tenacious of his rights, but everyone was not equally zealous to perform his duties. The dean was no autocrat, but only a chairman, while the visitor was often at a distance and had very limited rights of interference. Overlapping authorities caused confusion, and disputes about duties led to their not being performed. The great Minster at York, for instance, had a dean, a precentor, a chancellor and a treasurer; 36 prebendaries, 36 vicars choral, besides 36 chantry priests who lived together in St. William's College.[1] There were also clerks, acolytes, choristers, sacrists, bedes-men and others, most of them entrenched in freeholds, and therefore difficult to discipline and more difficult to dismiss. We do not know how many were normally resident;[2] but it is obvious that to organise and supervise such a body was wellnigh impossible.

Considering the circumstances, it is really surprising that the cathedrals were so well cared for. They were duly inspected and irregularities were reported and remain on record. The visitation of York Minster in 1519 reveals the following dilapidations and negligences.[3] It reads like the work of a lynx-eyed upper housemaid of a fault-finding disposition and a scolding tongue. The language need not be repeated. It is sufficient to tabulate the facts:

The clerk in his surplice is not always present with his torch when the Sacrament is renewed in the pyx.

There is a missal without clasps in danger of being ruined.

The candles before the statue of Our Lady are sometimes not lighted.

The reredos has not been dusted.

[1] Cutts, *Parish Priests, etc.*, 503.

[2] *York Historical Tracts*. Hamilton Thompson on "The Chapter". Several prebendaries were appointed by the Crown. The king's clerks were not usually resident. Others were ecclesiastical lawyers appointed by the Archbishop and belonged to his "family". *Vide* Austin in same volume.

[3] *York Fabric Rolls* (Surtees), 267.

The covering of the credence table is ragged and a disgrace.[1]

The sudary with which the acolyte presents the paten is dirty.

The books of the choir are in bad condition.

There is a chest in the choir which ought not to be there.

The hangings in the choir have been defiled by dogs[2] and the expectoration of priests.

The cloth for the reredos is of parti colours.[3]

The lectern in the chapter-house should be removed into the choir.

The oven for singing-bread should be moved into the chapter-house.

There are too few towels in the vestry.

The pipe of the vestry sink is stopped up.

The well in which St. Edwin was baptized is locked and not accessible to devout visitors.

Old vestments should be cut up for cushions.

Albs have been torn because the sleeves were made too narrow.

Vestments of the right colour[4] are not always worn.

The children's albs are frequently dirty.

There are two sets of vestments needing repair: the cost would not be great, but no one knows whose business it is or who should pay for it.

The lectern of the Gospel Book is broken.

Dust and cobwebs are to be found throughout the minster.

To those unacquainted with cathedral administration this list will appear formidable, but how glad a modern chapter would be if, at their monthly meeting, their clerk-of-works had nothing worse to report than one stopped-up drain. Deans and chapters have always been reproached for either locking up places which visitors most wanted to see, or of leaving them open to be injured or defiled. York must have had dozens of missals, but only one of them had broken clasps. This was an accident very likely to happen when books stood on a shelf with their backs inward. Anyone in a hurry pulled them out by their clasps : and sooner or later the clasps were broken. Then the vellum leaves of heavy books curled and crumpled.[5] York had hundreds of vestments,

[1] I assume that " the little awsterse " in connexion with the High Altar is the credence table. It may have been a " super-altar ", *i.e.* a portable stone for celebrations in unconsecrated places. Such altars were licensed to privileged persons and sometimes bequeathed to churches to be kept among their " jewells ". Micklethwaite, *Ornaments Rubric*, 35.

[2] The dog-whipper was inefficient : *The Booklet of the Mass*, Alcuin Club. In three out of thirty-three plates describing the ceremonies of the Mass, a man is seen whipping away a dog.

[3] This must be the Lenten veil, which was only raised at the reading of the Gospel and let down again at the *Sanctus*. It was usually white, but Feasey produces other instances where it was parti-coloured. *Holy Week Ceremonial*, 15. Cp. *Booklet of the Mass*, 60.

[4] The right colour was often a matter of dispute.

[5] Wordsworth and Littlehales, *Old Service Books*, 274.

and it is to the credit of the inspection that two sets were found needing minor repairs.[1] Vigilant sacrists to-day see that choristers' surplices are reasonably clean, but even they have not solved the problem how the buttons may be kept on their cassocks. Books in the choir handled by all and sundry soon become dirty, and even to-day, when carefully supervised church cleaners are armed with " Hoovers ", complaints are sometimes made of dust and dirt. We have got rid of dogs, and canons no longer spit, but a modern chapter might well dread the accusing eye of the Visitor of York Minster in 1519.

You do not discover the religion of a people in a cathedral church, for it exists to present an ideal of worship which may not be theirs. Its services are rendered with the same splendour whether a congregation be or be not present. It reminds us of what is due to the glory of God. It is not so much concerned with the edification of men. A parish church, on the other hand, belongs to the parishioners—it is their home; they participate in its worship; it expresses their devotion, reveals their interests, and defines their approach to God. This was especially true of the parish in the Middle Ages, though in some places there might be a resident rector who insisted on having his own way. Failing him, the parish council had the power to decide everything, and in it women voted as well as men, serfs with the free-born, for the church belonged to them all. Stow tells us that when St. Andrew's, Undershaft, was rebuilt in 1520, " Everyone put to his helping hand, some with their purses, and others with their bodies " : [2] and the value of this co-operation was not lessened because Stephen Jennings, a tailor, provided most of the money required.[3] The Church of St. Andrew's, Holborn, was rebuilt in 1446 largely by what was collected by men and women in boxes at ales, shootings and common meetings.[4] In three London parishes it was the custom for children to dance on May Day

[1] The inventory of the vestments in York Minster may be read in *York Fabric Rolls*, 212-235.

[2] Bishop Hobhouse, *Churchwardens' Accounts*, Somerset Record Society, iv.

[3] Stow, *Survey*, ed. 1603, 146.

[4] *V.C.H. London*, i. 244. Another instance is the way in which St. Andrew's, Plymouth, was enlarged. The town council closed all the taverns one day in each year. Each ward set up a booth in the churchyard. The inhabitants were invited to come with as many friends as possible, bringing such food as they liked, except bread and ale which they were to purchase on the spot. After ten of these picnics the new aisles were finished at the cost of £44 : 14 : 6. Mrs. Green, *Town Life in the XV Century*, i. 160.

and bring what they collected to church.[1] In London the churches were decorated with holly and ivy at Christmas, with palms, flowers, box and yew on Palm Sunday ; with birch, lilies and fennel at Midsummer ; and with garlands of roses and woodruff at Corpus Christi.[2]

The parishioners were responsible for the upkeep of the services, for providing and preserving the requisite ornaments, and for the repair to the fabric, excepting the chancel which belonged to the rector. It all cost a great deal of money, and they could have no collections for church expenses at the services, because any money offered at the altar went to the clergy. They had to rely on gifts and bequests, on guilds of pious people who became responsible for keeping the lights burning, and on the profits from entertainments. It is surprising how much religion had to do with the merry-making of the people. On certain vigils of saints bonfires were lighted in the streets, and the wealthier citizens set out tables before their houses and invited the passers-by to eat sweet cakes and drink wine. On Midsummer Eve and the Eve of St. Peter and St. Paul there was the Marching Watch, when the houses were decorated and illuminated, while men of all the wards, in all the bravery of their respective liveries, marched through the streets.[3] Stow writing in the reign of Elizabeth regretted those old days. Life had been more gay if people had not been so good. Religion had not been so serious but it affected more people ; and the churches had belonged to the people and not to the parson. In the country the church-warden had been the great man who organised everything. In the bigger towns he was often overshadowed by the guilds, and the guilds have to be studied if we would really understand the popular religion of the time.

III. *The Guilds*

Guilds were lay associations and for the most part altogether independent of clerical control. Their origin and object might be religious or secular, but the most secular were consecrated by religious observances. They show how religion leavened a work-a-day world. Tracing the history of particular guilds, we find how some of them started with a purely secular object and

[1] *V.C.H. London*, i. 243. [2] *Ibid.* [3] Stow, *Survey* (1603), 102, 103.

became in process of time social and religious fraternities ; how some which started as associations of poor men became wealthy and exclusive clubs ; and how some which started for the maintenance of a cult became the dominating power in municipal life.

At the beginning of the XVI century the great days of the guild merchant were over. By then, the guild merchant had in some places become one with the corporation, or only maintained as at Coventry a fictitious existence apart for financial reasons.[1] In other places, defeated by the craft guilds, it had ceased to have any municipal importance, and become a body of elderly and wealthy citizens who gave Gargantuan feasts, organised Corpus Christi processions, and took infinite care in making arrangements for one another's funerals.[2]

A trade or craft guild was formed to regulate wages and prices, to prevent undue competition, to maintain a standard of work, and to see that no alien dared to practise its particular mystery within the borders of the town.[3] It contained all the trade or craft, from the alderman employing many journeymen to the apprentice who was to receive " clothing, shoes, bedding, board and chastisement ".[4] The guild was ruthless to interlopers and those who cut prices. It maintained a stern discipline, not only over idle or rebellious apprentices, but over masters too much addicted to the trickery of trade. Yet a trade guild, so mundane in its objects, had not only a hall but a chapel. In the XV century especially, such guilds were building chapels down the aisles of the churches, destroying their symmetry from the outside even when they added to their picturesque appearance. The interiors were for the most part unspoilt, because of the

[1] Mrs. Green, *Town Life in the XV Century*, ii. 215-217. At Coventry the guild of the Holy Trinity was practically one with the corporation, but they kept their chests apart. When officers of the Exchequer demanded of the town dues and taxes, it could always be shown that the city had nothing, while of course the guild owed nothing.

[2] Grose, *Gild Merchant*, i. 117.

[3] Brentano, " Essay on the Origin and Development of Gilds " in *English Gilds*, E.E.T.S., cxiv. ff. Wyclif had not a single good word to say for guilds, and was especially severe on freemasons who will not allow one who hews stone to lay a wall, though he could do so to the profit of his master and without pain to himself. He accuses them of raising wages and preventing willing people from working for less ; he denounces them for not allowing those who wish to win to a knowledge of their craft ; and because they punish " them that freely help their neighbours ". He regarded each guild as a conspiracy " against the common profit of Christian men ", and therefore worthy of the greater excommunioation. *The Grete Sentence of Curs expounded* ; *vide* Winn's *Selections*, 104, and *English Works of Wyclif*, ed. by Arnold, iii. 333.

[4] Mrs. Green, *ut supra*, ii. 120 ft. n.

screens which separated the chapels from the main body of the church. In St. Michael's, Coventry, now so shapeless in appearance, there were once the chapels of the girdlers, drapers, dyers, cappers and mercers, while the marlers, tanners and butchers had their chapels attached to Holy Trinity, close at hand.[1] Each trade was dedicated to a saint, whose image was carried in the yearly procession. The artisan believed in his saint and in return for the candles he lighted in his honour expected his assistance in the workshop. It was a business partnership between earth and heaven, and brought this world and the next very near together. To-day, at the Lord Mayor's Show, the City companies go marching by in all bravery, but no saint is carried aloft and on the emblematic cars there is no appeal to God. At the Reformation trade and religion dissolved partnership. Henceforward in the workshop the motto is " Business is business ", while the Church is left for the parson and those who adhere to him.

The most numerous guilds were those that had been founded with a religious intent. They abounded in all parts of the country—more than 900 are known to have existed in Norfolk alone.[2] They appealed to all classes, from ploughmen upwards. Men and women alike belonged to them, but priests were generally excluded from membership, and for some unknown reason there was a guild to which no baker or his wife might belong.[3] Some guilds were founded for no other reason than to encourage devotion to some saint, or in honour of some mystery of the Faith. Guilds of the Holy Trinity, for instance, were fairly numerous ; and at York there was a guild of the Paternoster, to maintain an old play which set forth the goodness of the Lord's Prayer. In its rules the members were reminded that " those who remain in their sins are unable to call God their Father, and that they must in consequence restrict themselves to ' good and worthy businesses ' ".[4] It is a mistake to compare these guilds with our mutual benefit societies, for, though there is evidence that the members were kind to one another, the only mutual benefit contemplated in their foundation was the benefit

[1] Hamilton Thompson, *Growth of the English Parish Church*, 46, 50.

[2] Westlake, *Parish Gilds*, 122.

[3] Westlake, *Parish Gilds*.

[4] Miss Toulmin Smith, *English Gilds*, p. 37. Cf. Miss Toulmin Smith, *York Plays*, p. xxviii, where she notes Wyclif's reference to the Play in *De Officio Pastorali*, ch. xv.

to their souls after death.[1] Rich men could leave money for Masses to be said on their behalf, but many guilds originated as associations of poor men who desired to be remembered before God after their decease. The Masses prescribed by most rules were not to be said by the chaplain and his server alone, but were to be attended by the brethren, who were also required to be present at the funeral and yearly obit of the departed brother. They were sometimes required to say so many Paternosters or even the complete Psalter on his behalf.

There were also guilds for the better furnishing of the church, and one for the better support of a poor rector.[2] Some guilds undertook to maintain a school, or an alms-house, or to keep a bridge in repair. Nearly all of them kept lights burning before some image or before the rood in the church. Their object and activities were sufficiently varied, but they all represented the religion of the laity, and were nearly all under lay control. It was quite exceptional for a guild to be founded in co-operation with a rector, but such an instance occurs in St. Peter's, Cornhill, and it resulted in the rector having a voice in the appointment of the chaplain and seeing that he was useful in the church.[3] But when the masters of the guild of the Assumption in St. Margaret's, Westminster, took boat for London to find a priest for their brotherhood, they neither consulted their vicar, nor went in search of a spiritual director—they wanted a minister who would do as he was told, and probably found him in the nave of St. Paul's.[4]

In process of time some of these guilds became wealthy. They had in their chapels plate, ornaments and vestments. The inventories of the Boston guilds survive.[5] They also owned lands

[1] Toulmin Smith and F. J. Furnivall objected to the title of religious guilds, maintaining that they were only mutual benefit societies. Furnivall writes: " To have called these Religious because of their ornament of a Saint's name would have seemed to him [T. S.] and to me a monstrous contradiction ". Brentano agreed with them about the facts, but retained the name for convenience: *Development of Gilds*, p. lxxxvi. Mr. Westlake has, however, produced plentiful evidence to show that they were wrong. *Parish Gilds*, passim.

[2] Holy Trinity, Stamford, founded 1365. " Certain poor men noting the poverty of the Rector to be such that the Church in its feeble state scarcely provided for his maintenance, decided at their own charges to found a fraternity in augmentation of divine worship. Each one gives as he pleases to the Rector's maintenance, and the gild provides 16 candles before Trinity and has a feast at the rectory on Corpus Christi Day " (Westlake, *Parish Gilds*, 177).

[3] *Ibid*. 79.

[4] *Ibid*. 48.

[5] Peacock, *Church Furniture at the Period of the Reformation*, 185.

and houses. The Guild of Jesus in St. Paul's Cathedral had an income of over £400 (£8000) a year.[1] The time came when zealous Protestants, groaning over so much money being given to superstitious purposes, confiscated it all for their own enrichment.

In becoming rich these guilds were sometimes transformed in character. At Wisbech, for instance, a guild founded purely for devotion, first established an alms-house, then a school, then offered to keep the dykes in order, and finally became the civic authority in the town.[2] At Lichfield, by 1486, the Guild of St. Mary had gained complete control over the affairs of the city.[3] At Stratford-on-Avon, the Guild of the Holy Rood had been founded to maintain a college of poor priests, but went on to found a grammar-school where Shakespeare was educated, and exercised a dominating power over a wide neighbourhood.[4] At Norwich the Guild of St. George was founded to maintain the lights before the high altar, but in time became one with the corporation—the outgoing mayor becoming alderman of the guild, and all common councillors having a right to membership, if they would pay their share towards the annual feast.[5]

All these guilds, according to their wealth, contributed to the colour and pageantry of life. Perhaps it is also true to say that as the splendour of their processions and feasts increased, the devotion of the brethren diminished.[6] At Norwich one of the brethren represented St. George on horseback, clad in silver armour. He was attended by a sword-bearer, a banner bearer, by two carrying candles, and of course by a captive dragon, terrible to look upon but richly gilt. He was followed by the Lady of the Guild, representing St. Margaret in a robe made out of four yards of tawny and eight of crimson velvet. She also was attended by her dragon—the tame one. The other brethren followed on horseback, and each of the twenty-four aldermen was required to send a priest in a cope to give greater dignity to the procession. In their midst they carried their precious relic, an arm of St. George presented by Sir John Fastolf. They went to the cathedral to present their guild candle at the high altar:

[1] Sparrow Simpson, *Old St. Paul's*, 93.
[2] Westlake, *Parish Gilds*, 104-108.
[3] *Ibid.* 108, 109.
[4] Miss Toulmin Smith, *English Gilds*, xii.
[5] *Ibid.* 443.
[6] Westlake, 74.

they heard Mass and then proceeded to the Great Hall of the Bishop's Palace which they rented for their annual feast.[1]

Norwich was proud of its guild, and princes and nobles were proud to be enrolled in it. Norwich enjoyed its procession, and those privileged to partake of it enjoyed the feast. But it was a strange outcome of an association of poor folk who had agreed to combine their slender resources to keep one candle alight for ever in honour of our Lord. The candle had become an excuse for pageantry and ostentation. When the Reformation came it was put out, and I can imagine St. Bernard or St. Francis saying—it was time.

IV. *The Country Parishes*

If Trevisan is right in saying that the English assisted at Mass every day, he can only be right about the towns. In the country with its work and the distances, it must have been impossible. It is unlikely that many vicars celebrated every day, and they were under no obligation to do so. Langland tells us that men ought to labour,

> And on Sundays to cease, God's service to hear
> Both Matins and Mass ; and after meat in Church
> To hear their Evensong every man ought.
> Thus it belongeth for lord, for learned and lewd,
> Each Holy Day to hear wholly the Service.[2]

A parish priest was bound to say Matins, Lauds, Prime and Terce before his Mass, and the laity on Sundays were required to attend.[3] " Some of us laymen ", says Sir Thomas More, " think it a pain once in a week to rise so soon from sleep, and some to tarry so long fasting, as on the Sunday to come and hear out their matins."[4] But in *Dives and Pauper* no excuse is allowed unless for " messengers, pilgrims and wayfaring men ", and they are to " hear mass and matins if they can ".[5] We need not go so far as to suppose that this attendance was always quite voluntary. The Church had the power to deal with Sabbath-breakers and the profanation of holy days, as may be seen from

1 *Ibid.* 116-119.
2 Langland, *Piers Plowman*, C Text, x. 227. Cf. viii. 65.
3 Wordsworth, *Mediaeval Services*, 90.
4 More, *Apologye*, 116.
5 *Dives and Pauper*, quoted by Rock, *Church of Our Fathers*, iv. 163.

The Ecclesiastical Proceedings of the County of Durham.[1] In 1450 men convicted of working on Sundays and holy days were condemned to precede the Sunday processions as penitents and to receive two fustigations. In 1451, Isabella Hunter and Catherine Pykering, for washing linen on the festival of St. Mary Magdalene, were to receive two fustigations, each carrying a bundle of linen. Francis Gray was admonished to come to church on Sundays under penalty of fourpence, and on festivals under penalty of tenpence : the fines to be applied to the fabric of the Church of Durham. Thomas Kirkham and Thomas Hunter, for mowing a meadow on the feast of St. Oswald and receiving payment for it, were sentenced to precede the procession, each carrying a bottle of hay, to receive four whippings, and not to offend again under penalty of ten shillings. It was only by the exercise of such disciplinary powers that the Church maintained for the people days of social reunion—days for rest, worship and recreation. All laws limit freedom in some direction, but some laws have to be made in order to preserve a larger and more desirable liberty. It was not the poor who clamoured for the abolition of the excessive number of holy days.

On Sundays the whole parish came together—men from scattered farms and lonely granges tethered their horses by the churchyard wall. After Mass they fed in the church itself or in the churchyard, but in the XV century a well-equipped parish had a church-house.[2] After Evensong at three o'clock, one acting as "Robin Hood" led the young men to the butts. In the summertime were sports and dancing, the churchwardens providing the refreshments and defraying church expenses out of the profits.

The churchwardens were great people in the parish. In most cases one was changed every year and one was annually re-elected. With the aid of the church council they managed everything that had to do with the upkeep of the church ; and yearly there was an audit of the accounts. Croscombe in Somersetshire kept theirs with such a sense of drama that we can still participate in the excitement.[3] " Comyth in Robin Hoode and Lyttel

[1] Cutts, *Parish Priests, etc.*, 201.

[2] There were many church-houses in Gloucestershire. The one at Standish has been carefully restored and is now used for its original purpose. H. T. Lilley, *Hist. of Standish*, 95-100.

[3] Bishop Hobhouse, *Churchwardens' Accounts*, Somerset Record Society. Croscombe, *passim.*

John and presenteth XV shillings ". We can imagine the cheers. " Comyth in the yonglings and maidens " a little shamefacedly perhaps, but they have done well at Hocktide, and may be congratulated. " Comyth in the weavers ", and, for the third year running, " presenteth naught ". Was there a sense of depression, or had the weavers angry faces when somebody sniggered ? In spite of their failure there was always a balance ; and every year members of the six guilds were entrusted with one or two shillings out of the stock to keep the lights burning until fresh money came in. Croscombe in 1480 built a church-house for £13 : 2 : 11 and did well out of it. They also built a chapel dedicated to St. George which cost £29 : 11 : 8.

In early days the churchwardens began baking the holy loaf for distribution on Sundays. Then they took to brewing, and this led to *Ales* in church and churchyard until a church-house was built more suitable for such entertainments. A *Bid Ale* took place to help any case of distress : a *Bride Ale* to help a young couple to start in life together ; and a *Church Ale* to meet the expenses of the services. These feasts account for the fact that we find pots and pans, trenchers and spoons included in church inventories. We also find theatrical costumes for miracle plays, and a church with a good collection, like St. Peter in the East at Oxford, or Chelmsford, increased its revenues by hiring them out. Chelmsford had a marvellous wardrobe including " iii jyrkins, iii sloppes for devils " and " xxiii Bredes [Beards] and xxi hares [wigs] ".[1] In most country parishes there were archery competitions, organised by a " Robin Hood " and " Little John ", who also brought their profits to the church-wardens. There were also the collections made at Hocktide,[2] that is on the Monday and Tuesday after Low Sunday. On the Monday the young men went out into the streets with ropes and roped in the women : on the Tuesday the wives, or in some parishes the maidens, roped in the men : and in either case a small coin had to be paid for ransom. At this game the women

[1] Cox, *Churchwardens' Accounts*, 21, 277.

[2] The origin of Hocktide is obscure. Brand, *Popular Antiquities*, says that in the later Middle Ages it was supposed in some way to commemorate the slaughter of the Danes upon St. Brice's Day, 1001, or the death of Harthacnut. Cf. Chambers, *Mediaeval Stage*, i. 154-157. The custom is probably of earlier date. The etymology of the word is equally obscure. The *N.E.D.* gives several suggestions, but rejects them all. It does not mention Spelman's that it is from the German *hocken*, to bind, so the word may have some connexion with English *hook*.

were far the best and generally collected five times as much as the men. It must have been rather a boisterous lark, but the grave churchwardens of St. Edmund's, Salisbury, entered it in their accounts as "the devocyon of the people on Hoke Tuesday".[1]

How we answer the question "what have these junketings to do with the religion of the people?" will depend on how far we think that religion should interpenetrate the whole of life. In the Middle Ages most men did not think it incongruous that sports and dances should end in contributions to worship. There were indeed Puritans, even in those days, who thought that there could be little devotion in a people who would not support their church unless they received something in exchange for their offerings. On the other hand, there was something to be said for the men who offered the fruits of their pleasure in thanksgiving to God. The ordinary churchwarden probably did not bother his head with any such questionings. He had to get the money, and if anyone had challenged his conduct he would have justified himself somewhat as follows: "We are told that more crimes are committed on Sundays and holy days than on all the other days of the year. Squire and master maintain that the enforced idleness leads to 'execrable and abominable vices'.[2] If they are right we are surely to be commended for organising social gatherings—sports and feasts. It not only brings money into the church, but it brings the people also. It is because we are a Christian country that this is Merry England."[3] The churchwardens did not depend only on entertainments. They had many bequests, and some of them strange ones. Sometimes they were left a swarm of bees to produce not only honey but wax, sometimes sheep and sometimes cows which were let out to farmers. At Tintinhull in Somerset the churchwardens received 2s. from a farmer for "summering and wintering a cow",[4] and we are surprised to find in the accounts of St. Dunstan's, Canterbury, "for three-quarters of a cow", but it means that the animal had been leased for nine months.[5] People

[1] Cox, *Churchwardens' Accounts*, 64.

[2] Complaint of the Commons. Gee and Hardy, *Documents*, 150.

[3] We must not be misled by Barnabe, Googe's *Popish Kingdom*, 57-58, for this bitter Puritan was not born before 1540, and his poem is a translation from the Latin of Naogeorgus (Kirchmeyer), who speaks truthfully or otherwise of Germany and not of England.

[4] Bishop Hobhouse, *Churchwardens' Accounts*, 190.

[5] *Archaeologia Cantiana*, xvii. 141. Cp. *Bury Wills*, Camden Society, 44.

often left rings to the church, and it was usual for women to leave their wedding rings.[1] Many left clothing which was either used for coverings, made into vestments, or sold as rummage. At Croscombe, for instance, John Nelle's gown was bought by the Parson for 3s.[2]

Reading Bishop Hobhouse's *Churchwardens' Accounts* of four Somersetshire villages, none of which had a resident squire or rector, we marvel at the enthusiasm which the parishioners showed for their church. They were none of them rich : most of them lived in bare hovels, but like *Piers Plowman*, they thought it seemly " to kneel before Christ in a compass of gold ".[3] Pilton, for instance, was quite a small village and had but a single warden, but he has left us an inventory of the church. It had silver chalices, silver candlesticks, mazers and other ornaments, a wealth of vestments and more than twenty books. Tintinhull was even poorer, but we find in the accounts that the women washed all the altar linen and charged nothing. The village carpenter carved beautiful bench-ends which remain to-day, and the parishioners bought themselves a new Grail which cost them £2 : 3s., or some £43 of our money. When, however, they were commanded to buy the Great Bible, they pleaded poverty and paid for it by instalments. People who gave willingly and not of necessity would only give grudgingly towards what was not a gift but a tax.

Here is a list, probably incomplete, of what Yatton provided for the enrichment of their church :

		£	s.	d.
1451.	The Bells	£5	0	0
1457.	The Rood Screen	31	0	0[4]
1460.	New Service Books	5	6	8
1461.	Censer and Pyx	3	0	0
1481.	New Vestments	26	0	0
1482.	A Legenda	8	6	8
1485.	Extension of Churchyard	7	9	6
1490.	Silver Cruets	1	10	0
1499.	A Processional Cross	18	0	0
1526, 1527.	Organs	14	0	0
1534.	New Vestments	30	0	0

[1] Hobhouse, 22.
[2] *Ibid.*
[3] *Creed of Piers Plowman*, i. 123, which must not be confused with Langland's *Vision*.
[4] This was spread over several years, *vide* Hobhouse *passim* Bond, *Screens and Galleries*, makes the cost £27. Either he or I have miscounted the items.

They also built a church-house and prided themselves on paying salaries to the parish clerk, the organist and the sexton.

The actual extension of the churchyard only came to £3 : 6 : 8, but £1 : 13 : 4 was the fee for its consecration, and £2 : 16 : 8 was spent in entertaining the bishop and his retinue.

The Legenda was written on the spot.[1] The parish bought the vellum in quires, and hired the scribes, who were paid 6d. a day. They took two years to write the book, and the sheets written were inspected from time to time.

When Yatton first determined to have a new rood screen, what we should now call a committee was sent all round the country to report on neighbouring screens. After determining what they themselves wanted, standing trees were bought and cut down. It was not until these had seasoned that Crosse, the village carpenter, and his " child " (apprentice), could start on the work. It took several years to complete, and Crosse received a gratuity of 3d. when he set up the post of the rood loft. Also from time to time he received 2d. for beer " to make him well willed ". All the details may be traced in the accounts down to the price of nails and glue. At length it was finished, the rood was on high, the loft was splendidly gilt, and no less than eighty images adorned the screen. It is, as Mr. Bond says, almost inconceivable to us that it could have been made by a village carpenter, but there was then a tradition of craftsmanship and a love of artistic expression.[2] It died out after the Reformation because there was no employment for men like Crosse. An inferior carpenter could destroy. In Elizabeth's reign the man who took down the rood received 5d. and another 6d. for destroying the eighty images. The wages for sacrilege were not high.

All the money required for these objects was raised by the parish council and the churchwardens accounted to the parish council on how it was spent. The church was then a popular institution, and the churches then belonged to the people as

[1] In 1490 St. Dunstan's, Canterbury, had a new Legenda. Lady Roper gave a mark towards it and Mother Belser five, but the book cost £6 : 5 : 9½. The parish paid for 4½ dozen quires of vellum, 31s. 6d., and to the writer of 15 quires, 30s. Cooper in *Archaeologia Cantiana*, xvi. 297, 299.

[2] Bond, *Screens and Galleries*, 68.

they have not done since. After the great spoliation at the Reformation when the churches were robbed of the offerings of the poor, the poor ceased to take any interest in them and found for themselves new social centres in the village alehouses. For all they cared the parson might lock the church up from Sunday to Sunday and think of it as his own. Sir Christopher Trychay, who was Vicar of Morebath in Devon from 1520 to 1574, dared to write in his Parish Book: "When the church goods were sold without commission, no gifts were given to the church but all from the church. . . . By [from] the time of Edward VI the church ever decayed ".[1] To keep the churches from falling down legislation was required authorising the vestry to levy a church rate. It was reluctantly imposed and grudgingly paid.

The parish council was not like the vestry, which developed out of it, able to levy a poor rate, and it may surprise some that in all these churchwardens' accounts there is no record of collections for alleviating the distress of the poor. In these little villages there was probably no need for such collections. The population was stationary. Everyone knew all about everyone else, and people were inter-related. Everyone had his rights on the village common and his share in the common fields. Instead of unemployment the reeve probably found it difficult to get enough labour for the lord's domain. People had few wants, and there was no village shop to tempt the women into debt. Plowmen served from boyhood to old age on the same farm. When they could only totter about, no one thought of dismissing them. They might not receive wages, but no one grudged them food in the farm kitchen, or denied them straw on which to lie in the barn. Nobody was rich, and the poor have always been kind to one another.[2]

But if the church council distributed nothing in charity, they were much interested in the harmony of the parish. When feuds occurred and families quarrelled, the curate and some four elderly men were asked to arbitrate. If they effected a reconciliation or gave an award, the parties were charged, that if the

[1] Quoted Hobhouse, *Churchwardens' Accounts*, 218. Cp. 209.

[2] This would not be true of all districts. In some there was a floating population of vagabonds who were a menace to society. The laws that put down maintenance caused many to be turned adrift. Disbanded soldiers also found it hard to settle down; and in some places enclosures for sheep-farming broke up village life. Busch, *England under the Tudors*, 262 ff.

dispute broke out again, a sum of money would have to be paid to the churchwardens for the good of the church. Sometimes the council had to deal with a parishioner who was defrauding the church. Again arbitration was the first resort. So in the accounts of St. Dunstan's, Canterbury, we read: "Spent on the daying (arbitration)[1] between Baker and the parish iid ob".[2] Sometimes they were driven to legal proceedings. St. Dunstan's, Canterbury, sued Jeffery Peke for six years' rent of his house, which amounted to 2s., and it cost the churchwardens 2s. to get it. They had a second suit to recover three cows or their value from widow Belser and were successful: the cows were valued at 30s. and the costs came to 35s. 2d.; but they included "a potell of wine to Master Ramsay", and a dinner to the Bishop's Commissary. Of these costs the court only allowed them 15s. 8d. So they had some reason to complain that they would have done better if "Master John Roper Esquire" and his fellow arbitrators had acted betimes, and not by their delay involved the parish in legal proceedings.[3]

The parish church was not only the centre of worship but also of social life. It brought men together and made them feel one. It educated them quite unconsciously in self-government and independence. While the power of the manor court, with its insistence on feudal rights and the permanence of subjection, was everywhere decaying, the church council became the spontaneous mouthpiece for maintaining human rights and equal consideration.[4] In the constitution of the country it had as yet no legal existence—it developed differently in different parishes—but it was dominated by the idea that the christened formed one family, having one Father, the God who is over all.

The question now arises, Were the people, so zealous for their church and its adornment, ignorant of the faith for which it stood, and if not, how did the illiterate man receive instruction?

Already in this chapter I have spoken of the explanations of the Mass written in verse so that they could be easily memorised, and we may presume that the authors had reason to suppose that someone would teach them to the unlettered. For the teaching of the Faith and practice of the Church, as far back as 1281

[1] *N.E.D.*
[2] *Arch. Cantiana*, xvii. 141.
[3] *Ibid.* 146. Cf. xvi. 299-303.
[4] Hobhouse, *Churchwardens' Accounts*, Introduction.

Archbishop Peckham had ordered that four times every year the parish priest should expound the Creed, the Ten Commandments, the Gospel Precepts, the seven Works of Mercy, the seven Deadly Sins, the seven Virtues and the seven Sacraments of Grace.[1] They were to do so *vulgariter absque cujuslibet subtilitatis textura fantastica*,[2] and the archbishop by way of a model added a brief exposition of his own. In 1357, Cardinal Thoresby, Archbishop of York, issued similar injunctions, but he went further than Peckham in ordering the instruction to be given every Lord's Day. He also wrote a catechetical instruction in Latin, and had it translated and expounded by a monk named Gaytrige, Garryk or Gaytryk.[3] This was in the northern dialect. Another version still further expanded, in the language of the Midlands, was written by Wyclif who had been a friend of Thoresby. This was before he had adopted opinions at variance with the Church, but is in his terse and vigorous style and betrays his interest in moral conduct. The most "Wyclifite" sentence concerns Sunday:

> Hear thou God's service with reverence and devotion and say devoutly thy Paternoster, and thy Belief, and thine Ave Maria and other devout prayers, if thou can. And hear God's Law taught in thy mother's tongue, for that is better to thee than to hear many Masses. Afterwards eat and drink in measure, and thank God for his gift.[4]

How far the injunctions of Peckham and Thoresby were observed it is impossible to say, but John Myrc, writing in the XV century, assumes that priests will give similar instruction.[5] In the Bidding of the Bedes in the York Manuals the priest each Sunday asked the people to pray:

> For the Parson of this parish (and others) that have the cure of men's souls, that God give them grace well to teach their subjects, and

[1] Simmons and Nolloth, *Lay Folks' Catechism*, Introd. E.E.T.S. Cp. Cutts, *Parish Priests, etc.* 216-222.

[2] *Ibid.* p. 7.

[3] Gaytrige's Sermon has been printed by G. E. Perry for the E.E.T.S. (*Religious Pieces*, 1867). It only fills fourteen pages and expounds the Creed, Commandments, Sacraments, the Seven deeds of mercy and the Seven deadly sins.

[4] *Lay Folks' Catechism*, 41. This was not merely a Wyclifite opinion—Whitford the monk of Syon had certainly no Wyclifite tendencies; but he writes in *Werke for Householders*: "If there be a sermon any time in the day, let them be present, all that are not occupied in needful and lawful business: all other (occupations) laid aside, let them even keep the preaching, rather than the Mass, if perchance they may not hear both" (quoted Gasquet, *Eve of the Reformation*, 249).

[5] Myrc, *Instructions for Parish Priests*, 3.

the subjects well to work after haleful (wholesome) teaching, that both teachers and subjects may come to everlasting bliss.[1]

It is not without significance that the Yorkshire parish of Kirkby Malsherd in 1500 presented their parson at a visitation for not expounding the fundamental truths.[2] It proves that the people expected it and suggests that neighbouring parishes were more fortunate in their parsons.

The English people have always liked sermons, even long ones—Bishop Alcock preached for over two hours in St. Mary's, Cambridge—but they did not always get them, neither were they always satisfied with those they heard. It was no unusual answer to be made to Visitation enquiries that the parish priest preached as far as he knew how to do so—*quatenus novit*.[3]

To help unlearned and unready priests there were books like the *Homiliarius* and the *Liber Festivalis* of John Myrc. Both were translated into English and the latter was published by Caxton in 1483.[4]

But if the parish priest neglected preaching altogether, no one could well escape the wandering friars, who would hold forth in fields and market-places if they were denied the church.

[1] York Manual, quoted by Cutts, *Parish Priests, etc.* 208.

[2] *York Fabric Rolls*, 264 : " We also desire to have our Belief showed four times a year, as ye say we should have ". In one of his sermons Rypon, sub-deacon of Durham, says, " What punishment do the priests of to-day merit, who enter on the churches with the cure thereof, or rarely or never preach the Word of God ? Forsooth, neither do they preach a good life by their actions, which is called the preaching of an exemplary life. Assuredly they are worthy of the everlasting death of the soul, which is the death of Gehenna " (quoted by Owst, *Preaching in Med. England*, 47). Obviously sermons were expected and required. The preacher was denouncing the neglect of a well-recognised duty.

[3] Cutts, *Parish Priests, etc.* 286, 287.

[4] There is a XV-century MS. of the *Homiliarius* in English in the British Museum. Wordsworth and Littlehales, *Old Service Books*, 158. Gasquet, *Old English Bible*, 131, argues from the existence of such books that it was customary to sing the Gospel in Latin and English at High Mass. That was customary in France, but there is no evidence for it in England except some lines in *The Lay Folks' Mass Book*, 16, but they only appear in the B Text, which is nearest to the French original. On the other hand, Ellis, *Original Letters*, III Series, ii. 192, prints a letter written in 1531 to the Duke of Norfolk describing the Lutheran Mass at Nuremburg: " There the priest readeth softly the Gospel in Latin. In the mean space the deacon getteth into the pulpit, and readeth aloud the Gospel in the Almain tongue." The writer, probably Sir Thomas Boleyn, thought this worth reporting, because it was new to him. In 1537 *The Pystels and Gospels in English* were printed for general use ; and Lee, Archbishop of York, ordered that they should be used out of the English Bible during service (Burnet, *Reformation*, vi. 201). In 1538 Shaxton, Bishop of Salisbury, issued a similar injunction (*ibid.* 210). In 1542 Bonner, Bishop of London, followed suit (Wilkins, *Concilia*, iii. 866).

Their sermons were racy of the soil. They illustrated their teaching from the lives of the saints and enlivened them by stories from the *Gesta Romanorum*.[1] They pointed their morals by quoting popular proverbs and spiced their denunciations with coarse jibes.

The shriving pew or confessional was also a place of instruction. It gave the priest an opportunity of dealing intimately with the individual soul. He could question him about his faith as well as convict him of his sinfulness. Myrc instructs parish priests to ascertain if a penitent can say his Paternoster, Creed and Ave, and if he cannot, to give him such a penance that he will know them before he comes again.[2] He is to explain the Creed and Ten Commandments, but he is not to be hard on offenders :

> Better it is with penance lutte (light)
> Into Purgatory a man to put,
> Than with penance over much
> Send him to hell pit.[3]

The services for Baptism, Marriage and the Visitation of the Sick were partly in English, and there were also short English Litanies. The following occurs in a XV-century prymer :

> By Thy holy passion and most piteous death,
> Lord, deliver us,
> By thy blessed burying
> Lord, deliver us.
> . . . .
> In the hour of our death : help us, Lord,
> In the day of doom : deliver us, Lord.
>
> We sinners pray Thee hear us,
> That Thou give us peace and very concord
> We pray on Thee to hear us.
> . . . . . .
> Son of God, we pray Thee to hear us,
> Lamb of God, that doest away the sins of the world,
> Well hear us, Lord.[4]

Every Sunday at Mass there was the Bidding of the Bedes. It could be expanded or curtailed according to the occasion.

[1] *Gesta Romanorum*, a collection of stories for the help of preachers. Both Chaucer and Shakespeare were indebted to it.

[2] Myrc, *Instructions*, 25. [3] *Ibid*. 51.

[4] Wordsworth and Littlehales, *op. cit*. 52, 55. Quoted from B.M. MSS. 17011.

There was no fixed form, but all forms follow the same general plan. Prayers were first asked for the spirituality and spiritual necessities, then for the king, his government, the people and their welfare, for the sick and whole, and lastly for the dead.[1] A few extracts may be given from the *Festyvall*:

Ye shall kneel down on your knees, and lift up your hearts, making your prayers unto Almighty God.

. . . . . .

For all Dukes, Earls, Barons, Knights and Squires, and other Lords of the King's Council, which have any rule and governance of this land, that God give them grace so to counsel, rule and govern, that God be pleased, the land defended, and to the profit and salvation of all the realm.

. . . . . .

Also ye shall pray for all them that be sick or diseased of this parish, that God send them health the rather for our prayers. For all the women who be in Our Lady's bands and with child in this parish or in any other, that God send to them fair deliverance, to their children right shape, name and christendom, and to the mothers purification.

. . . . . .

And for all them that would be here and may not for sickness or travail, or any other lawful occupation, that they may have part in all the good deeds that shall be done here in this place or in any other place.

These are only selected sentences from a very lengthy Bidding. The Bidding in the *York Manual* is shorter and more simple. It was also broken up by antiphons, collects and responses. Again we select:

For all our good parishioners wheresoever they be, on water or on land, that God of His goodness save them from all manner of perils, and bring them safe where they would be in health of body and soul and also of goods.

. . . . . .

We shall also pray for all land tylland,[2] that God for His goodness and for His grace and through our good prayers maintain them that they may be saved from all evil winds and weathers and from all dreadful storms, that God send us corn and cattle for to live upon to God's pleasure and the welfare of our souls.

[1] Bede or bead = a prayer: *N.E.D.* The Sarum Form is printed by Maskell, *Monumenta Ritualia*; the York Form in the *Manual* edited by Raine for the Surtees Society. The *Festyvall* version is printed by F. E. Brightman, *The English Rite*, 1032.

[2] Tylland = tillage. The word is not in the *N.E.D.*

It will be seen that where the priest did his duty the illiterate had an opportunity of learning how to assist intelligently at Mass, the articles of his belief, the rules of Christian conduct, and what he should pray for. He was also called at stated times to listen to the Great Sentence or Greater Excommunication.

John Myrc says that it was read twice or thrice a year,[1] but Lyndwood tells us that it ought to be read four times: on the Sunday after Michaelmas, Mid-Lent Sunday, Trinity Sunday, and the Sunday after St. Peter in Chains. (August 1st.) It was to be read in church (though Lyndwood allows the churchyard) and with dreadful solemnity, the priest having cross, bell, book and lighted candle, *ut major auditoribus incutiatur timor*, says Lyndwood.[2] Myrc instructs:

> That shalt pronounce this hideous thing
> With cross and candle and bell knelling:
> Speak out redely for nought thou wonde [hesitate]
> That all may thee understonde.

There was no one form. That printed by Maskell[3] is rather in the form of an explanatory address, until it comes to the actual anathema. The form found in Myrc's Instruction is a regular commination beginning "By the authority of the Father, and the Son and the Holy Ghost . . . we accurse". Both deal with all sorts of misdeeds from murder to the withholding of tithes. After pronouncing the anathema the priest extinguished the candle, cast it down and spat on the ground, while the bell knelled out doom. Listening to this curse the rustic could be under no mistake—there were things which he must not do under penalty of separation from God and his fellows.[4]

All these means of instruction were open to the illiterate who lived in a parish where there was a diligent priest; but the illiterate are not always eager to learn and there must have been many neglected parishes at the beginning of the XVI century.

Many attributed powers and virtues to Church ordinances which the Church officially did not countenance, and this led to much superstition. The Church also, in order to popularise religion, had allowed a dubious crop of ceremonies and devotions to spring up, some of them silly and some of them childish. At

[1] Myrc, *Instructions*, 21-24.
[2] Lyndwood, 355.
[3] *Monumenta Ritualia*, III. 312, 330.
[4] *Ibid.* II. clxxi.

these the intelligent scoffed and the Reformers were to rage ; but neither troubled to understand or sympathise with the simple and the poor.

It is over eighty years since Dr. Rock published his delightful book, *The Church of Our Fathers*.[1] With much research and great learning he described the ceremonies of the mediaeval Church, their meaning and origins. He pictured for us a devout people who loved and understood their services, and left us wondering how the Reformation could have occurred. More recently Dr. Coulton, with even greater learning, has torn aside the veils of reticence, and revealed the dirt, disorder, cruelty and ignorance of the Middle Ages, and left us wondering how a system so corrupt could have survived so long. Perhaps if these scholars could transport us across the ages, each could take us to a parish which exactly verified his conclusions, and each would direct our attention to the facts that interested him.

We are in danger to-day of passing from a sentimental view of the Middle Ages seen from a sanctuary where the sun irradiates the stained-glass windows, to a realistic view of the Middle Ages as seen from a gutter on a gloomy day. We must be loyal to truth and not shut our eyes to unpleasing facts, but in transmitting the tradition we have received, we must not forget to conserve and emphasise all that is true and of good report. Above all in dealing with what is worst we should endeavour to understand.

V. *Ceremonial*

The churches were full of monuments, paintings, images and reliquaries. All the arts had been summoned to the aid of religion. The services were spectacular and dramatic ; but they had sometimes ceased to be seemly or appropriate, and their meaning was often liable to be misunderstood. There were people who used the Holy Bread as a charm, and others that believed Holy Water would of itself cleanse them from venial sins.[2] Rites had been so over-elaborated that they no longer made a direct appeal to the worshippers. There were many " dark and dumb ceremonies " which edified no one, and some

[1] The references in this book are to the edition by Hart and Bishop Frere.

[2] Aquinas, *Summa*, III. Q. lxxxvii. A. 3.

were neither dumb nor dark though their meaning and origin had been forgotten. Erasmus, for instance, tells us that on a certain day a stag's head on the point of a spear was brought into St. Paul's Cathedral by a rabble, who carried it to the high altar, blowing on hunting horns and behaving as if possessed with a Delian frenzy.[1] He did not know the tradition that St. Paul's was built on the site of a temple dedicated to Diana, or he might have connected the ceremony with the worship of the Delian goddess, and would certainly have been wrong. We know the origin of the custom ;[2] but we do not know the meaning of the horn dance at Abbots Bromley, nor whence that remote inland village obtained its horns of reindeer.[3] More than one ancient custom, like the yule log and the illuminated holly-bush at Christmas, date back to the dim gods of the misty North. Gregory the Great had written to Mellitus that feasts, unless repugnant to the Christian Faith, were not to be abolished but connected with the festivals of the Church.[4]

But we are not now concerned with the folklore of the people but with definitely Christian worship and how it was celebrated, how it developed and how it was degraded.

In the earlier Middle Ages God had naturally been thought of as the Overlord, and the Eucharist as an act of homage which the priest offered on behalf of the people for whom he was responsible. In a feudal society the Pope and emperor were said to hold of God directly, but everyone else did homage to someone and received homage from those beneath him—even the villein had rights over his child. In a feudal society a man was only concerned with his immediate lord who acted on behalf of those for whom he was responsible—the lord for his vassals,

[1] Erasmus, *Ecclesiastes*, fol. 51 (ed. 1535).

[2] The origin of the custom may be found in Strype's *Stow*, Bk. III. 164. "Sir William Bawd, Kt. . . . 1274 . . . granted to Marvy de Bosham, Dean of St. Paul's and the Chapter, that in consideration of 22 acres of land . . . within the Manor of Westly in Essex . . . he would, on the conversion of St. Paul, give them a good doe . . . and upon the Feast of St. Paul in summer a good buck, and offer the same at the High Altar, the same to be spent among the Canons Resident. The doe to be brought by one man, at the hour of the Procession to the High Altar ; and the bringer to have nothing. The buck to be brought by all his menay, and they are to receive 12d. and no more." Machyn, *Diary*, 141, commemorates the last time of the offering in 1557. Bonner attended in full pontificals, and all the parochial clergy were in copes. Forty horns were blowing round the buck's head.

[3] Plot, *Hist. of Staffordshire*, 434. Cf. Chambers, *Mediaeval Stage*, i. 166.

[4] St. Gregory, *Epistolae*, xi. 7.

the villein for his child. No one was independent but the excommunicate and the outlaw. So the priest was responsible for his flock and acted on their behalf. The services were rendered in their closed choirs with stately magnificence by Benedictines, or with the austere and self-conscious simplicity of reconciled sinners by Cistercians or Carthusians. The worship was rendered to God, and there was not much consideration for the edification of man.

The coming of the friars caused a revolution in the spiritual outlook. They thought not so much of the majesty and sovereignty of God, as of His exceeding loving-kindness in sending into the world His only-begotten Son. It was the incarnate Son, Very Man, Mary's little boy, who was the centre of their devotion ; and the altar was the place where he vouchsafed His Presence. They taught that He had come to redeem this world and claim it for God, that He had come loving men, sharing men's lot, and entering into their joys, their sorrows and pains, that He had come to preach a gospel to the poor. By preaching, by hymns and new devotions, they made religion interesting to the man in the street. They aimed at the consecration of the whole of life : they were so sure that this world as well as the next belonged to their Master. Their methods spread to the parish churches, were slowly adopted in cathedrals and even penetrated to the conservative cloisters. Religion was popularised.

A religion, however, that is becoming popular is in danger of being profaned. It is sad to think of what was originally childlike becoming childish, of bright fancies fading into silly superstitions, of spontaneous extravagances in speech being repeated as if they were dogmatic definitions, and spontaneous acts of extravagant devotion developing into a licensed disorder. A too great familiarity with sacred things may cause men to be flippant and irreverent ; and the holiest mysteries, when explained in vulgar terms, may cease to inspire wonder, so that any real sense of the supernatural is lost.

It was entirely right to teach men how to live by means of allegories, and to teach men by symbols to grasp spiritual truths. Allegories are analogies in action ; and symbolism is a visible shorthand by which we recognise truths that defy verbal definition. Both are justified by the belief of the unity of all things in God. But what was first an allegory may come to be regarded as a fact, and in the Middle Ages many such stories crept into the Breviary until " to lie like a second Nocturn " became a proverb.[1] Symbols also may be reverenced when men have forgotten for what they stood ; they may become mascots or charms, savouring of idolatry. Ceremonies also may be so elaborated, that their correct performance may become a complicated game and end in what the Reformers called " mummery ". At the beginning of the XVI century, parasites were strangling the fairest flowers in the ecclesiastical garden. Careful weeding and pruning was everywhere needed, but the Reformers found it easier to dig up the garden, and, having danced round a bonfire, to plant the bed anew with bitter herbs—medicinal no doubt.

The Reformers were intellectual and had a strident contempt for " the sottishly ignorant " and no consideration for their needs. They had a great work to perform in recalling men to a belief in the transcendent God, and a great protest to enforce against mechanical conceptions of worship. But they made a great mistake in believing that abstract words of five syllables had necessarily a greater spiritual content than concrete images. The poor in consequence were deprived of a religion which they could understand and practise.

Before the Reformation, children stole into church to see the crib, and say a prayer to Him who blessed the little ones. At Candlemas the congregation marched round the church with their lighted candles remembering the aged Simeon and in honour of Him Who is the Light of the World. All received ashes on Ash Wednesday that they might understand the defilement of sin, and remember that the day was coming when it would be said of them, " earth to earth, ashes to ashes, dust to dust ". On Maundy Thursday, great men washed the feet of the poor, typifying the reversal of human values in the light of the Incarnation. On Good Friday men crept to the Cross in humble adoration of Him Who had died for them. On Easter Eve the new fire was hallowed from which the Paschal candle was lighted, and the cold hearths of every home were kindled anew. At Rogationtide the fields were blessed and religion consecrated the daily toil. At Whitsuntide the dove descended

[1] Quoted by Pullan, *History of the Book of Common Prayer*, 154.

from the roof of the church, while clouds of incense perfumed the air. At Corpus Christi time were the glad processions of those rejoicing in Emmanuel, God with us. At Lammas the loaf, being the first fruits of the harvest, was presented as an act of thanksgiving to Him Who hears our prayer "Give us this day our daily bread". On All Hallows five boys in surplices with amices drawn over their heads chanted "*Venite omnes virgines sapientissimae*" in honour of those who had gone in to the marriage supper of the Lamb. On St. Nicholas Day or Holy Innocents a boy pontificated, reminding all of the command to turn and become as little children![1]

Such ceremonies were beautiful and cannot be called superstitious: but everything depended on how they were performed; and we must remember that the Reformers knew them as a working system. They were not everywhere celebrated with decorum, and a certain profanity was sometimes apparent. In the Middle Ages the line between the sacred and profane was undetermined. The men of that age had a practical instinct which led them to confuse the objects of this world and another. For instance, it was quite right that the parish should go in procession through the cornfields with the Blessed Sacrament to bless the fields and pray for the harvest. It was equally right perhaps that they should beat the bounds of the parish, and beat little boys at selected spots that they might remember them, and engage in joyous battles with the neighbouring parish at a disputed corner. What to our minds is inconceivable is that they should try to carry out both objects at the same time.

Perhaps we may best understand how a popular religion is liable to be degraded by reviewing some of the ceremonies of Holy Week and noting how they were sometimes and in some places spoilt.[2]

The service for Palm Sunday may be read in the Sarum Missal.[3] It is beautiful, scriptural, and the rubrics are appropriate, though to carry them out effectively a large staff of clergy would be required. At the moment we are concerned with the popular religion and have to think not of what was correct but of customary usage. After the blessing and distribution of the

[1] Rock, *Church of Our Fathers*, passim.

[2] Most of the following details are derived from Feasey, *Holy Week Ceremonial*, and from Tyrer, *Holy Week* (Alcuin Club).

[3] Warren, trans. of the *Sarum Missal*, i. 217, 229.

palms, the veil before the rood was raised, and the priest knelt to say *Ave Rex Noster*. Then the congregation formed itself into a procession and went outside the church. A tabernacle for the Blessed Sacrament and relics had been erected in the churchyard. The priests in charge of it advanced to meet the congregation, who sang Hosannah, and " Blessed is He that cometh in the Name of the Lord ". There were four stations at which the Gospel and antiphons were sung. At one of them, from an eminence, seven boys dressed as prophets sang the passage from Zechariah. The fourth station was before the Cross over against the south door, which was known as the Palm Cross and decorated with willows and flowers. At the west door a gallery was erected from whence boys sang Theodulph's hymn :

All glory, laud and honour
To Thee, Redeemer King.

Then the priests raised on high the shrine which contained the pyx and relics, and the people with bowed heads passed under it into the church to hear the Great Passion.

So far all was well, but it was a custom for a boy sometimes dressed as an angel to scatter from above the west porch cakes and flowers, so that the solemnity was spoilt by a scramble. Also comic relief was in some places provided by a wooden ass which was dragged along in the procession with a man walking behind and belabouring it with a whip. The whip was subsequently presented at the altar with a purse attached containing thirty pieces of silver.[1]

The Great Passion (St. Matthew xxvi., xxvii.) was sung from the rood loft. The tenor sang the narrative portions in recitative, the trebles sang the words of disciples and Jews in pricksong, and the bass the words of our Lord ; but our modern susceptibilities are somewhat shocked by finding in churchwardens' accounts how wine and beer were provided for the singers in the loft. Tenebrae was a most impressive service to

[1] The ass also had his part to play on the Feast of the Circumcision (*Fête des Fous*), when a woman with a child in her lap rode an ass in the procession in remembrance of the Flight into Egypt. With this was associated the *Prose de l'Âne*—

Orientis partibus
Adventavit asinus
Sarcinis optissimus
Hez, Sire, As'nes, Hez !

(Duncan, *The Story of the Carol*, 40)

signify the setting of the Sun of Righteousness and the darkness of the Jewish people who rejected our Lord. In dolorous tones the Lessons from the Book of Lamentations were read with the refrain, *Hierusalem*, *Hierusalem*, *convertere*, etc. One by one as the service proceeded the lights on the hearse were extinguished signifying " the manifold lights given by the Holy Prophets which at this time were darkened ". Only one light remained, to represent our Lord, and that was hidden behind the altar. The church was in darkness, there was a great stillness. Then the ceremoniarius used his clapper as a signal for the one light to be restored to typify the resurrection. But the whole service was spoilt when everyone arrived with his clapper; [1] and young people awaited, tense and eager, for the moment when they could make a noise.

On Maundy Thursday there was a reconciliation of penitents who had been driven out of the Church on Ash Wednesday. At the great west door of York Minster the archbishop sat to deal with offenders, and those who were obdurate were bound to the pillars and publicly whipped whatever their degree. In parish churches the usage was similar. Latimer speaks of " poor Magdalene under the board and in the belfry " [2] praying for readmission into the Church. On Maundy Thursday kings and great men washed the feet of the poor, but the poor did not want to have their feet washed or to minister to " The pride that aped humility ". In consequence they had to be well paid before they would submit to receive this act of charity.

On Good Friday a crucifix was brought down to the altar steps and laid on a cushion. Two priests sat beside it, and the people on their knees crept to kiss the Cross. *The Rationale of Ceremonial* [3] approved of the custom, " where we humble ourselves to Christ before the Cross, offering unto Him and kissing the Cross in memory of our redemption by Christ upon the Cross ". The king crept to the Cross and made his offering. At the same time he blessed the silver cramp rings which were supposed to derive their efficacy from Edward the Confessor's ring, which was kept in Westminster Abbey. The poor also crept to the Cross and made their humble offerings of eggs, bacon or apples.

[1] A clapper was used because no bell might be sounded in Holy Week. Tyrer, *Holy Week*, 71. For Tenebrae vide *Catholic Encyclopaedia*.

[2] Latimer, *Works*, i. 16.

[3] Cobb, *Rationale of Ceremonial*, Alcuin Club.

It so became possible for the Reformers to represent the ceremony as a device of the priests to get gain; and "to holde forth the Crosse for egges on Good Friday" became the subject of satire.[1]

On Good Friday afternoon the Crucifix, after being washed with wine and water, was wrapt in silk and solemnly buried with the Host in the Easter sepulchre, but in some places with misplaced realism the Host was enclosed in a wooden image which was called by the irreverent "Little Jack". The sepulchre was strewn with violets, tapers were lighted all round it, and watchers were appointed who were allowed to make a fire of coals to keep them warm through the night in the chilly church. At the barriers to the sepulchre stood a priest with a disciplining rod for any who cared to stretch out their hands for correction. Sir Thomas More tells of a lady "who wept ever for tender heart two days after when she talked of it, that the priest had on Good Friday with the discipline rod beaten her hard upon her lily-white hands".[2]

Very early on Easter morning at the sepulchre the liturgical drama of the resurrection was played. Three priests in dalmatics represented the three Marys and another represented the angel. The antiphons were beautiful and appropriate, but the ceremony became over-elaborate and too realistic, and was suppressed[3] not only in England, but in countries of the Roman obedience.

These notes on Holy Week have only been made to show how at the beginning of the XVI century a very beautiful ritual was liable to be debased in popular usage. There were then, as now, well-ordered parishes, but the abuses were sufficiently established to stir reforming zeal. Similar instances of degradation might be quoted throughout the year, but it may be sufficient to examine the history of the Boy Bishop.[4]

St. Nicholas was the patron saint of boys, and either on his feast, December 6th, or on Holy Innocents' Day, there was a Boy Bishop in the cathedrals and principal schools.[5] His

[1] Becon, *Works*, Parker Society. [2] *Apologye*, 114.

[3] Chambers, *Mediaeval Stage*, ii. 1-67.

[4] For the Boy Bishop see Rimbault in *Camden Society Miscellany*, vol. vii.; Rock, *Church of our Fathers*, vol. iv. 250-256; Chambers, *Mediaeval Stage*, i. 336-371.

[5] In most cathedrals on Holy Innocents' Day. In Bristol the Mayor attended in state at St. Nicholas Church on December 5th to hear evensong "and on the morrow to hire thiere masse and offer and hire the Bishop's sermon": Chambers, *Med. Stage*, i. 359. Cp. Hunt's *Bristol*, 110. At Winchester College the "Bishop" was to officiate on St. Nicholas' Day "and by no means on that of the Innocents". The same rule prevailed at Eton and King's College, Cambridge. Chambers, *op. cit.* i. 365.

episcopate took the place of the Feast of Fools, when the inferior clerks masqueraded in the vestments of their betters and burlesqued the services of the Church. This feast had been condemned and put down by ecclesiastical authority, but the ceremony of the Boy Bishop had been substituted in the hopes that children would be more amenable to control—a hope that was not in all places fulfilled, so that scandals in Germany caused the Council of Basle to forbid the custom.[1]

In England that condemnation had no effect : and in English cathedrals on St. Nicholas' or Holy Innocents' Day the senior chorister " if sufficiently handsome " was vested as a bishop and duly enthroned. The other choristers, St. Nicholas' clerks, occupied the stalls of dignitaries who sat humbly on the lower bench. A very beautiful service to follow the first evensong of Holy Innocents may be found in the *Sarum Processionale*.[2] Next day the boys conducted the service as far as the offertory,[3] and the Boy Bishop preached and blessed the people. There was something that was beautiful in this exaltation of childhood. There was a real belief that out of the mouth of babes and sucklings praise was perfected. It was good for reverend dignitaries to turn and become as little children at Christmastime while the children occupied their places. It was good that once a year the dean should bow the knee to receive the blessing of a boy.

At York, the Boy Bishop went on Visitation attended by a large retinue and was entertained at the great monasteries and given considerable sums of money.[4] At Exeter this was forbidden, and the " St. Nicholas " of Ottery St. Mary was not allowed to go outside the parish.

Rich vestments and ornaments were provided. We read of a white mitre embroidered with flowers and a crozier for the Boy

[1] *Catholic Encyclopaedia.* [2] *Camden Soc. Misc.* vii. Nos. 7 and 8.

[3] Maxwell-Lyte, Eton College, 156, quotes statute xxxi about the boys singing Mass *praeter secreta Missae*. Sparrow Simpson, *Old St. Paul's*, 85, quotes a statute of the cathedral which says, " Up to the more solemn part of the offertory ". Warton, *Hist. of Poetry*, ii. 531, says the boys of Winchester College performed the whole service. This was, of course, his mistake.

[4] The accounts of the Boy Bishop of York for 1396 are extant and are printed by Rimbault in *Camden Misc.* in an appendix. From the *Northumberland Household Book* we find that the Barn Bishops of Beverley and York each received 20s. from the Earl. In the *Durham Account Rolls* the Boy Bishop was called *Episcopus Eleemosynariae*. He received presents from almost all the officers of the abbey who entered the amounts in their account rolls. These sums varied from 20d. to 5s.

Bishop at St. Paul's. At York he had a cope of red velvet "with this scripture, 'the hye way is best'".[1] Archbishop Rotheram left to his Jesus College a mitre of gold for the "Barn Bishop"; while in the *Northumberland Household Book* may be seen a complete inventory of all that pertained to his office.[2]

Serious people took the ministrations of Boy Bishops seriously. For instance, Joan Symonds, who died in Coventry 1507, left—

> To the child Bishop for the time being my cloak of scarlet to make him a robe of on the condition that the Bishop with the children shall come to my husband's grave and mine, and there say *De Profundis* for my husband's soul and mine, the same day as they do at the grave of Thomas Wildgress in the Drapers' chapel.[3]

Colet[4] approved of the custom, for he ordained that the boys of St. Paul's school "shall every Childermas day come to Paul's Church and hear the Child Bishop's sermon, and after be at High Mass, and each of them offer a penny to the Child Bishop; and with them the Masters and Surveyors of the School". He went further and had a "St. Nicholas" of his own at St. Paul's School, for whom no less a person than Erasmus wrote his *Concio de Puero Jesu*.

Bishop Alcock wrote a sermon for the Boy Bishop,[5] and two others besides have survived.[6] One of them was preached in St. Paul's in 1497 and had evidently been written for the preacher. It is artificial in construction, and conceits; it parades scraps of classical learning, but illustrates its points by apt quotations from Scripture. When it attempts to be boyish it only reveals the facetious pedagogue. The other sermon was preached by John Stubs in the Cathedral Church of Gloucester in 1558, which was the last occasion for such orations. It also opens with some laboured divinity and reflections on the wickedness of heretics, ending with a short Bidding; but then

[1] Wordsworth, *Mediaeval Services*, 126. In 1472 the surplice of a Boy Bishop cost 5s., his cap in 1508 cost 1s. Rogers: *Agriculture and Prices*, iv. 582.

[2] *Northumberland Household Book*, 349.

[3] A. W. Reed, *Early Tudor Drama*, 4.

[4] Lupton, *Life of Colet*, 175, 176.

[5] *Sermo pro Episcopo puerorum*, by Alcock. Two editions of this sermon were printed by Wynkyn de Worde, and one copy of each survives—one at Stoneyhurst and one at C.C.C., Oxford. Gordon Duff, *Fifteenth Century English Books*, 4.

[6] Rimbault has edited these two sermons in *Camden Society Miscellany*, vii.

the style changes and we are aware that we have the authentic note of a boy. John Stubs, like many head-boys since, had very sound views on the value of corporal punishment, and feared that his juniors would not receive as much as he did of that salutary discipline. He is shocked at little choristers who come into choir forgetting to make their reverence, and instead of kneeling during service, "squat on their tails which lack twigging". He notices the language of street boys in which they must have been schooled at home, and the behaviour of grammar-school boys "as they leave school and go to their meals". "They are most ungracious grafts, ripe and ready for all lewd liberty".[1] He does not spare fathers and mothers who coddle their coaxing children, and do not study the thirtieth chapter of the Son of Sirach, which he finds too long to quote. He reproves schoolmasters who beat boys for breaking Priscian's head, a venial fault in Stubs' eyes, and neglect more serious offences. He ends, however, by apologising for his attempt "to reform my elders, I being so young in age as I am, and to reprove others wherein I am not clear myself, as some will judge who knew me in my childhood".

We may be quite sure that John Stubs carried out his duties of St. Nicholas with decorum, and saw to it that his clerks behaved themselves with propriety; but St. Nicholas and his clerks did not always come from cathedrals or collegiate churches with almonry schools and disciplined children. The custom had spread into parishes, and at Christmas-time the streets were alive with children dressed up in ecclesiastical garments of a sort, singing without any reverence scraps of church services, and knocking at doors with the hope of apples, nuts or even of halfpence. We need not be surprised that in 1541 Henry VIII, in suppressing the festival, said:

> Children be strangely decked and apparelled to counterfeit priests bishops and women; and so led with songs and dances from house to house, blessing the people and gathering of money; and boys do sing mass and preach in the pulpit, with much other unfitting and inconvenient usages, rather to the derision than any true glory of God, or honour of His saints.[2]

In Queen Mary's reign Bonner, Bishop of London, seems to

[1] Rivalry between the King's School, where the choristers are educated, and the Crypt School continued for centuries.

[2] Wilkins, *Concilia*, iii. 860.

have doubted about reviving the custom. On November 13th, 1554, he allowed it, but withdrew permission before St. Nicholas' Day, and was not everywhere obeyed.[1] Two years later "St. Nicholas went abroad in most parts of London, singing after the old fashion, and was received by many good people into their houses, and had as much good cheer as ever they had, in many places".[2] Elizabeth came to the throne and the custom was once more abolished. It was so utterly forgotten that less than a hundred years afterwards John Gregory,[3] on discovering the effigy in Salisbury Cathedral, "marvelled that a bishop should be so small, or a child so great in clothes". He searched and re-discovered the Boy Bishop, but it is very doubtful if the effigy that provoked his search had any connexion with a "St. Nicholas" who died young.

VI. *Miracle Plays*

If the ceremonies of the Church were liable to be debased, what is to be said of the miracle plays which were latterly altogether under lay control? Roughly speaking they flourished from 1350 to 1550, beginning, it is true, more than a century earlier and lingering long afterwards, dying one by one. The Whitsuntide plays at Chester were last performed in 1594,[4] while the parish play at Weston in Hampshire survived until 1680.[5]

All the arts had been cradled in the church or the cloister, but they early escaped from the limitations of their nurseries to find a varied expression in the world. So the religious plays began with the acted antiphons of Christmas and Easter, and were gradually elaborated and transformed.[6] From the church they passed to the churchyard; and then, when they drew large crowds from outside, they were taken over by the guilds and performed in the streets. The plays themselves, showing as they do a wide knowledge of Scripture, must in the first instance have been written by ecclesiastics, even if the Coventry cycle

[1] In 1555 the Child Bishop of St. Paul's sang to Queen Mary at St. James's the verses composed by Hugh Rhodes in her honour. Warton, *Hist. of Poetry*, III, 265.

[2] *Machyn's Diary*, Camden Soc., 75, 77, 121.

[3] John Gregory, 1607–1646. Wood, *Athenae Oxonienses*, iii. 205-207. The first edition of his *Posthuma* was published 1649, and his account of the Boy Bishop begins p. 95. A second edition in quarto was published 1671.

[4] Wright, *Chester Plays*, xix.

[5] Cox, *Churchwardens' Accounts*, 268.

[6] E. K. Chambers, *Mediaeval Stage*, vol. i. ch

did not come, as tradition said, from the Grey Friars. The Chester plays have been attributed to Ranulph Higden who died in 1364, and closely resemble in parts plays of French origin.[1] This, however, does not mean that the Church officially approved of them, and their relation to ecclesiastical authority is hard to determine. The Decretals[2] seem quite clear in forbidding all dramatic performances. Even minstrels and joculatores (tumblers and conjurers) are banned. The clergy might relieve their necessities, but must not look upon their shows and still less take part in them.[3] Archbishop Greenfield in 1312 held an enquiry at Ripon about clergy who transgressed these rules. Yet somehow or other ecclesiastical casuists must have got round their difficulties and proved to themselves that such representations as they wished to display were not covered by the prohibition.[4] No doubt there were grave churchmen from Grossetête onwards who continued to disapprove of them, for puritanism was very strong throughout the Middle Ages.[5] We are not surprised that Piers Plowman was never " at markets and miracles " ;[6] nor are we surprised that the Wife of Bath went merrily " to playes of myracles and to marriages ",[7] while " Joly Absolom ", the parish clerk, " who goeth with the censer on the holiday ",

> Sometymes to show his lightnesse and maistrye
> Playeth Herodes in a scaffold hye.[8]

This was very wrong. Clerks were of course forbidden to perform, but then we must remember that " Joly Absolom " disregarded more serious prohibitions.

[1] Pollard, *Miracle Plays*, xxi. [2] *Decretals*, Lateran Council, canon xvi.

[3] Chambers, *Mediaeval Stage*, i. 39.

[4] We find an early instance of such casuistry in Robert Manning's *Handlynge Synne*:

> Hyt is forebode hym yn the decree
> Miracles for to make or se :
> . . . . .
> He may in the Churches, through this reason
> Play the Resurrecyon
> . . . . .
> And he may play it withouten plight.

[5] Grossetête, *Epistolae*, 159, Rolls Series. For a sermon against the plays see Halliwell and Wright, *Reliquiae Antiquae*, ii. 45. A long quotation from it is given in A. W. Pollard, *Miracle Plays*, xxii. [6] *Piers Plowman's Creed*, 108.

[7] Chaucer, *Canterbury Tales*, Prologue. [8] *Ibid.* Miller's Tale.

Not only were clerks forbidden to act, but the great cycles of plays were entirely free from clerical control. It was the Mayor of York [1] who arranged which craft should be responsible for which play ; and it was he who issued a proclamation early in Lent that would-be players should appear before him and be approved. He required that they should be " sufficient in person and conning ", and that they should be " good players, well arrayed and openly speaking ". Pageant masters were then appointed, and there was plenty of time to rehearse before Corpus Christi Day.

It was the way of the crafts to grumble about the " pageant silver " [2] which they had to provide, yet they were constantly raising the cost of production by attempting to outvie one another. The pageants were also good for trade, for they brought many strangers into the town—Richard III, for instance, came to Coventry in 1484 [3] to see the plays. At the same time their object was religious, even if they were organised by laity, who were most unwilling that Church services should interfere with their good works. In 1485 Dr. William of Malton, a Franciscan friar, was summoned to York because the plays took place on Corpus Christi Day and made the Church procession impossible, so that the people were deprived of their indulgences granted by Urban IV. The friar was tactful—he declared the plays to be " good and most laudable " : he was eloquent on the subject of Corpus Christi Day : he was persuasive—and the people promised to defer their performances. Then the friar went away and his influence did not last. The laity reverted to their former date and the clergy had to be content.[4]

Archdeacon Rogers (*obiit* 1595), though he describes the last performance of the Chester plays, helps us to understand how they were performed :

These pageants [5] in carriages was a high place made like a house, with two rooms, being open at the top : the lower room they apparelled

[1] Miss Toulmin Smith, *York Plays*, xxxvii.

[2] Pageant silver, a rate on the members of the guild. It varied from 1d. to 4d. Pollard, *Miracle Plays*, v.

[3] Boas, *Shakespeare and his Predecessors*, 5.

[4] Coulton, *Art and the Reformation*, 393.

[5] Pageant, " A stage or platform on which scenes were acted or tableaux represented ; especially in early use, the moveable structure or carriage consisting of stage and stage machinery used in the open air performances of the mystery plays " (*N.E.D.*).

and dressed themselves, and the higher room they played: and they stood upon six wheels; and when they had done with one carriage in one place, they wheeled the same from one street to another.[1]

At York, however, some plays must have required both rooms for acting, for the action of two scenes was sometimes simultaneous. Again some scenes must have been played partly in the lower room and partly in the street, for there is a stage direction in the Coventry plays, "Here Erode ragis in thys pagond, and in the street also".[2] In the York play of the Temptation also the Devil evidently pushes through the crowd in order to reach the stage, for he begins, blustering—"Make room, be lyve and let me gang", when our Lord and two angels are above on the stage.[3] In some plays the action moves from one room to the other. So in the Coventry play we read, "Here they take Jesus and lead him in great haste to Herod: and the Herod scaffold shall unclose, showing Herod in estate, and all the Jews kneeling except Annas and Caiaphas".[4]

The players at York had to be ready in their places at half-past four in the morning, and were fined six shillings and eight-pence for being late. They were also fined for inefficient acting. The plays were only concluded at nightfall, and it is remarkable that forty-eight pageants could be shown and repeated in sixteen hours. There were twelve stations in different parts of the city, and on payment wealthy people could have a pageant before their doors. Pageants were moved during the day, but the same play might not be acted more than twice. It is difficult to discover the exact procedure.[5]

Besides the Digby Mysteries and many isolated plays and fragments, four great cycles have come down to us: those of York, Woodkirk (Townley), Chester and Coventry. They are all ultimately indebted to the *Cursor Mundi*,[6] a poem written about 1300. They follow its plan, starting from the Creation and ending with the Day of Judgment. They show a good deal of biblical knowledge and an acquaintance with the apocryphal gospels.

[1] *Harleian MSS.*, quoted by Wright, *Chester Plays*, I. xx.
[2] Sharp, *Pageants of Coventry*, 107.
[3] Toulmin-Smith, *York Plays*, 178.
[4] *Ludus Coventriae* (Shakespearean Soc.), 303.
[5] Toulmin-Smith, *York Plays*, xxxiii.
[6] *Cursor Mundi*, reprinted E.E.T.S. Pts. I-VI edited by Morris, Pt. VII edited by Hupe.

Sometimes in easy verse they follow the Gospel story very closely, and sometimes, as in the York Prologue [1] to the Annunciation, the author not only quotes from minor prophets but knows how theologians interpreted them. Laymen, however, had taken over the plays and made them their own. They had introduced much illustrative action and dialogue, and the plays as we have them admirably represent the popular mind in its crudity and strange lapses into the inappropriate. The plays are all the more interesting because they show how artisans and craftsmen brought the events of eternal significance into relation with their everyday life. Those who acted as shepherds of Bethlehem did not feel it was incongruous to declare their preference for Ely ale.[2] They are real shepherds and talk as such—that is, not at all in a refined manner. St. Joseph is a real carpenter and troubled by the demand of the king for an unexpected tax.[3] On the other hand, the kings who use French tags, the high priests and Pilate, who announces that he is ready to do justice in Parliament, are quite unreal, but they are as craftsmen thought of grand folk, having only seen them afar off, surrounded by their retainers.[4]

When the biblical narrative did not provide any dialogue or expressive action, the actors supplied the gap from their ordinary talk and daily experience. They were not to blame because they were altogether ignorant of oriental conditions. They were certainly not lacking in imagination. So to understand these plays we must throw ourselves back into the nursery world of make-believe. We must remember how one child will call to another, " Here are two apples. Let's pretend I am Adam. You may be Eve and Nurse must be Devil. Now Nurse, you begin like this. . . ." So the Garden of Eden may be re-enacted in the garden of a modern villa with surprising additions, expostulations from Nurse, and disconcerting realism. Details in the miracle plays we should also find to be disconcerting.[5]

As in nursery games, the scenery and properties were sometimes realistic and sometimes left much to the imagination. A

[1] Toulmin-Smith, *York Plays*.

[2] *Townley Mysteries*. Secunda Pastorum. In the Chester Play they drink Halton ale. Wright, *Chester Plays*, i. 123.

[3] Wright, *Chester Plays*. Salutations and Nativity, i. 106-107.

[4] Jusserand, *Literary Hist. of England*, i. 486, 487.

[5] *Ibid*. i. 471, 474.

placard was generally sufficient to tell the place of the action, and a brief pause was sufficient to indicate the flow of time. The actors announced themselves as " I am Abraham " or " I am Herod ". They were dressed in contemporary clothes, and contemporary clothes were symbolical of status. God Almighty was bearded and wore a tiara, a white cope and gloves.[1] Wicked kings wore a turban and swore by Mahound. High priests were vested as bishops and sat " in convocation ".[2] Doctors of the law wore round caps and furred gowns. Peasants and soldiers wore the dress of the day, and Mary Magdalene before her conversion was tricked out in overmuch finery. Angels went up to heaven and came down by real ladders, and the gloomy portal called Hell's-mouth was contrived to open and shut. Black, blue and red devils came out to claim the damned, while a clanging of unseen pots and pans signified the discord that prevailed within.[3]

In attempting to represent the supernatural, the heights of heaven or the depths of hell, there was little attempt to go beyond what may be seen or heard by ordinary folk. The ecstatic visions of mediaeval mystics were quite alien to the makers of miracle plays. They were content to be taught about devils by the gargoyles on the churches, and of the saints by the images in the niches below them. The devils were a little more grotesque and the saints a little sweeter than common folk usually are. In the division of good and bad both types became exaggerated ; but the lesson, and that was the important thing, was brought home in simple and often in dignified language. There were rewards for the righteous and there was wrath to come.

After all we have no celestial language, and visions are only understood by those who see them. What eye hath not seen nor ear heard can only be suggested by symbols. So when the Creator in the miracle play divided the light from the darkness, it was sufficient to show a cloth half white and half black. But from such naïve symbols the plays pass to the crudest realism. The *Crucifixio Christi* in the York play with its brutal insistence on imagined details is revolting and intolerable even in print.[4] Such a scene could only have been shown to a people

[1] God was represented at one time with a gilded face, but the gilding proved injurious and was abandoned. Pollard, *Miracle Plays*, xxvii.

[2] *Ibid.* xxvi.

[3] Jusserand, *Literary History of England*, i. 471, 475.

[4] Toulmin-Smith, *York Plays*.

thoroughly accustomed to torture and public executions. We shrink from physical horrors. Our forefathers crowded to them, missed not a detail of the brutality and pain, while they wept and howled aloud—purging their souls with pity and terror.

The astounding contrasts in the plays trouble the modern reader, but it was all consistent with life in a mediaeval city. It was not only in the pageants that contrasts were apparent ; life was a series of kaleidoscopic patterns. Splendour and squalor were combined in one view, and in the open life of the street everything seemed happening at once or in brisk succession. Men were moved to laughter or tears much quicker than they are to-day, and they laughed and cried much louder, sometimes passing from tears to laughter with a rapidity we should think indecent. Comic scenes, we know from Shakespeare, may heighten tragedy, and the Flood was none the less overwhelming because of the ludicrous scene describing

> The sorwe of Noe with his felawshipe
> Er he might get his wyf to shipe [1]

The mystery of the Incarnation was none the less real to the people who watched the Townley play because of the farcical scene of sheep-stealing. It was farce, but good farce. Everyone laughed and no one felt a shock when the theft was discovered and blows were exchanging, that angels should appear singing *Gloria in excelsis* with the result that there is peace on the stage and goodwill among the shepherds.[2]

We need not despise these improvisations, or even congratulate ourselves on our ignorance of the apocryphal gospels. The craftsmen themselves did not suppose that all their stories were true. In 1420 the masons of York did not wish to play *Fergus* because the story was not scriptural and caused more laughter than devotion, and because it came so late that daylight had almost gone.[3] It was just then that among the holiday crowds there would be many who were worse for drink, a fact that leads us to reflect on the religious value of the plays. If

[1] Chaucer, *Miller's Tale*. [2] *Townley Mysteries*.

[3] Coulton, *Life in the Middle Ages*, ii. 241, and *Art and the Reformation*, 394. Fergus was the English name for the prince of the priests, who attempted to overturn the bier of our Lady. The story is told in *The Golden Legend*, iv. 240 (Dent's edition), but Voragine tells us " It is called an Apocryphon ". Fergus was known as Belzenay in France.

religion is brought down into the street there is a risk of its being profaned ; but then it must be remembered that religion was intended for the men in the street. If the Gospel story is acted by rude and ignorant men, the representation will hardly commend itself to people of refined taste. In the miracle plays the Gospel story was shown to the poor in a way that they could understand, and those who saw it year by year must have known the main facts better than many educated people do to-day. It was none the less impressive because they could associate it with their daily life.

If serious-minded people are still shocked with the vulgarity which disfigures the miracle plays they should note the dubious taste of men with more pretentions to piety and culture. Lydgate, for instance, was a priest, a monk and something of a scholar. He had written in verse more than one paraphrase of the Mass, but this did not prevent his parodying his own work. It is true that his *Venus Mass*,[1] which is really addressed to Cupid, " the mighty God of Love ", ends with the Epistle, and it is also true that as erotic poetry it is without offence ; but to-day it is almost impossible to think of a religious man burlesquing his holiest rite.

Leaving morality plays and interludes for a later chapter, we may conclude this section by a reference to a parochial play, *Abraham and Isaac*.[2] The story follows closely on the narrative in Genesis and shows somewhat of the same simplicity and reserve. Abraham's unhesitating obedience is not qualified by any questioning of God's justice. The only question at issue is whether Abraham loves Isaac more than God. Abraham is sure God must be right, and that through the sacrifice Isaac himself is to be blessed. The author, however, concentrates attention on the immense tenderness with which the father prepares the boy for his fate, and the inconsequent variations of mood in Isaac's response. First he suggests that if he needs correction the rod should surely suffice. Death has hardly any meaning for him ; but he is quite clear that his mother must never be told the truth. He is quite ready to be a sacrifice, but grows impatient with his father's reiterated farewells. He

[1] Printed in Simmons, *Lay Folks' Mass Book*, 390, 395.

[2] First published by Miss Toulmin-Smith in 1866 from a MS. at Bromehall, Suffolk. A version in modern spelling was issued by the De la More Press in 1905.

cannot stand the tension. Will not his father strike? Then when the angel intervenes and there is a ram to be caught, he is for a moment an eager boy who brings it "full smart" to his father, saying to the ram:

> Though Thou be never so gentle and good
> Yet had I liever thou sheddest thy blood
> I-wis, sheep, than I.

It is only when his father bares the knife to slay the ram that the horror of death overtakes him and he is afraid. While Abraham pours out his thanksgiving, the boy is impatient to be gone—the "hill of vision" has become hateful to him, he wants to go home and talk to his mother.

In an epilogue "the Doctor" improves the occasion. God is to be obeyed even to our loss. Women must not grudge if God takes their little children to Himself, for He knows best. If they have faith like Abraham their stricken children may yet be spared.

This was a parish play.[1] There was no Lord Mayor to choose the actors, no competing guilds trying by elaboration to outvie their rivals, no gaping crowds coming to a spectacle and expecting to be amused. It was all quite simple; it suggests the countryside and country folk, though there is evidence that it was performed in London and Canterbury. It reveals a homely and religious temper better than the plays of the great cycles. Its humour is entirely English.[2]

VII. *Carols*

No account of popular religion before the Reformation would be complete without some reference to carols.[3] Most of those

[1] Chambers, *Mediaeval Stage*, ii. 130, thinks that it is a scene from a lost cycle; but, greatly daring, I have rejected this view.

[2] The blending of humour and pathos is so essentially English that we must forgive an accomplished French critic for thinking it silly: Jusserand, *Lit. Hist. of Engl. People*, i. 479. Apart from Abraham's references to the Blessed Trinity, I only found one line out of character. It is where Isaac says that he dreaded God more than death.

[3] Here we speak of popular carols. The poems set to music by Byrd, Gibbons and Henry Lawes are motets rather than carols: Grove, *Dict. of Music*. These, however, were so popular in the reign of Charles I, that an XVIII century etymologist suggested that the word *carol* was derived from *Carolus*.

that have been preserved date from the XV century, and it was then that they appealed to all classes. Afterwards Reformers disapproved of them, Puritans denounced them and musicians despised them. And yet many have survived—treasured in the memories of the poor.

The carol began in prehistoric times as a ring dance accompanied by song ; [1] and children to-day are going back to the childhood of the world when they play at " Ring a ring of roses " or " Here we go round the mulberry bush ". It is difficult to believe that these innocent pastimes can be traced back to pagan dances which the Church thought were of diabolic origin ; but the dances which the Church forbade were associated with nature-worship, and were celebrated at the winter solstice or in spring-time to propitiate the spirit of fertility. The gestures of the dance and the songs that they sang were often indecent ; and so was the resulting conduct which they were supposed to encourage or excuse.[2]

The Church failed in its attempt to suppress them, and only partly succeeded in trying to christianise them. The latter attempt was largely due to Franciscan influence.[3] St. Francis had loved the troubadours, and sent forth his Little Brothers to be *joculatores Dei*. He sent them to sweeten and purify God-given instincts which men had perverted or abused. The old nature-worship was consecrated when men were taught to venerate the Mother and the Child, and to see that a child, though born in a stable twixt the ox and the ass, was the hope of the world. Men understood the wailing of the Mother when the Son was crucified, and responded to the thought that death was the prelude to new life. All that was true in the old nature-worship was still more true in the Gospel story, and Christmas carols took the place of pagan song. Only by degrees did the one supersede the other. Much of the old pagan symbolism remained, but at length even the Holly Boy and Ivy Girl were supposed to have a Christian significance.

The round dance is easily understood. Those forming the circle either danced alone while the leader in their midst sang the stanzas, and then joined hands circling round him while

[1] *N.E.D.*

[2] Leighton Green, *English Carols*, Nos. 492, 493, illustrates the dangers of dancing at a later date.

[3] Leighton Green, cxxiii. ff.

they sang the burden; or they danced round him while the stanzas were being sung, and broke off to sing the burden. It was only necessary for the leader to know the carol; the burden could be picked up by the dancers; but it is the dance music and the burden that differentiate the carol from other songs.[1]

Young men and maidens still danced to Christmas carols in the time of Wyclif[2] and he gives the custom a modified approval; but the Church officially disapproved of dancing and in the XV century[3] carol dances seem to have died out. Many of the XV century carols were evidently intended to be sung round a table or at the fireside, but the music continued to suggest lively movement and the recurring burden is suggestive of a game.

Most carols are anonymous, but there are over a hundred by the Franciscan James Ryman[4] who flourished at the end of the XV century, and many more by the blind Augustinian, John Audelay,[5] of much the same date. Many, however, were composed by the people themselves, and we need not be misled by the prevalence of Latin verses.[6] They were all derived from liturgical proses or from the antiphones and hymns of the Breviary, which would be known to those who served the altar or sang in choirs, and would be recognisable by the people. Some carols may be due to *scholares vagantes* who earned hospitality during their vacations by singing songs proper to the season when they were required, or songs improper at any season if the company preferred them. Some of these macaronic verses carry on the sense very neatly. For instance:

Jesu, almighty king of bliss
Assumpsit carnem virginis:
He was and evermore is
Consors paterni luminis.[7]

[1] Leighton Green, *English Carols*, cxxxi.
[2] Matthews, *The English Works of John Wyclif*, 206.
[3] Coulton, *Five Centuries of Religion*, i. 531-538; ii. 401 ff. Dearmer, *Oxford Book of Carols*, quotes from St. Ouen's *Life of St. Eligius*, ii. 15: "Nullus in festivitate S. Johannis vel quibuslibet sanctorum solemnitatibus, solstitia aut ballationes vel saltationes aut caraules aut cantica exerceat".
[4] Ryman. A MS. in Cambridge Univ. Library used by Leighton Green.
[5] *Poems of John Audelay*, ed. by Ella Whiting, E.E.T.S., 1930.
[6] Leighton Green, *op. cit.* lx. ff.
[7] Leighton Green, *English Carols*, No. 3.

or James Ryman's carol beginning,

Upon a night an angel bright
Pastoribus apparuit
And anon right thro' God's might
Lux magna illis claruit.
For love of us (Scripture saith thus)
Nunc natus est Altissimus.[1]

Whatever the authorship of carols, the practice of carol-singing was originally of the people and gradually spread upwards until all classes received them. They were sung in village churchyards and in the streets of towns ; in village inns, farmhouse kitchens and manorial halls. Even a royal court did not disdain them. So when Henry VII in 1487 gave a Twelfth Night feast, "At the table in the middle of the Hall sat the Dean and those of the King's chapel, which incontinently after the King's first course sang a carol ".[2]

Carols should be distinguished from hymns. The primary object of a hymn is praise and, after that, aspiration. Carols on the other hand relate a past event as a reason for present rejoicing. Hymns are addressed to God ; carols to men.

Nowell, nowell, nowell, nowell,
Tidings glad I think to tell.

expresses the purpose of a carol-singer and his spirit of hilarity.[3] He intended to be noisy, for *nowell* in English was equivalent to *hurrah*, as *noël* in France was used for *vivat*.[4] This is strange, for Noël was the name of Christmas as early as the time of Charlemagne, but the Duke of Burgundy was welcomed with shouts of " Noël ! " when he entered Paris.[5]

Most of the carols have a great similarity. They insist on the virginity of Mary; they speak of Bethlehem that fair city, of the crib between the ox and the ass, of the shepherds and the angels' song, of the star which the wise men followed and of the offerings which they brought. They insist on the theological truths *Verbum caro factum est* and that the child was *Redemptor mundi*.

Sometimes a naïve imagination is concentrated on the story

[1] Leighton Green, *English Carols*.
[2] Leland, *Collectanea*, iv. 237.
[3] *N.E.D.*
[4] See the Dictionaries of Littré and Larousse.
[5] Monstrelet, *Chroniques*. In Johnes' trans. i. 129, *noël* is rendered *carol*.

and it is told from the point of view of the shepherd. There is one that may have been inspired by the miracle plays. As we read it we are back into old England :[1]

> The Shepherd upon a hill he sat ;
> He had on him his tabard and his hat,
> His tarbox, his pipe and his flagat,[2]
> His name was called jolly jolly Wat
> For he was a good herd's boy
> With hoy
> For in his pipe he made so much joy.

He heard the tidings from the angel, but before going to Bethlehem issues his instructions :

> Now must I go where Christ was born ;
> Farewell, I come again the morn ;
> Dog, keep well my sheep fro' the corn,
> And warn well, warroke,[3] when I blow my horn,
> For he was a good herd's boy, etc.

He finds our Lord in " a simple place " with the ox and the ass looking on. He makes his offerings

> Jesu, I offer thee here my pipe
> My skirt, my tarbox and my scrip ;
> Home to my fellows now will I skip
> And also look unto my sheep
> For he was a good herd's boy, etc.

The carol ends with farewells, our Lady speaking first :

> " Now farewell, mine own herdsman Wat."
> " Yes, for God, Lady, even so I'm that ;
> " Lull well Jesus in thy lap
> " And farewell Joseph with thy round cap."
> For he was a good herd's boy, etc.[4]

The good herd's boy has a sincere faith in his creed as he makes his humble and inappropriate offerings, and a real reverence, however awkwardly expressed, for a baby in his mother's arms. The same sentiment appears again and again in the Lullaby Carols, which are so tender that it is almost inconceivable that a man can have composed them, so certainly do they reveal a

[1] Leighton Green, No. 78. [2] Flagat = flageolet.
[3] Warroke = a stunted child. Wat's assistant.
[4] Cap is probably cape or cope. Some editors think the word was suggested by the halo in stained-glass windows.

mother's love. The carols of the Passion are inspired by the same sentiment ; they are almost exclusively concerned with the sorrow of the Mother on the death of her Son. Motherhood must have meant a great deal to the XV century English, and their religion was homely. In the bare hovels where they lived, they loved to think that the God of all the world had not disdained a stable, had come to share their hard lot and pay the penalty due for their many sins. The story touched their hearts and they felt that thanksgiving was best expressed in a festive spirit. One burden runs,

> Make we merry both lad and lass
> For now is the time of Christymas ;

and another,

> Now let us sing and merry be
> For Christ, our King, hath made us free.

So they not only sang *nowell* but *wassail* also, for wassail was the form of rejoicing which they understood. They were rude men, in touch with the earth and not at all heavenly minded; but they believed that our Lord had come to earth, lived on earth, and was fitly commemorated in an earthly manner.

There were many other carols sung at this time that had nothing to do with religion—carols that are political, amorous or profane. Some of them are very profane ; and this reminds us that if there was a popular religion in the Middle Ages there was also a popular irreligion.

Chapter IV

SUPERSTITIONS AND ABUSES

I. *Superstitions*

In the Middle Ages most men had a vivid belief in the supernatural, but all men were not good. It follows that with much real piety there was also much gross superstition, and occasional outbursts of wild and rebellious wickedness. God was blasphemed, the saints were cursed, the dead insulted. Bacchanalian dances took place at midnight in churchyards and even in churches.[1] Ribald parodies of Church services were enacted. Students at Christmas-time bawled bawdy songs about the streets,[2] and preachers who threatened men with the flames of purgatory were sometimes met with jeers and derision. Such deplorable profanity was spasmodic and occasional. It was the noisy protest of the young against the restraints which had been imposed upon them—the reckless proclamation of their freedom from control. They were like the naughty child of to-day who, beside himself with rage, breaks his favourite toys, strikes the mother whom he loves, and sobs " I don't care " from his place of penitence in the corner.

Such ebullitions of wickedness were not the results of unbelief. There is no savour in blasphemy where there is no belief in God. The men who cursed the saints meant to enrage them, just as those who practised black arts believed in the Devil.

The practice of demonolatry and witchcraft was not as prevalent in the Middle Ages as after the Reformation, but occult obscenities have had at all times an attraction for degenerate perverts. Men whispered filthy secrets about incubi and succubae;[3]

[1] Robert of Brunne, *Handlyng Synne*, ii. 9039 ff., takes over and expounds the legend of the sacrilegious dancers of Kölbigk, who for disturbing Mass were condemned to go on dancing for a year without stopping.

[2] For obscene songs at Christmas see Gascoigne, *Loci e Libro Veritatum*, 144. For the licentiousness at the festival note More's admission. *Dialoge*, Bk. II. ch. ii.

[3] For incubi and succubae see Reginald Scot, *Discovery of Witchcraft*, Bk. IV.; Summers, *Hist. of Witchcraft*, 89 ff.; *Encyc. of Rel. and Ethics*, iv. 631, v. 687.

they sold themselves to the Devil, said the Paternoster backwards and celebrated Black Masses. Again there is no evidences of unbelief. Those who celebrated Black Masses required a man in priest's orders that there might be an authentic Host to mishandle and insult.[1] But dealing as we are with popular religion, we are not concerned with abnormal wickedness beyond thinking how scared and credulous people crossed themselves devoutly at the mention of it. We are more concerned with the superstitions of irreligious people, who may have been stupid but were not abnormal.

In 1467 certain poor men in London stole pyxes out of the churches. One of them boasted, " I have ate nine Gods that were in the boxes for my supper ". Next day the locksmith, who helped them, went to Mass and could not see the Host. He then went from one church to another ; he went home and drank good ale and so to church again, but the Host he could not see. Soon afterwards he and his confederates were arrested and in Newgate he made his confession. After receiving absolution he could once more see the Host, and was executed rejoicing in our Lord's Presence. Gregory, the chronicler, thought it an edifying tale of sin and repentance. He thought also that it ought to convince heretics of the miracle in the Blessed Sacrament. He ends by quoting as scripture what was really an *obiter dictum* of Gregory the Great.[2]

Erasmus in one of his *Colloquies* tells the story of a shipwreck, and of the vows made by the panic-stricken passengers. One, an Englishman, promised mountains of gold to Our Lady of Walsingham if only he might be saved. Another, a Zeelander, kept on bawling to St. Christopher as if he were deaf, that he would give him a taper as tall as himself. When a friend reminded him that he could not afford such a gift, the Zeelander whispered, " You fool to think that I mean it. If I get ashore all right I shall not give him a tallow dip."[3] In writing this fictitious narrative, did Erasmus remember how he had twice vowed a poem in honour of St. Geneviève when he was sick, had twice recovered and not fulfilled his vow ? It was thirty-seven years after his first sickness that he published his *carmen votivum*.[4]

[1] Summers, *Hist. of Witchcraft*, 147.
[2] *Gregory's Chronicle*, Camden Society, 224, 225.
[3] Erasmus, *Colloquia*, i. 197 : *Naufragium*.
[4] Nichols, *Epistles of Erasmus*, i. 108.

For a third instance let us take the cult of St. Wilgefort, popularly known as the Maid Uncumber. Père Delehaye,[1] the Bollandist, numbers her among the saints who never existed. She had, however, a statùe in St. Paul's Cathedral, and was supposed to rid women of their husbands if they offered her oats.[2] *The Messenger* called Sir Thomas More's attention to this very unchristian cult, but he made light of it. First he obtained an admission that the oats offered in a year would not maintain " three geese and a gander " for a week, and then goes on :

Well, quod I, then the priests maintain not the matter for any covetise, and also, what the peevish women pray for they cannot hear. Howbeit if they pray but to be uncumbered, me seemeth no great harm nor unlawfulness therein. For that may they, by more means than one. They may be uncumbered if their husbands change their cumbrous conditions, or if they themselves peradventure change their cumbrous tongues, which is haply the cause of all their cumbrance. And finally, if they cannot be uncumbered but by death, yet it may be their own, and so their husbands safe enough.[3]

For Sir Thomas More it was all a matter of " three geese and a gander ", and not worth a prolonged cackle. He regarded it as many people to-day regard fortune-telling at a bazaar, pleading it is only a bit of fun that nobody takes seriously.

On the other hand, we may be much too easy-going with regard to superstition. There had been a time when Sir Thomas More had not treated fables so lightly. In presenting his translation of Lucian to Ruthall, Bishop of Durham, he had written :

There are those who think that they have done a lasting service to Christ, when they have invented a fable about some Saint, or a tragic description of Hell, which either melts an old woman to tears, or makes her blood run cold. There is scarcely any life of a Martyr or Virgin, in which some falsehood of this kind hath not been inserted ; an act of piety no doubt, considering the risk that Truth would be insufficient

[1] Coulton, *Five Centuries of Religion*, i. 546 ff. Delehaye, *Sanctus* (1927), 229.

[2] The statue represented a figure on a Cross, crowned, bearded and robed to the ankles. It was a copy of the Santo Volto at Lucca, and originally intended for the Christ ; but northern people, unaccustomed to these old crucifixes, invented the legend of St. Wilgefort. She was a daughter of the King of Portugal, who, in answer to prayer, was granted a beard that she might prove unattractive to a suitor. She then not only preserved her virginity, but was crucified for professing Christianity.

[3] More, *Dialoge*, Bk. II. ch. ii.

unless propped up with lies : Thus they have not scrupled to stain with fiction that religion, which was founded by Truth herself, and ought to consist of naked truth. They have failed to see that such fables are so far from aiding religion, that nothing can be more injurious to it. It is obvious, as Augustine himself observed, that where there is any scent of a lie, the authority of Truth is immediately weakened and destroyed.[1]

It is hard to believe that the man who wrote these sentences could really have regarded the cult of St. Uncumber with complacency ; but we have to remember that Sir Thomas More had been bred a lawyer and was accustomed to plead from his brief. In his controversy with Tyndale he was resolved not to leave him a leg to stand on, and when he could not justify what Tyndale condemned, he was still able to laugh him out of court.

In the three instances noted above, superstition and ignorance are allied with wickedness. In the last two instances magic has usurped the place of religion. The Zeelander who thought that he could cheat God and the saints, and the women who thought that they could obtain their wicked will by offering oats, alike believed that the favour of heaven could be bought, and that heaven was indifferent to morality. How far such superstition was prevalent it is impossible to say, but it was not far removed from other corruptions of sound doctrine. It was the indifference of the authorities to patent superstitions which made the Reformers so zealous in rooting up wheat and tares alike, being apparently unconscious that any wheat remained.

II. *The Cult of Our Lady*

The Church of the Middle Ages not only multiplied rites but promoted many cults. She knew that all men are not alike and therefore varied her appeal. She knew that many were ignorant and unintelligent, but she was content to make the best of them so long as they submitted to her rule. Submission to authority was the highest of all virtues in a feudal society, but when that was granted, men found the Church to be a tolerant and complacent mother. However systematic her theology, however

[1] Nichols, *Epistles of Erasmus*, i. 404.

precise her definitions, she was lax in practice: she did not restrain devotional extravagances and was not afraid of thaumaturgic excitement. It is not in consequence wonderful that many, in their religious life, lost all sense of proportion and pressed some truths to the falsehood of extremes. This is saddest when we contemplate how devotion to Mary passed into Mariolatry.

It might be thought that no praise or honour could be too great for the Holy Mother. God was well pleased with her and she was full of grace. The Holy Spirit overshadowed her; and she carried Jesus in her womb. As a child He was subject to her; and as a dying man He provided for her future. She was crowned with glory and honour, and all generations are directed to call her blessed.

Moreover, the devotion she has excited has been of untold benefit to the world.[1] It was through the exaltation of the Mother and the Child that innocence and purity came to be reverenced, that women acquired a new dignity and children a right to protection. All that was best in chivalry was inspired by this cult, though we have to admit that progress was partial and slow. Throughout the Middle Ages it is easy to find examples of the degradation of women and of the brutality of men. This is what we should expect. Ideals are received, accepted and reverenced; but they are only translated into life and action by slow degrees. When a shipwreck takes place to-day and the cry goes forth, "Women and children first!" strong men stand aside that the weak may be saved, because they are heirs to a tradition which has its origin in the devotion that mediaeval Europe paid to Mary and her Little Boy.

We need not in a chapter on popular religion think of the theological background, or of the bitter controversies of Dominicans and Franciscans concerning the Immaculate Conception;[2]

[1] This was the view of Lecky: *European Morals*, ii. 367.

[2] The Franciscans had a tale that the Blessed Virgin translated Duns Scotus to Paris from a place 300 miles distant, when she thought that the doctrine of the Immaculate Conception was in danger of being condemned. The story is referred to by Sir Thomas More in his *Letter to a Monk*, quoted by Bridgett, *Life of More*, 197. Harris, *Duns Scotus*, i. 10, has shown that Duns Scotus was scarcely so dogmatic on the Immaculate Conception as has been supposed. In his *Opus Oxoniense* he discusses three theories concerning the sinlessness of Mary, confesses that none knows which is right, but prefers the doctrine of the Immaculate Conception as most honourable to Our Lady.

but we ought to note that the stories of Joachin and Anna from the apocryphal gospels were generally accepted as historical narratives, and we ought to note how Mary's position changes in reference to her Son. St. Peter Damian, a man of fervid rhetoric and unbridled invective, wrote in the XI century of our Lady, *Accedit ad illud aureum Divinae Majestatis tribunal, non rogans sed imperans, domina non ancilla*, which suggests that the creature is superior to the Creator, though this was certainly more than the author meant. In the XIII century, Albertus Magnus, a sober theologian of encyclopaedic erudition, wrote: *Maria orat ut filia, jubet ut soror, imperat ut mater.*[1] Both writers were thinking of pictures and images, where the child is for ever in the mother's arms. It was natural so to represent her, for the child is the symbol of her glory and pre-eminence. But in pictures time has been arrested and a moment has become fixed. It is true that the mother controls her nursling, but she does not control a grown-up son. It is a bad mother who becomes a possessive parent, and would keep a growing boy tied to her apron-strings. Our Lady, the perfect mother, was not like that. Her glory and self-suppression are alike demonstrated at Cana of Galilee; when repulsed by her Son, she stood aside and said to the servants, " Whatsoever He saith unto you, do it ".

Having meditated on Our Lady's dominance over her Son, men naturally went on to think of her in opposition to Him. Our Lord came to represent justice and His mother triumphant pity. The vision of the red and white ladders was often told. They stretched to heaven. Our Lord leant over the top of one, His mother over the other. Those who tried to ascend by the red one to our Lord often fell off into hell. All those who ascended by the white one were received into heaven by Our Lady.[2] Who can imagine the shame and horror of the holiest and the humblest of God's creatures at finding her love for men contrasted with that of her Son to His manifest disadvantage?

It is difficult to read with patience the miracles of Our Lady, miscalled the Glories of Mary. A good many of them may be

[1] These two quotations may be found in Bishop Bull's *Works*, i. 101. Rashdall, *Universities*, i. 465, also quoting from Albertus, tells how he attributed to our Lord's Mother a knowledge of the *Trivium* and *Quadrivium*, and some acquaintance with Medicine, Law and Theology. ***Beatissima Virgo Bibliam et Sententias in summo habuit.***

[2] Pusey, *Truth and Office of the Church*, 103, 104 n.

found in *The Golden Legend* of Voragine,[1] which had a wide circulation in England during the XV century. The stories there are not so bad as in other collections. When we are told that a lecherous monk was condemned by Christ, but rescued by his mother on the ground that he always saluted her image, we feel that such conduct was not conducive to continence. Men in the Middle Ages had a great veneration for chastity as a wellnigh unattainable virtue, and combined it with a hope that the ever Virgin Mary would be indulgent to them in their vices. Many of the stories told of her pity reveal the moral standards of those who invented them, and nothing else. They are as unworthy of the Mother of God as the stories of the boy Jesus in the apocryphal *Gospel of the Infancy* are unworthy of Him.

The stories were no doubt told in order to encourage sinners to rely on Our Lady's intercessions, but the story of the scapular only shows a caprice of Our Lady in favour of the Order of Mount Carmel.[2] It was said that the Blessed Virgin brought the scapular to the Carmelites and promised, " Whosoever dies in this garment will not suffer everlasting fire ". This is salvation by magic. I am not concerned with the gloss on these words provided by the *Catholic Encyclopaedia*, which shows how people to-day in wearing the scapular may find in it a moral instrument of grace. I am concerned with the more literal-minded Middle Ages, when wicked men wore the scapular and trusted in it to pass straight through purgatory to heaven, saved by two strips of brown cloth. Such men had descended to the level of the man in the street who thinks to escape accidents and death thanks to the mascot affixed to his motor-car.

Many saints have witnessed to the value of the rosary as an aid to devotion, but even of that a superstitious use may be made. Sir Thomas More tells us how a Franciscan friar came to Coventry and conducted a mission there and in the neighbourhood, proclaiming that anyone who said the rosary daily could never be lost. The rector protested because " He found his

[1] Voragine, *Golden Legend*, Caxton's translation published by Dent, ii. 126 : iii. 25, 160 : v. 105. For other stories see Coulton, *Five Centuries of Religion*, vol. i. chs. ix., x., and pages 101 ff.

[2] The origin of the scapular is a matter of dispute. The vision of John XXII resulting in the Sabbatine privilege is apocryphal, and the Bull of 1322 is a forgery. The vision was attributed to St. Simeon Stock by Joannes Grossus in his *Viridarium* (1430), *vide* Coulton, *Five Centuries of Religion*, iii. 18. *Cath. Encycl.*, Sabbatine Privilege ; Scapular ; St. Simeon Stock. Cp. *D.N.B.* : St. Simeon Stock.

flock infected with such a disease that the very worst were especially addicted to the rosary for no other reason than that they promised themselves impunity in everything ". He was of course called " the enemy of Our Lady " and the controversy waxed warm. Sir Thomas writes :[1]

While the matter was at its hottest, it happened that I arrived at Coventry on a visit to my sister. I had scarcely got off my horse when the question was proposed to me, whether anyone could be damned who should daily recite the Rosary? I laughed at the foolish question, but was at once warned that I was doing a dangerous thing; that a most holy and learned father had preached against them who did so. I pooh-poohed the whole matter as no affair of mine. I was immediately invited to dinner, and accepted the invitation and went. There enters also an old friar with head bent, grave and grim; a boy follows him with books. I saw that I was in for a quarrel. We sat down and no time was lost; the question was at once proposed by my host. The friar answered just as he had preached. I said nothing; I do not like to meddle in odious and fruitless disputes. At last they asked my opinion. As I was obliged to speak, I told them what I thought, but only in a few words, and without emphasis. Then the friar pours out a long prepared speech which might have made two sermons. His whole argument being on certain miracles which he read from a Mariale[2] and from other books of that kind, which he had brought to table for greater authority. When at last he had come to an end, I modestly replied that he had said nothing in his whole discourse capable of convincing those who should not admit the truth of those miracles, which they might perhaps deny without abjuring the Christian faith, and even if they were perfectly true, they did not prove his point. For though you may easily find a king ready to pardon something in an enemy at the prayers of his mother, yet there is nowhere one so great a fool as to promulgate a law by which to encourage the audacity of his subjects against himself, by a promise of impunity to traitors, on condition of their paying a certain homage to his mother. Much was said on both sides, but I only succeeded in getting laughed at while he was extolled. The matter reached at last such a height through the depraved dispositions of men who, under colour of piety, favoured their own vices, that it could hardly be calmed down, though the bishop strove to do so with all his strength.

This story is enlightening and calls for several comments. The friar must have been an eloquent mission preacher, for many

[1] Bridgett, *Life of Sir Thomas More*, 97. The incident dated 1517 by Seebohm, *Oxford Reformers*, 416, was almost certainly ten years earlier. *Vide* Miss Routh, *Sir Thomas More*, 34.

[2] For the *Mariale* vide Coulton, *Five Centuries of Religion*, i. 501 ff. See also Pusey, *Truth and Office of the Church*, 103.

regarded him as coming with a message straight from heaven. He had evidently the gift we now associate with a revivalist. Then we note that his teaching was for the people a new message, something they had never heard before, so we cannot regard it as characteristic of the religious teaching at the time. The established authority, the rector, saw the danger of such teaching and protested against it. The bishop finally intervened; and as More approved of his doing so, we may conclude that he was on More's side. More had certainly no leanings towards Protestantism, and in the next paragraph to the one quoted advocates the salutation of Our Lady, and emphasises the value of her intercession; but at the same time he feels himself at liberty to doubt the miracles of the *Mariale*. There was no doubt at the time sufficient superstition and silly preaching to account for the reaction in the next generation when men refused to Our Lady the honour that was her due, and denied the value of her prayers. Wyclif had been wiser when he wrote:

> It is impossible for us to be crowned in heaven without Mary's good offices. She was the cause of Christ's Incarnation and Passion, and consequently of all the world's salvation.[1]

It is possible to make a vast collection of monstrous statements and silly fables from the last four centuries of the Middle Ages. It would be equally possible to compile an even larger book of the religious aberrations and silly stories of Protestant Europe; but it would be wrong to over-estimate their influence. The *Hours of Our Lady*[2] were most popular in England, and though those who do not believe in the communion of saints, and think it unlawful for men on earth to seek any intercourse with the saints in heaven might object to them, there is no line in the *Hours of Our Lady* open to the criticisms made above. The works of Richard Rolle, Walter Hilton and the Lady Julian of Norwich were the most widely read religious books of the XV century, and a devout Protestant can read them to-day for his edification.[3]

[1] Quoted by Lechler, *John Wyclif and English Precursors*, ii. 122.

[2] Littlehales, *The Prymer*, E.E.T.S., Pt. I.

[3] Rolle, indeed, in his youth wrote *Canticum Amoris*, a love poem to Our Lady which is sufficiently crude and extravagant: but in his later compositions there is no trace of the cult of Our Lady. See Miss Allen, *Writings of Richard Rolle*, 90. Was this typical of Yorkshire religion? From Raine, *Historians of the Church of*

The superstitions concerned with the Blessed Virgin were real enough. They appealed especially to the ignorant and the vicious. They were a source of weakness to the Church and a cause of the Reformation. They had arisen through men being encouraged to devote themselves to one cult, until they lost all sense of the proportion of the Faith, and forgot that the glory of Mary was her Son.

III. *The Saints*

If a lost sense of proportion accounts for popular misconceptions of the Blessed Virgin's place in the scheme of redemption, it is also true to say that it was her humanity which excited men's love. She was very woman, and there was in consequence a tendency to attribute to her whatever men thought to be womanlike. They imagined her as regal and dominant, beautiful and debonair. They attributed to her jealousies and unaccountable caprices. They deluded themselves into believing that she would ever be ready to cover up and condone the vices of her friends, and that she would not be above feminine wiles in getting her own way. So the Mary of the Gospels was obscured by the Madonna of legend, and the woman with whom God was well pleased was replaced by the woman who excites, captivates and enthralls a human lover. It is altogether a mistake to think that she was esteemed a goddess—she was always the woman who had power with God. It was on her human sympathy that men relied ; it was her womanliness that men loved, and in this sublimated eroticism there was not only evil but good.

York, Rolls Series, iii. 256, we learn that in 1343 " the services of the B.V.M. have been much disused in some of our churches ". From Raine's *Fasti Eboracenses*, 485, we learn that it was not until 1353 that Archbishop Thoresby built a Lady Chapel in the Minster where a daily Mass of Our Lady might be said. The following passage from Dame Julian's *Revelations of Divine Love*, 13, will illustrate how a recluse of Norwich regarded the cults of Our Lady and the saints : " We pray him [Our Lord] for His sweet Mother's love that Him bare ; and all the help we have of Her is of His goodness. And we pray for His holy Cross that He died on, and all the virtue and the help that we have of the Cross is of His goodness. And on the same wise, all the help that we have of special saints and all the blessed company of heaven, the dear worthy love and endless friendship that we have of them, it is of His goodness. For God of His goodness hath ordained means to help us, full fair and many : of which the chief and principal means is the blessed nature which He took of the Maid, with all the means which go afore and come after, which belong to our redemption and to endless salvation. Wherefore it pleaseth Him that we seek Him and worship Him through means, understanding that He is the goodness of all."

In the same way men did not think of the saints as spiritual beings in a far-off and inaccessible heaven, but as beings close at hand, still at work on earth, interested and active in the everyday concerns of life; who could be talked to, bargained with and propitiated with candles; who had power to reward their friends and might possibly bring evil on those who disregarded them.

The familiarity men felt for them was due to the number of their images in churches. There they were well-known conventional figures; dressed in contemporary costumes, and bearing symbols or emblems by which they might be easily recognised.[1] The Franciscans had taught men that everything that was visible should be regarded as symbolic of spiritual realities, but men reversed their teaching and brought heaven to earth by regarding these symbols as indicating their utility. The images of Crispin and Crispian were intended to teach men that even humble cobblers might aspire to heaven, but the cobbler who lighted candles in their honour thought—"These heavenly cobblers should help me to mend shoes". So St. Apollonia with her pincers and tooth might be invoked for toothache. The organ of St. Cecilia made her the patron to all musicians, and the stags of St. Hubert and St. Eustace called out the devotion of huntsmen, while St. Leonard with his broken fetters was the hope of all prisoners. St. Giles looked after cripples, St. Nicholas watched over boys, pickpockets and sailors, while St. Katherine cared for little girls and St. Osyth (properly Sytha) for women who had lost their keys.[2]

In the Middle Ages men thought of heaven as full of active personalities, and asked for the prayers of the saints as naturally as they asked for the prayers of their neighbours. They never paused to consider if the saints could hear them, for they believed that the saints were with our Lord. He, at least, was interested in all that concerned the children of men, and it was reasonable to suppose that those who were nearest to Him shared His interests.[3] Our Lord was indeed our "advocate with the Father", but His Body the Church had its part in the mediatorial kingdom. The whole Church

[1] Huizinga, *Waning of the Middle Ages*, ch. xii.: Religious Thought crystallising in Images. Ch. xv.: Symbolism in its Decline.

[2] St. Osyth, a Saxon princess, was often confused in England with St. Sytha, a domestic servant.

[3] Aquinas, *Summa*, Suppl. lxxii.

here and in heaven was one in Him. It is true that they shrank from a direct approach, and for this art was largely responsible. The awful doom pictures with our Lord throned upon the rainbow terrified many besides little Martin Luther. These men thought of Him as God Incarnate—as a consuming fire with eyes too holy to behold iniquity—and turned to seek for intercessors full of human pity.

People sometimes speak of the cults of the saints as a revival of polytheism,[1] but this is a mistake. The attraction of the saints was their full humanity—they were thought of as men and women by those who prayed to them—men and women in an exalted position and with extended powers. Moreover, the same men loved our Lord so long as they thought of Him as the baby in Mary's arms or as the man of sorrows nailed to the Cross. No books were more popular in the XV century than the Life of our Lord by Ludolphus Saxonicus, the Life wrongly attributed to St. Bonaventura, and the English version of it by Nicholas Love.[2] The Cradle and the Cross attracted: the Throne of Judgment repelled, and imagination failed to reconcile the impressions which pictures and images had made.

That gross superstition attended the worship of the saints even the Council of Trent could not deny,[3] but in reviewing popular customs and the flippant sayings of the streets it is difficult to determine how far these superstitions were really

[1] It is long since Heine wrote his delightful fantasia, *The Gods in Exile*. It was not intended to be taken seriously. More recently M. Saintyves has published a learned book, well documented and crammed with details—*Les Saints successeurs des dieux* (1907). Sometimes he attempts to prove too much. It was a happy thought of Boniface IV to rededicate the Pantheon to St. Mary and All Saints; but the saints were not the gods renamed, and only succeeded them in time. It was the practice of early missionaries to consecrate the old temples and sanctuaries to the One God, and some saints whom their converts were likely to revere. It is undeniable that the new saint sometimes attracted to himself the stories that had been told about the old divinities. This did not much affect the intention of the cult, though it gave rise to sundry superstitions. A better case can be made out for the saints as successors to the heroes, for heroism is alike in all religions. M. Saintyves writes (p. 94): "Le culte des héros et plus encore les cultes des saints sont infiniment supérieurs à toutes les vieilles formes du naturalisme primitif. Protestation reconnaissante de ce que nous devons aux générations passées, ils témoignent d'une intuition profonde de ce qu'il y a de religieux dans le sentiment de l'humaine solidarité. L'humanité est faite de plus de morts que de vivants, selon la belle pensée des anciens, et la méditation pieuse de la vie de ceux qui furent grands, ne saurait être ni ridicule ni méprisable."

[2] See below, Pt. II. ch. 3.

[3] *Canones et Decreta*, Sessio xxv. Positively the Church determined (i) the saints reigning with Christ offer their prayers for men, and (ii) that men may invoke them to pray for benefits from God, through Jesus Christ, our Lord.

influential in the lives of the people. To-day a man may be seen touching wood, but it does not follow that he has any real belief in the efficacy of his action. In the Middle Ages, however, faith in the supernatural was much stronger than it is to-day, and errors concerning the supernatural were in consequence much more deadly.

Errors crept in through men ignoring the distinction between direct petitions and requests for prayer. This distinction is insisted on in the Tridentine Catechism,[1] but had been forgotten by the pre-Reformation Church. In the Office for the Auxiliary Saints there was a prayer which begins—

> O God, Who hast distinguished thy chosen Saints. (George and his 13 companions) with special privileges before all others, that all those who in their need shall invoke their help shall obtain the salutary fulfilment of their prayers, according to the promise of Thy Grace.[2]

Strictly construed this would imply the abdication of divine power in favour of the fourteen saints ; and it was such teaching that naturally led men to bargain with the saints, promising them statues, chapels and candles if they would grant their desires. It also led disappointed votaries to attribute spite and mean passions when their requests were not granted. Error culminated when men came to think that the saint who could heal a disorder was also the author of it, and for instance that St. Roch would send a plague upon the people if he were not propitiated. So Erasmus, after describing the meekness of St. Francis under insults while on earth, makes one of his characters speak of his vindictiveness in heaven. He goes on :

> The Saints now that they are in heaven do not choose to be affronted. Was ever any man gentler than Cornelius, milder than Antony, or more patient than John the Baptist, while they lived upon the earth ? But now they are in heaven what dreadful diseases do they send among us, if we do not worship them as we should do.[3]

[1] *Tridentine Catechism*, Pt. IV. ch. vi. 3, 4. Cf. Bellarmine, *De Sanct. Beat.* i. 17 : " Non licet a sanctis petere ut nobis tanquam auctores divinorum beneficiorum, vel gratiam, aliaque ad beatitudinem media concedant ". He, however, allows a man to say " St. Peter save me " if he understands " by praying for me ".

[2] Huizinga, *Waning of the Middle Ages*, 155. The fourteen auxiliary saints were SS. Achatius, Giles, George, Christopher, Blaise, Cyriac, Denis, Erasmus, Eustace, Pantaleon, Vitus, Barbara, Katherine and Margaret. The office from which the above quotation comes was abolished after the Council of Trent. Cp. Rushforth, *Med. Christian Imagery*, 216, 217.

[3] Erasmus, *Exequiae Seraphicae : Colloquia* ii. 199.

England was proud, and rightly proud of her saints. The patriotic author who wrote the prologue to the *Nova Legenda Anglie* [1] maintained that there was no need for anyone to go on pilgrimage in foreign parts for the merits and examples of English saints were sufficient for all. Men could go on pilgrimage to St. Cuthbert at Durham, to St. John at Beverley, to the two St. Hughs at Lincoln,[2] to St. William at Norwich, to St. Etheldreda at Ely, to St. Edmund in the borough of his name, to St. Thomas at Canterbury, to St. Alban in his own town, to St. Swithin at Winchester, to St. Joseph of Arimathea at Glastonbury, to St. Thomas Cantilupe at Hereford, to St. Chad at Lichfield, or to many a smaller shrine. If men were sufficiently daring they might go and salute St. David in Pembrokeshire, and two pilgrimages to his shrine were said to be as meritorious as one *ad limina Apostolorum* at Rome; but this was because of the dangers by the way.[3]

The cult of a saint began at his tomb,[4] and it was the report of the miracles wrought there that determined his popularity. At Canterbury was the body of St. Augustine, who brought us baptism, but he was little regarded. At Canterbury was the body of St. Anselm,[5] one of the holiest men of the Middle Ages, but even the site of his grave was forgotten. Multitudes on the other hand flocked from all over Europe to the shrine of St. Thomas Beket and made their offerings. Those offerings in a single year reached the sum of £954 : 6 : 3, while not a penny was offered to Our Lord upon the Rood, and only £4 : 1 : 8 to the Blessed Virgin Mary.[6]

It is sometimes said that the clergy exploited the credulity of the people for their own profit, but this is far from a complete explanation. The clergy no doubt profited from a popular shrine,

[1] *Nova Legenda Anglie*, ed. by Horstman, i. 8.

[2] The shrine of Little St. Hugh, said to have been crucified by Jews, was more popular than that of the Great St. Hugh of Avalon. On the little St. Hugh and St. William of Norwich see Hutton, *English Saints*, 324-330.

[3] Calixtus II, 1119–1124, ordained that two pilgrimages to St. David's equalled one to Rome.

[4] Delehaye, *Sanctus*, 123.

[5] Anselm, it is true, was only canonised in the reign of Henry VII, and the king paid 1500 ducats for it. Hook, *Archbishops of Canterbury*, v. 460. The actual fees for the ceremony of canonisation are detailed in Morton's Register (Wilkins, *Concilia*, iii. 639), and amount to 799 ducats. The other 700 ducats were probably spent on petitioning the Pope and paying members of the curia to accept the proofs of sanctity.

[6] Forbes, *XXXIX Articles*, 381.

but the enthusiasm of the people was spontaneous, and this is proved by the unauthorised cults of the XV century. Thomas of Lancaster was a bad man ; but, owing to his sudden downfall and execution in 1322, his evil deeds were blotted out in a flood of pity. The little chapel on the hill at Pontefract became a shrine, miracles were reported to have occurred there, and it remained a rallying-point for the house of Lancaster down to the time of Robin of Redesdale in 1469.[1] Edward II, the enemy of Thomas of Lancaster, a few years later was barbarously murdered in Berkeley Castle, and attained to a reputation for sanctity by his death. Crowds of pilgrims flocked to his tomb in the Abbey of St. Peter at Gloucester, to its great enrichment, but nobody ever proposed his formal canonisation.[2] Richard Scrope, Archbishop of York, was indeed a holy man, but he perished in 1405 through rebelling against Henry IV. In vain the Government erected barriers to prevent access to his tomb, and the ecclesiastical authorities prohibited offerings to be made there. Scrope was a saint in the hearts of the people and they called him " The Glory of York ". More than half a century after his death the Northern Convocation petitioned, though in vain, for his canonisation.[3] York also was a centre of the cult of Henry VI, although Archbishop Booth issued a monition that his image was not to be venerated.[4] When Henry VII was king it was hoped that he would be canonised, but Bacon supposes that the Pope " put a difference between a saint and an innocent ".[5]

All these cults had a political significance, but far the most popular of uncanonised saints was :

Master John Schorn,
Gentleman born,
Who conjured the Devil into a boot.[6]

[1] Tout, *Pol. Hist. of Eng.*, 1216–1377, pp. 286, 303. It is noteworthy that Richard Rolle, *Incendium Amoris*, ch. 3, in Miss Comper's version, was probably thinking of Thomas of Lancaster when he wrote : " Truly all saints have not done miracles, either in their life or after their death; nor all damned have lacked miracles either in their life or after their death ".

[2] Tout, *ut supra*, 304.

[3] Solleway in *York Hist. Tracts*.

[4] The Monition is printed in *York Fabric Rolls*, 208. See also Hutton, *The English Saints*, 162-166.

[5] Bacon, *Henry VII*, 207.

[6] Sparrow Simpson collected all that was known about him and his cult and the result of his researches may be read in the *Journal of the British Archaeological Association*, vols. xxiii., xxv., xli. See also Coulton, *Five Centuries of Religion*, i. 545 ; *V C.H. Bucks*, sub Marston, and *Arch. Cantiana*, xiii. 115.

We know very little about him except that he became Rector of North Marston in 1290, and lived there until his death in 1314. As Buckinghamshire was a country of appropriated churches and wretchedly paid vicars, we imagine that "a gentleman born" was rare among the priests, and that resident rectors were not common. Schorn must have been eccentric or odd anecdotes would not have been attributed to him. How he conjured the Devil into a boot is unknown, but we suspect the story arose out of some edifying pleasantry, or perhaps because some gouty parishioner attributed his cure to his ministrations. When we are told that he struck the ground with a stick and discovered a spring, we suspect that he was a water diviner with a hazel twig. When we find that people who were troubled with agues and skin diseases sought his shrine, we imagine that in his lifetime he dosed his parishioners. The people must have loved him when living or they would not have venerated him when dead. From the village of Buckinghamshire his fame spread and his image appears on rood-screens in Suffolk and Devonshire. So popular did he become that Richard Beauchamp, Bishop of Salisbury and Dean of Windsor, bought up the advowson of North Marston and obtained leave from Sixtus IV in 1478 to remove his shrine to St. George's, Windsor, as it brought in a revenue of £500 a year.[1] In 1537 Dr. London sent up his picture from Marston to London for destruction, and St. George's Chapel soon after cleansed itself from what had become a superstitious cult.[2]

Master John Schorn was a secular priest and the saint of peasants. In both respects he was beneath the notice of monastic hagiologists. So no one wrote his life, though when promoted to Windsor he had his office in spite of the fact that he was not canonised.

It is to the monk John of Tynemouth, and Capgrave the Friar of Lynn, that we owe much of our knowledge of English saints and the way in which people regarded them. The compilers of the *Nova Legenda Anglie*[3] travelled far and wide to discover early records, and though they were unduly credulous, they have preserved much material of historical importance.

[1] The place of his shrine is now the Lincoln Chapel.

[2] Wright, *Suppression of the Monasteries*, 218. There was another statue of Schorn at Caversham; *ibid.* 224.

[3] *Vide supra*, 168.

They interspersed their lives with *Narrationes*. These are generally good tales but often irrelevant. They were intended to make the book more useful to preachers, and sermons were more or less popular according to the number of anecdotes that were told.

The *Nova Legenda Anglie* was written in Latin for the use of priests and religious, but *The Golden Legend* of Voragine was early translated into English and made a wider appeal.[1] Many of the stories are beautiful and many more are edifying. Some are dull, and there is a certain monotony due to the fact that men were more interested in what took place at the shrines than in what happened to the saints in their earthly lives. Marvels of course abound, but *ex hypothesi* saints were marvellous persons, and all marvels are not necessarily false. Some of these stories are quite true;[2] many record the true experience of witnesses, although we should interpret that experience differently;[3] many have grown in the telling out of all resemblance to their original form. Some again are due to an innocent imagination providing stories to explain pictures that were originally symbolic.[4] Some are entirely fictitious, and range from delightful parables[5] to silly and even repulsive fables concocted to order by uninspired hagiographical hacks. However, we need not be as hard as Sir Thomas More was on these fabulists. We should judge them not as antiquaries but as historical novelists. With scanty or no materials for a saint's life, they invented incidents to illustrate his sanctity, just as painters with no photographs to guide them delineated his features. The painters provided a beautiful and gracious figure which was not a portrait, and the writers provided miracles appropriate to the character and his circumstances.

In the Middle Ages men were avid for miracles and quite uncritical in accepting them. The men of the Renaissance were quite as uncritical in rejecting them altogether. After the Reformation men were quite as credulous, though their taste for rarities had changed. They were no longer interested in

[1] Miss Greenwood, *Camb. Hist. of Eng. Lit.*, ii. 333, prefers the earlier English version of *The Golden Legend* to that printed by Caxton. So does R. W. Chambers, *Continuity of English Prose*, cxxiii., in Harpsfield's *More*.

[2] St. Martin and his cloak.

[3] The trance of St. Thomas Aquinas before the crucifix at Naples.

[4] *St. George and the Dragon*. See Coulton, *Art and the Reformation*, 281 ff., for how the story of St. Nicholas and the resurrection of the boys grew up.

[5] St. Christopher is one of the most beautiful.

saints, but had become interested in monsters and monstrosities, and were ready to swallow with open mouth the most unlikely of travellers' tales. The men who accepted as gospel truth everything contained in Pliny's *Natural History* were no more intelligent than those who accepted unreservedly the whole of the *Acta Sanctorum*.

Some of the stories told of saints were of pagan origin, or were adaptations from the folklore of the people. Exceptional people attract tales to themselves, just as an acknowledged wit becomes the heir to the witticisms of his forefathers. When, however, we have admitted all this, we are still certain that the cult of the saints is quite distinct from the worship once offered at pagan shrines. The amatory adventures of the Olympian deities have no connexion with the ascetic extravagances of men who esteemed self-sacrifice the highest law of life.[1]

The childish simplicity of many of the stories also rendered them offensive to the new age. With the revival of learning men were growing up, and were like modern boys of fourteen, vastly superior and contemptuous of those nursery tales which they once loved and may love again. In their day these nursery tales had an educative value, and no one is wise who would dissociate himself from his past. The *Lives of the Saints* had often been written for very simple folk; but they crystallised ideals and inspired men with thoughts of high endeavour. So we hate the superstitions which the Church tolerated in the XV century, because they made a Reformation necessary; and we deplore a Reformation which deprived our people of so large a part of their Christian heritage.

When we have denounced with Sir Thomas More all the lies and absurdities which disfigured the mediaeval hagiologies,

[1] In the second part of Saintyves' book—*Les Saints successeurs des dieux*—he brings together a great deal of evidence to prove that Christian stories have been derived from heathen sources. Some of his instances—the minority—cannot be denied: direct borrowing is proved. Many of his instances only illustrate the fact that story-tellers dealing with the same subject-matter are apt to write in the same way. We are familiar with this in modern novels. Some of his instances are very far-fetched in more senses than one. When we study what everyone admits to be true history, we find that parallels abound. This is what we should expect: for though it may be true that history never repeats itself exactly, so that no one can foretell the future, it is equally true that history is a series of repetitions, so that with our personal experience of life we are able to understand past ages. Parallels abound because humanity is always the same: they are never exact, as no two people are ever exactly alike.

and when we have deprecated the superstitions and extravagances arising from them, the fact remains that in the real lives of the saints we have an inheritance of inestimable value.

Many were men of heroic faith who withstood tyrants: many renounced ease and pleasure in aspiring to know God: many carried on stoutly a war against the sins of the flesh: many out of weakness were made strong. They did not claim any right to a good time, or think that increasing comfort was a proof of progress, or that wealth was a sign of the divine approval. It was not the Catholic saints who reversed the Beatitude and taught "Blessed are the rich, for theirs is the Kingdom of Heaven".

The *Lives of the Saints* have other lessons to teach of meekness, modesty and simplicity; of kindliness to men and flaming love for God. There were among them men drawn from all classes—women and little children, the innocent and many forgiven sinners. Their very eccentricities make them memorable and picturesque. Their relations to animals read like fairy stories,[1] but some of them may be true; for men of peace may enter into the promises of Isaiah. In some ways and to some degree they reflected the beauty and perfection of Christ.

The day came when their pictures were defaced, their images broken, their legends torn up, and when there was no one to teach the children their old and glorious traditions: and we understand how this was possible when we consider some of the facts alluded to above.

Hugh Latimer, indeed, did not object to images so long as they were used "to be laymen's books for remembrance of heavenly things"; and of the saints he wrote: "I never denied that they might be worshipped and be our mediators, though not by way of redemption (for so Christ alone is a whole Mediator both for them and for us), yet by the way of intercession".[2] This accords admirably with the definition of Trent and the teaching of the Tridentine Catechism,[3] but the definition and teaching came too late. For what we lost in England the Pre-Reformation Church must bear the blame.

[1] Lecky, *European Morals*, ii. 168-171.

[2] Foxe, *A. & M.*, vii. 474.

[3] *Canones et Decreta*, Sessio xxv., and *Catechismus Concilii Tridentini*, Pt. III. c. 2. 29.

IV. *Images*

The saints were extremely popular in England until the outbreak of the Reformation and were altogether forgotten two generations later. This may cause surprise, because in spite of disapproval a belief in fairies, goblins and demons has persisted century after century—but a belief in the earth spirits springs from contact with nature, and a belief in the saints from familiarity with art.

A lonely man in a dark room heard a door creak and was full of ghostly tremours: a maiden "fancy free" saw fairies dancing in a wood mid the flickering lights: a man who had stayed too long in the ale-house saw spectres in the churchyard on his way home: a servant called on to explain a disaster in the dairy put the blame on "the little people". Sinners shuddered at the hooting of an owl, and were frightened at the clatter of a storm; they heard conscience calling in the whispering leaves, and fiends mocking in an unexpected echo. Nature, sometimes friendly and sometimes menacing, will always waken some response in sensitive souls.

The saints on the other hand were human—that was their attraction. They were represented in concrete images and were made as life-like as possible. They were to be contemplated and had a definite story attached to them. The man who saluted one of them and lighted a candle in his honour, at least knew his name and his fame and how he might be expected to help. But when the images were destroyed the memory of the saints soon faded away. They were then only people in books which few people read; and the new preachers told no anecdotes about them.

There was much to be said in favour of images—the poor man's books; but devotion to them had passed all bounds and led to deplorable superstition. In the *Summa Theologia* of St. Thomas Aquinas you may read, *Cum Christus latriae adoratione sit adorandus, imago quoque eadem adoratione adorandus est,*[1] a conclusion that some commentators have tried to explain away. He further taught, *Crux Christi est adoranda adoratione latriae,*[2] a conclusion which very many theologians, including

[1] *Summa,* III. Q. xx. A. 4.

[2] *Summa,* III. Q. xxv. A. 8. For an attempt to explain it away see Bossuet, *Lettres sur l'adoration de la croix.*

Bellarmine, deny. Aquinas, however, had very little influence on English theology before the Reformation,[1] and we are glad to find in the humble works of English priests a more moderate attitude. Myrc in his *Festival* wrote :

Men should learn by images whom they should worship and follow. To do God's worship to images is forbidden. Therefore when thou comest to the Church, first, behold God's Body under the form of bread upon the altar ; and thank Him that he vouchsafe every day to come from the holy heaven above for the health of thy soul. Look upon the Cross, and thereby have mind of the passion he suffered for thee. Then on the images of the holy saints ; not believing on them, but that by the sight of them thou mayest have mind on them, that be in heaven : and so to follow their life as much as thou mayest.[2]

So Richard Rolle writes : " To images is praising due, that is for them of whom they are images, for that intent only are they to be venerated ".[3] So *Dives and Pauper*, after explaining the distinction between *dulia* and *latria*, says, " Whoso doth any divine service that is called *latria* to any creature or any image . . . he doth idolatry ".[4]

The official English teaching may best be learned from the Constitutions of Archbishop Arundel issued in 1408 :

From henceforth let it be taught commonly and preached by all that the Cross and the image of the Crucified, and the rest of the images of the Saints, in memory and honour of those whom they figure, as also their places and relics, ought to be venerated with processions, bendings of the knee, bowings of the body, incensings, kissings, offerings, lightings of candles and pilgrimages, together with all other manners and forms whatsoever as hath been accustomed to be done in our predecessors time ".[5]

This very comprehensive admonition is yet far " on the hither side of idolatry ", but it raises the question, Did such practices tend that way ? When men made pilgrimages to salute a special image, and when an image became renowned for the miracles done for its votaries, was it not inevitable that men should come to think that the image had virtue in itself ? Sir Thomas More attempts to reassure *The Messenger* on this point :

[1] Aquinas in England, *vide* Pt. II. ch. 2.
[2] Myrc, *Festival*, quoted by Strype, *Eccles. Mem.* I. i. 214.
[3] *Short Treatises*, ed. by Perry, E.E.T.S., p. 10.
[4] *Dives and Pauper*, quoted Rock, *Church of Our Fathers*, iii. 286.
[5] Quoted Gibson, *XXXIX Articles*, 561.

I trust that there be no man so mad or woman neither, but that they know quick men from dead stones, and tree from flesh and bone. And when they prefer, as ye spake of, our Lady of one pilgrimage before our Lady at another, or one Rood before another, or make their invocations and vows some to the one and some to the other, I ween it easy to perceive that they mean none other, but that Our Lord and our Lady sheweth more miracles at the one than the other.

He challenges *The Messenger* to take the simple woman, and

If ye ask her whether it was Our Lady of Ipswich or Our Lady of Walsingham that stood by the Cross at Christ's passion, she will, I warrant you, make answer that neither or both. And if you demand of her further, "Which lady, then?" She will answer, "None image but Our Lady that is in Heaven." And this I have proved often, and ye may when you will and find it true, except it be in one so very a fool, that God will give her leave to believe what she list.[1]

We find sweeping accusations of idolatry when we turn to Protestant authors, but they do not always define the word and often leave the impression that they regarded as idolatrous any sign of reverence to anybody or anything, unless it were to "a godly prince", that is to a prince who agreed with themselves. This justifies us in scrutinising their evidence, but there is much that we cannot reject; and most of them, though prejudiced, are honest witnesses. Their witness has this further importance. They were not strangers liable to misunderstand the meaning of an alien faith, but they were men brought up in the Church; and, if they were mistaken, the blame must largely fall on those who instructed them. Everyone did not defend image worship with the intelligence of Sir Thomas More, or hold such moderate views as Myrc in his *Festival*. For instance, Cardinal Gasquet quotes from a sermon in defence of image worship preached by Roger Edgeworth in the reign of Queen Mary:

An image is a similitude of a natural thing that has been, is, or may be. An idol is a similitude of what never was or may be.[2]

Christ was crucified and St. Paul was beheaded, therefore neither a crucifix nor an image of St. Paul with a sword can be an idol! It would also seem to follow that all idolatry is impossible, for no one can make a *similitude* of nothing. Further, supposing the word *similitude* is not pressed, the statue of Peter Pan is not necessarily an idol because "he never was or may be".

[1] *Dialoge*, Bk. II. ch. ii.

[2] Gasquet, *Eve of the Reformation*, 258.

Apart from idolatry, and there was probably more of it than Sir Thomas More imagined, we are bound to admit that there were many superstitions. They may not have been definitely fostered by the Church, but she regarded them with a complacent tolerance. Besides, a popular shrine meant large offerings from which the clergy benefited; also, there was naturally a tendency to be jealous of its interests and to magnify its religious importance. The question which remains to be considered is, Did it lead to fraud? The accusation was often made against the clergy as guardians of images and relics. As regards images, I do not think it can be proved, but it is well to consider what we know about Our Lady of Worcester, Our Lady of Cardigan and the Rood of Grace at Boxley in Kent.

At Worcester there was a very famous statue. The legend ran, according to Bale, that the Blessed Virgin appeared to Egwin and ordered him to make an image of herself, as she wished to be worshipped in Worcester.[1] As Egwin was bishop from 693 to 717, the statue should have been eight hundred years old and have survived two fires which at different times gutted the cathedral. Then there is the other legend, according to William Thomas, that when the statue was taken down and disrobed it was found to be the image of a bishop ten feet high. This very tall story I venture to disbelieve. It occurs first in *Il Pellegrino Inglese*,[2] a dialogue written in 1552 by William Thomas, whom Bishop Ridley described as "an ungodly man".[3] The object of his book was to convince Italians of the virtues of Henry VIII and the necessity of his righteous reformation. It was appropriately dedicated to Pietro Aretino, the most licentious poet and the most reckless libeller of his time. Had this story been true, Latimer, who took down the statue, would have mentioned it to Cromwell when he wrote:[4]

> I trust your Lordship will bestow our great Sibyll to some good purpose, *ut pereat memoria cum sonitu*. She hath been the Devil's instrument to bring many, I fear, to eternal fire: and she herself, with her old sister of Walsingham, her young sister of Ipswich, with

[1] Bale, *Summarium* Cent. 709, quoted by Val Green, *Hist. of Worcester*, i. 95.

[2] *Il Pellegrino Inglese* was translated and published by Froude in 1871 as *The Pilgrim*. William Thomas is the sole source of the story, and Herbert (*Henry VIII*, 496), Burnet (*Reformation*, i. 386), Collier (*Eccles. Hist.*, ii. 149) and Staveley (*Romish Horseleech*, 79) rely on him. For Thomas's Life see *D.N.B.*

[3] Strype, *Eccles. Mem.* III. i. 282.

[4] Latimer, *Works*, ii. 395.

their other two sisters of Doncaster and Penrice, would make a jolly muster in Smithfield : they would not be all day in burning.[1]

But there is still better evidence of its falsity. When the image had been stripped of all its adornments, a citizen went and kissed it, saying to the bystanders, " Ye that be disposed to, offer—the figure is no worse than it was before ".[2]

The next story is of Our Lady of Cardigan. She was supposed to have been found at the mouth of the Teifi with the child in her lap and a burning taper in her hand. The legend proceeds that she was moved to Christ Church, Cardigan, but returned four times of her own accord to the place where she was first found. Finally, St. Mary's Cardigan was built. The taper she held in her hand continued to burn without diminution for nine years until a Welshman forswearing himself, it went out and could never be relighted. This legend had been handed down from a dim past, and in its ultimate form may be regarded as an old-wives' tale ; but John Frodsam confessed that as the Welsh were always stealing the wax, he had substituted a taper of painted wood which satisfied the purposes of devotion.[3] In spite of Barlow's representing this as an imposture, there is no evidence of fraudulent intent.[4]

We pass on to the famous Rood of Grace at Boxley in Kent. This was a mechanical image that could be made to bow its head, open its mouth and roll its eyes. It was taken down before the commissioners arrived ; but one Geoffrey Chamber saw the possibility of what we should now call " a stunt ".[5] It was taken to Maidstone and exposed as a cheat in the market-place : it was taken to London and exposed on a scaffold at Paul's Cross while Bishop Hilsey preached a sermon on the perils of idolatry and iniquities of monks.[6] It was afterwards destroyed by the

[1] Our Lady of Worcester was burnt at Worcester, the other images at Chelsea. Wriothesley, *Chronicle*, 83.

[2] Froude, *Hist. of England*, iii. 237, quotes from MS. in S.P.O., II Series, vol. xlvi.

[3] Wright, *Suppression of Monasteries*, 186. Fr. Thurston in his article on "Relics" in *Cath. Encycl.* calls attention " to the prominence given to the taking of oaths on relics in the various Welsh codes, founded on the laws of Howel the Good ".

[4] Froude, *Hist. of England*, iii. 287.

[5] Gairdner, *Lollardy and the Reformation*, ii. 123-132.

[6] *Ibid.* ii. 173. The Letters of Finch and Partridge (Parker Society, *Original Letters*, 606, 608) only tell us what an anonymous German merchant had heard in London.

mob and Walter Gray wrote about it in one of his popular ballads :

> For the rood of grace
> Hath lost his place
> And is rubbed in the gall ;
> His false devotion
> Hath lost promotion
> And is broken in pieces small.
>
> He was made to joggle
> His eyes to goggle :
> He could bend his brows and frown
> With his head he could nod
> As a proper young God
> His chafts would go up and down.[1]

Cromwell knew the value of ballads for propagandist purposes ; and it was seen that the exposure was properly written up with picturesque details added, besides moving accounts of the king's sorrow at such wickedness, and of the people's rage at being so shamefully abused. Nothing was omitted that would commend itself to those who organise similar demonstrations in the anti-God campaign of the Soviet. But there is no evidence that any deception was intended or practised. The monk who had made it long ago probably saw no harm in doing so. People came and gaped at it as they continue to gape at the moving figures of the clock at Wells. Then we may suppose it got out of order and was no longer used, because Chamber acknowledges its fame was of the past, that the machinery was of old wire and rotten sticks, and that the monks professed ignorance of how it worked.[2] Lastly, while Hilsey was preaching his eloquent sermon at St. Paul's Cross, he must have known of a similar mechanical image in St. Paul's Cathedral. That concerned the Resurrection, and the image could put its legs out of the sepulchre, raise its hands to bless and turn its head. No one, however, just then was attacking secular cathedrals, and

[1] Chafts, a north country word for jaws. N.E.D.

[2] Froude, *Hist. of England*, iii. 288, could not resist the temptation of adding to the story details of a dramatic nature in the discovery of the so-called fraud : " It happened that a rationalistic commissioner looking closely, discovered symptoms of motion at the back of the figure ", and so discovered the imposture of the monks. But the rood had been taken down before Southwell, the commissioner, arrived, and he found it on the ground—" a monstrous sight ".

Protestant historians since have not dared to impute fraud to deans like Colet and Pace.

These mechanical toys used for sacred purposes are offensive to our taste, and it is of course possible that a child or very ignorant person may have been deceived, or that a neighbour may have bragged unadvisedly in another shire about the wonders of his own rood ; but there is no evidence to substantiate the charge of deliberate imposture.

V. *Relics*

The men of the Middle Ages needed concrete and tangible symbols of that supernatural world in which they devoutly believed. Things and places were not merely hallowed by their associations, were not merely indications of the unseen, but were instruments of spiritual power or localised spheres of sanctity. So if devotion to the saints largely depended on their images, it depended still more upon their relics.

The veneration of relics is natural and primitive. When Polycarp was burnt, the brethren gathered up his bones as " more precious than jewels ", and bestowed them in a safe place, that year by year they might celebrate the martyr's heavenly birthday.[1] Everyone has treasured mementoes of dead friends ; all Christians have reverenced the bodies of the dead ; the greatest buildings in the world are monuments and tombs.

It is also quite natural, as every museum testifies, to collect memorials of the past ; and when religious interests were dominant, as in the Middle Ages, the treasuries of the churches were the museums of the people. Men were then as willing to give vast sums for a relic of St. Mary Magdalene as they are now ready to give vast sums for a relic of Nell Gwyn or Lady Hamilton. The spirit of the collector is the same ; the persons in whom he is interested are different.

It is just because of this natural veneration, and this mania for collecting rarities, that the temptation arose to exploit the ignorant by selling sham memorials and faked curios. As early as the end of the IV century, St. Augustine denounces men who, in the habit of monks, wandered about North Africa selling

[1] Lightfoot, *Apostolic Fathers*, Pt. II. i. 454.

spurious relics,[1] and at the end of the XIV century Chaucer tells us of pardoners wandering about England with their fardels stuffed with " pigges bones ".[2] In the Dark Ages the trade had been brisk and body-snatchers had had a glorious time. Later, wily Levantines palmed off on innocent Crusaders ridiculous relics with grotesque histories, which were brought home, reverently received and placed in jewelled reliquaries. They had been bought in good faith, were received in good faith, and faith sometimes wrought miracles by their means. Very few people can believe to-day that the Crown of Thorns is an authentic relic;[3] but no one suspects the veracity of Pascal when he vouches for the sudden healing of his little niece after being touched with the holy thorn.[4]

Men were very easily satisfied with what was not evidence. When Erasmus enquired at Walsingham how they knew that they had the Virgin's milk, he was scornfully referred to the record of how they came by it. That record may have been true ; but it only showed that an unknown nun in Constantinople had vouched for it. Erasmus thought the incident amusing ; but there is also something pathetic in such simplicity.[5]

A childlike simplicity, a passionate desire to collect, a reverence for holy things and a superstitious dread of the consequences of unbelief alike contributed to the ready acceptance of the strangest relics. If seven cities claimed to be the birthplace of Homer, it sometimes happened that seven cities claimed to have the tomb of one saint. It was on the multiplicity of the same relics that Calvin harped in his treatise on the subject,[6] and men were left with the alternative of believing in the crass ignorance of the clergy or their designing knavery. Ignorance there was, and also knavery ; but in most cases it is probable that legends grew up naturally without any consciousness of deceit.

At some famous shrines a trade went on in models of its principal attraction. Pilgrims bought them and took them home. In their wills they left them to their parish church and in a

[1] St. Augustine, *De op. Monach.*, ch. xxviii, quoted by Thurston, *Cath. Encycl.*, article " Relics ".

[2] Chaucer, *Canterbury Tales*, Prologue.

[3] Mandeville, *Travels*, ch. 2, speaks of the Crown of Thorns—" half is at Paris, and the other half at Constantinople ". The compiler, copying from many books, is neat in providing similar explanations.

[4] Sainte-Beuve, *Port Royal*, tries to find a natural explanation.

[5] Erasmus, *Peregrinatio : Colloquia* i. 349.

[6] Calvin, *Treatise on Relics*.

generation or so they were believed to be originals.[1] So there was a famous girdle of Our Lady at Aix-la-Chapelle, and another like it at Westminster Abbey, and ten more in England alone. Secondly, there was a theory, undefined, that anything which had been in contact with a relic possessed some of its virtue and might be esteemed a relic itself. So the cramp rings distributed on Maundy Thursday derived their efficacy not merely from the royal blessing, but because they had been touched by the ring of Edward the Confessor. Thirdly, there was the horrible custom, prohibited by Gregory the Great, of dismembering the bodies of the saints. St. Richard of Chichester, for instance, was divided so as to provide two stations for the pilgrims.[2] When you are shown a silver head of a saint, and the sacristan assures you that it contains the skull, he may be mistaken. It may be that only a very small fragment is within ; but no one is so temerarious as to look. Many relics are of microscopic proportions. They may be genuine, but they do not justify the claim to the possession of the body.

That certain relics should have been multiplied, and their veneration tolerated in different places, is certainly no credit to the Church. For instance, Baldwin II of Constantinople sold what was reputed to be the lance of Longinus which pierced our Saviour, for a great sum, to Louis IX.[3] At Nuremberg was another lance of Longinus, and Baron Rozmital in 1465, setting out on his pilgrimage, had his ring touched with this spear because it was a certain remedy against any " sideaches or attacks ".[4] In 1491 the sultan Bajazet sent the head of a third lance to Innocent VIII as part of the price for not allowing his rebellious brother, Djem, to escape. It was received with pomp by the Cardinal Borgia, afterwards Alexander VI, and is venerated in St. Peter's to this day.[5] There was another in a little chapel at Caversham, not the gift of an infidel, but brought by a one-winged angel from heaven. It would be interesting to know how this story arose, but Caversham had a strange collec-

[1] Thurston, *Cath. Encycl.*, article " Relics ".

[2] Bede Jarrett, *Cath. Encycl.*, article " Pilgrimages ".

[3] Gibbon, *Decline and Fall*, xi. 280.

[4] Cust, *Gentlemen Errant*, 11.

[5] Creighton, *Papacy*, iii. 151. The author of *Mandeville's Travels* attempts an explanation : " The spear shaft hath the Emperor of Almaine, but the head is at Paris. And, nevertheless, the Emperor of Constantinople saith that he hath the spear head ; and I have oftentimes seen it, but it is greater than that of Paris."

tion of relics—a part of "The holy halter" with which Judas hanged himself, the dagger with which Henry VI was slain, and another dagger which despatched Edward the martyr king.[1] The harbouring of such curiosities, though all of them fakes, seems to have been innocent, and to have had no more religious significance than the preservation of Guy Fawkes' lantern in the Ashmolean at Oxford. This excuse cannot always be made, for the superstitions connected with some relics were of such a nature that we can understand how good men impatiently demanded their destruction.

St. Thomas Aquinas ingeniously accounts for the miracles which occurred at shrines by saying that as we love and honour the bodies of the saints which were once temples of the Holy Ghost, so God likewise loves them and honours their remains by working miracles in their presence.[2] But this is not how the people thought of relics. They came to think of them as charms or talismans, as things with marvellous properties; and the personalities of the saints were forgotten. Excessive reverence led to superstition and superstition led to irreverence—men dismembered the bodies of the saints and applied their relics to unhallowed uses.[3]

Superstition in regard to relics cannot be denied, but it does not follow that there was any conscious imposture. Such an accusation, however, has been frequently made, especially in regard to the Holy Blood of Hayles; and it is in consequence right that the evidence should be examined.

A crystal vase possessed by the Abbey of Hayles was supposed to contain the blood of our Lord shed on Calvary.[4]

[1] Wright, *Suppression of Monasteries*, 221-225.

[2] Aquinas, *Summa*, III. Q. xxv. A. 6.

[3] Huizinga, *Waning of the Middle Ages*, 150, writes: "The Spirit of the XV century did not differ much from that of the Umbrian peasants, who about the year 1000, wished to kill St. Romuald, the hermit, in order to make sure of his precious bones, or of the monks of Fossanuova, who, after St. Thomas Aquinas had died in their monastery, in fear of losing the relic, did not shrink from decapitating, boiling and preserving the body. During the lying-in-state of St. Elizabeth of Hungary in 1231, a crowd of worshippers came and cut off or tore in strips the linen, enveloping her face; they cut off the hair, the nails, and even the nipples. In 1392, King Charles V of France, on the occasion of a solemn feast, was seen to distribute ribs of his ancestor, St. Louis; to Pierre D'Ailly, and to his uncles, Berry and Burgundy, he gave entire ribs; to the prelates one bone to divide between them, which they proceeded to do after the meal."

[4] There were relics of the precious Blood in Westminster Abbey, at Ashridge in Kent, at Bruges, and many other places. St. Thomas Aquinas denied the possibility

The relic was not invented by its owners, for it was purchased in 1267 by Edmund, son of Richard, Earl of Cornwall, from Florenz V, Count of Holland, whose father had brought it from the Holy Land, authenticated by Pantaleon, Patriarch of Jerusalem, who subsequently became Pope Urban IV.[1] Edmund presented the relic to Hayles in 1270, and it acquired a great reputation throughout the country.[2] It was said that no one could see the blood if he were in mortal sin, and that therefore he must be shriven before approaching the relic. Latimer, in a letter to Morice in 1533, tells how people "came by flocks" to see it, believing that the sight "certified them that they be of clean life, and in state of salvation without spot of sin, which doth bolden them to many things".[3] In fact, the belief gave rise to a dangerous superstition.

In February 1538 Bishop Hilsey in denouncing the Rood of Grace at Paul's Cross referred to the Holy Blood at Hayles. He said that twenty years before at Oxford he had heard the confession of a miller's wife. She had told him of her relations with the Abbot of Hayles and of the jewels she had received from him, but said that when he offered her one which she knew had hung near the Holy Blood she was afraid. Whereupon the abbot said, "Tush! thou art a fool, it is but duck's blood".[4]

This is the sort of tale which a government would desire to spread in order to justify their spoliation of monasteries; but though the bishop called on God to damn him if his story were not true, we may disregard it. A priest who breaks the seal of the confessional does not inspire confidence, and if he related what he heard, his informant may not have been truthful. The abbot, who was dead, may have said the words, but if he did so he was a liar, for it certainly was not duck's blood.

The abbot, Stephen Segar, who was a royal chaplain [5] and

of any such relic of Calvary, but supposed that the relics shown in churches came miraculously from some image. *Summa*, III. Q. liv. A. 2. Subsequently, Dominicans and Franciscans were bitterly opposed on this subject; and in 1464 argued the question for three days before Pius II, who then silenced them and refused to give a decision. Wadding, *Anal. Minor.*, xiii. 58, 206.

[1] St. Clair Baddeley, *Glos. and Bristol Arch. Soc.*, xxiii. 276 ff. See further his book, *A Cotswold Shrine*.

[2] It has been suggested that the proverb "As sure as God is in Gloucestershire" is a reference to this relic.

[3] Latimer, *Works*, ii. 364.

[4] Wriothesley, *Chronicle*, i. 75, 76.

[5] *L. & P.*, xii. 1. 1323 (Gairdner).

a friend of Cromwell's, journeyed to London and asked for a commission. He protested that the liquid had never been renewed to his knowledge, and that the same monk had kept it for forty years.[1] On returning home he wrote a letter stating that he did not himself believe in the relic, and asking leave to demolish the shrine, adding that the silver and gold in it was only worth from £30 to £40.[2] On hearing this, Latimer wrote to Cromwell, suggesting that " The ' Bloody Abbot ' meant to appropriate the jewels to himself ".[3] Cromwell, however, needed no such warning; he had seen that Layton had the abbot's bond for £500 that he would alienate none of the abbey goods, and he also had his private undertaking to surrender the abbey whenever required.[4] The abbot, who " thanked God that he lived in an age of enlightenment ",[5] had his eyes wide open to his own advancement, and also to the dangers that beset his position.

Cromwell appointed a commission consisting of Latimer, the abbot, the Prior of Worcester, Holbeche, and a squire named Tracy: they met on October 4th, 1538. They found the relic to be enclosed in a round beryl, and they opened it in the presence of a great multitude. Within was a little glass which contained an unctuous coloured gum; as seen through the glass, it was red like blood; but when taken out it was like glistening amber; and it stuck to the glass like bird-lime. The commissioners reported accordingly, and on October 28th Latimer was again at Hayles, and wrote to Cromwell that he had been " bolting and sifting " the matter all the forenoon. He repeats the evidence of the commission, and confesses that he had got no further. We may conclude that however false the relic was, there is no evidence that anyone had ever tampered with it.[6]

But in 1552 that imaginative Welshman, William Thomas, gave the following account in *Il Pellegrino Inglese*,[7] and he has

[1] *Ibid.* xiii. 1. 347.
[2] *Ibid.* xiii. 2. 408.
[3] *Ibid.* xiii. 2. 186.
[4] *Ibid.* xiii. 2. 481.
[5] Stephen Segar did well for himself. He obtained a pension of £100 a year (£2000 of our money), and the use of Coscombe House. He is buried at Halifax, where his brother was Vicar. St. Clair Baddeley, *Glos. and Bristol Arch. Soc.*, xxii. 160.
[6] Latimer, *Works*, ii. 407.
[7] *The Pilgrim*, edited by Froude, 38. Adair in *Tudor Studies* (1924) has a very interesting article on Thomas and tries to make the best of him.

been quoted as the authority on the subject by Lord Herbert and Burnet : [1]

> And what blood, trow you, was this ? These monks (for there were two especially and secretly appointed to this office) every Saturday killed a duck and revived therewith this consecrated blood as they themselves confessed, not only in secret, but also openly and before an approved audience.

Not content with this invention, he tells us that the crystal which contained the relics was opaque on one side and transparent on the other, and that the transparent side was not shown to a rich man until in his dread of damnation he had paid for many Masses and given great alms.

VI. *Miracles*

Sanctity was attested by miracles, and miracles were a prelude to canonisation. A man was not canonised until he was dead, and most of the miracles took place at his tomb. Relics in consequence assumed an undue importance until people tended to forget the saintly life, and thought only of the wonder-working bones.

Many miracles attributed to saints were not as good as fairy stories, because they were just as untrue and not so interesting. Some of them also are of such a nature that devout people are glad to think that they never occurred. On the other hand, many were true ; and for some there is plentiful evidence.[2] Some miracles have only become fabulous stories in the process of repetition. Some can easily be explained by natural causes, and some can not. About a great many a wise man will suspend judgment.

If by a miracle we mean something that happens which can best be explained by the direct intervention of God, it follows that we must first believe in a God Who is free to act before a miracle can be perceived. From day to day many marvellous and unexpected things happen, but the modern man extolls his luck, assigns the cause to chance, or prattles about coincidence. He thinks himself in consequence ever so much more intelligent than the poor people who said their

[1] Lord Herbert of Cherbury, *Henry VIII*, 496 ; Burnet, *Reformation*, i. 385.

[2] E. A. Abbott, *On the Miracles of St. Thomas of Canterbury.*

prayers, expected God to act, and, obtaining their desires, gave God thanks. After all, the Protestant who says his prayers, and has experienced answers to prayer, is not in a position to argue that miracles have ceased.

Miracles, we may believe with St. Augustine,[1] are never *contra naturam* ; but we know how we can adapt the laws of nature to serve our own purposes, and if there is a God it is absurd to suppose that he is inferior to us in this respect.[2] When further we consider our ignorance of nature, we are unwise in asserting that anything is impossible to Him who knows all. Theists believe that God is ever working in the world, but He is not a mere mechanic, and His world is not a machine. It is when the unexpected happens in answer to prayer, or to fulfil some moral purpose, that we naturally think of personality within the Godhead, and realise that He is not merely a First Principle, but a Being free to act in the universe which He has made.

Stories of mediaeval miracles that would have been laughed at a hundred years ago present no difficulties to-day. Sir Thomas More tells us of his own experience about a hysterical girl who was cured when laid before the image of Our Lady of Ipswich.[3] No scientist to-day would deny the possibility of such a story being true. A hundred years ago Protestant historians made fun of the belief that St. Francis received the stigmata, but non-Catholic professors to-day are ready with an explanation of the fact.[4] Can we, however, believe the Friar Caserta,[5] and his story about the crucifix at Naples? He tells that while he watched St. Thomas Aquinas praying, he heard a voice from the crucifix say, *Bene scripsisti de Me, Thoma ; quam ergo mercedem recipies*, and St. Thomas replied, *Non aliam nisi Te*. I think we may assume that Caserta was a truthful man, who relates what he actually experienced. I see no difficulty in believing that the colloquy with our Lord really took place, but I do not for that reason feel it necessary to believe that a painted board was provided with organs of speech.

[1] St. Augustine, *Contra Faustum*, xxvi. 3.
[2] J. S. Mill, *Three Essays*, 227, acknowledges the validity of this argument.
[3] More, *Dialoge*, Bk. I. ch. xvi. [4] Sabatier, *St. François d'Assise*, 330.
[5] Originally related in the contemporary Life of Tacco, but is to be found in the Lives of St. Thomas, e.g. *Golden Legend*, vii. 157, or Alban Butler, *Lives of the Saints*, iii. 49.

There are people who think that when an explanation can be given they have escaped from a miracle, and that when, with our present knowledge, no explanation can be given, they are justified in unbelief. An explanation of how an event happened does not affect an argument about who caused it, and it would be absurd to disbelieve in certain phenomena in the natural world because scientists are at present baffled in their attempts to explain them. In dealing with miracles we have to ask, Is the evidence sufficient to convince an unprejudiced man : and is the miracle of such a nature as to be consistent with what we know otherwise about the righteousness and holiness of God ?

It is true that an ill-regulated appetite for the marvellous led men to accept the illusions of the hysterical and insane, to believe in absurdities and in miracles that had no moral purpose. The doctrine of the Roman Church that sanctity is revealed by miracles led to many assertions being made in the Middle Ages that would not bear the scrutiny of the authorities to-day. A holy man died, his friends and admirers believed him to be a saint, and in consequence expected miracles. A man invoked the dead man for help in a bargain. He was successful and his success was magnified into a miracle. A man had a dream that his departed friend was in heaven, and it was accounted a vision and a revelation. An enemy of the holy man when alive came to grief, and it was supposed to be the vengeance of the holy man ; but the argument *post hoc, propter hoc* may be fallacious. Pecock protested that " pretensed miracles " and " pretensed visions " were but a slender thread to draw so great a conclusion as that a man was a saint.[1]

A readiness to believe also sometimes led to deliberate imposture. Sir Thomas More,[2] for instance, tells us that when Humphrey, Duke of Gloucester, visited St. Albans, a man was led by his wife up to the shrine, and declared that, having been blind, he had received his sight. The Duke questioned both him and his wife, and they both attested blindness from birth. The Duke, looking at him, said, " I don't believe you can see well now. Tell me the colour of my gown." The man did so. The Duke then asked the colour of other people's gowns and received correct answers. Finally he committed him

[1] Pecock, *Repressor*, Rolls Series.

[2] *Dialoge*, Bk. I. ch. xiv.

to the stocks as an impostor, for the sudden gift of sight would not have allowed him to know immediately how colours were named.

The Messenger immediately capped the tale with a nastier one which Sir Thomas also accepted as likely, but he summed up judicially:

> Miracles we find largely reported in the godly books of St. Gregory, St. Augustine, St. Jerome, St. Eusebius, St. Basil, St. Chrysostom and many other holy doctors of Christ's Church whose books were not unwritten this thousand year. And when ye say that of miracles many be now-a-days feigned, so may it be that some were then also: but neither then nor now neither were all feigned.

The Reformers rightly raging against the superstitions of the people, and with plentiful material for the exposure of imposture, denounced as lies all miracles subsequent to the Acts of the Apostles. Their descendants brought up in limited unbelief have seen that on their fathers' principles logic demanded that they should renounce all miracles whatsoever. The time has come for us to review the evidence with the open mind and balanced judgment of Sir Thomas More.

VII. *Pilgrimages*

People who believed in holy places, relics and miracles, naturally wished to travel and see things for themselves. Superior people might sneer at pilgrims, and satirists might make merry at their expense, but they did not decline in numbers until the shrines in England were destroyed and it was no longer possible to obtain a licence for visiting the shrines abroad.

Men became pilgrims for a variety of reasons, good and bad. Some went barefoot and some in luxury, some went in search of heaven and some to see the world. Some went bewailing their sins, and some exulting in holiday freedom. Some merited respect and admiration, and some the scornful denunciation of reformers.

In the Early Church martyrs on their way to death claimed the privilege to absolve penitents; and they were the last hope that the excommunicate had of being restored to the communion of the Church. Then it was thought that if the prayers of these righteous men were so availing on earth, they must be even more availing when the righteous men had reached to heaven. It was at the spot on which they suffered or by the tomb in which their bodies lay that men felt nearest to them.

Sometimes priests enjoined men in proof of penitence to go "naked in pilgrimages or barefoot".[1] Sometimes a penitent on his own account braved perilous journeys and begged his way, that at least he should expiate as far as possible his sins, and not seek an easy pardon. If the Middle Ages abounded in violent crimes they abounded also in heroic penances.

As the veneration of relics seemed to be justified by the report of miracles, men began to localise the sources of physical and spiritual health, and sought shrines as people to-day seek well-advertised health resorts, and enquired of saints with the same simple-mindedness as men now enquire of the fashionable physician. Physicians in those days did not inspire as much confidence as the saints, and on the little pewter flasks to be bought at Beket's shrine were stamped the legend: *Optimus aegrorum medicus fit Thoma bonorum.*[2]

People made vows that they would return thanks at some particular shrine if they obtained their object or escaped from some danger. In 1513 Sir Arthur Plantagenet in peril of shipwreck, vowed to our Lady of Walsingham that if he was spared he would eat neither flesh nor fish until he had saluted her image.[3] Later, Admiral Howard wrote to Henry VIII that he has given Plantagenet leave of absence from his ship in order that he might fulfil his vow. In the same year Katherine of Aragon wrote to tell her husband of the victory on Flodden Field, and added, "And now to our Lady of Walsingham that I promised so long ago to see".[4]

Many sought places of hallowed memories in much the same

[1] Chaucer, *Persone's Tale*, Pt. I.

[2] Jusserand, *English Wayfaring Life in the Middle Ages*, 338. Brewer, *Henry VIII*, i. 240, writes: "Pilgrimages to St. Thomas of Canterbury, in April and May, a month or six weeks ride on horseback over fresh fields and salt downs, change of diet and change of air, worked wonders for exhausted frames and overcharged digestions: and 'The blissful martyr', St. Thomas had the credit, and richly deserved it, 'of helping them that were sick', more effectually than the best leach in all the shires of broad England." In 1517 Wolsey went to Walsingham to correct the weakness of his stomach. *Ibid.* i. 242.

[3] *L. & P.*, i. 3903.

[4] *Ibid.*

spirit as people to-day make pilgrimages to the battlefields of Flanders to see where their loved ones died and plant flowers for remembrance on their graves. The Holy Land had an especial attraction for them, thinking like the imaginary Sir John Mandeville:

> Well may that land be called delectable and a fructuous land, that was be-bled and moisted with the precious blood of Our Lord Jesus Christ; the which is the same land which Our Lord be-height us in heritage.[1]

This land, so dear to Christians, was however their lost heritage, and it is not surprising that warlike pilgrims should wish to recover it by force. The Crusades provoked a genuine enthusiasm, and their failure a lasting regret. Men still dreamed of a crusade to come and Shakespeare makes Henry IV say he would go

> As far as to the sepulchre of Christ. . . .
> To chase these pagans in those holy fields,
> Over whose acres walked those blessed feet,
> Which fourteen hundred years ago were nail'd
> For our advantage to the bitter cross.[2]

Great numbers regarded pilgrimages as holiday jaunts, and religion as an excuse for making them. They went to see new sights, to meet and mix with new people, to get away from the humdrum life of their little towns, and they expected to enjoy themselves. They were not very devout, but they were not unbelieving. They said their prayers, made their offerings and listened with open mouths to the stories of sacristans. They bought little tokens to pin in their hats, and went home to outdo the sacristans when telling of the wonders they had seen.[3] Chaucer has described a typical crowd—men and women of all classes—good-natured on the whole and tolerant. The Carpenter's tale did not shock them, the Rime of St. Thomas did not bore anyone but mine host, and they listened with respect to the very long sermon of the Persone on penance and the seven deadly sins.[4] They had no doubt hired their horses at the Tabard inn and changed them at Rochester, a

[1] *Travels of Sir John Mandeville*, Prologue.
[2] *Henry IV*, Pt. I. Act I. Sc. 1.
[3] Brent, "Pilgrim Signs" in *Arch. Cantiana*, XIII. 111 ff.
[4] Chaucer, *Canterbury Tales*, passim.

shilling being paid for each stage. The horses were branded in a prominent manner, lest rogues should be tempted to deviate from the way and appropriate them. Rogues are certain to be found on all roads and in all places where strangers congregate.[1]

Lastly, there were those whom we may call professional pilgrims—spiritual tramps always on the road from shrine to shrine, and living on what they might pick up by the way. They were to be found all over Europe, decorated with Canterbury bells, with the palms of Jerusalem, the scallop shells of Compostella, and the vernicle which might betoken Genoa or Rome, because both cities claimed to possess the sudary of St. Veronica. The palmer wore a loose frock, often patched with crosses, and broad-brimmed hat sometimes fastened by strings beneath his chin, and sometimes hanging by the strings behind his back. From his girdle hung his bowl and the scrip which might contain food and might contain relics. In his hand he carried his pilgrim staff with a round nob at one end and shod with iron at the other.[2] There is an appropriate service for dismissing pilgrims in the Sarum Missal with special blessings of the scrip and staff. On the delivery of the latter, the priest said:

> Receive this staff for the support of thy journey and for the labour of thy pilgrimage; that thou mayest be able to overcome all the hosts of the enemy, and to arrive in safety at the threshold of the saints, whither thou desirest to go, etc.[3]

These staves were sometimes misused. At Chichester in 1478 such a fight took place among pilgrims in their attempt to reach the shrine of St. Richard that one man was killed, and Bishop Storey had to issue injunctions that no staves should be carried in future when approaching the saint.[4] Pilgrims going to Jerusalem carried a cross instead of a staff. At one time such pilgrims were branded with a cross, but this was ultimately forbidden by canon law.

Many palmers or pilgrims were no doubt quite genuine in their devotion:

> They bare with them no maner of thynge
> That was worth a farthynge
> Cattell, golde ne fe;

[1] Jusserand, *Eng. Wayfaring Life*, 348.
[2] Heath, *Pilgrim Life in the Middle Ages*, 134.
[3] Warren, *Translation of the Sarum Missal*, ii. 170.
[4] *V.C.H. Sussex*, ii. 49, 50.

But mekely they asked theyre meate
Where that they myght it gette
For Saynct Charytie.[1]

But as time went on these pious vagabonds

Went forth on their way with many unwise tales,
And haven leave to lie all their life time.[2]

The tales they told of foreign lands and strange places earned them a place in the chimney-corner, and the temptation to romance must have been wellnigh irresistible.

Some were men of loose lives and deserved the condemnation of the Dominican, John Bromyard, who was Chancellor of Cambridge, and a great opponent of the Lollards :

There are some that keep their pilgrimages not for God but for the devil. They who sin more freely when away from home, or who go on pilgrimage to succeed in inordinate and foolish love—those who spend their time on the road on evil and uncharitable conversation may indeed say, *peregrinamus a Domino*, they make their pilgrimage away from God to the Devil.[3]

These words apply not only to palmers but to pilgrims in general, and they are confirmed by the judgment of Thomas à Kempis, that " they who go often on pilgrimages, seldom become holy ".[4]

The place of pilgrimage had sometimes ceased to be a place of sanctity. Walsingham, for instance, was the most disorderly religious house in Norfolk when Bishop Goldwell visited it in 1494. Twenty years later Bishop Nix found that the prior lived a scandalous life and had stolen the treasures of the chapel for his own use ; that the canons had broken into the prior's cellar by night and were often found drunk and quarrelling in the taverns of the town ; that the boys were rebellious and undisciplined. The prior was forced to resign and a man from outside took his place, but he had to call in the suffragan bishop to help him before he could restore order.[5]

If the morals of Walsingham were bad, Rome had an infamous reputation. The harlot in the Colloquy of Erasmus says,

[1] The Ballad of Syr Isumbras, quoted by Bede Jarrett in his article on " Pilgrimages " in the *Catholic Encyclopaedia*.

[2] Langland, *Piers Plowman*, i. 49.

[3] Quoted Bede Jarrett. *Ibid.*

[4] *Imitatio Christi*, i. ch. 23.

[5] Jessopp in *V.C.H. Norfolk*, ii. 396.

" People were wont to come from there worse than they went ", and the good young man answers that he only escaped temptation because he took with him " a book instead of a bottle—the New Testament with Erasmus' paraphrase ".[1]

In spite of criticism from so many quarters, the popularity of pilgrimages continued unabated. Guilds at Coventry, Maidstone and York provided board and lodgings for poor pilgrims, and Ludlow had an ancient guild of palmers.[2] The New Inn at Gloucester, the Bell at Tewkesbury and the George at Glastonbury were founded for their accommodation. Several guilds at Lincoln were obliged to attend one of their members, intending a pilgrimage as far as the city gate, and every brother was bound to give him a halfpenny if going to Rome or a penny if going to Jerusalem.[3] It was also esteemed meritorious if those unable to make a pilgrimage paid someone else to make it on their behalf. Sir Thomas Tuddenham of Norfolk, for example, sent John Capgrave, who on returning home wrote *The Solace of Pilgrims*.[4]

Many English pilgrims went to salute Our Lady of Boulogne[5] and the head of St. John the Baptist[6] at Amiens. They were easily accessible. It took longer to visit the Three Kings of

[1] Erasmus, *Coll.*: *Scorti et Adolescentis*.

[2] Barnard, *Companion to the Middle Ages*, 208.

[3] Jusserand, *Wayfaring Life*, 350.

[4] *The Solace of Pilgrims*, 1450, was first published by C. A. Mills (O.U.P.) in 1911, with very valuable notes. Capgrave used as his guide-book *Mirabilia Urbis Romae*, which has now been edited, and translated by Nichols as *The Marvels of Rome*. But Capgrave was no mere copyist. He saw things for himself, and made his own observations. He was very accurate in copying inscriptions. As this can be proved from those that remain, he is a good authority for those which have perished. A very different book was *The Stacyons of Rome*. Two versions of this were edited by Furnivall for E.E.T.S. The first (1866) is in *Political, Religious and Love Poems*. The second (1867) is bound with *The Pilgrim Ship*. The author is anxious to point out how many years' remission from purgatory may be gained by a visit to the City:

> " He that will his soul leach [cure]
> Listeneth to me and I will teach,
> Pardon is the soul bote [cure],
> At greatest Rome there is the rote [root]."

Adam of Usk's experiences in Rome are interesting: *vide* his *Chronicle*, edited by Maunde Thompson (R.H.S.).

[5] Wife of Bath had been to Rome, Boulogne, Compostella and Cologne. Chaucer, Prologue, *Piers Plowman*, xii. 37. B Text mentions Rome and Rocamadour.

[6] St. John the Baptist's Head. The hinder part was said to be at Constantinople, the forepart in Rome, the jaws at Genoa, and the whole at Amiens. The author of *Mandeville's Travels*, p. 72: " I wot never, but God knoweth: but in what wise that men worship it, the blessed Saint John holds him apaid ".

Cologne, or Our Lady of Rocamadour in Guienne, though the latter remained a popular shrine owing to the fact that Guienne had so long belonged to the English Crown and that trade with Bordeaux was continuous. It was more difficult to visit St. James of Compostella, but no other foreign pilgrimage was so popular with the English. In a single year 2400 licences were issued to visit that shrine. When William Wey [1] was there in 1456 there were in Corunna harbour 80 ships *cum topcastellis* and only 4 *sine topcastellis*. Of these ships 32 were English.[2] The voyage, which with luck took nearly a week, was a test of endurance. A hundred or more pilgrims were packed on a very limited deck : most of them were ill ; and all were frequently disturbed by unsympathetic sailors, while the captain cried,

> Haul the Bowline ! now vere the sheet !
> Cook, make ready anon our meat,
> Our pilgrims have no lust to eat,
> I pray God give them rest.[3]

On reaching Compostella they were rewarded by taking part in the most splendid ceremonies ; and saw the image of St. James incongruously decorated with the crown of the Saracenic King of Granada, captured in battle. When Wey was there four Englishmen carried the canopy over the Blessed Sacrament in procession, and the English alone had a sermon in their own tongue. It was preached by a Franciscan who was a bachelor in theology.[4]

If the pilgrimage by sea to Compostella was uncomfortable, it was less dangerous than by land. Andrew Boorde says, " I had rather go five times to Rome out of England, than one to Compostella ; by water it is no pain, but by land it is the greatest journey an Englishman may go ". He himself accompanied a party of nine, English and Scottish, from Orleans ; and the nine all died on the way back, " by eating of fruit and drinking of water ". Boorde, the only survivor, on reaching Aquitaine " did kiss the ground for joy ".[5]

[1] *Arch. Cantiana*, xiii. 112.
[2] *The Itineraries of William Wey*, Roxburgh Club, 154.
[3] *The Pilgrim Ship*, E.E.T.S., edited by Furnivall; quoted Jusserand, *Wayfaring Life*, 371.
[4] Wey, *Itineraries*.
[5] Boorde, *Dyetary*, 1542, E.E.T.S., 205, 206.

Not many pilgrims from England during the XV century went as far as Jerusalem. One of the few was John Tiptoft, Earl of Worcester, equally famed for his learning and his cruelty. Another was William Wey,[1] Fellow of Eton, who has left accounts of his two pilgrimages to Palestine. He did not, like Tiptoft, go with a great train, but he was apparently a man of wealth, with an eye to his comfort and a determination that he would not be swindled if he could help it. We learn from his *Itineraries* the precision that was necessary in bargaining with the padrone of a Venetian galley, of the articles and stores that should be laid in for the voyage, and of where money could be changed to the best advantage. He knew it was advisable to secure an upper berth, and how quick one ought to be to obtain the best donkey in Jaffa where first come was first served, and late arrivals had only Hobson's choice.

Wey was a practical man, but also most devout. He was shriven before arriving at Jaffa, and sang *Vrbs beata Jerusalem, in faburthyn.*[2] It was three days before the Saracens would allow his company to land. Then they knelt on the shore and sang *Christus resurgens* and went on their way singing and hearing Mass at the various holy sites. Wey had come to Palestine to determine certain perplexities he had felt in reading the Bible, and resolved them all to his own satisfaction. He was of an enquiring and even critical disposition; and yet was very credulous, to our thinking. Here are his verses about Siloam:

There is a well a little thence
There Our Lady Christ's clothes did cleanse;
Above that is a water by it one
That healed the blinde man
Fast by, against the law
Manasses to death did Esias saw,

[1] Wey, *Itineraries*, passim. Cf. Boorde, *Dyetary*, 219, 221. Wynkin de Worde, *Information for Pilgrims*. In the last-named book we learn: "In the seven and twentieth month of June, there passed from Venice under sail, out of the haven of Venice, at the sun going down, certain pilgrims towards Jerusalem in a ship of a merchant of Venice, called Moroson. The patron of the said ship was called Luke Mantell. To the number of 46 pilgrims, every man paying, some more and some less, as they might accord with the patron. Some that might pay well payed 32 ducats, and some 26 and 24 for meat and drink and passage to Port Jaffa." *The Information* has not been reprinted, and the unique copy is in the Advocates' Library at Edinburgh. See Gordon-Duff, *Fifteenth Century Books*, 62.

[2] *In faburthyn = cum nota.* The word is compounded of the musical notation *fa* and the word *burthen* so often associated with song.

And high from thence a field there is
Ycleped *Ager Sanguinis*,
But for them that Latin lack
It is called Acheldmac.[1]

Later in life Wey became a monk at Edyngton, where he built a chapel on the model of the Holy Sepulchre, and furnished it with the little treasures he had brought from the Holy Land. He also made a map of Palestine, seven feet long, which is very largely accurate; and painted little scenes of events that had happened in different places. William Wey was not only a great traveller but a scholar—a devout man of common sense; but he seems to belong to an altogether different world to Erasmus, and yet Erasmus was on pilgrimage only half a century later.

In 1512[2] Erasmus paid a first visit to Walsingham, offering to Our Lady a Greek ode. He tells her how the poet,

Bringing these verses, all he has,
Asks in reward for his most humble gift,
That greatest blessing, purity of heart
And full remission of his many sins.[3]

Fourteen years later, when possessed by a different spirit, he published his Colloquy, *Peregrinatio religionis ergo*. In it he tells of another visit some years later, but he never stayed for long in England after 1514, and we may have our suspicions that the visit never took place. Anyhow, the narrative is fictitious, although it must have had sufficient verisimilitude to be accepted by his contemporaries. The same criticism may be made of his visit to Canterbury with Colet. This was probably earlier than 1512, before he went to Cambridge, and was written up and embellished years afterwards when Colet was dead, and Erasmus wished to ridicule pilgrimages and hold monks up to scorn. As told, we almost see the impatient contempt of Colet and hear the snigger of Erasmus; while we sympathise with the hot discomfort of the sacristan, dimly aware that his oft-repeated patter was despised. It is dramatic enough, a masterly description of

[1] Wey's Latin is much better than his doggerel verses.

[2] Dr. Allen has settled the date of *Ep*. 262, which mentions the visit to Walsingham. Seebohm, *Oxford Reformers*, 272-275, is wrong about the date, and I hope he is also wrong in regarding the poem as a profane joke.

[3] Quoted Jessopp, *V.C.H. Norfolk*, ii. 397.

what did not occur. On the real day Erasmus, who spoke no English, walked behind Colet, observant but silent: and Colet probably remembered that he had relics much more questionable if much less profitable in his cathedral church of St. Paul.

Erasmus apologised to Wolsey for the many things he had said about pilgrimages in the *Colloquies*. He explained that he was only anxious that men "should not go visiting St. James at Compostella, leaving behind their wives and children who depend on them, and many other things too numerous to mention, which the priests themselves in their sermons should point out to them".[1] This was merely to say what Reynard the Fox says in the French version translated by M. Jusserand:

> There is in the world many a good man who has never been to Rome. Such an one has come back from the seven saints worse than ever he was. I mean to take my way home, and I shall live by my labour and seek honest earnings. I shall be charitable to poor people.[2]

The times were changing fast. Good men were no longer thinking of how they might get to heaven, but how they should live on earth. Domestic duties and honest earnings were mounting in the scale of virtues. They were coming to be estimated more highly than adventures after holiness. Also among the pious, the *Devotio moderna* of Hilton and Thomas à Kempis was spreading. Men were turning from a religion of external worship to listen to the voice of God speaking within, so Hilton says:

> It needeth not to run to Rome, nor to Jerusalem to seek Christ there, but turn thy thoughts into thine own soul where He is hid, as the Prophet saith, *Soothly thou art an hid God*, and seek Him there.[3]

Pilgrimages remained as popular as ever, but they were ceasing to attract the more devout.

VIII. *Purgatory*

We cannot conclude our account of popular religion before the Reformation without speaking of purgatory. We are not,

[1] Quoted Mangan, *Erasmus*, ii. 148. In Allen's ed. of the Letters, *Ep.* 1696, the date is 1526.

[2] Jusserand, *Wayfaring Life*, 352. The French in Appendix, 455.

[3] Hilton, *Scale of Perfection*, Bk. I. ch. 49.

however, concerned with the writings of Dante and St. Catherine of Genoa,[1] or with the Decrees of Trent,[2] but with the popular teaching of the time, the abuses to which it gave rise, and with the accusations made against the clergy.

There are several passages in Holy Scripture which suggest that the dead may pass through stages of purification and progress on their way to God. Reason tells us that very few can leave this world fit for the Beatific Vision, while justice suggests that forgiveness should be associated with penance.

The Early Church, preoccupied with the thought of our Lord's almost immediate return, could only think of the dead as under the altar, crying " O Lord, how long ! " The little band of expectant and heroic martyrs, face to face with a heathen and hostile world, were not called upon to consider the fate of less ardent Christians. Questions concerning the intermediate state did not become pressing until there was a mixed multitude of baptized Christians who died without manifest signs of grace. Many of them, not markedly devout and with conspicuous failings, were none the less kind, lovable and believing. It became impossible to believe that a good God would consign them to a hell of everlasting torment. Probation might indeed end with death, but that did not preclude the possibility of progress and purification afterwards ; and, if such a belief cannot be proved, there is much in Holy Scripture to countenance it, and nothing to prevent its being entertained. In consequence, the Church has ever prayed :

> Remember, O Lord, the Souls of Thy servants, and handmaidens, who have gone before us with the sign of faith, and sleep the sleep of peace ; to them, O Lord, and to all who rest in Christ, we pray that Thou wouldest grant a place of refreshment, light and peace.[3]

Remembering how the Church has prayed, it is startling to read how Sir Thomas More,[4] who heard Mass every day, thought the souls of the departed cried to living men :

[1] St. Catherine of Genoa, *Treatise on Purgatory*, edited by Cardinal Manning. Cf. von Hügel, *Mystical Element in Religion*, ii. 230-246.

[2] *Canones et Decreta : Concilia Tridentini*, Sessio xxv. There is a purgatory, and the souls there retained are relieved by the suffrages of the faithful and chiefly by the acceptable sacrifice of the Mass. . . . Those things which tend to a certain kind of curiosity and superstition are to be prohibited as scandals and stumbling-blocks to the faithful.

[3] Canon of the Mass.

[4] More, " Supplication of Souls ", *Works*, 337 ; quoted by Forbes, *XXXIX Articles*, 311.

If ye pity the poor, there is none so poor as we, that have not a brat [1] to put upon our backs. If ye pity the blind, there is none so blind as we, which are here in the dark, saving for sights unpleasant, and loathsome, till some comfort come. If ye pity the lame, there is none so lame as we, that can neither creep one foot out of the fire, nor have one hand at liberty to defend our face from the flame. Finally, if ye pity any man in pain, never knew you pain comparable to ours; whose fire as far passeth in heat all the fires that ever burned on earth, as the hottest of all that passed a feigned fire painted on a wall. If ever ye lay sick, or thought the night long and longed for day, while every hour seemed longer than five, bethink you then what a long night we sely souls endure, that lie sleepless, restless, burning and broiling in the dark fire one long night of many days, of many weeks, of many years together. You walter, peradventure, and tolter in sickness from side to side, and find little rest in any part of the bed; we lie bound to the brands, and cannot lift up our heads. You have your physicians with you, that sometimes cure and heal you, no physic will help our pain, nor no plaisters cool our heat. Your keepers do you great ease, and put you in good comfort; our keepers are such as God keep you from — cruel, doomed sprites, odious, envious and hateful, despiteous enemies and despiteful tormentors, and their company more terrible and grievous to us than is the pain itself: and the intolerable torment that they do us, wherewith from top to toe they cease not continually to tear us.

Sir Thomas More wrote this horrible paragraph in the hope of persuading men to pray that their dead friends might enjoy refreshment, light and peace, but he has piled up his images in such a way that we receive a wrong impression about God and purgatory—a wrong impression that was only too prevalent in his day. It is conceivable that a loving God will chastise His children with severity, and that His children, by willing acceptance of that chastisement, may be purged from sin. It is conceivable that stern discipline may be necessary before careless sinners may become steadfast in virtue. It is conceivable that sinners enduring penance may be sustained by our sympathy and support. It is even conceivable that their sufferings may be shortened by our intercession, God associating us with Himself in His mercy. But it is inconceivable that a good God should go on tormenting His children because other people will not say Masses or buy indulgences on their behalf.

It is well to remember how the belief in the horrors of

[1] Brat = a cloth used as an upper garment, usually of a makeshift nature. *N.E.D.*

purgatory arose. The Dark Ages were barbarous and cruel, and men were accustomed to inflict and endure pain as a matter of course. Their sins were of the body—violence, sexual lust and excess in eating and drinking. Their penances were appropriate—self-flagellation, fasting, and the mortification of natural desires. What they thought right to inflict on themselves, they thought a good God and a better Judge would inflict with even greater severity. As time went on the penitential discipline was relaxed, men became more indulgent to themselves, and even a little kinder to one another ; but the doctrine of purgatory did not change, because men thought it had been confirmed by revelations.

These supposed revelations were mostly reported by monks or nuns who mistook disordered dreams for visions. Rigorists in creed and practice, their fantasies came of overmuch fasting and of morbid introspection. Scrupulous about trivial actions, they were apt to dream of the horrible punishments which they dreaded when awake. A dead friar appeared to tell one of his brethren, " I am much tortured, because when others watered their wine, I drank mine pure in order that I might sleep ". The Blessed Virgin, who should have remembered that her Son had compassion on her when He was dying upon the Cross, came to tell a friar how another brother was grievously punished because on his deathbed he had looked with carnal compassion on his weeping kinsfolk. A monk to whom had been vouchsafed a vision of purgatory was able to tell a laughing brother exactly how he would suffer for his levity in another world. Preachers asserted that it was better to do a hundred years of hard penance in the body than to burn in purgatory for a single day : and that to be in purgatory but the twinkling of an eye was more grievous than any torment St. Lawrence suffered upon his gridiron.[1]

If such awful punishments awaited the cloistered for their venial faults, imagination could not conceive of anything worse for those living lives of brutality in the world ; but men of the world were apt to close their eyes and refuse to contemplate distant prospects of appalling retribution. Sometimes indeed revivalist preachers succeeded. A man was convicted of sin, convinced of purgatorial fires and experienced conversion.

[1] Coulton, *Five Centuries of Religion*, i. 74.

Often eloquent preachers became quite popular. In the Middle Ages there were many like the evangelicals of a hundred years ago who were thrilled by sermons about hell, while they had assurance that the flames were not for them—the elect, the already saved.

Abelard and the Victorines did much to develop a belief in purgatory [1]; and we must not forget that the doctrine permitted men to hope that at long last great sinners might be saved. The belief opened a way of co-operation between the living and the dead, and made the one mystical Body of Christ, here and in the world beyond, a reality to the ordinary man. If the saints can help us by their prayers, so we by prayers can help the souls in purgatory. The bereaved did not feel that it was best to forget their loved ones or brood in dull despair over memories of the past. Their dead were still alive and had need of them. They could help them on their way to refreshment, light and peace.

Men who had lived in sin, when sickness came and death drew near, sought an escape from judgment to come. It was then that they made legal indentures with abbeys that their obits might be kept, endowed chantries that a priest might sing for their souls, desired others to be pilgrims on their behalf or earn indulgences which might be placed to their credit. Conscience made cowards of them, and superstition prompted them to buy respite from the punishment which they felt that they deserved. This mechanical method of attempting to obtain salvation had no support in the teaching of the Church; but the theory of "satisfactory" Masses, and the fact that they were paid for, no doubt encouraged superstition and made "Purgatory Pickpurse" a byword. Latimer said:

> It was a pleasant fiction, and from the beginning so profitable to the feigners of it, that almost, I dare boldly say, there hath been no emperor that hath gotten more by taxes and tallages of them that were alive, than these [friars], the very and right begotten men of the world, got by dead men's tributes and gifts.[2]

[1] Kirk, *Vision of God*, 513, 514.

[2] Latimer, *Works*, i. 50. Cp. Lecky, *European Morals*, ii. 235: "Whatever may be thought of its other aspects, it is impossible to avoid recognising in this teaching [about Purgatory] a masterly skill in the adaptation of means to ends, which almost arises to artistic beauty. A system which deputed its minister to go to the unhappy widow in the first hour of her anguish and desolation, to tell her that he, who was

Whatever may be said against the practical system, this is a double calumny. The Church certainly did not invent purgatory in order to extort money, and Latimer was in a position to know how poor the mendicant orders were found to be when they were dissolved. The calumny arose out of the fact that men had been encouraged to make charitable bequests for the good of their souls, and that there were a multitude of " soul priests " who earned a miserable living by saying Masses for particular people. That the sacraments of the Church were sold at a price was the root evil, though if a man founded a chantry and wished it to be served in perpetuity, it seemed only right that he should endow it. Whether he did right in founding it depended on his motive, and there were plenty of people to impute a bad one. Even to-day disappointed heirs will suggest that a testator who makes charitable bequests was hoping to buy heaven, and are quite ready to accuse a clergyman of undue influence if there is any chance of upsetting the will.

dearer to her than all the world besides, was now burning in a fire, and that he could only be relieved by a gift of money to the priests, was assuredly of its kind not without extraordinary merits." On which it is only necessary to say—the Church never deputed anyone to go on any such errand, and never taught that money given to priests would ensure relief in purgatory. Hundreds of mediaeval wills have survived, and very few of them contain gifts to priests who were not relatives.

CHAPTER V

ECONOMIC AND SOCIAL CHANGES

I. *The Abbeys*

SCANDALS among the clergy and superstitions among the people no doubt called for reformation ; but they were not the only causes of the Reformation that occurred. The mediaeval system was everywhere breaking up ; social and economic changes were taking place ; and perfectly orthodox people were asking, " Ought the monasteries to be preserved ? " The ordinary man complained that the abbeys absorbed too much of the national wealth and contributed too little to the national prosperity.[1] He resented the privileges of the abbeys and asserted that they were enjoyed at the expense of the community. He condemned their principle of seclusion, maintaining that the country had a claim to the co-operation of all its citizens. England had owed much to the abbeys in the past, but the day for their destruction was at hand.

Abbeys have been described as hives of industry, cradles of the arts, havens of peace, schools of discipline, homes of praise and prayer, and beacons illuminating the dangers of this world and directing men to safety in a world beyond ; but the most extravagant of apologists would not so describe the abbeys of the XV century. The monks had lost their fervour of devotion ; they no longer laboured with their hands, they produced nothing to speak of in the way of art or literature, and they were lax in

[1] This attitude was by no means new in the XVI century. Stow, *Annals*, 330, tells of the variance between clergy and laity at the Parliament of Coventry in 1406 : " The Knights affirming that they had, oftentimes going forth with the King against rebels and enemies, not only spent largely their goods, with and for the King, but also had got their bodies in great danger and jeopardies, where in the mean season the clerks sat idle at home and helped the King never a whit. But Thomas Arundel, Archbishop of Canterbury, made answer, that the clergy did always give the King as much as the lay people did, considering that they did oftener give the King Tenths than the laity gave Fifteenths. And moreover, that more of their tenants did serve the King in his wars, than the tenants of the laity. And besides this, they prayed day and night for the prosperity of the King and of all them that faithfully served him."

the observance of their rule. They could justly plead that after nine hundred years much of it was obsolete, and that in taking vows they had only bound themselves to observe the rules of the cloister life which had become customary.[1]

The outside world thought them idle, and " abbey lubber "[2] was a term of reproach which they probably did not deserve. The daily round of services was kept up in the choir, if not always at the canonical hours. Much time had to be spent in estate management, and the litigation it necessitated both in the king's courts and at Rome. It was no light work to provision the great houses with food, drink, oil, wax, fuel and clothing ; to see that repairs were attended to, and to supervise workmen and servants. There were novices to be trained in the cloister and choristers in the almonry ; the sick had to be cared for in the infirmary, visitors had to be entertained in the guesten house, and alms had to be distributed at the abbey gate. In a fairly well-ordered monastery there was plenty to do ; but it is pertinent to ask who benefited by all these activities but the monks themselves ; and, if others received benefits, were they sufficient to justify the vast wealth of the monasteries ?

They had become possessed of great estates and much tithe. In consequence they were envied, although they were nearly always in debt and financial difficulties.[3] They were heavily taxed both by Pope and King, who required to be paid in coin. Ready money was scarce, and in order to meet the demands they were driven to usurers who only lent at unconscionable rates. Benefactions too often took the form of enriching the abbey church or the erection of new buildings, which added to the cost of upkeep and often entailed other obligations. On their estates they were for the most part easy landlords, content with customary rents.[4] They made bad bargains in granting corrodies, while kings and

[1] Chaucer in his Prologue speaks of his monk—

> The reule of Seint Maure and of Seint Beneit,
> Because that it was old and soundele streit,
> This like monk lette olde thinges pace,
> And held after the newe world the trace.

[2] Abbey-lubber properly was used for a hanger-on at the abbey ; but by the XVI century it had come to be used of a monk.

[3] Coulton, *Five Centuries of Religion*, iii. *passim*.

[4] Denton, *Fifteenth Century*, 147, states that the monastic lands being better cultivated, often paid higher rents. Rogers, *Agriculture and Prices*, iv., says that the monks were easy landlords.

the descendants of founders would often insist on corrodies being given to persons nominated by themselves.[1] "They were," says Trevisan, "obliged to keep many poor gentlemen, who were left beggars" in consequence of the law of primogeniture.[2]

The monks were largely recruited from the families of tenants on the abbey estates.[3] It was good business for a farmer to make his second son a monk, for from the monastery he might help his elder brother on the land. It was usual for a novice to enter religion at the age of sixteen, and we may imagine a boy tempted by a dream that he might be abbot or prior, although he could only have a reasonable expectation of being an obedientiary. The life was quiet, sheltered and secure: it called for no strenuous endeavour, but provided plentiful employment. The religious ceremonial was splendid and varied; and a young novice soon became proud of his church and jealous of its fame. He looked forward to the day when he should say his first Mass and receive *exennia* that he might make merry with his friends.[4] In a good monastery the life was a happy one, and there is no reason to question the genuine religion of the inmates, even though there was nothing heroic about it.

The old enthusiasm for the self-renouncing life of the cloister had passed away. The day of asceticism had passed; and the monks, in ceasing to be rigorists, had ceased to excite the admiration of the world outside. Only two monasteries were founded in the XV century, and Henry VII was the patron of the Observant Friars. The numbers of the monks were dwindling; and this was not entirely due to lack of vocations, but was largely the result of straitened circumstances. When the monks worked with their

[1] *Italian Relation*, 51: "If the abbeys founded by the Crown do not actually pay money to the King, they are obliged to pay the expenses of one, two or three gentlemen, and as many horses with their keep, at the pleasure of His Majesty, because whenever the King wishes to bestow an easy life upon one of his servants, he makes one of these monasteries pay his expenses." See also Baskerville, *English Monks*, etc. 65.

[2] Baskerville, 61; "The younger sons of the gentry had a fine opportunity for advancing their careers by taking service under an abbot or prior. Every religious house had a crowd of persons of the squire class, wearing its livery, administering its estates, presiding over its manorial courts, acting as stewards, bailiffs, gentlemen farmers, etc. . . . A whole crowd of gentlemen had clothing, board and lodging free in every religious house." In the *Complaynt of Roderick Mors* we are told that the monks would have given more in alms, "if they had not had so many mens' horses to feed, and had not been overcharged with such idle gentlemen as were never out of the abbeys".

[3] Pearce, *Monks of Westminster*, 38.

[4] *Ibid.* 21, 22.

own hands and shared a communal life, numbers were important for most men could contribute in labour more than they cost to keep, but when monks lived on their endowments and enjoyed stipends from them, it was natural that they should limit their numbers as far as possible in hard times.[1] It was this decline in numbers which made men wonder if monasteries any longer supplied a need.

Each Benedictine monastery was a self-contained unit ; and the congregations established by the fourth Lateran Council rarely interfered in its internal affairs, and had no machinery to make such interference effective.[2] The dilapidations of a negligent abbot might ruin his house ; a weak prior might be fatal to all discipline ; an immoral monk might corrupt the younger members of the community. Most monasteries had their ups and downs ; sometimes the tone was good and the discipline strict ; sometimes it was lax and the monks disorderly. From time to time there were terrible scandals, which are duly noted in chronicles, while the greater number of orderly houses did nothing to occasion remark. Sexual immorality was occasional—probably no great house was altogether or for any length of time entirely free from it ; but its extent was exaggerated by suspicion and the nasty gossip of the cloister.[3] Over-eating and over-drinking were much more common. The monk was often an epicure :

> A fat swan loved he best of any roast,[4]

and mediaeval preachers dilate on *Gula* with gusto. It was not, however, the irregularities of the monks which made

[1] Coulton, *Five Centuries of Religion*, iii. 542.

[2] *Catholic Encyclopaedia*, " Benedictines ". The statement in the text does not mean that the general chapters did not issue statutes or conduct visitations. Pantin, *Chapters of the English Black Monks*, 3 vols. (C.S.), prints the results of several visitations in vol. iii. In vol. ii. he prints the statutes suggested by Henry V for the reform of the Order. The chapter, however, preferred statutes drawn up by the Abbot of St. Albans. They were admirable, but it is probable that the statutory monk was as hard to find as the economic man.

[3] Gossip was one of the evils prevalent in the cloister. Sir Thomas More writing to a monk says : " Are there not many who if they omitted a verse of their office would think it a crime to be expiated by many tears, and who have not the least scruple to take part in caluminous gossip, longer than their longest prayers ? " Quoted Bridgett, *Blessed Thomas More*, 101.

[4] Chaucer, *Prologue*. Swans were esteemed a great delicacy. They cost 6s. 8d. each when a chicken cost 4d. and a fat goose 10d. Rogers, *Agriculture and Prices*, iv. 343.

them unpopular, but their corporate selfishness. They were for ever insisting on their rights, and sometimes forging charters to maintain them. They were full of *esprit de corps* and could always plead like the monks of Coventry that they would not surrender the rights of their Church "for fear of blemishing their conscience".[1] Tyndale wrote:

> They will lose nothing. Why? It is God's, not theirs. It is St. Hubert's rents, St. Alban's lands, St. Edmond's rights, St. Peter's patrimony, say they, and none of ours.[2]

The secular clergy disliked monks for their appropriation of rectories; and the bishops found them obstructive when they ventured to hold visitations. Where towns had grown up about them as at St. Albans, Abingdon,[3] Reading and Bury St. Edmunds, they were continually at feud with the people. They hated friars and friars reciprocated their hatred. They clung to Rome, because Rome was too far away to exercise supervision. Monasteries gloried in their independence and did not recognise their consequent weakness. They were isolated corporations which the State, when it wanted, could easily suppress. Only in the North was there any strong popular feeling in their favour.

The monks who were promoted to the higher offices in the monasteries had mostly been trained in the "nurseries" at Oxford and Cambridge, and gloried in the title of *Magister*.[4] Such men were the champions of the Old Learning, and ready to denounce the *Poets* for their revolt against academic tradition. Monastic parlours were perhaps not very unlike Oxford common rooms before the Oriel Noetics began to call in question both the university and the universe.

The men of the New Learning were not slow to defend themselves. Sir Thomas More in his *Letter to a Monk* has very unpleasant strictures on monastic reading and criticism;[5] and

[1] Miss Dormer Harris, *Coventry*, 46.

[2] Tyndale, *Obedience of a Christian Man*, 236.

[3] Langland, *Piers Plowman*, B text, x. 366, seems to have had a special grudge against the Abbot of Abingdon, for he prophesies,

> Then shall the Abbot of Abingdon and all his issue for ever
> Have a knock of a king, and incurable wound.

[4] Pantin, *op. cit.* iii., ix., states how the English Black Monks, from the XIII century onwards, insisted on study and maintained their establishments at the universities.

[5] Bridgett, 94.

Starkey thought that monastic endowments might be better employed. He even suggested that the great abbeys of St. Albans and Westminster should be turned into public schools for the sons of noblemen.[1] Wolsey suppressed many small monastic establishments to found his great college at Oxford and his school at Ipswich. He employed one Thomas Cromwell, and trained him for work which he was soon to do on a larger scale for another and more rapacious master.

There had been a time when kings could rejoice in the extent of monastic estates, because they were areas of comparative peace in a turbulent world and acted as buffer states between militant barons. It was generally of advantage to kings that the spiritual peers formed a majority in the House of Lords. It was more to his advantage that there were bodies from whom he could extort large sums of money without exciting national ill-will. But the day came when, through the senseless extravagance of Henry VIII, the treasury was empty; and he proceeded to kill the goose that laid the golden eggs. He also wished to endow a new aristocracy, but not out of crown lands. Having proclaimed himself Supreme Head of the Church, he soon found that the abbeys were too independent, and too detached from the life of the nation to have any place in his new England.[2]

The methods adopted for their suppression were odious and the waste of wealth and of artistic treasures was lamentable; but monasticism had served its purpose, and at this time did not appeal even to the devout. Considering its vast landed possessions it was inevitable that some change should be made. If Henry VIII had not quarrelled with the Pope,[3] he might, like Francis I, have made a concordat by which he could bestow abbeys *in commendam*.[4] The abbeys in England

[1] Starkey, i. 187. It is noteworthy that Martin V had endowed the University of Pavia by suppressing many monasteries. Gascoigne, 4.

[2] Coulton, *Five Centuries of Religion*, iii. 443.

[3] By the Pragmatic Sanction of Bourges the Pope was deprived of annates, reservations and expectations, while the Church in France obtained a certain freedom in electing to ecclesiastical posts. By the Concordat of 1516 Dr. Kitchin (*Hist. of France*, ii. 181) says, " the king presented to the Pope the wealth of the Church and the Pope handed over to the King its independence ". The Pope really made a bad bargain, for the king obtained the right to appoint, with few exceptions, to all bishoprics, abbeys and benefices.

[4] The practice of holding abbeys *in commendam* never obtained in England. Wolsey holding the Abbey of St. Albans is the one exception. It never existed in

would have then decayed as they did in France, while their revenues were spent at court by royal favourites. If Charles I had had, like Louis XIV, an immense amount of patronage to bestow that could only be held for life, there would have been no Civil war, but there might have been at the end of the XVIII century a reign of "terror".

II. *Agriculture*

In the country districts there was little or no opposition to the Church, though many of the parishes were served by ill-paid vicars, and rich rectors were often absentees. Professor Thorold Rogers has corrected the gloomy picture in Denton's book,[1] and assures us that "the XV century and early years of the XVI were the golden age of the husbandman, the artisan and the labourer",[2] though he admits that the labourer was paid in money when prices were high, and in kind when they were low. The rosy view of the period is borne out by the memory of Bishop Latimer:

> My father was a yeoman, and had no lands of his own, only he had a farm of three or four pounds a year at the uttermost; and hereupon he tilled so much as kept half a dozen men. He had walk for a hundred sheep; and my mother milked twenty kine. He was able and did find the King a harness, with himself and his horse, while he came to the place that he should receive the King's wages. I can remember that I buckled his harness when he went to Blackheath field. He kept me to school, or else I had not been able to have preached before the King's majesty now. He married my sisters with five pounds or twenty nobles a piece, so that he brought them up in godliness and fear of God. He kept hospitality for his poor neighbours, and some alms he gave to the poor. And all this he did of the said farm, where he that now hath it payeth sixteen pounds by year or more, and is not able to do anything for his prince, for himself, nor for his children, or give a cup of drink to the poor.[3]

Some fifteen years before Latimer was born, *i.e.* in 1485, Sir

Belgium and was discontinued in Germany. In Italy Leo X, while still in his cradle, was abbot of sixteen monasteries, including Monte Cassino. The Council of Trent—Sessions xxi. 8 and xxiv. 2—tried its best to prevent this abuse, but the French monarchy was too strong for its edicts on this subject to have any effect: Montalembert, *Monks of the West* (English trans.), i. 104.

[1] Denton, *Fifteenth Century*, passim.

[2] Rogers, *Agriculture and Prices*, iv. 23, 490.

[3] Latimer, *Works*, i. 101.

John Fortescue had written for the exiled Prince Edward, son of Henry VI, whom he hoped would be king, a picture of English felicity which was perhaps a little highly coloured :

England . . . surpasses all other countries in fertility. There are fields and pastures enclosed by hedges and ditches, planted with trees, so as to be a defence to herds of sheep and cattle against the storm and the heat. The pastures are generally watered, so that the animals that are enclosed in them need no keeper day or night. There are no beasts of prey, and sheep can lie by night unwatched in their folds and so enrich the soil. Hence the people of that country are not weighted by heavy labour, but breathe freely like those patriarchs, who chose rather to feed cattle than oppress themselves with the anxieties of husbandry. Moreover, the same country is so dotted and filled with land-owners, that hardly a hamlet in it is without knight, esquire or franklin, who is not enriched with good property.[1]

Nearly thirty years later, Trevisan reports :

Agriculture is not practised in this country beyond what is required for the consumption of the people ; because were they to plough and sow all the land that was capable of cultivation, they might sell a quantity of grain to the surrounding countries . . . above all they have an enormous number of sheep, which yield them quantities of wool of the best quality.[2]

He also states, " there are four thousand parks in England, all enclosed with timber fences ".[3] Parks had existed since the days of Canute and sporting rights were strictly preserved. There were also the extensive royal forests and chaces with their own laws. Further, the custom was growing up for the wealthier farmers to buy up the strips of the common fields and enclose them. Fitzherbert, who wrote on husbandry about 1521, approved of these enclosures. The hedges protected the cattle in the winter and protected growing crops from cattle, and saved the farmer from paying wages to swineherds and shepherds.[4] From the farmers' point of view he was no doubt right, but labour-saving expedients always begin by throwing men out of employment and the French critic in the *Débat des Héraulx d'Armes* says :

In England some one man keepeth in his hands two or three farms, and where hath been six or eight persons in every farm, he keepeth only a shepherd or wretched herdman and his wife.[5]

[1] Fortescue, *De Laudibus*, ch. 29 ; quoted in Rogers, iv. 748.
[2] *Italian Relations*, 10.
[3] *Ibid*. 39. [4] Rogers, iv. 40 ff. [5] Quoted *ibid*. iv. 513.

Fitzherbert in advocating enclosed fields did not intend the decrease of tillage, neither was he defending the appropriations of wastes and commons by the lord of the manor ; but sheep-farming was so much more profitable than anything else that there was a temptation to enclose whole tracts of land for this purpose, turning the inhabitants out of their houses.[1] It was against this evil that the Act against Enclosures was directed. Sir Thomas More wrote :

> Your sheep that were wont to be so meek and tame and so small, now, as I hear say, be become so great devourers and so wild, that they eat up and swallow down the very men themselves. They consume, destroy and devour whole fields, houses and cities. For look in what parts of the realm both grow the finest and therefore dearest wool, there noblemen and gentlemen—yea, and certain abbots, holy men no doubt—not contenting themselves with the yearly revenues and profits, that were to grow to their forefathers and predecessors of their lands, nor being content that they live in rest and pleasure nothing profiting, yea much noying the weal public ; leave no ground for tillage, they enclose all in pastures : they pluck down towns, and leave nothing standing, but only the Church to make a sheephouse. And as though you lost no small quantity of ground by forests, chaces, lands and parks, these good holy men turn all dwelling places and all glebeland into desolation and wilderness.[2]

The animus against abbots is here unmistakeable, and More at any rate did not foresee what would happen when monastic estates passed into lay hands.[3] The covetous had long had their eyes on monastic property. As early as 1410 the Lollards had pointed out that " the landed estates of the bishops, abbots and priors would suffice to endow fifteen earls, 1500 knights, 6200 squires and 100 hospitals ".[4] The proposal had not been for-

[1] The first Act against enclosures is 4 Henry VII. cap. 19 (1489). The second and more drastic Act was in 1515, four months after the publication of *Utopia*. It was followed by a Royal Commission and many enclosures were destroyed. Ashley, *Econ. Hist.*, Pt. II. 282.

[2] *Utopia*, 51. Cunningham, *Eng. Ind. and Commerce*, i. 445, quotes an Inquisition printed in Dugdale's *Warwickshire*. Henry Smith had enclosed land at Stratton Baskerville " by means whereof the Church grew to such ruin, that it was of no other use than for the shelter of cattle, being with the churchyard wretchedly profaned ".

[3] Cunningham, i. 530, writes : " Mr. Leadham's statistics show that the ecclesiastical houses had pressed on the system of enclosure, with consequent eviction, nearly if not quite as fast as their lay brethren. Still there seems to have been a slight preference in their favour, and as resident proprietors they performed duties which were less carefully attended to, when their property was confiscated and passed into the hands of new men."

[4] Stow, *Annals*, 338.

gotten, and was reiterated by Simon Fish and Tyndale.[1] There were many that were hungry for land, and such suggestions did not fall on deaf ears.

It was not only because agriculturists were prosperous that men hankered after land. The Englishman has always been more at home in the country than in the town ; and this, again, is not merely from his delight in nature or his passion for field sports, but because he desires a permanent home in which he can be interested and leave to his children—taking a pride in his domain, and perhaps enjoying the thought that he is responsible for inherited dependents. Many a young man at the court of Henry VIII hoped to found a family, for the fortune-seekers were no longer celibate ecclesiastics ; and many a merchant or rich craftsman wished for land and the social status which it conferred [2] Caxton, who had lived so long in the Low Countries, was puzzled by the fact that there were in London so few old burgher families.[3] Starkey thought that men ought to be compelled to live in towns, when he noted how the larger houses were often ruinous and deserted.[4] Lord mayors like Thomas Knolles, 1410, Nicholas Wotton, 1415, Geoffrey Boleyn, 1457, and Ralph Josselyn, 1466, were the ancestors of county families.[5] How else was the rich merchant to invest his wealth ? There were many usurers in the XV century, but usury was not respectable. Hoards of money might be lost in a day, by robbery, fire or riot ; or, apart from these accidents, were spent without recall. By the purchase of land a permanent revenue was assured, and whatever chances came, land did not disappear. Men in consequence wanted land, and thought the abbeys had too much of it. It was not possible in a community rapidly acquiring riches that the most desirable commodity should be locked up in mortmain.

III. *The Towns*

The towns had been growing in prosperity throughout the XV century and were for the most part quite uninterested in the

[1] *Supplication for Beggars* and *Obedience of a Christian Man.*

[2] As early as 1420, Poggio had noted that Englishmen considered it disgraceful to live in towns, and judged the degree of a man's nobility by the extent of his estates. He had himself known a wealthy merchant who, having invested his money in land, was admitted into the highest circles. Einstein, *Italian Renaissance in England*, 221.

[3] *Prologues*, ed. by Crotch, 77.

[4] Starkey, *England*, 177.

[5] Kingsford, *Prejudice and Promise*, 121.

dynastic quarrel of York and Lancaster. It is true that after the battle of Wakefield and the march of Margaret of Anjou upon London, the towns of the Midlands and South took up arms. An excited ballad-writer tells us :

> The wolf came from Worcester, full sure he thought to bite ;
> The dragon came from Gloucester, he bent his tail to smite ;
> The Griffen came from Leicester, flying in a tyte ;
> The George came from Nottingham, with spear for to fight.[1]

Bristol [2] joined up under their banner of the Ship and Coventry under the Black Ram, while the largest contingent came from London. The bloody battle of Towton, fought on Palm Sunday in a snowstorm, gave Edward of York a crown, but the citizens who fought so stoutly for him were not interested in his claim. They fought to revenge the invasion of the Northern army that had sacked Grantham, Stamford, Peterborough, Huntingdon and St. Albans, and would have sacked London but for the scruples of Henry VI, who was set free at St. Albans in time to ruin his own cause.[3] Towton was a battle between North and South, between feudalism and commerce, and was the one battle in which most of the towns were concerned. Bristol,[4] however, was consistently Yorkist, thanks to the influence of Canynges ; Canterbury was Lancastrian, and the Cinque Ports were loyal to the disloyal Warwick. Londoners were divided in their sympathies. They fought for Edward in 1460, and cheered Henry when he was restored in 1470, though Stockton, the prudent lord mayor, conscious that " the times were queasy, feigned himself sick, and kept his house a great season ".[5] With these exceptions the towns remained neutral ; not one of them stood a siege, and all of them were ready to open their gates and welcome a victorious army.

During this time of disorder the central government had ceased to function with any success ; but the municipal governments were active in regulating the lives of citizens. Behind their stone walls and town ditches, these municipalities became more and more self-contained units, while each had laws and customs peculiar to itself.

[1] Quoted Miss Harris, *Coventry*, 133.
[2] Hunt, *Bristol*, 99.
[3] Oman, *Pol. Hist.* iv. 403.
[4] Hunt, *Bristol*, 97.
[5] Fabyan, *Chronicle*, 660 (1811 ed.).

It was through the discussions at town meetings that Englishmen became politically-minded ; and it was because those who passed resolutions had to carry them out that Englishmen became realists in politics. The towns were small ; everyone was known, and it was difficult to evade regulations regarding trade, wages, and prices or escape from obligations to keep order. No one could safely decline the honour of being mayor, bailiff or town clerk, or refuse the unpleasant duties of sergeant, tax-collector or common constable.[1] In Romney a citizen refusing office was turned out of his house, which was sealed up until he repented. At Sandwich he was forbidden to bake or brew ; and, if he did, the commons could take his bread and beer to their own use. Every freeman had to have his arms, and be ready to defend the town from enemies without, or to preserve order within the walls. Public works were carried out by the forced labour of the whole community, although a rich man was usually allowed to pay a deputy to perform his service. In some towns the number of freemen was strictly limited, in some there was great readiness to receive suitable strangers, and in all towns there was a population who had no civic rights. Some were countrymen who had come to the town seeking work or wishing to escape from bondage, and some were well-to-do people who were willing to forgo rights so long as they could escape from responsibilities. Among the freemen there was plenty of *esprit de corps*, a jealous regard for their privileges and independence, and sometimes a corporate selfishness which rivalled that of the abbeys.

The right to manage their own affairs was won by each town separately, and all of them were not equally successful. Towns on the royal demesne were the first to become free,[2] for kings were so often in want of money, and charters were readily granted in exchange for it. Towns belonging to feudal lords could also usually purchase their freedom,[3] and did so as soon as they were strong enough not to need the lord's protection. Towns belonging to bishops generally struggled in vain, for a bishop could not alienate the property of his see, and he was usually a better man of business than a lay baron. The long struggles between the town of Bishop's

[1] Mrs. Green, *Town Life*, 188.

[2] Mrs. Green, i. ch. vii.

[3] *Ibid.* i. ch. viii.

Lynn [1] and the Bishop of Norwich, were for rights and not because of wrongs. The town was prosperous and had little to complain of. The same perhaps may be said of Romney, though there also the fight went on and Cranmer was the last archbishop who refused to enfranchise the town [2]

Bishops did not live in the towns, and were not always in touch with their officers. In consequence, the burghers assumed independence in one direction or another, and pleaded custom in the law courts when their encroachments were discovered. It was different where towns were possessed by abbeys, for the monks were always on the spot, were for ever interfering, and would never surrender the least of their rights. Bury St. Edmunds [3] had a calamitous history. At one time a Guild of Youth defied the monks, but were so rash and riotous that their elders for once sided with the abbot. On another occasion the burghers broke into the abbey, burnt its muniments, and compelled the abbot to grant them the rights of a free community ; but their triumph was short-lived. They were subdued by the forces of the abbot and the king, and made to renounce the privileges they had gained.[4] St. Albans obtained a royal charter, but tore it up in despair as they found it impossible to contend with the abbot. Cirencester had a similar experience, although it had been granted special privileges by Henry IV for the service which the citizens had rendered him when they dragged the earls of Kent and Salisbury out of the abbey and beheaded them in the market-place.[5] Reading was more fortunate, for it had once been a royal borough and preserved many of its rights, but it could not progress ; and a legal judgment of 1508 merely endorsed one given two hundred and fifty years before. In these long disputes the faults were by no means all on one side ; but if we remember that there was continual friction we shall understand why the towns were not sorry when their abbeys were dissolved.

Only a few towns belonged wholly to abbeys ; but most of

[1] Mrs. Green i. 287-294. Bishop's Lynn=King's Lynn.

[2] *Ibid.* i. 408, 409.

[3] *Ibid.* i. 296, 298. See further Miss Lobel's *Bury St. Edmunds*, ch. iii. The rising of the Guild of Youth took place in 1264, the more serious rebellions in 1357 and 1381 ; but the disputes were continuous, and proceedings begun in the Star Chamber in 1514 had not been concluded when the abbey was dissolved and the town ruined.

[4] Mrs. Green, i. 295.

[5] *Ibid.* i. 299-308.

the large towns had abbeys within their boundaries or just outside their walls. The abbeys made the maintenance of order difficult because it was so easy to escape into the "Liberties",[1] where the city authorities could not intrude. They sometimes made the city insecure, for an abbey, as at Winchester, might command one of the gates. They made trade regulations ineffective, because recalcitrant craftsmen might set up within the precincts and defy the city fathers.

Canterbury[2] had to contend with its archbishop, with the Abbot of St. Augustine's and the Prior of Christ Church—the last being the most formidable opponent. City and prior fought over meadows, mills and markets, sometimes before the courts and sometimes with bows and arrows; but city and prior had a common interest in the pilgrims who brought trade into the town and offerings to the cathedral. Just before the dissolution, the mayor won the last contest by removing the market away from the abbey gate, and depriving the prior's tenants in the precincts from opening shops, which were not under the mayor's control although they faced the market.

Winchester[3] was not so fortunate. The great Fair of St. Giles belonged to the bishop and during the fair he had the right to close all the shops in the city, so that the city lost by the fair and the bishop shared in the profits made by those who came to sell. This was only one of Winchester's grievances, and in 1450 the city petitioned the Crown saying that it could no longer pay the king's taxes owing to the depopulation that had taken place.

Exeter[4] on the other hand, thanks to an energetic mayor,

[1] In *Tudor Studies* Miss Jeffries Davis has described the many Liberties within the City of London; and Miss Thornley has shown what a nuisance the Sanctuary of St. Martin le Grand was to the authorities.

[2] Mrs. Green, i. 371-382.

[3] *Ibid.* i. 323-330. In their petition to the king they state that 997 houses were empty and eleven streets had fallen down. They attribute their decay to frequent plagues and withdrawals of citizens. In half the city the Mayor had no authority. The great convent of St. Swithin, the cathedral, and the bishop's palace were free from control, also the royal castle, while the queen's stalls were free from taxes. The bishop took tolls of all merchandise on the river, and nearly all the cloth-workers migrated into the bishop's street. St. Swithin's had many houses within its precincts. Cp. Kitchen, *Winchester*, 174, who proves that the petition of the citizens greatly exaggerates their destitution, and also the number of empty houses.

[4] *Ibid.* i. 340-368. Based on *Shillingford Papers*, published by the Camden Society.

Shillingford, whose letters have survived, put up a gallant fight against both bishop and chapter—both sides quoting precedents that went back to the time of Vespasian, and both sides giving bribes, which carried more weight.

Coventry [1] was divided into the Earl's Half and the Prior's Half, and although the prior obtained a lease of the Earl's Half, the inhabitants of each part insisted on their particular customs and privileges.

At Bristol [2] the prior of St. Augustine's was still contending for his rights on College Green when the dissolution took place. In Bristol as in other places there was no love lost between the monks and the corporation.

It is usual to blame the monks for their greed and to applaud the sturdy burghers struggling for civil freedom ; but this is unfair. The monks were stubborn Englishmen, as were the burghers ; and both sides preferred to be ruined by lawyers rather than surrender what they believed to be their rights. It was the system that was at fault, a system for which neither side was responsible ; and the system had had its justification in the past. There was a time when the abbeys could not have existed without freedom from outside control. There came a time when the towns could not grow and prosper while these privileged bodies retained their powers. The abbeys were dissolved, and the only towns that remained with rival authorities were Oxford and Cambridge. In them Town and Gown rows carried on a tradition of the Middle Ages to a time almost within living memory.

Townsfolk in the XV century were naturally hostile to ecclesiastical authorities ; but they were, as we have noted, exceedingly devout. In many towns the citizens pulled down the old churches and built better ones, adorned with all the treasures they could procure. But having built them they meant to manage them themselves. As they were often lay rectors this was quite possible. The vicars they appointed were their servants ; so even to-day the finances of Canynges' wonderful Church of St. Mary Redcliff are administered by a select vestry of which the vicar is not *ex officio* a member. At Plymouth, where the guild and the corporation were one body, they decreed what vestments should be worn at St. Andrew's and when. Only "the second blue

[1] Miss Harris, *Coventry*, 56-66.

[2] Hunt, *Bristol*, 118.

copes " might be used at the funerals of those who left less than twenty shillings to the church.[1]

Being business men they collected for church expenses as they collected for the expenses of the town. The sergeants were sent to levy the dues for " blessed bread " or wax for " trendylls ".[2] They kept careful accounts and noted how much it cost the town to provide a scuttle of coal for the new fire at Easter.

They were strictly orthodox in intention, but they were very parochially-minded. They knew their duties as Christians, they had listened to much moral exhortation, and they treasured many stories from the Gospels and the *Acta Sanctorum* ; but they knew very little of the theological background to their religion and were vague about the doctrine of the Catholic Church, which everyone had taken for granted.

But if they were strictly orthodox, the long struggle of three hundred years with ecclesiastical authorities had resulted in the merchants having an anti-clerical bias : and when they went abroad their prejudices were confirmed, for in many places the Church was more secularised than it was in England. It is not then surprising that English merchants at Antwerp, or in the Baltic ports of the Hanseatic League, should listen to the new Lutheran teaching and cease to be orthodox. They then smuggled Lutheran books into England, and formed secret societies for the dissemination of Lutheran opinions. Protestantism entered England at the ports, and the Reformation, in so far as it was a religious movement, was of middle-class origin : it was the most important result of international commerce.

IV. *Mediaeval Economics*

The Church of the Middle Ages cannot be said to have formulated any system of economics, but it laid down rules for the conduct of merchants, tradesmen and artisans. It was not concerned with the production of wealth, but much interested in its distribution ; it was not concerned with how money could be made, but with the morals of those who made it.[3] It insisted

[1] Mrs. Green, i. 158. [2] Trendle = a hoop for wax tapers. *N.E.D.*

[3] Cunningham, *English Industry and Commerce*, i. 251. "The discipline of penance, and the canons which were enforced in the ecclesiastical courts, were framed not with reference to burghal prosperity, but in the hope of detecting and suppressing the greed for gain."

on asking "Is it just?" and not "Will it pay?" It insisted that the welfare of the community should come first, and that self-interest was an unworthy motive. It legislated for men as they ought to be, and not as they were. It taught that avarice and covetousness were sins and that contentment was a virtue; whereas the modern man regards the accumulation of riches as an end in itself, and discontent as a valuable incentive to exertion. However, as society became more complex much of the earlier teaching of the Church had to be modified; and it was the Reformation that revolutionised men's ideas on the ethics of industry. The Protestant nations then started on their way to commercial prosperity and have proved that "the children of this world are in their generation wiser than the children of light".

The modern economist argues from facts as they are, the mediaeval Church from theological dogmas. The modern state protects contracts and punishes frauds; the mediaeval Church was concerned with persons—with sinners and their correction. Public opinion to-day tolerates anything that is not contrary to law and rather admires those who are clever enough to evade it; but we must not forget that the mediaeval Church provided a system of casuistry, often sophistical, for the relief of tender consciences in doubtful situations.

In the feudal system there was no recognised place for the trader, and the mediaeval Church regarded the merchant as engaged in a base if necessary calling. St. Thomas Aquinas was prepared to justify the merchant if he was not moved by the lust for gain but was striving to serve the community, and was content with a modest reward for his labour.[1] Theologians were afraid lest "the cares of this world and the deceitfulness of riches might choke the Word of God and render it unfruitful". Fascinated by the thought of the Pentecostal Church which had all things in common, they inclined to a theoretical approval of communism, "*Dulcissima rerum possessio communis est*"; and regretted that it could only be realised in a monastery. Gratian wrote: *Communis enim usus omnium, quae sunt in hoc mundo, omnibus hominibus esse debuit.*[2] But facts did not correspond with the theory, and when we come to St. Antonio of Florence

[1] *Summa Theol.* II. ii. Q. lxxvii. A. 4.

[2] *Decretum*, Pt. II. c. xii. Gratian appeals not only to the Acts but also to Plato.

in the XV century, he admits that private property is necessary in a fallen world, and that men work more and dispute less when this is recognised. He, however, desires that it should be shared by as many as possible, and that those possessing it should be charitable.[1]

But even when admitting the possession of private property the canonists differed from the civilians and denied any absolute ownership. This allowed them in the interests of morals to deny man's claim : " I can do as I like with mine own ".[2] On the other hand they taught that while everyone had a right to a just recompense for his labours, everyone having food and raiment ought to be therewith content. Hoarding or even saving they branded as the sin of avarice ; it was also a sin against the community, for money was intended for use, and the man who withdrew it from circulation [3] was engrossing for himself what was meant for all—not using it himself and preventing its use by the poor who had need of it. Later, in the Middle Ages, writers came to see that there were years of abundant harvests and years of scarcity, and that there was something to be said for the prudent man who thought of the future. They also recognised that many men died in the prime of life, and that provision should be made for widows and orphans. So the doctrine ultimately ran that a man had a right to save sufficient to maintain himself and his family in the state proper to his condition in life.

This could be the better defined when the classes were separated by clear-cut distinctions and men believed in the fixity of status. According to the Divine purpose, it was taught, one man had been born a prince, another a gentleman, a third a villein ; and for each there was an appropriate standard of living. Each ought to accept his lot with its rights and duties as coming from God,[4] and would find that " godliness with contentment is great gain ". In spite of this teaching on the

[1] Tãwnay, *Religion and the Rise of Capitalism*, 32.

[2] Ashley's *Economic History*, ii. 387, 388.

[3] It must be remembered that there was a very insufficient supply of coins throughout the Middle Ages.

[4] Ashley, *Econ. Hist.* ii. 389, quotes Chaucer's parson : " God ordained that some men should be more high in estate and degree, and some folk more low, and everyone should be served in his estate and in his degree ". Also Wyclif : " a man should wit to what estate a man is called of God, and after the office of this state serve his God truly, as the diverse members serve the body in their kind ". Wyclif divided men into " priests, gentlemen and labourers ", or into " clerks, lords and commons ".

fixity of status, it was the Church that kept open the one way to advancement; and in the Church the son of a churl might become a cardinal.

Conceiving of society as a body in which some members were more honourable than others, theologians emphasised the fact that no man liveth to himself alone, and that we are all members one of another. In consequence, the welfare of the community was of more importance than the profit of the individual. It was for the protection of the community that laws were passed against forestalling, engrossing and regrating. All the necessaries of life had to be sold in the open market or at any rate at market prices. The mayor fixed the price of bread and beer, weighed the bread and tasted the liquor. We smile at this over-regulation of trade, but in days when the necessities of life could only be drawn from a restricted area and transport was slow and precarious, it would have been possible for a wealthy man to buy up the whole supply before market day and refuse to part with it except at famine prices. In our own day there has been an attempt to "corner" the wheat supply of the world, which luckily failed. Had it and similar enterprises succeeded, there would soon have been legislation quite as drastic as that of the Middle Ages.[1] Further, we have not yet outgrown the necessity for laws against false weights and measures, against the adulteration of food and against coining. The invention of the milled edge has now made obsolete the crimes of clipping and sweating coins, which went on until late in the XVII century.

From the text "Whatsoever ye would that men should do to you, do ye even so to them" theologians investigated the ethics of trading. It was clear that no one liked to give more for a thing than it was worth, and no one liked to sell at a loss, and therefore everyone should ask and should pay a just price. It was at first thought possible that a just price might be arrived at by taking into consideration the cost of material and the time spent on it in labour.[2] The theory broke down directly people began to ask questions. What was the just price of a unique object or of goods for which there was a great demand and a limited supply, or of goods brought from a distance which had passed through many hands? Were there not great

[1] Ashley, *Econ. Hist.* i. 184, 185.

[2] *Ibid.* i. 138.

differences in the quality of the materials and in the skill of the craftsman ; and ought not such differences to be taken into account ? As a matter of fact the regulation of prices was left to the guilds,[1] who tried by their own regulations to ensure uniformity of output ; but everyone had heard even if he did not heed, that a tradesman should be satisfied with a moderate profit, should consider what was the just price and not how much he could get for the things he had to sell.

If the Church set itself against excessive profits and condemned all forms of speculative trading, it was still more definite on the subject of usury. The argument against it was based on Luke vi. 35, and fortified by the fallacious dictum of Aristotle that money does not breed.[2] There was a good deal of papal legislation on the subject before 1311,[3] when Clement V, at the Council of Vienne, declared all secular legislation in favour of usury to be null and void, and branded as heresy the belief that usury was not sinful. Canonists were very careful in safeguarding this law. A man was a usurer who received his money back with a present paid in kind. A man was a usurer who asked a higher price if he was allowing the buyer credit. A man was a usurer who lent money expecting some advantage in return. However, in the course of time numerous distinctions and modifications were found to be necessary. A man might be put to trouble and expense in coming to demand repayment, and if so, he had a right to compensation. A man might find himself in financial difficulties if the debtor did not refund the money on the appointed day, and Aquinas agreed that he had a right to damages. Delay on the debtor's part might prevent the creditor from using the money to his own advantage and his claim to consideration was ultimately allowed, although Aquinas wrote " a man cannot sell what he has not got ".[4] Again, a family might have a common stock, and might all receive dividends, though

[1] *Ibid.* i. 195 : " the Gilds were not altogether without check : for the wards of Candlestick Street and Walbrook presented the Weavers before the King's Justices on the charge that ' by confedracy and conspiracy in the Church of St. Margaret Pattens, they ordained among themselves for weaving each cloth they should take sixpence more than anciently they had been wont ' ; and it would appear, though the record is imperfect, that they were bound to return to the old charges ".

[2] The metaphor of Aristotle passed into the common speech. The Merchant of Venice taunts Shylock with desiring " a breed from barren metal ".

[3] Ashley, i. 159. Alexander III at the third Lateran Council deprived a usurer of communion during life and of Christian burial after death.

[4] *Summa,* II. ii. Q. lxxviii. AA. 1, 2. See Ashley's explanation, ii. 397-403.

all had not taken part in the work. Again, a man might entrust his money to a merchant and share in the profits of a venture if he had also shared in the risks of loss. More dubious was the case of a man who lent money to a landowner and received the lease of a farm at a nominal rent, which he enjoyed until the money was repaid. By the end of the XV century, thanks to Gabriel Biel [1] and St. Antonio of Florence,[2] the decree had been so whittled away that any respectable capitalist could accept it.

The laws forbidding usury hardly affected the development of commerce, for few merchants can have been so optimistic as to hope for a profit if they had to borrow money at 60 per cent.[3] It was wealthy ecclesiastics or great lords who were the victims of the Lombard bankers, because they might be called on to pay large sums of money to the Pope or the king which could only be obtained from bankers owing to the scarcity of coin in the country. The Crusades could never have taken place if the Jews had not been willing to finance the knights who went to fight for the Cross, charging 45 per cent in interest.[4] Nobody blamed them, because though usury was a damnable sin, the Jews were damned already. It is true that the kings pillaged the Jews and obtained more than half of the fruits of usury; but that did not trouble the mediaeval conscience, for it was thought obviously right that Christian kings should spoil infidels.[5] The Jews were the king's chattels; and when they were expelled, they were succeeded by the Pope's vassals, who required 60 per cent on loans.[6] Dante placed the moneylenders of Cahors in hell; [7] but Innocent IV styled them "the peculiar [speciales] children of the Church".[8] Grossetête rebuked the Lombards, and died lamenting their extortions. Peckham could only be induced to

[1] Gabriel Biel, vide *Cath. Encycl.*

[2] St. Antonio, *vide* Tãwnay, 40, 41, etc.

[3] Cunningham, i. 258-263, does not think that the regulations hindered commerce.

[4] According to Maimonides, a Jew who lent to a Christian was bound by his religion to charge interest (*E.R.E.*, *sub* "Usury"). On the sufferings of the Jews during the Crusades *vide* Hyamson, *Jews in England*, 18-22.

[5] Mediaeval monarchs objected to the conversion of the Jews as that brought them under the Canon Law. Some kings, it is asserted, demanded compensation for every Jew who was converted. *E.R.E.*, "Usury".

[6] Tãwnay, 29.

[7] *Inferno*, canto xi. Cahors was so notorious for its usurers that Causine became the name of a usurer.

[8] Matthew Paris under 1253.

pay them by a threat of excommunication, and he reminded Nicholas III that " by your Holiness' special decree it would be my duty to take strong measures against such lenders ".[1] The papal Camera could not carry on without these international bankers, and the bankers had the Camera in their power, so that they did as they liked, sure of papal connivance.[2] It was significant that when Londoners quarrelled with Scotch merchants they could think of nothing worse to call them than Pope's men.[3]

The Lombard bankers only dealt with a small class ; and their general unpopularity was due to the fact that they were supposed to export great quantities of coin out of the realm.

The indignation of the people was more excited against the petty usurer who victimised the peasant who had lost his cow, the craftsman whose tools had been stolen, the silly youth who wished to anticipate his inheritance and the reckless optimist who believed that something was sure to turn up. Moneylenders have always been unpopular, so that no one enters on the trade who cherishes his reputation ; and this was especially true in the Middle Ages when it was everywhere believed that all usurers would be damned. Preachers denounced their sin in public and confessors exhorted their penitents :

> Usure and okere that beth al on,
> Teche hem that they use non ;
> That ys a synne fulle grevus
> By-fore oure Lord swete Jhesus.[4]

At the same time it was obvious then as now that people who had no savings and were living with a small margin for contingencies would at times need to borrow, and that the number of people willing to lend without security and without interest is very limited. Abroad, the Franciscans established *Montes Pietatis*, to advance small sums to the poor. At first, this was done gratuitously, but it was then found necessary to make a small charge to cover expenses, and the Dominicans accused the rival order of usury. Leo X, by a Bull in 1515, decided in

[1] The Pope's men of course repudiated the charge of usury. They lent money gratuitously for a very short time and then charged 10 per cent every two months to cover expenses in demanding it. Ashley, i. 99.

[2] Lunt, *Papal Revenues*, ch. vi.

[3] Pickthorn, *Henry VIII*, 111.

[4] Myrc, *Instructions to Parish Priests*, 12. In his form for the Great Curse, usurers are included, 22. And more is said on the subject under Avarice, 39.

favour of the Franciscans, defining usury as "gain to be acquired from the use of a thing not in itself fruitful, without labour, expense or risk on the part of the lender".[1] There were no *Montes Pietatis* in England, but the universities had chests from which they relieved impecunious scholars, and in which they retained their pledges—chiefly books containing unproductive learning.[2]

In 1341 a law was passed that

> The King and his heirs shall have the cognizance of usurers dead, and the Ordinaries of Holy Church shall have the cognizance of usurers living, as to them pertaineth, to compel them by the censures of Holy Church for their sin to make restitution of the usuries they have taken, against the laws of Holy Church.[3]

The laity, at any rate in London, were not content with the way in which the ecclesiastical courts did their work, for in 1365 they obtained a writ from Edward III empowering two aldermen and four common councillors to seek for and punish those engaged in "the horrible vice and knavery of usury and malechevance".[4] This led to an ordinance which concerned itself not merely with the usurers but with the brokers who arranged the loan. The latter were to be imprisoned for a year and after a second conviction made to forswear the city, being conducted to the gates "with their heads uncovered, unshod and without girdle, upon horses without saddles".[5] In 1377 there is on record the interesting case of Richard Cornwall and Walter Southous. The former had borrowed for three months £10 on good security from Walter Southous through the medium of Italian brokers to whom he had lawfully paid a commission. When he came to pay at the appointed time, Walter Southous said the loan was of £12. The case came into court; and apparently Southous contended that he had made no contract with Cornwall, but was merely collecting the debt of £12 due to a Lombard who had left the country. The jury

[1] Lecky, *Hist. of Rationalism*, ii. 259. Cp. Ashley, ii. 451.

[2] Rashdall, *Universities*, ii. 350.

[3] Quoted Ashley, i. 196.

[4] *Liber Albus*, ed. by Riley, 318, 319.

[5] *Ibid.* 339 ff. Cunningham, i. 360-366, comments at length on the case; and concludes that while the verdict was natural at the time, it was certainly unjust. On the other hand, it seems that there was an evident conspiracy to evade the law. We have only a summary of the case; and it is well to remember that the jury had heard the witnesses and knew Walter Southous.

did not believe him ; and he went to prison, losing his money and having to pay a fine of £2 to the Guildhall.

London was at least fifty years in advance of other towns ; but it is clear that towards the end of the reign of Edward III the citizens, even when they agreed with the Church, preferred to manage their own affairs in their own way. That spirit was spreading throughout the XV century, and with it a dislike of the Courts Christian and their interference. When the Reformation came, Henry VIII could rely on the anti-clerical bias of town burgesses. Business was to be freed from a moral code founded on theological dogmas.

The canonists were ideally right, for if there be a God who is Lord of all, and if His will has been revealed, His law should govern all and be applicable to everything. Though this may be true, yet as knowledge grew and life became more complex, it was found that neither canonist nor theologian was competent for his task. When it became impossible that a man should know everything, specialists became a necessity and the sciences had to be studied separately. When the unity of the Church was destroyed, there was no longer a body that could correlate the results of fresh knowledge. Each science went its own way, and no science more completely revolutionised old conceptions than the science of political economy.

Good as well as evil resulted from the change. New virtues such as thrift, diligence and self-reliance were insisted on ; and a path to progress was discovered which might lead to plenty, prosperity and power ; men were encouraged to develop their resources and to save their surplus that fresh enterprises might be undertaken. The mediaeval Church had been socialistic and static—it taught that each man had his allotted place and his duty to the society in which he found himself. The new teachers were individualistic and progressive—they encouraged competition, and argued that a man's first duty was to himself—that he should strive to better his position in the world. When we consider the advance which has been made under a system of free competition, we cannot altogether condemn it. When we consider the consequent evils which to-day menace our civilisation, we may well regret that the Church of the XVI century was powerless to provide men with a system of social morality.

For this failure the Reformers were not directly responsible, except in so far as they emphasised individual faith and neglected to emphasise corporate charity. The English Reformers at any rate were thoroughly mediaeval in their attitude to gain and covetousness. No Franciscan friar ever denounced greed and rapacity more vehemently than preachers like Lever and Latimer, or more bravely resisted the oppression and exploitation of the poor. But they could no longer appeal to a moral law which had a recognised authority to maintain it. Morality had become a matter for the individual conscience and private opinion. Some will blame the Reformers, because they shattered the unity of Christendom ; and some will blame the Popes, who, claiming universal authority, only used it to forward Italian interests. The Church had so dismally failed to justify her moral claims that men may be excused if they did not perceive the potential value of a visible catholicity.

V. *Manners*

The commercial classes at the close of the Middle Ages were no longer content with the humble rôle assigned them by St. Thomas Aquinas. They were becoming conscious that the welfare of the country depended more on the way they peacefully penetrated foreign lands than on the spectacular invasions of armed forces. The cities of Italy had long freed themselves from feudal intervention. The cities of the Low Countries had fought and conquered feudal superiors. It was now England's turn to become a commercial nation. Henry VII understood the situation ; and the *Intercursus Magnus* was his greatest achievement. Henry VIII when young went to war in the romantic spirit ; but he soon learnt that the possession of wool was of more value than the possession of Tournay or Guines. The Church did not understand. Her organisation had been assimilated to that of feudalism ; and she went on contending for rights that were undoubtedly hers, and undoubtedly out of date. She was allied to the old caste which had been for ages dominant ; she shared their prejudices and did not approve of the middle classes then increasing in prosperity and rising in power. A similar fate overtook the Church at the end of the XIX century. The middle classes had then been for a long time dominant ;

the clergy were for the most part drawn from them ; and so the Church found it difficult to understand or sympathise with the aspirations of Labour—she did not know how to appeal to a semi-educated proletariat.

In many ways the Church was losing what had been her established position in the world. For instance, all the arts had once been cultivated in the monasteries, but this was no longer so. The famous embroidery—*Opus Anglicanum*—no longer came from nunneries, but from shops. The carved images of saints were wrought in London and so were the canopies of tombs. The stones were packed and sent into the provinces to be put together by local masons who were sometimes incompetent.[1] The miniature paintings which adorned MSS. had been executed in the abbey *scriptorium*, but were now being painted by limners in the city. The Church for a long time remained the best patron of the arts and crafts ; but wealthy merchants wished to emulate in their homes what they had seen at Antwerp and at Bruges, and the taste for luxury soon spread to castles and manor-houses. The artists who had worked to supply the needs of the religious were equally willing to decorate the houses of the wealthy, and art became secularised. London, especially, was famous for its silver plate. Trevisan tells us that he counted fifty-two goldsmiths' shops as he walked up the Strand to St. Paul's and that all the cities of Italy together could not make so great a display.[2]

The English had a great love of pageantry, but had once been satisfied by the ceremonial in the churches and by the processions of the guilds through the streets. But the Church lost its attraction when the Court and City entered into competition. They introduced novelties, their shows were more varied, and they might be enjoyed without reverence and without constraint. Hall loved to chronicle the strange dresses, the dances, masks and allegorical devices, and the reckless expenditure of a young king with nearly two millions of money to throw away.

Never was a court more gay, and never was a king more popular than Henry VIII at the beginning of his reign. He was then the wealthiest monarch in Christendom, and the most popular. He was also the finest athlete of his time. He tired out eight horses a day when hunting. He could overthrow his stoutest

[1] Coulton, *Art and the Reformation*, 204. [2] *Italian Relation*, 42.

knights in the lists. He could shoot an arrow further than any of his archers. He could jump, wrestle and throw the bar with the best. If in these popular sports he excelled he was equally good at tennis. " It is the prettiest thing in the world ", wrote Falier, the Venetian envoy, " to see him play, his fair skin glowing through a shirt of the finest texture." [1]

He was not withdrawn from his people in majestic isolation ; he courted publicity, and with an all-consuming vanity wanted to be seen and to be admired. Standing a head and shoulders above most of his subjects, with quick wits and a hearty manner, he mixed freely among crowds—a king by nature as well as by birth. At one of his pageants all the performers had sewn on their costumes their devices in letters of gold. At the conclusion of the performance the king made a gift of the letters, which the onlookers took as a gift to themselves. There was a rush to secure them in which the king himself was stripped down to his doublet and hose, but he enjoyed the romp and went home laughing. A shipmate went to a goldsmith with such letters as he had secured, and sold them for £3 : 14 : 8, or more than £70 of our money.[2]

How could the people fail to adore a king so entirely one with themselves and yet so conspicuously their superior, who mixed with them so familiarly while clad in cloth of gold. " Love for the King," wrote a Venetian, " is universal with all who see him, for His Highness does not seem a person of this world, but one descended from heaven." [3] The popular attitude to him was very little on " the hither side of idolatry "—was he not God's vice-regent upon earth, the Lord's anointed who could do no wrong, so that even the victims of his cruelty and injustice professed their love and loyalty to him on the scaffold ? It is terrible to look forward from this bright beginning to the gloomy and suspicious monster who could remember with grim satisfaction that " he had never spared a man in his anger nor a woman in his lust ".

Such a king naturally attracted to him the brilliant young men of the country. They came for the most part not from the castles of the old nobility, but from the manor-houses of knights

[1] Falier, quoted by Gurney-Salter, *Tudor England through Venetian Eyes*, and by Pollard, *Henry VIII*, 29.

[2] Hall, 519.

[3] Quoted Pollard, *Henry VIII*, 26.

and squires. They may have read the *Eclogues* of Barclay [1] on the discomforts of the court and the disappointments of courtiers, but they did not heed nor believe him. For them, the court of Henry was the land of promise. The young men were fortune-seekers who were not to be contented with a "bowge at court".[2] They did not indeed mean to be diligent clerks, to enter holy orders and attain to bishoprics; they wanted to enjoy the Golden Age and hoped for wealth through the favour of their master. To obtain that, they had to be expert in arms and sports and not uneducated. The king spoke Latin and French fluently and understood Spanish and Italian. He also played upon the recorders, the flute and virginals, and composed madrigals, Masses and anthems.[3] He delighted in the conversation of the learned, and those who lived with him had to be accomplished and intelligent. Dullness and pedantry were abhorred and the men of the old learning were laughed at.[4] These young men were not religious, but they followed their king to his frequent devotions, and listened deferentially while he and Wolsey discussed the Thomist theology.[5] When the king became anti-clerical, so did they; and the king saw to it that they obtained seats in his Reforming parliaments. Such courtiers were a new class in England—well-born and well-educated adventurers with an eye on the main chance. Some of them perished on scaffolds and some received exceeding great rewards. Year by year there were more recruits arriving at court and fewer churchmen employed in State affairs. By the end of the reign there was a new aristocracy and a bankrupt State.

[1] The *Eclogues* of Alexander Barclay, ed. by Miss White, E.E.T.S., 1928.

[2] Bowge at court, court rations. See Skelton's poem.

[3] Barclay, *Eclogues*, ii. 328:

> Minstrels and singers be in the court likewise
> And that of the best and of the French guise.

The singers were, however, English. Henry VIII imported Memo, the Italian, and made his court listen to his playing for four hours at a stretch.

[4] That gentlemen should have their sons grounded in the arts and letters was the new fashion. Starkey, *England*, still complains that many country gentlemen were more fit to train hounds than heirs. Pace, *De Fructu* (preface), tells of a gentleman with whom he disputed, who declared that he would rather his son was hanged than that he studied letters, for all learned men were beggars. "It becomes the sons of gentlemen to blow the horn correctly, to hunt with skill, and carry a hawk gracefully and train him."

[5] On Henry VIII, interest in School Divinity and Aquinas, see Lord Herbert of Cherbury, *Henry VIII*, 13, 33, 94, 349.

A brilliant court is more often renowned for its manners than its morals, and the court of Henry VIII was no exception; but in his time the same insistence on manners rather than morals was characteristic of the whole country. The citizens in the town had their code, and all believed that

> In hall or chamber or where thou gone
> Nurture and manners maketh man.[1]

An effort was made to establish this thesis by religious sanctions:

> For clerkés that the seven artés con
> Seyn that courtesy from heaven came
> When Gabriel our Lady grette
> And Elizabeth with Mary met.
> All virtues are closed in courtesy
> And all vices in villainy.[2]

The clerks, appealed to, did not recognise that manners may become the conventions of a caste and badges of exclusiveness, that they are often artificial, and at the best are sorry substitutes for moral principles. When manners are preferred to morals, a book on etiquette is of more value than a sermon, and a gentleman usher is of more consequence than a priest.

Manners in England were never so elaborate as those at the court of Burgundy,[3] which impressed John Paston when he attended Margaret of York on her marriage with Charles the Bold. Of that court he wrote to his mother, "I heard never of none like to it, save King Arthur's", and later in the same letter, speaking of the citizens, he says, "By my troth, they are the goodliest fellowship that ever I came among, and best men to behave them and most like gentlemen".[4]

However, by the report of foreigners English manners were good. In 1517 the papal nuncio, Chieregato, wrote to Isabella D'Este:

> The wealth and civilization of the world are here, and those who call the English barbarians appear to me to render themselves such.

[1] *Manners and Meals*, E.E.T.S., 14. [2] *Ibid.* 16.
[3] Court of Burgundy; see Huizinga.
[4] *Paston Letters*, No. 585. For Manners at the Court of Burgundy, see Huizinga, *Waning of the Middle Ages*.

I here perceive very elegant manners, extreme decorum, very great politeness.[1]

Trevisan observes :

> In addition to their civil speeches, they have the incredible courtesy of remaining with their heads uncovered with an admirable grace while they talk to each other.[2]

All the witnesses agree on the freedom of intercourse permitted to women ; and Erasmus in 1499, while still young, was ravished by the kisses he received from young ladies. He wrote to Andrelinus :

> If you were once to taste them and find how delicate and fragrant they are, you would certainly desire not for ten years only like Solon, but till death to be a sojourner in England.[3]

At other times Erasmus had plenty to say about the dirty condition of English houses—of filthy floors and bad ventilation ; of surly inn-keepers and knavish carriers ; and of the drink he found disgusting—beer. Erasmus was a man of moods. When he had been kissed and flattered everything was rose-coloured : when he was peevish and unwell everything was detestable ; but in either mood he is important to the historian, if we remember that what he describes so vividly and with such precise detail is an actual and recent experience. But his generalisations from it are to be accepted with caution. English homes were no doubt not so clean as those in Holland, and one floor may have been as filthy as the one he describes, but all floors were not like it.[4] If we look up the history of the words *besom* and *broom* in the *New English Dictionary* we find that the former can be traced back to the year 1000, and that both words have a continuous history. The inference is certain : brooms were used.

In his *Encomium Moriae*[5] he tells that the English prided themselves on the beauty of their women, on their music and on their well-appointed tables. Trevisan[6] doubtfully admits the

[1] Quoted by Miss Gurney-Salter, *Tudor England through Venetian Eyes*, 125.
[2] *Italian Relations*, 22.
[3] Erasmus, *Ep.* 103.
[4] *Ep.* 1532. Erasmus' letter to Francis on filthy English rooms.
[5] *Encomium Moriae*, ii. 346 : " forma, musica et lautae mensae ".
[6] *Italian Relations*, 20.

first claim; Giustiniani[1] is enthusiastic about the second, while the third we feel must have been justified after reading John Russell's *Book of Nurture*.[2] John Russell had been usher to Humphrey, Duke of Gloucester, and in his extreme old age wrote a book of instruction for servants, for the humble pantler, as well as for him who aspired to be a lord's chamberlain.[3] From this book we may learn how the tables were furnished, what food was prepared, and how it was carved and served with the appropriate sauces. We also learn about the ordering of the guests, and the impropriety of placing the Mayor of London at the same table with the Mayor of Queenborough.[4]

John Russell wrote of a ducal household, but there are a great many manuals of instruction designed for the middle classes, and they also deal very largely with table manners. Many of them were written in verse for children to learn by heart. They teach such elementary rules as you must not wipe your nose on the tablecloth.[5] The manners otherwise advocated make for decency, though we are sometimes puzzled, as when Corderius declares, " It is a wild and rude thing to lean upon your elbows ".[6] But even when most conventional, these rules no doubt made intercourse with equals and also with superiors agreeable to all parties. They deprecate eccentricities and over-emphasis, maintaining that

A measurable mean way is best for all.[7]

These treatises assumed that good manners level all classes, and the author of *The Lyttele Childrenes Lytil Book* had no doubt that anyone who followed his rules might frequent any company, and that all would say on his departure, " a gentleman was here ".[8]

[1] Giustiniani in 1515 wrote that " the King's choristers are really divine rather than human . . . as for the counter-bass voices, I do not think that they have their equal in the world " (quoted Gurney-Salter, 124). Wolsey was thought to have a finer orchestra. Henry VIII borrowed it and made it play all night without a rest. The Shalma-player died a few days afterwards, " but whether it was with extreme labour of blowing, or by poison (as some judged) because they (Wolsey's minstrels) were commended by the King more than his own ", Stow does not determine. *Annals*, 535.

[2] *Book of Nurture*, printed in *Manners and Meals*.

[3] It is noteworthy that in the minute regulations for laying the table and for handling of food there is no mention of a fork. The first fork (forpix) we hear of in England belonged to a citizen of York in 1443. *Plumpton Correspondence*, xxxiv.

[4] *Manners and Meals*, 192.

[5] *Ibid.* 14.

[6] Corderius, quoted by Mrs. Field, *The Child and His Book*.

[7] *Manners and Meals*, 10.

[8] *Ibid.* 22.

It is evident that the middle classes were growing in self-confidence and self-respect. One of the treatises teaches : " Be not too meek or men will hold thee for a fool ".[1] There was indeed much of such teaching, with the result that many young people became assertive and uppish, thinking too much of themselves. A satirist writes :

> Now every boy will counterfeit a Knight
> Report himself as good as he.[2]

Such young people were very unpleasing to an old-fashioned man like Caxton.[3] They were still more unpleasing to the Church, which was also old-fashioned. The Church was in consequence out of touch with the new age. It could not be otherwise, when for centuries it had harped on the virtue of humility and the duty of submission.

VI. *The Home*

We cannot understand the changes of the XVI century without noting the growing importance of the home and home life. There was no longer a conflict between the ideals of the cloister and the hearth ; for very few felt a vocation for the cloister, and many, like Sir Thomas More, were called of God to serve Him, by caring for aged parents and by bringing up children in the way of righteousness.

This ideal of home life was hardly possible until there was a numerous and prosperous middle class. The great barons thought much of their families and alliances, of their blood and of their quarterings ; but moving as they did from castle to castle and living always in public amid a host of retainers, they had few opportunities of cultivating the intimacies of home life. Their children were put out to nurse ; and the little son of an earl was more at home in the house of his foster-parents than in the hall of his father.

Among the poor the family tie was very strong. Children were the poor man's only possessions. From an early age they contributed by their labour to his support, and were his only hope of protection when he grew old or was disabled. But the

[1] *Ibid.* 304. [2] Quoted by Mrs. Green, *Town Life*, ii. 11.
[3] Caxton, *Prologues, etc.*, 78.

bare and squalid houses in which the poor lived were hardly homes. They were at best shelters from the weather, places to eat and sleep in, while social life was out of doors, or in that parish church which they shared with their neighbours.

Our modern conception of a home is a middle-class ideal. It presupposes a separate house permanently occupied. It presupposes furniture and the mementoes of at least three generations. The family within the home, of different ages and sexes, constitutes a true social unit, with order, subordination and customs peculiar to itself; but the essence of a home is this—it is a joint possession, so that the youngest member speaks of it as " mine ". Such homes were being founded by squires in manor-houses and yeomen in farms, as well as by merchants, lawyers and tradesmen in the cities. The home was the central fact in the child's experience; it provided a woman with a satisfying sphere for her activities; while the man desired the reputation of a good housekeeper, that was one who showed hospitality to his poorer neighbours and to the chance traveller who came his way.

These homes were built up on arranged marriages. Only widows and widowers were free to make an unfettered choice. Wards, both male and female, were sold while under age to the highest bidder, with the sole protection that they might subsequently sue their guardian for damages if he had compelled them to marry anyone to the disparagement of their rank.[1] Parents regarded the marriage of their children as within their province, and satisfactory settlements were of the first importance. We have a great deal of information about the mercenary marriages of the Paston family; and then we note that most of the marriages turned out well. Even the refractory Elizabeth, who was " beaten once a week and sometimes twice in one day and had her head broken in two or three places ",[2] was unwilling to change her condition unless the proposed husband would make her " a reasonable jointure ". While all this was so, it is clear that the inclinations of sons and daughters were often considered; and it was even then possible for Margery Paston [3] to make a love-match with Richard Calle, a dependant of the

[1] *Paston Letters*, No. 72. See further, Gairdner's summary of the wardship of Stephen Scrope, who " was bought and sold as a beast ". *Introd.* clxxv.

[2] *Ibid.* No. 71.

[3] *Ibid.* Nos. 617, etc.

family, though "good heed" was taken that "Sister Anne"[1] did not follow her example and marry John Pamping. William Paston, when a boy at Eton, saw a girl who attracted him, and asked his elder brother to look her over and make enquiries if her prospects were as good as he had been told. At fifteen he was thinking of matrimony, and not afraid to make his wishes known; but he was prudent and recognised that marriage meant money as well as romance.[2] Wise parents, no doubt, for the most part made suitable marriages for their children. The bride and bridegroom were generally too young to know their own minds. They lived together, and love was the result of matrimony if not its cause.

Trevisan tells us that he had never known an Englishman to be in love; but Trevisan did not understand the English character. His idea of a lover was an eloquent Romeo, but Romeos are infrequent in England. For the ordinary Englishman the woman he loves is sacred, and he would consider it a profanation to talk about her in the presence of a foreigner.

Trevisan is equally misleading when he writes:

> The want of affection in the English is strongly manifested towards their children, for after having kept them at home till they arrive at the age of seven or nine years at the utmost, they send them out, both males and females, to hard service in the houses of other people . . . and in inquiring the reason of this severity, they answered that they did it that they might learn better manners.[3]

The answer was correct, but his deduction from it was false. There were in those days three courses of education. If it was intended that a boy should be a clerk he went to school; if it was intended that he should be a courtier he became a page; and if it was intended that he should follow a trade he was bound an apprentice. No one in those days wished to prolong the period of childhood. Parents then desired that their children should grow up as rapidly as possible. Sir John Paston[4] was censured for keeping his eldest son too long at home, and Erasmus reproved mothers who deferred sending their children to school until they were seven or even ten.[5] I think we must also take into

[1] *Ibid.* No. 753.
[2] *Ibid.* No. 827.
[3] *Italian Relations*, 24.
[4] *Paston Letters*, No. 325, etc.
[5] See Quotations from *Declamatio* in Mrs. Field, *Child and His Book*, 137.

account the tendency to pet and spoil young children until they became unmanageable.

The view that there was a tendency to spoil children is borne out by the protests of the moralists. Dudley in his *Tree of Commonwealth* writes :

> Let not the feminine pity of your wives destroy your children : pomp them not at home in furred coats : and their shirts to be warmed against their uprising : and suffer them not to lie in their beds till ten of the clock : and then a warm breakfast ere their hands be washed.[1]

The author of the *Babees Book* dedicated his rhymes to " sweet children for whose love I write ".[2] Sometimes there is a note of playfulness even in *Symon's Lesson of Wysedom* for children. For instance he writes :

> Learn as fast as thou may and can
> For our bishop is an oldé man,
> And therefore thou must learn fast
> If thou wilt be a bishop when he is past.[3]

And Symon was a great believer in the birch and fully convinced

> He hateth the child that spareth the rod.[4]

but we need not believe that the little bundle of twigs in the hands of most mothers was a very formidable weapon. Richard Whytford in his *Werke for Householders*,[5] warns parents that they must " defer the correction of their children " when they are " chafed and vexed " with them, and only punish them " with the charity of Our Lord ".

[1] The tendency to spoil children caused Erasmus (*Enchiridion*, c. 14) to write : " Certainly there is no hate more cruel than is this hate, when the foolish fathers and mothers favour the vices of their children : the common saying is, how tenderly love they their children ; but I pray thee how cruelly hate they their children ; which (while they follow their own affections) regard not at all the wealth of their children. What other wisheth to us our most hateful enemy, than that we here sinning unpunished shall fall into eternal punishment." Lupset (*An Exhortation to Young Men*, 235) writes to his ex-pupil Withypoll, that when he was a boy he had refrained from showing his love " for long have I been taught, that the master never hurteth his scholar more, than when he uttereth and showeth by cherishing and cockering, the love that he beareth to his scholars ". Both Erasmus and Lupset were protesting against the customs of their age.

[2] *Manners and Meals*, 8. [3] *Ibid*. 401. [4] *Ibid*. 402.

[5] *Werke for Householders*, quoted by Miss Robinson, *In a Mediaeval Library*, 127-128.

When on the contrary you chide, bawl, curse and with ungodly words rebuke or strike with hastiness to revenge your own cause or appetite, you shall render the persons more stubborn and stiff hearted and engender in them a hatred towards you.

Whytford, however, was all in favour of whipping children and wrote a prayer for them to say to their mothers each morning :

If I lie, back-bite or steal
If I will curse, scorn, mock or swear,
If I chide, fight, strive or threat,
Then am I worthy to be beat.
Good mother or mistress mine,
If any of these nine
I trespass to your Knowyng ;
With a new rod and a fine
Early naked before I dine
Amend me with a scourging.

Whytford goes on, " If they deserve it fulfil then their petition " ; but we may be certain that the child, who put his hands together and prettily made his prayer, was much more often drawn to his mother's knee and kissed than turned across her knee and whipped.

From Whytford we pass to his friend Sir Thomas More, the pattern parent for all time, who wrote to remind his children how he had fed them with fruit and cakes, how he had clothed them in silken attire, and how, if he had flogged them at all, it had been with the tail of a peacock.[1] And yet Sir Thomas More was a natural disciplinarian, and in his happy home there was a strict decorum, a healthy religion, and diligent study which was not inconsistent with toys and pets and lots of fun.

Erasmus, who had never known what it was to have a home of his own, wrote to Ulrich von Hutten and Budaeus about the household at Bucklersbury[2] as if it were the revelation of a new life in a new world. More was indeed singular in his views on female education, and was still more singular in his personal charm ; but he hated eccentricity and was not singular in the ordering of his house. That was managed by his " shrewd wife ", a very conventional lady. It was shared by his aged

[1] More, *Epigrammata* ; quoted Bridgett, *Sir Thomas More*, 135, and Chambers, *Sir Thomas More*, 179.

[2] Erasmus, *Epp.* 999, 1233.

father, Sir John More, a very conservative old gentleman. More's children, wards and dependants were instructed in the New Learning, but they lived in the world, entertained guests, and conformed to the customs of their class. In hundreds of English homes there was the same ideal; but at Bucklersbury and afterwards at Chelsea the ideal was for once realised.

The ideal of the home was of middle-class origin: it had sprung up independently of the Church and it was to find its expression in the best of English institutions. The family had always been important, but the home gave the family a local habitation, common possessions and associations which resulted in a real unity. What the church in the Middle Ages had meant to the parish, that the home became for the family. The idea of both is the same; but for obvious reasons the Church had not recognised this. The Church had laid down rigorous laws concerning marriage and insisted on its sacramental character; but she had regarded chastity as the highest of all virtues and asceticism as the only road to the attainment of sanctity. Sir Thomas More was not alone in showing that it was possible to consecrate home life to the glory of God; but it was left for the Reformers, in violent reaction against the Church, to exalt the married state. We should be grateful for their teaching, because they stabilised social life, even when we deplore that they could not understand how all men have not the same vocation. Paul was a celibate and Peter a married man, but both built up the Kingdom of God. The Church of the Middle Ages taught men to renounce this world in seeking for another: the Reformed Church taught that in the other world the work done here will be crowned. The teaching of both is true, if we remember that both people and circumstances vary.

CHAPTER VI

POLITICAL CHANGES

I. *Introduction*

HOW the Reformation came about cannot be understood if we restrict ourselves to thinking of it as a religious movement. It was not due merely to ecclesiastical abuses or to popular superstitions—real as they were. It was also due to political and social changes for which the Church was and was not responsible.

The papal claims to universal dominion had to be settled some day; but no one expected decisive events like the Concordat of Francis I with Leo X, the sack of Rome by the troops of Charles V, and the Act of Supremacy passed by the subservient Parliament of Henry VIII. The rising spirit of nationalism was destroying the conception of Christendom, but men were shocked when the Pope consented to oblige the Grand Signor by keeping Djem as a hostage in Rome and when Francis I made an alliance with the unspeakable Turk. The discovery of America and the new trade routes converted England into a commercial power, and international competition inflamed the English hatred of foreigners. Under administrative centralisation, the feudal jurisdictions and the power of the great abbeys were waning, while greedy courtiers and rich citizens were hungry for land. It was an age of discovery, and ages of discovery are ages of unsettlement; but during this unsettlement the Church was conservative—it was bound up with the old order of society, and identified with its social theories and ideals. It was out of touch with secular progress, and blind to the necessity of adapting itself to new conditions. The best men were desirous of reforms, but they hoped to carry them out on old lines. They looked to the past rather than to the future. They were unaware that an old world was dying, and that a new world was growing up—eager to enter on its inheritance.

Contemporaries rarely understand the tendencies of their time. They are like those who arrive on the seashore at the turn of the tide and do not know which way it is flowing. Contemporaries cannot know the outcome of what is happening about them—they are only conscious that there are conflicting forces and many cross-currents. Changes also often come so imperceptibly that a man heeds them no more than he heeds the gradual transformation of his own body from year to year. It needs a serious illness to convince him that he is no longer the man he was. It needed the Reformation to convince the Church that she had endangered her existence by neglecting symptoms of disease and decay.

II. *The New Monarchy*

The Lancastrian kings failed, not because they were tyrannical and oppressive, but because, under the constitutional system they had adopted, order could not be maintained. Notwithstanding Fortescue's enthusiasm for the *Dominium regale et politicum*, it was impossible to make it work. The executive was not strong enough to carry into effect the legislative enactments, legal judgments could not be enforced, and under a free constitution the rights of the people were contemptuously disregarded by "over-mighty subjects". The Yorkists, who claimed to rule by hereditary right, were never more than the triumphant leaders of a faction. Strong and ruthless, they destroyed their enemies without respect for law or tradition. They were dictators in a time of emergency, and their despotism had so far an excuse.[1] With Henry VII a new order came into existence. By his marriage he united the Roses, by his commercial treaties he conciliated the towns, by his heavy-handed justice he suppressed disorder; and he always observed legal forms in his most arbitrary acts. He brought the nation peace and prosperity; he responded to the nation's desire for stability; he became the first national king. He was not regarded as the feudal overlord or the paramount proprietor of the land, but as king and representative of the people; his interests were their interests, his greatness their greatness, and obedience to the Crown became almost the sole political virtue. No Dominion

[1] Stubbs, *Const. Hist.* iii. 291.

can exist for long that depends entirely on force. Dominion is hallowed by tradition, is sustained by moral obligation, and becomes imperative when it is supposed to be by divine appointment and providence. Sovereignty, it was felt, must lie somewhere. The civilians had attributed it to the Emperor, canonists had attributed it to the Pope, but, fostered by common lawyers, there gradually grew up under the Tudors a belief in the divine right of kings.[1]

Under the Plantagenets there were three almost equal powers —the Crown, the Church and the Baronage. The union of two of them might coerce the third ; but the interests of any two did not for long coincide. They formed a trinity of powers in one state, but they were rarely altogether at one.

When Henry VII assumed the crown, the power of the baronage was broken. For more than a hundred years the peers had been diminishing in numbers through war, forfeiture and the marriage of heiresses who carried their honours into other families. Many peers had been impoverished during the civil wars, and their power as a class was at an end. There remained indeed a few peers who were enormously rich ; but they were so few that they were isolated in the State and could one by one be destroyed. As a class, also, the old nobility was degenerate. The Florentine Ubaldini writes, that while the people were tall and strong, the lords were little of stature and feeble of frame. This was perhaps due to the custom of premature marriage ; and premature marriage was due to the fear that the child might inherit while still a minor, and that the Crown might sell him or her in marriage to the highest bidder.[2]

When Henry VII assumed the crown the power of the Church was undermined. This was partly due to the Pope being much more interested in securing the political support of the king than in championing the rights of the clergy. It was partly due to the fact that as the king had the right to nominate bishops, the leading positions in the Church were bestowed on his officials.[3] It was partly due to the fact that as non-resident bishops summoned no synods, the Church as a corporate body had ceased to exercise much influence in the State. It was partly due to the fact that the people, though devout, were only

[1] Figgis, *Divine Right of Kings*, 32-36.

[2] Denton, *Fifteenth Century*, 260, 261.

[3] Stubbs, *Const. Hist.* iii. 565.

parochially-minded : the Church as an institution had ceased to make an appeal.

The king, then, stood alone without rivals : the king had brought peace and there was no one to question his prerogatives. Sir John Fineux, the Chief Justice, who remembered Lancastrian days, had been convinced of the need of a strong executive. He wrote :

The prince's prerogative and the subject's privileges are solid felicities together, and but empty notions asunder. That people is beyond precedent free and beyond comparison happy who restrain not their sovereign's power so far to do them harm, as he hath none left him to do them good.[1]

If Fineux was convinced that a strong king would be of advantage to the people, a generation later Gardiner was convinced that obedience to the king—whatever he commanded—was a religious duty :

For who ever denied that the prince ought to be obeyed ? It is most certain that he who will not obey the prince, is worthy to die for it : as it is comprehended in the Old Law and also confirmed in the New Law. But we must see, will he say, that the king do not pass the limits appointed him,—as though there must be an arbiter for the ordering of his limits. . . . What manner of limits are those that ye tell me of, seeing that the Scripture hath none such ? But generally speaking of obedience, which the subject is bound to do unto the prince, the wife unto the husband, or the servant to the master, it hath not added one syllable of exception, but only hath preserved the obedience due to God safe and whole that we should not hearken unto any man's word in all the world against God.[2]

After all, Gardiner did recognise an exception which nullifies much that he had previously said. It was left for William Tyndale, in his Lutheran zeal for the godly prince, to state the autocrat's claim most clearly :

God hath made the King in every realm judge over all ; and over him there is no judge. He that judgeth the King judges God ; and he that layeth hands on the King layeth hand on God ; and he that resisteth the King resisteth God, and damneth God's law and ordinance. If the subjects sin, they must be brought to the King's judgment. If the King sin, he must be reserved unto the judgment, wrath and

[1] Quoted *D.N.B.*, " Fineux ".
[2] *De Vera Obedientia*, Janelle's ed., 99.

vengeance of God. And as it is to resist the King, so is it to resist his officer, which is set or sent to execute the King's commandment.[1]

A wise man like Sir Thomas More saw the danger of attributing to the king uncontrolled power, and in relinquishing office advised Thomas Cromwell—

> You are now entered into the service of a most noble, wise and liberal prince; if you will follow my poor advice, you shall, in grave counsel-giving unto his Grace, ever tell him what he ought to do, and never what he is able to do.[2]

From these quotations it must not be supposed that the Tudor despotism was due to any theory about the nature of sovereign power. Its encroachments on the older constitutional system were quite haphazard. The Tudor kings were strong men resolute to have their own way, and they were intelligent enough to adopt the means that were available. If these means were likely to raise doubts in the minds of their subjects, they had to be justified, preferably on religious grounds; but the Tudors never disturbed institutions in the interest of any theory. Henry VII had no objection to appeals to Rome, neither had Henry VIII until the failure of his own. It was only then that he was convinced how necessary it was, that over all persons and in all causes he should be supreme.

III. *Papal Sovereignty*

There were at the close of the Middle Ages two theories concerning the authority of the Church. According to one the Pope was an autocrat who defined the Faith and decreed Law, while bishops were only his deputies, with no power of initiative or independence. According to the other view, the Catholic Church was a federation of national churches under the presidency of the Pope, whose duty it was to summon General Councils in order that the united episcopate might decide vexed questions. There were three theories concerning the relations of Church and State. First that the Emperor and the Pope had co-ordinate authority, each being supreme in his own sphere. Secondly, that the Emperor represented the majesty of

[1] Tyndale, *Obedience of a Christian Man*, 177.

[2] Roper, *Life of More*, 153.

God, and that the Pope had specified spiritual duties within the empire. Thirdly that the Pope was possessed of two swords —spiritual and temporal—emperors and kings being subject to his correction.

The academic view of the relations of Church and State was no doubt influenced by St. Augustine's *De Civitate Dei*. The saint wrote at a time when society was mostly pagan, and he developed his argument by way of contrasts. As the world became Christian, a fusion of Church and State should have taken place ; but at any rate in Western Europe the distinction remained as clear-cut as ever. It had, however, to be differently stated. Everyone now belonged to both Church and State and vowed obedience to both. The Emperor and the Pope equally derived their power from God. They ruled the same people, but each was restricted to his own sphere. Stephen of Tournay states the theory quite plainly :

> In the same City and under the same King there are two peoples, and corresponding to the two peoples two ways of life, corresponding to the two ways of life two authorities, and corresponding to the two authorities two orders of jurisdiction. The City is the Church, the King is Christ. The two peoples are the two orders of the Church, the clergy and laity. The two ways of life are the spiritual and the carnal. The two authorities are the priesthood and the kingship. The two jurisdictions are the divine and human laws. Give to each his due and all things will agree.[1]

As, however, there was no agreement on what was due to each authority and as spiritual and temporal rights could not be disentangled, this theory was never translated into fact, but remained a thesis for endless disputations in the schools. It was never indeed entirely surrendered ; for until the middle of the XVII century Church and State were one body and everyone was required to be a loyal member of both. As a theory it was embalmed by Dante in his *De Monarchia*,[2] a book that was written after the failure of the Emperor Henry VII. It is not quite true to say that this book is an " epitaph rather than a

[1] Stephen of Tournay was a XII century canonist, and the quotation comes from his Introduction to his *Summa Decretorum*. I owe the quotation to A. J. Carlyle, *Med. Pol. Theory*, ii. 198.

[2] For appreciation of Dante's *De Monarchia*—Bryce, *Holy Roman Empire*, 263 ; Lane-Poole, *Illustrations of Mediaeval Thought*, 262 ; Creighton, *Papacy*, i. 30 ; Figgis, *From Gerson to Grotius*, 27.

prophecy ", for in it may be found the germ of Cavour's ideal of a Free Church in a Free State. Dante wrote to prove that sovereignty exists to preserve for all men spiritual freedom, a truth that is still imperfectly realised ; and that there are divine laws which a secular power is incompetent to administer —a truth that the totalitarian state denies. Dante tried to keep the balance even between the respective jurisdiction of Pope and Emperor, but recognised that the question of precedence was bound to arise. He decided in favour of the Pope, for " since earthly happiness is subordinated to eternal, let Caesar show towards Peter the reverence wherewith a first-born son honours his father ".

Both before and after Dante, civilian lawyers maintained the supremacy of the Emperor, and in their books reduced the powers of the Pope to defining the articles of the Faith, to reforming the morals of the clergy, and setting an example of apostolic poverty becoming in the successor of St. Peter. But the proclamation of the imperial supremacy was only a *brutum fulmen*, and the Popes were not attracted by the rôle assigned them. The canonists, on the other hand, basing their theory on the Donation of Constantine and the Decretals of Isidore, and unaware that the Donation was a fiction and the Decretals forgeries, maintained that the Pope had two swords, the temporal and the spiritual, so that kings owed him obedience.

Apart from what was thought to be history, the papal theory was founded on the principle that as spirit is superior to matter, so the Church as a spiritual kingdom ought not to be controlled by an earthly monarch ; [1] but it is obvious that the Church of the Middle Ages was not merely a spiritual kingdom, and it was arguable that, if the powers that be are ordained of God, monarchs might be informed by the Spirit. The Popes were right in their contention that faith and thought ought to be free from the constraint of physical force ; but they found that they could only exercise that freedom themselves if they were possessed of temporal power ; and having obtained

[1] J. S. Mill quotes from Guizot : " The separation of temporal and spiritual power is founded on the idea that material force has no right, no hold over the mind, over conviction, over truth " ; and then adds, " Enormous as have been the sins of the Catholic Church in the way of religious intolerance, her assertion of this principle has done more for human freedom than all the fires she has ever kindled have done to destroy it " (*Dissertations and Discussions*, ii. 243).

it, they could not resist the temptation to persecute others, although by so doing they destroyed the argument for the freedom that they claimed.

It was their claim to universal sovereignty that involved them in most of their difficulties, although it is a mistake to suppose that, apart from the imperialist lawyers, it aroused much opposition. Kings freely acknowledged papal claims and often disregarded them in their actions.[1] When they conflicted with their own rights they were apt to treat Popes as they were treated by their own barons, who also had rights which were jealously conserved. In the Middle Ages there was a network of rights,[2] depending on custom or on charters, on status or office, on tenure, inheritance or conquest. Such rights could not always be reconciled one with another, but they continued to be asserted when they could not be maintained; they were acknowledged when they were not respected; they were pleaded in the law courts and evaded by legal fictions. We need not in consequence imagine that opposition to the Pope meant any repudiation of papal claims, or that papal concessions to powerful kings meant anything more than that some claim was for the time in abeyance. Rights were held to be inalienable in their nature, even when their enforcement had to be postponed to a more convenient season.

The Popes had triumphed over the empire, but they were often thwarted by the kings of England and France.

John might do homage for his kingdom and promise to pay a small tribute to the Pope; but Parliament might subsequently discover that no action of his could be binding on his successor, and that England had never been his to give away. The Pope might command Edward I to cease from war with Scotland on the ground that Scotland was subject to the Holy See; but Edward could reply that he held his lands immediately from God, and his Council might add that he was unable to alienate Scotland, for the King of England was *ipso facto* lord of the land. It will be seen that John, however unwillingly, fully acknowledged papal claims; it should also be clear that the other two incidents did not raise the question of papal rights, but disputed

[1] Montalembert, *Monks of the West* (E.T.), i. 152: "The Church has never seen her authority more contested than in the Middle Ages, even by those who recognised it most dutifully in theory".

[2] Stubbs, *Lectures on Med. and Mod. Hist.*, 209, 210.

the facts which occasioned the claims to be made. It was only as kings became more powerful and nations more self-conscious that these claims became an embarrassment to the Papacy, for the Pope might be called on to enforce them when he knew that he would be successfully defied.

Even in the spiritual sphere the papal ideal could not be entirely realised. The Popes attempted to centralise everything at Rome. They wished to rule the Church by *Legati a Latere*, they wished the clergy to be an international body, and they wished their own law to be administered in a uniform manner throughout Europe. The kings of England, however, from William the Conqueror onwards, would not allow a *Legatus a Latere* to enter their kingdom without their permission, which was not easily granted.[1] The archbishops as *Legati Nati* were unsatisfactory makeshifts, for they were in closer touch with the king than with the Pope. The friars, having no possessions but many papal privileges, formed to some extent an international body ; but the rest of the clergy, *possessioners* as the friars called them, were compelled not only by birth and language but by the property which they held to identify their interests with the State, while alien priories were often confiscated in time of war. No doubt a universal Church, standing for peace and concord, required a clergy not bound in allegiance to princes who were frequently at war with one another ; but no such Church existed. The Popes were only too ready to form leagues and enter into political alliances in order to preserve or extend their frontiers. They hired mercenaries to fight for them and used the spiritual weapon of excommunication to ensure their material gain. Neither the unity of the Church nor the peace of Christendom were advanced by a Pope like Julius II.

There was some friction during the XV century, but the kings of England had need of papal recognition, and the Popes had need of English money, so that there was a good deal of give and take. Martin V complained, " It is not the Pope but the King of England who governs the Church in his dominions " ; [2] but Martin could still humiliate Chichele and advance Beaufort, even if he could not get the Statute of Provisors repealed.[3] He provided Richard Fleming to the see of

[1] Makower, *Const. Hist. of C. of E.* 232.

[2] Quoted Pickthorn, *Henry VIII*, 105.

[3] Capes, *Ch. Hist.* 170-174.

York, but he soon found it advisable to retranslate "Richard of York"[1] back to the see of Lincoln. A papal collector who published Bulls which had not been authorised by the Government was imprisoned for his irregularity. When Pius II demanded a subsidy from the clergy for his crusade, Convocation replied that the king would not allow taxation, but had no objection to collections being made throughout the country for so pious a purpose.[2] On the other hand, Lollardy and the alleged atrocities of the Bohemians had frightened all classes, and not merely the bishops, into a respectful orthodoxy. No one could have been more submissive than Henry VI, while Beaufort, Kemp, Bourchier and Morton became Cardinals for services rendered.

On the whole, throughout the XV century the Popes increased in power, and no one could have approved their claims more absolutely than Sir John Fortescue, the loyal Chief Justice of the devout Henry VI:

> Christ is King of all the world, and the Pope is His vicar upon earth, to whom all earthly powers are subject, even to the kissing of his feet. . . . Kings are subject to the Pope not only in their persons but in their temporalities. He may compel them to rule their subjects justly, and punish them if they do not, as Popes have done both to Kings and Emperors before now. Christ the Lord of all the earth hath placed in the hands of the Pope, His vicar, both swords, and he is *Rex et Sacerdos*.[3]

Sir John Fortescue did not live long enough to give his opinion on the Alum case in 1486. The Pope derived a considerable revenue by exporting alum from the Papal States[4] to England and Flanders where it was required by manufacturers of cloth.[5] A Florentine ship with a cargo of alum was seized by pirates in the Channel, and the Pope promptly excommunicated them. The Council decided that restitution should be made, but debated at length if the Pope had the right to punish the king's subjects, as the case was within the cognizance of the king's

[1] Capes, *Ch. Hist.* 200. Cp. Puller, *Orders and Jurisdiction*, 177.

[2] Wilkins, *Concilia*, iii. 587 ff.

[3] Fortescue, *Works*, 113, 116; quoted by Plummer in his Introd. to the *Governance of England*. Maitland, *Canon Law*, 48: "In the XV century a lawyer might prostrate himself before the papal omnipotence, and yet mean but little by the more extravagant of his phrases".

[4] Lunt, *Papal Revenues*, i. 60 *et passim*.

[5] *Year Book*, 1 Henry VII, printed in Williams, *England under the Early Tudors*, 183: summarised Pickthorn, *Henry VII*, 181.

courts. Hussey referred to the fact that in the reign of Edward IV a papal legate was refused admittance into the kingdom until he had taken an oath that he had brought nothing with him prejudicial to the Crown. The Chief Justice quoted the precedent of Edward I referred to above, and the Bishop of London remembered how Humphrey Duke of Gloucester had thrown papal letters into the fire ; but they came to no decision. This was lucky, as at a later date Henry VII was only too pleased that the Pope should excommunicate the supporters of Perkin Warbeck. In 1497 the Milanese ambassador wrote :

> The Pope is entitled to much praise, for he loves the King cordially, and strengthens his power by ecclesiastical censures so that at all times rebels are excommunicated. The efficacy of these censures is now felt by the Cornishmen, who are in this trouble that all who eat grain garnered since the rebellion, or drink beer brewed from this year's crops, die as if they had taken poison, and hence it is publicly reported that the King is under the direct protection of Almighty God.[1]

Henry VII also received leave for Morton to visit the exempt monasteries and to curtail the privileges of sanctuary. He also obtained a dispensation for the second marriage of Catherine of Aragon which enabled him to retain her dowry and cement his alliance with Spain.

Henry VIII began his reign by posing as the champion of the Papacy which involved him in two useless wars. He wrote the book which earned him the title of Defender of the Faith ; and when Sir Thomas More besought him to modify what he had written in defence of papal authority, he replied, " We are so much bounden unto the See of Rome, that we cannot do too much honour to it ".[2]

The time came when he did not feel " so much bounden to the see of Rome ", and reconsidered his views on papal power. He had twitted Luther with having written " they sinned damnably who did not obey the Pope ", and " that excommunication is a medicine to be suffered with patience and obedience " ; and asked what new spectacles had Luther got that he now saw things so differently.[3] A few years later this contemptuous critic refused obedience, and did not patiently

[1] *C. S. P. Milan*, 540, in Williams, 185. [2] Roper, *Life of More*, 189.
[3] *Assertion of the Seven Sacraments*, 4-8.

receive excommunication. He did not find the testimony of antiquity or the concurrence of the saints so convincing. He was seeking other precedents and he discovered that

> This realm of England is an Empire . . . governed by one supreme Head and King, having the dignity and royal estate of the imperial crown of the same, unto whom a body politic, compact of all sorts and degrees of people, divided in terms and by names of spiritualty and temporalty, be bounden and ought to bear, next to God, a natural and humble obedience.[1]

This was an overstatement, not borne out by " the sundry old authentic histories and chronicles " to which the preamble of the Act appeals ; but it was a declaration in harmony with the nationalist spirit that was then so strong. The claims of Innocent III and Boniface VIII could no longer be sustained. Excommunications had been pronounced so indiscriminately that, except for Cornishmen, they had lost their terror. Neither Charles V nor Francis I was in the least likely to risk anything for the Pope unless it might be turned to their own profit. The day of inalienable rights was passing away. It was the day of accommodations, treaties and contracts. But for the Divorce, Henry might, like Francis I, have concluded with the Pope a Treaty of Perpetual Peace ; but this would not have prevented a Reformation movement in England, and might, as in France, have entailed a series of religious wars.

IV. *Local Independence*

Much more interesting than the Pope's claim to universal dominion is the study of how far there was local self-government in the Church and how the idea of national churches grew up.

From the days of Charlemagne, that *Episcopus episcoporum*, until the Reformation there was a constant struggle between a desire for local independence and the need of a central authority ; and in the earlier period the local powers were strong. It could hardly have been otherwise when Europe was divided into many nations, and when in each country Church and State were co-extensive. The bishops were territorial magnates, who often

[1] Gee and Hardy, *Documents*, 187.

held office under the king, and their interests were closely bound up with the country where they dwelt. Inevitably for the English bishops the *Ecclesia Anglicana* was an entity, in communion and in alliance with other entities overseas, while the Pope was the overlord with whom it was most desirable to remain on good terms. The theory was feudal and fitted the Church into the framework of a feudal society.

Everyone, clergy and laity alike, acknowledged papal supremacy, for it was necessary when powers were evenly balanced that there should be an external authority with whom it was possible to lodge an appeal. St. Anselm was quite right in insisting on papal investiture, for the spiritual existence of the Church was at stake. St. Thomas Beket was right in withstanding the Constitutions of Clarendon, for it was then most necessary to preserve the liberties of the clergy. Neither could have been successful had there been no Pope. The Pope in distant Rome preserved the Church from irreligious kings and baronial ruffians. On the other hand, the Pope was useful to kings. In the XII and XIII centuries the *Ecclesia Anglicana* was nearly always on the side of popular liberties, and the king had to look to Rome for support. Innocent III absolved John from his oath to observe Magna Carta; and Alexander IV absolved Henry III from his oath to observe the Provisions of Oxford.[1] The Lancastrian kings, owing to their defective title, found papal recognition of value both at home and abroad, and so did Henry VII. There were always occasions when the Pope could help in settling international difficulties.

Churchmen and kings alike were glad that there was a Pope to help in time of need, but churchmen and kings alike were always ready to resent his unsolicited interference—they even sometimes co-operated in resisting his encroachments. When contests arose sometimes the Pope won and sometimes the king. For instance, when John refused to receive Langton as archbishop and retained the temporalities of Canterbury, Innocent III laid the land under an interdict, and the fears of the people, deprived of the sacraments, compelled the king to give way. When Boniface VIII forbade the clergy to pay taxes,

[1] The canonists maintained that the Pope did not absolve a man from his oath, but declared that he was absolved, the oath *ab initio* being null and void. *Vide* Carlyle, *Med. Pol. Theory*, ii. 202.

Edward I replied by making the clergy outlaws—putting them outside his protection ; and the decree of Boniface became a dead letter.[1]

It is possible to exaggerate the significance of these disputes. Protestant historians have done so in an attempt to prove that there was a strong anti-papal feeling in England throughout the Middle Ages. This is not true, and the disputes can be best understood if we compare them with the disputes which sometimes take place between a county council and some office in Whitehall. The county councillors have local knowledge, are unwilling to incur extra expenditure, and sometimes have prejudices due to a too provincial outlook. The civil servants at Whitehall have a wider outlook, but a natural desire to simplify their work by imposing uniform rules without much consideration of local conditions or local resources. No one denies the supremacy of the central office, but the local body can often put up a very good fight, and is by no means always defeated.

When the Pope was at Avignon under French domination, and England was at war with France, it was natural that there should be a certain unpopularity attached to the person if not to the office of the Pope. When the Great Schism occurred, each nation chose which Pope it would obey, England acknowledging one and France another.[2] This was a terrible blow to papal pretensions and prestige. Charles V of France for five years withdrew his obedience from both claimants and acted as Pope himself, while the orthodox University of Paris debated whether a Pope was necessary to the Church. The Cardinal D'Ailly, a moderating influence, maintained that the Pope was only the chief minister of the Church, *ministeraliter exercens administrative dispensans*.[3]

When the Council of Constance assembled it was decided to vote by nations, and the federal character of the Church seemed to be established. The Pope was acknowledged as the head of

[1] Boniface VIII gave way but tried to save his face in a Bull dated March 12th, 1301, in which he says that he left to the king what the latter had collected through *Impositiones et exactiones illicitas* from the clergy, and freed him from all penalties incurred in consequence of such exactions. Makower, 39.

[2] Selden, *Table Talk*, 87 : "The Papists call our religion a Parliamentary religion ; but there was once, I am sure, a Parliamentary Pope. Pope Urban was made Pope in England by Act of Parliament against Pope Clement."

[3] Bruce, *Age of Schism*, 124.

the Church in ordinary circumstances and for administrative purposes, but the Council decreed that—

> A General Council could not be dissolved or prorogued by the Pope . . . that everyone, even the Pope, must obey the Council in matters concerning the Faith and extirpation of heresy, and that it had authority over the Pope as over all Christians.[1]

It really looked as if the Papacy, so overwhelming under Innocent III, was going to end as a constitutional monarchy; but the complete failure of the Councils of Constance and Basle to reform the Church proved that the time for a federal constitution had not come; while the unwillingness of the triumphant Papacy to undertake reform necessitated the Reformation.

Had the Council of Basle been composed of men intent on the peace and reform of the Church it might have accomplished much; but the men who came together for peace and reform were the representatives of many nations sent by their respective governments to further or to safeguard national interests. The rising spirit of nationalism in France, Spain, Germany and England prevented real co-operation; and none of these nations, restive under papal interference, was prepared to submit to the dictation of a body that comprised so many of their enemies and rivals. In those days it was impossible that a League of Nations should flourish without a head, and the Pope was unwilling to further the projects of a council which had determined to curtail his powers. The council only succeeded in leaving a memory of its claims and ideals.

This council failed, but that was no reason why a future council should not succeed, and appeals to such a council were frequently made. It was still regarded as the ultimate authority. Even Sir Thomas More, who died for the spiritual freedom of the Church and the unity of Christendom, wrote to Cromwell shortly before his execution, maintaining the rights of the Pope, but adding, " Yet never thought I the Pope above a General Council ".[2]

Starkey in his dialogue between Lupset and Pole put into the mouth of the latter his belief that the Pope was a usurping tyrant " who defineth all and dispenseth all at his own liberty ".

[1] *Ibid.* 167. Cp. Figgis, *From Gerson to Grotius.*
[2] Strype, *Eccles. Mem.* I. ii. 104.

He would have him held to be head of the Church because that authority had been given him by a General Council, but he would not allow

> any cause to be sued out of the realm except causes of schism in the Faith which pertains to the dissolution of the Catholic and Christian faith. Such causes we would reserve to him as head appointed by common authority; and as for all other controversies, I would that they should be defined at home in our country.[1]

Sir Thomas More believed that an administrative head was necessary for the external unity of Christendom, and he was undoubtedly right; but an administrative head may allow its members to function with considerable freedom. It may also be argued that neither an administrative head nor an external unity, however desirable, are necessary to the life of the Church. The autocephalous churches of the East are illustrative of this fact. Accepting the Cyprianic view—*Episcopatus unus est, cujus a singulis in solidum pars tenetur*—[2] it is possible to maintain the federal conception of the Church, and if this be granted it follows that any particular church may separate without losing its identity. The Church of England did so and has survived. Other nations have tried to maintain the federal idea within the Church of Rome and failed. We think of the Spanish bishops at the Council of Trent in the XVI century, of Gallicanism in France in the XVII century, of Febronianism in Austria in the XVIII century, of German opposition at the Vatican Council in the XIX century, and of the Ultramontane victory in 1870.

V. *Canon Law*

The *Corpus Juris Canonici* derived its authority from the Pope, but it was the *Jus Commune* of all Europe, and there was no other law that dealt with ecclesiastical rights and duties, or with private and social morals. The Provincial Constitutions were meagre in the extreme, although Lyndwood's commentary covers the ground relevant to England; but the importance of the *Provinciale* lies in the commentary rather than in the texts, and the commentary is derived from the Corpus and from the works of canonists upon it.

The ecclesiastical courts had ceased to be popular, but they

[1] Starkey, *England*, 199.
[2] *De Unitate Ecclesiae*, cap. 5.

were not regarded as foreign except by heretical litigants like Richard Hunne. For over four hundred years the canon law had been administered by English lawyers in the Courts Christian of England; and the law so administered was not altogether independent of the royal power.[1] No papal Bull could be received or published in England without the consent of the king.[2] A writ of prohibition might issue from the king's courts forbidding a Court Christian to meddle with particular cases, and such writs were frequent during the first half of the XV century.[3] All canonists admitted the validity of immemorial custom even when contrary to the papal law unless it had been forbidden in express terms.[4] The most important of such customs concerned annates, advowsons,[5] the naves of churches[6] and wills, but Lyndwood refers to such small differences as the date of the beginning of winter,[7] the custom of the province of Canterbury in following the Use of Sarum rather than that of the metropolitan Church,[8] and the use of a hanging pyx instead of a tabernacle for the reservation of the Blessed Sacrament.[9]

Nearly two centuries before Lyndwood, Bracton[10] had stated quite clearly that the Pope had ordinary jurisdiction in spiritual matters over everyone, and that the king within his realm had ordinary jurisdiction in temporal affairs;[11] but it was not easy

[1] Maitland, *Canon Law*, 48: "Our canonists obtain an intellectual luxury at a cheap rate when they place the *Plenitudo potestatis* in a pope whose bulls, if like to be troublesome, will never reach their hands, but will be impounded by a secular power, for whose doings they are not responsible."

[2] Makower, 235. Cp. Pickthorn, *Henry VII*, 181. It is noteworthy that Queen Mary in 1557 ordered the seizure of papal Bulls directed against Cardinal Pole.

[3] Ogle, *Canon Law*. This was probably due to disputed interpretations of the Statute of Praemunire. *Vide* Wilkins, *Concilia*, iii. 533, 540, 556.

[4] Lyndwood, *Provinciale*, 13a: *injugendo mandamus* defines such custom "quae non est contra fidem vel contra bonos mores, ac quae est pia erga Deum ac Ecclesiam". The *Decretal* teaches that the custom must be *rationabilis* as well as *praescriptive*. In Sext it is laid down that customs are not annulled by contrary positive legislation unless expressly mentioned in the subsequent law. Lyndwood thought the custom should be immemorial. Later canonists were content with ten years. Rome to-day decrees that prescriptive right is established in forty years. On *Consuetudo* see *Codex*, edited by Cardinal Gasparri. *Canons*, 25-30.

[5] For annates, advowsons and wills *vide supra*, 17, 39-40.

[6] By English law, parishioners are responsible for the upkeep of naves. Lyndwood, 53a: *Reparatio*.

[7] *Ibid*. 194a: *Hyeme*.

[8] *Ibid*. 104a: *Usum Sarum*.

[9] *Ibid*. 148a: *cum clausura*.

[10] Bracton, quoted Maitland, *Canon Law*, 106.

[11] Pickthorn, *Henry VII*, 181; quoted from *Year Book*, 21 Henry VII.: "It seems that the King cannot be called Parson by Act of Parliament, for no temporal act can cause a temporal act to make a temporal man to have spiritual jurisdiction. For if it was ordained by Act etc. that such a one should not tender tithes to his curate,

to decide what was temporal and what was spiritual. It might be thought that a cure of souls was certainly within the sphere of a spiritual court. So it was, but advowsons were private property and all questions relating to them were within the cognizance of the king's courts. The Statute of Provisors had then this legal justification. It was passed to prevent the Pope from interfering with rights which could only be determined by a tribunal where he had no authority. Again there was an undisputed right for anyone to appeal to the Pope ; but the king had the indubitable right to forbid anyone from leaving or from entering his dominions. The Pope might pronounce a valid sentence on any case brought before him, but the king might punish anyone for seeking abroad what might be to the king's damage or to the discredit of his jurisdiction ; hence the Statute of Praemunire. In ordinary cases the kings had no objection to appeals to Rome ; the objection came from the Courts Christian of England because of the loss of fees.

There was a great deal to be said in favour of a final court of appeal, and very little to be said for the Curia as a court of first instance ; but the Pope claimed to be the Universal Ordinary, and there were canonists ready to justify his claim. Maitland quotes from Tancred as follows :

> Normally the competent judge is the Judge Ordinary of the defendant's domicile ; but Rome is the common fatherland of all, as we learn from the *Digest* ; and the Pope is Judge Ordinary of all men, as we learn from the *Decretum*.[1]

It suited some to open their cases in a place where they were not known. It also saved them from appealing from one court to another, and it sometimes saved them in time and expense. But it was obvious that most of the cases could not be tried at Rome, because of the impossibility of transporting witnesses or of understanding local conditions. The Pope in consequence commissioned delegates to hear cases in England ; and litigants raced to Rome not to secure a verdict, but to see that the delegates appointed were not unfavourable to them.[2] So it

the act would be void, for concerning such a thing as touches nearly the spirituality, such temporal act cannot make any ordinance." So argued a sergeant, and the Chief Justice agreed, " A temporal act without the assent of the Supreme Head [the Pope] cannot make the King a Parson ".

[1] Maitland, *Canon Law*, 104.

[2] *Ibid.* 11 ff.

came to pass that the majority of the cases were decided in England by English canonists—the Pope recognising their competence to act on his behalf. The time came when Henry VIII used this fact to his own advantage, and abolished appeals to Rome on the ground that the Spiritualty

> always hath been reputed and also found of that sort, that both for knowledge, integrity and sufficiency of number, it hath always been thought, and is also at this hour sufficient and meet of itself, without any intermeddling of any exterior person or persons, to declare and determine all such doubts, and to administer all such offices and duties as to their rooms spiritual doth appertain.[1]

As a matter of fact, apart from questions of marriage, the number of appeals had been growing less, and thanks to Archbishop Warham, more and more cases were initiated and concluded in this country. The law might be of papal origin, but justice was administered by an Englishman. It was a fatal day for the Papacy when Leo X appointed Wolsey *Legatus à Latere*. The claims of a distant Pope had only affected a very few, but when his deputy set up his legatine court at Westminster many had reason to be afraid. The English Courts Christian were superseded, and when Warham tried to assert his rights as *Legatus Natus*, Wolsey, being also Lord Chancellor, threatened him with a writ of *praemunire*. Wolsey fell, and the bishops recovered their jurisdiction. They preferred Henry who interfered with their authority, to Wolsey who had extinguished it.[2] The Divorce was unpopular, but the people were amazed when Henry, King of England, was cited to appear in person before the Cardinals, Wolsey and Campeggio. They agreed with Suffolk when he said, " Now I see that the old said saw is true, that never a legate did good in England ".[3] Their amazement turned to fury when the case was revoked to Rome,[4] for nationalism was rampant in England, and Englishmen were easily persuaded that the Pope as a foreigner had no claims on their allegiance.

VI. *Nationalism*

As feudalism decayed great nations came into existence under powerful kings who thought but little of Christendom,

[1] Gee and Hardy, *Documents*, 108.
[2] Pollard, *Wolsey*, 215.
[3] Hall, 758.
[4] Brewer, *Henry VIII*, ii. 365, 366.

but much of fortifying their frontiers. By the end of the XV century England was a conscious unity; France and Spain had arrived at a political unity; Germany was inflamed with a national ideal which was to be frustrated by the Reformation; and Machiavelli was dreaming of a time when Italy should be more than a geographical expression.

In England this unity had been of very slow growth. There had always been an intense local patriotism,[1] but it was centuries before England became one. There were Angles and Saxons and Danes; there were the Celtic fringes; and there were aristocrats more proud of Norman blood than of being true-born Englishmen. The villeins, bound to the soil, knew very little of anything that happened a few miles from their hamlets. The freeholders depending on their own exertions to supply their primary needs, rarely left home, unless obliged to follow their immediate lord in those baronial wars which antagonised neighbouring districts. In the University of Oxford, North and South were separate "nations" and created disorder by their continual conflicts. Language and pronunciation varied so much that the men of one shire could not make themselves understood in another. The Lancashire lad had very little in common with the man of Kent, though he probably had an improper curiosity concerning his tail.[2]

But all through the Middle Ages forces making for unity were at work. The Church, as organised in great dioceses, brought men together, while judges on their circuits were a recurrent reminder that there was a central power. When foreign wars occurred, and the feudal array with its limited obligations was useless, paid soldiers were gathered from all over England and became comrades as they shared in victories and defeats. Knights of the shire and burgesses may have come unwillingly to parliaments, but they returned home with a wider outlook. As lawyers became busy at Westminster, country gentlemen had often to spend term time in London. As towns arose and trade

[1] Coulton, *Five Centuries of Religion*, iii. 3: "Nationalism was strong in the Middle Ages, even when the rival 'nations' were only neighbouring towns or villages".

[2] Polydore Vergil, 284 (ed. Leyden, 1644), tells how the men of Strood cut off the tail of Beket's horse, and that their descendants were ever afterwards born with tails. Lambarde, *Perambulation of Kent* (1826 reprint), 356 ff., devotes six pages to the refutation of this calumny.

increased, so did intercommunications. The time came when the Cotswold sheepmaster was interested in the London market and the staple at Calais. The Black Death and the resulting scarcity of labour led to the enfranchisement of many villeins in spite of manorial courts and the statutes of labourers. Wandering friars by their preaching helped to standardise the language, while wandering ballad-singers provided the people with a common tradition. After the Wars of the Roses, the power of the great barons was broken. The king alone remained and he was supported by the squires and wealthy citizens, who stood for peace and order. They were men with plenty of public spirit but with very limited interests. England meant much to them, but they were not interested in Christendom.

In the earlier centuries, when there was only a local patriotism, Christendom had been a reality to the upper classes and the clergy. The feudal system had been fairly uniform throughout Western Europe; the conventions of chivalry had made intercourse agreeable; and the science of heraldry had provided knights with a passport everywhere. The kings of England for a long time held many fiefs on the Continent, and for a hundred years maintained their right to the crown of France. The great baronial families were of foreign origin, spoke French among themselves, sometimes had French possessions or made French marriages,—they belonged to an international caste. The bishops looked to Rome for protection from the king; the great abbeys looked to Rome for protection from the bishops; and the king looked to Rome to keep the Church in order. General councils were attended by kings and princes as well as by ecclesiastics, and were by no means confined to the discussion of theological problems. The canon law dealt with all questions of public and private morality; and English archdeacons qualified for their offices by studying at Bologna or Padua. The civil law was studied throughout Europe, and was generally appealed to, though often in vain, in international disputes. Learning also knew no frontiers. Oxford and Paris were cosmopolitan universities, and students wandered from one *Studium Generale* to another, with Latin as a common language, dignified by degrees that were reciprocally recognised. Commerce was almost entirely in the hands of the Hanseatic League, of Venice and Genoa, who obtained rights and established depôts and factories in many countries. On them England depended for luxuries and foreign goods, though English pirates sometimes forestalled the market by attacking merchantmen on their way up the Channel. Henry V tried to suppress this piracy, not out of any regard for foreign traders, but because it was so necessary for him to keep the narrow seas open for communications with the Continent.[1]

The change came in the next reign when France was definitely lost and the king had to concentrate on national interests. The loss of France was ultimately a blessing, but at first its consequences seemed disastrous. The fighting lords came home at the head of armed bands, brutalised by the long war and incapable of peaceful labour. The evils of maintenance and livery were multiplied, and the over-mighty subject was a menace to the country ; but the mutual slaughter and vindictive confiscations of the Wars of the Roses destroyed feudalism.[2] The sons of the semi-independent magnates were gradually transformed into accomplished courtiers. The Tudor kings marked down the heads of the old feudal families with Plantagenet blood in their veins for destruction as opportunity offered ; and the new nobility, created by the king and dependent upon him, were neither provincial in their patriotism nor European in their outlook.

England also by the end of the XV century had become a commercial nation. Edward IV did not disdain to engage in trade himself.[3] Henry VII's diplomacy was largely employed in negotiating with the Netherlands, the Hanseatic League and Venice.[4] The English merchant adventurers naturally resented the fact that the privileges accorded to the Steelyard in London were not reciprocated in the ports of Lubeck and Hamburg ; and they rejoiced that in the tariff war with Venice England secured all the advantages. In London and Bristol there grew

[1] For English pirates, see Kingsford, *Prejudice and Promise*, 78-106.

[2] Green, *Hist. of English People*, ii. 7, writes : " In the one Bill of Attainder which followed Towten twelve great nobles and more than a hundred knights and squires were stript of their estates to the King's profit. Nearly a fifth of the land is said to have passed into the royal possession at one period or another during the Civil War." This may be true, but we must allow for the fact that many estates were subsequently restored.

[3] *Ibid.* ii. 8 : " His ships freighted with tin, wool and cloth made the name of the Merchant King famous in the ports of Italy and Greece ". This again is somewhat of an exaggeration. Cp. *Prejudice and Promise*.

[4] Busch, *England under the Tudors*, 147-159.

up a hatred of foreigners, and Evil May Day was only an outstanding incident.[1]

England had achieved her unity earlier than France ; and her unity was more real as she had no debateable frontiers and was shut in by the narrow seas. Her unity moreover did not altogether depend on the personalities of kings, but on the spirit of an insular people. They loved their land and were proud of their independence, they hated foreigners and were very pleased with themselves. Trevisan with some amusement writes :

> The English are great lovers of themselves and everything belonging to them ; they think that there are no other men but themselves and no other world but England ; and whenever they see a handsome foreigner they say that " he looks like an Englishman ", and that " it is a great pity that he should not be an Englishman " : and when they partake of any delicacy, they ask him, " whether such a thing is made in his country ".[2]

This intense nationalism is reflected in the attitude of England to the Western Church. The Statute of Provisors was not strictly enforced, but it removed the incentive which young men had formerly had to study at Paris or journey to Rome in the hope of securing preferment in England. The English clergy were in consequence becoming insular. Oxford also had ceased to be a centre of European culture, and was no longer a rival to Paris but only a rival to Cambridge, then growing into importance. The Church courts had once been popular, but had acquired an evil repute, so that Richard Hunne could describe them as " foreign tribunals ". Wolsey's exercise of legatine power increased the unpopularity of papal authority. It was in consequence easy to excite prejudice against the Papacy and men were ready to believe that the Pope's power was due to usurpations too long permitted. While becoming a united nation the English had ceased to be good Europeans.

[1] Hall, 588, 589.

[2] *Italian Relation*, 20. Creighton, *Hist. Lectures, etc.* 232, quotes this passage and illustrates it by a passage from the diplomatist, Sir Robert Wingfield : " As the English nation has always surpassed the French in valour and good faith (I do not wish to speak invidiously), so it cannot be judged inferior to it either in antiquity and dignity, or in the size of its territory, or in its learning and capacity ".

PART II

THE TENDENCIES OF THE TIME ACCOUNTED FOR

CHAPTER I

THE HISTORY OF LOLLARDY

I. *John Wyclif*

It is usual to speak of John Wyclif as the Morning Star of the Reformation,[1] but it is well to ask, With what limitations has he a right to that title ? To answer that question we must review the history of Lollardy and try to determine its doctrines and their prevalence in the early years of the XVI century.

Wyclif was a Yorkshireman, honest, hard headed and combative by nature, before Oxford had trained him to be a subtle controversialist. He had succeeded FitzRalph, Archbishop of Armagh, as head of the secular priests who opposed the Franciscans in the University.[2] His academic speculations involved the relations of the Church to the State, and the limitations of temporal and spiritual power. He was in consequence drawn into public life, became a royal chaplain, championed the cause of the king against the Pope, and was a diplomatist at Bruges. Finding his country ruined by taxation due to the war, and her credit destroyed by repudiated loans, he saw but one remedy—the plundering of the Church, which was over-rich. This was not only in accordance with his academic speculations, but appealed to him on practical and moral grounds. Being a man of simple tastes, he hated the luxury of the clergy, and was full of moral indignation at the abuses which were only too patent. Then controversy led him to consider the popular beliefs which supported the existing system, and his hard common sense rendered him intolerant of all superstitions, however innocent and childlike. He went back to the Gospel and identified the Church of his day with Judaism in the time of our Lord. He was called " the Evangelic Doctor " ; and believed that religion could only survive when the Church was poor. In these contentions he

[1] Bale, *Summarium*, Cent. iv. 154, was apparently the first who gave Wyclif this title.

[2] *Fasciculi Zizaniorum*, edited by Shirley, R.S., p. liii.

had the support of great men with greedy eyes on Church estates, and of needy scholars at the University disappointed about preferment. The best brains at Oxford—Repyngdon, Aston, Hereford and Purvey—were also at his service. The chancellor and proctors protected him as far as they dared ; and there was a time when Friar Stokes, his opponent, went in fear of his life.[1]

It is impossible to construct a coherent system of theology out of his writings. Like all controversialists, he was driven to attack and defend positions he would not himself have chosen. Besides, while the Latin works are indubitably his,[2] it is very uncertain how far he was responsible for the English works which go by his name. Yet, the English works are more important if we would understand the Lollardy of the XV century.

In the Latin works, Wyclif is a cautious Augustinian,[3] much influenced by Archbishop Bradwardine,[4] whose work *De Causa Dei contra Pelagium* remained the standard work on Grace until well on into the XVII century. In the English works we read : " Each man that shall be damned is damned for his own guilt ; and each man that shall be saved is saved by his own merit ".[5] What would Luther or Calvin have said to that ? Yet it suggests the standpoint of the XV century Lollards, who were frankly Pelagians. A generation after Wyclif many of them had denied Original Sin, repudiated the sacraments of Baptism, Holy Communion, Penance and Matrimony, and the keeping of Sundays and holy days.[6]

This development of his teaching would no doubt have staggered Wyclif ; and it is very doubtful if he would have approved of some practical applications of his doctrine of Grace. It is true that the Lollards of the XV century were unable to read *De Dominio Divino* or *De Dominio Civili*, and would not

[1] *Fasciculi Zizaniorum*, 299 ff.

[2] *Ch. Q. Rev.* xix. 61.

[3] Rashdall, " Wyclif ", *D.N.B.*

[4] Bradwardine, 1290–1335. So in Chaucer's *Nun's Priest's Tale* we read,

> But I ne cannot boult it to the bren
> As can the holy Doctour Saint Austin,
> Or Boece or the Bishop Bradwardine.

As late as 1618 Sir Henry Savile edited the *De Causa Dei*.

[5] Sermon, " The Gospel on the Chairing of Saint Peter ", in Winns' *Selections*, 95. Parson's *Three Conversions of England*, Pt. III 186. He is delighted to quote Luther and Melanchthon's disparaging remarks about Wyclif.

[6] Walsingham, ii. 252, 253.

have understood them had they been available. But all through the centuries men have been influenced by great books which they have not read ; and ideas are never so potent as when they have been translated into the ordinary speech, and summed up in popular slogans. Dominion for Wyclif implied a lord and subjects. God, he argued, was Lord of all things, and men held what they had directly and immediately of Him. There were no mesne lords. Such a theory ultimately led to a denial of a mediatorial Church and a mediating priesthood. In feudal language he was anticipating what Luther meant when he spoke of justification by faith alone. Wyclif writes :

> All leadership of man, natural or civil, is conferred upon him by God, as the prime author, in consideration of his returning continually to God the service due unto Him : but by the fact that a man through omission or commission becomes guilty of mortal sin, he defrauds his Lord-in-Chief of the said service, and by consequence ensures forfeiture : wherefore . . . he is rightly deprived of all lordship whatsoever.[1]

This argument was used to invalidate the sacraments celebrated by priests in mortal sin, and to justify the confiscation of the property of a negligent Church ; but it was soon seen to be equally cogent when applied to laymen, their rights and possessions. Again, following St. Augustine on the negative character of evil, he says : " Sin is nothing ; and men, when they sin, become nothing ". On the other hand, " the faithful man hath the whole world of riches ; for him all things work together for good ". Each faithful man is therefore lord of the universe ; and it follows that all faithful men must hold their goods in common. So he interprets " Charity (*i.e.* Grace) seeketh not her own—seeketh not to be a proprietor ".[2]

Wyclif was perfectly aware that his theories could not be reconciled with the life about him ; so he argued that all governments were the result of the Fall and due to the usurpation of Satan. As God submitted to this, so should we ; and the conclusion is that God ought to obey the Devil in this world. Probably by this paradox he intended no more than that we should render to all their due, remembering that Christ ministered to Iscariot, acknowledged the authority of Caiaphas and allowed Himself to be tempted by the Devil.[3]

[1] Quoted Lane Poole, *Illustrations of the History of Mediaeval Thought*, 294.
[2] *Ibid.* 292-296. [3] F. D. Matthew, *Eng. Works of Wyclif*, xxxvi.

However revolutionary his ideas might be, Wyclif meant to restrict their application to the Church and not to extend them to the State ; and however convinced he was of his theories, he was not like St. Francis, ready to strip himself of his advantages and wed Poverty as a bride. He saw the evils of pluralities and non-residence ; but he was himself a pluralist and for most of his life an absentee.[1] He denounced papal provisions, but he accepted one from Gregory XI,[2] and was very angry when Urban VI refused to confirm the grant. Moreover, he went bail for a large amount so that a friend might go to Avignon in search of a second benefice.[3] He maintained that no priest should be entangled in affairs of state ; but he was long engaged in politics, and it was the Bad Parliament and not the Good which had his support. He worked very well with the friars so long as he was attached to John of Gaunt, and only discovered their manifold iniquities when that alliance was at an end.[4] He wished the churches to be poor, plain and without adornments ; but he retained his rich benefice, ministered in his " painted church ", and died in possession of all his emoluments. Though his life was to this extent a contradiction of his creed, he no more perceived it than wealthy communists perceive a like inconsistency to-day. He longed for change, he worked for change, he was willing to use his position to promote change ; but, until change should come, he felt justified in adapting himself to the conditions of life about him.

How was the change, which he desired, to be brought about ? Only by making the will of God better known, and the will of God, he thought, was plainly revealed in Holy Scripture. But how was a people, especially the illiterate, to learn the Scriptures ? Only by preachers sent out expressly to expound its literal sense. An English Bible and the Poor Preachers were to convert the world power into the Kingdom of God.

It is strange that Wyclif, " the Great Clerk ", the learned theologian and master of distinctions, should show such contempt for the *mixtim theologi* (motley theologians)[5] and their learned commentaries. How came he to believe so wholeheartedly that the Bible was its own interpreter, and alone

[1] Jenkins, *C.Q.R.*, cvi. 64 ff.
[2] *Ibid.* 67-69.
[3] Workman, *John Wyclif*, i. 243.
[4] *Ibid.* i. 283 ; ii. 43, 44.
[5] Lechler, *John Wickliffe*, ii. 24.

necessary for salvation ?[1] Perhaps after all his triumphs in disputation, and his successful defence of strange paradoxes, he had come to doubt the value of learning and the validity of his exquisite conclusions—that is the nemesis which lies in wait for controversialists.[2] But it is perhaps more true to say that Wyclif was not primarily interested in dogmatics, was less interested in ascetic and devotional theology, and had a profound contempt for the allegorical interpretation of Scripture then so prevalent. Poetry, mysticism and other-worldliness were alien to him. He was fundamentally, and in spite of his learning, the plain man and he wished to be a social reformer. He thought that he found in the Bible a vivid condemnation of the world as he knew it. He found in it also plain directions for life, and devoutly believed that conduct was nine-tenths of religion. Wyclif was at heart a pragmatical Englishman.

Reading the Bible in this spirit he became convinced that the New Testament was " open to the understanding of simple men in the points that be most needful for salvation ", and that " no man was so rude a scholar, but that he might learn from the words of the Gospel according to his simplicity ".[3] It was only necessary that he should have it in the tongue wherein he was born. That was his right, for

> The Holy Ghost gave to the Apostles wit on Whit Sunday for to know all manner of languages to teach the people God's law thereby: and God would that the people were taught God's law in divers tongues.[4]

That Wyclif and his friends, Nicholas Hereford and John Purvey, should translate the Scriptures was, from the ecclesiastical standpoint, quite unobjectionable. Wyclif knew that the French had a version in the vernacular,[5] and Purvey tells of a Flemish version that had been ultimately approved by the Pope.[6] Wyclif's version was made from the Vulgate, and even Netter of Walden did not impugn its accuracy, while there was

[1] *Ibid.* for Wyclif's views on scriptural interpretation, ii. 28-31.

[2] *Ibid.* ii. 2, quotes from *De Veritate Sacrae Scripturae* : " I acknowledge that oft times for the sake of vainglory, I departed from the teaching of Scripture, both in what I maintained and what I opposed, when my double aim was to acquire a dazzling fame among the people and to lay bare the pride of the Sophists ".

[3] Workman, ii. 151.

[4] *De Officio Pastorali*, ch. xv., in Matthew, *English Works*, 429.

[5] *Ibid.*

[6] Purvey's *Prologue* ; Winn's *Selections*, 21.

nothing of heretical pravity in Purvey's prologue.[1] Why then was it banned? Because so many did not read it for their souls' edification, but in order to find texts and instances whereby they might condemn the Church and the social order. In the Bible they found an arsenal of maledictions against priests, lawyers, judges and kings. It is not in consequence surprising that the bishops were driven to forbid the book to all who were not licensed to read it by a competent spiritual authority.

With the Bible or parts of it, and with tracts from the prolific pen of Wyclif, the Poor Preachers went forth not so much to proclaim a gospel as to prepare for a reformation. There was no lack of preaching at the time, and no lack of Scripture in the sermons, but they were not calculated to upset the world.[2] Apart from friars, preachers needed a licence from the bishop, but Wyclif maintained that Christ was sufficient authority, and that a licence might come immediately from Him.[3] This was undeniable, but it hardly justified Wyclif in assuming Christ's power and licensing men himself. He was not, however, the first or last heretic who has identified himself with God.

His action has been compared with that of St. Francis ; but St. Francis was as humble as Wyclif was proud.[4] St. Francis sent forth his Little Brethren to teach the poor that God loved them ; Wyclif sent forth the Poor Preachers to tell the poor how evil the rich priests were. He supplied them with a variety of forcible expressions. He writes of " stinking friars " ; he calls the bishops " horned fiends ", the Pope " a sinful idiot " and the cardinals " incarnate devils " ; he describes the monks as " gluttonous idolaters committing whoredom with the devil ", and the parish priests as " idolatrous leprous and simoniacal heretics ".[5] In the schools he was a subtle disputant, in the market-place a pungent pamphleteer : but it is only fair to add that his opponents paid him back in his own coin.

Such preaching pained the pious soul of Walter Hilton in his retirement at Thurgarton. He writes :

[1] *C.Q.R.*, Jan. 1901.

[2] Owst, *Preaching in Mediaeval England*. Sermons denouncing ecclesiastical abuses were generally in Latin and preached at synods and visitations. Sermons in the vernacular were concerned with the sins of the people.

[3] " Sermon on Dai of oon Evangelist ", Winn's *Selections*, 31-34.

[4] Workman, ii. 201, 214.

[5] Capes, *Ch. Hist.* 124, culled these flowers of rhetoric from Wyclif's works.

The words that they show by preaching sound all to backbiting and to striving and to discord, making reproving of states and persons; and yet say they that all this is charity and zeal for righteousness. But it is not sooth, for St. James, the Apostle, saith that *where'er envy is and flitting, there is unstableness and all evil work.* And therefore that cunning (knowledge) that bringeth forth such sins cometh not from the Father of Light that is God, but is earthly, beastly and fiendish.[1]

The Poor Preachers may have been scurrilous fanatics; but they were sincere, and sincerity ensured them success. They had been inspired by Wyclif with a hatred of iniquity and a zeal for social righteousness. The abuses they denounced were real and well known to their hearers; and they may be excused if they exaggerated their prevalence or refused to consider what might be said on the other side. Sometimes they had to skip from one diocese to another in order to escape from episcopal officials; but the bishops, if we except Courtenay and De Spenser, were indifferent—like their successors, they were accustomed to abuse. The Poor Preachers also at first had powerful lay support. Knights with their armed retainers protected them on their village greens while they denounced the rector or an adjacent abbey. The motives of these knights were no doubt mixed. Some, like the courtiers of Henry VIII, had greedy eyes on Church lands, and were easily persuaded that the Church would be more spiritual if disendowed, and the parochial clergy more useful if entirely dependent on themselves. But there were others of whom the pseudo-Knighton, who hated Lollardy, said: "They had a zeal for God, but not according to knowledge".[2] These men were thrilled in hearing the scriptures in homely language, and received it gladly, rejoicing Wyclif's heart:

O comfort is of knights that they savoren much the Gospel of Christ's life. For afterwards, if God wole, their lordship shall be taken from priests, and so the staff that maketh them hardy against Christ and His law.[3]

[1] Walter Hilton, *Scale of Perfection*, Bk. II. ch. xxvi. Chaucer's Parson in the *Canterbury Tales* (Pt. II. *sub ira*) is equally emphatic. "Lo, what saith St. Augustine 'there is nothing so like the Devil's child as he that often chideth.' . . . Now cometh the sin of them that sow and make discord among folk; which is a sin that Christ hateth utterly, and no wonder it is; for he died to make concord. And more shame do they to Christ than did they that Him crucified, for God loveth better that friendship be among folk than he did His own Body, which He gave for unity."

[2] Knighton, ii. 181.

[3] "Sermon on the Gospel of Many Martirs", Winn's *Selections*, 18.

Wyclif was himself, by inheritance, lord of a manor. He came of the lesser gentry, and however socialistic his theories might be, he could not escape from the outlook of his class. Dr. Workman translates from the *De Dominio Civili* :

> Oh ! how happy and fertile England would be if every parish church had as of yore a saintly rector residing with his family ; if every manor had a just lord residing with his wife and children : then there would not be so much arable land lying fallow and so great a dearth of cattle.[1]

Such admirable sentiments might have proceeded from the hero in one of Miss Charlotte Yonge's novels. They are central in the old English tradition ; but they were not shared by the Poor Preachers, who were more concerned with the wrongs of villeins, and were fascinated by the doctrine of the community of goods.

When the Peasant Revolt was suppressed in 1381, Wyclif, notwithstanding his social antecedents, did not act as Luther did when the peasants revolted in Germany. He deprecated the outbreak, but he spoke out with courage on the oppressions suffered by the poor and extenuated as far as possible the crimes committed—even the murder of Archbishop Sudbury. On the other hand he was sensitive to the accusation that the rising was due to what his Poor Priests had taught.

> Some men that ben out of charity slander Poor Priests with this error, that servants or tenants may lawfully with-hold rents and service from their lords when lords be openly wicked in their living.[2]

It is evident then that the accusation had been made before Wyclif's death ; and directly after the revolt Courtenay carried a Bill penalising unlicensed preachers. A generation later Netter of Walden asserted that the Lollards were the prime movers in the rising ; and a confession of John Ball, probably spurious, was published to that effect.[3] In one sense Netter was right. The ideas of Wyclif had been leavening the masses, though they gave expression to them in terms he had never intended to be used.[4]

The fermentation went on throughout the reign of Richard II ; and the social unrest became every year more dangerous. Truthfully or not, it was generally attributed to Lollard teaching ; and scaremongers blamed the bishops for not extirpating the heresy. The bishops, however, could do very little as the

[1] Workman, i. 264.
[2] Winn's *Selections*, 101.
[3] *Fasciculi Zizaniorum*, 272-274.
[4] Workman, ii. 246.

Lollards had powerful friends at court, and among them John de Montacute,[1] third Earl of Salisbury, that elegant amateur in novelties whom Froissart so admired, and to whom Christine de Pisan sent her son for education.

II. *Lollard Persecutions*

When Henry IV seized the crown, the opposition to the Lollards became violent. Arundel, the restored Archbishop of Canterbury, was prepared to take action against them ; and Convocation petitioned that they might be suppressed. The House of Commons also took action in a petition, not so prolix but quite as insistent. The result was that the Act *De Haeretico Comburendo* was passed in 1401. It had all the demerits of legislation passed in panic, and Sawtre was burnt before the Bill became law because the authorities were in such a hurry to make an example.

The Act really made but little difference. It was too drastic and affected too many people to be put in force. In the Unlearned Parliament at Coventry in 1404, and in the Parliament at Worcester in 1405, the Lollards were at any rate a strong minority ; and in later parliaments proposals were made for the confiscation of Church property with a view to lessening taxation. In 1406, on the other hand, the orthodox retaliated in a long petition setting forth the detestable principles of the Lollards and how easily they might be applied to all forms of private property. In 1410, the Lollards not only proposed the disendowment of the Church, but drew up an elaborate scheme for dealing with her possessions. In the same parliament other members agitated for stricter laws against heretics. The bishops were accused of negligence ; for the Act of *De Haeretico Comburendo* had been passed in 1401, and no one had suffered under it. Such was the state of public feeling when Badby, the tailor of Evesham, was tried and burnt in March 1410.[2]

In 1414 was the dangerous conspiracy of that unbending Lollard, Sir John Oldcastle, Lord Cobham. He was a popular man of great wealth, and a soldier of unbounded audacity.

[1] Montacute, *D.N.B.*

[2] Fuller, *Worthies*, London, 204, is wrong in stating that Badby suffered about 1401 ; Foxe, *A. & M.* iii. 325, has the correct date, March 1409/10.

Henry V, who had been his friend, had attempted to convert him in August 1403, without success. He was arrested the following month, and defied the ecclesiastical court. When he was convicted of heresy, the king intervened that he might have fifty days' respite, and it was perhaps with the king's connivance that he escaped from the Tower. If so, he was ungrateful, for he at once began to organise an insurrection. Small bands of Lollards were soon moving through the country towards London. It was hoped that 20,000 armed men would arrive at St. Giles-in-the-Fields soon after midnight on January 7th, 1414. Someone, however, betrayed the place of rendezvous ; and Henry, nothing if not prompt, shut the city gates so that the London contingent could not come out. He, with men-at-arms, was on the ground when the first bands arrived, and they mistaking in the darkness the royal forces for friends, were quickly surprised and disarmed. The rest was easy. The conspiracy had been dangerous, but ended in a fiasco. A revolution had been averted and only thirty-eight people suffered death.

It is not altogether surprising that later in the year a further Act against the Lollards was passed. By it Justices of the Peace might on their own authority arrest persons defamed for heresy, and hand them over to the ordinaries of the ecclesiastical courts. This Act compelled the bishops to try suspected heretics ; and under this Act most of the burnings took place.[1]

In reviewing these facts I cannot accept the legend of Foxe, though endorsed by Professor Trevelyan, of an ignorant, brutal and bigoted priesthood persecuting pious people because of their superior enlightenment. The Professor appeals to the heresy trials which are on record, and triumphantly tells us that they contain no political charges.[2] Of course they do not, for an ecclesiastical court could not take cognizance of anything political. They had to restrict themselves to heresy ; and the heresy with which they were most concerned was connected with the sacrament of the altar.

In Wyclif's [3] earlier works there are speculations about the blessed sacrament and the possibility of a " mathematical body " ; but when he wrote *De Dominio Civili* in 1377 he still

[1] Stubbs, *Const. Hist.* iii. 391, 392.

[2] Trevelyan, *Age of Wyclif*, 340, App. 370. For Lollard teaching about the community of goods, see trials of Garrenter and Monk, Wilkins, *Concilia*, iii. 493-503.

[3] Matthew, *English Works*, xxiii.

believed in transubstantiation. In his *Confessio*, 1381,[1] he had given up that belief. In his *De Apostasia* (1381–1382) he writes, " Christ is at once God and Man, so the Sacrament is at once the Body of Christ and bread—bread and wine naturally, the Body and Blood sacramentally ".[2] This is consubstantiation. In *The Wycket*, if *The Wycket* be by him, he writes, "A sacrament is no more to say, but a sign or mind of a thing past ". It was *The Wycket*[3] which became the vade-mecum of Lollards.

In his Latin works he had never denied the Real Presence, though in speaking of it he availed himself of ambiguous distinctions and sheltered himself behind so orthodox a writer as Hugo of St. Victor.[4] His objection to transubstantiation was based on the impossibility of accidents existing apart from substance : an objection which St. Thomas Aquinas had perceived long before, and for which he had not provided a very convincing answer.[5] The difficulty is really a verbal one, for it does not necessarily arise if we substitute the modern words, appearances and reality for accidents and substance.[6]

Whatever we may think of the doctrine of transubstantiation, we must deplore the time at which the discussion was reopened. It drove the ignorant but would-be orthodox to express their faith in crude terms which the Lateran Fathers had meant to exclude. It drove the ignorant but proudly unorthodox into equally crude negations—while intending to oppose materialistic conceptions, they emptied the Sacrament of any spiritual content.

Some writers have suggested that Wyclif's[7] purpose was to cut at the root of sacerdotal power, which depended on the belief that priests alone could consecrate the bread and wine to be the Body and Blood of our Lord ; and that the opposition was only alarmed lest their revenues might disappear if men no longer valued the offering for the living and the dead. This is quite gratuitously to attribute base motives to both parties. Wyclif was an honest man who followed his argument unmindful of consequences. Even his adversaries saw this. Nicholas Love, the pious Carthusian of Mount Grace, wrote :

[1] *Fasc. Ziz.* 115 ff.
[2] Quoted Workman, ii. 38. Cp. *Fasc. Ziz.* 122.
[3] Workman, ii. 39. For authorship of *Wycket* see Lechler, ii. 219, 325, 330. For its continued circulation see Strype, *Memorials*, I. ii. 53, 65 ; More, *Apologye*, 186 ; Foxe, *A. & M.* iv. 226, 241.
[4] *Confessio*, *Fasc. Ziz.* 123.
[5] *Summa*, III. Q. lxxv. A. 5.
[6] Batiffol, *Eucharistie*, 486.
[7] Trevelyan, *Age of Wyclif*, 170 ; Lane Poole in Trail's *Social England*, ii. 170.

> Through his great learning and knowledge of philosophy he was deceived, in that he gave more credence to the doctrine of Aristotle, that standeth only in natural reason of man, than he did to the doctrine of the Holy Church and the true doctors thereof touching this precious sacrament.[1]

We have no reason to believe that his opponents were not equally honest. They may not have understood as well as he did Aristotle and the principles of Realism, but perhaps they had a clearer perception of the consequences of his teaching on the religion of the people. For them it was the Mass that mattered, and how much it mattered writers with nearly four centuries of Protestantism behind them fail to understand. It was the Lord's own service, and the central fact in man's worship. It brought our Lord to His people, and focussed their attention on Him. It bridged the gulf between this world and the next, the living and the dead. In Jesus, believed to be present, the communion of saints became a reality. In a world of inequality and discord, the value of the individual soul was vindicated at the altar. There and there alone distinctions of race, class and culture were transcended, and men were one. The action of the liturgy was intelligible to all, even though the language was in an unknown tongue. It was something all had in common. There was nothing to take its place—there never has been nor will be. It was not merely the dignity of the priesthood that was at stake, but the honour that all men owed to God's presence. It was not merely the wealth of the Church that was threatened, but the worshipping community. The soul of the nation was in jeopardy.

Did Wyclif's learned friends ultimately understand this ? We do not know ; but anyhow they recanted. Philip Repyngdon died a cardinal of the Roman Church ; John Aston wrote a refutation of his heresies, but I cannot find that he ever persecuted the faith he had once professed.[2] Nicholas Hereford, after thinking things out first in an English prison and then in another at Rome, submitted to authority, was restored to his chancellorship, obtained fresh preferment, and sat in judgment on his erstwhile

[1] Nicholas Love, *The Mirror of the Blessed Life of Jesus Christ*, 316. Rashdall, *D.N.B.*, says in very different language much the same thing.

[2] Bale, *Summarium*, Cent. iv. col. 170, says of Aston : " Wickliffi optimi viri discipulus firmus perseveravit ad exitum. Vir vere Apostolicus et pius ". Foxe also thought the same, probably misled by Bale, *A. & M.* iii. 258. But his recantation can be read in *Fasc. Ziz.* 231 ; also in Knighton, ii. 171.

associate, Walter Brut.[1] Fleming, the pert young regent at Oxford, whom an exasperated Arundel wished that he could " swap with a rod ", lived to be a bishop of Lincoln,[2] and carried out the decree of the Council of Constance, by exhuming and burning the remains of Wyclif. Even Purvey, Wyclif's closest friend, abjured him and obtained a benefice; then, like other rectors, quarrelled with his parishioners over tithes;[3] but he at least could not cease from writing, with the consequence that he was soon in trouble again, left his living and disappears from history. The cause of Lollardy was afterwards sustained by the unlettered poor.

This is exemplified by the case of Badby.[4] He was a tailor of Evesham, and was condemned as a heretic by the Bishop of Worcester early in 1409, but given a year for reconsideration. He apparently escaped from the diocese and found work in London,[5] but was once more arrested in March 1409/1410, and tried before Archbishop Arundel and a strong court of bishops and theologians. The Archbishop was very patient translating the Latin, and trying to explain in simple language what the doctrine of the Church really was. Badby was contemptuous of any learning but his own, and unafraid of the awful fate he was courting. His mind was quite clear. " If priests could make the bread to be the Body of Christ, then there were 20,000 Gods in England every morning, and he believed only in One." When faced with the words of institution, he replied that " if he had heard Christ say, This is my Body, he should say *Christ spoke amiss* ". The Archbishop gave him another three days before passing sentence, but he then declared that " a spider and a toad were superior to the consecrated host, and more worthy of reverence, for they were alive ".[6] The Archbishop had no option. He declared the man a heretic, and handed him over to the secular power with an earnest petition that his life might be spared. In the then state of public opinion this was impossible,

[1] The Lollards called him the Master of the Nicolaitains. Foxe, *A. & M.* iii. 188.

[2] Wylie, *Hist. of the Reign of Henry IV*, iii. 435.

[3] Foxe, *A. & M.* iii. 257.

[4] The best and most accurate account is in Wylie, *Hist. of Henry IV*, iii. 437-440. He gives all the authorities.

[5] Fuller, *Worthies*, London, 204, describes him as " an artificer in Blackfriars, London ".

[6] Badby probably misunderstood Wyclif's arguments. *English Works*, 357. Cp. Matthew's footnotes, 526.

but the Prince of Wales himself came to Smithfield to see if by exhortation and promises he could not induce him to withdraw from " dangerous labyrinths of doctrine ". He spoke in vain, but when the fire was lighted and Badby cried for mercy, the Prince ordered the blazing faggots to be swept away, the man to be released from bonds and laid on the ground. Once more the Prince offered him life and a pension, but Badby sat up and said that he would rather burn. He was, in consequence, covered with a barrel and burnt to ashes. " The tailor ", says Sir Charles Oman,[1] " showed higher heroism than that which won Agincourt." We agree ; but for the future victor of Agincourt something should be said. A prince had come to a tailor to save, if it were possible, his life in this world, and, as the prince thought, his life in the world to come.[2] And we should not think evil of his unwilling persecutors. The Bishop of Worcester must have connived at his evasion, and the Archbishop of Canterbury [3] interceded on his behalf.

When we read this and other lamentable stories we honour the heroism of those who died for their faith, we hate the law under which they suffered, but we dare not condemn the judges. Neither should Protestant writers make party capital out of these horrors. They should remember that, with Bishop Latimer's expressed approval,[4] more Anabaptists were burned under Henry VIII than Lollards in the XV century [5]—Anabaptists being indistinguishable from Lollards except in name. Neither should superior persons be too contemptuous of an age when good men were punished, for we have seen politicians of undoubted good-will trying to keep the Mahatma Ghandi out of prison, and failing to do so. We ought to pity the ecclesiastical rulers who had to deal with fanatics impervious to reason ; while we pity the suffering fanatics, who in the way of unreason, witnessed so bravely to the supremacy of conscience. Some seventeen people were burned to death in England for heresy during the XV century, while a great number were summoned, recanted and walked in penitential processions carrying faggots.

[1] Oman, *Pol. Hist. of England*, iv. 223.

[2] Hoccleve, *Regement of Princes*, E.E.T.S., 11-13, sounded the Prince's praise.

[3] Lechler, 453, speaks of Arundel's " hypocritical request that he might not be put to death ". Stubbs, *Const. Hist.* iii. 390, is also doubtful of Arundel's sincerity.

[4] Latimer, *Sermons*, 160.

[5] Dixon, *Ch. Hist.* i. 40.

But the persecution was very intermittent ;[1] and in most times and places Lollardy was blatant. Had it not been so, we could not account for Pecock's famous book, *The Repression of Overmuch Blaming of the Clergy*, a book written in popular language in answer to popular criticism. All through the century bishops needed to be reminded that it was their duty to suppress heresy.

It was not only from *The Wycket*, *The Lantern of Life* or *The Regimen of the Church*—all of them attributed to Wyclif—that the Lollards derived their strange opinions, but from that Bible which Wyclif believed to be its own interpreter. Some taught that the Jewish Sabbath ought to be kept, and some that pork ought not to be eaten, and some that pork was a suitable meal for a Friday in Lent. Some maintained, arguing from Abel, that men should only offer animals to God. Some, in their desire for forbidden knowledge, obtained not only the Scriptures but books of sorcery.[2] Some said that there was no sacrament except marriage, and some that marriage was not a sacrament. Some said that no bastard could be saved, and some that sexual sin was of little consequence. Some said that a child's baptism was invalid if either the priest or one of the sponsors was in mortal sin ; some repudiated baptism. Some denounced war and capital punishment and approached the doctrines of the Quakers, and some objected to singing in church. They quoted I Peter iv. 12 as forbidding pilgrimages : and from I Corinthians xiv. 28 derived their title. They were " the known " people who would be saved.[3]

The Lollards had very little in common beyond a rooted hatred of the priesthood, a keen relish for ecclesiastical scandals, and a fervent belief that every scripture was for private interpretation. But we must not judge of the movement by its eccentrics. There were many who had revolted from the scandals in the Church ; many also were filled with a desire to read the Scriptures in the only language which they understood. That was good, even when the desire was stimulated by the thought that " stolen waters are sweet ", and even though the slaking of the thirst filled them with a sense of secret superiority. We have only a feeling of disgust when we read in Foxe of the ribald Nicholas

[1] Stubbs, *Const. Hist.* iii. 394. [2] Barclay, *Ship of Fools*, i. 195.
[3] Capes, *Ch. Hist.* 192.

Canon, and marvel that his profanity was so lightly punished.[1] We have but little sympathy for the truculent Margery Backster, who believed that the devils who fell from heaven with Lucifer had entered into the images of the Church.[2] We feel quite differently for Nicholas Belward of Norfolk, who bought in London a New Testament for four marks and forty pence, which probably represented a lifetime's savings, and studied it diligently with William White and Margery his wife, sometimes carrying it to the house of Thomas Moore, because he had a servant, John Pert, who could read well.[3] These humble people were no doubt seekers after God.

III. *Reginald Pecock*

Many wrote books to confound the Lollards, but Reginald Pecock (1395–1460) wrote to convert them. " He hoped ", says Gairdner, " to reconcile Lollards to the Church by better arguments than the fires of Smithfield."[4] In his *Treatise on Faith* he writes :

> The clergy shall be condemned at the last day if by clear wit they draw not men into consent of true faith otherwise than by fire and sword and hangment, although I will not deny these second means to be lawful, provided the former be first used.[5]

Having been a parish priest in London before becoming Bishop of St. Asaph, he knew the arguments of the Lollards, states them fairly, and then appeals not to authority but to reason.[6]

Unfortunately he attempted to defend the indefensible—the unpreaching prelates and their absenteeism, the misapplied wealth of the church, the simoniacal contracts with the Pope, and the superstitious worship offered to images. A bishop, he argued, should devote himself to the deep problems of theology, and might leave to lesser men the elementary instruction of the people.[7] Again, it was charitable to suppose that a bishop out-

[1] Foxe, *A. & M.* iii. 599. [2] *Ibid.* iii. 596. [3] *Ibid.* iii. 597.

[4] Gairdner, *Lollardy and the Reformation*, i. 203.

[5] *Book of Faith*, edited by Morison, 139.

[6] In the *Book of Faith*, 202, he tells us how he had often spoken with the men who were esteemed " Dukes " among the Lollards, and " they have loved me because I would patiently hear their evidence, and their motives without exprobation ".

[7] Pecock's *Abbreviator* printed with *Repressor*, ii. 616, 617.

side his diocese was engaged on the wider interests of the Church and people. It was true that many misapplied the wealth of the Church ; but that was no reason for confiscation, for they were only tenants for life, and their successors might spend the money to advantage.[1] It was impossible that any money paid to the Pope should involve simony, for the Pope was lord of all and any money paid to him was his own.[2] A man might believe that an image sweated, winked, spoke, heard prayers and worked miracles, but he was no idolater unless he believed that the image was God.[3] He turned with a smile on those who asserted that the Franciscans were hypocrites, because, forbidden to touch money, they counted it with a stick, and asked, " Does counting it with a stick make them love money more ? "[4] He met the Bible men who wanted scriptural authority for everything by reminding them that in Holy Scripture only Aaron and his sons are commanded to wear breeches, and then comes the poignant question, How about the brewing of ale ?[5]

Yet Pecock was not without sympathy for the Bible men. He acknowledges that the Bible, especially the historical parts of the Old and New Testament, " is miche delectable and sweet, and draweth the readers into a devotion and love to God, and from love and deinté of the world ". But this does not excuse a conceit which despises learning and instruction.

Pecock himself was a thorough-going rationalist. He acknowledges indeed that from the Bible we learn some mysteries which transcend reason—the nature of God, the Incarnation and Redemption—" but ", he adds, " we believe the Revelation when we see that it is reasonable ". Otherwise the Bible bears witness to the Law of Kind (nature) ; and, should there seem to be any conflict, the Bible must be harmonised with the Law of Kind, while the Law of Kind must not be forced into conformity with our understanding of Scripture.[6] Again he writes :

[1] Sermon at Paul's Cross ; Babington's Introd. xvi.

[2] *Repressor*, i. 153, 154.

[3] *Ibid.* ii. 558, 559.

[4] *Ibid.* i. 118, 120.

[5] *Ibid.* i. 66.

[6] *Ibid.* i. 25, 26. He had a great contempt for the common method of proving doctrines from isolated texts of Scripture interpreted in a metaphorical sense. In this he had been anticipated by du Bois (*c.* 1300), who had written : " It is no doubt usual among professors of theology to take a double sense in the words of Scripture, the literal or historical, and the mystical or spiritual : but for the purpose of argument none but the former can be valid ". Quoted Lane-Poole, *Illustr. of Med. Thought*, 261.

It belongeth not to any Scripture to ground any governance or deed of service of God, or any Law of God or any truth which men's nature by reason may find, learn or know.[1]

And again :

If any man be feared that he trespass to God if he makes over-little of Holy Scripture which is the outward writing of the Old Testament and the New, I ask why he is not afeared lest he make over-little and apprise over-little the inward scripture of the before-spoken Law of King, written by God himself in man's soul, when he made man's soul to his image and likeness ?[2]

This, taken alone, might be interpreted in the Quaker sense of the Inward Light, but nothing was further from Pecock's thought. He abhorred mysteries and identifies God's gift of reason with the logical faculty, proclaiming it supreme.[3] The Law of Kind is recognised by " the doom of reason ", but before that doom can be pronounced the facts must be known. This necessitates the study of moral and natural philosophy. Then if the rules of logic are observed the doom is final. He saw the answer to this—knowledge is limited and reasoning fallible, but he was not abashed. He says that hearing and sight are both defective, but we are bound to use them and trust them.[4] The same is true of reason, and he adds, " God will forgive involuntary error ".[5] He would have agreed with Bishop Butler about reason ; " We have no other faculty to judge of anything, including Revelation ".[6]

Pecock therefore has no belief in the plenary inspiration of the poor humble man who reads his Bible. How could he be humble if he despised the aid of " substantial clerks, well learned in logic and moral philosophy " ?[7] He claimed for himself the right of private judgment, because he believed himself competent to exercise it, but he was not prepared to extend that right to the unlearned, for then " men should accord together as dogs do in a market place when each of them teareth other's coat ".[8] He

[1] *Repressor*, i. 10. Pecock's sentence has been abbreviated.

[2] *Ibid.* i. 51.

[3] *Book of Faith*, 174 : " A syllogism . . . having two premises openly true and to be granted, is so strong and so mighty in all kinds of matters, though all the angels in heaven would say that his conclusion was not true, yet we should leave the angels saying, and trust more to the truth of his syllogism ".

[4] *Repressor*, i. 73. [5] *Ibid.* i. 75. [6] Butler, *Analogy*, Pt. II. ch. iii.

[7] *Repressor*, i. 85. [8] *Ibid.* i. 85, 86.

twits the Lollards with their schisms. Are there not among them those known as doctor-mongers, opinion-mongers and neutrals?[1] They claim indeed that God will reveal Himself to "the true livers in His law", "but", says Pecock, "it is notorious that some of their most influential leaders are vicious men".[2]

A year after publishing *The Repressor*, Pecock was translated to Chichester and was soon engaged on *A Treatise on Faith*. In this book he made it clear that if he did not believe in the infallible Bible, still less did he believe in an infallible Church. His leading thought he expresses as follows:

> It was a shameful thing for the Christian church to hold such a faith for substance of its salvation, and yet not to suffer it to be examined: it were imputing a villainy to Christ that would give such a faith to his people, into which faith he would his people should turn all other people, and yet could not allow his faith to be full tried.[3]

Faith, he maintained, was only probable, opinional and rarely sciential in this life.[4] Probability was our guide in life; but it was right to follow a teacher, who may fail, in so far as it is not known that he has failed.[5] On the other hand, General Councils have erred and the Fathers have disagreed. Pecock, when asking for reasons, was not to be put off with authorities. When opposing divines quoted the Fathers he replied, "Pooh! You are just as good teachers as they, and may just as well quote yourselves."[6] Again, he said of St. Jerome:

> Certes, his tongue is not the key of heaven or of earth, neither had power to make anything true or false, or otherwise then he could find it to be true or false in Doom of Reason or of Holy Scripture.[7]

He disagreed with the dictum of Gregory the Great: *Fides non habet meritum cui ratio humana praebet experimentum.*[8] This

[1] *Ibid.* i. 87. [2] *Ibid.* i. 103.

[3] *Book of Faith*, 132. Cp. *Folewer to the Donet*, ed. by Hitchcock, Pt. I. ch. xiv.

[4] *Book of Faith*, 140 ff.

[5] *Ibid.* 113. In the *Folewer to the Donet*, 62, he writes: "Faith is a knowing whereby we assent to anything as to truth, for as much as we have sure evidence greater than to the contrary, that it is told and affirmed to us to be true, by him of whom we have sure evidence, or notable likely evidence, greater than to the contrary, that therein he not lied". In his *Reule of Christen Religion*, edited by Greet, 117, he teaches how we ought to be satisfied with probable truth as a guide for life.

[6] Gascoigne, *Loci e Libro Veritatum*, 217; *Repressor*, ii. 623.

[7] *Repressor*, ii. 335.

[8] Gascoigne, 210; *Book of Faith*, 145.

was bad enough, but to his contemporaries what was far worse, he scoffed at Duns Scotus. The Subtle Doctor had admitted that our Lord's descent into hell could not be proved by Scripture, but declared it was of faith because the apostles had put the article into the creed. Pecock replied that the apostles did not write the creed which goes by their name, and that the article was not in the creed when St. Augustine lived, and in consequence the opinion of Scotus could not be maintained.[1] The restless brain of Pecock was never content. He even wrote a new creed, but it has not survived.[2]

It will be seen that Pecock may have been orthodox ; but his defence of orthodoxy was not on orthodox lines. He was a witty Welshman, quick to defend a truth or expose an error ; dexterous when maintaining a bad cause, and ready to forgive anything but an *ignoratio elenchi*. We imagine him to have been a kindly man, for there is no word of bitterness in any of his writings. He certainly understood how to talk to the gallery ; and, being excessively vain, he expected them to wonder, laugh and applaud.[3] Intellectual arrogance was his ruin. Lords in the Council and unlearned bishops hated him for his all too patent sense of his own superiority.

It was an indiscreet letter to the Lord Mayor, Canning, on a political question that brought about his ruin ; but it was never convenient to try a bishop for treason, so he was handed over to Archbishop Bourchier, who summoned him to appear with his books as one defamed for heresy. At first he was truculent and demanded to be tried by his peers in disputation and not by prelates unskilled in the schools. But very soon his courage failed and he collapsed. He even listened meekly to the reproofs of George Neville, who had by papal dispensation been appointed to the see of Exeter when far below the canonical age.

It was not long before the Archbishop informed his " dear brother, Master Reginald ", that "he was like all heretics blinded by the light of his own understanding " and that " the time had come when he must recant or burn ".[4] Pecock, quite rightly,

[1] Babington, Introd. lxxi. Cp. *Book of Faith*, 303-305.

[2] Gascoigne, *Loci e Libro Veritatum*, 214.

[3] An amusing instance of Pecock's belief in himself is to be found in *The Foleuer*, 81 : " If thou wilt have stronger witness to the purpose than is the witness of Aristotle, look then, my son, into a sermon I made in Latin to the clergy ".

[4] Babington, *Introduction*, xliv.

was not prepared to die for what were, after all, opinions rather than convictions, and so he braced himself to accept the disgrace. He recanted many things which he had never taught,[1] and two propositions which were long afterwards affirmed to be true by the Council of Trent. He afterwards at Paul's Cross, in the presence of the multitude, cast three of his folios and eleven quartos into the fire, exclaiming against his own pride and presumption. He was then sent to prison, but managed to appeal to the Pope. Calixtus III ordered that he should be reinstated ; but he was in the power of his enemies, and they compelled him to resign. Pius II—and no man had better reasons for forgiving literary indiscretions—tried to save him, and ordered that he should be sent to Rome. But the Pope was disobeyed, and Pecock died in the monastery at Thorney, having been confined in " a secret close chamber " with " one sad person to make his fire and bed ".[2] We do not suppose that his famous *Repressor* converted many Lollards, but it had all the merits required for a " best seller ", and a bitter chronicler remarks that " many infected by his pestiferous teaching remained in error ".[3] A little later Edward IV wrote to Sixtus IV that Pecock's writings were multiplied, and that not only the laity but churchmen and scholastic graduates scarcely studied anything else.[4] He had to be suppressed, and he was suppressed so successfully that this stalwart opponent of the Lollards is included by Foxe among his martyrs, and the *Index Expurgatorius* of Madrid described him as a Lutheran Professor of Oxford.[5]

[1] Recantation in Wilkins, *Concilia*, iii. 576. [2] Babington, lvii.

[3] *Three Fifteenth-Century Chronicles*, 168.

[4] *C. S. P. Venetian*, i. 451. Quoted by Hitchcock, *The Donet*, xxv. By the early statutes of King's College, Cambridge, every scholar at the end of his year of probation had to promise that he would never favour the errors of John Wyclif and Reginald Pecock, and a similar promise had to be made at Queens' College, Cambridge. Mullinger, *Hist. of Cambridge*, i. 296.

[5] Capes, *Ch. Hist.* 216. How completely Pecock was suppressed may be seen from the fact that Foxe, *A. & M.* iii. 731, did not know that he wrote against the Lollards. He prints Bourchier's citation and Pecock's recantation, adding an article about the Blessed Sacrament composed apparently by himself. For the rest he translates verbally from Bale's *Index Britanniae Scriptorum*, 337, and Bale depends entirely on Pecock's enemy, Gascoigne. Hall, 237, is even more ignorant. He thought Pecock got into trouble by lecturing at Oxford against Annates and Peter's Pence. Parsons, the Jesuit, *Three Conversions of England*, Pt. III., Calendar, Feb. 11th, has the date twenty years wrong, and says that Pecock denied " three express articles of the Creed ". This too is untrue. Pecock rejected the Descent into Hell on critical grounds. He also affirmed that while we say I believe *in* God—Father, Son and Holy Ghost, we only say we believe the Holy Catholic Church and the Communion of

His case has been worth considering at length, for it shows us bibliolaters confronted by a rationalist, and the Church rooted, however unintelligently, in an age-long tradition. The Church condemned Wyclif and condemned Pecock. Both were learned—abler and better men than their opponents—and yet in both cases the Church was right. Wyclif had ample justification for denouncing the ecclesiastical abuses of his time, but Lollardy would have destroyed the Church. Pecock had ample justification for upholding the claims of reason, but by claiming that all questions were open for discussion he was imperilling the historic faith and undermining the authority of the Church as a teaching body with a gospel to deliver. The Church, after all, exists for other purposes than to be a debating society.

IV. *Lollard Survivals*

The Wars of the Roses gave the chroniclers something more exciting to write about than the vagaries of Lollards, but that does not prove that Lollardy was extinct. Without organisation, learning or leaders of distinction there was little for history to record. The ordinary Englishman hated heresy; and there was periodical alarm at the supposed increase of heretics, and the dangers that might be anticipated. Lollards were chiefly concentrated in London and the eastern counties, but they appear sporadically elsewhere. There was a carpenter in Somerset who believed that " a sinful man may never be damned through his sinful living, for then Christ must needs damn his own flesh and blood which he took of Mary the Virgin ", and there were two Wiltshire clerics who abjured the usual negations.[1] In 1498 there was the heretic at Canterbury whom Henry VII converted, and to whom he gave a noble. About him the chronicler writes :

> This year in the beginning of May, the king being at Canterbury, was burnt an heretic, a priest, which by the king's exhortation before his death was converted from his erroneous opinions and died a Christian man : whereof his grace got great honour.[2]

On which Fuller comments, " If the king's converts had no

Saints ; but this distinction is approved in the *Tridentine Catechism*, " de Symbolo," ix. 23.

[1] Jenkins, Morton's Register, *Tudor Studies*, 47.

[2] Kingsford, *Chronicles of London*, 222. Gairdner, *Lollardy and the Reformation*, i. 274, 275, points out that the man must have been burnt a week or ten days after the king left Canterbury.

better encouragement, this was the first he made and the last he was likely to make ".[1]

A year later the ambassador of Ludovico Sforza wrote from London of a new sect of heretics who declared "baptism unnecessary for the children of Christians, marriage a superfluous rite, and the sacrament of the altar a fiction", but he adds, "the bishops have begun to persecute them ".[2]

Notwithstanding the cases of cruelty reported by Foxe at Amersham and elsewhere,[3] Bacon was right in saying that proceedings against heretics were "rare in this king's reign and rather by penance than by fire ".[4]

At the beginning of the reign of Henry VIII, Fitzjames, Bishop of London, began a heresy hunt in which he discovered Hunne's Bible with all its "naughty" annotations.[5] Foxe tells us of forty confessors between 1509 and 1527 in the London diocese, which included Essex; but he only tells us of heretics who would be accounted orthodox when Elizabeth was queen. There were, he naïvely remarks, other and odious charges which he did not believe to be true, and would not weary his readers by repeating. The forty all abjured and did penance, by standing with faggots on their shoulders before Paul's Cross during sermon time, except Sweeting and Brewster, who were burnt as relapsed heretics.[6] This was in 1511, and in the course of a gossiping letter Ammonius wrote from London to Erasmus with sprightly exaggeration:

> I do not wonder that the price of faggots has gone up, for many heretics furnish a daily holocaust, and yet more spring up to take their place. And, so please you, the brother of my man Thomas—more a stick than a man—has not only started a sect, but has disciples.[7]

And Erasmus, loving warmth and yearning for a Dutch stove, wrote from Cambridge to say that with winter upon us he will hate heretics the more for raising the price of fuel.[8] Neither man was serious nor particularly interested; but we note that a burning had "news value"—neither man would have mentioned a hanging, for men were hanged every day.

[1] Fuller, *Church Hist.* Bk. XV. 155.

[2] *The Venetian Calendar*, i. 799. Quoted Gairdner, *Lollardy and the Reformation*, i. 274, 275.

[3] Foxe, *A. & M.* iv. 123 ff.

[4] Bacon, *Henry VII*, 135.

[5] More, *Dialogue*, Bk. III. ch. xv.

[6] Foxe, *A. & M.* iv. 18.

[7] Erasmus, *Ep.* 239.

[8] *Ep.* 240.

Writing in 1533, Sir Thomas More tells Saint German that if he omits the dioceses of London and Lincoln he will not find four persons punished for heresy in five years, and in most dioceses not five in fifteen years, and not one handed over to the secular arm in twenty years. He acknowledges that in the London diocese twice as many heretics had been punished as in the rest of England, but he challenges Saint German to prove that any one of them suffered unjustly.[1]

The diocese of Lincoln in those days included the counties of Lincoln, Leicester, Rutland, Northampton, Oxford, Buckingham, Huntingdon, Bedford and part of Hertford. In 1521 John Longland became bishop. He was a pious, energetic man, a preacher, a reformer of abuses and a hater of heresy. He found the county of Buckingham in a sad state. Nearly all the livings were appropriated and the vicars were wretchedly paid. Church life was at a low ebb, and Lollardy abounded. He obtained royal letters to all mayors, sheriffs and constables that they should co-operate with him in the suppression of heresy.[2] Foxe gives us a list of fifty heretics who abjured and of four relapsed heretics who were burnt, and thinks that there were two others. All that can be said for certain is that one was burnt, that he too abjured at the stake and died, as the vicar of the parish said, " a Christian man ". Subsequently Longland sent more than one man to the stake. He also greatly raised the religious life in the county, so that, at his second visitation, the words *omnia bene* are applied to many parishes which had been scandalous. How, then, are we to regard him ? Very much as we regard a judge of assize to-day who puts on the black cap and condemns a criminal to death. Four hundred years hence men may regard capital punishment as we regard the burning of heretics ; but the men then will be wrong if they stigmatise our present judges as inhuman monsters. No one need suppose that Longland liked burning heretics. To hand a relapsed heretic over to the secular authorities was no doubt painful to him, but he had a duty to perform and a law to administer.[3]

[1] More, *Apologye*, 129, 130. Cp. 167.

[2] Up to 1616 sheriffs of Buckingham promised to enquire after and apprehend Lollards. In 1616 Sir Edward Coke became sheriff and altered the oath. Aubrey, *Brief Lives*, i. 178.

[3] Foxe, *A. & M.* iv. 219-246, gives very full particulars which he professes to have derived from Longland's Register, carefully quoting the folio where each fact

Longland was a persecutor, and so was Fitzjames, but apart from them there seems to have been very little persecuting of Lollards on the eve of the Reformation. That, however, does not help us to know how many Lollards there were, or how much sympathy they excited ; and it is, I believe, an error to suppose that the sect was all but extinct. Sir Thomas More, for instance, in his *Apologye*, tells us of an attempt made by " a hundred men or above " to rescue a " known heretic " from the ordinary, and this implies that Lollards must have been fairly numerous.[1]

When Tunstall, as Bishop of London, arrested " old father Hacker, alias Ebb " in 1527, the Lutheran movement had been going ten years in Germany, but the movement in which Hacker was a leader had a far longer history.[2] He saved himself by betraying his disciples ; and they, arrested in turn, denounced others. We thus become acquainted with a society of known people with ramifications extending from London to Norwich. We also have light on the connexion between Lollardy and Protestantism. One Hiller was introduced to the apostate Friar Barron and showed him his old Wyclifite books, " which books the said friar did little regard and made a twyte of ". The friar was a good salesman and Hiller, in consequence, paid three shillings and fourpence for Tyndale's edition of the Gospels. It was the Bible which was the link between Lollardy and the Reformation.

may be found. Longland's Register exists, complete and in good condition, but not one of the facts is there. Foxe must therefore be referring to some other book no longer extant, and his facts cannot be checked (*vide V. C. H. Bucks*, i. 301). Foxe also gives many details which were told him on the spot forty years later ; but they may be viewed with suspicion. We know how an intelligent peasantry would respond to the invitation, when they heard of a kind gentleman staying at the inn, with money in his pocket and a desire to sup on horrors. We can safely disregard the story that Scrivener's children were compelled to light the fire that consumed their father. How many were burnt ? Sir Thomas More, *Apologye*, 105, writing ten years later, says *one*. Foxe, writing forty years later, says four certainly, and probably two others. He does not profess to find these facts in the Register. Fuller, *Worthies: Bucks*, writing with Foxe before him, only tells of one, Scrivener. His next entry is concerned with another of Foxe's martyrs, and shows that he was alive many years afterwards. Lollard leaders had many aliases, and it is possible that Foxe's various informants told him the story of one man under different names.

[1] More, *Apologye*, 178. Skelton refers to them in *Colyn Cloute* (Dyce ed., i. 332) :

And some of them barke,
Clatter and carpe
Of that heresy arte
Called Wiclevista,
The develysshe dogmatista.

[2] Strype, *Memorials*, I. ii. 50-65.

It may be concluded that the proportion of Lollards to the population was much the same as the proportion of Communists to the population to-day. In other respects there are analogies between the two parties. The Lollards were mostly poor men of the artisan class, but they had a few secret supporters who were wealthy merchants or tradesmen. For the most part the ordinary Englishman knew about them, shook his head sadly when they were mentioned, and left them alone. Just as now someone starts a scare about the subversive propaganda in Communist Sunday schools, so before the Reformation someone worked up suspicion of the evil designs of the Lollards. Then there would be raids, a search for papers and prohibited books, and an examination of those detected. Sometimes there were outbursts of fury against Lollards for their profanity, indecent behaviour in church, demonstrations against popular worship, or sacrilege. Generally it was the more innocent members of the sect who were tried and punished on such occasions : the more guilty got away. Lollards no doubt rejoiced when they heard of what Luther was doing in Germany, just as Communists rejoice over what they hear of happenings in Russia. No doubt they were ready to receive and shelter emissaries from Germany ; but I do not suppose that they were interested in Lutheran theology, which was quite alien to their own, for they symbolised with Luther's enemies, the Anabaptists. It was the same class which provided most of the victims in Queen Mary's reign. They were the true descendants of the Lollards. They did not die for Lutheranism or Calvinism. They died protesting against the existence of a Church and priesthood. They died maintaining that the Bible in the vernacular was all that was necessary for salvation. They died for the principle that of that Bible every man was his own and sufficient interpreter.

CHAPTER II

THE HISTORY OF SCHOLASTICISM

I. *The Rediscovery of Aristotle*

IT is necessary to know about Lollardy in order to understand the response that was made to the English Reformers. It is necessary to know something of scholasticism, if we would understand why theology in the early XVI century was entirely out of touch with the spirit of the age. Why did renaissance scholars view the schoolmen with such contempt, and why did the Reformers hate them with so much venom ? Why was there no living school of theology at either Oxford or Cambridge able to cope with the new knowledge ? Why were the men of the Old Learning so narrow-minded and bigoted ? Were they being loyal to their tradition ?

To answer these questions we shall have to go rather far afield, for scholasticism was cosmopolitan, and we cannot think of the English schoolmen in isolation. We shall also have to go far back and start with the XIII century, if we would understand how the intellectual triumphs of that age led to the defeats which the schoolmen suffered at the hands of humanists and reformers.

When the great schoolmen arose in the XIII century they were the saviours of Christian philosophy—we might almost say, the saviours of the Christian religion. If it is true that the ignorant were then ready to believe anything that gave them a thrill of surprise, it was equally true that there were superior people who prided themselves on disbelieving most things, however well attested. The Albigenses were given over to a Manicheism which was sapping the moral bases of society, and the disciples of Joachim of Flore were expecting a new dispensation and an apocalyptic communism. There was a steady influx of Jewish and Arabian books on science and philosophy ; and there were enthusiastic modernists ready to jettison much of the Christian faith in order to accommodate what remained with the new enlightenment. Paris was crowded with scholars eager to hear and tell some new thing. Pious people were satisfied with the mysticism derived from St. Bernard and the Victorines, while traditionalists insisted on the supreme authority of St. Augustine. St. Bonaventura, who, of all the schoolmen, was most in sympathy with the past, wrote : " The word of wisdom was given to Plato ; to Aristotle the word of knowledge . . . but the word both of wisdom and knowledge was given by the Holy Ghost to Augustine ".[1]

The scholasticism with which we are concerned was due to the recovery of Aristotle. Up to the XIII century only his works on logic had been known, though inaccurate information had filtered into Western Europe from Arabic and Jewish sources. The first translations were also interpolated and came to Paris with the commentaries of Averroes. Grossetête, while Chancellor of Oxford, had the *Ethics* translated from the Greek under his supervision. James of Venice was responsible for the *De Anima* ; but it was later, thanks to the inspiration of St. Thomas Aquinas, that William of Moerbeke and Henry of Brabant produced a complete Aristotle in Latin.[2]

The Church was at first suspicious of this new knowledge, coming as it originally did from infidel writers. In 1210 a Council at Paris, summoned by Peter of Corbeil, Archbishop of Sens, forbade anyone in public or private to read the natural philosophy of Aristotle or the *Commentaries* of Averroes. In 1215 the Papal Legate, Robert de Courçon, allowed the *Ethics* to be read, but not the *Physics* or *Metaphysics*. As the prohibition was disregarded, in 1228 Gregory IX wrote *ad magistros Theologiae Parisienses*, accusing them of setting up the image of Antiochus in the Temple of God, and daring to strengthen the faith by arguments of reason, " for Faith has no merit when Reason furnishes it with proof ". Three years later the octogenarian Pope had changed his mind, and discovered that the " books

[1] *Sermo Anecdota*, 80, 81. Quoted by Gilson, *Études de philosophie médiévale*, 81, and by D'Arcy, *Aquinas*, 18.

[2] Mullinger, *Hist. of Cambridge*, i. 95, writes concerning these translations : " If the versions from the Greek by James of Venice, John of Basingstoke and William of Moerbeke were painful from their extreme literalness, those from the Arabic by Herman the German, Adelard of Bath and Michael Scot, lay under the still more serious defect of having been filtered through the medium of some half-dozen preceding versions. It is an ascertained fact that the Arabic translations were invariably made from Hebrew and Syriac manuscripts."

of natural philosophy, forbidden by the Provincial Council at Paris, are said to contain both useful and useless matter". He therefore commissioned William of Auxerre and Stephen of Provins to examine the said books and give their approval to correct versions. He also directed the Abbot of St. Victor and the Prior of the Dominicans to absolve those who had incurred ecclesiastical censures by disobeying the previous prohibitions. In 1237 all censures were withdrawn, and soon some knowledge of the *Physics* and *Metaphysics* was required of all students in arts. In 1245 Hales produced his *Summa*; a little later Albertus Magnus was lecturing at Cologne; a little later again St. Thomas was dominant in Paris. But even then conservatives like Tempier, Bishop of Paris, continued to rage; and it is well to remember that Hales, Albertus and Aquinas had to fight for their new learning in the XIII century, as Le Fevre, Reuchlin and Erasmus had to fight for theirs at a later date. The situation at both times was much the same. There were the wild men, intoxicated with their new learning, staggering towards a precipice of unbelief; there were the conservatives who saw the dangers very clearly, and not so clearly the value of the New Learning; and there were the wise men, prepared with due discrimination to claim the New Learning for the Church and use it for the more confirmation of the faith.[1]

Alexander of Hales and his pupil Albertus Magnus made heroic efforts to reduce their knowledge into a system; but neither of them had such an orderly mind or such a masterly grasp of essentials as St. Thomas Aquinas, who, never resting, never hastening, built up a coherent system of theology and philosophy which survives to-day.

Looking back on this XIII century scholasticism, Dr. Hort writes: "It is the most consistent and hopeful attempt ever made to set up Christian faith as the ruling principle in all departments of human activity".[2] More recently Dr. Whitehead has acknowledged the great debt which modern civilisation owes

[1] Lacey, *Wayfaring Essays*, 147-153; de Wulf, *Mediaeval Philosophy*, i. 248, 249; Harris, *Duns Scotus*, i. 55-60; Rashdall, *Universities*, i. 356-361. It is not without significance that between 1228 and 1231 Michael Scot had deserted Frederick II and been received with great distincton at Rome. Michael had dedicated his translation of the *De Anima* to Stephen of Provins, and Gregory IX made the said Stephen one of the censors.

[2] Hort, *Hulsean Lectures*, 74.

to the schoolmen, who taught men how to discipline their thought and classify their knowledge.[1] Naturally he deplores their neglect of mathematics and their unquestioning acceptance of Aristotelian physics, but for this they were not to blame. Indeed, it should be remembered that Albertus wrote *Oportet experimentum non in uno modo, sed secundum omnes circumstantias probare*, and repeatedly encouraged scholars to observe for themselves.[2] St. Thomas also had at times a prudent scepticism about the finality of Greek science, and, writing of the Ptolemaic system, says: "The hypotheses of the astrologers are not necessarily true; in employing them they seem to explain the facts, but no one is forced to believe that they are right; perhaps some scheme that is still unknown to man can serve to explain all the appearances of the stellar universe."[3]

The schoolmen often suffer reproach because their thought has always a theological bias; but this was inevitable in the XIII century. Theology had been more studied than any other science; its terms were better defined; its implications were better thought out, and it was the one subject on which the schoolmen had an adequate library—the works of the Fathers. Theology was in consequence dominant—the queen of sciences; and there was a resolute endeavour to bring all knowledge into conformity with her conclusions. This was not, in practice, consistent with freedom of investigation, although both Albertus and St. Thomas desired that each science should be pursued independently. Moreover in their desire for a synthesis they were right; and if there be a God and He has revealed Himself, it is obvious that there never will be a satisfactory explanation of the universe which leaves Him and His revelation out of account. It is equally obvious that God's revelation will never be completely understood until it is interpreted in the light of all the facts. The schoolmen did maintain that all truth belongs of right to Christian thought as the spoils of the Egyptians to the Hebrews. St. Thomas quotes more than once the dictum of St. Ambrose, *Omne verum a quocumque dicatur, a Spiritu sancto est*;[4] Roger

[1] Whitehead, *Adventures of Ideas*, 137-138, 149, 152.

[2] Quoted de Wulf, *Mediaeval Philosophy*, i. 295.

[3] *De Coelo et Mundo*, ii. 17. This is a stock quotation. Taylor, *Phil. Studies*, 244; De Wulf, *Med. Phil.* ii. 19; D'Arcy, *Aquinas*, 57.

[4] Maritain, *Introd. to Philosophy*, 97.

Bacon wrote, *Oportet theologum scire omnia* ; [1] and Albertus at least attempted the impossible. He wrote not only on theology, philosophy and ethics, but also on logic, psychology, politics, physiology, physics, natural history and chemistry ; and at the end of his labours was happily unaware of how much there was to be known. Roger Bacon guessed aright : " Future generations will know much that we are ignorant of, and the time will come when our successors will wonder that we were so blind to things obvious to them ".[2]

Not only was their creed fixed and defined, but most schoolmen believed in the verbal inspiration of every verse in the Bible, and were inclined to mistake oriental imagery for facts.[3] Roger Bacon went further, and believed that all knowledge was contained in Holy Scripture, and that every new discovery had been anticipated in the sacred text. For instance, he quotes (Ecclesiasticus xliii. 4), " a man blowing a furnace is in works of heat ; but the sun three times [*tripliciter*] more, burning up the mountains " ; then he interprets *tripliciter* " in a threefold manner ", and concludes that his author knew all about the incidence of the sun's rays, and the laws of reflexion and refraction.[4]

The schoolmen also were as much hampered as helped by the other authors whom they accepted. As champions of Aristotelianism they were unwilling to admit that *The Philosopher*, their master, ever erred in any matter of human wisdom ; [5] as devout sons of the Church they considered it temerarious to

[1] Bacon, *Opus Minus*, 358. Quoted Little, *Roger Bacon*, 25.

[2] Bacon, *Compendium Studii Philosophiae*, 426. Quoted Little, *Roger Bacon*, 18.

[3] This is not true of St. Thomas. *Summa*, I. Q. lxviii. A. 1 : " Since Holy Scripture can be explained in a multiplicity of senses, we should adhere to a particular explanation only in such a measure as to be ready to abandon it, if it be proved with certainty to be false, lest Holy Scripture be exposed to the ridicule of unbelievers and an obstacle be placed to their believing ". *Ibid.* I. Q. lxv. A. 3 : " As however this theory [of the waters above the firmament] can be shown to be false by solid reasons, it cannot be held to be the sense of Scripture. It should rather be considered that Moses was speaking to ignorant people, and that out of condescension for their weakness, he put before them only such things as are apparent to the senses." For St. Thomas as an interpreter of Holy Scripture see Pope in *Manchester Essays*, and McNabb, *From a Friar's Cell*, 236-251.

[4] Bacon, *Opus Majus*. Quoted Little, *Roger Bacon*, 25.

[5] " The Aristotelian *Corpus* supplied the Middle Ages with an organised body of scientific knowledge far in advance of anything which Western culture had hitherto known, and consequently it was accepted as the last word of human wisdom " (Dawson, *Mediaeval Religion*, 79).

contradict St. Augustine; and they never doubted the authenticity of the works of Dionysius the Areopagite.[1] They honestly tried to harmonise their very discordant authorities, and their many distinctions and intricate explanations render most of them hard to read.

Considering their limitations it is natural for the modern freethinker to describe the schoolman as working with his mind in chains;[2] but in reality, after accepting what was believed to be knowledge and bowing to the masters who went before him, he was a daring rationalist intent only on finding fresh truth. After all, the man who rises every morning believing everything is an open question, never gets anywhere. All fruitful thinking starts from assured premises, and the most fruitful thinking comes from men who dare to accept data which are hard to reconcile. Such thinking calls for distinctions, and distinctions may be unduly multiplied, but they train the mind in exact thought. It may be that truth is not best discovered by disputation; but in using syllogisms, disputants are compelled to define their terms. Such a disputant may misunderstand his opponent, but he has not the chance of misrepresenting him; and the mediaeval schoolman was under no temptation to do so. He sought the glory of providing a complete refutation of a proposition that everyone thought had been demonstrated. He appealed to an audience which appreciated logic and had little respect for the arts of oratory.[3]

It was an age when books were few but well conned; when instruction was given orally and memories were cultivated; when scholars did not pass examinations, but were continually tested by disputations. When Aquinas taught at Paris, it was customary for a professor in Advent and Lent to announce that he and his pupils would maintain their theses against all comers. An intellectual tournament took place. The Bishop of Paris sometimes presided, and on one occasion at least the king, St.

[1] The *Divine Hierarchies* and the *Divine Names*. Thomas de Vio alone among the schoolmen had doubts about these works. The best account known to me of Dionysius is in Westcott, *Religious Thought in the West*.

[2] Bury, *History of Freedom of Thought*, ch. iii., " Reason in Chains ".

[3] Rashdall, *Universities*, 365. " By the time of Aquinas, it was felt that the better the imaginary opponents' case can be stated, the more credit there is in refuting it. The Scholar's intellectual enjoyment of thirty ingenious arguments against the immortality of the soul was not diminished by thirty-six equally ingenious arguments with which the attack would immediately be met."

Louis. Scholars from all the schools crowded to the debates ; for days together objections and rejoinders would be hazarded, and every tyro had an opportunity to distinguish himself. The professor himself dealt with the weightier objections, and finally wrote out his judgments, which were copied and distributed as *Quaestiones Quodlibetales*.[1]

Sometimes the debates waxed warm, as when Peckham attacked Aquinas ; but it was Peckham who became excited, while the saint maintained his calm and courtesy. In the evening we are told he would retire to his convent, and " was even more tranquil in his soul than in his words ". Only on one occasion did the fierce blood of his Norman Sicilian ancestors boil over, and that was in his last great conflict with Siger of Brabant, the champion of Averroes—a man who claimed to be orthodox, who was undoubtedly sincere and therefore dangerous.[2] St. Thomas concludes :

> Behold our refutation of the error. It is not based on documents of faith, but on the reasons and statements of philosophers themselves. If anyone there be, who boastfully taking pride in his supposed wisdom, wishes to challenge what we have written, let him not do it in some corner, or before children who are powerless to decide on such difficult matters. Let him reply openly if he dare. He shall find me there confronting him, and not only my negligible self, but many another whose study is truth. We shall do battle with his errors, or bring a cure to his ignorance.[3]

The students at Paris nicknamed Aquinas " The Dumb Ox ", so great was his bulk and so remarkable his taciturnity ; but it will be seen from the above quotation that the Ox could bellow. Otherwise he was not ineptly named. He had the strength of an ox, the patience of an ox, and wide-open contemplative eyes. All through life he was bearing the burden of innumerable

[1] D'Arcy, *Aquinas*, 29.

[2] Siger of Brabant played a great part in the University of Paris. When he was condemned there he appealed to the Pope ; but, before his case could be heard, he was assassinated at Orvieto by his own *clericus* who had gone mad. Dante not only places Siger in Paradise, but makes Aquinas pronounce his eulogy. *Paradiso*, canto x.

[3] Quoted D'Arcy, *Aquinas*, 46. Concerning this controversy, A. E. Taylor, *Phil. Studies*, 232, writes : " On the merits of this controversy it seems to me unmistakeable that the Averroist receives, what is a rare thing in a metaphysical controversy, a direct and crushing defeat, which makes the reading of the Essay a delight to anyone who can appreciate the art of mental warfare ".

doubts as he moved slowly but steadily forward to the vision of God.[1]

II. *From Aquinas to Cusanus*

The following notes are designed to show the different standpoints of the leading schoolmen, and to illustrate their teaching on points that became burning questions at the Reformation. They are also designed to trace how scholasticism which started to reconcile faith and reason, ended by accepting the dictum that what was true in philosophy might be false in theology. Those who acquiesced in such a conclusion confessed that scholasticism had failed.

When St. Thomas Aquinas died in 1274 at the age of forty-eight, his disciples thought that the work had been accomplished. His two great *Summas* were massive and impressive, coherent and apparently conclusive. He had vindicated the Christian faith at the bar of reason, and every objection seemed to have been anticipated and answered. He had done this as an intellectualist who was quite certain " that the end of man is the contemplation of the Truth ".

> And to this end all other activities seem to be directed. For perfect contemplation we require bodily health, which is secured to all by such artificial contrivances as are necessary to life. We require freedom from the perturbations of the passions—a goal obtained by the moral virtues and by prudence. We require freedom from external perturbations—a freedom at which the entire organisation of civil government aims. So if you look at the matter rightly, all human occupations seem to be devoted to the needs of those who contemplate the Truth.[2]

For St. Thomas the contemplative life meant the life of the student. Man's business was to know and to think, but he recognised that in this life man could only approximate to the truth. He confessed that it transcended the capacity of faith and reason alike, while Grace only afforded a partial illumination. Truth would only be realised in the Beatific Vision (*Lumen gloriae*), and even then man's contemplation would not result in comprehension. He would still be a creature of finite capacity in the presence of an infinite God.[3]

[1] There are over 3000 articles in the *Summa Theologica*, and some 10,000 objections are stated and answered.

[2] *Contra Gentiles*, iii. 37.

[3] *Summa*, I. Q. xii. Cp. *Contra Gentiles*, iii. 51, 55.

Meantime on this earth he had two sources of information—God's creation and God's revelation of Himself.[1] Creation could be explored, and assuming One Mind and a rational order, an advance in knowledge might be attained by arguments from analogy. Revelation had to be accepted, then shown to be reasonable, and finally by analogy related to other knowledge. He followed Albertus in separating philosophy from theology; but he believed that in the end knowledge from both sources must agree, for God cannot contradict Himself, or teach in the natural order anything that is inconsistent with His revelation. At the same time he utters a warning to unlearned dogmatists:

> Nothing may be asserted as true that is opposed to the truth of Faith—to revealed dogmas. But neither is it permissible to take whatever we hold as true and present it as an article of Faith, for the truth of our Faith becomes a matter of ridicule among the infidels, if any Catholic, not gifted with the necessary scientific learning, presents as a dogma what scientific examination shows to be false.[2]

He esteemed reason to be man's highest gift, because it enables him to think God's thoughts afresh. He believed in a rational religion, ultimately based on accurate and detailed knowledge, capable of verification by intellectual processes. He viewed with suspicion the intuitions of mystics. He denied that man had any innate ideas.[3] He would have repudiated Newman's *illative sense* and endorsed the axiom of Leibnitz, *Nihil est in intellectu quod non prius fuerit in sensu*.[4] If his eyes were always turned up to heaven, his feet were firmly planted on the earth. In happy phrase, Dr. Kirk calls him "an otherworldly humanist",[5] for while he championed the dignity of man and the natural law, he never doubted that they depend on the supernatural order.

He rejected St. Anselm's[6] ontological proof for the existence of God, being more interested in what man may know than in

[1] *Contra Gentiles*, i. 3-6. In iv. 1 he writes: "There is a threefold knowledge that man may have of divine things. The first is ascent through creatures to the knowledge of God by the natural light of reason. The second is the descent of divine Truth by revelation to us, Truth exceeding human understanding, Truth accepted, not as demonstrated, but as really delivered for belief. The third is an elevation of the human mind to a perfect insight into things revealed."

[2] *De Potentia*, i. Quoted D'Arcy, *Aquinas*, 30.

[3] *Summa*, I. Q. lxxxiv. A. 3.

[4] *Ibid.* III. Q. lx. A. 4.

[5] Kirk, *Vision of God*, 379.

[6] Out of fifteen leading schoolmen of the XIII century, St. Thomas and Richard Middleton alone rejected St. Anselm's argument. Taylor, *Phil. Studies*, 233.

what he cannot imagine. Starting from the world perceived by the senses, he argued for the necessity of a First Cause—the unmoved Mover of the Universe. He argued also from the unity and order of the world to the Universal Mind. No one was more convinced than Aquinas that he lived in a kingdom of ends. All the sciences he ranged in order of dignity according to the ends they have to serve ; all were further related the one to the other ; and all must find their complete explanation in God. For St. Thomas there is a hierarchy of being from God Who is pure Act to the *prima materia* [1] which is mere potentiality, a potentiality which only becomes actual when united with form. Man stands midway on the ladder of God's creation ; below him are the irrational creatures, above him are the celestial hosts. Man is an animal endowed with reason, at the head of the natural order and in touch with the supernatural : the latter he can know partly from revelation and partly by arguments from analogy.[2]

His doctrine of " two worlds " is worked out with great care. He notes that each stage of existence mirrors in some degree what is above it, and reflects further somewhat of the divine nature. He notes also that each higher stage fulfils and completes what was imperfect in the stage below, so that man, aware of his own limitations and incompleteness, can yet conceive of what an angel must be like. With the aid of analogy he can go further in determining stages in the supernatural order, for St. Thomas can imagine no missing rungs in the ladder of existence, no gap as it stretches up to God.

No one was ever more convinced than St. Thomas of the all-pervading power of God, that all things proceed from Him, are sustained by Him, and tend to a perfect end.[3] He was equally

[1] *Matter* (the Aristotelian ὕλη) could neither be seen, handled nor known. Until allied with *Form* it was mere potentiality. *Form* (μορφή) was the principle by which a thing is what it is—apart from *Matter* an idea, combined with *Matter* an actuality.

[2] In the last century it was the fashion to ridicule the angelology of Aquinas. See Lamb's *Works* (ed. Lucas), vi. 117, vii. 816 ; D'Israeli, *Curiosities of Literature*, i. 63-66 ; Seebohm, *Oxford Reformers*, 109-110. In the present century Professor A. E. Taylor, *Phil. Studies*, 246, writes : " The ' this worldly ' and ' the other worldly ' are not juxtaposed, the one is subordinated to the other in virtue of definite guiding principles clearly laid down, and the relations of the superior to the subordinate are made logically transparent. To my mind the clarity which is brought into the treatment of this supreme problem of the Eternal and the Secular is the best proof of all of the genuine originality of the Thomistic thought, and of its perennial significance for all generations of men."

[3] *Contra Gentiles*, iii. 64, 68.

convinced of the freedom of the human will ; that men can rebel against God and are responsible for their actions. He saw that belief in predestination was the inevitable corollary if there is an unchangeable God with a rational purpose and power to accomplish it. He saw also that unless freedom of will is admitted it is impossible to speak of men being virtuous or of God being just.[1] He had the courage to maintain both truths, derived respectively from his metaphysics and his psychology. He tried desperately, but was not altogether successful in reconciling them.

It is easy to understand that though a man is free to will and act, God may overrule what he does and determine the consequences. Judas, for instance, was a traitor and deserved a traitor's doom, though the outcome of his treason was the redemption of the world. A reply is not so easy when someone points out that God was responsible for the being of Judas, foreknew his treason, and might have prevented it, but did not do so. To this St. Thomas would have replied, first, that it was only by the exercise of his free will that Judas could have attained to God, and that therefore had he been deprived of his freedom he would have been a lost soul,[2] punished for a crime he had not committed ; secondly, that though God was responsible for the being of Judas, He was not responsible for his sin which was due to defects in secondary causes.[3] If anyone rejoined, but God is ultimately responsible for the *defects*, St. Thomas answered, " No ! God is the author of all that is, but evil has no real existence. It arises from a defect or privation of good." He went further to justify such privation : " it is even as the silent pause gives sweetness to the chant ".[4] He replied to the question of Boethius, " If there be a God, whence comes evil ? " by saying that the question was wrongly asked, for " there would be no evil if the order of good was removed, the privation of which is evil : and there were no such order of good if there were no God ".[5] This inadequate view of evil as negative he derived from St. Augustine, and he derived from him also an inadequate view of sin as arising from concupiscence, perverted desire, rather

[1] *Ibid.* iii. 73. [2] *Ibid.* iii. 73. [3] *Ibid.* iii. 66, 71.

[4] *Ibid.* iii. 71. Browning expresses the same thought in Abt. Vogler :

The evil is null, is naught, is silence implying sound. . . .
Why else was the pause prolonged, but that singing might issue thence !
Why rushed the discords in, but that harmony might be prized !

[5] *Contra Gentiles*, iii 71.

than from a rebellious will ; and yet St. Thomas is dominated by the thought of law and is emphatic on the virtue of obedience.

Man, he teaches, is under a *Lex Naturalis* which must be obeyed for his own well-being, and for the preservation of society. He goes on to consider positive law,[1] and finds that it is valid when it implements or safeguards the *Lex Naturalis*,[2] and further should be obeyed when it does not contradict it. But man does not only belong to the natural order, but also to the supernatural ; and since the loss of original righteousness, man can only fulfil its obligations by a gift of grace. He does not restrict grace to the fruits of the Incarnation ; for him it is always and everywhere due to God's love for His creatures.[3] In consequence he is not compelled, like Luther and Calvin, to regard fallen humanity as a mass of perdition or to declare that heathen virtues were splendid vices altogether displeasing to God. Grace for him is always a gift, and not something that can be earned or deserved. No one can claim it as a right, and no one can question God's justice when He punishes one and pardons another for the same offence. All have sinned and deserved punishment, and the damned receive no more than they deserve ; but every judge retains the prerogative to pardon ; and so God by punishment makes His justice manifest, and in pardoning reveals His mercy.[4] Being a gift, grace is not irresistible : it can be accepted or declined ; and so he does not fall into the subsequent error of Calvin that men will be saved by a divine fiat in spite of themselves. He guards also against the idea of an arbitrary and capricious Deity when he speaks of grace *de congruo* or even *de condigno*. A gift is none the less a gift, because the giver considers the needs and desires of the recipient. A judge no less shows mercy, because it is the result of compassion for a penitent offender. St. Thomas can allow a degree of merit while he repudiates all idea of desert. Grace for him is the free gift of a God " Who gives more than we desire or deserve ".[5]

Although believing that sin originates in concupiscence,

[1] *Summa*, II. i. Q xciv.
[2] *Ibid*. II. i. Q. xcv. 96.
[3] *Ibid*. III. Q. lxii. A. 1 : " Grace is related to sacraments as genus to species ".
[4] *Expositio in Ep. Divi Pauli*. Rom. ix. Quotations in Sanday and Headlam, *Romans*, I.C.C.
[5] A and B both deserve punishment, but A is penitent and may be pardoned. He receives grace *de congruo*. A and B are both aware of their limitations. A is content but B desires to transcend them. B may receive grace *de condigno*.

there is no Manichean taint in the teaching of St. Thomas. For him man is composed of body and soul, and they are not distinct entities, but related to one another as matter is to form and act to potentiality.[1] As he believed in the unity of God and the unity of nature, so he believed in the unity of man. It followed that a man might not despise his body, or be indifferent to his surroundings. His passions were to be disciplined but not extinguished. St. Thomas believed that generation would have taken place if man had remained in a state of innocence; and the sensible pleasure in marriage would not have been less, "for the purer the nature the greater would have been the sensible pleasure".[2] He knew that it was wicked for men to live upon the level of brutes; he taught that it was presumptuous of men to try to live as if they were angels. Men, like all other creatures, should turn to their Creator, but the best homage they can offer Him is through obedience to the nature with which He has endowed them.[3]

It is not in contradiction of this teaching that St. Thomas, in dealing with ethics, first of all considers the theological virtues of faith, hope and charity. According to him they are only received through an infusion of grace, but for St. Thomas a true humanity is always a God-aided humanity; and this is equally apparent when he deals with the cardinal virtues of prudence, justice, temperance and fortitude, for the *Lex Naturalis* is also of God. In considering the natural virtues he is sometimes said to have incorporated the whole of Aristotle's *Ethics*, but he often transforms the teaching of his master by Christian assumptions; in places he corrects him, and he adds much that he had never dreamed of.[4] Aristotle would indeed have been surprised at the

[1] *Summa*, I. Q. lxxv. A.A. 3, 4. 4; III. Q. ii. A. 1: "Naturae quidem, secundum quod anima unitur corpori, fiat una natura, sicut ex actu et potentia, vel materia et forma". The doctrine so stated involved Aquinas in difficulties especially when considering what happened at death. D'Arcy, *Aquinas*, 209. Harris in *Legacy of the Middle Ages*, 244, writes: "At death the union of *form* and *matter* is dissolved and the individual destroyed. What then of immortality? The soul, says St. Thomas, is a *separable form*, it can continue to exist as an individual without *matter*. Surely a very strange conclusion, and one which directly contradicts the fundamental thesis of Aristotelianism, namely, that the individual which is the real, is the compound of *form* and *matter*. In fact St. Thomas' *anima separata* is a philosophical monstrosity." See further *Summa*, I. Q. lxxxiv. A.A. 3, 7, and I. Q. xc. A. 4. See also Gilson's comments. *Études de philosophie médiévale*, 109-112.

[2] *Summa*, I. Q. xcviii. A. 2.

[3] Kirk, *Vision of God*, 384.

[4] Maritain, *Introd. to Philosophy*, 99, goes so far as to say, "Between Aristotle as viewed in himself and Aristotle viewed in the writings of St. Thomas is the

questions concerning prayer and worship discussed under justice,[1] and he would hardly have consented to the articles on humility.[2] Though St. Thomas finds a place for magnanimity and magnificence, the μεγαλόψυχος [3] is transfigured beyond recognition. There is little in common between the prig solicitous to act in a way becoming his magnificence, and the saint inwardly troubled lest he should prove unworthy of his high vocation as a son of God.

The first part of the *Summa* deals with God and His creatures ; the second part deals with man and his conduct ; and the third part deals with the God-Man, what He has done on our behalf and how He communicates Himself to us through the sacraments of the Church.

St. Thomas believed that the Incarnation [4] would not have taken place had there been no sin. He believed that by sin man had sold himself into bondage and could only be redeemed by sacrifice. Therefore the atonement is central in his theology, and the incarnation is the means by which it was brought about. That atonement is available for us, because through sacraments we become participators of the divine nature ; and because when joined with the Lord as members of His mystical Body the Church, we can offer with Him, our Head, the one sacrifice for the sins of the world.

In treating of the sacraments, he does not use the word *symbols*, consecrated by the use of the Fathers and Victorines. He retains the word *signs*, but is careful to insist that they effect what they signify. He introduces the word *instruments* ; [5] and did not decide the question, since so hotly debated, Are the instruments of grace physical or moral ? [6]

The instruments of grace, he teaches, are of value from the prime agent who uses them, that is God. He illustrates his doctrine by an axe which is suitable for cleaving wood, but unable of itself to do anything apart from the workman. He further distinguishes instruments : they are either joined as the hand is to the body, or separate as a stick. Christ is the united

difference which exists between a city seen by the flare of a torchlight procession, and the same city bathed in the light of the morning sun ".

[1] *Summa*, II. ii. QQ. lxxxi-lxxxiv.

[2] *Ibid.* II. ii. Q. clxi.

[3] *Ibid.* II. ii. QQ. cxxxii-cxxxv.

[4] *Ibid.* III. Q. i. A. 5.

[5] *Ibid.* III. Q. lxii. AA. 1, 3, 5.

[6] A. L. Lilley, *The Sacraments*, 101, 108.

instrument, the sacraments the separable instruments, and so the saving grace of the sacraments is derived from our Lord's Divinity through the human nature which He has assumed.

This idea of instrumentality runs through the whole of the teaching of St. Thomas. For him the whole world was God's instrument. To understand its purpose was his aim ; to be himself used by God was his desire. Grace was one of the means for his enlightenment, a means by which his mind might correspond with God. He looked forward to the marriage gifts of the soul in heaven—vision, comprehension and fruition—and found that they fulfil all that the theological virtues had led to—vision, the reward of faith ; comprehension, the reward of hope ; and fruition, the reward of charity.[1]

St. Thomas though an intellectualist was singularly free from arrogance. He thought so continually of God that he could not but remain humble. Beneath all his passionless reasoning there is but one desire, to face the facts and find the truth. Those who think of him as a logical machine should remember that he wrote the eucharistic hymns in the office for Corpus Christi, and that the *Divine Comedy* of Dante dramatises his theology. The mystics Eckhart and Tauler were nourished on his works, and St. Bonaventura from early manhood was his familiar friend.

St. Bonaventura was three years older than St. Thomas, and for a few months survived him. He represented at its best the Franciscan spirit, as St. Thomas represents at its best Dominican zeal for orthodoxy. For seven years they taught together at Paris ; together they contended with William St. Amour for the rights of the mendicants in the university ; and when the Pope decreed in their favour, they received their long-deferred doctorates on the same day. They were friends who on many points were content to disagree. They never attacked one another ; and Dante was happily inspired when he makes Aquinas in heaven celebrate the sanctity of St. Francis, and Bonaventura the sanctity of St. Dominic.[2]

St. Thomas was an intellectualist and the champion of

[1] *Summa*, Suppl. Q. xcv. A. 5. The compiler of the Supplement derived this from St. Thomas on the *Sentences*. The connexion of hope and comprehension is at first puzzling, but Peter Lombard writes : " Hope is the certain expectation of future bliss, coming from the Grace of God and from preceding merit ". Quoted by Wicksteed in a note on Dante's *Paradiso*, canto xxv.

[2] *Paradiso*, cantos xi., xii.

reason ; St. Bonaventura was a mystic and the champion of faith. St. Thomas regarded the contemplation of truth as the end of man ; St. Bonaventura, love. St. Thomas was an Aristotelian who incorporated in his system much from St. Augustine ; St. Bonaventura [1] was an Augustinian who used the recovered Aristotle with caution and some reserves. St. Thomas remained a student all his life, never becoming even a prior ; St. Bonaventura became General of his Order at a time when the Observants and the Relaxed were in conflict. He was immersed in affairs and had constantly to be travelling. It is amazing how he found time to write as much as he did.

He is the author of lengthy Commentaries on the *Sentences* of Peter Lombard, but is best known as the author of the *Breviloquium* and the *Itinerarium mentis in Deum*. The first was placed by Lord Acton among the hundred best books in the world, but M. Gilson evidently regards the second as its superior.[2] The *Breviloquium* is a handbook of theology and starts with considering God and the Blessed Trinity. It goes on to deal with creation, the corruption caused by sin, the incarnation, the Holy Spirit, the sacraments and the last four things. The *Itinerarium* reverses the process and describes the ascent of the soul to God. Man, being a sinner, can only start on the way by praying for repentance and a spirit of submission to what justice requires. On the first stage of ascent he seeks and finds vestiges of God in the world about him ; in the second stage of ascent by the contemplation of his own soul he seeks and finds the image of God within him ; in the third stage he rises to a direct knowledge of God and becomes a partaker of the Divine Nature, " not supremely in the absolute sense, but supremely in respect to himself ".[3]

He rejects a belief in innate ideas so far as the world of sense is concerned, although he allows for innate habitudes. As regards the other world, he believes that everyone from birth has the witness of God within him ; and, where St. Thomas argues from analogy, he depends upon intuitions.[4] He not only teaches that

[1] Hauréau, *Phil. scholastique*, ii. 219, overstates St. Bonaventura's indifference to the peripatetic philosophy.

[2] Gilson, *La Phil. au moyen âge*, ch. vi., and *Études de phil. médiévale*, 80 ff.

[3] Quoted Evelyn Underhill, *Mysticism*, 131.

[4] Gilson, *Études*, 91.

the certitudes of faith are prior to reason, but that they are superior to it. He teaches as St. Anselm, that man must believe before he can hope to understand.[1] This, he says, is not to depreciate reason, for there is no more profound joy for the soul than to understand what it believes.[2]

St. Bonaventura is equally clear with Hugo of St. Victor[3] that no one can know *what* God is ; but that no one can ignore the fact of His existence. Men are aware of Him by nature, they may learn much *about* Him, and if they require reasonable proof they should find the ontological argument of St. Anselm conclusive. As God is, and all things proceed from Him, all enquiries should start with Him. It is futile to discuss or try to understand what is imperfect and relative apart from some concept of what is perfect and absolute. About God, St. Bonaventura[4] was as certain as St. Paul that " of Him and through Him and to Him are all things " ; and about man's end he is as certain as St. Augustine, *Nata est anima ad percipiendum bonum infinitum, quod Deus est ; ideo eo solo debet quiescere et eo frui.*[5]

In his doctrine of creation he varies from St. Thomas[6] because he cannot believe that the *materia prima* is mere potentiality. If it were, it is difficult to see how it could be related to the God Who is pure act. He believed, in consequence, that it contains *rationes seminales* ; and in consequence he is under no temptation, like St. Thomas, to believe in the eternity of matter. But it is not in these arguments that one perceives the real difference between the two saints. In contemplation of the external world, St. Bonaventura does not think so much of the purpose of things as of their beauty. The world for St. Thomas was a wonderful machine adapted to certain ends, while St. Bonaventura, as a true son of St. Francis, bowed down in rapture because the world in its beauty spoke to him of God.

[1] St. Anselm, *Proslogion*, i. 1.

[2] Gilson, *Études*, 78.

[3] Hugo of St. Victor, *De Sacramentis*, I. iii. 1, quoted by Harris, *Duns Scotus*, ii. 173.

[4] Gilson, *Phil. au moyen âge*, 149.

[5] *In Sent*, i. 3. 2 ; quoted by Gilson, *Études*, 78, and by Harris, *Duns Scotus*, ii. 166. Cp. St. Augustine, *Confessiones*, i. 1.

[6] *Summa*, I. Q. lxvi. A. 1 : " *Creationis enim terminus est in actu. Ipsum autem quod est in actu, est forma. Dicere igitur materiam praecedere sine forma est dicere ens in actu sine actu, quod implicat contradictionem.*" The inference would be that matter without form is uncreated and eternal. St. Thomas would reply that they always co-existed.

In considering the nature of man he disagreed with St. Thomas about its simplicity. He believed that body and soul were alike endowed with matter and form ; and so believing, escaped the difficulty which St. Thomas found in accounting for the soul's survival at death. At the same time, he rejected the platonising theory that the soul is related to the body as a boatman to his boat ; for the body is much more than the instrument of the soul.[1] Man on the earth is a real entity, however composite ; and this belief was possible for St. Bonaventura because, unlike St. Thomas, he recognised the possibility of a plurality of forms.

St. Bonaventura did not contend for the rights of the body in the same way as St. Thomas ; but his real argument is clear, and he strengthens his case by the importance he attributes to the emotions. The body for him was proved to be sacred because the Word had become flesh ; and the human life of Our Lord is the inspiration of all his work. For him Christ is all. He comes down from the Father of Lights, and by His Light makes all things clear. In the body He provided for man's need ; He was and is the infallible mind interpreting the immutable truth which can be summed up in the words—God is Love.

He agreed with St. Thomas when he wrote of the sacraments that " they contain within themselves the healing truth and grace which they present, and in presenting confer what they promise " ;[2] but he did not believe with St. Thomas that they were physical causes of grace. Also he did not regard them so much as divine instruments for the adornment of the soul, as opportunities for divine companionship. This led him to formulate a doctrine which is known as Occasionalism, which regards the sacrament as having no virtue apart from its appointed use, and while being used in the appointed way ; so that a lost Host or a Host consumed by an infidel, would not in any sense be the Body of Our Lord.[3] This theory was silently dropped by the later Franciscans ; but it has been revived to-day by those who deprecate extra-liturgical devotions to the Blessed Sacrament.

St. Thomas and St. Bonaventura each went his own way and

[1] Quotations in Harris's *Duns Scotus*, i. 163.

[2] *Breviloquium*.

[3] Lilley, *Sacraments*, 95. Darwell Stone, *Hist. of the Eucharist*, i. 335, only refers incidentally to this theory.

did not criticise each other. St. Thomas, however, had critics in plenty—Kilwardby, Peckham, Middleton and Duns Scotus, all of them Oxford men. In M. Gilson's phrase, "Oxford came to undo what Paris had done ".[1]

It is difficult to write about Duns Scotus, for practically nothing is known of his life, and there is no accepted canon of his writings—works accepted by Dr. Harris are rejected by M. de Wulf.[2] Neither is there any agreement about the order in which his books were written ; and, as he is not always consistent with himself, there are many points on which it is impossible to ascertain what was his final opinion. He died young, his work unfinished, and it may be that the disciples who systematised his teaching were not always accurate in presenting his thought.

M. Gilson [3] credits him with attempting a synthesis between the Aristotelian and Augustinian schools, but he admits that he was far too original a thinker to prove an ideal mediator. He did not, according to Dr. Minges,[4] differ from St. Thomas as much as has been supposed. Another critic says he was not so much concerned with the doctrines of St. Thomas as with the arguments with which he supported them.[5] But this is not the whole truth. Scotus was doubtless a ruthless logician ; he was also a constructive thinker.

No one will deny that he found weak spots in the armour of St. Thomas ; and, having been trained at Oxford, which was then addicted to mathematics, he had stricter views than St. Thomas as to what constituted a demonstration. Conclusions which St. Thomas claimed to have proved, Scotus regarded as only probable. He went so far as to deny that theology was capable of being a science in the strict sense of the word, but he allowed it to be called a practical science, because theologians pursued a practical end—the knowledge of God. He admitted that theology provided the mind with immutable truths, but they were only known by revelation. He transferred to the domain of the faith such subjects as the omnipotence of God, creation and

[1] Gilson, *Phil. au moyen âge*, 226.
[2] Harris, *Duns Scotus*, i. 361-375 ; De Wulf, *Mediaeval Philosophy*, ii. 70-71.
[3] Gilson, *Phil. au moyen âge*, 225.
[4] Minges, *Cath. Encycl.*, article " Duns Scotus ".
[5] Turner in *Cath. Encycl.*, article "Scholasticism". So Prantl, quoted by Harris, *Duns Scotus*, 269, says : " Duns Scotus and Kant were critics who disputed more or less the arguments for the theorems of natural theology . . . but did not deny the theorems themselves ".

the immortality of the soul. He widened the gap between faith and reason.[1]

Duns Scotus,[2] being a mathematician, was concerned to prove that the conception of infinity was natural and therefore true. He goes on, " if we believe in infinity, there must be infinite being, and an Infinite Being is God ". It is this idea of God's infinity that dominates all his thought. He regretted that he was compelled to use a negative word when speaking of the divine perfections, but human language had no other term to express the transcendence of those finite qualities which we know. He does not seem to have faced the logical difficulty of linking up this conception of God with the finite universe and the finitude of man.

He agreed with St. Bonaventura about creation in time and also about plurality of forms. He also made popular the idea of *formalities*, that is, the correct concepts of those who view an object for a particular reason or from a particular standpoint. As he attributed reality to his multiplied forms and some sort of reality to his formalities, he opened the way for his successors to hypostasise any abstract term—so in time it came to pass that words superseded things, and philosophy tended to become a game of logic, and had no relation to vital thought and the world of experience.

Scotus had no doubt concerning the reality of universals. So he argued that Plato and Socrates agree together more than Socrates and an ass. Socrates, Plato and the ass are numerically the same, but Socrates and Plato have something in common—humanity. Taking this for granted, Scotus is much more concerned with the problem of individualism. Philosophers hitherto had been overmuch concerned with *quidditas*, what a thing is ; Scotus invented the hideous term *haecceitas* to stand for the differentia of particular things. For instance, *Plato is a man*, and mankind is his quiddity ; but if we speak of *this man Plato*, Platonism is his *haecceity*.

Everyone admits that the individual is the real and that all knowledge starts from particulars ; but some are more interested in assigning an object to a class, and some in noting the distinction of the object within the class. Scotus was interested in individuation. He was interested in men as individuals, and this

[1] Minges, *Cath. Encycl.*, and Harris, *Duns Scotus*, i. 90 ff.

[2] Gilson, *Phil. au moyen âge*, 234 ; Harris, *Duns Scotus*, i. 176, 177.

was in line with the importance he assigned to a free will in God and man.

If St. Thomas thought first of truth, and St. Bonaventura of love, Duns Scotus gave the primacy to the will. Will, he maintained, was prior to intellect, which may influence but does not determine it ; as men often act in defiance of their better judgment.[1] If St. Thomas,[2] as some think, in his view of an ordered universe moving to a predestined end, came at times very near to the heresy of Gottschalk, afterwards revived by Calvin, others think that Scotus in his libertarianism approached the forbidden frontiers of Pelagius. Both schoolmen were, however, saved from heresy by the tradition of the Church which holds its creed as an indiscerptible whole, and administers the sacraments which maintain the balance between grace and freedom. In the sacraments grace is given ; it may be accepted and used.

Scotus taught that God's will is perfectly free, though it is impossible to think of Him contradicting Himself. By His will He decrees what is right and what is wrong, and His will is always and everywhere supreme. He states these truths sometimes in such a paradoxical form that morality and goodness seem to be thought of as the result of arbitrary decisions by an irresponsible being.

Man, he maintains, because he is created in God's image, is likewise free. He will not even allow that he is bound by his past —by his habits, circumstances and character. God might, but will not, constrain him. He then reconciles his belief in the universality of divine causation and his belief in the complete freedom of the human will by a reference to God's foreknowledge. Man is free to act and responsible for his actions ; but God from all eternity knew what he would choose to do, and planned human history in the light of that knowledge.[3]

Scotus by his emphasis on individuality and free will was quite unconsciously preparing the way for a revolution. In the Middle Ages society had been stable and unprogressive from its

[1] De Wulf, *Mediaeval Philosophy*, ii. 83.

[2] On pages 304-306 I have admitted the predestinarian views of St. Thomas, but have emphasised also his views on free will, and noted his failure to reconcile them. I gather that the Bishop of Gloucester, *Christian Theology*, 202-205, would agree with me. But there are passages in St. Thomas which, taken alone, would show him a complete determinist. See quotations in N. P. Williams, *Fall and Original Sin*, 404, 405, and in Rashdall, *Idea of Atonement*, 379.

[3] N. P. Williams, *The Fall and Original Sin*, 414-415.

adherence to a few general principles. It had stood for solidarity in thought, faith and institutions ; the world, the Church and man were all regarded as static ; rights and functions were duly determined. An insistence on the incalculable human will led to confusion, change and progress. The time was coming when men could claim the right to think for themselves, and do what they liked ; when they could justify their resistance to authority both in Church and State. No one would have reprobated such conduct more vehemently than Duns Scotus, a man of Franciscan piety. He was scattering seed from which came an altogether unexpected crop.

His theology also had a character of its own. He tended to minimise the Fall. It was due to Adam's inordinate love of Eve and unwillingness to be parted from her. He minimised also its effect : man was not in consequence a mass of perdition, but was only deprived of his supernatural endowments, and they were restored in Christ. The natural man, therefore, living in accord with the law of his being, could still perform acts which merited the divine approval ; and though the heathen and the unbaptized could not enter heaven, he did not regard Limbo as an unattractive place. He thought that there would be no pain or sadness there, and that the inhabitants would still know God through His works and take pleasure in the knowledge.[1]

He did not believe like St. Thomas that, had there been no sin and no need of redemption, there would have been no Incarnation, men attaining to the Beatific Vision in some other way. He taught that God, in creating, intended to perfect His work, and that his work could only attain perfection when it was perfectly united with and perfectly expressed by the Incarnate Word. This involved more than the immanence of God in nature, for men are persons, and the Word had to enter into a personal relationship in order to unite Himself with them, and this began to be realised when the Word became flesh and dwelt among us. The Incarnation, then, is due to the absolute Will of God ; but the manner in which it took place and the cross to which it led may be assigned to God's contingent Will and was determined by the sin of man.[2]

[1] N. P. Williams, *The Fall and Original Sin*, 408 ff. Cp. Rashdall, *Idea of Atonement*, 389.

[2] *Vide* Maynard Smith, *Atonement*, 168. Cp. Westcott, "Gospel of Creation", in his *Epistles of St. John*.

This view of the Incarnation reacted on his teaching about the sacraments. He thought of them first of all as the gifts of a loving God. He came, says Vacant, very near to denying the sacrifice of the Mass, and opened the way for Protestant opinions.[1] At any rate, he distinguished very clearly between the sacrifice of the Cross and the offering made in the Mass. He taught that in the Mass our Lord was passive, and that the offering was made by the Church militant. If this were right, the Church being a finite body, the offering could only have a finite value. Secondly, our Lord being passive in the hands of the Church, the Church could assign the virtue of any celebration to any particular object she desired. This teaching led to a vast multiplication of Masses, and to the abuses connected with "satisfactory" Masses, against which not only Cranmer but Tunstall and Gardiner protested.[2]

If Scotus criticised St. Thomas, they still had much in common. If he widened the gap between faith and reason, it was only in deference to a rigorous logic. He was still loyal to the faith of the schoolman that a synthesis was to be found. William of Ockham, on the other hand, was actively hostile to his predecessors, and even when he accepts the doctrines of Duns Scotus, he presses them to the falsehood of extremes.

The life of William of Ockham has been rewritten of late years from the material provided by modern research. We are now told that he was born in 1300 and not in 1280, so he cannot have been the pupil of Scotus who died in 1308.[3] He was never a Fellow of Merton, but joined the Franciscan Order as a boy, and was lecturing for it in Oxford from 1320 to 1324. He was a Bachelor of Divinity who never became a doctor, which accounts for his being called *Venerabilis Inceptor*. He was not Provincial of his order in 1322. It was William of Nottingham who held that position and distinguished himself at the chapter at Pisa.[4] Ockham never taught in Paris, but in 1324 was summoned to Avignon to answer objections to his lectures on the Sentences. A

[1] Vacant, *Hist. de la conception du sacrifice de la messe*, 49. Cf. Darwell Stone, *Hist. of the Eucharist*, i. 343-344; Kidd, *Later Med. Doctrine of the Sacrifice of the Mass*, 48, 102.

[2] For Tunstall: Burnet, *Reformation*, v. 209. For Gardiner: Dixon, *Ch. Hist.* iii. 263, 264.

[3] De Wulf, *Mediaeval Philosophy*, ii. 176.

[4] William of Nottingham died at Leicester in 1336. He wrote commentaries on the Four Gospels. Bale, *Index Brit. Script.* 140.

cardinal discovered fifty-one errors in his work, but Ockham by his *invincible* logic escaped condemnation. In 1328 he upheld the cause of the *spiritual* friars who were being persecuted by John XXII. He was imprisoned at Avignon but escaped to Pisa, where he approached Louis of Bavaria, saying, *O Imperator, defende me gladio et ego te defendam calamo.*[1] In 1330 he was excommunicated by John XXII, and in 1332 retaliated by exposing the Pope's errors concerning the saints and the Beatific Vision.[2] His book was a success. The University of Paris censured the Pope's teaching; Philip the Fair expostulated with his Holiness; while Louis of Bavaria made it the pretext for invading Italy to depose a heterodox Pope.[3] But in 1334 John XXII died. Ockham spent the last twenty years of his life at Munich in continual controversies, but is supposed to have been reconciled to his order and to the Papacy before he died.[4]

Ockham's opposition to the Papacy began in defence of his order, or rather of a party within it. He was proud to be numbered among the persecuted Fraticelli with their ideal of absolute poverty. It was natural for him to go on and denounce the wealth and temporal power of the Popes, arguing that Christ only gave spiritual jurisdiction to St. Peter, and that St. Peter could confer no more on his successors. Any powers that the Pope had beyond this had been received from human grants or were usurpations acquiesced in by indolent princes.[5] The true source of temporal authority had to be discovered; and Ockham found that the plenitude of power was in the emperor. Finally, he defended Louis of Bavaria when he dissolved, *proprio motu*, the marriage of Margaret Maultasch, heiress of the Tyrol, with John, Prince of Bohemia, and granted her a dispensation to marry his own son in spite of their consanguinity.[6]

[1] The story first appears in Tritheim, *De Scriptoribus Ecclesiasticis*, 1494. See Lane-Poole, *D.N.B.*, article "Ockham".

[2] The importance of the controversy was due to the fact that, had the Pope's views been accepted, the cults of Our Lady and the saints would have had no logical ground. Ockham's book was *De Dogmatibus Papae Johannis XXII*. He subsequently wrote *Compendium Errorum Papae*, making John, who was then dead, responsible for seventy errors and seven heresies.

[3] Creighton, *Papacy*, i. 42.

[4] Asserted by Wadding and Tritheim and denied by Raynaldus. *Vide* Lane-Poole in *D.N.B.*

[5] Creighton, *Papacy*, i. 36. In a fuller discussion of Ockham's views see Lane-Poole, *Illustrations of the Hist. of Med. Thought*, ch. ix.

[6] Creighton, *Papacy*, i. 43, 44.

Ockham, the political thinker, will be of importance when we consider how Henry VIII seceded from the papal obedience, but here it is only necessary to think of him as a schoolman. He hated the abstractions of the Scotists, and his logic had a " razor " edge as he applied the maxim *entia non sunt multiplicanda praeter necessitatem.*[1] He even denied that the concept of cause had any reality outside the mind. For him the individual thing was alone real. It was to be observed, analysed and tested without any preconceptions ; and so he may be considered as the prophet of modern science.

He introduced a moderate nominalism ; but while denying the reality of universals, he admitted their convenience when thinking. Humanity, for instance, may not exist, but it is useful to have a concept of it when an unknown man is mentioned. Such concepts he called *terms*. They were not arrived at by acts of intelligence, but were due to a confused memory of repeated sensations. As only the individual is real, these composite pictures of a decaying memory were very far removed from reality ; and bewildered opponents complained that he had made it impossible to demonstrate the existence of the external world or the being of God.[2]

Though observed facts alone had any reality, *terms* were necessary if observed facts were to be discussed ; but as the terms were only hypothetical, all argument was *ex supposito*. Granted an hypothesis, Ockham was prepared to attack or defend it, and to deduce all the consequences of holding it ; but the discovery of a new fact might necessitate the finding of a new term, and the process would have to begin all over again. The only thing he never doubted was the validity of his own logic ; and in logic his adversaries found him invincible.

As terms only originated in the memory of sensations, the supra-sensible was beyond the scope of the human intellect, and man, apart from revelation, was incapable of knowing anything of God. For Ockham the ordered universe of St. Thomas was dissolved, the arguments from analogy had no meaning, and the scheme of Natural Theology had collapsed. Ockham transferred all the articles of religion to the province of faith, and regarded the gulf between religion and science as fixed and impassible.

[1] The famous " razor " is not to be found *totidem verbis* in his works.

[2] De Wulf, *Mediaeval Philosophy*, ii. 238.

He accepted the dictum of his friend Jean de Jandun,[1] " what is true in philosophy may be false in theology " ; but those who accepted this doctrine of the " two truths " were bound to confess that scholasticism had failed.

Ockham's position, whatever we may think of it, is at least intelligible. There were facts that suggested hypotheses to the natural philosopher, and he should ponder them apart from extraneous considerations, and be free to follow the argument where it led. There were other facts which had been revealed, and the theologian was free to interpret them, and assert as true any doctrines which could be deduced from them. He was, though he did not know it, opening the door to much superstition.

Ockham declared that revelation was infallible, and by revelation he meant Holy Scripture and the mind of the Church. As, however, he maintained that Popes had erred, Councils had erred, the Fathers had erred, and the Doctors of the Church had erred, it must remain doubtful how he thought the infallible mind was to be discovered. This is of less importance as he says elsewhere, " Whatever the Church of Rome believes, this alone and nothing different I believe either explicitly or implicitly ".[2] He professes his faith in all the articles of the creed, in transubstantiation, in the immaculate conception of the Blessed Virgin, in the miracles and cults of the saints. All these doctrines he thinks can be clearly deduced from the revelation he has accepted ; but he adds, they cannot be demonstrated by man, and are in themselves so highly improbable that men restricted to reason would pronounce them false.

With his dislike for general laws and pronounced individualism, he conceives of God as an entirely arbitrary being.

[1] For Jean de Jandun see Gilson, *Études de phil. méd.* 364. Unfortunately, the dictum of Jean de Jandun became a commonplace among educated men, and enabled them to express belief in endless superstitions that their reason rejected. Rastell, *Gentleness and Nobility*, makes a plea for reason in argument with opponents :

> " Then they will alege some auctoryte
> Of the lawes or elles of devynite
> Whiche in no wyse men may denye,
> And yet knowe well that of phylozophy
> The pryncyples oft contraryant be
> Onto the very grounds of devynite."

Quoted A. W. Reed, *Early Tudor Drama*, 109.

[2] Quoted Darwell Stone, *Hist. of Eucharist*, i. 364.

Man's morality, he believes, had no justification beyond the divine fiat ; and God made acts good and evil as He chose. He could conceive of God saving the wicked, damning the Blessed Virgin, or commanding men to hate Himself. He accepted the Incarnation. God became man, but he thought that He might, had he chosen, just as well have become an ox or a log.[1] He thought very clearly on the supremacy of God's Will, but not so clearly on the divine character, and still less about how far human nature reflects the divine image.

On transubstantiation he writes :

> The substance of bread and wine ceases to be, and the accidents alone remain, and under them the Body of Christ begins to be. This is clear to the Church by some revelation as I suppose, and therefore the Church has so decided.

But he goes on that—

> the substance of bread and wine might remain in the same place, while under the same species is the Body of Christ, is very reasonable though the Church has decided against it.[2]

That is consubstantiation, and we wonder if Martin Luther was indebted to William of Ockham for the suggestion. He was certainly brought up on Ockham's works, and at times proclaimed himself an Ockhamist.[3]

There are other things that Luther may have learnt from Ockham in the Ockhamist university of Erfurt. One is his belief in " the Godly Prince ", and another is his belief that the Church had no authority in secular affairs. From Ockham he may have learnt to separate religion from worldly learning, though Ockham would not have countenanced his contempt for the latter. From Ockham he may have learnt that faith does not come by reasoning, but has its source in the Holy Scriptures and the mind of the Church. Luther accepted the Holy Scriptures and failing to discover the mind of the Church, found the witness to the faith in his own heart, which led him to propound the comfortable doctrine of assurance which Aquinas had foreseen and denied.[4]

[1] *Centiloquium Theologicum*, Conclusions v. and vi. Quotations in Rashdall, *Idea of Atonement*, 388.

[2] Quoted Darwell Stone, *Hist. of Eucharist*, i. 364.

[3] For Luther's Ockhamist education see Boehmer, *Luther*, and Fife, *The Young Luther*.

[4] *Summa*, I. Q. xxiii. A. 1.

It was, however, Gabriel Biel, " the last of the scholastics ",[1] whom Luther learnt almost by heart and subsequently learnt to hate. Biel died at Tubingen in 1495, and is chiefly remembered for his exaggerated views on the sacrifice of the Mass and the restricted value that he placed on the sacrament of penance. He was also a pioneer in the study of political economy. Long before he died, new knowledge and a new outlook were causing men to grope after a new reconciliation between science and theology; and Nicholas of Cusa stands midway between the Aristotelian renaissance of the XIII century and that pagan renaissance which is sometimes called the rediscovery of the world.

Nicholas [2] was born in 1401 at Cues in the diocese of Treves, the son of a prosperous boatman. He went to school at Deventer, where, like Thomas à Kempis and Erasmus, he was taught by the Brethren of the Common Life. He afterwards studied at Heidelberg, Padua and Cologne, and graduated in both law and theology. He went to the Council of Basle, attached to the family of Cardinal Caesarini, and wrote *De Concordantia Catholica* which became the text-book of the reforming party.[3] He afterwards seceded to the Pope; and, according to Aeneas Sylvius, became " the Hercules of the Eugenists ". He was then sent to Constantinople to heal the schism between East and West. On his return he accompanied the Greeks to Ferrara and played a leading part at the Council of Florence. He was more than once a legate in Germany and encountered much opposition in his attempts to reform the monasteries. He was made a cardinal by Nicholas V, and Bishop of Brixen. In administering his diocese he became involved in a quarrel with Sigismond, Count of Tyrol, who seized him, shut him up in prison, and permanently ruined his health by ill-treatment. Pius II excommunicated the Count, who, however, only made his submission after the Cardinal's death. Nicholas died at Todi in 1464, while actively assisting Pius II in his proposed crusade against the Turks.

[1] For Biel's Life see *Catholic Encycl.* For his views on the Eucharistic Sacrifice see Darwell Stone, *Hist. of Eucharist*, i. 388-391, who quotes passages which show how far he was in line with Catholic tradition; and Kidd, *Later Mediaeval Theories of the Sacrifice of the Mass*, who quotes passages at variance with the best traditions.

[2] Nicholas of Cusa. For his life see *Catholic Encyclopaedia*, Pastor: *History of Popes*, ii. 104-137. Scattered references in Creighton, *Papacy*, and Gregorovius, *Rome in the Middle Ages*.

[3] For an admirable account of the *Concordantia* see Figgis, *From Gerson to Grotius*, 58-60.

In the intervals of his busy life he composed many books on law, theology and mysticism—on grammar and on mathematics. He knew Greek, Hebrew and some Arabic, and was in close correspondence with the humanists of the Italian Renaissance. The more he knew the more he was convinced of how much was still unknown ; and he had no respect for systems which claimed to explain God and the universe on an inadequate basis of facts. He distrusted the syllogistic method, and did not believe that any advance in knowledge could be made by logic. In his *Docta Ignorantia* he maintained that the right attitude of man to God and the universe was one of *wonder* ; and that only those who waited patiently in the darkness would receive light. He believed that men arrived at understanding not by a process of reasoning but by an immediate intuition which God vouchsafed to the humble. He demonstrated that though reason cannot tolerate contradictions, contradictions or rather opposites everywhere abounded. He assumes that these *coincidentia oppositorum* will find their reconciliation in God. For him God is the Infinite, the One and All. He enfolds all things in Himself and unfolds Himself in all things. This is perilously near to Pantheism, but he escaped from it because his conception of infinity was apart from space. He argued that longer or shorter, more or less, were irrelevant in considering infinity ; and that mind occupied no point in space. In consequence God may be identified with the absolute maximum or the lowest possible minimum. There is further no logical separation between a finite being spatially conceived and an infinite being conceived as an idea. For Nicholas as for Plato it was the idea which was real. In this way the incarnation may be understood—how in Jesus dwelt the fullness of the Godhead bodily.[1]

As a mathematician and astronomer[2] he is memorable in the

[1] I have relied on de Wulf, *Mediaeval Philosophy*, and E. F. Jacob, *Bulletin of the John Rylands Library*, xiv. No. 2. The best book on the subject is apparently Van Steenberghe, *Le Cardinal de Cusa*.

[2] Nicholas of Cusa was not only a mathematician but was fond of illustrating his theological works by mathematical paradoxes. Being a practical man he was much concerned with the reform of the Calendar, just as his rival Regiomontanus, also a practical man, is best remembered for his *Ephemerides*, the first nautical almanac. As an astronomer Nicholas maintained that the earth was one of the stars and was not the centre of the universe, that the poles were not fixed, but that the earth revolved daily, and was otherwise in continual movement. He also discovered that the orbits of the planets were not circular, and in other ways anticipated Copernicus, who was born nine years after his death. Leonardo da Vinci had a great admiration for

history of science, as a mystic he had much in common with Pascal and Malebranche; as a speculative thinker he may be compared to Hegel;[1]—but all his books were written with a view to his own age. He loved the rediscovered classics and the monuments of ancient art; he was at home in the court of Nicholas V, and associated with scholars like Poggio and Lorenzo Valla. He noted the dangers of the reviving paganism, and tried to claim the New Learning for Christ. He was only too conscious that the degenerate Thomists and Scotists of his day made no appeal to the scholars and poets. He believed that a new synthesis might be found in studying the works of the Neo-Platonists and Dionysius the Areopagite. He failed in his immediate object because the humanists, intoxicated with the rediscovery of this world and its beauty, had no time to think of another and no interest in metaphysics or religion. He founded no sect, but select souls were inspired by his writings; and the tradition of his teaching survived. Le Fevre edited his works and published them in France. In England, Grocyn, Colet and More may be thought of as his disciples, even though they only knew him through later men like Ficino and Pico da Mirandola.

III. *Oxford and Scholasticism*

Scholasticism was cosmopolitan and its disputes were current throughout Europe. Men travelled from university to university, vagabonds of learning, and it was said that "Sundry schools make subtle clerks".[2] Bohemian scholars of Oxford carried Wyclif's works to Prague and Vienna; and Filargo, a native of Candia in Crete, after studying in Italy and in Paris, graduated

his mathematical treatises, and much later Giordano Bruno spoke of him as "the divine Cusanus". It is noteworthy that Nicholas was the friend of three Popes and that Giordano Bruno was burnt in the Piazza dei Fiori at Rome in 1600. Freedom of thought had suffered a check through the Reformation.

[1] Von Hügel, *Mystical Element in Religion*, ii. 331.

[2] Chaucer, *The Merchant's Tale*. Barclay in his version of *The Ship of Fools* did not agree (i. 145):

"One rennyth to almayn another unto fraunce
To parys [Paris], padway [Padua], Lumbardy or Spayne;
Another to Bonony [Bologna], Rome or Orleance;
To Cayne [Caen], to Tolous, Athenys or Colayne [Cologne];
And at the last retourneth home agayne
More ignorant, blynder and gretter folys
Then they were when they first went to the scolys."

as a Bachelor of Theology at Oxford. He subsequently became Archbishop of Milan and Pope Alexander V.[1]

Throughout the scholastic period Paris was the centre from which knowledge of theology and philosophy radiated ; but few of the great schoolmen were Parisians and many of them came from England. Fuller boasts, " If Britain first received her Christianity from Rome, Italy received her school divinity from Britain " ; and he justifies the brag by quoting Alexander Minutianus, *Scholastica Theologia ab Anglis et in Anglia sumpsit exordium, fecit incrementum, pervenit ad perfectionem.*[2] The consideration of the following list affords some reason for his contention.

Alexander of Hales, *Doctor Irrefragibilis* (*d.* 1245),[3] was a Prebendary of St. Paul's and Archdeacon of Coventry before he became a Franciscan friar and went to teach theology in Paris. There he wrote his vast *Summa*, which Roger Bacon said weighed as much as a horse ".

Robert Grossetête (*d.* 1253), Bishop of Lincoln and Chancellor of Oxford, "was", said Bacon, "an expert in all sciences". He knew some Greek and Hebrew, translated *The Testaments of the Twelve Patriarchs*,[4] and supervised the first translation from the Greek of Aristotle's *Ethics*.

Adam de Marisco, *Doctor Illustris* (*d.* 1257), was a Franciscan and a great friend of Grossetête.[5] He spent most of his life in Oxford. Roger Bacon says " He was perfect in all wisdom ".

Roger Bacon, *Doctor Admirabilis* (1214–1294), was a Franciscan often in trouble with the authorities of his own order. He was imprisoned by them for long periods, but protected by

[1] Filargo, Pope 1409–1410. Gregorovius, *Rome in the Middle Ages*, vii. 606 ff. Henry IV addressed a letter to him reminding him of his studies in Oxford. Maxwell-Lyte, *Oxford*, 301. For an account of his scholastic views, de Wulfe, *Med. Phil.* ii. 196-198.

[2] Fuller, *Ch. Hist.* III. vii. 15. Aldus, who hated the schoolmen, in publishing Linacre's edition of *The Sphere* by Proclus, hoped that he might receive more works of the same value from England, " whence formerly there had issued a barbarous and rude literature which threatened the Italian sanctuary of knowledge ". Quoted by Einstein, *Italian Renaissance in England*, 37.

[3] Roger Bacon denied that Hales himself wrote the *Summa. Opus Minus*, 326. Quoted by de Wulf, i. 346 footnote.

[4] It was brought to England from Greece by John of Basingstoke.

[5] De Wulf, *Med. Phil.* i. 259, is probably wrong in thinking that he first taught in Paris. See dates of his life in *D.N.B.*

more than one Pope, though not by the Franciscan Nicholas IV. His life was passed in Oxford and Paris.

Robert Kilwardby, Archbishop of Canterbury and afterwards Cardinal Bishop of Porto (*d.* 1279), taught in Paris and Oxford. Though a Dominican he opposed St. Thomas Aquinas. His *De Ortu* is said to be the most remarkable book of the Middle Ages on the classification of the sciences.[1]

John Peckham, Archbishop of Canterbury (*d.* 1292), was a Franciscan educated at Oxford. He taught in Paris, Oxford and Rome. Such was his reputation that the cardinals uncovered in his presence. He opposed St. Thomas in Paris and caused his works to be censured at Oxford.[2]

Richard Middleton, *Doctor Solidus* (*fl.* 1280), was a Franciscan educated at Oxford. He spent most of his life at Paris and died at Toulouse. Duns Scotus is said to have been his pupil.

Duns Scotus, *Doctor Subtilis* (1263–1308), was a Franciscan educated at Oxford. He taught in Oxford, Paris and Cologne.

William of Ockham, *Venerabilis Inceptor* (1300–1349), was a Franciscan who taught in Oxford and Avignon. He spent the last twenty years of his life at Munich.

Walter Burley, *Doctor Perspicuus* (1275–1345), was a secular priest who went from Oxford to Paris and from Paris to Oxford. He was a pupil of Duns Scotus and a friend of Ockham, but subsequently attacked them both. He was the one schoolman with pretensions to an elegant style.

John Baconthorpe, *Doctor Resolutus* (*d.* 1346), was a Carmelite who taught chiefly in Oxford, though he visited Paris and Rome. In the latter place he was not well received. He defended the philosophy of Averroes against the Thomists and tried to show that it was capable of a Christian interpretation.

Richard FitzRalph, Chancellor of Oxford and Archbishop of Armagh (*d.* 1360), was the friend of Baconthorpe and shared his enthusiasm for Averroes. He was an opponent of the Franciscans and went to Avignon to denounce them.

Thomas Bradwardine, *Doctor Profundus* (1290–1349), taught in Oxford. He was the foremost mathematician of his

[1] De Wulf, *Med. Phil.* i 392. Gilson, *Études de phil. méd.* 120, says that in 1277 he condemned thirty propositions drawn from the works of St. Thomas.

[2] For explanations of the dissent of Peckham and Kilwardby see Gilson, *Études de phil. méd.* 109-122, and Tout, *St. Thomas in History*, Manchester Lectures, 23-25.

age. He revived Augustinian views of Grace in an extreme form.

Robert Holcot (*d.* 1349) was a Dominican and friend of Bradwardine. He wrote on scholastic subjects and also commentaries. De Wulf reckons him among the Ockhamists, but on many points he disagreed with his master.[1]

John Wyclif, *Doctor Evangelicus* (1324–1389), wrote on logic, metaphysics, ethics and theology, and after being the glory of Oxford, was the cause of her decline as a home of sound learning.

No other nation in Europe during the XIII and XIV centuries produced so many distinguished thinkers.[2] Besides those mentioned above, it was Haymo of Feversham who transferred the little Franciscan school at St. Denis to Paris where it became so famous.[3] William of St. Giles, another Englishman, was the first Dominican doctor in Paris. Peter the Irishman taught Aquinas in Naples. Albertus Magnus repeatedly acknowledged his indebtedness to Hales, whom St. Bonaventura called *Magister et Pater*.[4]

While most of these schoolmen taught in Paris at some time or other, Oxford claimed to be the equal of that university, and strove to convince the world of the fact. In 1318 Edward II wrote to John XXII that Oxford was an older university than Paris, and that Paris owed its origin to Oxford scholars.[5] Such was the belief in England, but it was not well founded. In 1322 the chancellor of Oxford maintained before the Pope that his university was no whit inferior to Paris; but he failed to secure for her equal privileges. Richard de Bury, a man of letters rather than a schoolman, was certain about the superiority of Oxford; and he knew both universities well. He concludes:

Minerva deserted Athens for Rome. Then, having given the slip to the Parisians, she has at last happily reached Britain, the most

[1] Holcot, now so little known, had once a European reputation. His scholastic works were published at Lyons in 1505.

[2] Haymo. See Little in *Cam. Med. Hist.* vi.

[3] Peter the Irishman. See De Wulf, *Med. Phil.* ii. 3. Michael Scot and also Alfred the Englishman had also been prominent at the court of Naples when Aquinas was an infant.

[4] De Wulf, *Med. Phil.* i. 363. In 1165 Clement IV nominated St. Bonaventura to the See of York, but he declined the honour. *Cath. Encycl.*

[5] Maxwell-Lyte, *Oxford*, 97. The idea that the University of Paris developed out of the Palace School presided over by Alcuin is exploded. Cf. Rashdall, *Universities*, i. 273.

renowned of islands, or rather the microcosm, that she may show herself indebted to Greeks and Barbarians.[1]

There was a temporary decline in numbers at Paris in the middle of the XIV century,[2] probably owing to wars and tumults ; but by the end of the century she was once more supreme under the great chancellors Pierre d'Ailly and Gerson. Paris played a great part in Europe throughout the Conciliar period, while Oxford dwindled in numbers and reputation. It is true that at Constance, Robert Hallam, Bishop of Salisbury, who had once been chancellor of Oxford, was the right-hand man of the Emperor Sigismund ; but he represented his king and not his university. He is reported to have said that John XXIII ought to be burnt for his iniquitous life, and that John Huss ought not to be burnt for his heretical opinions.[3] At Basle and Florence Oxford was not represented and had ceased to count.[4]

There is no doubt that in the XV century Oxford declined in numbers, though no reliance can be placed on mediaeval statistics. William of Rishanger [5] states that in the reign of Henry III there were 15,000 students in Oxford. In 1357 FitzRalph told the Pope that in his young days there had been 30,000 students and that they had been reduced to 6000.[6] A generation later Wyclif wrote that there had been 60,000 students and were only 3000.[7] These estimates are alike ridiculous —the men of the Middle Ages could not count, but the state-

[1] Richard de Bury, *Philobiblon*, ch. ix. Lane-Poole, *D.N.B.*, states that Holcot, Bradwardine and FitzRalph had all been members of his " family ".

[2] Rashdall, *Universities*, ii. 586, quoted from the Paris Chartulary, " *nimium est illa scholarium multitudo contracta et Parisiense studium incredibiliter diminuatum* ".

[3] Milman, *Latin Christianity*, viii. 250, 263, 299. At an earlier date Hallam was largely responsible for the election of Alexander V. Capes, *Ch. Hist.* 165.

[4] Oxford was invited to send theologians to Basle, but declined on the score of expense. Eugenius IV invited them to Ferrara, but the English bishops refused to contribute anything to help a poor university. Brodrick in Clark's *Oxford Colleges*, 162, writes that Abenden was Oxford's representative at Constance, but Anthony à Wood was unaware of the fact. He also states that Kemp, afterwards Archbishop of Canterbury, represented the university at Basle. The *D.N.B* tells us that Kemp was appointed to represent the king, and did not go. Kemp's movements are well known and his visit to Basle is impossible. John Langdon and Thomas Brown, successively bishops of Rochester, did represent England at the Council. *V.C.H. Kent*, ii. 59.

[5] Rishanger, *Chronicon*, Camden Soc. 22.

[6] FitzRalph, *Defensorium Curatorum*.

[7] Wyclif, *De Ecclesia* (Loserth's ed.), 374.

ments are very good evidence for a decline in numbers.[1] The Black Death would account for a great falling-off in Wyclif's day, but there was no increase afterwards. In 1438, according to a petition of the University of Oxford, there were but 1000 students, and for this no doubt Lollardy was in part responsible.[2]

We do not know the truth about the famous letter of October 1406, vouching for the orthodoxy of Wyclif.[3] Huss produced it at Constance with the University seal attached. The adventurous Peter Payne [4] may have stolen the University seal and forged the letter, as Gascoigne afterwards asserted; [5] or, as Maxwell-Lyte suggests,[6] it may have been the result of a snap vote obtained during the long vacation; but anyhow, it implicated Oxford in Lollardy. In consequence the prudent and the pious may have sent their sons to Cambridge; and it is certain that during the XV century, Cambridge, from being a university of no importance, grew to equal Oxford in numbers, and perhaps to surpass her in reputation.[7]

Wyclif, by leaving the schools for the market-place, had convinced the world that ideas might be dangerous, and the world in self-defence sought to suppress them. As early as February 1397, the Southern House of Convocation complained of the heresies freely preached at Oxford; and Archbishop Arundel announced his intention of "visiting" the University. He had instead himself to go into exile, and the Lollards enjoyed a breathing-space. Reinstated by Henry IV, Arundel held a Provincial Council at Oxford, which condemned the Wyclifite Bible, and ordained that no book hereafter should be read in any college or hall until it had been examined and approved by twelve delegates appointed by the Archbishop, and that no copy of the said book should be sold until it had been collated with the approved MS., which was to be kept in the University chest.

[1] On the whole question see Rashdall, *Universities*, ii. ch. xiii.

[2] Wilkins, *Concilia*, iii. 528. Mallet, *Oxford*, i. 139, quotes from *Epistolae Academicae*, 156. He also notes how Mr. Salter believes that, omitting choir boys and servants, the number was only 620: undergraduates 300, bachelors 100, regents 70, non-regents 150. The University, however, included everyone from the Yellow-Beak, aged ten, to the grey-beard aged seventy. It also included cooks, servants, scribes, parchmenters, bookbinders and the families of students. Wylie, *Henry IV*, iii. 407, produces evidence for students arriving with wives and families.

[3] Wilkins, *Concilia*, iii. 36.

[4] Peter Payne. See *D.N.B.*

[5] Gascoigne, *Loci e Libro Veritatum*, 20.

[6] Maxwell-Lyte, *Oxford*, 280.

[7] Rashdall, *Universities*, ii. 522, 523.

Convocation desired the University to appoint twelve masters to examine Wyclif's works. The University at first refused, but Arundel insisted, with the result that the appointed censors by a large majority discovered 267 errors. Then all scholars, graduates and undergraduates were made to swear that they would forsake such errors, and a great bonfire was made at Carfax of Wyclif's works.[1] In 1411 Arundel again gave notice that he could "visit" the University; but the University pleaded that it was exempt from his jurisdiction by a Bull of Boniface IX. None the less, Arundel came to Oxford; and the proctors, Byrche and Brent, barred St. Mary's against him. He proclaimed an interdict which was disregarded; and the students with arms pressed into the streets, so that the Archbishop and his followers were compelled to withdraw. He then appealed to the King, who summoned the chancellor and proctors to London and ordered them to resign. They did so, but the regents of the University promptly re-elected them. The Prince of Wales, afterwards Henry V, then intervened, and in the end the University was forced to submit.[2]

It was inevitable that Oxford should cease to be a cosmopolitan university and should become a national institution; but the date of the change may be fixed as 1411, when Arundel triumphed. It is true that in 1479 Sixtus IV renewed the Bull of Boniface IX which Parliament had declared invalid, and John XXIII had revoked;[3] but his action came too late. It did not even occasion a protest, as it had no effect, for Oxford by that time was the faithful and obedient servant of Church and King. Her chancellors were no longer elected to guard her liberties against the Bishop of Lincoln, but were for the most part people of importance, living elsewhere, and not particularly interested in her internal concerns. Her degrees no longer had a European repute, as too often they were conferred by "graces" in obedience to royal commands. Freedom of thought had been stamped out. No longer could Averroists like FitzRalph and Baconthorpe startle respectable ecclesiastics; no longer could a Wyclif trouble statesmen by indiscreet speculations on the social fabric. If Oxford was still to provide a home for sound learning it was on condition that she should discipline with severity her

[1] Maxwell-Lyte, *Oxford*, 294. [2] Mallet, *Oxford*, i. 238, 239.
[3] Maxwell-Lyte, *Oxford*, 325.

more original sons. In such an atmosphere, theology and philosophy became more and more academic ; and when the Reformation came there were no scholars of the Old Learning who could appeal to the people in a language that they understood.

If Oxford in the time of her decay produced no great thinkers neither did Cambridge in the days of her growth. In the first three-quarters of the XV century she was content to stand in the old ways ; and this is clear from the library catalogues which have survived at Peterhouse, Trinity Hall, Pembroke, Queens' and St. Catherine's.[1] They possessed the works of St. Anselm, Albertus Magnus, Aquinas, Hales, Bonaventura, Boethius, Duns Scotus, Burley, Holcot, Langton, John of Salisbury, Grossetête and Richard Middleton. They had also FitzRalph's attack on the Franciscans and Woodford's reply. The four Latin Doctors, SS. Ambrose, Augustine, Jerome and Gregory, were represented by some of their works. They had also some of the Victorines, and the Commentaries of Nicholas of Lyra. They had no Greek books, no Latin books of the Golden Age, only one treatise of Avicenna, and very few books on Logic. Light literature was represented by the rhyming chronicles of Layamon, and Richard of Gloucester, which were recited round the fire in college halls on festival nights.[2]

The general check to intellectual progress was not entirely due to the ecclesiastical dread of heresy. The Statute of Provisors of 1390 had had unforeseen results.[3] It had been passed to prevent the Pope from bestowing lucrative benefices on non-resident foreigners ; but the Pope had also been wont to provide for scholars, and the universities had forwarded to him year by year a list of those deserving promotion. Kings, nobles and other patrons bestowed their livings on friends and dependants, or on people useful to themselves ; [4] and scholars naturally complained

[1] Mullinger, *Cambridge*, i. 325.

[2] So at Oxford, William of Wykeham in his statutes for New College permitted, on festivals and winter nights, when there was a fire in hall, fellows to indulge in singing, or reading " poems, chronicles of the realm and wonders of the world ". Clark, *Oxford Colleges*, 158.

[3] There had been previous Acts of Provisors in 1357 and 1365.

[4] Barraclough, *Papal Provisions*, 145 : " In some cases where a bishop had not as much patronage as he desired, he asked the pope to provide for people whom he nominated ". P. 171 : " Many a bishop was willing to dispose of his rights to the benefices within his jurisdiction, in favour of the pope, if only to avoid the pressure of the magnates and royal officials ". P. 45 : " It must be emphasised that the pope did not usually interfere with livings in lay patronage, although in canonical theory

when they found themselves debarred from preferment.[1] In 1392 and 1404 graduates were exempted from the statute, the Commons declaring that the non-advancement of scholars led to heresies in respect to God and to rebellion against the king. This exemption did not benefit the universities, for the Pope naturally refused to oblige Parliament so long as the "execrable" statute limiting his prerogative was in force.[2] In 1417 the warden of New College persuaded Convocation to decree that benefices over 60 marks in annual revenue should be reserved for doctors, and those worth 50 marks a year were to go to licentiates in law or medicine, or to bachelors in theology. To prevent evasion those who received their degrees "by grace" were not to be eligible. Unfortunately all matters of advowson and patronage were within the purview of the common law,[3] and the vote of Convocation only registered a pious opinion of what ought to be.

But if scholars had nothing to hope for in England if they studied theology, the same thing was true in other countries. Aeneas Sylvius said, "Only Justinian and Hippocrates fill the purse". A XV century vocabulary says, "*Theologia est animae pabulum, leges sunt egenis remedium*"; while one of the *Obscure Men* quotes:

> Dat Galienus opes et sanctio Justiniani,
> Ex aliis paleas, ex istis collige grana.[4]

The complaint indeed had been heard long before the Statute of Provisors. Roger Bacon had written:

they fell within the plenitude of his power". This fact is illustrated by a story told by Watson, *Cam. Med. Hist.* vi. 557. Robert Thweng, a northern knight, when a foreigner was intruded into his living at Upleatham, raised a riot, burned the barns of alien ecclesiastics and gave their goods to the poor. Henry III sent him to Rome, and Gregory IX acknowledged his claim to the patronage, and deprived the intruder.

[1] Hocclere, *Regement of Princes*, 190:

> "Worthy clerks famous
> In Oxford and Cambridge also
> Stonde unadvanced. Whereas the vicious
> Favelle hath churches and prebends mo
> Than God is pleased with."

For the shameless abuse of patronage and simony see Gascoigne, 2, 20, 49, 208.

[2] Capes, *Ch. Hist.* 169 and 172.

[3] Maitland, *Canon Law*, 62, 63, etc.

[4] These quotations are derived from Stokes' edition of the *Epistolae Obscurorum Virorum*, 170. There is a better reading of the verse: *Dat Justinianus honores.*

Every man of superior talent, possessing an aptitude for theology and philosophy, betakes himself to Civil Law, because he sees its professors enriched and honoured by all prelates and princes.

Holcot maintained that the civilians looked down on the theologians as Hagar looked down on her barren mistress; while Richard de Bury, who as a Prince Bishop had little to complain of personally, defied the lawyers, who might be the friends of the world, but were certainly the enemies of God.[1]

The fear of heresy, the Statute of Provisors and the lucrative study of the law all contributed to the decline of theology, but these causes were not so important as the nature of the theology taught. By the XV century the inspiration of scholasticism was exhausted. Through the dissidence of the sects it had decayed.

IV. *Decline of Scholasticism*

There had been a time when a Pope consulted Hales as an oracle; when St. Louis sat at the feet of Aquinas, and the courtiers of Charles of Anjou flocked to his lectures in Naples; when cardinals unbonneted in the presence of Peckham; when Baconthorpe, seeking glory, challenged all disputants in Rome and was discomfited; when the dialectical triumphs of Duns Scotus were the talk of Europe—but in the XV century scholasticism was out of touch with the spirit of the age; and the schoolmen wrangled among themselves, while nobody cared.

In the XIII century thought had been free for all who accepted the creed; but in the XV century thought was no longer free, because the later schoolmen were in bondage to their predecessors. The great schoolmen in one sense had been only too successful. They had become authorities to be studied and not criticised—that is to say, not criticised by their disciples; for each of them was hailed as the founder by a sect which strove for victory; and no sect sought for or desired to discover the reconciling truth.

In 1287 the Dominicans in a General Chapter decreed that all their friars should promote and defend the writings of St. Thomas Aquinas, and that those who failed to do so should not be allowed to teach.[2] In consequence, while Dominicans remained

[1] These quotations are derived from Mullinger, *Cambridge*, i. 214.

[2] Little, *Cam. Med. Hist.* vi.

learned and industrious, they ceased to produce original work and contented themselves with writing commentaries on their author. Paris remained the stronghold of Thomism, with Cologne as a subsidiary fort. At Oxford Thomism did not count. The censures of Kilwardby and Peckham were never rescinded. The Dominicans at Oxford concentrated on biblical exegesis.

The Franciscans were generally loyal to Duns Scotus, though in their convent at Oxford they were divided—half of them being Ockhamists. In the University, the Northern Nation was for Scotus and the Southern for Ockham. They had in consequence one more excuse for brawls both in the schools and in the streets.[1]

Clement VI induced the University of Paris to condemn Ockham's works in 1346, and Louis XI, for some unknown reason, banned his books in 1476; but in Germany, outside Cologne, Ockham was supreme. In 1425 the Prince Elector called on some masters of Cologne to justify their conduct in accepting as guides the old-fashioned doctors Albertus and Thomas, and neglecting the modern masters, Ockham and his disciples.[2] He did not like his university to be old-fashioned; but the Dominicans were too strong for him, and retained their pre-eminence until the days of Ortwin and Pfefferkorn.

The result of this sectarianism was that the later schoolman was bound to assume that his chosen master had solved all the weightier problems of philosophy and theology, so that it only remained for him to propound fresh problems, which might be solved on the same principles and make his master's system more complete. When Dr. Inge writes: "Scholasticism became a mummified philosophy, in which there were no problems to solve and a great many pundits to consult",[3] he is more epigrammatic than correct. Scholasticism decayed because the problems were too many, and because no schoolman would consult, or at any rate consider, any pundit but his own.

A later schoolman had also a pious duty to perform in safe-

[1] De Wulf, *Med. Phil.* ii. 216, 217.

[2] *Ibid.* ii. 203-205. Vienna, Erfurt and Heidelberg were nominalist universities. In Prague and Cracow nominalism preponderated. *Ibid.* ii. 288, 289. The universities of Salamanca and Coimbra were Ockhamist, and his teaching was strongly supported in Venice and Bologna. Heidelberg was open to a realist in the days of the Obscure Men. Vide *Epistolae*, i. 46.

[3] Inge, *Outspoken Essays*, i. 237.

guarding his master on those points at which he was most liable to be attacked. This led to the multiplication of distinctions, which were often of a verbal nature and always complicated the problem to be discussed. Erasmus wrote : " It is impossible to bind such schoolmen down to anything, so skilful are they in evading a conclusion by means of a distinction ".[1]

The later schoolmen lived in retirement, poring over crabbed texts, speculating with audacity on things beyond human ken, hazarding opinions which could only be debated by those who had been trained in their special studies, caring not at all if laymen were uninterested, and certainly not expecting them to understand. In controversy with their equals they could take much for granted, and concentrate on points of difference. In doing so, they inevitably lost all sense of proportion and magnified the importance of abstruse problems. A century later Bishop Andrewes warned a Reformed Church against falling into a like error :

> A false conceit is crept into the minds of men, that the points of religion that be manifest to be certain petty points. These, yea, these be great and none but these, that have great disputes about them. It is not so. Those that are necessary God hath made plain ; those that are not plain not necessary.[2]

The fiercest controversies of the later schoolmen were on points not necessary to be believed nor easily to be understood. Sir Thomas More declared that he might as soon obtain bodily nourishment by milking a he goat into a sieve as spiritual nourishment by reading the schoolmen.[3]

Nothing was ultimately more fatal to scholasticism than the number of its students who were adepts in formal logic.[4] In 1512 Chunrad Pschlacher had published his *Compendiarius Parvorum Logicalium* in which he says, " *Dialectica est ars*

[1] Erasmus, *Encomium Moriae*, ii. 261. Chaloner, the Tudor translator, gives this very free rendering : " they find out so many evasions, that all the art of man cannot bind them so fast, but that an easy distinction shall give them a starting-hole to escape the scandal of being baffled ".

[2] Andrewes, *Sermon on Nativity*, iii. See *Sermons*, ii. 35.

[3] Pace, *De Fructu*, 83, quotes this quip. More, in describing the attainments of the Utopians, writes (*Utopia*, 185) : " They have not devised one of all those rules of restrictions, amplifications and suppositions, very wittily invented in the small Logicals, which here our children in every place do learn ". His translator, Ralph Robynson, writes in the margin : " In this place seemeth to be a nipping taunt ".

[4] Lupton, *Life of Colet*, 42.

artium, scientia scientiarum, ad omnia methodorum principia viam habens", and about that declaration all schoolmen were in entire agreement. An Englishman, William Shyreswood, early in the XIII century published his *Parva Logicalia*; and a little later Petrus Hispanus (John XXI) his *Summulae Logicales*. They were both manuals for conducting debates, adding very little to the science of logic, but giving easy instruction in the art of practising it.[1] Men learnt to rejoice in disputing for its own sake, and in furnishing proofs for what was patently absurd. There is the pleasing story of the young student fresh from Paris who proved to his father that the six eggs provided for their common meal were in reality twelve. The father was unable to detect any fallacy in the reasoning; but he ate the six eggs on the table and left his son the six he had created by his logical learning.[2] No doubt such dialectics sharpened men's wits but they did not satisfy men's appetites, and became in time a bar to progress in knowledge.[3] As early as the XII century, John of Salisbury had uttered his warning that logic was a barren study to men who knew nothing else.[4]

Here it is to be noted that many of the conundrums which have brought the schoolmen into contempt were only propounded in order to provide exercises in mental agility. We need not believe that Wyclif intended us to take him literally when he described schoolmen disputing "Whether men in bliss wear clothes? Whether any man was saved when Pharaoh's army were drowned? What was the name of Toby's dog? What Christ wrote on the ground when the woman was taken in adultery?"[5] We should read his satire as we should read a

[1] These two books were supposed by Mullinger and Prantl to have been translated from the Greek of Psellus, and in consequence they speak of "Byzantine logic". Lane-Poole (*D.N.B.*, "Ockham"), on the other hand, believes that Psellus translated the *Summulae* into Greek. Mullinger, *Cambridge*, i. 297, maintains that Shyreswood's book is superior to that of John XXI.

[2] This oft-repeated story dates back to Giraldus Cambrensis.

[3] Barclay's version of *Ship of Fools*, i. 145:

> "I wyll not say but that it is expedient
> The to know of logyke the crafte and connynge
> For by argument it makyth evydent
> Miche obscurenes, sometyme enlumynynge
> The mind: and sharpynge the wyt in mony a thynge:
> And yet oft by it a thynge playne leight and pure
> Is made diffuse, unknowen, hard and obscure."

[4] Rashdall, *Universities*, i. 67.

[5] Quoted Wylie, *Henry IV*, 421.

" General Knowledge Paper " in *Punch*, intended to ridicule the questions set by schoolmasters for small boys to answer in their holidays. It was not St. Thomas Aquinas, as is sometimes stated, who asked, " How many angels could dance on the point of a needle without jostling one another ? " That problem occurred to the author of *The Memoirs of Martinus Scriblerus* : [1] but Martinus never existed and the " point of his needle " is a joke.

At the beginning of the XVI century there was a great revival of enthusiasm for classical antiquity. Men were enthralled by the poets and historians of Rome. They were reading Plato in Ficino's translations ;[2] and they found philosophy as written by Cicero easier to understand than the subtleties of Duns Scotus. They despised the old discipline of the schools, and treated with contempt the wisdom of their fathers. Above all they sneered at the barbarous latinity of the university professors of theology, which was none the less superior both in vocabulary and syntax to the Latin talked in the law courts. Erasmus ridiculed the pretensions of both professions. Of the theologians he says :

> They deny that it accords with the dignity of Sacred Studies, that its professors should be forced to obey the rules of pedagogues. Behold the majesty of theologians. They have the right to speak incorrectly and share that privilege with many cobblers.[3]

Erasmus was fastidious ; but it is not necessary to conclude from his *Encomium* that university professors spoke no better Latin than the " obscure " correspondents of Ortwin. They no doubt despised the refinements of the humanists, used words in a sense not recognised in the classics, and constructions which would have surprised the Augustan age ; but Latin was still a living language, and living languages develop, are sometimes debased,

[1] *The Memoirs of Martinus Scriblerus*, ch. vii. The memoirs were intended to ridicule antiquaries and metaphysicians. The author was probably Dr. Arbuthnot, although they first appear in the 1741 edition of the *Works* of Pope.

[2] *Platonis opera omnia, Latine de versione Marsilii Ficini*. Venetis, 1491.

[3] *Encomium Moriae*, ii. 366. Cp. *Epistolae Obscurorum Virorum*, ii. 28 : "Johan Pfefferkorn in the present Tractate writes like a Theologian : and Theologians pay no heed to Grammar, for they belong to another faculty ". Barclay in his version of *The Ship of Fools*, i. 144, writes :

> " Yet many are besy in logyke and in lawe,
> Whenall theyre gramer is skarsly worth a strawe."

but never remain through the centuries the same. The Latin of the schoolmen was not beautiful and lacked distinction ; but it was serviceable and enabled St. Thomas and others to express their meaning with the utmost brevity, clearness and precision. Their metaphysical terms were certainly uncouth ; but classical Latin had no equivalents for words in Aristotle. The schoolmen at least invented terms which represented all too literally their master's Greek.[1]

It was not only that logic chopping was distasteful to the humanists, and that for them bad grammar was the sin that damned, but that they thought advancing knowledge had rendered the old *Summas* out of date. Some of the scholastic assumptions were no longer tenable. This would not have mattered if they had been assumed for purposes of illustration ; but most of the scholastic reasoning was deductive, and a whole chain of syllogisms lost their validity when the fact on which they depended was disproved. In the first half of the XVI century there was a chorus of scholars all over Europe shouting " Down with the Aristotelians ", but there was scarcely one of them qualified to challenge the truth of Aristotelian physics or metaphysics. Were they, then, the victims of prejudice or merely jealous because the men of the Old Learning monopolised all the best paid posts in the universities ? No ! the real opposition arose from the fact that the scholars were certain that scholasticism did not provide a wide enough basis for the widening interests and culture of the new age. Fuller compares the schoolmen to citizens of London, who having little land, enlarged their houses by building additional storeys. " So ", he says, " the Schoolmen . . . lacking the latitude of general learning and languages, thought to enlarge their active minds by building up." [2] Fuller was not a friendly critic, and he did not really appreciate the altitude which certain schoolmen had reached. They had at least

[1] *Advancement of Learning*, Bk. ii. iv. 2 : " The Schoolmen took the liberty to coin and frame new terms of art to express their own sense, and to avoid circuit of speech, without regard to the pureness, pleasantness, and (as I may call it) lawfulness of the phrase or word ". But the schoolmen only extended a vocabulary which dates back a very long way. Rand, *Founders of the Middle Ages*, 144, quotes Valla as saying, " Boethius was the first to teach us to speak like barbarians ". Turner in his article on " Scholasticism " (*Catholic Encyclopaedia*) emphasises the point I have made in the text ; and long before, Hallam, *Literature of Europe*, i. 18, had written, " It was as impossible to write metaphysics in good Latin, as the modern naturalists have found it to describe plants and animals ".

[2] Fuller, *Ch. Hist*. Bk. III. Cent. xiv. 24.

defined all the questions which are of perennial interest to philosophers. This was no small achievement, and it was none the less a real one because they so often studied the questions in the interests of theology.[1]

At the beginning of the XVI century, however, interest in metaphysics was exhausted. For a variety of reasons it was only the simple and immediate facts of experience which interested men. Natural science was born, though it was but an infant of days; and the Old Learning was flouted and overthrown by humanism, which had reached an elegant adolescence—being as vain as a peacock of its plumage and having a more melodious cry.

Rhetoric took the place of logic, and men studied the arts of persuasion while escaping from the rigours of proof. The age of reason was over, and the controversies of the Reformation were largely fought out over questions of fact. It was the age of the *Nuremburg Chronicle*, of the *Centuries of Magdeburg* and *The Annals of Baronius*. Archbishop Parker collected historical documents and relied on their evidence to confute the claims of Rome. The Italian divines at the Council of Trent complained of the constant appeal to authorities and precedents. They said it was " a novity and a condemning of school divinity, which in all difficulties useth reason "—but they appealed to the examples of St. Thomas and St. Bonaventura in vain. Even the Papacy had for the time repudiated its appeal to reason and its belief in an infallible logic.[2]

This distrust of reason recurs from time to time and passes away. Even lawyers, opportunists and pragmatists are driven to adopt some philosophy. Scholasticism was certain to reappear in new forms. All through the troublous times the Sorbonne remained loyal to St. Thomas, while Louvain divided her allegiance between him and Duns Scotus. Protestantism in Germany was soon promulgating a scholasticism of her own on narrower lines. Hooker in England was learning from Aquinas

[1] Harnack, *Hist. of Dogma*, vi. 226, writes: " From the doctrine of God, there grew up the doctrines of thought and will; from the doctrine of the Trinity the doctrine of the cosmos; and from the doctrine of the sacraments the doctrine of space ".

[2] Sarpi, *Hist. of the Council of Trent*; quoted by Whitehead, *Science and the Modern World*, p. 13. At the Council of Trent the *Summa* of St. Thomas was accepted as a text-book and St. Bonaventura was freely quoted: but they were appealed to as authorities who settled points which might no longer be discussed.

how to defend the claims of reason and law. Suarez in Spain and Bellarmine in Italy were reviving the old scholastic method, and presenting old and new conclusions appropriate to their own time. But all this does not concern us at present. We have aimed at showing what scholasticism was and why it failed in the days before the Reformation ; why there were so few theologians to combat the Reformers, why those theologians were pedants who had lost the ear of the people and become Aunt Sallies for the irreverent scholars of the Renaissance.

CHAPTER III

THE ENGLISH MYSTICS

1. *Popularity of Mystical Books*

THE Lollards attacked the Church as an institution—her wealth and power. The humanists attacked her theology, which had become arid, sophistical and out-of-date. The mystics attacked no one, but unintentionally sapped the foundations of a sacerdotal Church which expressed itself in sacraments and social ordinances.

The great mystics belonged to the XIV century, but their works were never more popular than on the eve of the Reformation. They provided the spiritual food on which devout people of the early XVI century were nourished, and we cannot understand the period aright unless we take them into account. There are more MSS. of Richard Rolle extant than those of any other English mediaeval writer.[1] The Carthusians of London and Sheen and the Brigittines of Syon were busy in multiplying copies of mystical works.[2] The early printers entered into competition with them in order to supply a popular demand. In 1483 one of the first books printed at Oxford by Theoderic Root was Richard Rolle's *Explanation of Job*.[3] In the early XVI century Wynkyn de Worde published three other books which he ascribed to Rolle, though none of them was in fact written by him.[4] In 1510 two more works of Rolle were printed at Paris, and in 1533

[1] Miss Hope Allen has herself examined 400 MSS. of Rolle. *Vide* her index of them : *Writings of Richard Rolle*, 563-567.

[2] Sweden still possesses some seven important Rolle MSS. derived from the Brigittines of Syon. Miss Allen, *op. cit.* 49, 567. The Douce MS. of *The Cloud of the Unknowing* was copied by William Tregose (*d.* 1514) of the London Charterhouse. The Harleian MS. of the same work was also written in the Charterhouse. The Parkminster MS. was written by William Exmoor, the Carthusian martyr. *The Scale of Perfection* was transcribed by Green, a Carthusian of Sheen (A. W. Reed, Foreword to *Works of Walter Hilton*). Methley, a Carthusian of Mount Grace, translated *The Mirror of Simple Souls* and *The Cloud of the Unknowing* into Latin.

[3] Gordon-Duff, *Fifteenth Century English Books*, 101.

[4] One of them was Henry Suso's *De Aeterna Sapientia.* Wynkyn de Worde entitled it *Hours of the Name of Jesus*. So did Notary. Both ascribed it to Rolle.

another at Antwerp: they were probably intended for the English market. In 1535 and 1536 his Latin works were published at Cologne by Johan Faber of Heilbron, a zealous opponent of Lutheranism. Rolle was certainly regarded as orthodox, though Horstman [1] treats him as a precursor of the Reformation, because he denounced scandals and did not love the *Religiosi*.[2] It was just because he was orthodox that Lollards were tempted to interpolate his works, and tried to shelter their own tracts under his venerated name.

It is to Margaret Beaufort's [3] initiative that we owe the first printed editions of Hilton's *Scale of Perfection*, of the anonymous *Mirror of Simple Souls*, and of the *Imitatio Christi* of Thomas à Kempis; but the printers found them profitable and went on issuing editions after her death. In 1490 Wynkyn de Worde published *The Scale of Perfection*, because

> This mighty Princess hath commanded me
> To imprint this book, her grace for to deserve.[4]

Julian Notary produced an edition in 1507, Pepwell another in 1521 and Wynkyn de Worde two more, one in 1521 and another in 1533.

Margaret Beaufort herself translated *The Mirror of Simple Souls* [5] from the French, although there was already a translation a century old which Richard Methley (*c.* 1451) had turned into Latin. Four editions of this work are known between 1507 and 1526.

John Dygon, a recluse of Sheen, began to write a copy of the *Imitatio Christi* [6] in 1441, and it was finished by another hand. This was three years before Thomas à Kempis made his final revision. An English translation soon followed; but William Atkinson translated it anew for Margaret Beaufort. Pynson

[1] Horstman, *Yorkshire Writers*: Richard Rolle of Hampole.

[2] In his *Melum* Rolle complains of persecution by the *Religious*, and Miss Allen, *op. cit.* 123, 476, thinks he refers to the Cistercians of Rievaulx and Byland. In 1327 monks were unpopular throughout England. It was the year when there were risings against the abbeys of St. Albans, Bury St. Edmunds, Abingdon, Dunstable, Feversham and Winchester. *Op. cit.* 479. Dom Noetinger on the other hand, in his preface to *Le Feu d'amour*, xliii ff., thinks that Rolle refers to the friars and finds that his words are echoes from William Saint-Amour.

[3] Cooper, *Margaret Richmond*, 87, 108.

[4] Gordon-Duff, *Fifteenth Century Books*.

[5] *Mirror of Simple Souls*, ed. by Miss Kirchberger (Orchard Books).

[6] Bigg, Introduction to *Imitatio* (Methuen).

published this in 1503, and Wynkyn de Worde in 1517.[1] It was superseded by the translation of Richard Whitford, " the Wretch of Syon ", whose version was first printed in 1556 by Cracow, though made long before.

Wynkyn de Worde in 1501 and Pepwell in 1520 printed a little book which purports to be " taken out " of Margery Kempe's *Contemplations*.[2] Caxton in 1486 and 1490 published *The Mirror of the Blessed Life of Jesus Christ* [3] by the Carthusian Nicholas Love as the *Speculum Vitae Christi* of St. Bonaventura ; and five years later Wynkyn de Worde and Pynson produced editions of the same work. Caxton also published *The Cordiale : memorare novissima* and several other devotional works. There are three editions before 1500 of Bishop Alcock's *Mons Perfectionis* by Wynkyn de Worde and Pynson, two editions of *The Abbey of the Holy Ghost*,[4] and one of *The Chastening of God's Children* ; while for those who did not care for distinctly mystical works there was Caxton's edition of *The Golden Legend*, *Dives and Pauper*,[5] and no less than twenty-four editions of works by John Myrc.

Professor Chambers [6] has recently pointed out the immense importance of this literature for determining the development of English prose ; but it is still more important for a proper understanding of the religious thoughts of devout people at the beginning of the XVI century. It was the literature of the middle classes, when the schoolmen were only read by professed theologians, and Chaucer and Malory were the delight of gay courtiers and fair ladies.[7]

[1] *D.N.B.* " In style and feeling the finest rendering into English of the famous original." Dr. Bigg, Introd. p. 3, preferred that of the Jesuit Anthony Hoskyns. Most people to-day would prefer that of Dr. Bigg.

[2] Edmund Gardner has printed these pages in his *Cell of Self Knowledge*.

[3] The Quaracchi editors have rejected the *Speculum*. It is not by St. Bonaventura. Nicholas Love's version is scarcely a translation. He expands and curtails his author as he thinks fit. The passage that Pourrat, *La Spiritualité chrétienne*, ii. 278-283, thinks most worthy of quotation is not in Love. The dates given for editions are those in Gordon-Duff, *op. cit.*, which differs from those in the Orchard version.

[4] *The Abbey of the Holy Ghost* has been reprinted by G. Perry, *Religious Pieces*, E.E.T.S., 1867.

[5] Gordon-Duff, *op. cit.*

[6] Chambers, *Continuity of English Prose*, passim.

[7] Caxton, Prologue to his *King Arthur*. *Vide* Crotch, *Prologues and Epilogues*, E.E.T.S., 92.

II. *Hermits and Anchorites*

On the Continent[1] mystics for the most part belonged to the religious orders, but in England they were solitaries and recluses. Monks with estates to administer, establishments to maintain, infirmaries to look after and guest-houses to keep up, found it difficult to keep the minimum requirements of their rule, and the constant succession of their services. In the cloister and dormitory being never alone, they had little opportunity for private devotion, and most had little inclination for mystical contemplation. The friars were constantly on the move ; they lived with the people, preached to the people, and were always busy, perhaps too busy, with other people's concerns. They were for the most part as little detached from the world as a modern "social worker" ; and though they may have embraced a life of poverty to ensure freedom from worldly cares, they soon discovered that mendicants only throve by practising the arts of ingratiation. In consequence the cultivation of the interior life was left to hermits and anchorites. These must not be confused.

> For some flee from the world and enclose themselves in walls
> And steken them in stones, and little will they speaken—
> To fly such occasions as folly will finden—
> And these we clepen ancres in the common speech.
> Also in contemplation there are many others,
> That drawen them to deserts and endure much pain ;
> By herbs, roots, and fruit live they for their God's love ;
> And this manner of folk men call hermits.[2]

No book was more popular in monastic refectories than the *Collations of Cassian* ; but hermits, unless originally monks, were not likely to hear about the Fathers of the Desert ;[3] and they followed a native tradition ultimately derived from St. Cuthbert and St. Guthlac. Some were men who longed to escape from a wicked and boisterous world into solitude, seeking a peace which comes from God only. Some were men who were impatient of

[1] SS. Anselm and Bernard were monks ; St. Bonaventura was a Franciscan ; Eckhart, Tauler and Suso were Dominicans ; Ruysbroek was first a secular priest and afterwards a canon regular ; Gerson was Chancellor of Paris, and a man of affairs ; and Thomas à Kempis was an Augustinian canon.

[2] Wright, *Political Songs*, ii. 64, where the verses are printed in sixteen short lines.

[3] Rolle did know about the Fathers of the Desert. See footnotes to Noetinger's translation of the *Incendium Amoris* (*Le Feu d'amour*).

any restraint, who could not be bound by external rules, and were restless when confined to particular places. Such men chose some cave or hut for a home, but claimed the right to roam at will. Many said like Richard Rolle, " I have loved a certain wilderness, and chose to live away from men ".[1]

Alexander IV, by a Bull dated April 13th, 1256, had endeavoured to unite all hermits under the rule of St. Augustine ; [2] but this Bull was never published in England, and Langland could describe one as

> I 'habited as an hermit : an order by himself :
> Religion sans Rule or reasonable obedience.[3]

Richard Rolle wrote : " To God above a hermit owes obedience ; he is his own Abbot and Prior, and the Master of the Cloister of his heart ".[4] He goes on to say that out of courtesy he should acquaint his bishop with his manner of life ; and in order that his sins may be forgiven, he should chose some elderly monk or rector for his confessor ; but it is evident that neither bishop nor confessor was to direct his life.

It is not surprising that ecclesiastical officials looked on hermits with suspicion and disfavour. They did not approve of men under no authority, who tramped the roads and lived on alms. They knew that some had adopted the habit as a cloak for their evil lives, and that Perkin Warbeck was not the only one who tried to escape from justice in a hermit's garb. Even genuine hermits gave trouble. Sometimes they preached without a licence ; sometimes, like William of Swinderby, they preached heresy and talked sedition ; [5] sometimes they ventured to prophesy even before kings. John hanged Peter the Wise of Pontefract, and Henry IV beheaded the White Hermit of England, while Henry V listened to the denunciations of the French hermit and let him go free. Most hermits, however, restricted their activities to good works. Some lived in deserted chapels and served them ; some kept beacons alight on dangerous headlands ; some

[1] Rolle, *Incendium Amoris*. Chiefly I depend on Miss Comper's version, *The Fire of Love* ; occasionally on Misyn's trans. in E.E.T.S.

[2] Noetinger, Preface, *Le Feu d'amour*, xvii.

[3] *Piers Plowman*, B Text, xiii. 265.

[4] *Regula Heremitarum*, f. 73. Quoted by Miss Allen, *Writings of Richard Rolle*, 327.

[5] Cp. the accounts in Gairdner, *Lollardy and the Reformation*, i. 28-38, and Owst, *Preaching in Mediaeval England*, 121-129.

emulated St. Christopher in carrying people over fords ; some acted as guides through wild country ; and some became oracles of the countryside.[1] All professed to live for the contemplation of God, and Rolle was right when he said, " Great is the hermit's life if it is greatly done ".[2]

Little is known, but much has been written about the life of Richard Rolle. Apart from scattered references in his own works, we have only the Lessons in the Office [3] drawn up thirty years after his death, when there was some hope that he might be canonised. He was born about 1297, not far from Pickering in Yorkshire.[4] He was probably an awkward boy who found it hard to get on with others—a boy with a vehement temper, impatient of all restraint, but with an insistent conscience—a boy who could never escape from a consciousness of God. He went to Oxford at an early age, probably as the companion of his patron, Thomas Nevill,[5] the son of Lord Nevill of Raby,[6] who was already a boy archdeacon amply endowed. At Oxford Rolle acquired a copious and curious Latin vocabulary, but took no interest in scholastic disputations : he was even then devoted to the Scriptures.[7] He tells us that his adolescence was impure; and, when eighteen, he suddenly left Oxford, perhaps in the hope of escaping temptation.[8] If so, he did not find himself safe at home in a Yorkshire dale, but ran away to be a hermit, after, in boyish fashion, adapting some of his sister's clothes, that he might dress himself for the part.[9] In this, as in all else, he acknowledged no authority but his own conscience, and it is not surprising that his conduct was often misunderstood. For a time he was befriended

[1] Miss Clay, *Hermits and Anchorites*, passim.

[2] *Incendium Amoris*, i. ch. 13.

[3] The *Officium* was printed by Canon Perry for the E.E.T.S. in a revised form in 1921. Miss Comper only translated three of the nine Lessons.

[4] Thornton-le-Dale is most probable, though some favour Thornton-le-Street.

[5] Rashdall, *Universities*, ii. 625, wrote : " The rich man lived in a hostel of his own with a numerous ' familia ', including poorer but well-born youths, who dressed like him and acted as his ' socii ' or humble companions ".

[6] For Nevill see Miss Allen, *Writings of Richard Rolle*, 444 ff.

[7] The *Officium* (Perry ed., xxiv.) tells us that he desired to learn the Scriptures rather than physics and secular knowledge : and at Oxford he had the opportunity, for Grossetête had established a daily lecture on the Bible. In the *Incendium Amoris*, 13, he writes : " I offer this book to be seen, not to philosophers and wise men of this world, nor to great divines lapped in infinite questions, but unto the boisterous and untaught, who more long to love God than to know many things, for truly not disputing but working is to be known and loved ".

[8] *Incendium Amoris*, i. ch. 12.

[9] *Officium*.

by a squire named Dalton and his wife;[1] but he quarrelled with the former, was disapproved of by his bishop, was persecuted by monks and frequently had to change his abode. He sometimes entered into manor-houses and ate what was set before him,[2] partly, he explains, to satisfy his hunger and partly out of good manners ; but critics watching him said that he cared too much for delicate food. This annoyed him ; but he was equally annoyed when fed on mouldy bread and scraps. He went and sat on the village ale bench, craving fellowship with his " even christian " ; and this was turned to his reproach. He approached women, who repulsed him, misunderstanding his intentions ; and in telling his experiences he cries, " This truly happened unto me, because I sought their salvation ".[3] He had come out of his solitude to win souls, and found himself everywhere an object of suspicion.

It was two years and eight months after adopting the hermit's life that he had had his first mystical experience : " I felt within me a merry and unknown heat. . . . I was expert it was not from a creature but from my Maker, because I found it grew hotter and more glad." [4] This interior glow was for him a revelation of the love of God. A year and three months later, while sitting in a chapel, he heard the heavenly choir : " The songs of everlasting praise and the sweetness of unseen melody, which may not be heard or known, but to him who received it : and it behoveth him to be clean, eschewing the things of earth ".[5] It was for him a foretaste of heaven. Destitute and scorned by the religious, he wished all to know of his divine consolations, and wrote his *Melum*, a long book in alliterative Latin. It was meant to confound his enemies, but they must have marvelled most of all at his fantastic style.[6]

[1] For Dalton see Miss Allen, *op. cit.*

[2] *Incendium Amoris*, i. ch. 11.

[3] *Ibid.* i. ch. 12.

[4] *Ibid.* i. ch. 15. In both his Latin and English Psalters he protests that in speaking of this heat he is not using a metaphor. Miss Allen, *op. cit.* 180.

[5] In the Second Consideration of the Stigma, *Little Flowers of St. Francis*, there is a similar experience : " Then appeared unto him an angel in great splendour, who had a viol in his left hand and in his right hand a bow ; and while St. Francis was stupefied at the vision, the angel drew the bow once across the viol, and immediately there was heard such sweet melody that his soul was enchanted with sweetness, and he lost all bodily sense ; insomuch that, as he afterwards related to his companions, he thought that if an angel had drawn the bow a second time across the strings, his soul through excessive sweetness would have parted from his body ".

[6] In the opening chapter of *The Melum* he explains himself thus : " *Liquide loquor non timeo temptantes, non tales in turbine trucidabuntur, Silere non scio, sic caritas me coget, ut cuncti cognoscant quod capax consisto cantabilis clamoris, et*

It was soon after this that Miss Allen thinks that he may have gone to stay at the Sorbonne.[1] There would have been nothing inconsistent in his doing so, for he maintained that " it is not ill for hermits to leave cells for a reasonable cause, and afterwards if it accord to return to them again ".[2] The Sorbonne at the time specialised in biblical exegesis and pastoral theology. It was then the stronghold of the secular clergy ; and it may have been in Paris that Rolle was ordained a priest.[3] His later books reveal that he had become a theologian with a considerable knowledge of the Scriptures. He was also able to quote the Fathers ; though perhaps he relied on Peter Lombard or on commonplace books compiled by others.

If he studied in Paris, it was that he might be guarded against self-deception in his life of contemplation. He never wavered in his purpose to fulfil what he believed to be the calling of God. He spent long years on the wild moors of Richmondshire, and learnt there the sweetness of communion with God in the peace of summer days, and the educational value of stern discipline when exposed to the wintry blasts. Sometimes he dwelt in a cell, sometimes he wandered, and at intervals wrote his commentaries and tracts with a celerity which is commemorated in the *Officium.*

sonum suscipio celicum insignem, dum discedere dilexi a divitum dolore et sancte subsistere, solitarie sedendo, canens et calidus, ac jubilans jugiter ". Quoted by Miss Allen, *op. cit.* 117. Some years later in simpler language he justifies his writings : " *Non igitur ex arrogantia aut ex superbia loquimur, sed misericordiam Dei ac bonitatem ejus in nobis attestamur* ". The *Canticles* quoted by Miss Allen, 164.

[1] Dom Noetinger in *The Month*, January 1926, maintained that Rolle went from Oxford direct to Paris, took the degree of doctor (as Pits, *De Rebus Anglicis*, says he did), and became a hermit when of mature age. He quotes certain XVII century notes purporting to be derived from the lost archives of the Sorbonne ; but as they speak of Richard of Hampole their authenticity is doubtful, for it was only in later life that he was associated with that place. Secondly, as Miss Allen points out, his early works were crude ; and it is only in his later works that he shows himself a theologian. Dom Noetinger is not convinced, and in his preface to *Le Feu d'amour* emphasises a quotation in which Rolle speaks of himself when *adolescens* and when *juvenis*. A man was *adolescens* between eighteen and thirty, *juvenis* between thirty and forty. Lewis and Short, *Latin Dictionary*, says a man was *juvenis* between twenty and forty, but the word was used very loosely. Du Cange, *Glossarium*, ed. 1884, only supports Noetinger with one quotation. Rolle no doubt followed English usage. Trevisa, translating *Bartholomeus Anglicus*, writes, " Adolescentia duryth the thyrd vii year " (quoted *N.E.D.*). It is noteworthy that in the *Melum*, Rolle in different places speaks of himself as *puer*, *juvenculus* and *juvenis*.

[2] *Incendium Amoris*, i. ch. 15.

[3] Dom Noetinger has convinced me that Rolle was a priest. Orders would be necessary for a Socius of the Sorbonne. Rolle could hardly have obtained them in England as he did not belong to an order, and was without *title* or patrimony.

He was assured that God was very Love, and he lived to make that wonderful love known to others ; but he was awkward with men, because, as he said, *non feci sicut ipsi fecerunt.*[1] Yet even among men he had his disciples, and wrote *Judica me, Deus* for a friendly parish priest, and *Emendatio Vitae* for William Stokes, a Doctor of Divinity.

With women he was more successful,[2] and for the last nine years of his life he made his headquarters in a wood near the Cistercian nunnery of Hampole, and became director to the inmates. For a nun at Yedingham he wrote *Ego Dormio*, and for a nun at Hampole, Margaret Kirkby, he wrote *The Form of Living* and his English Psalter. A year before his death Margaret was enclosed as an anchoress at Laten, and for fifty years she survived her director.[3]

From his books we may judge that Rolle, as he grew older, grew more mellow. His Latin became more normal, and he expressed himself in English with direct simplicity and force. By prayer, fasting and mortifications he had conquered the unruly flesh and subdued his passionate temper, and had learnt that his extreme sensitiveness was an aid to humility. The wayward and extravagant boy had become a saintly man ; but it was through self-discipline and grace, and not by submitting to external control. He died in 1349, the year of the Black Death.

If hermits loved to roam in wildernesses, anchorites, enclosed in small houses abutting on a church, chose to be examples of recollection and detachment in the busiest haunts. There was an anker called Symon at All Hallows, London Wall, who wrote out his meditations at the beginning of the XVI century, which were published with the imprimatur of Bishop FitzJames.[4] There had been a succession of anchorites at St. Margaret's, Westminster, another place of public resort. There was an anchoress at St. Nicholas, Worcester, opposite the city cross ; and the last of these was ejected with difficulty by Thomas Cromwell's

[1] *Melum* ; quoted by Miss Hodgson, *Sanity of Mysticism.* Cp. a passage in *Amatores Mundi* quoted by Miss Allen, *op. cit.* 205.

[2] In the *Incendium* he admits that the friendship of women is allowable but dangerous.

[3] For Margaret Kirkby see Miss Allen, *op. cit.* 502-511.

[4] *The Fruyte of Redemptyon*, printed by Wynkyn de Worde 1514, 1530, 1532 (Miss Clay, *Hermits and Anchorites*, 180). The colophon states that the Bishop had " studiously read and overseen " the book, and commended it " to the true servants of sweet Jesus " (A. W. Reed, *Early Tudor Drama*, 163).

commissioners.[1] Dame Julian was enclosed for more than forty years in the busy city of Norwich ; and Dame Margery Kempe ended her long life enclosed at King's Lynn.

The wandering hermit by the conditions of his life found any rule hard to keep ; and many like Rolle became hermits because they could brook no restraint, and could only develop on their own lines. The anchorite, on the other hand, had no desire for freedom, and his life of seclusion was only possible by having a rule that demanded all his time. There are many who love monotony, provided that they have something definite to do, and obtain as much satisfaction by punctually observing rules as other people do by breaking them.

Charles Kingsley has described the anchorite [2] as a morbid fanatic immured in a bare and filthy cell, as cut off from all human interests and driven by superstition to seek in renunciation the salvation of a self-centred soul. On the other hand, Miss Clay [3] insists that the life of the anchorite was regarded as a career and not as the abdication of all careers. The anchoress was encouraged to work and to keep herself and her room tidy. She was served by one or sometimes by two attendants. She was not vowed to poverty, but was often the recipient of small legacies and other gifts. She practised abstinence, but was warned against fasting to the injury of her health. Her other mortifications were self-chosen. Some anchorites were no doubt very ascetic ; but most of them lived quiet lives with a daily round of devotion. Some perhaps became sour and fretful, having mistaken their vocation ; some approached the cheerful optimism of Dame Julian of Norwich.

There were several rules written for anchorites. The earliest is that written by Ælred,[4] Abbot of Rievaulx, for his own sister. Very little later comes the *Ancren Riwle*,[5] which was continually

[1] Miss Clay, *op. cit.* 184. " There was an Ancres with hom I had not a lyttil besyness to have her grant to come oute, but owte she is." Commissioners' *Report*, Worcester.

[2] Kingsley, *Hermits*, 330.

[3] Miss Clay, *Hermits and Anchorites*, 85.

[4] Ælred, *Institutio Inclusarum*.

[5] The *Ancren Riwle* was formerly attributed to Richard Poore, Bishop of Salisbury, but dates do not admit of his authorship. It was apparently composed about 1135 for Emma, Gunhilda and Christina, ladies who had waited on Queen Maud, the wife of Henry I. No MS. of this original has survived, but it has to be assumed from personal details in subsequent versions. In 1200 there was a new version designed for a larger community. In 1230 there was a French translation made from a composite text. In 1300 Simon of Ghent, Bishop of Salisbury, translated it into

copied, adapted and modified up to the XV century. Rolle's *Form of Living* written for Margaret Kirkby, Hilton's *Scale of Perfection* written for a woman " closid in a hous ", and the XV century *Book for Recluses* are devotional treatises and not rules.

Anchorites and anchoresses were licensed by the bishop ; and there was an office for enclosing them. They lived for the most part in two rooms. One had a window looking into the church so that they could see the altar, and the other had a window looking into the street, covered with a blind of black cloth having a white cross in the centre. They took part in the Church services ; they read and meditated ; they worked at making their own clothes, repairing vestments or making garments for the poor ; they were forbidden to " make purses to gain friends therewith and blodbendes of silk ".[1] It was thought inadvisable that they should own cows, as they opened the way to worldly distractions and might lead to friction with the hayward. They might keep a cat. " An anchorite must not become a schoolmistress, or turn her house into a school for children. Her maiden may, however, take any little girl, concerning whom it might be doubtful whether she should learn among boys ; but an anchoress ought to give her thoughts to God only ".[2] All anchoresses did not observe this prohibition or Ælred would not have written—

> Let not boys or girls approach thee. There are some recluses who undertake the teaching of girls and turn their cell into a school. She sits at the window and they settle down in the porch. She watches them one by one, and according as each behaves, now she is angry, now she laughs, now she threatens, now she beats them, now she coaxes them, now she kisses them, now she calls a weeping child to come nearer to be beaten ; she strokes her face, she draws up her head, and eagerly embracing her, calls her now daughter, now darling.[3]

Two other temptations beset the anchoress—the one came from " sitting too long at her parlour window ", and the other

Latin for the nuns of Tarrent. Later in the XIV century there was a further revision, a copy of which is in the Pepysian Library. In the XIV and XV centuries devotional writers borrowed from it : Chambers, *Continuity of English Prose*, xcviii. It was translated for the Camden Society by James Morton. There is a revised edition with an Introduction by Cardinal Gasquet in *The Mediaeval Library*.

[1] Blodbendes should be *brodbends*. Brod = embroidered and bend = scarf. See *N.E.D.* under *brod* and *bend*. Neither Blodbend nor Brodbend is in the dictionary.

[2] *Ancren Riwle*, 318, 319.

[3] *Institutio Inclusarum*, ch. vii. Quoted by Miss Clay.

came from her maid. It was a common saying that "almost every anchoress hath an old woman to feed her ears".[1] The *Ancren Riwle*, speaking of the maid, insists that "she be very plain and of sufficient age", that she should only go where she was sent, should sing her prayers on her way, and not stop to talk with either man or woman.[2] The window was a greater difficulty, because many came to consult the anker or anchoress, and charity forbade them not to help. Walter Hilton gave them sound advice which we abbreviate:

> If a man come and tell his dis-ease, comfort him gladly; but if he fall to idle tales, feed not his speech. If a priest come wishing to teach thee, hear him with reverence; but do not try to teach him, for it falleth not to thee to teach a priest. Speak meekly to a man who bringeth thee alms. Do not reprove men unless you know that they will take it well, keep silence as much as you can, and that will relieve you from a press of callers.[3]

All anchoresses did not follow these counsels. Many loved to talk and gloried in edifying others. The *Ancren Riwle* tells us about them:

> Some one is so learned and of such wise speech, that she would have him (the caller) know it. She sits and talks to him, and gives him word for word, and becomes a preceptor who should be an anchoress, and teaches him who has come to teach her: and would by her own account soon be celebrated and known among the wise—known she is well; for from the very circumstance she thinketh herself to be reputed wise, he understands that she is a fool; for she hunteth after praise and catches reproof. For at last when he is gone away he will say, "This anchoress is a great talker".[4]

It is obvious that anchoresses were after all human and subject to human frailties. Had they all been candidates for sanctity, the many warnings in the rule would have been inappropriate. Some, no doubt, had mistaken their vocation, a few gave occasion to scandal, but the great majority were devout women happy in a round of religious duties. They kept their rule, but recognised that it admitted of exceptions; and perhaps their consciences were not much troubled if they spent an occasional half-hour at their parlour window hearing the news and lamenting the sins of the wicked world outside.

[1] *Ancren Riwle*, 67.
[2] *Ibid.* 320.
[3] *Scale of Perfection*, i. ch. 83.
[4] *Ancren Riwle*, p. 51.

Christina, the recluse of Markyate, had been the counsellor of kings as different as Stephen and Henry II; Loretta, once Countess of Leicester, and for fifty years the recluse of Hackington, was consulted both by Henry III and her great-nephew, Simon de Montfort.[1] Her sister Annora, the widow of Hugh Mortimer, was enclosed at Iffley. Margaret Kirkby was a young nun who became an anchoress. Julian of Norwich went straight from a convent school to her solitary cell. Margery Kempe had been the mother of fourteen children, and made the long pilgrimage to Jerusalem before she had herself enclosed, and spent her last years in writing her autobiography and meditations.[2] The successive anchorites at Westminster were drawn from the cloister; and many of the greater monasteries had their Reclusorium.

The enclosure was for life; but again there were exceptions. Margaret Kirkby was twice moved, and Thomas Scrope or Bradley had a varied experience. He first dwelt in an ankerhold belonging to the Carmelites at Norwich, but he came out of it in 1425 to be a mission preacher. Clad in sackcloth with a girdle of iron fetters, he went through the streets crying, "The New Jerusalem, the Bride of the Lamb, should shortly come down from heaven". His conduct scandalised the provincial of the Carmelites, and Bradley was once more sealed in his cell. Twenty-five years later he was dispensed from his vows and consecrated as Bishop of Dromore, was presented to several Norfolk livings and acted as assistant to the Bishop of Norwich. In 1457 he resigned, gave away all his possessions, and became once more a mission preacher, walking with bare feet from one Norfolk village to another, teaching the ten commandments. He died in 1491 wellnigh a hundred years old.[3]

The life of an anker does not seem to have been prejudicial to health. Loretta must have been over eighty when she died; Dame Julian of Norwich lived for forty years after her

[1] For Loretta see F. M. Powick in *Christian Life in the Middle Ages*, 147-168. She was much concerned in the coming of the friars. Thomas of Eccleston, *De Adventu*, 55, says: "She nourished the friars in all things, as a mother her sons, by winning for them in a wise way the goodwill of magnates and prelates, by whom she was held in the highest esteem".

[2] See Miss Allen's communication to *The Times*, December 27th, 1934, on the discovery of the autobiography.

[3] Miss Clay, *Hermits and Anchorites*, 163-164. Cp. Owst, *Preaching in Mediaeval England*, 118-121.

"Shewings"; and an anker at Westminster, who was sixty years enclosed, was a reputed centenarian at the time of his death. Neither did the life lead to idiocy, as Kingsley supposed. Several ankers were the counsellors of kings. It was in an anker at Westminster that Richard II trusted; and the anker foretold his downfall. It was to an anker at Westminster that Henry V repaired on the day of his accession to receive absolution for his past sins and advice as to his future conduct. Henry VIII and Katherine of Aragon both testified their respect for solitaries in the early years of the XVI century.

Such people were of varied character. Some had a passion for holiness and were happy, like Dame Julian, in the revelations of divine love. Some were introspective, self-tormentors, who found in pain the physical excitement for which they craved. Some brooded over their sins until they became the victims of hallucinations. Those who aimed highest had to endure the worst temptations. They were brave men and women, on a steep path, struggling through darkness up the mount to God.

We only know that Walter Hilton was once an Augustinian canon of Thurgarton, and it is an inference that he became an anchorite. He wrote with the lucidity of a scholar, and with a scholar's contempt for illiterate preachers. Otherwise he shows a spirit of sweet reasonableness. He knew enough of the world to know that all men are not alike, and that God has many servants to do His will in a variety of ways. So great was his reputation in England after his death, that it was natural to attribute to him the authorship of the *Imitatio Christi* which was circulating in England as *Musica Ecclesiastica*.[1]

By the beginning of the XVI century the *Imitatio Christi* had become by adoption an English book. Written by a monk confined in a cloister, it has gone into all the world and found a home everywhere. Intended for devout recluses it has fascinated men living busy lives, and convinced sad unbelievers that spiritual experience is a reality for some men if not for them.

Thomas à Kempis was born about 1380, and educated, like Erasmus at a later date, by the Brethren of the Common Life at Deventer. In 1400 he entered the Augustinian convent of the Agnetenberg near Zwolle in Holland; and he died a nonagenarian in 1471, having only once for three years left his remote

[1] Dom Noetinger, Introduction to *The Scale of Perfection*, viii., ix.

retreat. In a beautiful script he had copied and recopied the whole Bible ; he had also copied a variety of devotional works. In his leisure he had polished and repolished his own book until it reflected his exquisite refinement. " There are ", said Dr. Bigg,[1] " constant rhymes, like the tinkling of bells, running through the melody of his prose ". " But ", he adds, " this is only true of the first two books." Another life would have been necessary to bring the two last to the same standard of perfection ; but the whole exhales the perfume of the cloister garth, and shows how much wisdom may be stored in a house of quiet. The author was at one with the peace of his surroundings, and according to an English mystic, " In that soul that is most occupied in thoughts of peace hath God made his dwelling place ".[2]

There was peace in the Agnetenberg at Zwolle, but there was little peace outside its walls. While men treasured the *Imitatio* as a legacy of the Middle Ages, they ceased to respect the lives which made such books possible. The Reformation came ; and the anchorite, wedded to accustomed forms, was unable to survive in a world of change. The hermit was equally unlucky—he had ever claimed a freedom for himself which included freedom of speech, and this became impossible in an age which punished verbal treason. Hugh Lathbury, a hermit of Bristol, was imprisoned in 1530 for hoping that Katherine of Aragon might be queen again.[3] Three years later the hermit of Chesterfield asked, " If it were right to hang, draw and quarter a man who defaced the king's arms, what ought to be done to the man who pulled down churches and destroyed the images of the saints ? " The Derbyshire justices thought it best that the hermit should answer his own question before Cromwell's commissioners. Christopher Warrener, a recluse of Canterbury,[4] was accused unjustly of complicity with Elizabeth Barton, the Maid of Kent. He met with no sympathy when he confessed that she had been to see him, and that he regarded her as a nuisance as she interrupted his meditations.[5] It came to pass that any slander, however improbable, was readily believed against solitaries, when for political reasons suspicions were excited. In 1530 Joachim de

[1] Bigg, *Wayside Sketches*, 140.
[2] " Discovery of Spirits " in Edmund Gardner's *Cell of Self Knowledge*, 165.
[3] *Letters and Papers*, viii. No. 809.
[4] Miss Clay, *Hermits and Anchorites*, 165. [5] *Ibid.* 54.

Vaux commemorated the peace with England by building a hermitage at Dover which might serve as a lighthouse. A few years later the hermit who tended it was waylaid and almost beaten to death—the rumour running that he was signalling to the king's enemies. In the bustling social life of the time, the ideal of the solitary had become an anachronism and his disinterested service aroused suspicion. Men had once valued the prayers of anchorites, but the life of prayer was meaningless to the new advocates of preaching. So Becon wrote :

> Judith, when time required, came out of her closet to do good to others. Our Recluses never come out of their lobbies, sink or swim the people. Judith put herself in jeopardy to do good to the common country. Our Recluses are unprofitable clods of the earth, doing good to no man.[1]

III. *The English Mystics*

Wyclif,[2] an impatient pragmatist, had no respect for priests who devoted themselves to contemplation. He accuses them of being either hypocrites or self-deluded ; he dismisses the records of ecstasies and visions as self-originated dreams or fantasies. He insists that our Lord came to preach and live an active life ; that the often-quoted text, " Mary hath chosen the better part ",[3] was not applicable, because Mary was only a woman and it was her duty to listen to sermons ; that St. Paul's exhortation, to " pray without ceasing ", was not to be interpreted of spoken words ; that a Christian's duty lay in good works and points of charity ; and that contemplation was only proper for the life of heaven.

Many may sympathise with such teaching ; but it is one-sided. Richard Rolle was more broad-minded when he taught that each man had his own vocation, and that no two vocations are the same. He admits that " there are many active men better than some contemplatives ", although he immediately adds, " the best contemplatives are better than the best active ".[4]

[1] Becon, *Reliques of Rome*, 54.

[2] " Of feyned contemplatif lif ", in F. D. Matthew, *The English Works of John Wyclif*, E.E.T.S., 188 ff.

[3] *The Cloud of the Unknowing*, ch. xviii. " As Martha complained then on Mary her sister, right so yet unto this day all actives complain of contemplatives."

[4] *Incendium Amoris*, I. ch. xxi. Cp. I. ch. vii. Rolle agrees with St. Thomas, *Summa*, P. II. ii. Q. clxxxii. A. 2.

Walter Hilton, an enthusiast for the contemplative life, none the less wrote an excellent little book for devout living in the world. He is perhaps a little condescending when he writes :

> Active life alone belongeth to worldly men and women which are lewd, fleshly and boisterous in knowing of ghostly occupation ; for they feel no savour in devotion by fervour of love as other men do, nor have they any skill in it. And yet nevertheless they have dread of God and of the pains of hell, and therefore flee sin ; and they have desire for to please God and for to come to heaven ; and they have goodwill to their even Christians. Unto these men it is needful and speedful to use the works of active life, as busily as they may, for help of themselves and of their even Christians ; for they can do naught else.[1]

A little later he is more explicit :

> He that for the love of God in contemplation leaveth the love of his even Christian, and doth not to them as he ought when he is bounden thereto ; he fulfilleth not charity. Also in the contrary wise, whoso hath more regard to works of active life and to business of the world, that for love of his even Christian he leaveth ghostly occupation utterly after that God disposeth him thereto, he fulfilleth not fully charity.[2]

Few men may be called to the contemplative life, and those who rashly enter upon it are exposed to many dangers ; but there is no higher adventure than the search after God. No one blames an enthusiastic astronomer who shuts himself in an observatory, who denies himself the ordinary pleasures of life, who spends long nights in vigil, and finally discovers a new star. Why, then, should men be so contemptuous of one who shuts himself up in a cell, freeing himself from all distractions, that by concentration and attention he may learn of God ? Both astronomy and religion need specialists if knowledge is to increase.[3] Specialists, it is true, have deliberately limited the range of their study ; but however narrow they may themselves be, their discoveries may have a wide significance when contributed to the pool of general knowledge.

Naturally specialists are particularly liable to lose their sense

[1] Hilton, *Minor Works* (Orchard Books), Op. I. ch. iii.

[2] *Ibid.* Op. I. ch. v.

[3] Bigg, *Wayside Sketches*, 135 : " We need a special class of students of God, of men and women, whose primary and absorbing interest it is to work out the spiritual life in all its purity and integrity. They will be an unworldly and impractical race—all great students and artists are so. They are theorists and idealists. But theories and ideas, however abstract they may appear, have, if solid, surprising practical results."

of proportion, and it should occasion no surprise that the mystic in his solitary cell, concentrating on the interior life, should sometimes be unmindful that men have social duties. It was this one-sidedness which provoked Milman to write his eloquent attack on the *Imitatio Christi*.[1] Thomas à Kempis was for him a self-absorbed monk who cared for nothing " but the purification and elevation of his own soul ". He describes his book as " absolutely selfish in its aim as in its acts ", as presenting self-culture as an end in itself, or at best as a means of attaining to heaven. This is unjust. Thomas à Kempis was a specialist. He knew very little of the world, but a great deal about one human heart—his own. He wrote of what he knew ; and he is no more to be condemned for not treating of the social aspects of Christianity than a writer on pure mathematics is to be condemned for not being interested in cricket. He can scarcely be described as self-absorbed, for there is no taint of egoism in his work, which was evidently inspired by the desire to help others on the way to holiness. Let us admit that he was a specialist, with the limitations of a specialist, and be grateful for what he has taught us of the spiritual life. As a matter of fact, the chorus of human gratitude is still swelling after nearly half a millennium. No one dare say that the long life of seclusion in the cloister of Zwolle was wasted, even when bound to admit that there are aspects of religion to which he was blind.

All mystics retire into themselves to find God ; and in judging them we have to ask, Are they God-centred or self-centred ? There are many types of mystics to-day ; and there were as many in the XIV century.

First of all let us think of Rolle. He desired to know God rather than to save his soul. He knew that by searching he could not find God, and that he must wait until God should reveal Himself ; but he could prepare for the revelation by getting free from all distractions, by repenting of his sins, by disciplining himself, and by meditation on the demands of scripture. Ultimately the revelation came to him and he entered on the higher life of contemplation. He writes :

Some think contemplation is the knowledge of deep mysteries : others that it is the state of total concentration on spiritual things : others again that it is an elevation of mind which makes the soul dead

[1] Milman, *Latin Christianity*, ix. 163 ff.

to all fleshly desires. All these, no doubt, are true in their measures; but to me it seems that contemplation is joyous song of God's love.

The rest of Rolle's life was "a joyous song"; but he did not wish to sing it alone. The more he loved God, the more he loved his fellow Christians: He was so full of that love that he forgot himself, and his early desire for self-vindication. The four chapters on Love in *The Form of Living* are lyrical utterances in spite of the author's endeavours to expound his subject in a reasoned and reasonable manner.[2]

Secondly, there are those who have experienced an instantaneous conversion in the midst of their sins, who have felt the mighty hand of their God upon them with a compulsion impossible to resist. We are not concerned with the explanations of modern psychologists, but will quote from *The Cloud of the Unknowing* the mediaeval explanation, although it is far from being satisfactory:

I trow that Our Lord, as specially and as oft—yea, and more specially and more oft—will vouchsafe to work holiness in those that have been customary sinners, than in some others that never grieved Him greatly in comparison with them. And this will He do, because He would be seen of all merciful and almighty, and because He would be seen to work as He liketh, when He liketh and where He liketh.[3]

Such converts could not forget themselves, for they were themselves the evidence of God's mercy; and it was by remembering what they had been that they were led to adoration.

The third type of converts were the sick souls—men convicted of sin, and in terror of judgment, who had tried to reform, failed and almost despaired; who had themselves felt the inrush of forgiveness with a sense of freedom that justified them in saying, "We are saved". Such men are much concerned about themselves before conversion, and afterwards are apt to remain self-centred. They are tempted to divide men into the saved and the unsaved, and to think that all the saved must have experienced a like conversion. They feel that their salvation separates them from their fellows, and makes them censorious about those who indulge in pleasures that they have renounced. Their

[1] Rolle, *Emendatio Vitae*, ch. xii.

[2] Rolle, *Form of Living*, ch. vii. to x. In Heseltine, *Selected Works of Richard Rolle*. Cp. *Emendatio Vitae*, ch. xi., in Miss Comper's version.

[3] *The Cloud of the Unknowing*, ch. xxxiv.

conversions have been real; but Walter Hilton, who knew such men, speaks of them as "dupes of the Fiend". "They are seen", he says, "between two black raining clouds; the one cloud is presumption and highing of themselves, and the other cloud is down-putting and lowering of their even Christians".[1]

Men of this self-centred type have been more numerous since the Reformation than before. They are usually the fruits of revivalist preaching; and in the Middle Ages the converts of revivalists worked off their excitement in dangerous pilgrimages and heroic flagellations. The mystics of whom we are writing had nothing to do with revivalists, and were sworn foes to all that savoured of publicity; but they all entered on the *Purgative Way*, and would have found it difficult to conceive of a religion which did not involve asceticism.

Asceticism of some sort is a necessity for a healthy life. A man soon discovers that unlimited self-indulgence is neither good for his body nor for his soul. He, at least, sees that it is wise to be temperate in all things. He may not be religious, but he wants to be physically fit and well.

A man with greater moral earnestness perceives the weakness of his will, his liability to certain temptations, and the impossibility of doing the things that he would. In his desire to be master of himself he resolves to avoid occasions of falling, or to penalise himself when he falls. He may not be religious, but he desires to vindicate his manhood. Such self-discipline is good if it does not become an unhealthy obsession. In the Middle Ages many were dualists, and there were countless examples of those who strove to subdue the flesh, who had a morbid desire for suffering and a perverted pleasure in testing their capacity to endure pain. *The Ancren Riwle*[2] in places illustrates this, while the life of Blessed Henry Suso[3] shows his curious ingenuity in devising instruments of self-torture. The anonymous author of *The Discerning of Spirits* warns men that the Devil may lead them to be proud of their austerities, and may also lead them "to the open reproving of other men's defaults, which they have not the office for to do".[4] This warning was not required by men like Suso. All

[1] Hilton, *Scale of Perfection*, ii. ch. xxviii.

[2] *Ancren Riwle*, 289, 290.

[3] William James, *Varieties of Religious Experience*, 306-310.

[4] One of the ancient tracts published by Pepwell, 1521. Reprinted by Gardner, *Cell of Self Knowledge*. Cp. a letter of St. Catherine of Siena to William Flete, the

mystics insist on humility ; and for humility Blessed Henry Suso was a pattern.

Apart from physical well-being and moral mastery, many have become ascetics in order to devote themselves to concentrated attention on the Spirit of God. They have striven to kill all earthly desires and to renounce all interest in this world. They have even renounced reason in order to be more receptive of supernatural teaching. The authors of *The Cloud of the Unknowing* [1] and *The Mirror of Simple Souls* both advocate this self-emptying as a prelude to divine knowledge. They ignored the fact that man is incapable of receiving any supernatural knowledge that cannot be related by analogy to his own experience. They ignored also the fact that the more heaven is desired, the more important becomes the way to it. This world has an intensified significance when it is regarded as a preparation for another.[2]

Christian asceticism has more usually its root in penitence. A man punishes himself, or voluntarily submits to punishment in an ardent desire to do what he can to expiate his sins by enduring an equivalent recompense. Ordinary men accepted hard penances, hoping to escape from worse penalties in purgatory or hell ; but the mystics endured them from an overwhelming sense that they had by their sins hurt our Lord. " I am not worthy ", says à Kempis, " but to be scourged and punished : because grievously and often I have offended Thee : and in many things have greatly sinned." [3]

In the Middle Ages the Church was one, and devout people felt that they were members one of another, so that it entered into the heart of recluses that by their mortifications they could make some reparation for the sins of men in the world, filling up that which was behindhand of the sufferings of Christ. This is expressed in a very naïve way by Dame Margery Kempe, who was willing " to be hacked as small as flesh to the pot, so that I

English Hermit. " They often mar their perfection by making themselves judges of those who are not going the same way as they are going " (quoted Gardner, *op. cit.* 52).

[1] *The Cloud of the Unknowing*, chs. xliii., xliv.

[2] Inge, *Lectures on Mysticism*, 34 : " All conclusions about the world above us, which are not based on the analogy of our own mental experience, are either false or meaningless ". *Ibid.* 24 : " Whatever view of reality deepens our sense of the tremendous issues of life in this world wherein we move, is for us nearer the truth, than any view which diminishes that sense ".

[3] *Imitatio Christi*, iv. ch. 52.

could by Thy death save them all from damnation ". Throughout the *Colloquy* our Lord praises her willingness, but restrains her eagerness to suffer. He is represented as saying, " Daughter, if thou knewest how sweet thy love is to Me, thou wouldest never do other things but love Me with all thy heart ".[1]

But the great desire of the mystics was to be conformed to our Lord in His sufferings and passion. Dame Julian of Norwich desired three gifts of God. " The first was mind of His passion ; the second was bodily sickness in youth, at thirty years of age ; the third was to have of God's gift three wounds . . . the wound of very contrition, the wound of kind (*i.e.* natural) compassion, and the wound of steadfast longing after God ".[2] She had her desires. In 1373, when thirty years of age, she was so sick that all thought she would die. Then she had her fifteen *Shewings, The Revelations of Divine Love.* She recovered and lived more than forty years afterwards, perfecting her contrition, extending her compassion, and ever in more hopeful love, longing for the Lord, Who had revealed Himself in his " Blissful Passion ".

To speak of the " Blissful Passion " seems strange to us who cannot read the Gospel account without pain, and would certainly avert our eyes with horror from visions in which Dame Julian rejoiced. She, however, concentrated on each terrible detail, and did not view it as a modern pacifist or humanitarian. For her the sacrifice was splendid—she thrilled at the heroic patience it exemplified, and the consuming love which was its cause. It was the vision of Calvary which inspired her optimism, and convinced her that in spite of everything, " all is well and shall be well ".

The second stage in the mystic's progress was the *Illuminative Way*, which began with meditation and ended with contemplation. It began with discursive prayer and ended with the prayer of quiet. In the first stage thought was exercised, in the second self was forgotten ; and in the third the soul was simply receptive and had passed into the *Unitive Way*.

Rolle [3] is emphatic in urging men to read the Bible, but suggests that " hard sayings may be left to disputers, and witty men, used for a long time in Holy Scriptures ". Apart from

[1] Printed in Gardner's *Cell of Self Knowledge*, 53-57.
[2] *The Revelations of Divine Love*, Miss Warrack's version, ch. ii.
[3] Rolle, *Emendatio Vitae*.

other commentaries he wrote two on the Psalter, claiming no originality, but confessing that all was derived from holy doctors.[1] With equal modesty the author of *The Cloud of the Unknowing*[2] refused to quote lest he should be tempted " to curiosity and display of knowledge ".

The reading of the Bible was no doubt generally restricted to clerks ; but all could meditate on the well-known facts of our Lord's life,[3] and never was there greater devotion to the humanity of our Lord. Hilton said, " We must live under the shadow of his humanity as long as we are here below ".[4] Nicholas Love, at the beginning of his *Mirror of the Blessed Jesus*, quoted as from St. Bernard the saying that " for simple souls, contemplation of the Manhood of Christ is more natural, more profitable, and more secure than is high contemplation of His Godhead ".[5] It was for simple souls that he wrote his book, often following the Gospel story word for word, often inserting apocryphal matter, and sometimes writing like an imaginative child who makes up stories for himself about his hero. Here is his description of how our Lord took leave of His mother when He started on His mission :

" Dear Mother, it is now high time that I should go to glorify and make known My Father, and also to show myself to the world, and to seek the salvation of souls, since My Father hath ordained and sent me into the world for this end. Wherefore, dear Mother, be of good cheer, for I shall soon come back to thee." And therewith that sovereign Master of Meekness, kneeling down before his mother, lowly asked her blessing. And she, also kneeling, and clasping Him devoutly in her arms, with weeping, said thus : " My blessed Son, since Thou wilt go now with Thy Father's blessing and mine, think of me and have in mind to come back to me ".[6]

[1] Prologue to the English Psalter, quoted by Miss Hodgson, *Sanity of Mysticism*, 156.

[2] *The Cloud of the Unknowing*, ch. lxx.

[3] Rolle, *Incendium Amoris*, ch. xxvi., writes : " Nothing is merrier than Jesus to sing, nothing more delightful than Jesus to hear. Hearing it truly mirthes the mind and song uplifts it."

[4] Hilton, *Scale of Perfection*, ii. ch. xxx. Cp. i. ch. xxxv.

[5] The quotation, as the editor notes, comes from the *Epistola ad fratres Montis Dei*, falsely attributed to St. Bernard, and now assigned to William of St. Thierry. It has recently been translated by Shewing and published by Sheed and Ward as *The Golden Epistle*. The Epistle was denounced by Gerson for its false teaching ; but Nicholas Love and the author of *The Mirror of Simple Souls* were indebted to it. The latter exaggerated its more daring statements. *Vide* Miss Kirchberger's introduction to *The Mirror*, xliv-xlvii.

[6] *The Mirror of the Blessed Jesus*, ch. xiv.

Nicholas Love was not in the strict sense a mystic, and mysticism properly begins when a man passes from the external teaching and sinks into his own soul to find God there. Hilton explains how we were made in God's image, and that He is within us, but we must find Him ; how He may be lost like the treasure in the field, like the coin lost in the house, like the Christ asleep in the tempest-tossed boat. He concludes :

> He is there though He be lost from thee ; but thou art not in Him until thou hast found Him. This then was His mercy, that He would not suffer Himself to be lost, only where He may be found.[1]

Such introversion must not be confused with introspection. The latter is concerned with self-analysis and betokens a self-centred life. The mystic on the other hand concentrated on one object—God. He was filled with a great desire to know Him. He had perhaps, like the woman in the parable, to sweep diligently ere the dust and dirt defiling the soul was removed, and the coin stamped with the king's image was found. Rolle said, " Contemplative sweetness is not gotten, but with full great labour ; and with joy untold it is possessed ".[2] Dame Julian approached the subject from the other side :

> Our soul is kindly rooted in God in endless love : and therefore if we will have knowledge of our soul and communing and dalliance therewith, it behoveth to seek unto Our Lord God in whom it is enclosed.[3]

The belief in the hidden God within, and direction by the inner light, had its dangers. Men were tempted to mistake their own thoughts, desires and fantasies for divine revelations.[4] Walter Hilton warned men against trusting in visions received waking or sleeping, for they may come from a good angel or from a bad one. Men must try the spirits whether they be of God, and must always remember that visions are of secondary importance in the life of contemplation.[5] The true contemplative life, he said, " lieth in perfect love and charity felt inwardly by ghostly virtue, and by soothfast knowing of God and ghostly things ".[6]

[1] Hilton, *Scale of Perfection*, i. ch. xlix.
[2] Rolle, *Emendatio Vitae*, ch. xii.
[3] *Revelations of Divine Love*, 135.
[4] Pourrat, *La Spiritualité chrétienne*, ii. 446.
[5] Hilton, *Scale of Perfection*, i. ch. x.
[6] *Ibid.* i. ch. iii.

Mystics have at all times been tempted to some form of gnosticism, and to believe themselves initiates possessed of hidden knowledge. This tendency becomes more noticeable as we approach the Reformation period—Cornelius Agrippa, Reuchlin, Pico della Mirandola and Paracelsus were all interested in magic; but even the XIV century had devotees of the occult; and the author of *The Cloud of the Unknowing* speaks with contempt of those who

> stare in the stars, as if they would be above the moon, and hearken if they shall hear any angel sing out of heaven. These men will sometimes, with the curiosity of their imagination, pierce the planets; and make a hole in the firmament to look in thereat. . . . Yet all this is but deceit seem it never so holy, for in this time they have souls full empty of any real devotion. Much vanity and falsehood is in their hearts, caused by their curious working: insomuch that oft-times the devil feigneth quaint sounds in their ears, quaint lights and shinings in their eyes, and wonderful smells in their noses; and all is but falsehood.[1]

Visions, he maintained, might be real, but were never sent by God to satisfy an idle curiosity. Dame Julian wrote: "I saw soothly in Our Lord's teaching, the more we busy us to know His secret counsels . . . the further we shall be from knowing thereof".[2] Visions were to be prized for their spiritual value, and not because of their extraordinary nature. Further, they were to be tested by Scripture. Richard of St. Victor wrote:

> Even if you think that you have been taken up into the high mountain apart, even if you think that you see Christ transfigured, do not be ready to believe anything that you see in Him, or hear from Him, unless Moses and Elias run to meet Him. I hold all that in suspicion, which the authority of Scripture does not confirm, nor do I receive Christ in His clarification unless Moses and Elias are talking with Him.[3]

These mystics then make no claim to possess esoteric knowledge. They do claim that their eyes have been opened to understand what every man might know. They claim that while most men

[1] *Cloud of the Unknowing*, ch. lvii.

[2] *Revelations of Divine Love*, 69.

[3] Richard of St. Victor, *Benjamin Minor*, cap. 181; quoted Gardner, *Cell of Self Knowledge*, xv. Only ten chapters of this book were published by Pepwell in 1521. Richard is claimed as a native by both Ireland and Scotland. He died in 1173. For him Benjamin was the type of the contemplative, because of the Vulgate reading—Ps. lxvii. 28. *Ibi Benjamin adolescentulus in mentis excessu.* He argues that at the birth of Benjamin Rachel dies. Therefore Rachel stands for failing reason.

looked at the world through the smoked-glasses of convention and prejudice, they saw things as they were, saw them as God sees them, saw them in relation to eternity.

What the opening of the ghostly eye is, said Hilton, the greatest clerk on earth cannot imagine by his wit, nor fully tell by his tongue. For it may not be got by study, nor through man's travail only, but principally by grace of the Holy Ghost, and with travail of man.[1]

It is God's response to man's desire for Him ; and it is man's reward for patient continuance in the art of contemplation. To the opened eye, " Reason is turned into light, and the will into love ".[2] Love is the source of understanding and " Perfect love maketh God and the Soul to be as if they were one thing ".[3] It is a mystical union like marriage, so " in this oneing is the marriage made betwixt God and the soul, that shall never be broken ".[4]

Dame Julian expresses the same thought in a somewhat different way :

For as the body is clad in the cloth and the flesh in the skin, and the bones in the flesh, and the heart in the whole, so are we, soul and body, clad in the goodness of God and enclosed, Yea, and more homely ; for all these may waste and wear away, but the goodness of God is ever whole.[5]

Rolle is equally clear and refused to exaggerate the attainments of the Contemplatives :

The fire of love lies in their hearts and burns therein, and makes them clean of all earthly filth ; and forthwith they are contemplative and ravished in love. For contemplation is a sight, and they see into heaven with their ghostly eye. But thou shalt know that no men have perfect sight of heaven whilst they are living bodily here. But as soon as they die they are brought before God and see Him face to face and eye to eye, and dwell with bliss without end. For Him they sought and Him they desired, and Him they loved with all their might.[6]

All these mystics had experienced ecstasy or rapture, but they recognised its occasional nature. Hilton writes :

[1] Hilton, *Scale of Perfection*, ii. ch. xl.
[2] *Ibid.* i. ch. xiv.
[3] Hilton, *Minor Works*, Cp. i. ch. viii.
[4] Hilton, *Scale of Perfection*, i. ch. viii.
[5] *Revelations of Divine Love*, ch. xi.
[6] Rolle, *Form of Living* (Heseltine's Version, ch. xii.).

> The common grace lasteth whole whatsoever a man do, so long as his will and intent is true to God. . . . Special grace, felt through the unseeable presence of God, that maketh the soul a perfect lover, lasteth not ever alike whole in the highness of feeling, but changeably cometh and goeth.[1]

A man is to keep such a favour " privy—except it be to his confessor " ; to " meek himself " and wait until it come again.[2]

Nothing is more remarkable in these mystics than their gaiety. They had lived hard lives and denied themselves all relaxation, they had suffered from misunderstandings, they had persevered through dreary wildernesses of spiritual dryness and known the sense of dereliction in the night of the soul ; but they had always been sure that the dawn would break, and that the Sun of Righteousness would rise with healing in His wings. They wrote to witness that their faith had not been in vain. The romantic Rolle went on his way singing ; the cheerful Dame Julian found our Lord both homely and courteous ; the sober Hilton was full of quiet thankfulness. Their perplexities were resolved, so that Dame Julian was convinced that " sin is behovable ",[3] and the author of *The Mirror of Simple Souls* could bid farewell to the virtues [4]—statements which can only be understood if read in their context. The first mystic had been convinced that all things work together for good ; and the second had experienced the enfranchisement which St. Paul had felt when freed from the Law—he need no longer fuss and worry about his conduct, but loving God might do as he liked.

The other remarkable fact about these mystics is that, unlike some on the Continent, they are not obsessed with a sense of the Devil's power or terror-struck with the thought of hell. Dame Julian indeed was perplexed when thinking of a place of torment and asked that she might be shown it, and so understand how, in spite of it, all is well. Her petition was denied : she was only shown her own sins, and encouraged to have faith in the teaching of the Church which somehow some day would be reconciled with her optimism. In one of her " Shewings " she saw our Lord

[1] Hilton, *Scale of Perfection*, ii. ch. xli.

[2] *Ibid.* i. ch. vi.

[3] *Revelations of Divine Love*, 56.

[4] *Mirror of Simple Souls*, Div. iii. ch. iii. On this statement see the comments of Mrs. Herman, *Value and Meaning of Mysticism*, 79, and Miss Underhill, *Mysticism*, 219.

overcoming the fiend—" For this sight I laughed heartily ".[1] On another occasion, when she doubted of her visions, she dreamed of the Devil, and felt that it served her right, though she is careful to state that it was only a dream.[2]

In *The Cloud of the Unknowing* we are told, " the Devil hath his contemplatives as God has His ",[3] and visions of the Devil are the reward of those who seek occult knowledge. " The holy, on the other hand ", said Hilton, " have nothing to fear ".

It is full fair contemplation of the fiend in a clean soul, where grace bringeth the fiend to the sight of the soul as a clumsy caitiff bound with the might of Jesus that he might not hurt any. . . . There is no creature as unmighty as he is, and therefore it is great cowardice that men dread him so much.[4]

The English, unlike some continental mystics, are all definite on the heinous nature of sin, though they found it difficult to account for it. Most followed the Neo-Platonist theory that was mediated for them through St. Augustine ; that evil was only the privation of good, and sin the acquiescence in that privation. The varied statements of Dame Julian in this connexion are interesting :

I saw God in a point, that is to say, in my understanding, by which sight I saw that He is in all things. I beheld and considered, seeing and knowing in sight, with a soft dread, and thought, *What is sin?* . . . I saw not sin, for I believe it hath no manner of substance, and no part in being. . . . Yet sin is the cause of all pain. . . . Sin is the sharpest scourge that any chosen soul may be smitten with. . . . There is no harder hell than sin. . . . We should choose all the pains of earth, purgatory and hell rather than choose sin. . . . Sin is in sooth vile, and more painful than hell, without likeness, for it is contrary to our fair nature. . . . But sin hindereth not God's working. . . . It occasions the revelation of God's mercy. . . . It teacheth the saint humility. . . . It is the cause

[1] *Revelations of Divine Love*, 32.

[2] *Revelations of Divine Love*, 165 : " And in my sleep at the beginning, methought the fiend set him on my throat, putting forth a visage full near my face, like a young man's, and it was wondrous long and lean, and I saw never such. The colour was red like the tilestone when it is new burnt, with black spots therein like black freckles, fresher than the tilestone. His hair was red as rust, clipped in front, with full locks hanging on the temples. He grinned on me with a malicious semblance, showing white teeth ; and so much methought it the more horrible. Body and hands had he none shapely ; but with his paws he held me in the throat, and would have strangled me, but he might not."

[3] *Cloud of the Unknowing*, ch. xlv.

[4] *Scale of Perfection*, ii. ch. xlv.

of Christ's pains, and we have lastingly matter for joy, for endless love made Him suffer. . . . He triumphs and all is well.[1]

Dame Julian was scarcely a systematic thinker. She grasped such truths as came to her, and did not trouble to reconcile them with one another. Had she been convicted of inconsistency, she would have professed herself an unlettered woman with due humility, but would none the less have adhered to her own experience.[2]

All these mystics trusted to their intuitions. They believed in the inner light, and that a still, small voice came from a source external to themselves. They were free to accept the light and obey the voice, just as they were free to accept the temptations of the world, the flesh and the devil. They also had " to try the spirits whether they were of God ".

It may be seen that each thought that cometh in our hearts whether it be good or evil, it is not evermore the speech of our own spirit ; but the consent to the thought, whatsoever it be, that is even of our own spirit.[3]

IV. *Dangers of Mysticism*

All mystics have but one object, to know God ; but they seek Him in different ways, and all ways have their own danger. Some are inspired by the contemplation of nature and sink into pantheistic error ; some are so enthralled by ceremonial and ritual that they elaborate an unreal symbolism ; some with an unchecked fancy accept dreams as private revelations and become puffed up with gnostic pride ; some seek for God mirrored in their own souls, and become the victims of auto-suggestion and suffer from hallucinations.

None of the English mystics were symbolists, and none of them were much addicted to speculative thought. They relate spiritual experience which some may not think credible ; but they were all notably sane. Some were hermits living an open-air life, and some were anchorites with a specified round of religious duties. They were not neurotic people, like Elizabeth Barton, the Maid of Kent, or enthusiastic cranks with a heresy to ventilate.

Perhaps it may be true to say that they were not nature

[1] *Revelations of Divine Love*, 26, 56, 79, 83, 124, 157.
[2] Von Hügel, *Mystical Element in Religion*, ii. 294.
[3] Gardner, *Cell of Self Knowledge*, 132.

mystics, though Rolle loved the wilderness and the sense of freedom he enjoyed on the Yorkshire moors. He also loved the song of birds, although his references to the nightingale have probably a literary origin.[1] Hilton rather grudgingly admits that the world may be a revelation of God :

It is fair looking with the inner eye on Jesus in bodily creatures to see His might, His wisdom and His goodness in ordinances of this kind ; but it is much fairer looking on Jesus in ghostly creatures.[2]

Though not nature mystics, our authors were free from all taint of manicheism. Dame Julian is quite clear on the relation of nature to Grace :

Nature is all good and fair in itself, and Grace was sent out to save Nature and destroy sin, and bring Nature to the blessed point from whence it came. . . . Thus are Nature and Grace of one accord : for Grace is God as Nature is God, He is two in manner of working, but one in love ; and neither of these worketh without the other, and they are not disparted.[3]

It should be clear from what has gone before that if these mystics aimed at union with God, they never dreamed of absorption into God. They had no tendency to pantheism, and no desire for a permanent condition of " naked nothingness ".[4] They were saved from both these errors by their conception of Love.[5] Love implies a lover and a beloved one, a giving and a response. Love also quickens all the faculties of the lover, and irradiates not only the beloved object, but also all that he sees. Love points the way not to annihilation, but to the fullness of life.

This is true even of the authors of *The Mirror of Simple Souls* and *The Cloud of the Unknowing*. They speak at length of stripping themselves of human knowledge and of earthly interests and of all desires on their way to God ; but it is possible

[1] Miss Hodgson, *Sanity of Mysticism*, has explored Rolle's country and insists on the influence it had on his works. She has perhaps overstated a good case.

[2] *Scale of Perfection*, ii. ch. xlv.

[3] *Revelations of Divine Love*, 157.

[4] After the author of *The Mirror of Simple Souls*, Div. xx. ch. ii., has described that she " has nothing withholden in naughting herself and is forbidden all work ", Methley, who translated the treatise into Latin, remarks: " If this soul never did any work, she could not have written this book, so we must understand her as describing a short time—when she was in prayer ".

[5] Mrs. Herman, *Meaning and Value of Mysticism*, 298-300.

that they meant little more than a modern scientist means when he says that in the pursuit of new knowledge a man must free himself from all preconceptions and approach his subject with an open mind. *The Mirror of Simple Souls* is full of flouts and jeers directed against reason, but it may be argued that the writer's sarcasms are really aimed at the syllogistic method—she is only contending that knowledge cannot be increased by chopping logic. When both authors profess that, by entering into the dark cloud of the Unknowing, they become aware of the ineffable God and have no language in which to express their experience, they are still persons in contact with a Person—God is not for them an abstraction [1]—while following the negative way of the pseudo-Dionysius they still inconsistently believe, as he did, in the incarnation ; and after asserting that nothing can be affirmed of the Godhead, they accept our Lord in his manhood as the revelation of the Father.[2]

It is possible to vindicate the orthodoxy of these authors ; but it is impossible to deny that their teaching was dangerous and liable to be misunderstood. Miss Underhill admits that *The Mirror of Simple Souls* is " a piece of mystical literature of an advanced kind, often fringing the borders of orthodoxy ".[3] There is, however, no doubt about the faith of the other mystics under consideration. They would all have echoed the words of Dame Julian, " I yield me to my Mother, Holy Church, as a simple child oweth ".[4] The author of *The Cloud* had nothing but contempt for heretics, " who cry and whine in their throats, so greedy be they and hasty to say what they think ",[5] while Walter Hilton, a quiet man and a scholar, was disgusted by noisy

[1] *Mirror of Simple Souls*, Div. iii. ch. xxii. : " There is none other but He, which may not be known. . . . He only is my God that none can one word of say, nor all they of Paradise one only point attain nor understand, for all the knowing that they have of Him."

[2] Westcott, *Religious Thought in the West*, 159-160, thus contrasts the affirmative and negative ways : " According to the one, everything which *is* may be affirmed of God, because so far as it is, it exists in Him. According to the other way, everything, so far as we are cognizant of it, may be denied of God, because our conception introduces the element of limitation, which cannot be applied to Him. Thus on the one hand He *is* Wisdom, Love, Truth and Light, because the absolute ideas belonging to these words are included in His Being ; and on the other hand He is *not* Wisdom, *not* Love, *not* Truth, *not* Light, because He is raised infinitely above the notions with which the words are necessarily connected by men."

[3] Miss Underhill, *Mysticism*, 462.

[4] *Revelations of Divine Love*, 98.

[5] *The Cloud of the Unknowing*, ch. liii.

disputants who disturbed men's faith.[1] These mystics took the Church for granted with her creed and sacraments ; and her witness preserved them from the extravagances of mystics of a later date. None the less they were not interested in the Church as an institution, nor with the social implications of Christianity. Specialists in all that concerned the interior life, they had the limitations of specialists. If writers from Wyclif to Dean Milman have been one-sided in condemning them, they were themselves one-sided as guides to life.

As solitaries they could help a soul in trouble, but they had no gospel for the world at large. As solitaries they were ill-fitted to be guides for conduct in courts, camps or counting-houses ; while they did not perceive that organisation and continuity were necessary if the Church were to fulfil her mission. Some mystics made such a sharp distinction between the spiritual and secular that their readers were tempted to make a fatal separation of religion from business, and to think that they could be pursued apart. They were further tempted to believe that religion consisted solely in the relation of the soul to God, leaving their neighbours out of account. This, as we have seen, was not the teaching of Rolle or Walter Hilton, and would not have been directly taught by the others. It arose from an over-emphasis on the interior life. They all in some degree forgot that there was a Kingdom of God ; that the Church existed to leaven the mass and discipline the wicked ; that she had duties to perform for many imperfect people.

There was another danger implicit in mysticism, due to a depreciation of reason and a contempt for learning. Thomas à Kempis writes quite truly :

When thou hast learned and read many things, thou must ever return to the beginning, *I am He that teacheth man knowledge* ; and I bestow a clearer understanding on little children, than can be taught to man.[2]

It is not necessary to dispute his saying :

Far nobler is that learning which trickles down from above from divine influence, than that which is painfully amassed by the wit of men.[3]

[1] Hilton, *Scale of Perfection*, ii. ch. xxvi.
[2] *Imitatio Christi*, iv. ch. 43. [3] *Ibid.* iv. ch. 21.

But the constant repetition of such teaching tended to dissociate the life of devotion from the duty of study, while reason was cast down from her throne of judgment.

Many taught to rely on their intuitions felt no necessity to try the Spirits whether they were of God ; they forgot that Christianity is an historical religion, and that the Holy Ghost, in Whom they trusted, has been guiding the Church through the ages towards the truth. In their exaltation of the spiritual nature of religion they were inclined to minimise the value of outward observances, until Sir Thomas More was driven to believe that their hearts were inspired by a devilish device to destroy the devotion of ordinary men.[1]

This was certainly not the aim of the mystics under consideration ; but their books were read by men who found in them an excuse for neglecting their duties. Mystical treatises were popular, theological works were not, so that when the XVI century dawned there was an unbalanced presentment of the faith.

The genuine mystics were full of joy because they had come into immediate contact with God. They had passed beyond believing in a creed to intercourse with a Person. They knew that God loved them and they responded to that love. Nothing else mattered. They were not always conscious of His presence ; but they were quite sure that He had come to them and would come to them again. When with Him they wanted nothing else, could think of nothing else, and afterwards they had nothing else to talk about.

They have recorded their experience and it is of inestimable value for those who receive it humbly, who accept the evidence of experts and do not delude themselves into thinking that they can become experts at second-hand. When such books are popular, as they were at the beginning of the XVI century, presumptuous persons, having mastered the language of the saints, might think that they shared in their exaltation ; and having noted the freedom to which the saints had attained by a life of discipline, might imagine that they could assume a like freedom, without doing anything to earn it. Because a saint has passed beyond believing in a creed to the knowledge of a Person, it does not follow that an ordinary man does not need to know the

[1] *Dialogue*, i. ch. ii.

dogmas in which the Church has formularised her age-long experience. Because a saint has reached a stage where love alone dictates his conduct, an ordinary man is not excused from cultivating the virtues. Because a saint has become indifferent to the pains and pleasures of earthly life, neither the saint nor the ordinary man is free from the duties that lie close at hand. There is no greater danger to the spiritual life than the over-stimulation of the emotions, the indulgence in cloudy speculations, and the unrealities of pietistic talk. The genuine mystics were fully alive to these dangers, the pseudo-mystics were not. It was the pseudo-mystic who was tempted to despise the Church, neglect the sacraments, and congratulate himself on believing in the religion of the heart.

There is indeed no positive evidence that these books inclined men to receive the doctrines of the Reformers, although it is true that the works of Rolle were largely interpolated by the Lollards, as was also *The Prick of Conscience* [1] once attributed to him. The Carthusians, who had been so diligent in transcribing these mystical treatises, died as martyrs for the unity of Christendom and the sovereignty of Christ ; while those who escaped abroad took with them their precious books, which were edited and republished a century later by Augustine Baker [2] and Serenus de Cressy.[3] On the other hand, when Wynkyn de Worde in 1525 printed a new book called *The Image of Love* by an Observant Friar and Bachelor of Divinity named John Ryckes, he was brought before the Vicar General and charged with publishing an heretical work. In the XIII, XIV or XV centuries the book would have been considered a fair specimen of Franciscan piety, contrasting the image which the soul discovered of the Love of God with the jewel-bedecked images to be found in the churches ; but in 1525 such reflections were thought to be

[1] *The Prick of Conscience*, reprinted by the Philological Society 1862–1864, was not by Rolle, though it was long thought to be his principal work. Miss Allen, *Writings of Richard Rolle*, 15, 372 ff. The interpolations are examined 387 ff.

[2] Augustine Baker (1575–1641) was born in Monmouthshire, joined the Roman Church in 1605 and became a Benedictine. He wrote to Sir Richard Cotton, " There were many good English books of old time ", and asked his correspondent to send some of them to the nuns at Cambrai (Ellis, *Original Letters*, II Series, iii. 256-258). He edited *The Cloud of the Unknowing*, and wrote a commentary on it.

[3] Serenus de Cressy (1605–1674) was born in Yorkshire. A Fellow of Merton, he joined the Roman Church 1646, and became a Benedictine. He was afterwards chaplain to Catherine of Braganza. He edited *The Scale of Perfection* and *The Revelations of Divine Love*.

dangerous ; passages were quoted from the book by people like More's *Messenger* ; and it was suppressed, though the pious and orthodox nuns of Syon bought sixty copies.[1]

Luther [2] in his early years owed a great deal to Eckhart, Tauler and the *Theologia Germanica*, but he had nothing but contempt for Carlstadt and Frank, who were ever speaking of " Spirit, Spirit, Spirit and cared not for Bible, sacrament and preaching ".[3] Protestants, having proclaimed the right of private judgment, had enough incentives to division without admitting the solvent of mysticism ; and in consequence for two generations the mystical approach to God was only followed by anabaptist sects. The same was true in England ; but it does not follow that mysticism had done nothing to prepare men's minds for the Reformation.

The mystics had emphasised personal rather than corporate religion, and the cultivation of the interior life divorced from external practice. They had stressed the possibility of an immediate approach to God, until their followers failed to see the value of a mediatorial Church and a sacerdotal ministry. They had relied on intuition rather than on reason, on the inner light and not on an authoritative tradition ; and they had no wish to reconcile their spiritual enlightenment with human learning. The English mystics would have repudiated the Reformers with indignation, and the Reformers would have denied any indebtedness to the mystics ; but the mystics had done much to prepare the soil and create the atmosphere in which the new ideas could grow and breathe.

[1] A. W. Reed, *Early Tudor Drama*, 166-168.
[2] Fife, *Young Luther*, 197-201.
[3] Quoted by Inge, *Christian Mysticism*, 196.

CHAPTER IV

THE LITERATURE OF THE PEOPLE

I. *Moralists and Moralities*

THE mystics produced works of devotion for serious-minded people ; but the moralists appealed to the crowd. Conduct has always been insisted on by religious teachers in England ; and in tracts, sermons and interludes the public has been invited to follow the way of righteousness and contemplate the horrors of sin. The mediaeval literature on these subjects is far from being uniformly dull. It abounds in illustrations, anecdotes and parables, and often contains character sketches equal to those of modern essayists.

Wandering preachers, friars, palmers and pardoners collected and held audiences by telling them stories about what they had heard or imagined or seen. When personal reminiscences were exhausted, they fell back on the *Bestiaries*[1] for parables, told stories out of the *Gesta Romanorum*, and imparted information derived from " the Gothic Pliny ", Bartholomaeus Anglicus,[2] whom Trevisa had translated into English. A dose of moralising was the powder in the jam, and the audience was not critical. After all, they knew the difference between right and wrong without being told : but they had few opportunities of learning about anything outside their own village or little town except what they learnt from itinerant preachers.

Sermons carefully planned were preached at synods, visitations and on other great occasions. They were generally in Latin, and were concerned with clerical failings and ecclesiastical

[1] *Bestiaries* contained accounts of fabulous beasts and also fables like those of Aesop.

[2] Warton, *Hist. of Poetry*, ii. 393, calls Bartholomaeus " the Gothic Pliny ". He was an English Franciscan who wrote in the first half of the XII century. His book *De Proprietatibus Rerum* was read everywhere and translated into French, Dutch and Spanish. Trevisa made the first translation into English, and Batman, chaplain to Archbishop Parker, the last. Spenser, Marlowe, Ben Jonson and Drayton borrowed from it. Recently a volume of selections has been edited by Robert Steele and published in the *Mediaeval Library*, with an introduction by William Morris.

abuses. From the days of Bromyard [1] and Rypon [2] to the days of Colet and Latimer, they provided opportunities for much plain speaking and a good deal of fervent rhetoric. There were also during Lent in all the larger churches courses of sermons which usually dealt with the seven deadly sins, so that prospective penitents might make good confessions before Easter. Under various headings, with many subdivisions, the wickedness of the world was analysed, and the sins of individuals were laid bare, not without gleams of humour and sometimes with biting satire. Such sermons were popular, for the frailties of human nature are always interesting; they were also easy to write, for they required no learning beyond what might be picked up in the street. Dr. Owst says, " Once let the mediaeval homilist get astride the vices, and then the virtues which ever accompany them, and he may be safely trusted to gallop triumphantly to his conclusion ".[3]

A revived interest in these sermons has led some to emphasise unduly the seamier side of mediaeval life. Sins are always noticeable and call for remark; respectability is taken for granted, and cannot be made interesting. If anyone to-day advertised a course of sermons on the *Sins of Society*, he might be sure of a crowded congregation; and the congregation would assemble not because they knew all about them, but because they hoped for shocking revelations.[4]

Sometimes the mediaeval moralist attempted to teach

[1] John Bromyard, Dominican, was Chancellor of the University of Cambridge in 1380, and was a great opponent of Wyclif. He wrote many books besides sermons and is frequently quoted by Coulton, *Five Centuries of Religion*, and by Owst, *Preaching in Mediaeval England*.

[2] Robert Rypon was sub-prior of Durham. Cardinal Gasquet, *Old English Bible*..., refers to his unpublished sermons to prove that the parish priests preached regularly to their people. This assertion led Dr. Owst to read the MS. and he found that the author continually denounced the parochial clergy, who " know not how to expound a single article of the faith nor one precept of the Decalogue ". He quotes a number of passages; but we need not take Rypon too literally. First, he was a monk criticising the secular clergy; secondly, he was a monk of Durham, and the clergy of the Northern Counties were notoriously ignorant; and, thirdly, he was extremely rhetorical. Owst's quotations may be read in *Preaching in Mediaeval England*, 28 ff.

[3] Owst, *Preaching in Mediaeval England*, 322.

[4] Dean Church, *Dante and Other Essays*, 128, writes: " No age is blind to practical abuses, or silent on them; and, when the Middle Ages complained, they did so with a full voiced and clamorous rhetoric, which greedily seized on every topic of vilification within its reach . . . but it by no means implied unsettled faith, or a revolutionary design ".

spiritual truth by homely analogies. Here is a passage from the XV century *Chastening of God's Children*, borrowed in substance from the much older *Ancren Riwle*:

> When Our Lord suffereth us to be tempted in our beginning, he playeth with us as a mother with the child, which sometimes fleeth away and hideth her, and suffereth the child to weep and cry, and busily to seek her with sobbing and weeping; but then cometh the mother suddenly with merry cheer and laughing, beclipping her child and kissing, and wipeth away the tears. Thus fareth Our Lord with us, as for a time He withdraweth His grace and favour from us. Insomuch that in His absence we be all cold and dry, sweetness have we none nor savour in devotion.[1]

Some of the sketches in the *Ancren Riwle* have almost a dramatic character. It would be hard to better the following description of a slanderer:

> He casts down his head, and begins to sigh before he says anything, and makes sad cheer, and moralises long without coming to the point, that he may be the better believed. But when it all comes forth; then is it yellow poison. "Alas, and woe is me, that he or she hath fallen into such repute. Enough did I try, but I could do no good herein. It is long ago I knew it, but I should not have said a word. Now however it is known abroad and I cannot gainsay it. They say that it is bad and yet it is worse than they say. Grieved and sorry I am that I must say it; but indeed it is so, and that is much sorrow. For many things he or she is greatly to be praised, but not for this. No man can defend them."[2]

Here is another extract showing the same gift of dramatic presentment:

> No seduction is so perfidious as that which is in a plaintive strain; as if one spake thus: "I would rather suffer death than indulge an impure thought with regard to you; but had I sworn it, I could not help loving you; and yet I am grieved that you know it. But yet forgive me that I have told you of it; and, though I go mad, thou shalt never after this know how it is with me."—And she forgives him, because he speaks thus fair, and then they talk of other matters. . . . He afterwards seeketh an opportunity to break his promise, and swears that necessity forces him to do it; and thus the evil grows, the longer the worse; but no enmity is so bad as false friendship.[3]

This dramatic way of teaching of morals is in England a persistent tradition. We can trace it from the *Ancren Riwle* to

[1] *The Chastising of God's Children*, quoted by Chambers, *Continuity of English Prose*, c.

[2] *Ancren Riwle*, 66, 67. Cp. Chambers, *op. cit.* xcvii.

[3] *Ibid.* 73.

the sermons of Wyclif and Bromyard, to the stories told by Sir Thomas More and the conversations invented by Foxe, to the *Characters* of Overbury and Earle, to incidents in the *Pilgrim's Progress*, to the Essays of Addison and Steele, to the portraits in Law's *Serious Call*, until we come to the *Roundabout Papers* of William Makepeace Thackeray. Ethical treatises are apt to be dull, and moralising is resented unless it is illustrated in action ; and then it is most effective when the moralist deals with permanent types, so that each reader may verify their truth in his own experience.

Argument in the Middle Ages took a semi-dramatic form and was conducted by means of dialogues. Many of them are famous. St. Anselm wrote his *Cur Deus Homo* to justify the Atonement. *The Clerk and the Knight* in the XIV century dealt with the limitations of the Spiritual Power.[1] *Doctor and Student* for nearly three centuries was regarded as a legal text-book.[2] In his *Colloquies* Erasmus set out to teach boys Latin, but ended by discussing the manners of men ; while Sir Thomas More in a Dialogue with the Messenger endeavoured to refute the opinions of Protestants.

In the XV century these two literary conventions had a further development in the morality plays which were the rude precursors of our serious dramas and problem novels. They also appealed to people who refuse to receive instruction unless the virtues and vices are personified.

The morality plays are for the most part dull ; but in the XV century they were not thought so, and they supplied a need. The miracle plays required scenery, many actors and a great deal of organisation. The characters in them were well known and had to conform to a story that was also known. The Morality, on the other hand, required no pageants, and few actors. It could be performed in any church or churchyard or in the hall or garden of a great house. Moreover, as the plot was not known beforehand, there was an added attraction—it admitted of surprise.

[1] *Disputatio inter clericum et militem* was a French work, written about 1296 in favour of Philip the Fair, after the publication of *Clericis laicos* by Boniface VIII. It was translated by Trevisa, whose version has been edited by G. J. Perry for the E.E.T.S. It was printed by Berthelet in both Latin and English in 1533. A good account of it may be read in Janelle, *L'Angleterre catholique à la veille du schisme*, 261 ff.

[2] *Doctor and Student*, by Christopher Saint German, 1st edition, 1531 (Berthelet) ; last edition, 1815. Lowndes, *Bibliographer's Manual*.

This is not true of the earliest known Morality, *The Castle of Perseverance*,[1] which was probably produced about 1401 and was more ambitious than most of its successors, for it necessitated a Castle for Human Nature and four scaffolds raised against it, North, South, East and West, for the World, the Flesh, the Devil and God. Besides these there are, on the one hand, the Seven Deadly Sins who are made to speak in sprightly verse; and on the other hand Contrition, Confession, Mercy, Justice, Truth and Peace. The author never for a moment forgets that he is a moral teacher; his play follows on the same lines as the mediaeval sermon; his characters are only abstractions, yet they are sometimes cleverly contrasted; and his plot moves forward to its charitable conclusion. Human Nature had fallen into many temptations. Justice says, " Let hym drynke as he brewit ": Mercy appeals to the passion of Christ; and *Pater sedens in trono* accepts the plea.

The miracle play started with the Creation and ended with the Day of Judgment. The earlier Moralities started with the cradle and ended with the tomb. In the Middle Ages men liked to be reminded that " the paths of glory lead but to the grave ". After the Reformation they welcomed stories of difficulties and disaster, but insisted that the hero and heroine should ultimately marry and live happily ever after. They ceased to be obsessed with the thought of death.

How real that obsession was in the Middle Ages may be illustrated by *Everyman*,[2] the best known of all morality plays, although the intention of the author was to exalt the priesthood and proclaim the value of the sacraments. Everyman is told that he must die, and finds himself deserted by friends and kinsmen. He has to die alone. Goods, in whom he had trusted and thought his servant, jeers at him. He was but lent; he passes from one to another, and " his love is contrary to the love everlasting ".

> My condition is man's soul to kill
> If I save one, a thousand do I spill. . . .
> For when thou art dead and gone, this is my guise
> Another to deceive in this same wise.

[1] A. W. Pollard, *Miracle Plays*, Introd. xlv ff., Text 64 ff.

[2] *Everyman* is a XV-century translation of a Dutch play, *Elkerlijk*. Pollard, *op. cit.* 202. It was printed by Pynson and John Skot. Many modern reprints have been issued since the revived interest in the work.

Everyman turns to Good Deeds, but Good Deeds declares himself overwhelmed by Everyman's sin. He introduces him, however, to Knowledge, who brings him to confession, to penance and to the sacraments of the Church. Everyman is then at peace, but he has still to face the loss of all his powers. Beauty fades away, Strength departs from him, Discretion deserts him, Five Wits fail him : and Good Deeds only remains to go before him to the throne of judgment. The play is admirably constructed, while there is humour in the speeches ; we are made to pity Everyman.

It was partly due to the uncertainty of life in the XV century, and partly due to the way in which purgatory was preached and painted, that the thought of death possessed men's minds. The devil in the Middle Ages was often a comic figure, with his horns and hoofs, his hairy body and long tail ; but Death is always horribly presented as a dancing skeleton, gruesome, ghastly and grinning. The thought of death accompanied by a belief in judgment to come may restrain men from evil and be an inspiration to moral endeavour ; but where there is no real belief in a future life it may induce a spirit of hopeless defiance and find its expression in simulated scorn. A healthy-minded man does not allow his mind to dwell on horrors ; a morbid man often finds a perverted pleasure in contemplating them. If there was much of promise in the XV century, there was also much that was decadent. *The Dance of Death* illustrates that decadence in an effective manner.

The Dance of Death[1] had its origin in France, when the country was being torn asunder by civil wars and devastated by English invaders. It was actually danced at Besançon and elsewhere, and was more horrible and fascinating than any morality play. It was painted on the walls of the churchyard of the Holy Innocents at Paris ; it was there that Lydgate saw it in 1426 and translated the verses which described the pictures. The Archbishop of Canterbury had the dance painted in the great hall of his palace at Croydon ; and Jankin Carpenter, Recorder of London, built a new cloister for St. Paul's Cathedral which was decorated with similar pictures and Lydgate's verses. It was one of the sights of London ; and men found a sardonic satisfaction in contemplating Death as the great leveller of the manifold

[1] Lydgate, *The Dance of Death*, edited by Warren and White, E.E.T.S.

inequalities of the world. Here was a pope, grasping the keys of eternal life, seized by Death, and here was Death dancing away with a rheumatic plowman. Here was a king whose wrath meant death to others, himself the victim of the indiscriminating Terror. Here was a young man in his wasteful prodigality and here the usurer who thinks to hold him in his toils, both being danced off by the Death who jeers at both. Here the minstrel becomes aware " that all be not merry that otherwhile dance ", and the little child repeats the platitude, " As soon dieth a young man as an old ".

It was all very grisly and unpleasant, but it led Sir Thomas More to moralise :

> We were never so greatly moved by the beholding of the Dance of Death pictured in Pauls, as we shall feel ourselves stirred and altered by the feeling of that imagination in our hearts And no marvel, for these pictures express only the loathly figure of our dead bony bodies, bitten away the flesh ; which though it be ugly to behold, yet neither the light thereof, nor the sight of all the dead heads in the charnel-house, nor the apparition of any ghost is half so grisly as the deep-conceived fantasy of death in his nature, by the lively imagination graven in thine heart.

Entertaining himself that " deep conceived fantasy ", he has no patience with the man who dreams of " so many torches, so many tapers, so many black gowns, so many merry mourners laughing under black hoods, and a gay hearse ". He reminds such a man that " He will not stand at a window and see how worshipfully he shall be brought to church ". He asks him rather to contemplate his death-bed :

> When a rabble of fleshly friends, or rather of flesh flies, skip about thy bed and thy sick body, like ravens about thy corpse, now almost carrion, crying to thee on every side, What shall I have ? Then shall come thy children and cry for their parts ; then shall come thy sweet wife, and where in thy health haply she spake thee not one sweet word in six weeks, now shall she call thee sweet husband and weep with much work, and ask thee what shall she have ; then shall thine executors ask for the keys, and ask what money is owing thee, ask what substance thou hast, and ask where thy money lieth. And while thou liest in that case, their words shall be so tedious that thou wilt wish all that they ask for were upon a red fire, so that thou mightest lie one half-hour to rest.

But these discomforts are as nothing to the imagined horrors of the dying, when lying in thy bed, thy head shooting, thy back aching, thy veins beating, thy heart panting, thy throat rattling, thy flesh trembling, thy mouth gaping, thy nose sharpening, thy legs cooling, thy fingers fumbling, thy breath shortening, all thy strength failing, thy life vanishing and thy death drawing on.[1]

These sombre reflections were written by Sir Thomas More when he was forty-two years of age, and in the heyday of his reputation. After writing them he may have returned to the cheerful circle of his family and heard John Heywood read one of his " mad merry plays ". Sir Thomas recognised that there was a time to be grave and a time to play the fool ; he was no foe to innocent merriment ; but, while sometimes flippant as a controversialist, he was never profane, and never attempted to commend religion and morals by pandering to the irreverence of the vulgar.

On the other hand, in order to attract the mob, the dull morality play was enlivened by the introduction of the Vice.[2] This precursor of the harlequin bounded on the stage with a wooden lath instead of a sword, and by his gags and antics diverted the audience. He had been introduced that he might bring Virtue into relief ; but the more successful he was, the less was Virtue regarded. This was the more to be regretted in an age when men received most of their instruction through the eye —through ceremonial in the churches, through pageants in the streets, and through interludes in the halls of the mighty. Nothing remained sacred and the spirit of irreverence spread.

The reformers duly recognised the possibilities of the stage for propaganda purposes. John Bale, for instance, wrote *John the Baptist*, evidently thinking of himself as the prophet, and of canonists and theologians as scribes and pharisees.[3] He also wrote *King John*,[4] in which the monarch is represented as a

[1] *Novissima.* Sir Thomas More's Works, ed. by Campbell and Reed, i. 468-470.

[2] The Vice. *Vide* Pollard, *English Miracle Plays*, liii. ; Jusserand, *Literary Hist of English People*, i. 491 ff.

[3] Bale, *John the Baptist*, reprint in *Harleian Miscellany*, i. 102 ff.

[4] For *King John* vide Pollard, *op. cit.* lvi. 146 ff., 202 ff. *King John* was first produced in the reign of Edward VI, and was republished with complimentary allusions to Queen Elizabeth. The virtues of King John were first discovered by Simon Fish, *Supplication for Beggars* ; they were emphasised by Tyndale, *Practice of Prelates*, 295, and then by Bale. Having been excommunicated by the Pope, he came to be regarded as a Protestant hero. Shakespeare, *King John*, Act III. Sc. 1, puts into his mouth a defiance of Rome. Holinshed, *History*, ii. 339 (1807 ed.),

virtuous prince to whom had been entrusted " a sword for to correct all vice " ; who tried to reform the Church, but was excommunicated by a wicked pope, and poisoned by a still more wicked monk. So history subserved the political situation ; but had King John been able to see the play, how he would have laughed !

II. *William Caxton*

The moralists hitherto discussed were either clerical or under clerical influence; but with the invention of printing the lay moralist had his opportunity; and, though at first he could only hope to appeal to the important few, he was soon to command a wider public than could be reached from any pulpit. From Caxton to the present day, self-constituted censors have dealt with the manners and morals of society without any reference to the Church and sometimes in defiance of her decrees. Others have found in current events matter for moral reflections ; and lay sermons are often quite as platitudinous as those by men commissioned to insist on a defined code.

William Caxton was born about 1420 in the Weald of Kent, and was bound when fourteen to Robert Large, a mercer of London who was Mayor in 1439 and died in 1441, leaving his young apprentice twenty marks. For the next thirty years Caxton lived on the Continent. He became Warden of the English Mercers at Bruges, and Governor of the Merchant Adventurers. Later he was attached to the court of Margaret, Duchess of Burgundy. He collected books which he translated ; and finally he learnt the new mystery of printing at Cologne. His first attempts were produced abroad, but in 1476 he settled in the Almonry at Westminster, perhaps coming home to be near an aged father.[1] He was much more than a printer, for many of the

regrets that previous historians had been prejudiced against the king, who " had a princely heart in him ". In a ballad to Elizabeth we read :

> " Have you not rede of good Kyng John
> How by them he was undone ?
> The Bishop of Canterbury, that wicked man,
> Accused him to the Court of Rome :
> They enterdyted his lande, as the cronicle sayeth, Lady, Lady,
> A monk poysoned him to his death, most dere Lady."

Harleian Miscellany, x. 262.

[1] Caxton established himself at Westminster. In 1478 a William Caxton, who may have been his father, was buried in St. Margaret's, Westminster : Crotch,

books he published were translated by him ; all of them show his editorial care, and for most of them he wrote prologues and epilogues. He was an enthusiast for standardising the English language ; he also strove to enrich its vocabulary and was perhaps a little too fond of inkhorn terms. But before all else he was a moralist. He was an elderly man of varied experience who had succeeded in life, and felt himself not only competent to give good advice, but in a position to prove the value of right conduct.

His first didactic work was *The Game of Chess moralized*. It was a description of life as illustrated by the game. It had been written originally in Latin by Jacobus de Cresollis, but there were two French versions, and Caxton used them both.[1] The book was printed abroad in 1475 and dedicated to George, Duke of Clarence, who is said to have been drowned in wine. Two years later he published *The Dictes and Sayengs of the Philosophers*, from a translation made by Lord Scales when at sea on a pilgrimage to St. James of Compostella. Lord Scales tells us in his own prologue, " Every human creature by the suffrance of Our Lord God is born and ordained to be subject and thrall unto the storms of fortune ".[2] He thought that he had weathered his own storms, and did not foresee that ten years later he would perish on a scaffold. In 1478 Chaucer's translation of the *Consolatio Philosophiae* was printed, and Caxton tells us in his prologue that Boethius " made this book for his own comfort

Prologues and Epilogues of Caxton, cv. In 1474 a Richard Caxton became a novice in the Abbey, said his first Mass in 1478, rose to be fourth prior in 1498, was custos and treasurer of the Abbey manors, and died in 1504 : Pearce, *Monks of Westminster*, 165. An Oliver Caxton had been buried in St. Margaret's 1465 (Crotch). We can trace the progress of Caxton's business. In 1476 he rented one shop from the Abbey for 10s. per annum ; in 1483 he rented a second for 2s. 6d. per annum. In 1486 a third was assigned to him, apparently without payment. In 1488 he payed 4d. for an extra shop during the week while Parliament was sitting : Crotch, ciii.

[1] Hoccleve, *Regement of Princes*, E.E.T.S., 77, borrowed largely from the Dominican, Jacobus de Cresollis.

[2] Crotch, *Prologues*, ciii. While awaiting execution at Pontefract in 1483, Scales wrote the ballad printed in Ritson, *Ancient Songs and Ballads*, 149. I quote the first and last verses :

Sum what musyng,
And more morning,
In remembring
  The unstedyfastnes,
The world being
Of such whelyng
Me contrarieng,
  What may I gesse ?

My lyfe was lent
To me on intent ;
It is ny spent ;
  Welcome fortune :
But I ne went
Thus to be shent,
But she hit ment,
  Such is her wont.

. . . rehersing . . . how Philosophy appeared to him, showing the mutability of this transitory life ; and also informing him how fortune and hope should be understood with the predestination and prescience of God, *as much as may and is possible to be known naturally* ".[1] In 1481 he published a translation of Cicero, *de Senectute*, made some twenty years before for the octogenarian Sir John Fastolf. With it he published a translation of the *de Amicitia* made by Tiptoft, Earl of Worcester, and also the *Declamation of Noblesse*[2] which Tiptoft had translated from Bonaccorso. To the latter he prefixed a eulogy on the earl and a lament for his execution in 1470.[3] Caxton can only have known about this Italianate Englishman as an elegant scholar and patron of letters. He did not know him as the Constable who administered Paduan Law and impaled his victims.[4] In 1481 Caxton published *The Mirror of the World*, which a rich citizen wished to present to that Lord Hastings[5] who with little space for preparation had to lay his head upon a block ; while in 1484 he dedicated his *Order of Chivalry* to Richard III with a prayer that he might be victorious over all his enemies.[6] So, Clarence, Scales, Tiptoft, Hastings and Richard III were all associated with the Caxton Press ; and it is not surprising that in his Prologue to *The Royal Book*, 1488, he should write : " When I remember and take heed of the conversation of us that live in this wretched life, in which is no surety or stable abiding. . . . In which you may see at eye all is but vanity ; and that men repute

[1] Crotch, *ibid.* 36. It will be seen that Caxton understood his author better than some critics, who have doubted whether Boethius was really a Christian. The theological works are now admittedly his, and perhaps made the Arian Theoderic suspicious of a man so pronouncedly orthodox. But Boethius kept his theology and philosophy distinct. In the *De Consolatione* he tried as far as is possible *naturally*, *i.e.* without the aid of revelation, to reconcile his belief in universal causality with the fickleness of fortune. For Boethius see Gibbon, *Decline and Fall*, vii. 43 ff. (1820 ed.) ; Rand, *Founders of the Middle Ages* ; and W. P. Ker, *Dark Ages*. Chaucer's translation has been reprinted for E.E.T.S. with an introduction by Richard Morris.

[2] *The Declamation of Noblesse* provided Henry Medwall with the plot of his play *Fulgens and Lucreece*. It has been edited by F. S. Boas in *Five Pre-Shakespearean Comedies* (World Classics).

[3] Crotch, *Prologues*, etc. *Tullius on Friendship*, 45; *The Declamation of Noblesse*, 47

[4] Creighton, *Hist. Lectures*, etc., 199: " Tiptoft is a conspicuous example of that truth, so often taught and so constantly disregarded, that when a scholar takes to politics, his scholarship does not save him from occasionally losing his head ".

[5] Crotch, *Prologues*, etc 52.

[6] *Ibid.* 84.

for wisest and greatest among princes in a moment are overthrown and brought to nought."[1]

For a century—from Caxton to Spenser—the lay moralist harped upon mutability, on the changes and chances of this mortal life.[2] They reflected the sense of insecurity which all men felt; and they made change more possible because they taught all men to expect it. Only in a world without plans and with no settled outlook would it have been possible to carry through the break with Rome, the Reformation under Edward VI, the reaction under Mary, and the settlement under Elizabeth, which was not regarded at the time as having settled anything.

This world of constant change affected people in various ways. Few proved themselves to be "antique Romans" after the order of Boethius. Many regarded themselves as bound to Fortune's wheel,[3] or accepting life in the spirit of a gambler, grasped at every momentary pleasure, rushed into any adventure, and were reckless about the consequences. The prudent regarded life as a waiting game, and were prepared to accommodate themselves to what they did not like in the confident expectation that all would soon be reversed. The pious dismally chanted "vanity of vanities, all is vanity", and turning from an evil world, contemplated the eternal order, where "there remaineth a Sabbath rest for the people of God".

It is strange how few had any idea of progress. Christians indeed prayed, *Thy Kingdom come*; but they must sometimes have asked themselves if that prayer was answered by the encroachments of the Papacy. A few scholars were alive with zeal for the advancement of learning, believing that with the increase of knowledge all men would become good. A few

[1] *Ibid.* 100, 101.

[2] Cp. The last stanza of the *Faery Queen*:

"Then gin I thinke on that which Nature sayd,
Of that same time when no more change shall be.
But stedfast rest of all things firmely stayd
Upon the pillours of Eternity,
That is contrayre to *Mutabilitie*:
For all that moveth doth in *Change* delight:
But thenceforth all shall rest Eternally
With Him that is the God of Sabbaoth bright:
O that great Sabbaoth God, graunt me that Sabbaoth's sight."

[3] The wheel of Fortune was a favourite theme of the moralists. See *The Prick of Conscience*; Lydgate's *Fall of Princes*, Bk. VII.; Hawes' *Pastime of Pleasure*, cant. i.; Barclay, *Shyp of Folys*.

merchant adventurers thought that the discoveries of a new world would redress the failures of the old, and that prosperity would result from new markets and an increase of trade. A few Dominican and Jesuit missionaries, later in the century, were boldly to claim the world for Christ and teach that true progress could only be made when the Gospel was accepted. They were far in advance of their age. The great majority looked wistfully to the past—to a Saturnian realm or to a Primitive Church,[1] when everything was as it should be. The Saturnian realm was undiscoverable, notwithstanding Ralph Hythloday's reports of *Utopia* ; but there were plenty of people who thought they knew all about the Primitive Church and how it might be restored. They went to work as XIX-century architects started on ancient buildings by destroying all developments without considering their beauty or their worth.

Meantime those who possessed power, position or wealth were only concerned with securing some measure of stability. No one questions the amazing ability with which Henry VIII and Elizabeth maintained themselves in the midst of danger, but neither of them looked very far ahead. To face the difficulties of the day and to take precautions against the morrow was the most that they could do. They both had a highly developed instinct for self-preservation, though both constantly imperilled their safety by satisfying some immediate desire. Their acts of reckless daring alternating with acts of consummate prudence make them interesting to our age, but did not add to the stability of their own.

When not concerned in proving that all is vanity, the lay moralist was insisting on the importance of correct behaviour. This may seem at first inconsistent, but by instinct they were right, for by laying down a standard of conduct they were making

[1] Lydgate, *Fall of Princes* (Bk. VII., E.E.T.S., 808), has much to say about the Golden Age, when Saturn reigned. I quote two verses :

> " Fortitude then stood steadfast in his might,
> Defended widows ; cherished chastity ;
> Knighthood in prowess gave so clear a light
> Girt with his sword of truth and equity.
>
> That golden world could lovë God and deede
> All the seven deeds of mercy for to use :
> The rich was ready to do almës dede ;
> Who asked harbour, men did not him refuse."

a valuable contribution to the stability they so passionately desired.

In 1483 Caxton published *Caton*,[1] which he thought to be " the best book to be taught to young children in school ", and he quotes the authority of Poggio, who esteemed it as " a noble book and a virtuous, and such one that men may eschew all vices and ensue virtues ".[2] Caxton thought it the more necessary because

> I cannot judge the cause, but fairer nor wiser nor bet bespoken children in their young days are nowhere than they are in London ; but at their riping there is no kernel nor good corn found, but chaff for the most part.[3]

Caxton is not the only elderly man who has delighted to pet attractive little children and found boys and girls from fourteen to sixteen troublesome. Perhaps some of them learnt from *The Caton* to behave themselves in the presence of their elders.

The book which the Knight of the Tower, La Tour Landry,[4] made for his daughters had been popular in England long before 1484, when Caxton printed it in a new translation made by himself. It contains a great number of stories with appropriate morals. The morals are usually but not always excellent, and some of the stories would not have been considered suitable for a Victorian schoolroom. Caxton, however, thought the book " necessary to every gentlewoman of what estate she be ",[5] and he was probably right ; for social conditions did not admit of reticence being observed. Very likely he read the book to his daughter Elizabeth, then aged thirteen ; but if so, the warnings did not save her from an unfortunate marriage, and her

[1] The book ascribed in the Middle Ages to Cato was not written by him. It consists of 146 proverbs each in a couple of hexameters. Miss Waddell, *Wandering Scholars*, xx., says, " Cato is the father of the Copybook headline, and very valuable to students writing home, even more so to the less scholarly parent making suitable reply ". If Poggio in the XV century did not know that it was spurious, Alexander of Neckham in the XII century was better informed.

[2] Poggio Bracciolini (1380–1459) was an industrious scholar who travelled over Europe, including England, in search of MSS., and discovered Tacitus in Germany. His original works were not like the *Cato* and did not tend to edification.

[3] Crotch, *Prologues*, etc., 78. *Vide supra*, 235, 238.

[4] The original book was written by Geoffrey de la Tour Landry in 1371. Caxton's version has never been reprinted in its entirety, but Thomas Wright edited an earlier translation of the book in 1868 for the E.E.T.S. In 1902 Miss Rawlings published about half of Caxton's translation, omitting the coarser and more tedious chapters.

[5] Crotch, *Prologues*, etc., 86.

matrimonial difficulties were finally dealt with in an ecclesiastical court.[1]

Having provided for the instruction of boys and girls, Caxton produced *The Order of Chivalry*, " which book is not necessary for every common man, but to noble gentlemen that by their virtue intend to come and enter into the noble order of chivalry".[2] In his prologue he makes an impassioned appeal to knights who do nothing but sleep and take their ease, go to bagnios and play at dice, to fit themselves for their calling, and especially to read about the knights of olden time. He advises them to read Froissart, but he does not advertise the *Polychronicon* of Ralph Higden, which he had printed, or puff the *Morte d'Arthur*, then preparing for publication.

In 1487 he published his *Book of Good Manners*, translated from the French, and intended for the common people that they should not behave as " brute beasts ".[3] It is largely made up of texts from Scripture and sentences from saints and doctors of the Church ; but it is essentially a book compiled by a layman for laymen, and commends such morality as laymen accept.

Caxton himself was a devout man ; but these books are significant, because, while in no sense hostile to the Church, they are independent of her ; they are free from theological teaching, though they rest on the validity of Christian assumptions which were then taken for granted.

III. *The Satirists*

It is necessary to take the satirists into account ; but it is easy to exaggerate their importance. There have been mordant satirists—decadents scourging a decadent society—men impotent to construct and hopeless of reform, who could only snarl and sneer and snap, but could not bite. England, however, in the early XVI century produced no such satirists. The English were not decadent, they were for the most part too full-blooded and boisterous. They had almost forgotten their own satirists of an

[1] Crotch, *Prologues*, etc., cxix., cxxvii., cxxxix.

[2] *Ibid.* 80, 81. *The Book of Chivalry* was written by Ramon Lull about 1274. There were several French versions, also a Latin. In 1456 Sir Gilbert Hay translated it for the Scots. In 1484 Caxton translated it from the French. It has been edited by Byles for the E.E.T.S. (1926). *Vide* Alison Peers, *Ramon Lull*, 120-124.

[3] *Ibid.* 99.

earlier time, if we except the playful satire of Chaucer's tales and Gower's *Confessio Amantis*. It is notable that *The Vision of Piers Plowman* was not printed until 1550, when Crowley thought it might be useful as Protestant propaganda, as showing that even in the far-off days of Edward III " it pleased God to open the eyes of many to see His truth ".[1] Gower's *Vox Clamantis* was in Latin verse and had in consequence no propagandist value, while it did not interest scholars, who shuddered at its false quantities. It was first printed by the Roxburgh Club in 1850. *The Complaint of the Plowman* and *Jack Upland*[2] were Lollard satires, only read by those who dared to possess prohibited books, and so cannot have influenced public opinion in the early years of Henry VIII.

On the other hand, Englishmen rejoiced in what Bishop Hall subsequently called " toothless satires "—humorous reflections on things in general, and especially on the frailties and eccentricities of mankind. The most popular of such books was *The Ship of Fools* which was published in 1509 under the distinguished patronage of Margaret Beaufort, Countess of Richmond, the king's grandmother. The *Ship* may have been first constructed in Germany, but in the English version it was manned by an English crew.

Sebastian Brandt, born 1458, was a Doctor of Laws, an Imperial Counsellor and Syndic to the Senate of Strasburg. He composed his *Narrenschiff* in leisure hours, published it in 1494, and enjoyed its far-reaching success. Locher in 1497 translated it into Latin and it was then re-translated into French, Dutch and English. Tritheim compared the author to Dante ; and Hutten acclaimed him as the lawgiver to German poets. Erasmus and Reuchlin delighted in the work ; so did mechanics in Strasburg and Basle ; while preachers pillaged it for their topical sermons. It dealt with subjects common to everyone, and satirised types whom everybody knew. It made no claim to be clever ; it was content to be always sane. It was really too commonplace to rank with great literature ; but because it was commonplace it appealed to all classes ; and for the same reason it continues to interest the historian of social life and manners.

[1] Skeat, edition of *Piers the Plowman*, II. lxxii.

[2] Wright, *Political Songs and Poems*, " Complaint of the Ploughman ", i. 305-306 ; " Jack Upland," ii. 16-39.

Pynson published in 1509 an English version—*The Shyp of Folys*,[1] by Alexander Barclay, then a canon of Ottery St. Mary. It is not a literal translation, for English instances are substituted for German, and Barclay himself composed many "Envoys" to his author. He apologises for his style, saying, "My speech is rude, and my terms common and rural";[2] but in consequence he reached a wider public. He is not addicted to pleonasms or to far-fetched figures of speech; but he has great facility in writing verse, and occasionally produces a good line or a deft characterisation. He condemns the wicked in plain terms, but there is no venom in his sketches; and he is on the whole a genial advocate of virtue. Neither the clergy nor the laity suffer too severely under his lash, but he sees clerics and laymen alike at sea in a crazy boat with Folly at the helm, drifting on to the rocks and heedless of their fate.

John Heywood[3] was a wit rather than a satirist, and his interludes are farces and not indictments. He was a stout Catholic; he got into trouble for plotting against Cranmer, and in his old age accepted poverty and exile rather than deny his faith. He married Joan Rastell, the niece of Sir Thomas More, and was the father of two distinguished Jesuits. He probably owed his advancement at court to Sir Thomas, and some of his Interludes may have been first performed in More's house or garden.[4] Mr. A. W. Reed goes further and suspects that Sir Thomas himself wrote *The Pardoner and the Friar*.[5] Heywood, at any rate, intended no more harm to the Church of his day than the author of *The Private Secretary* intended to the Church of the XIX century; but as the *Private Secretary* was a recognisable caricature of a certain type of Anglican curate, so Heywood's Parson, Friar, Pardoner and Palmer were recognisable caricatures of people in his own day.

The Four P's[6] is the title of one of his interludes. They

[1] *The Shyp of Folys*, edited by Jamieson, 2 vols. [2] *Ibid*. i. 1.

[3] A. W. Reed, *Early Tudor Drama*; A. W. Pollard, *English Miracle Plays*.

[4] Puttenham, *Art of English Poesie*, 51: "These new comedies or civil interludes were played in open pavillions or tents of linen cloth or leather, half displayed that the people might see". Medwall, a chaplain to Archbishop Morton, wrote Interludes, and from *The Northumberland Household Book* we learn that the chaplain who could produce Interludes received higher pay.

[5] The greater part of *The Pardoner and the Friar* is printed in Fairholt's Introduction to *Wit and Folly* (Percy Society, 1846).

[6] It has been edited by F. S Boas in *Five Pre-Shakespearean Comedies* (World Classics).

stand for the Pardoner, the Palmer, the Poticary and the Pedlar. Each of the first three claims that he helps men to heaven more surely than the others and is eloquent in his own self-praise. The Pedlar suggests that instead of abusing one another they ought to join forces for their common object. To this they assent, but cannot agree who shall be chief. At last they decide that he who proves himself the greatest liar shall be leader; and the Pedlar awards that position to the Palmer, who said that in all his many travels he had never met with a woman out of temper. This, however, only leads to fresh wrangling until the Pedlar sums up by saying, "No man hath lost, nor no man hath won". He thinks the Palmer right if he goes on pilgrimage for the love of Christ; and that the Pardoner is right if for the love of his neighbour he strives to free him from his sins. They are both wrong when each, with his own virtue, despises the other. Here the Poticary interposes that he "uses no virtues at all", and the Pedlar finds in his truthfulness a sign of grace. We suspect the Pedlar of agreeing with the Poticary that the relics and pardons of Palmer and Pardoner were alike counterfeit, but he concludes that there is a place for relics, pardons and the apothecary's art in the "Church Universal". In this he no doubt voiced a general opinion. The Palmer, Pardoner and Poticary before him were obvious cheats ready to compete in lying; but palmers, pardoners and apothecaries need not be cheats, and such men with right motives might be useful in the world.

The Four P's was probably written in 1520; and the More household were just then interested in liars, for had they not all been taken in by "Edyth, the lyeing wydow which still lyveth"?[1] Walter Smith, More's servant, wrote a poem on her twelve merry jests which was published in 1525; but if we wish to read the justification of triumphant lying we have to go back to *Reynard the Foxe*, and there we shall find the satirical spirit dominant.

No one knows how the story of Reynard the Fox[2] originated.

[1] *The Twelve Merry Gestes of Edyth, the lying Widow* was written by Walter Smith and published by John Rastell. The adventurous lady had pretended to be a widow with means. Alington and Roper had contended who should secure her for one of their dependants; Smith, a third suitor, revenged himself in rhymes. A. W. Reed, *Early Tudor Drama*.

[2] Caxton's edition of *Reynard the Fox* has been edited and reprinted by Thoms for the Percy Society and by Arber in his series of reprints. Thoms writes in his Introduction: "If the story of Reynard had its origin, as it undoubtedly had, among

It is, as Thomas Carlyle said, "A European performance", and it was five hundred years at least before it attained a standardised form. Its wit, invention and daring irreverence suggests a Gallican source, and reminds us of how the game of Gab was played in Norman castles. There men vied who should make the wildest boast, who should say the wickedest thing, who should tell the most prodigious lie ; who, in short, should best attain to the level of the Fox, the example for all time of joyous and successful wrong-doing.

For the Fox nothing is sacred and no man is true ; honesty is humbug and simplicity is ridiculous. It is only by lies and craft that success is possible in this life ; but the lies must be plausible—lies with circumstance ; and the story is a handbook to how they should be told. So Reynard is able to devour the Weak, flatter the Great and outwit the Strong. The reader ranges himself inevitably on Reynard's side, because he feels that he must be on the side of intelligence against stupidity. Besides, the stupidity of the Lion, the Bear and the Wolf do not call for compassion, while the simplicity of the Hare and the Ram only excite contempt.

the Germans . . . still if we would point out the soil on which during the XII and XIII centuries it was most assiduously cultivated, we must place our finger on the North of France. In the Norman French poems we find many rich and pure streams of this dearly prized romance." I am not so sure about the Germanic origin. The first known version of the tale is *Fabella Lupina*, written by Nivardus, a monk of St. Peter at Ghent, between 1148 and 1160. Richard Cœur de Lion refers to Reynard and Isengrin in one of his *Sirventes*. At the beginning of the XIII century a prose version of the story was written by Peter of Saint Cloud, and at the end of the century the story was told in verse by Jacquemars de Gielée of Lille. At the beginning of the XIV century, Philip the Fair had the story acted before him ; and in his version Reynard became Pope and still preyed upon poultry. Jusserand, *Hist. of English Literature*, i. 147-152, shows how the French version was more true to animal life, and in quoting the French version of Chanticleer and the dead hen demonstrates its superiority to other versions. There was a German version by Heinrich der Ghiseven late in the XII century, and a Flemish version by William de Matso about 1250. There were also English versions. Humphrey, Duke of Gloucester, had one which is now in the Bibliothèque Nationale in Paris. *Reynard* was first printed in Dutch at Gouda in 1479. Caxton translated it from the Dutch and printed his version in 1481. A German, calling himself Heinrich von Alkmaar, turned the story into verse and published it at Lubeck in 1498. This last Hallam in his *Literature of Europe* thought was the earliest edition, but in his second edition (i. 136) corrected his blunder. Carlyle, *Misc. Essays*, ii. 145-151, who had not read Caxton, thought that Alkmaar found the story " in a state of dry bones " and " blowing upon it with the breath of genius, raised it up into a consistent fable ". As a matter of fact the Alkmaar version follows the Dutch very closely even in the additions. So does Goethe in his hexameters, and so does Mr. Ainslie in his spirited translation of Goethe ; but even Mr. Ainslie does not seem to have read Caxton.

The first part of the story is told with infinite gaiety ; but the second part has been to some extent spoilt by interpolations. The late XV century did not, as Carlyle thought, create a consistent fable but marred one already made. Among the additions we may note the Fox's apology for lying, and his reference to bishops and rich priests who did not practise what they preached. We may add the report of the Ape upon the courts of Rome, where the concubine of Cardinal Puregold could ensure the verdict for which she was paid ; also the veiled account of robber barons who sit in judgment on small thieves and send them to the gallows. Some of the fables, good in themselves, are awkwardly introduced, and Caxton ended his book with irrelevant paragraphs on the love of money being the root of all evil. These insertions spoil to some extent the artistry of the story, but they are significant of the public opinion at the time, and therefore important to the historian. Caxton feared that they were too outspoken and thought it prudent to say, " If anything be said or written herein, that may grieve or displease any man, blame not me but the Fox, for they be his words not mine ".[1]

The book is to be enjoyed as literature—to moralise on it would show a lack of humour, if some, without humour, had not hailed it as a secular Bible.[2] It is really the legacy of the profane spirit which went mocking all things good down the centuries of the Middle Ages—the spirit that reveals itself in the gargoyles outside churches and lurks beneath the stalls of monkish choirs. The faithful were not disturbed by its activities. It reminded them of the necessary truth that there is something ludicrous in sin, and that those who go in the way of folly, sooner or later, are certain to be tricked. It was when in the XVI century religion was divorced from life that the Fox and all he stood for became independent. He ceased to mock, and gravely claimed to represent wisdom. So the Fox became the oracle for statecraft ; the exponent of the principle that all is fair in love and war ; the judge who declares that success and wealth, however gained, need no justification ; that fools exist for the witty to defraud.

[1] Crotch, *Prologues*, etc., 62.

[2] Carlyle, *Misc. Essays*, ii. 149. "Among the Germans, *Reinecke Fuchs* was long a House-Book, and universal Best-Companion : it has been lectured on in Universities, quoted in Imperial Council-halls ; it lay on the toilette of Princesses ; and was thumbed to pieces on the bench of the Artisan ; we hear of grave men ranking it only next to the Bible."

Everything in a book may be excused except dullness, and there is no dull page in *Reynard the Fox* ; but in life dullness must be tolerated, and bright wits are far from an excuse for everything.

Reynard the Fox is sometimes coarse : but it was written in a plain-speaking age. Reynard, however, had a clean mind as well as a bright intelligence ; but the same cannot be said for Skelton, who is sometimes obscene and often nasty.[1] *The Merrie Tales* about him are some of them true, some of them exaggerated and some of them extravagant inventions, but they were all fathered on Skelton and are evidence of the repute in which he was held.

He was born about 1460, and first comes into notice as the translator of classical authors and as a Latin poet.[2] He received a laurel crown from three universities—Oxford, Cambridge and Louvain. He was tutor to Henry VIII, and after obtaining holy orders, was appointed to the rectory of Diss in Norfolk. He retained this benefice until his death, although he was suspended by Bishop Nix because of his irregular life. He continued to hang about the court, and has described his fellow parasites in a poem, designating them by such names as Favelle, Dissimulation and Riot.[3] They are not, however, abstractions but accurately observed personalities. He wrote panegyrics on Wolsey and expected a prebend from him which he did not obtain. Then he bespattered him with abuse in *Why come ye nat to Court?*—the boldest satire of the time. Wolsey thought the author had better come to York House, and sent officers to arrest him ; but Skelton found the sanctuary door at Westminster open and went inside. He never dared to come out again, and died six years later in 1529, just before the fall of the Cardinal.

Skelton[4] wrote correct Latin verse and had a great command

[1] George Saintsbury, *Social England*, iii. 101, writes of Skelton's *Tunning of Elynnor Rumming* as " anticipating and bettering Smollett at his filthiest, but full of master strokes ".

[2] Skelton, *Poetical Works*, edited by Alexander Dyce, 2 vols., 1843.

[3] *Bowge at Court*, *i.e.* court rations : *N.E.D.* Puttenham, *Art of English Poesie*, 70 : " With a good allowance of dyet, a bouche at court as we used to call it ". Favelle = flatterer.

[4] Skelton's scholarship impressed Caxton. In his preface to *Eneydos*, 1490 (see Crotch, 109), he writes, " He hath translated the Epistles of Tully, and the Book of Diodorus Siculus, and divers other works out of Latin into English, not in rude and old language, but in polished and ornate terms craftily, as he that hath read Virgil, Ovid, Tully, and all the other poets and orators to me unknown ". None of these translations have survived, and critics have accepted the judgment of Erasmus on

of broad Saxon. He was a scholar with a taste for low company, and how well he knew it may be seen in *The Tunning of Elynnor Rumming*, which he wrote with evident gusto and quite unnecessary detail. He never knew when to stop; and poems flowed out of him in a torrent of words—airy fancies, bad jokes, quaint conceits and pure nonsense, scraps of French and Latin, follow one another in any sort of order. They seem the work of a genius who was drunk. Yet the genius is there, and Skelton is right in saying—

> Though my rhyme be ragged
> Tattered and jagged . . .
> It hath some pith.[1]

Catullus in eighteen lines had bemoaned a dead sparrow dear to his mistress; and Skelton in 1382 lines does the same thing. *Phylip Sparowe* is his best work; it shows his exuberant fancy, and in it he forgets to play the buffoon. The same cannot be said for *Ware, Hawk!* which was written against a parson who let slip his hawk in Diss church with the result that the blood of a slain pigeon defiled the altar. Skelton did well to be angry, and some of his invective is much to the point; but he overshot his mark when he compared the sporting parson to Nero, Jesabel, Julian the Apostate and Nestorius: and the reader is not unduly impressed when he reads:

> Yet the Souden nor the Turke
> Wrought never such a worke,
> For to let theyr hawkés fly
> In the Church of Saint Sophy.[2]

There is no lack of venom in his satire upon Wolsey. It could only have been written by a man who had lost his temper and was perfectly reckless in his accusations. Wolsey was at many points open to attack; but it must be remembered that *this* attack was made by a man who had sung the Cardinal's praises in the hope of promotion. In *Colyn Clout* the intention of the author is obscure. His rustic hero pours out complaints about

Skeltonum, unum Britannicarum litterarum lumen ac decus (*Ep.* 104, od. Allen). These words, however, were written in 1499 when Erasmus was contriving to live by flattering great people and their dependants. He was writing to Henry VIII, then a boy nine years of age, and could be certain that his tutor would read them. Skelton was no doubt a scholar, but we must not over-estimate the testimony of Erasmus.

[1] Skelton, *Works*, i. 313. [2] *Ibid.* i. 162.

the Church, and states that he is only repeating what people say. The author then in his own person protests :

With language thus poluted
Holy Churche is bruted
And shamfully confuted.
My penne now wylle I sharpe,
And wrest up my harpe
With sharpe twynkyng trebelles
Against all such rebelles
That labours so to confounde
And brynge the Church to the grounde.[1]

However, he does not fulfil his promise, but continues to attack the clergy, some for their out-of-date theology, and some for their Lutheran sympathies, and then returns to the poor, who say

The Church hath too mykel
And they have too lytell.[2]

He enlarges on the pride of prelates and their luxury. He becomes so interested in describing the naked goddesses in their tapestries that he forgets for a time that he is a satirist. Sometimes in the midst of this farrago he speaks of reforms that were necessary. For instance, he writes :

Ye bysshops of estates
Shulde open the brode gates
Of your spiritual charge,
And com forth at large,
Lyke lanterns of lyght,
In the peoples syght,
In pulpits autentyke
In the wele publyke.[3]

Wolsey tried to suppress these poems, but they were printed and circulated. Men enjoyed reading them and probably quoted them as freely as modern historians, but they did not take them so seriously because Skelton was a well-known man, and his reputation was none too good. Skelton had a lively wit and had a real gift for satire ; but he was a man of loose life, a loose tongue and an excitable temper. In everything he was excessive, and his criticism of the Church, like his attack on Wolsey, failed to be effective because of its overstatement.

It would, I think, be true to say that these satirists had little

[1] Skelton, *Works*, i. 330. [2] *Ibid.* i. 332. [3] *Ibid.* i. 338.

or no influence in preparing for the Reformation; but they testify to a freedom of thought and a freedom of speech in pre-Reformation days for which men were afterwards punished. The only satirist who clearly influenced the Reformers was Erasmus. Nearly every educated person in Europe read his *Encomium Moriae*, and it was speedily translated for the uneducated. Leo X and his cardinals laughed over it and thought it most excellent fooling. Northern Europe took it seriously and quoted it as though it had been a legal indictment. How Erasmus wished it to be understood, none can say. Perhaps he had no definite intention. He certainly did not wish to precipitate a revolution; and yet Melchior Adam was only exaggerating a little when he wrote, *Erasmus Pontifici Romano plus nocuit jocando, quam Lutherus stomachando.*[1]

IV. *Ballads*

The satirists appealed to townsmen who knew many men of various callings, and appreciated a neat label for them, or a libel upon them. Ballads, on the other hand, appealed to town and country alike. In town, for a year, they were sung or shouted by every prentice lad, and then forgotten; in the country they lingered longer, and were taught by hoarse old men to grandsons with treble voices. In the process of transmission they have suffered many changes and it is often impossible to determine their date. Some we only know from the broadsides of illiterate printers in the XVII century, some have been adapted with a didactic intent, and some have been remodelled for political reasons. Some again have been "improved" by elegant scholars like Bishop Percy; and some have been taken down phonetically from the lips of some village gaffer, so that we have them in their final stage of corruption. Yet, notwithstanding all the literary and linguistic uncertainties, the ballads reveal the spirit which animated the forgotten dead—the ordinary man and woman of the buried past.[2]

[1] Quoted Mark Pattison, *Ency. Brit.* (8th ed.).

[2] The most complete collection of *English and Scotch Ballads* is that of Professor Child (5 vols., Riverside Press). The Percy *Reliques of Ancient Poetry* (3 vols.) was first published in 1765. References here are to the corrected edition of 1775. Ritson, *Ancient Songs and Ballads*, was published in 1790. References are to Hazlitt's reprint of 1877. Ritson, *Robin Hood* (2 vols.), was published 1795. The best selection of ballads is Allingham's *Ballad Book* (G.T.S.).

There was no connexion between the minstrels, who were honourably entertained in the courts of princes, and the ballad-singers, who were more at home on a village green.[1] The minstrels were for the most part French, and their songs were French or of French origin. They chanted the knightly deeds of Charlemagne, Roland and Arthur, and were often as lengthy and wearisome as the Poet of the *Rime of Sir Thopas*.[2] The ballad-singers, on the other hand, fiddled their way from village to village and sang for their supper on the village ale-bench or in the inglenook of some yeoman's homestead. They knew what their audience liked to hear ; and, in supplying it, confirmed their taste.

The political ballads of the Middle Ages may have had great influence on current opinion, but their vogue was brief. Laurence Minot wrote of the wars of Edward III, and was full of patriotic fury against French and Scots.[3] His songs were written down in the XV century, but they had long before ceased to be popular. The Scot had never troubled the Midland shires, and the English peasant had no desire to fight in foreign parts—though none excelled the English bowman when face to face with an enemy. The bowmen won the battles, but kings and knights were commemorated in the ballads. This is true of *Our King went forth to Normandie*,[4] and of that other ballad of Agincourt printed in Wright's *Political Songs*.[5] In consequence the English peasant preferred the fabulous exploits of Guy of Warwick and of Bevis of Southampton to those of the Black Prince or Henry V. The reason is obvious. The boy, seated on a stool before the fire, could picture himself slaying a dragon, but could not imagine how he could maintain his " just claim " to the crown of France.

It was different on the Borders of Scotland, where raiding and reiving never ceased though the kings of England and

[1] On this point Ritson was right (*Ancient Songs*, i.-xxxiii.) and Percy wrong (*Reliques*, I. xix.-lxxxvii.). Padelford, *Cambridge Hist. of Eng. Lit.* ii. 375, finds between the minstrels and the ballad-singers, the *Scholares Vagantes*, those irresponsible college graduates and light-hearted vagabonds who were equally at home in alehouse, in hall, in market-place or in cloister, and who could sing with equal spirit a ribald and saucy love-song, a convivial glee, a Christmas carol, a hymn to the Virgin, or a doleful lay on the instability of life and the fickleness of riches.

[2] *Canterbury Tales*.

[3] Wright, *Political Poems and Songs*, i. 58-91.

[4] Percy, *Reliques*, ii. 25 ; ballad with music in Fuller-Maitland, *English Carols of the XV Century*, p. 15.

[5] Wright, *op. cit.* ii. 123.

Scotland were sometimes at peace. The heroes of Border ballads belonged to families known to all—they were Percies and Scropes, Douglases and Buccleuchs. The lesser people, meriting song, had household names like Kinmont Willie,[1] Johnny Armstrong[2] and Parcy Reed.[3] They lived in a world where it could be said of Hotspur: "He kills me six or seven Scots at a breakfast, washes his hands and says to his wife, 'Fie upon this quiet life, I want work'".[4] Fighting was the business of such men; and they were stirred to action by listening to ballads extolling the valour of their fathers, or excited to make reprisals in hearing about the exploits of the Scots. There was little ill-feeling, for the enemies respected one another. So without malice they went forth gaily to prove their manhood—to slay or to be slain. All this is exemplified in the *Ballad of Chevy Chase*.[5] The Percy had sworn that he would hunt in Scotland, and went to chase the deer attended by 1500 archers. The Douglas had sworn that he would repel the trespassers, and went to meet them with 2000 men.

> Hardier men of heart and hand
> Were not in Christianté.

The leaders wished to settle who was superior in single combat, but the followers on both sides were unwilling to be lookers-on and a general conflict ensued. Percy sought out Douglas and after a great fight killed him. Then,

> The Percy leanèd on his brand
> And saw the Douglas dee,
> He took the dead man by the hand
> And said, woe is me for thee.
>
> To have saved thy life I would have parted with
> My lands for yearés three,
> For a better man of heart and hand
> Was not in all the north countrie.

Directly afterwards Sir Hugh Montgomery slew Percy and was

[1] Scott, *Minstrelsy of the Scottish Border* (Henderson's edition, ii. 39). Scott acknowledges that he has rewritten *Kinmont Willie*. Child, iii. 469; Allingham, 271.

[2] *Johnny Armstrong*. Child, iii. 362; Ritson, 331; Allingham, 103.

[3] *Parcy Reed*. Child, iv. 24 and 520; Allingham, 34.

[4] Shakespeare, *Henry IV*, Pt. I. Act II. Sc. 4.

[5] *Chevy Chase*. Child, iii. 303, and iv. 502; Percy, i. 1; Ritson, 92; Allingham, 148. The later version is in Percy, i. 251.

himself slain by an English archer ; but the battle went on until only 53 English and 55 Scots remained alive. The ballad-singer thought it a glorious fight, fought to a finish, and concluded with a prayer for his audience,

> God send us all good ending.

The author of the later version concludes with a different prayer :

> God save the King, and bless this land
> In plenty, joy and peace ;
> And grant henceforth that foul debate
> 'Twixt noblemen may cease.[1]

The men of the Midlands, with no national animosities to cherish but with the same love for a man of his hands, and with the same respect for lawless independence, found a hero in Robin Hood, who represented to them all what they would have liked to be. Whether any such person ever existed is doubtful. The attempts to determine his date have failed ; the pedigree provided by Stukeley and endorsed by Ritson is of no value ;[2] but the arguments by which he would be resolved into a solar myth are ridiculous. There had been plenty of outlaws from the days of the Conquest to the days of the Tudors, and they naturally took refuge in the forests. Hereward the Wake, the Disinherited after the battle of Evesham, Adam Gurdon in the Chiltern beechwoods, and Robin of Redesdale all belong to history. Robin Hood gradually attracted to himself the stories which were told of such people ; he also inherited the tales told of Northern worthies like Adam Bell and Clym of the Clough. His legend originated in the counties of Nottingham, Derby and York, but as his supposed exploits multiplied, the range of his supposed activities was extended. We are told of his shooting an arrow into the roof of Ludlow Church, of his practising archery in Somerset, while Cumberland claims him as a native of her shire. This is not surprising ; for the travelling ballad-singers

[1] It was the earlier version that Sir Philip Sidney approved : " I never heard the old song of Percy and Douglas, but I found not my heart moved more than with a trumpet : and yet it is sung by some blind crowder, with no rougher voice, than rude style ; which being so evil apparelled in the dust and cobweb of that uncivil age, what would it work, trimmed in the gorgeous eloquence of Pindar ? " (Sidney, " Defence of Poesie ", *Works*, Feuillerat's ed., iii. 24.)

[2] Ritson, *Robin Hood*, I. xxi., xxii.

found that it was good business to introduce a little local colour into their songs.

Robin Hood was an outlaw who delighted in the freedom of the greenwood. He was not a fugitive skulking from justice, and he was not an embittered Ishmael with his hand against every man. He was a jolly companion who took the ups and downs of life with good temper, who was always ready to jest with his victims. If he robbed the rich, he gave to the poor ; if he fought the sheriff of Nottingham and other oppressors, he succoured the oppressed and earned the title of " a very gentle thief ". *Gentle* here means gentlemanly, for both Robin and his merry men might be rough, though they were never cruel. They stood for sturdy independence, generosity and justice : they stood for the open-air life, for field sports and skill in archery, for rough games and practical jokes. They provided the countryman with an ideal, though he never thought in consequence of leaving his chimney-corner for life in the greenwood. In the ballads the forest was always green ; there were never bare branches dripping moisture; there was no frost and snow, no starvation and no rags. The merry men had always a venison pasty for their dinner ; they wore feathers in their caps and were clad in Lincoln green. It was a banished duke in a play who sought the forest of Arden that he might " live like the old Robin Hood of England ". Very young men might flock to him that " they might fleet the time carelessly as they did in the golden world ";[1] but even such a duke discovered that

> The season's difference, as the icy fang
> And churlish chiding of the winter's wind,[2]

made him shrink with cold. The peasant, listening to the ballad-singer, knew all that beforehand. He had no love for an outlaw's life ; but he loved Robin Hood. Robin Hood was English and reveals to us what an Englishman of the Middle Ages really admired, and how he judged the society in which he lived.

Robin Hood had no respect for bishops, fat abbots, or even for the cellarer of St. Mary's Abbey.[3] Neither had the countryman, so he chuckled as he heard of their being despoiled. On the other hand, Robin could contend on equal terms with the Curtal

[1] *As You Like It*, Act I. Sc. 1. [2] *Ibid.* Act II. Sc. 2.
[3] Ritson, *Robin Hood*, ii. 258.

Friar, and must needs have a chaplain of his own, Friar Tuck.[1] This is significant. There has never been much anti-clericalism in England, but countrymen have ever been willing to think evil of dignitaries, magnifying their wealth and minimising the duties they are called on to perform. On the other hand, they often admire the curate almost as poor as themselves, and think that if everybody had his rights he would be Archbishop of Canterbury. Such men also respect their rector, and perhaps like him the more if he is not too clerical. Friar Tuck represents a type of cleric well known in England and nowhere else. He accepts his creed, and is not altogether unmindful of his duties. He is easy-going, large-hearted, no precisian in speech or conduct, and apt to pride himself on damning humbug. He gives more thought to his glebe than his sermons, and prefers field sports to ecclesiastical ceremonial. Such men have done little for the furtherance of religion, but on the whole, they have had a healthy influence on rural life.

In the Robin Hood ballads we have reference to the "Christ Who died on rood" and to "His Mother dear", for whom the outlaw professes a real devotion. This takes practical form in his attitude towards women.

> Robyn loved Our Dear Lady ;
> For doute of dedely synne
> Wolde he never do company harme
> That any woman was ynne.[2]

Even when the wicked Prioress of Kirkley had bled him almost to death, he will not allow Little John to avenge him, saying,

> I never hurt woman in all my life,
> Nor man in woman's company.[3]

Whatever the morals of the countryside may have been, the creed of the countryside was sound—they believed in constancy and honest love. This comes out quite clearly in the other ballads

[1] How far back the fame of Friar Tuck goes is brought home to us by the fact that a real outlaw adopted the name. Stow, *Annals*, 352 B, under 1417 writes : "One, by his counterfeit name called Friar Tuck, with many another malefactor, committed many robberies in the countries of Surrey and Sussex, whereupon the King sent out his writs for their apprehension".

[2] Child, iii. 39 ; Ritson, *Robin Hood*, i. 4 ; Allingham, 160.

[3] Child, iii. 102 ; Ritson, *Robin Hood*, ii. 186 ; Allingham, 283.

that were popular in the *Bailiff's Daughter of Islington*,[1] in *Pretty Bessie of Bednall Green*,[2] in *The Patient Grizell*[3] and in the *Not Brown Maid*.[4] These heroines of the English people would not commend themselves to the epicene champions of women's rights, but they were women worthy of men's devotion —women who knew that true love may be measured by its capacity for sacrifice.

The first literary reference to Robin Hood comes in *Piers Plowman*,[5] where we learn that some knew rimes of Robin Hood better than their Paternoster. A century later Barclay says of many,

> No scripture think they so true nor good
> As is a foolish geste of Robin Hood.[6]

But moralists could not destroy his popularity; and in 1495 Wynkyn de Worde raised him to the dignity of print by publishing *The Lytell Geste*.[7] Later Chettle and others wrote plays about him; but his fame continued to depend on ballads which were not only sung by itinerant minstrels, but printed in Broadsides and sold at fairs. Country parishes appointed someone to represent Robin Hood and superintend their May Day games.[8] The villagers thought him a more important person than their bishop, as Latimer discovered to his great chagrin, when he sent notice to a certain parish of his intention to preach, and found the church locked on his arrival. He was told,

> "Sir, this is a busy day with us, we cannot hear you: it is Robin Hood's Day. The parish have gone abroad to gather for Robin Hood. I pray you let them not." . . . I thought my rochet should have been regarded, but it would not serve: it was fain to give place to Robin Hood's men.[9]

"It is no laughing matter", said the angry bishop, but he had only

[1] Child, ii. 426; Percy, *Reliques*, iii. 132; Ritson, *Ancient Songs*, 265; Allingham, 156. [2] Percy, ii. 162. [3] Percy, i. 184.

[4] Arnold, *Chronicle*; Percy, ii. 27.

[5] Langland, *Piers the Plowman*, C Text, vii. 11.

[6] Barclay, *Shyp of Folys*, i. 72. Cp. *Eclogues*, xxvii.

[7] Ritson, *Robin Hood*, i. li.

[8] Hall, *Chronicle*, 582, tells how Henry VIII went a-Maying with his Court and how they were surrounded by Robin Hood and his merry men (the Royal Archers disguised), and led into the Greenwood where a feast was prepared for them.

[9] Latimer, *Sermons*, i. 208. Latimer represented the new age. Tyndale, translating Deut. xi. 19: "Talks of them (God's words) when thou sittest in thine house," adds a gloss, "Talks of robynhod, says our prelates."

given a day's notice, and the churchwardens probably depended on the Robin Hood collections to cover church expenses for the year.

Ballads dealing with love stories were numerous, simple and sentimental. All the men were brave, and most of the maidens were tender and true, except the scornful *Barbara Allen* [1] who was held up as an awful example. There is an insistence on the vicissitudes of fortune, but a prejudice in favour of a happy ending, which distinguishes English ballads from those of Scotland, and distinguishes the outlook of the common people from the experience of their betters. The comic spirit did not intrude itself very often, though the *Tottenham Tournament* [2] is an excellent burlesque, funny even to-day, but how much more funny when the allusions did not need an explanation!

Originally these ballads had no didactic purpose ; they were the spontaneous outpouring of unpremeditated art, yet they reflect the character of the people and unconsciously determined their conduct. They were popular, and the time came when propagandists saw that the ballad form might be used to further religious and political opinions ; that they might even have a more immediate influence than sermons or royal proclamations.

There was a tendency at the end of the XV century to re-write ballads in the interest of religious devotion on the principle that the Devil should not have all the best tunes. There is, for instance, a poetic dialogue called *Jesus and Maria* which is really beautiful, but it parodies verse by verse the *Not Brown Maid*. The author was no doubt a man of pious intentions, even if he mistook the value of associated ideas.[3]

When the Reformation came, both sides wrote ballads ; and true religion suffered from the profanity and vulgarity of hack writers who had no religion of their own, but a clear perception of what their patrons wished them to attack. These ballads no longer depended on the taste and memory of the wandering singer ; they were in print and could be sold for a penny. They

[1] Child, ii. 276 ; Percy, iii. 124 ; Allingham, 243.

[2] Percy, ii. 13 ; Ritson, 75.

[3] Rimbault, *Ancient Poetical Tracts* (Percy Soc., 1842), 34. This parodying of secular songs and rewriting them for the pious had long been common in France. About 200 *chansons pieuses* have survived that are obvious imitations of *pastourelles*. In Germany Luther used popular tunes for religious purposes. Leighton Green, *The Early English Carols*, cxviii.

were read as well as sung, and they excited prejudice as much as they obscured truth.

Hack writers also began to discover new themes for ballads, and strove to satisfy that curiosity for the abnormal which took possession of the world when the supernatural was so largely suppressed. So we have the scene of the shepherdesses inspecting the pack of Autolycus, and being recommended a ballad " to a very doleful tune, how a usurer's wife was brought to bed of twenty money bags at a burthen, and how she longed to eat adders'-heads and toads carbonadoed ".[1]

The credulity is the same, but we may prefer the self-confessed rogue Autolycus to the lying Pardoner with his relics,

> Nay, Sirs, behold here may ye see
> The great toe of the Trinity.[2]

We may also prefer the innocent credulity of the Shepherdesses asking, " Is it true, think you ? " to the nasty scoffs of the Poticary in *The Four P's*. Notwithstanding the licence of the Elizabethan stage, the audience of Shakespeare would not have tolerated the jests of the catholic Heywood. England changed much during the XVI century—in some respects it improved, and it is not a fact that the ballads of love and hardihood were altogether superseded by those having a pseudo-scientific interest.

V. *Romance*

What ballads were to the homestead, romances were to the castle, and from the romances we may discover somewhat of the mental, moral and religious outlook of the people for whom they were written—people who were living artificial lives, whose only interests were in love and war, who disguised and to some extent refined their vices by the use of symbolism and allegory.

In the Middle Ages many great ladies lived a secluded life.[3] They could not often leave home and they had little to do. Only a few of them were capable of managing a castle with a host of retainers, and their husbands were often away in court or camp. So the provisioning of the castle, the discipline of its inmates,

[1] *Winter's Tale*, Act IV. Sc. 4.

[2] *The Four P's*, p. 9, in Boas's *Five Pre-Shakespearean Comedies*.

[3] For the life of ladies in feudal times *vide* Wright's *Womankind in Western Europe* ; Warre-Cornish, *Chivalry* ; Eileen Power in *Legacy of the Middle Ages*.

and the management of the estates were left to officials, while the great lady lived in her bower. Her children were often put out to nurse and brought up by foster-parents, until they were old enough to be sent to court or some other great house where they might be trained in arms and courtesy, while the lady herself was waited on by the children of her friends. She could hunt or hawk or sit in the walled-in pleasaunce and listen to the song of birds.[1] She could play at chess and tables, or, being more active, at blind-man's-buff, hide-and-seek and forfeits. She spent much time with her maidens in embroidery ; and, while the embroiderers worked, they asked one another riddles or told stories. Sometimes a minstrel visited the castle,[2] and the inmates were content to listen for hours to a new voice chanting the adventures of some paladin of chivalry ; but the visits of a minstrel were rare, and a page was petted who could tell a good story with graceful and appropriate action. The great lady herself told stories—it was a recognised accomplishment. Such stories were not always edifying, and rarely as well told as those by Fiammetta, Filopena and Elisa in the *Decamerone*.

When books were multiplied and reading became general, the art of recitation tended to disappear ; then a gentlewoman sat on a cushion at her lady's feet and read, perhaps for the tenth time, the one romance in the house—possibly written on parchment and glorious with illuminated capitals. *The Canterbury Tales* were at one time popular, although even then Gower was reckoned the equal of Chaucer, but both were superseded by Lydgate, the monk of Bury, and at the end of the XV century he was the fashionable poet. Stephen Hawes in his *Pastime of Pleasure* speaks of him as " the flower of eloquence " and as " the chief original of my learning ".[3] Caxton with more perspicacity declared that Chaucer " excelleth in my opinion all other writers . . . he writeth no void words ", and there is in him " the picked grain of sentence ",[4] that is, the selected fruit of a ripened judgment. Lydgate, however, was a poet if not a great

[1] *Vide* Chaucer, *The Romaunt of the Rose*, etc.

[2] Some great lords kept their own minstrels. John of Gaunt had a band at Tutbury who held a court and elected one to be their king : Plot, *Staffordshire*, 435. These minstrels in the absence of their lords wandered about the country. It would seem that Lydd (H.M.C.v. 518) at different times entertained the minstrels of most great peers : Mrs. Green, *Town Life in XV Century*, 147.

[3] Hawes, *Pastime of Pleasure*, i. xx., xlvii.

[4] Crotch, *Prologues and Epilogues of Caxton*, 69.

one. He had considerable powers of description ; and was fertile in invention. He may still be enjoyed in selections, but there is too much of him. There are over 36,000 lines in his *Fall of Princes*[1] and 30,000 in his *Troye Book*.[2] They appealed to people with abundant leisure. Bishop Alcock believed that they tended to the "encrease of virtue and the oppression of vice",[3] perhaps contrasting them with other romances, for instance, with the *Romaunt of the Rose*.

In considering this famous book it is well to remember that the rich and idle are seldom continent. The fair and frail ladies and their carpet knights talked much of the imperious claims of love and the urge of nature when they meant to satisfy physical impulses. They could not distinguish between Eros and Agape any more than the contemporary theologians. St. Bernard out of the Canticles expounded the mystical love of Christ for His Church, using the language of sexual desire, but sublimating it to express a spiritual devotion. Jean de Meun discovered that the Canticles were a series of love poems offered by Solomon to Pharaoh's daughter ; and, fortified by a sacred text, proceeded to give a mystical justification for sexual excesses.

The love of allegory suggested the title, for the *Rose* was the emblem of Our Lady. Dante regarding her as the representative of the Church Triumphant, saw that the snow-white rose in heaven was the throng of saints for whom Christ died—they were like petals opening out from a heart of gold.[4] His elder contemporary, Jean de Meun, accepting Mary as the representative woman, saw the red rose on earth—it had the fragrance of all-fair womanhood and it was there for men to pluck and to ravish.[5]

[1] *The Fall of Princes*, by Lydgate, edited by Bergen (E.E.T.S., 4 vols.). It is a translation into verse of a prose work by Boccaccio.

[2] *Troye Book*, ed. by Bergen (E.E.T.S., 4 vols.).

[3] Quoted in *D.N.B* under Lydgate.

[4] Dante, *Paradiso*, xxx., xxxi. ; Gardner, *Dante's Ten Heavens*, 273, writes: "By making the glory of the Blessed take the form of the Rose, which is also the emblem of Mary, the poet to some extent identifies her glory and triumphs with that of the Church Triumphant". There are several Carols of the Rose (Leighton Green, *Early Eng. Carols*, 130-132). The best known begins,

> "There is no more of such virtue
> As is the rose that bare Jesu
> Allelluya."

[5] Only the 7700 lines printed in Chaucer's *Works* are in English ; but there are good analyses of the whole poem in Morley, *English Writers*, vol. iv. ; in Wright, *Womankind in Western Europe* ; and in Huizinga, *Waning of the Middle Ages*.

Chivalry had as its ideal, loyalty to one lady and reverence for all women, but when the *Romaunt of the Rose* appeared, the devout lover content to serve, was being supplanted by the lover who was an amateur experimenting in emotions, and he in turn was to give place to the gallant who boasted of his conquests. The self-conscious lover was no longer concerned with his obligations to a lady, but was skilful in the arts of seduction. Love was for him a sport, a pursuit, and woman was the quarry.

Guillaume de Lorris, who wrote the first part of the poem about 1237, was at least decent. L'Amant finds by a fair river the walled-in garden of Deduit (Pleasure); and Deduit has for wife Liesse (Joy); and for his companions Leisure and Riches.

From the garden Old Age, Poverty, Avarice and Vilanie (the villein class) are shut out—Love is not for them.[1] Idleness, beautifully arrayed, opens the gate; Mirth and Beauty are dancing, and the God of Love is there. L'Amant wandering in the garden sees the Rose; and Love tracks him down, wounds him with his five arrows and seals up his heart. L'Amant then swears homage to Love, and is warned how agitating such a service will be, but is given rules for final success. His first trespasses in the garden are unfortunate, but at length Bel-Accueil (Fair Reception) brings him into the presence of the Rose and Venus permits him to kiss her. Then Jealousy (the husband) intervenes, imprisons Bel-Accueil,[2] and erects a fortress about the Rose with four gates and four warders, Wicked-Tongue, Danger, Dread and Shame, the proper guardians of Chastity. Throughout we hear much of the longings, sighs and torments of L'Amant, but he never seems to give a thought to the welfare of the Rose, whom he so ardently desires to possess.

[1] Neither Guillaume nor Jean had much class prejudice. The former is translated by Chaucer, ll. 2191 ff.:

> " But who so is vertuous,
> And in his port not outrageous,
> When such one thou seest thee beforne,
> Though he be not gentle borne,
> Thou maiest well seine this in sooth,
> That he is gentle, because he doth
> As longeth to a gentleman."

Similar teaching is put into the mouth of Nature by Jean de Meun.

[2] Bel-Accueil is somewhat disguised in the Chaucer as Bialacoil.

Guillaume de Lorris had some doubts about his own fantasy, for he makes Reason to expostulate with L'Amant, asking him to reflect that he is young, has been foolish, and that Idleness is to blame. She shows him that a way of escape is open to him, even though it may involve self-chastisement. To this L'Amant has no better reply than that honour compels him to be faithful to the Rose.

Guillaume de Lorris died, his poem unfinished ; and for forty years it remained almost unknown until Jean de Meun published it, adding over 14,000 lines of his own. Guillaume had planted a pleasant garden for dalliance, and Jean introduced into it a rabble of lewd and mocking spirits through whom he could express his views on women and his disbelief in chastity.

> All are, have been or will be
> Unchaste, in fact or in will.

Reason appears again, not to [illegible] on youthful folly, but to denounce the female sex and advocate male friendships. Later L'Ami attacks the marriage state and laments an age of Saturn when all women were common. L'Amant, however, perseveres in his attempt to win the Rose. He tries to employ Folle-Largesse but finds he is not rich enough for bribery. He does employ Faux Semblant (deceit) on the principle that all is fair in love and war. The King of Love comes to his aid with all his barons. They assault the castle and are repulsed. Then L'Amant goes to Cythera to implore the help of Venus, who declares that she will abolish chastity among women. Next, an embassy has to be sent to Nature, remotely busy in the renewal of the world. She sends her high priest Genius ; and he, vested as a bishop, excommunicates all who resist the dictates of Love. Finally, the King of Love tosses his torch into the castle and it capitulates. L'Amant plucks the Rose while Genius preaches a licentious sermon on the evils of sex repression.

Such was the book which was regarded as a breviary by a corrupt aristocracy for more than two centuries. It was translated into many languages, and churchmen were not ashamed to write commentaries upon it. Even at the end of the XV century[1] Jean Molinet tells us that its verses were as current as proverbs, and lest it should fall out of fashion in the XVI century

[1] Huizinga, *Waning of the Middle Ages*, 106.

Clément Marot carefully modernised the French.[1] Gerson, indeed, had denounced it; and Christine de Pisan had protested on behalf of her sex. Gontier Col was scandalised by her attack and wrote to assure her that—

Master Jean de Meun, a true Catholic, a solemn master and doctor in holy theology, a very profound and excellent philosopher, knowing all that is capable of being known to the human understanding, whose glory and renown lives and will live for ages to come, by the grace of God and work of Nature, made and compiled this book of the Rose.[2]

That, to some people, is its further condemnation. It was written by a scholar, a theologian and a priest, by one who could insinuate obscenities while using the language of the liturgy, who could put into the mouths of Venus and Nature references to the mysteries of the Faith and use them in illustration of impurities.

How far the *Romaunt* was popular in England it is impossible to say. We know that Chaucer translated some of it, for Deschamps congratulated him on having "planted the Rose Tree in the angelic land, Angleterre".[3] There are many allusions to all parts of the *Romaunt* in Chaucer, Gower, Hoccleve, Lydgate and Hawes; but all these writers were well acquainted with French. Professor Skeat thinks that there were many translations, because the three fragments printed by Thynne in his edition of Chaucer's *Works* are by three different authors, the first of them being possibly by Chaucer himself.[4] Apart from these fragments the supposed translations have perished, if indeed they ever existed, and Thynne's version is only supported

[1] Clément Marot (1495–1544) translated the Psalms into French. While in prison for his Protestant opinions he modernised the *Roman de Rose*. He fled for his life to Geneva because of his Protestantism; and fled for his life from Geneva, as Calvin had no toleration for his licentious life.

[2] Quoted Wright, *Womankind in Western Europe*, 149.

[3] The poem by Deschamps is printed in Skeat's *Chaucer*, i. p. lvii.

[4] The third fragment translated in Northern England contains the long attack on the Friars by Faux Semblant:

"As William seynt Amour wolde preche
And ofte wolde dispute and teche" (l. 6765).

When we remember that Saint Amour's attack was on such saints as Aquinas and Bonaventura, we know that he was a false witness and we need not give overmuch credence to his contemporary and disciple Jean de Meun. On the other hand that an Englishman in the North of England 150 years later chose to translate this passage against the friars indicates a dislike of the mendicant orders at that date in the North of England.

by one XV century MS.[1] Is it not possible that the *Romaunt* was best known in court circles where French was understood, and that there was no demand for a complete English translation of such a very un-English work? The English took their vices seriously and not with cynical gaiety; they often defied the moral law, but did not make a mockery of virtue.

The English, however, delighted in allegories just as much as their neighbours on the Continent. For them Lydgate wrote his *Temple of Glass*,[2] and for them Stephen Hawes, the young poet at the court of Henry VII, wrote his *Pastime of Pleasure*[3] and his *Example of Virtue*.[4] In the former Grand Amour sets out to woo La Bel Pucell, and longs to be worthy of so great a prize. He begins by acquiring the seven liberal arts, patiently listening to the Lady Grammar's discourse on the noun substantive. It is not until he reaches the Tower of Music that he meets his sweetheart in a garden, and offers her his love with boyish modesty and fervour. The maid is slow in accepting him, and then her relatives carry her away into a far country, leaving the lover to complete his education in geometry and astronomy. He then attends the Tower of Chivalry, is trained in arms by Minerva, and receives the accolade from the centaur Melizius, after instructions in the obligations of knighthood. Thus equipped he sets out to find La Bel Pucell, but is hindered by the dwarf Gobelieve, who has no respect for women, but brings comic relief, and relief from the rhyme royal into the poem. After this interlude Grand Amour slays the giant with three heads, who represents the world, the flesh and the devil, and afterwards another monster with seven heads, representing the seven deadly sins. No wonder the Lady Perseverance approves of him, and Venus sends a letter in his favour to La Bel Pucell. He has, however, still to cross a dolorous wilderness before he sees the towers of his lady's palace on an island. Even then he almost loses sight and strength through a metal monster called Privy Malice, but he finally, by the aid of Pallas, reaches La Bel Pucell, and they are duly married according to the *Lex Ecclesiae*. Here the poem should have ended, but

[1] Thynne's edition of Chaucer was published in 1532. It was the first collected edition of all the works attributed to him.

[2] *The Temple of Glass* had been attributed to Hawes, but Hawes himself quotes it as by Lydgate.

[3] *The Pastime of Pleasure* was printed by Southey, *English Poets*, 1831.

[4] *The Example of Virtue*. See *Cam. Hist. of Eng. Lit.* II.

Hawes looks far ahead and sees Old Age, Policy and Avarice approaching. Grand Amour is only saved on his deathbed and his epitaph concludes with the immortal lines :

For though the day be never so long
At last the bell ringeth to evensong.

Hawes, it will be understood, was full of moral fervour, and confessed that he could not conceive of real poetry being divorced from morality. He thought that some poets were not read because their morals were obscured in such a cloud of words and had no suspicion that his own *aromatyke fume* was inconsistent with clarity. He was himself well educated and had travelled : he was at once a child of the Renaissance and an impenitent reactionary. He loved to dream of the May mornings, the bird-haunted gardens, the magical palaces and fair ladies of the older poets. He loved also the old knightly ideals and regarded life as an endless adventure. For him there were still giants to be overcome and maidens in need of protection. In the prosaic court of Henry VII he and many beside him longed to escape into that world of chivalry which had never existed.

At the same time Hawes believed that learning was necessary for the equipment of a gentleman, and was therefore a generation in advance of his time, though Baldassare Castiglione[1] had come on an embassy to England and displayed in his own person the perfections of a courtier. Young Englishmen, however, were more responsive to the mediaeval ideal. They were reacting from all that they had heard of the brutality and treason which characterised the Wars of the Roses and were seeking for a higher standard of life in an entirely fabulous past. They were not yet sufficiently refined to appreciate the niceties and delicacies of *Il Cortegiano*; but they found what they wanted in the romance of *Morte d'Arthur* which was published by Caxton in 1485. Hawes and his friends would certainly have agreed with Caxton about the merits of Malory's book :

wherein they shall find many joyous and pleasant histories, and noble and renowned acts of humanity : gentleness and chivalry. For herein

[1] Baldassare Castiglione, 1468–1529. *Vide* Courthope, *Hist. of English Poetry*, ii. 18, and Einstein, *It. Renaissance in England*, 187. He came to England when Henry VII conferred the Order of the Garter on the Duke of Mantua and acted as his proxy at the installation. He wrote an account of England to his mother (*Lettere* xiii., xiv., xxvii.). His famous book *Il Cortegiano* was translated by Sir Thomas Hoby, and it became the Vade-mecum of Elizabeth's courtiers.

may be seen all noble chivalry, courtesy, nobility, friendliness, hardiness, love, friendship, cowardice, murder, hate, virtue and sin.[1]

Sir Thomas Malory was a Lancastrian knight who was exempted from the general pardon of Edward IV. He is supposed to have written his great book in prison, but if so, he was not debarred from the use of a considerable library. The book was finished in the ninth year of Edward IV (March 3rd, 1469–March 2nd, 1470) and the author was shortly afterwards buried in the Church of the Grey Friars near to Newgate.[2]

He freely acknowledges his indebtedness to French authors, but his book is much more than a compilation. He selected what pleased him ; and if his episodes are not always consistent one with another, there is a consistency of style and outlook ; and the author reveals himself as a man of very human sympathies, with a passion for loyalty and a veneration for those who are chaste.

If Malory's body was in prison his mind was free to create a wonderful dreamland. There you could ride down forest glades and find a fair meadow fit for jousting. There you would sometimes come upon a wayside cross, or a chapel with lights burning and an altar vested for Mass. Within there might be a tomb or a dead knight laid out for burial, raising questions which sometimes are and sometimes are not answered. There were no poor in his land, no labourers, no craftsmen, no children and no homes. It was a land populated by knights, squires and their damosels ; by monsters, giants and the enemies of mankind. The knights have splendid armour, can shiver countless lances, and are never long without a horse. There are mysterious ships that sail without a crew and reach the desired haven. There are castles and abbeys where knights are entertained ; but they make their confessions to hermits in their cells or to recluses at their windows. There are also dwarfs and monsters, recreant knights and alluring women, Merlin, a magician, and Morgan de Fey, who learnt her unhallowed arts in a nunnery.[3] The Questing Beast appears for a moment and disappears for ever ; he belongs to the unsubstantial fabric of a dream.[4] It is all in dreamland and the dreams change and recur ; they are much concerned with perils and with all the temptations that flesh is heir to.

[1] Crotch, *Prologues*, etc., 94.
[2] Christ Church, Newgate Street.
[3] *Morte d'Arthur*, Bk. I. ch. 2.
[4] *Ibid*. Bk. I. chs. 19, 20

It is the book of an old man with a boy's heart—in love with adventure. His knights go pricking to and fro, having no plans, but ready to give the unexpected " a frolic welcome." There is no particular purpose in their expeditions until all vow themselves on that high feast of Pentecost to seek the Holy Grail, and leave Arthur weeping as they disperse.[1]

The Holy Grail is an allegory. It is one of many in the book ; but we can hardly follow Kenelm Digby, who would allegorise the whole. For him the quest of the Holy Grail is "the highway of Our Lord Jesus Christ", the Round Table is the perfect faith, the Siege Perilous is the seat of Christ at the last supper, the enchanted castles are the strongholds of Satan, the lions and dragons are the demons of temptation, the deeds of arms are acts of charity, the crusade to Jerusalem is the quest for the celestial city, the beauty of the knight in armour is holiness, and the fair ladies are the virtues and Christian graces.[2]

Few who read the book for themselves will accept such an interpretation. None of the allegories is long sustained, the episodes often follow one another with the inconsequence of a dream. Folklore and legend make their contributions, and there is much that is of the earth earthy about the stories. It would be impossible to christianize Merlin, who, it will be noted, made the table to represent the round world, while the Siege Perilous was especially designed for one who should come. Besides, though the background of the book is dreamland, though the knights follow romantic conventions and perform incredible feats, they are real people with human passions and with no resemblance to plaster saints—even Galahad is not an abstraction.

The author was evidently a devout man—a devout soldier. He knew a good many Bible stories in a haphazard way, and could quote a good many texts from scripture. He must have listened to many sermons, but there is no evidence that he had read the Bible. He believed in the Mass, in confession and in the efficacy of the last rites of the Church ; but, and it is strange in the XV century, there are no references to Our Lady, or the saints, while he knew that it was possible to produce counterfeit Bulls of the Pope. His knights practise their religion, while the holy hermits who shrive the penitent, both in their severity

[1] *Morte d'Arthur*, Bk. XIV. ch. 8.

[2] Kenelm Digby, *Broadstone of Honour*, Godetridas.

and their compassion, are models for those who would save souls.

Passing from one extreme to another we should note the severe judgment of Roger Ascham on *Morte d'Arthur* :

> The whole of which book standeth in two special points, in open slaughter and bold bawdry. In which book those be counted the noblest knights that do kill most men without any quarrel, and commit foulest adulteries by subtlest shifts ; as Sir Lancelot, with the wife of King Arthur his master ; Sir Tristram, with the wife of King Mark, his uncle ; Sir Lamerocke, with the wife of King Lote, that was his own aunt. This is good stuff for wise men to laugh at, or honest men to take pleasure at : yet I know when God's Bible was banished the Court, and *Morte d'Arthur* received in the princes' chamber.[1]

This is very unintelligent criticism, and no better than that of secularist lecturers on the Old Testament. It is the more surprising as coming from a scholar who professed admiration for Homer. Long before Malory wrote, the stories of Lancelot and Tristram were the common property of Europe. He could only tell them anew in his own way, and he understood the stories better than Ascham. Tristram and Lancelot were very great lovers ; and, although their love was illicit, they were loyal servants of their ladies. All the elements of tragedy contribute to their downfall, and granting their characters there is a certain inevitability in the result. Malory treats them with understanding and compassion, but he does not extenuate their sin. They may have been men after the heart of a soldier, but he does not set them forth as examples. He treats with reverence Sir Galahad, the maiden knight, Sir Bors and Sir Percival : Sir Percival is all the more an example, because he so nearly succumbed to the fascination of the Lady of the Ship.[2]

Malory did not set out to write a moral treatise any more than he set out to write a spiritual allegory. He set out to write from French sources a complete history of Arthur and his knights, but the stories suffered a certain transmutation while passing through his mind. It is possible to think of him as a man with a high moral standard, who had lived most of his life in a very lax society. He does not falsify what had been his own experience of life, amply corroborated as it was by his authorities ;

[1] Ascham, *Scholemaster*. Giles ed. of *Ascham's Works*, iii. 159.

[2] *Morte d'Arthur*, Bk. XIV. chs. 8-10.

and yet both he and his authorities recognised that there was a moral governor of the universe, and that even in this life retribution was to be expected. Arthur's adultery with Morgawse, early in the book, leads to the birth of Mordred the traitor, who kills Arthur at the end. Lancelot recognises that after his life of vainglory he cannot hope to achieve the Holy Grail, though his repentance is sincere and he wears a hair shirt. Lancelot and Guenevere weeping over Arthur, whom they had loved and betrayed, know that they must part. The man asks for one last kiss and is refused.[1] Both go their way to expiate as far as possible their sin by austerities. Both know that in yielding to temptation they have wrecked the whole system of knight-errantry in their world.

Ascham's other accusation, "those be counted the best knights who kill most men without any quarrel", is equally untrue. Many of the encounters in the book were no more serious than a boxing match, and boxing matches have been known to end in regrettable fatalities. Many of the encounters were provoked and some were due to misunderstandings as when the brothers Balin and Balan[2] slew one another. The fact remains that knights of the Round Table were vowed to redress wrongs and protect the weak, and that they stood for courage and courtesy, for hardihood and fair play. Sometimes this sense of fair play is shown in a way that would exercise a casuist. For instance Sir Gaheris discovers Sir Lamorak in bed with his widowed mother. He kills his mother, who has dishonoured the family not for the first time, but he lets the knight go free, because he is in his shirt and cannot defend himself.[3]

A pacifist may read with regret a passage like the following:

> Therewithal came King Arthur but with few people, and slew on the left hand and on the right, that well nigh there escaped no man, but all were slain to the number of thirty thousand. And when the battle was ended, the king kneeled down and thanked God meekly.[4]

To a soldier believing in his righteous cause such conduct was quite appropriate.

Another incident may be quoted—Sir Percival, Sir Bors and Sir Galahad kill the knights who had attacked them unprovoked. Then the tale goes on:

[1] *Morte d'Arthur*, Bk. XXI. ch. 9. [2] *Ibid.* Bk. II. ch. 18.
[3] *Ibid.* Bk. X. ch. 24. [4] *Ibid.* Bk. IV. ch. 3.

So when they beheld the great multitude of people which they had slain, they held themselves great sinners. "Certainly", said Sir Bors, "I ween an God had loved them, we should not have had power to slay them thus; but they have done so much against Our Lord, that He will not suffer them to reign any longer." "Say ye not so", said Sir Galahad, "for if they misdid against God, the vengeance is not ours, but to Him which hath power thereof." [1]

A holy man then arrived who assures them of the wickedness of the knights and of the great deliverance they had wrought for the oppressed people. Sir Galahad then agrees with Sir Bors: "Certainly an it had not pleased Our Lord, never would we have killed so many men in so little a while".

The book is chiefly concerned with love and war because they were the principal interests of the people for whom it was written. It was, as Ascham says, to be found in the chamber of princes. It appealed to a section of society which was not very numerous, so that only two editions of the *Morte d'Arthur* were printed in the XV century, whereas in the same period fifteen editions of the *Golden Legend* were sold. Among ordinary people the saints were much more popular than the knights.

The world of Malory's dream was a world lying in wickedness, with a band of very imperfect men trying to set things right. They fail completely owing to their imperfections and double-mindedness. Galahad alone could heal the Maimed King with the Blood of the Saviour and he alone achieved the Holy Grail.[2] Huizinga has noted the pessimism which prevailed among the upper classes at the end of the Middle Ages. Feudalism was waning fast.[3] So Galahad, having seen the vision of the Grail for a moment, longs to die that he may enjoy the bliss of that moment for evermore. He sees a world in need of a reformation, and longs to escape from it. He has no faith in the future, and no vision of a reformation which might be at hand.

VI. *Some Generalisations*

It is difficult to determine what influence all this literature had on the minds of the people, or how far it reflected what they were thinking. It is still more difficult to assess the evidence it offers concerning religion and morals.

[1] *Ibid.* Bk. XVII. ch. 8.
[2] *Morte d'Arthur*, Bk. XVII, ch. 21.
[3] Huizinga, *Waning of the Middle Ages*, 22 ff.

There were then, as at all times, a multitude of bad people in need of conversion ; and there were some very plain-spoken prophets of doom to call their sins to remembrance. Such prophets no doubt spoke from experience, and much that they said was true ; but perhaps, like Elijah, they were apt to forget that there were yet seven thousand who had not bowed the knee to Baal.

The satirists loved to expose acknowledged evils, and took malicious pleasure in revealing the seamy side, when there was another which had a seemly appearance. They cannot be dismissed as of no importance, because the scandals must have been to some extent patent or the satirists would not have obtained a hearing ; and the imputed evil, even when false, must have been of such a nature that many would believe it.

The satirists appealed to citizens who were growing in wealth and importance. They lived close together and were always meeting to discuss their common rights or their divergent interests. In the close-packed streets where everyone knew everyone else, gossip was prevalent and criticism unrestrained. Men and women welcomed satire. It armed them with biting sentences that could be applied to their neighbour. A satire on the clergy justified their own irreligion ; while a satire on the wealthy filled the envious with a sense of their own superiority.

The ballads belonged to the countryside, and were sung at village festivities. The people who sang them were, for the most part, healthy-minded, simple, sentimental and untroubled with thought. Their lives were very hard, their poverty was often extreme ; but they took the world as they found it, made the most of holidays, and everyone was jolly as the ale went round.

The romances are more important, because they provided reading for the ruling class. From them we gather it was the fashion to dwell on a golden past, to sigh for escape into " faery lands forlorn ", and to glorify " the snows of yester-year ". Yet in this literature of the disillusioned there was, in spite of its authors, somewhat of promise for the future. *Morte d'Arthur* and the *Golden Legend* professed to preserve the old ideals ; and the ideals so preserved were capable of inspiring action in the future. It is well that some should idealise the past, for a sense of continuity is requisite for ordered progress. No nation can, with safety, make an entirely new start; and it is always as necessary to conserve old values as to create new ones. The young men who see visions need to be balanced by the old men who dream dreams ; and it was because this balance was maintained that the Reformation in England was not altogether a revolution ; and that the Church was able to bring out of the treasure house things new and old.

At the beginning of the XVI century the conservatives did not desire progress but stability. They wanted existing rights to be maintained, the old laws to be administered, and everyone, from the villein upwards, to be kept in his place. Yet they knew that the feudal system was in ruins, that the old hierarchical constitution of society was no more, and that the Church was no longer an independent power that could champion the weak in the presence of kings. They saw changes in all directions and were afraid. Hawes, himself a conservative, tried to inspire hope.

> Drive despair away,
> And live in hope which shall do you good.
> Joy cometh after when the payne is past ;
> Be ye pacient and sobre in mood :
> To wepe and waile, all is for you in waste ;
> Was never payne, but it had joy at last
> In the fayre morrowe.[1]

There were others who were not conservatives, and who did not need this consolation—kings, no longer pretending rights, but intent on conquests ; merchants challenging the ascendancy of the military caste ; and smart young men seeking a career free from the restrictions imposed on a celibate priesthood. Travellers were discovering new worlds, and scholars were rediscovering an old civilisation, while the printing press was broadcasting knowledge of both. Ulrich von Hutten could exclaim, *O saeculum ! O Literae ! juvat vivere*,[2] and Erasmus when fifty-one could wish that he were younger, so certain was he of the golden age at hand.[3] He dreamed of an age of sweet reasonableness, when the faith would be clarified by the New Learning. The Reformation, however, came with violence and he lived long enough to be disappointed.

[1] *Pastime of Pleasure*,

[2] Quoted by Huizinga, *Waning of the Middle Ages*, 22.

[3] Erasmus, *Epistola*, 541 (Allen's ed.), Feb. 1517. " Sed tamen in praesentia pene libeat aliquantisper rejuvenescere non ob aliud nisi quod videam futurum ut propediem aureum quoddam saeculum exoriatur ".

CHAPTER V

HUMANISM

I. *The Ferment of the Renaissance*

THE last chapter closed with the promise of a new day, dreaded by the conservative majority, and impatiently awaited by a handful of humanists. The conservatives were impotent, because they were pessimists ; the humanists were dangerous because they were eager, active and hopeful. When the day dawned the apprehensions of the conservatives were justified, and the humanists found that they were not to enjoy sweetness and light. It was a stormy and dark day ; but the storm cleared the air, and the resulting flood, if it destroyed much that was precious, also swept away many festering impurities. In the long run, Christendom, including the Church of Rome, was in a healthier condition after the Reformation.

It was a wonderful age. Christendom was still one and scholars were cosmopolitan. This is perhaps best illustrated by the letters that Erasmus wrote and the letters that were written to him ; but it is well to remember that those we think of as contemporaries were not all of the same age.

When Henry VIII ascended the throne in 1509, Cardinal Ximenes was 74,[1] and the Complutensian Polyglot, on which he and his scholars at Alcala were engaged, was not completed for another eight years. Leonardo da Vinci was 57 ; Reuchlin, 54 ; and Le Fevre, 45. These three were suspected of heresy. Erasmus, who wrote his *Enchiridion* for a Christian soldier, was 42 ; and Machiavelli, who wrote *The Art of War* for a Medici prince, was two years younger. Budaeus was 38—a busy diplomatist and the best Greek scholar in Europe. Copernicus, aged 36, was quietly studying the heavens from the palace of his uncle, the Bishop of Heilberg.[2] Pietro Bembo, also 36, was the complete Ciceronian, attempting, as a papal secretary, to deal with ecclesiastical affairs

[1] Hefele, *Life of Cardinal Ximenes*, Eng. trans. ch. xi.
[2] Jourdan, *Stress of Change*, ch. ix.

without compromising his literary conscience. Ariosto at 35 had just produced his comedy *Suppositi*[1] at the Ferrara carnival, notwithstanding the tragic happenings in the family of D'Este. Michelangelo was 34 and at the height of his fame, while Sadoleto was 32, and not yet engaged in a religious revival. Raphael, Luther and Rabelais were alike 26; but Raphael alone was famous, while Luther and Rabelais were still confined in their respective cloisters. Zwingli, aged 25, was a schoolmaster at Glarus, and about to be a militant chaplain of Swiss mercenaries. Julius Caesar Scaliger was the favourite squire of the Emperor Maximilian—a soldier and not yet a scholar of renown. The ex-page of Ferdinand the Catholic, Ignatius Loyola, aged 18, was also a soldier, gallant and gay. Ulrich von Hutten was a turbulent youth of 21; Pietro Aretino was a dirty-minded boy of 17; and Philip Melanchthon was a lovable child, aged 12. All these men who were going to be famous men, and were living lives for the most part remote from one another; but none of them were solitaries. Each was surrounded by lesser men, friends and foes, who, if they are now forgotten, none the less contributed to the foundations of the modern world.

The Church was ill prepared for the changes that were to come. Her apologetics were out of date, and had never been designed to meet the attacks of biblical and historical criticism. Mediaeval theologians, for instance, had never concerned themselves with the doctrine of the Church. The Church so obviously was, that no one thought it necessary to provide a rationale for its existence.[2] The subject of the Church was left to the canonists, who were chiefly concerned in defining its power and determining the mode of its operations. When men arose, who declared that the Church was an invisible body and that its members were only known to God, the canonists were dumbfounded and the theologians were uncertain how they should refute the new doctrine.[3]

Historical criticism was also confusing the minds of scholars.

[1] E. G. Gardner, *Dukes and Poets of Ferrara*, 522-544.

[2] In Billuart's useful index to the *Summa* of St. Thomas Aquinas (Paris, 1856) there are eight entries under *Ecclesia*, four under *Papa*, and 338 under *Angelus*.

[3] The doctrine of the Invisible Church derives from Luther, although he believed also in a visible Church as defined at Augsburg. Cranmer, if he was responsible for the XIII Articles, puts the two senses in which the Church might be understood one after the other, without any attempt to relate them (Jenkyns, *Remains of Cranmer*, I. xxi., and Hardwick, XXXIX *Articles*, 31 ff. and 262).

In the first half of the XV century, when Alfonso of Naples was at variance with Eugenius IV, Lorenzo Valla [1] delighted his patron by proving that the Donation of Constantine was a fiction.[2] Just after the middle of the century the cardinals Nicolas of Cusa and Turrecremata were expressing doubts, only too well founded, about the earlier Isidorean Decretals.[3] Lorenzo Valla had denied the authenticity of the works of Dionysius the Areopagite, and had ridiculed the legend that the Creed had been composed by the Twelve Apostles, each of them contributing one of the Articles. He had, like Roger Bacon[4] a century and a half before, called attention to the corruption in many texts of the Vulgate, and he had written notes on the New Testament, which Erasmus first edited and subsequently appropriated. These critical works were certainly not endorsed by the Church, and ordinary folk would never have heard of them if they had not been denounced by Franciscan preachers. Pecock had read Valla ; John Free commended his works ; Grocyn set out to refute his views on Dionysius, but in studying his opponent was convinced and retracted.[5] Erasmus, when a mere lad, had the opportunity for reading Valla [6] in that monastery which he afterwards sometimes described as a home of obscurantism. The New Learning was penetrating to the most unlikely places and was causing alarm and intellectual unrest. To-day there is no need to appeal to the Forged Decretals if you wish to maintain Petrine claims ; and it is easy to understand how the Pope had a right to " St. Peter's patrimony " apart from the Donation of Constantine. No one now thinks that the truth and authority of the

[1] For Lorenzo Valla cp. Symonds, *Revival of Learning*, 186-190 ; Sandys, *Classical Scholarship*, ii. 66-70 ; Hallam, *Lit. of Europe*, i. 147-150 ; Gregorovius, *Rome in the Middle Ages*, vii. 569 ff.

[2] The Donation of Constantine was re-edited by Ulrich von Hutten and dedicated with a satirical preface to Leo X (Gregorovius, vii. 573). It was published in an English translation, 1534.

[3] Isidorean Decretals. See False Decretals in the *Cath. Encycl.* For their history see H. C. Lea, *Studies in Ch. Hist.* The official edition of the *Corpus Juris* upheld the genuine character of the False Decretals as late as 1580 : *Cath. Encycl.* The last serious defence of this historical character was written in 1628. Holdsworth, *Hist. of English Law*, ii. 139.

[4] Little, *Essay on Roger Bacon* (Hertz Trust), 23-25.

[5] Erasmus tells the story in his reply to the censures of the Sorbonne on his denial that the Areopagite was the author of the Dionysian works (*Declarationes ad Censuras Fac. Theol. Paris*). He tells the story again in his commentary on Acts xviii. 34. Montague Burrows, *O.H.S. Collectanea*, ii. 356.

[6] *Epp.* 20, 23. 25, 26, 29.

creed depends upon the acceptance of an absurd legend, or that the authority of the Vulgate is compromised because many corrupt readings had crept into many manuscripts. But to the people of the early XVI century the new knowledge came as a shock. It seemed to render everything insecure—the authority of the Church, the inspiration of the Creed, and the finality of the appeal to Scripture. The New Learning was to people then what the Higher Criticism was to people in the last generation. The faithful were dismayed and the irreligious were jubilant. Some said, " If the critics are right, my faith is vain ", and others said, " The critics are right, and I no longer need believe anything ". At the beginning of the XVI century the English were conspicuously orthodox, and so were the English exponents of the New Learning; but those whom they taught were not always ready to accept the moderation of their teachers. The younger men had been encouraged to desire a reformation of the Church, and in reforming what was old they found an excuse for introducing much that was new; and so it came to pass that the Oxford Reformers were succeeded by revolutionaries. A few years passed away and " the Greeks " were fighting with " the Trojans" at Oxford, while at Cambridge the disciples of Erasmus were reading Martin Luther.

But the Renaissance was not only concerned with critical scholarship; it was also a frank revival of paganism. Italian artists had awakened to the beauty of the world, and especially to recognise the beauty of the human form. Italian humanists had discovered the beauty of Virgilian verses and the splendour of Ciceronian rhetoric. They had meditated on the ruins of Rome and become idolatrous before classical statues which they thought were Greek, though most of them dated from the age of the Antonines. From these survivals of literature and art they had been led to imagine that there had once been a Golden Age when everyone enjoyed the fullness of life and was free to follow the dictates of nature. In the light of this vision they condemned their immediate past as a time of Gothic barbarism, and derided the inhibitions of Christian morality as the kill-joy precepts of gloomy monks.

The humanists had eaten of the Tree of Knowledge, and were resolved to be as gods and discern for themselves what was good and what was evil. They claimed freedom to think for themselves and express their thoughts, and they despised all authorities not written in classical Latin. They claimed the right to follow their own impulses, to gratify their senses and to enjoy life. Their works were often licentious; [1] they glorified the lusts of the flesh and defended the worst forms of sexual perversion. In 1500 this teaching had little or no influence in England. It was half a century later that the proverb arose, "The Italianate Englishman is a devil incarnate"; [2] and it was later still that Harrison described the Elizabethan courtiers as the best educated and worst-living men in the world.[3]

No age, however, is as bad as bad men describe it; and Italy in the XV century was not altogether as wicked as might be thought from reading some of its literature. At the beginning of the century St. Catherine of Siena was active; and at the close, St. Catherine of Genoa. In the middle of the century St. Bernardino was preaching; [4] a little later St. Antonio was a great influence in Florence; and at the end Savonarola was prophesying in the Duomo. The response these saints met with proves that the Italians were not wholly given over to the world, the flesh and the Devil. Fra Angelico lived in a cloister, but he painted for men outside who could appreciate the purity of his little angels. Vittorino da Feltre,[5] among the humanists, in the middle of the century, conducted a school at Mantua devoted to religion and sound learning, while Castiglione and Guarino wrote for courtiers who were certainly not degenerate. Ficino, with a lamp always burning before a bust of Plato, translated the works of that philosopher and Plotinus, before he was converted by the preaching of Savonarola. Pico della Mirandola, who burnt his love poems, was spell-bound by the same great Dominican, and attempted to reconcile the teaching of Genesis with the *Timaeus*; [6] and from Cusanus to Sadoleto and Contarini

[1] Symonds, *Revival of Learning*, *passim*; Villari, *Machiavelli*, ch. i.

[2] Ascham, *Works*, iii. 159-167; Harrison, *Description of England* (New Shakspere Soc.), i. 120.

[3] Harrison, *op. cit.* Pt. I. 271: "Our common courtiers for the most part are the best learned and endued with excellent gifts, so are many of them the worst men, that any man shall either hear or read of".

[4] St. Bernardino. *Life*, by Thureau-Dangin, translated by Baronin von Hügel (Medici Society, 1911).

[5] Vittorino da Feltre. Jebb, *Romanes Lecture*, 16-20.

[6] Pater's appreciation of Pico in his *Renaissance* is well known. For an account of the *Heptaplus* see J. M. Riggs' introduction to More's translation of Pico's life, pp. xiv-xx.

there were many who tried to relate the New Learning to the Christian faith.

England at the beginning of the XVI century was receiving more good than evil from Italy : Colet had been converted by friars in Italy, and had probably listened to the apocalyptic thundering of Savonarola.[1] Barclay freely adapted the *Eclogues* of Aeneas Sylvius; and the *Eclogues* of Giovanni Battista Mantuano were translated by schoolboys who had to be more literal than Barclay for fear of the rod. More translated the life of Pico della Mirandola and caught somewhat of the inspiration which came from the Platonic Academy. Had he never read Plato's *Republic* he could not have written his *Utopia.* Plato was the philosopher of the English humanists and they did not think of him as the master of Aristotle but as his opponent. With his aid the English humanists went forth to defeat the schoolmen, professed disciples of Aristotle. They ridiculed the traditional teaching of the schools and in so doing unintentionally opened the way for the Reformation.

The New Learning was spreading rapidly, thanks to the printing-press, the possibilities of which had begun to be understood. When printing was invented, the books first produced were for the most part bibles, breviaries, books of devotion and lives of the saints. They were wanted by people who could not afford written copies, while the rich patron and book collector regarded them as our fathers regarded a typewritten letter.[2] Then printers like Aldus at Venice, Fröben at Basle, and Gryphaeus at Lyons produced texts edited by the first scholars in Europe.

Such works caused men to over-value the printed page, and to assume that manuscripts no longer had any importance. It is regrettable that when More sent Grynaeus to Oxford, the University were only too glad that he should take away manuscripts. Why should they keep them when there were printed editions ? [3]

Before the invention of printing, men were free to criticise

[1] Erasmus, *Ep.* 1211, Allen's ed., iv. 521 ; Seebohm, *Oxford Reformers*, 17, 18 ; Lupton, *Life of Colet*, 52. The last notes how Colet in his Lectures on the Romans introduced a long extract from the *Theologia Platonica* of Ficino.

[2] Vespasiano regarded printing with the contempt of one who was a connoisseur in penmanship, and in describing the magnificent library of the Duke of Urbino, assures us that it was not profaned by a single printed book. *Memoirs of Vespasiano da Bestichi*, trans. by W. G. and E. Waters.

[3] Miss Routh, *Sir Thomas More*, 146.

the Church in Latin, and the ecclesiastical authorities were only occasionally disturbed. Such criticisms circulated among scholars and were duly answered according to the rules of logic. An ambitious young man offered to maintain some daring thesis or attack some scholar with an established reputation. A controversy ensued and the language was violent, but it only provided intellectual excitement for a leisured class. The printing-press changed all this. The men who were in earnest soon learnt to write for the people, and the men who were half in earnest were apt to be taken too seriously. The battledore and shuttlecock of mediaeval disputations ceased, and the controversies of the Reformation were more like an exchange of cannon shot. The cultured Leo X thought the multiplication of books would be for the advantage of mankind and that literature—

> not only led to the ornament and guidance of human life, but was applicable and useful to every particular situation; in adversity consolatory, in prosperity pleasing and honourable; insomuch that without them we should be deprived of all the grace of life and all the polish of social intercourse.[1]

He was thinking of the books he had read with Politian in his youth and not of the theses propounded by Martin Luther. "Another monkish quarrel",[2] was his contemptuous comment when he heard of them; but because of the printing-press the quarrel divided Europe into two hostile camps.

Rabelais [3] thought that the printing-press had been invented by divine inspiration as an instrument for man's betterment, and that the Devil had suggested artillery to defeat God's purpose. He did not foresee how the Devil might use the printing-press to foment wars, and that men would fight more fiercely for ideas than for material gain. Neither did the men of the New Learning in England foresee this. They were men of peace—Colet dared to denounce war in a sermon when Henry VIII was on the eve of starting on an expedition in France; [4] Erasmus wrote *Bellum*, a pacifist tract, in a somewhat belligerent spirit; [5] and More

[1] Quoted Jebb, *Romanes Lect.* 9.

[2] Creighton, *Papacy*, v. 69.

[3] Rabelais, *Pantagruel*, Bk. II. ch. 8.

[4] Lupton, *Life of Colet*, 189-190. Henry VIII found his explanation quite satisfactory. So perhaps Colet hedged in the royal presence.

[5] *Bellum*. My edition is Halle, 1724. The tract consists of a commentary on the proverb *Dulce bellum inexpertis*.

assured the world that his Utopians did not regard the soldier as following an honourable profession.[1] They all thought that learning would fill men's hearts with a spirit of sweet reasonableness ; but they taught the Reformers, and the Reformation led to the wars of Religion and proved that ideas are more explosive than gunpowder.

Rabelais was prescient but perhaps premature in what he says about artillery. Henry VII had his train of artillery, but England for the most part went on fighting in the old way—the Battle of Spurs was won by charging horsemen, and the battle of Flodden by the bowmen of Cheshire. England, however, was behind the times :[2] Professional soldiers, commanding drilled troops, were revolutionising the art of war. The Italian Condottieri had for a century studied strategy, and conducted their campaigns as if they were playing chess. The campaigns were not much more dangerous than chess, for a general who was outmanœuvred usually capitulated, and often allied himself with the old friend he had been hired to fight, forfeiting the pay he would have received for a victory.[3]

At the end of the century Italy was invaded by the French, the Swiss and the Spaniards. The Italians were horrified by soldiers who killed people, sacked cities, did not know the first thing about strategy and tactics, and broke every rule of the game ; but the Italians were intelligent ; they studied the methods of their invaders, they consulted Livy, and in Machiavelli they found an admirable exponent and critic of the new art of war.

It is significant that the dialogue between Cosimo Rucellai and Fabritio Colonna [4] takes place in a garden after a banquet while some are sitting in an arbour and some are lying on the grass. They know exactly when cavalry should be used ; what are the merits of the Swiss phalanx, and how it might be broken ; the defects in the equipment of the Spanish infantry, and how they might be rectified by adopting that of the Roman legionary. They dispute about fortifications and entrenchments ; but notwithstanding the enthusiasm of Fabritio we are aware at the end

[1] *Utopia*, 243. The Utopians, however, used mercenaries to fight for them, just as Henry VII hired Swiss.

[2] Oman, *Art of War in the Middle Ages* (1885), 122.

[3] Macaulay, *Essay on Machiavelli*.

[4] *Works of Nicholas Machiavel*, trans. into English, 1675, pp. 435-523. Cp. Villari, *Machiavelli*, ii. ch. 8.

that Machiavelli is doubtful whether the Italians have stomach enough to fight. His book was not translated into English until the reign of Elizabeth,[1] when Whitehorne dedicated his version to the Queen " as the first-fruits of a poor soldier's study ". The young Englishman at the beginning of the XVI century was not particularly interested in war. Those who were adventurous thought more of the discoveries by Portugal and Spain.

If war on a great scale was demoralising Europe, the geographical discoveries of the time were unsettling men's minds, although they had no conception of the real changes which would result. We know that, when Diaz rounded the Cape and Vasco da Gama returned from Calicut, the commercial supremacy of Genoa and Venice was doomed ; that, when Columbus discovered America and Amerigo Vespucci rounded the Horn, the future lay with the nations upon the Atlantic seaboard ; that, when gold flowed from the Indies and slaves were brought from Guinea, the economic conditions of the Middle Ages had to be revolutionised ; but in the early years of the XVI century men hardly perceived these consequences, and yet their minds were disturbed.

Europeans had so long been shut in by the Mohammedan barrier that they had come to think of themselves as the world. The nations might be constantly at war ; but they had related interests, shared a common culture, professed a common religion and looked to a common centre. The Roman Empire was a tradition, and for all the nations Rome was the capital of the world. Some had read the travels of Marco Polo, and more had delighted in the marvels of the fictitious Mandeville, but they read these books as we read of voyages to the moon or of visitors from Mars—they were interesting but in no sense relevant to their lives. The Portuguese and Spanish discoveries, on the other hand, opened up new worlds, and made men understand the limitations of their experience. There were vast continents with innumerable people to whom Christianity had never been proclaimed. Was Rome after all the capital of the world, or was Christianity only a local religion ? Thanks to that delusive faculty, the imagination, it was the size of the new continents and the distances that could be travelled that seemed to dwarf for a time the importance of Europe. The men of the XVI

[1] Einstein, *Italian Renaissance in England*, 96.

century felt, like the men of the XIX—who had been brought up in heliocentric conceptions—felt when they grasped the fact that they lived on an insignificant planet in a tenth-rate solar system.

The Pope, indeed, had no misgivings about his universal sovereignty. He bestowed on Portugal Africa and the East, and on Spain all that lay west of the Azores. He was not paralysed by his imagination, neither was he making himself ridiculous. He was following a practical instinct—he saw that for the peace of his world at that time it was better that the fleets of two maritime nations should sail in different directions. He overlooked the fact that English and Dutch adventurers might also wish to explore and might become fanatically anti-papal when in conflict with Spanish claims.

Henry VII paid no regard to the Pope's donation. He might have had the honour of commissioning Columbus but for a series of accidents.[1] As it was :

> When news was brought that Don Christopher Colonus Genuese had discovered the coasts of India, whereof was great talk in all the court of Henry VII who then reigned, in so much that all men with great admiration affirmed it to be a thing to be more divine than human to sail by the West into the East where spices grew.[2]

So wrote Sebastian Cabot in his old age. In his youth Henry had commissioned his father, John Cabot, his brothers and himself to go forth and " to set up our banners and ensigns in every village, town, castle, isle and mainland of them newly found ".[3] The Cabots, and not Columbus, were the first to reach the mainland of America ; but they only discovered the rock-bound coast of Labrador and the Island of Newfoundland.[4] They did not find the isle of spices, nor did Robert Thorne and Hugh Eliot who followed them. The zeal for exploration declined, because the Bristol merchants who had financed the expeditions were not satisfied with such profits as might be derived from three savages " clothed in beasts' skins, who ate raw flesh and were in their demeanour like brute beasts " ; but John Rastell lamented the

[1] Busch, *England under the Tudors*, 161, 162. *Vide* Gairdner's notes, 359.

[2] Hakluyt, *Principal Voyages*, v. 86.

[3] *Ibid.* v. 83.

[4] Sebastian Cabot in his old age was not a very truthful person, and he seems to have taken credit to himself for discoveries made by his father. *D.N.B.*

chance that had been missed of teaching the brutish tribes "to know of men the manner and also to know God their Maker".[1]

The many discoveries at the end of the XV century enlarged men's views, but disturbed their mental balance. The flood of new knowledge made men despise their teachers and think that the Old Learning was no longer of any account. They were eager to see and know, but there was so much that was new that they were constantly distracted and followed a wayward course. They were like boys let out of school, running hither and thither, ready to defy authority, but with no settled plans for the exercise of their freedom. A good example of this spirit of enterprise and lack of stability may be found in the career of John Rastell, the brother-in-law of Sir Thomas More.[2]

He was, according to Wood,[3] educated at Oxford and then joined the Middle Temple and was called to the Bar. Shortly after marrying Elizabeth More in 1504 he succeeded his father as coroner of Coventry and might have settled down to a respectable existence in the city to which his family belonged. But after a few years he entered the service of Sir Edward Belknap and was for two years a soldier in France. In 1514 he was again in London, practising at the Bar and starting a printing-press. From this press came immense folios containing his *Abridgement of the Statutes* and also a little book of *The Merry Jests of the Widow Edith*.[4] He printed More's *Supplication of Souls* and his own *Pastime of the People*,[5] a dull history book with very quaint woodcuts. In 1517 he fitted out a ship to explore the New World with his chief printer as second in command. However, he never got further than Waterford, for his sailing-master cheated him and the crew mutinied. He next took to devising pageants and was commissioned to design the banqueting-hall for the Field of the Cloth of Gold. He afterwards built a stage in the garden of his house at Finsbury and wrote the interludes that were acted there. He then turned his attention to theology and wrote a Dialogue to establish the doctrine of Purgatory by pure reason without any appeal to Scripture or ecclesiastical authority. To his book Frith replied. Rastell set out gaily to convert Frith;

[1] *Four Elements*, by John Rastell, quoted by *C. Mod. H.* ii. 51.
[2] A. W. Reed, *Early Tudor Drama*, ch. 1.
[3] *Athenae Oxonienses*, i. 100.
[4] *Vide supra*, 391.
[5] *The Pastime of the People* was reprinted 1811 by Rivingtons, etc.

and Frith converted him. As a Protestant he attached himself to Cromwell and sat in the Reformation Parliament as member for Dunheved in Cornwall. However, he disapproved so strongly of paying tithes that Cromwell clapt him into the Fleet prison, where he died in 1536. Obviously he was a man of many parts who never continued in one stay. He was, however, typical of a restless age that was to express itself in many changes during the Reformation.

II. *XV-Century Humanism in England*

The Renaissance in England was a century later than the Renaissance in Italy, but there had been continual intercourse between the two countries, and there had been many precursors of Colet, Erasmus and More.

Thousands of pilgrims *ad limina Apostolorum* crossed the Alps in the XV century. They went to earn indulgences, but they picked up knowledge by the way. Capgrave, for instance, was able on his return to write the *Solace of Pilgrims* ; and he had found that solace in studying with intelligence the antiquities of Rome.[1]

Scores of archdeacons and would-be archdeacons studied at Bologna and Padua, and some did not confine their attention to the Decretals and Justinian. Proctors for the king or archbishop were often passing to and fro, and there were many English notaries practising in the papal courts. Lastly, there were young men eager to see the world, who enjoyed the profusion of Italian despots ; and scholars who had heard tell of the New Learning, and regarded Italy as the fount of knowledge.[2]

Not only did Englishmen go to Italy, but Italians came to England in search of preferment or in search of manuscripts ; as papal collectors, or in the way of trade.[3] Poggio, who had been introduced to Beaufort at the Council of Constance, came in 1420 hoping to find a munificent patron, and perhaps also to find manuscripts like those he discovered at St. Gall. Beaufort

[1] *Solace of Pilgrims. Vide supra*, 194.

[2] There was an English " nation " at Bologna, English rectors at Vicenza and Vercelli, while the Registers at Padua contain a great number of English names. Rashdall, *Universities*, i. 157, and ii. 4.

[3] Italian merchants at Bristol are said to have persuaded John Free to go to Italy ; but it was an Englishman, William Grey, who paid his expenses.

only offered him a small benefice, and such libraries as he examined yielded nothing that interested him. He writes :

> I visited many convents ; they were full of books by modern doctors, whom we should not think worthy even to be heard.[1]

Aeneas Sylvius was more fortunate, for he found in the sacristy of St. Paul's a history which, according to the colophon, had been written six hundred years before.

> The writer of the history was noted as the Greek Thucydides, whom we know by report to have been famous. I found, however, no translator's name.[2]

The earlier Italian scholars were a little contemptuous of Englishmen. Petrarch, for instance, found that omnivorous reader, Richard de Bury, somewhat of an amateur, and he was disappointed in a Northerner who could give him no information about Ultima Thule.[3] Leonardo Bruno, while commending an English monk, named Thomas, writes: "He loved the humanities so far as one of his nationality could understand them ".[4] Yet Bekyngton was a considerable scholar,[5] and Aeneas Sylvius in a somewhat patronising letter approved the Latin of Adam Molyneux. The man, however, whom Adam was accused of murdering, excited Italian admiration.[6] Humphrey, Duke of Gloucester, is acclaimed by Italian scholars as *Litteratissimus*, and addressed in prefaces, which were duly paid for, as *Immortalis Princeps*.[7]

This selfish, unprincipled profligate, who all but ruined England, had a redeeming virtue—a genuine love of letters and learned men. Antonio Beccaria of Verona was one of his secretaries and collected books on his behalf ; another, with the assumed name of Titus Livius of Forli, styled himself his " poet and orator ", and had a commission to write the Life of Henry V.[8] Leonardo Bruno at first dedicated to him his translation of

[1] *Ep.* 43. Quoted Hallam, *Lit. of Europe*, i. 110.
[2] Quoted by Creighton, *Hist. Lects.* etc. 198.
[3] Blakiston, *Trinity Coll. Oxford*, p. 7. Cp. Creighton, *Hist. Lects.* 193, 194.
[4] Einstein, *Italian Renaissance in England*, 15.
[5] Bekyngton Correspondence. Rolls Series.
[6] *D.N.B.* (Molyneux) refers to Aeneas Sylvius, *Ep.* 80, 186, and to *De Europa*, 443. Cp. Creighton, *op. cit.* 197.
[7] Einstein, *op. cit.* 7.
[8] Thomas Hearn printed the *Life of Henry V.*

Aristotle's *Politics*, but withdrew the dedication when a suitable acknowledgment was not received. Piero Candido was more fortunate with his translation of the first five books of Plato's *Republic*; but then he compared the Duke to Caesar and Augustus, and the Duke was equally flattering to the scholar. Gloucester did not neglect literary Englishmen. He was the patron of Pecock, Capgrave and Lydgate. He is, however, more famous as a book collector, and most famous as the founder of the library at Oxford.[1]

Oxford had been the home of the scholastic theology, but it was poorly furnished with classical texts. Thomas de Cobham, Bishop of Worcester, was building a library adjoining St. Mary's in 1327. He left his books to the University, but he died in debt. Adam de Brome bought the books for £50, intending them for Oriel; but the scholars of the University raided the college and carried them off for the common use.[2] They were not many in number and only filled two chests. A few years later in 1345, Richard de Bury left to Durham College the large library which he had collected during his many embassies to different parts of Europe, but he too died in debt, so that many of his books were sold and only a few of them reached their destination.[3] The real founder of the University library was Humphrey, Duke of Gloucester. His benefactions extended over more than thirty years, and a grateful University, given to hyperbole, assured him—

> previously there had been, it is true, a university at Oxford; but study there was none, for there were no books; now, however, through your gifts, we too can discern the secrets of learning.[4]

Apart from flattery and exaggeration, this and other letters show that Oxford was beginning to despise its great tradition of skill in philosophy and theology, and had come to believe that the faculty of arts was alone worth cultivating. It is noteworthy that, though Gloucester's library contained Wyclif's Bible, it had otherwise little theology and none of the schoolmen. It contained translations of Arabic authors on medicine and astrology; translations of Aristotle and Plato; most of the Latin poets as well as Quintilian, Seneca and Cicero; five volumes of Boccaccio,

[1] Einstein, *op. cit.* ch. i.
[2] Pearce, *Thomas de Cobham*, 246-248.
[3] Blakiston, *Trin. Coll. Oxon*, 7.
[4] Quoted Einstein, *op. cit.* 10.

seven of Petrarch and two of Dante. The day for lay education had dawned.[1]

The new books at Oxford no doubt inspired men to seek the land from which they came ; but we must not forget the archdeacons who went to study law and learnt in Italy to have a wider outlook. One of them, Andrew Hollis, was King's Proctor in Rome, and became a Protonotary Apostolic to Eugenius IV. On his way home he stayed eighteen months in Florence ; and Vespasiano da Besticci, who called him Ols, wrote that he was devout and charitable, and might have been a bishop or even a cardinal if he had not fled from all earthly honours. He bought so large a library in Florence, presumably from Vespasiano, that it had to be sent to England by sea. He then went home himself, and retired with his books to a benefice in the country and " became dead to the world for the love of God ".[2] So far Vespasiano—but perhaps he exaggerates his retirement. At any rate Hollis was Archdeacon of Anglesea from 1427 to 1450, and Chancellor of Salisbury from 1445 to 1470. He held prebends in St. Asaph, Lichfield, Southwell and York, and was Rector of St. Dunstan's in London and of Davenham in Cheshire.[3]

A wandering scholar who was even better endowed was William Grey, a son of Lord Grey of Conder.[4] He belonged to Balliol and had been Chancellor of Oxford (1440–1442) before he started on his travels. He first studied theology at Cologne, and lived so magnificently that the burghers were unwilling to part with so profitable a guest, and he had to escape from the city disguised as an Irish pilgrim. He then studied at Florence, Padua and under Guarino at Ferrara. After being made King's Proctor he went to Rome, was a friend of Bessarion and a favourite of Nicholas V, who provided him to the see of Ely. At home he lived for the most part in his splendid palace in Holborn, enjoying the garden famed for its strawberries, and surrounded by scholars vocal in his praise. He died in 1478 and

[1] Maxwell-Lyte, *Oxford*, 321. It is interesting to compare this library with that formed by Charles V and Charles VI of France. 843 volumes from it were purchased by John, Duke of Bedford, in 1425, and dispersed at his death ten years later. For some notes on its contents see Darwin, *Louis D'Orleans*, Appendix F.

[2] Vespasiano da Besticci, *Memoirs*, translated by W. G. and E. Waters (Routledge, 1926), 206-208.

[3] *Ibid.* 5. (Le Neve, *Fasti*, 30, calls him Hulles, and 268, Holes.)

[4] Besticci. Cp. Creighton, *Hist. Lects.* 201 ; Einstein, *op. cit.* 19 ff.

left more than 200 manuscripts to his old college. One hundred and fifty-two of them are still there, though most of them are in a mutilated condition, for they had been adorned with miniatures painted by Florentine artists, and readers have found the temptation to cut them out irresistible.

John Tiptoft [1] was also of Balliol; and at the age of twenty-two, after being created Earl of Worcester, he started as a pilgrim to Jerusalem. Returning to Venice, he spent three years in Italy, partly in Florence where he loved to wander unattended, and partly at Ferrara as a pupil of Guarino. He then went to Rome and made an oration before Pius II, who is said to have wept for joy because of his graceful Latinity. He bought so many books that Vespasiano speaks of his despoiling Italy to enrich England. But Tiptoft not only learnt from scholars the art of rhetoric, but from Italian despots their methods of government, so that on returning to England his cruelties as Constable made his name a byword. When he was executed in 1470, Fuller says, "then did the axe at one blow cut off more learning in England than was left in the heads of all the surviving nobility": [2] but the books from which the learning came were stored in Oxford until they were dispersed or destroyed, like those of Duke Humphrey, by the Vandals of the Reformation.

Robert Flemming,[3] also of Balliol, became Dean of Lincoln, and it is said that he started on his travels because he could not control his turbulent chapter. He stayed in Italy many years, being first a student with Guarino and afterwards a protonotary to Sixtus IV. He had a villa at Tivoli, where he wrote verses in honour of Sixtus and published them as *Lucubrationes Tiburtinae*. His great friend was Platina—a very dubious character, who wrote the *Lives of the Popes*; and he may have belonged to the Roman Academy of Pomponius Laetus—a very pagan society which ultimately was suppressed. He collected many books and presented some of them to Lincoln College, Oxford, which had been founded by his uncle, and he left them also a Greek and Latin Dictionary which he had compiled himself.

Grey and Tiptoft were great men who travelled with splendid

[1] Tiptoft. *Vide supra*, 384; *Vespasiano Memoirs*, *D.N.B.* etc.

[2] Fuller, *Worthies*, Cambridgeshire, i. 155 (1662 ed.).

[3] For Flemming, Free and Gunthorp, *vide D.N.B.* Creighton, *Hist. Lects.* 202-203; Einstein, *op. cit.* 17-23.

retinues: Flemming was a well-to-do man able to provide for himself; John Free and his friend Gunthorp, both Fellows of Balliol, were poor men who depended on the liberality of Grey. John Free started for Ferrara with ten pounds. He spent four of them on the way, and soon after his arrival he had to pawn his books with the Jews until he could receive further supplies from his patron. He was probably the greatest of the English scholars at this time. He not only learnt Greek but graduated as a doctor of medicine and a doctor of civil law. He wrote a book on botany. When Guarino died at the age of ninety, he was deputed to make his funeral oration; when the admirers of Petrarch lamented the monkish rhymes in which he was commemorated, Free was asked to compose a new epitaph more worthy of the poet; when Grey's nephew died in Italy, he wrote the bishop a letter of consolation full of classical quotations and with little reference to the Christian hope. When Tiptoft came to Padua he joined his retinue and went with him to Rome. Pius II recognised his merits as a classical scholar, and provided him to the see of Bath and Wells, but he died before he was consecrated.

Gunthorpe also managed to thrive in Italy and collected books. He was a rhetorician; and when he came home was employed by Edward IV to write Latin orations and complimentary letters. He became Dean of Wells and rebuilt the deanery, ornamenting it with all sorts of guns. By his will he distributed his books between Oxford and Cambridge and gave to his Cathedral church a silver image of the Virgin which weighed 143 ounces.[1]

All these men were wandering stars. They went to Italy and elsewhere for the purpose of self-culture, and they did very little to improve the education of England except through the books which they left to colleges. It was otherwise with Selling, who founded a school at Canterbury.

William Selling, as a young man, had been sent to Canterbury College at Oxford, and was still *in statu pupillari* in 1450.[2] In 1464 the Convent of Christ Church, Canterbury, gave him leave of absence for three years to study in any university, and in 1467 he and his fellow monk, Walter Hadley, became doctors

[1] Warton, *Hist. of Poetry*, ii. 555.

[2] Tanner, quoting no authority, states that he was at All Souls, and he has been followed by Warton and other writers, but his 1450 letter to Prior Goldstone shows that this is incorrect. Vide *Christ Church Letters* (Camden Soc.), xiii.

of divinity at Bologna.[1] They did not at once return home, for in 1468 the convent granted letters of fraternity to Johanita Bely, who had entertained them at Venice. In 1469 Selling was ordered to proceed to Rome in order to obtain the issue of indulgences for those who should attend the jubilee celebrations in honour of St. Thomas Beket. In 1471 he became Chancellor of Christ Church, Canterbury, and a year later Prior. He acquired a great store of Latin and Greek manuscripts, and built a library for them. He opened a school and taught in it himself. Linacre was his most brilliant pupil. Linacre was sent up to Oxford and became a Fellow of All Souls, but Selling took him with him when he went on an embassy to Rome in 1486, and on his return left him at Florence to study under Politian. It must not be supposed that he was always so successful as a teacher, for there is a pitiful letter from one of his old pupils, Richard Selling, then at Oxford, to say that he had failed in his arts course and wanted to study law. He was probably allowed to do so, for he subsequently became chancellor of the monastery.[2]

The new knowledge was derived from Italy, but it had to be grafted on the native stock before it could become fruitful in this country; and the distinctive character of English humanism was due to the preparatory work that had been done in the grammar-schools and colleges of the XV century. We should not forget the great foundations of Winchester and Eton, Magdalen College at Oxford with its school attached, and God's House at Cambridge which Byngham founded for the express purpose of training grammar-school masters.[3]

William of Wykeham in founding his two colleges of Winchester and New College, wished them to be allied, but he made them independent. Winchester had its own warden and fellows, and the school they were to keep was the reason for their existence. The education of boys in grammar, or, as we should say, in humane letters, was what the founder had at heart. He was only too well aware that boys were going up to the university far too young, insufficiently grounded to benefit by the lectures,

[1] *Christ Church Letters*, xxxiii. The dates from the Canterbury Registers clearly disprove the *D.N.B.* contention that Selling only went to Italy after he became prior. Compare *Letters*, x. and xxx., and note Selling's progress in Latin composition. The burning of his library was due to the Visitors of Henry VIII.

[2] For Richard Selling—*Ch. Ch. Letters*, xxix., and Introd. p. xvii.

[3] Leach, *Mediaeval Schools*, 257.

and with far too many opportunities for getting into mischief. So he planted his school at Winchester and not at Oxford, and the boys were to remain there until they were nineteen, and then to proceed to New College for the severely scholastic course he had planned.[1] The result was that all Wykehamists were primarily grammarians and that some Wykehamists retained a love of humane letters. Wykeham had been careful to preclude the possibility of his college becoming subject to monastic control, and he did not confine his school to the training of ecclesiastics. As a statesman he was aware of the need for a better educated laity, but as a bishop he desired that the laity should be Christian. Grammar he regarded as the key which unlocked the Holy Scriptures, and as the gate to the liberal sciences which led up to theology, the mistress of all knowledge. Wykeham himself in education as in all else was an old-fashioned conservative,[2] and in drawing up his statutes he was indebted to those of Merton and Queens'; but it was because he made his school independent of the college that it achieved its success. At both school and college he established the connexion between religion and sound learning, which was to differentiate the English Renaissance from that of Germany and Italy. Italian scholars despised theology, while Luther and his followers for the most part decried human learning.[3]

About 1465 an Italian named Cornelio Vitelli came to Oxford, and Thomas Chandler, Warden of New College,[4]

[1] On New College Studies see Rashdall in *Clark's Oxford Colleges*, 159 ff.

[2] Leach, *op. cit.* 204-208.

[3] As early as 1520, Erasmus writing to Reuchlin (*Ep.* 1155) fears that Lutheranism and *Bonae Litterae* may be found to be incompatible. Writing to Pirkheimer in 1528 he was sure of it (*Ep.* 1977) : " Ubicunque regnat Lutheranismus, ibi litterarum est interitus ; et tamen hoc genus hominum maxime litteris alitur ". It is noteworthy that Reuchlin, Mutianus Rufus and Crotus Rubianus all reverted to Catholicism because they thought it more favourable to intellectual freedom (Beard, *Hibbert's Lectures*, 337). Melanchthon remained a humanist to the end, and in 1557 bewailed the decline of letters and science in Germany. Luther, once a humanist, came to believe that when everyone had a Bible no other literature would be required. In order that all might read the Bible he was a strenuous advocate for primary schools not only for boys but also for girls (Boehmer, *Luther*, 238, 239). Later the Strasburg reformers issued a declaration in which they said : " Perish the graces of the Latin language, perish the marvels of learning, which obscure the glories of Christ : the word of Christ saves us, the word of others destroy us " (quoted Elliott-Binns, *Hulsean Lectures*, 53).

[4] Thomas Chandler, a Wykehamist and friend of Bekyngton, was Warden of New College from 1454 to 1474, and Chancellor of the University from 1457 to 1461, and from 1472 to 1479. In 1462 he published his *Collocutiones*, and Leland admits

received him with an oration and made him praelector of his college. Erasmus in his *Ciceronianus* speaks disrespectfully of Vitelli's Latin style ; [1] but Vitelli knew some Greek and was able to impart it to William Grocyn, who came from Winchester to Oxford the same year. Grocyn has been styled by Hallam " the patriarch of English learning " ; [2] he was really the link between mediaeval and modern scholarship. For some years he was Reader in Divinity at Magdalen, and his library was well stocked with the works of Aquinas, Scotus and Ockham. He also possessed many of the Fathers, most of the Latin poets and prose writers, and, such was his appetite for universal erudition, he had a copy of Vegetius' *De re Militari*.[3] Warham came up from Winchester four years after him and was his friend until his death. William Latimer, William Lily, Linacre and Colet were all of them probably his pupils, and certainly his friends. He had the gift of attracting the young. He did not go to Italy until 1489, when he was forty-three years old, and possessed very definite opinions and immense knowledge. His young friend Linacre was already in Florence, sharing in the studies of Giovanni de Medici, thanks to the magnificent Lorenzo.[4] William Latimer and Colet at intervals followed their master to Italy, and the former long afterwards, in writing to Erasmus, told him how assiduously Grocyn had studied Greek under Politian and Chalcondylas.[5] But Grocyn resisted the attractions of the Platonic Academy, though he bought the works of Ficino. He remained an Aristotelian, and when, some years later, he was writing to Aldus, he congratulated him on his edition of Aristotle, adding : " I think the difference between these great philosophers Aristotle and Plato, is simply that between a man of science and a man of myths ".[6]

These Englishmen were in Florence during the turbulent religious revival due to the preaching of Savonarola.[7] Politian,

that he wrote Latin correctly both in verse and prose. Montague Burrows in *O.H.S. Collectanea*, ii. 338-342.

[1] Vitelli stayed in Oxford until he went to teach in Paris in 1489.

[2] Hallam, *Lit. of Europe*, i. 276.

[3] For Grocyn's Library, *O.H.S. Collectanea*, ii. 319-324.

[4] Linacre reminded Giovanni de Medici (Leo X) of their early association when he dedicated his *Galen* to him.

[5] Erasmus, *Ep.* 520.

[6] *O.H.S. Collectanea*, ii. 351.

[7] Savonarola was preaching in Florence between 1489 and 1498. Linacre was in Italy from 1486 to 1493 ; Grocyn from 1489 to 1491 ; Latimer from 1490 to 1506 ; Colet from 1493 to 1496.

Ficino, Pico, and Botticelli all became disciples of the friar, and the magnificent Lorenzo sought comfort from him on his deathbed, though he received none, for the friar was inexorable.[1] It is not suggested that the Englishmen were carried away by this wave of religious excitement. Grocyn was a mature man and a dogmatic theologian. Linacre was a shrewd man with any amount of practical common sense. He, we know, proceeded to Padua in order that he might study medicine. Latimer was a quiet man, diffident and reserved, who probably shrank from all demonstrations of an emotional kind. Only Colet, and we cannot be sure that he was in Florence, afterwards showed somewhat of the puritan austerity and somewhat of the prophetic fire of Savonarola. They were, however, all of them religious men who had been brought up in a religious atmosphere, and they found in Italy that, for the moment, religion was of paramount interest. When they returned to England they did not dissociate humanism from religion, as they might have been tempted to do had they visited Italy in any other decade of the XV century.

III. *Erasmus in Oxford*

Grocyn[2] on his return hired rooms in Exeter college and began once more to teach. In the following year (1492) Cardinal Morton, Archbishop of Canterbury, sent his favourite page to Canterbury Hall " for his furtherance in learning ". This page was Thomas More, aged fourteen, who came up very short of pocket money but with any amount of brains. His father only allowed him to stay up for two years, because he believed that wealth was more necessary than learning, and that the study of the common law was likely to prove more profitable than the study of the classics.[3] Imaginative historians describe how Grocyn, Linacre and Colet puzzled over Greek texts aided by the marvellous boy ; but this is all nonsense.[4] Colet, who was

[1] Savonarola refused absolution to Lorenzo on his deathbed as he would not restore the liberties of Florence. Villari, *Savonarola*, 146-149.

[2] *O.H.S. Collectanea*, ii.

[3] Miss Routh, *Thomas More*.

[4] Cardinal Gasquet, *Eve of the Reformation*, 27, has the following note : " Sir Thomas More writing to Colet says : ' I pass my time here at [Oxford] with Grocyn, Linacre and [George] Lilly ; the first, as you know, the only master of my life, when you are absent ; the second the director of my studies ; the third the dearest companion in all the affairs of life ' (Stapleton, *Tres Thomae*, 165). Another constant companion

starting to Italy in a few months, may have commended his little friend to Grocyn, that is, if the Colet and More families knew one another, as they probably did. Linacre, returning from Italy as a doctor of Padua in 1493, was, according to Wood,[1] incorporated at Oxford and read a "shagling" lecture;[2] but he settled in London, and it was probably in London and not in Oxford that he made the acquaintance of More. Everyone, however, who met "Young More" loved him and talked about him. Erasmus had heard such talk before he met him by chance in 1499 at the dinner-table of Sir John Say.[3] When the young man, aged twenty-one, joined in the conversation, Erasmus exclaimed, *Tu es Morus aut nullus*,[4] and More replied, *Tu es Erasmus aut diabolus*—a reply that was neither witty nor polite and only comes to us through Cresacre More. Erasmus, however, was attracted to More, and even forgave him when he introduced him, unprepared, to the royal nursery at Eltham, and presented him to that redoubtable little boy who was to be Henry VIII. More and his friend Arnold had complimentary verses to offer to the children; and Erasmus, having none, had for three days to wrestle with an unwilling muse in order to repair the omission.[5]

After meeting Grocyn, Linacre and More in London, Erasmus went to Oxford, where he was entertained at St. Mary's College[6] by Richard Charnock, a prior of his own order of Augustinian canons. He spent three pleasant months at the

of More at Oxford was Cuthbert Tunstall, etc." So far the Cardinal, but the letter was not written at Oxford in 1492 but in London 1504–1505. It begins by stating that More had just met Colet's servant in the law courts. It goes on to rally him on remaining among the orchards of his country parish at Stepney, when he was so wanted in his pulpit in St. Paul's. Colet became Dean in 1504 and resigned Stepney in 1506. George Lily was not born when More was at Oxford, nor was his father William Lily then resident there. Tunstall was at Balliol for a few months in the year before More went up to Oxford, and then migrated to King's Hall, Cambridge.

[1] Wood, *Athenae Oxonienses*, i. 43.

[2] A "shagling" lecture was one permitted but not authorised by the University N.E.D.

[3] This is probable, because Sir John Say was the father-in-law of Lord Mountjoy, who had brought Erasmus to England. Mountjoy was a minor and his wife a child. He lived with his father-in-law who was a friend of the Mores. Sir John More and his son were subsequently Sir John Say's trustees. Nichol's *Letters of Erasmus*, i. 200.

[4] The story comes from Cresacre More's *Life of Sir Thomas*, 83 (1726 ed.). Its historicity is doubted by R. W. Chambers, *Sir Thomas More*, 76.

[5] Allen, *Erasmus to Botzheim*, i. 6. Cp. *Ep.* 113

[6] Frewen Hall is on the site of St. Mary's College.

University and enlarged the circle of his acquaintance with English scholars. Brumus (which may be a copyist's error for Grocyn) [1] had written to Colet in his praise, and Colet at once addressed him in a polite letter of welcome which met with a somewhat extravagant reply. Erasmus also made the acquaintance of Sixtin,[2] a Dutchman like himself, but beneficed in England, and probably of John Claymond, then of Magdalen, to whom he afterwards dedicated his translations from St. Chrysostom. Erasmus was impressed by the spirit of religious seriousness which he found in Oxford and also by the lack of pedantry. He went to hear Colet lecture on the Epistle to the Romans, and learnt from him a new approach to the Scriptures; [3] but he was not yet prepared to desert his career as a humanist and devote himself to the exposition of the Bible, as Colet urged him to do. He describes a dinner party at Oxford when "the good cheer would have satisfied Epicurus, and the table-talk would have pleased Pythagoras".[4] At the head of the table sat Colet, "assertor and champion of the old theology"; on his right sat Charnock, "high priest of the Graces"; on his left a young man who had that day preached the Latin sermon and who "was a man of modesty as well as learning". Erasmus sat next to him, "that the banquet might not be without a poet"; while a "cheerful and witty lawyer", whom he calls Philip, sat opposite. There were several others present, and Dr. Allen, who thinks the dinner was at Magdalen,[5] suggests that Wolsey may have been among the guests—he was then master of Magdalen College School. In conversation they chanced to discuss what exactly was the sin for which Cain was rejected; and when Erasmus thought that the dispute was becoming too serious for a banquet, he enlivened it with an apologue which he afterwards elaborated for the benefit of Sixtin. He had, while at Oxford, a more serious controversy with Colet on the interpretation of the Agony in Gethsemane,[6] when he advocated the conventional view that the human nature of our Lord shrank from the pain that He foresaw, while Colet, following St. Jerome, thought that our Lord's agony was due to His compassion for the Jews, who were about to incur such awful guilt.

[1] Allen, *Erasmi Epistolae*, i. 242.
[2] *Ibid.* i. 261.
[3] *Ep.* 108. Also 108 in Nichols' translation.
[4] *Ep.* 113.
[5] Allen, i. 268. Cp. Lupton, *Life of Colet*, 94.
[6] *Epp.* 109, 110, 111, 112.

Erasmus at this time was not very serious-minded, but he was an observant person ; sceptical and flippant himself, he was quick to detect and expose unreality in others ; but he never at any time failed to recognise the utter sincerity of Colet. He wrote to Colet letters unlike those that he wrote to anyone else. He knew Colet's contempt for the schoolmen, but still regarded him as the champion of orthodoxy. Neither he nor Colet foresaw the influence that the theology of Colet, when interpreted by Erasmus, would have on the Reformation.

Erasmus on this first visit was pleased with England, and with his own reception; and to different correspondents he confided such impressions as they would appreciate. To the volatile Faustus Andrelinus he wrote :

> We have made progress in England. The Erasmus you once knew is now become almost a sportsman, no bad rider, a courtier of some practice, bows with politeness, smiles with grace, and all this in spite of himself. If you are wise you will fly over here. . . . To take one attraction out of many : there are nymphs here with divine features, so gentle and kind, that you may well prefer them to your Camenae. . . . The rest of my story we will laugh over together, for I hope to see you before long.[1]

To the serious student, Robert Fisher, studying in Italy, he wrote :

> I never liked anything so much before,—I find the climate both pleasant and wholesome ; and I have met with so much kindness, and so much learning, not hackneyed and trivial, but deep, accurate, ancient, Latin and Greek, that, but for the curiosity of seeing it, I do not now so much care for Italy. When I hear my Colet, I seem to be listening to Plato himself. In Grocyn, who does not marvel at such a perfect round of learning. What can be more acute, profound and delicate than the judgment of Linacre ? What has Nature ever created more gentle, more sweet, more happy than the genius of More ? I need not go through the list. It is marvellous how general and abundant is the harvest of general learning in this country, to which you ought all the sooner to return.[2]

Erasmus was indeed happy in his friends, but we have to remember that in 1499 he was not a celebrity, and his friends, so important in his own eyes, were people of no importance to the rest of England. He did not at this time know Warham, Fox, Fisher, FitzJames and Smythe, scholars who had already

[1] *Ep.* 103 ; trans. by Nichols, i. 203.

[2] *Ep.* 118 ; trans. in Nichols, i. 226.

attained to positions of power. On his second visit, from 1505 to 1506, he was presented by Grocyn to Warham, who scarcely valued sufficiently the dedication of his *Hecuba*; [1] he made the acquaintance of Fisher, and dedicated another of his works to Fox, hoping to be noticed and rewarded because he knew Richard Whitford, the Bishop's chaplain.[2] By then he was becoming famous and his friends were becoming influential.

It is evident that the New Learning was not really new when Henry VIII came to the throne: but it had hitherto been an academic possession of which the ordinary man knew nothing. Suddenly there were men who could popularise this learning, and were eager to do so. They were the prophets of a new age; and what they taught went to the heads of the unlearned like new wine. Intoxicated young men began to despise all that they had hitherto reverenced, and to be quite sure that change meant progress and all that was new must be true.

This may not be so apparent if we do not keep in mind the ages of those who were prominent at this time, or soon to be prominent. In 1509 Grocyn was 63, the father of the scholars. The patrons of learning were: Richard Fox, 61; William Warham, 59; and John Fisher, 50.[3] William Latimer and Thomas Linacre were alike 49; Colet was 42, and William Lily a year younger. They were all men with established reputations. The rising stars were: Tunstall, 35; Wolsey, 34; More, 31;[4]

[1] Allen, *Epp. Erasmi*, i. p. 5.

[2] *Epp.* 187, 191.

[3] The age of Fisher is disputed. The *D.N.B.* believes that he was born in 1459. Bridgett, *Blessed John Fisher*, 7 ff., and Van Ortrey, *Analecta Bollandiana*, x. 202, argue for 1469. The evidence is not conclusive either way, but I believe *D.N.B* is right. He matriculated at Cambridge 1483, and was B.A. 1487. This favours the 1469 date. Wolsey was a bachelor at fifteen. But we must remember Erasmus was a bachelor at twenty-nine. He became commissary or vice-chancellor of Cambridge in 1501, which favours the earlier date for his birth. He became a bishop in 1505, and there is a sermon attributed to him in which he speaks of himself as consecrated, *Qui paucos annos habuerim*, but the attribution of the sermon is disputed. Gairdner, *Letters and Papers of Richard and Henry VII*, attributes it to Blyth, Bishop of Salisbury. Holbein painted his portrait two years before his death, and it is inscribed in *anno aetatis*, 74. This seems conclusive, as Fisher must have supplied the information. The Papal Nuncio, writing on the day of his death, says, "the English call him a valetudinarian of ninety, reckoning him 25 years older than he is". This should not be pressed to mean more than that the current talk about his age was exaggerated. His contemporaries regarded him as aged. It is difficult to imagine that he was younger than Colet and Erasmus and only nine years older than More.

[4] There has been a dispute whether More was born 1478 or 1480. R. W. Chambers, *Sir Thomas More*, 48-49, seems to have determined this controversy in favour of 1478.

and Pace, 27. The men yet unknown were : Stephen Gardiner, 26 ; William Tyndale, 25 ; Hugh Latimer and Thomas Cromwell, 24 ; Cranmer and Croke, 20. The bright little boys were Thomas Lupset, aged 12 ; Thomas Elyot and Starkey, 10 ; and Reginald Pole, 9. The last was a pupil of William Latimer.

It should be noted that Grocyn, William Latimer, Linacre, Colet, Lily, Tunstall, Pace, Lupset, Starkey and Pole all studied in Italian universities. They went to Italy in order to complete the education they had received in England ; and the Italians confessed that, after themselves, none spoke Latin more correctly. When they returned they seemed to have absorbed what was best in Italian culture without contaminating their native piety. Fifty years later, both learning and religion were imported from Germany and Switzerland ; theologians received them with becoming meekness ; but educated men, who were not theologians, ignored Teutonic culture and sought for inspiration in the lighter literature of France, Italy and Spain.

IV. *Erasmus in London and Cambridge*

When Henry VIII ascended the throne in 1509, More wrote Latin verses to celebrate the advent of the Golden Age ; and Lord Mountjoy invited Erasmus to come once more to England,[1] where he had twice been disappointed of preferment, assuring him that with a new king all was changed. " The heavens laugh, the earth exults, all things are full of milk, of honey and of nectar. Avarice is expelled the country : Liberality scatters wealth with bounteous hands."[2] He is sure that the king will be especially lavish to scholars, and pictures him greeting Erasmus with a line from Martial.

Accipe divitias et vatum maximus esto[3]

Erasmus may or may not have believed that Henry VIII was familiar with Martial ; but he was certain that Mountjoy had not composed the letter above his name. Mountjoy had been his pupil and he knew the extent of his Latinity. So he wrote on the top of the sheet " Andreas Ammonius " in order that posterity might not be deceived.

[1] Erasmus visited England in 1499, in 1505–1506 and from 1509 to 1514. He also came on flying visits, 1515, 1516, 1517.

[2] Erasmus, *Ep.* 215.

[3] Martial, Bk. VIII. *Ep.* 56.

Erasmus had been for three years in Italy. He had taken a doctor's degree at Turin ; had studied at Bologna ; and had worked for the printing-press of Aldus at Venice.[1] He had been to Rome, where cardinals like Riario and Grimani had been civil ; but he had only been fed with promises.[2] No doubt he might have obtained an official appointment, but he was not prepared to barter his freedom for the emoluments of an office. Erasmus wanted money down, and enough of it to enable him to live his own life and do his own work with comfort. He was quite shameless in writing begging letters, a prince of mendicants ; but his servility went no further. He never felt the least obligation to those who supplied his needs. We must not blame him. There was no endowment of research, and the universities were becoming merely places of instruction and ceasing to be homes for the learned. Besides, at this time many of the universities were hostile to the New Learning, and defiant young men, who called themselves poets, refused to frequent them or take degrees,[3] preferring to be servant pupils to a distinguished scholar.[4] Their masters found the proximity of a good printer more advantageous than a professorial chair, and they could make more money by correcting classical texts for the press than by teaching those for whom the texts were prepared. Most scholars, however, dreamed of some munificent Maecenas who would reward their golden eloquence with golden coin. They preferred that he should be a king, and so a fit subject for immortal verse. They were not ashamed

> To heap the shrine of luxury and pride
> With incense kindled at the Muses' flame.

When Lord Mountjoy wrote that Henry VIII desired to be surrounded by scholars, Erasmus packed up and came to England, only to be disappointed. He understood all the arts

[1] Erasmus complained that Aldus and his father-in-law Asolanus starved him, and he revenged himself in the colloquy *Opulentia Sordida*. Julius Caesar Scaliger in his attack on Erasmus tells how the frugal Italians were scandalised by the Dutchman's appetite for food and drink. Mangan, *Erasmus of Rotterdam*, i. 245-258 ; Nichols, *Epp. of Erasmus*, i. 447-448.

[2] Nichols, *op. cit.* i. 454 and 460-462.

[3] *Epistolae Obscurorum Virorum*, ii. *Ep.* 46.

[4] Croke, afterwards Professor of Greek at Leipzig and Cambridge, was servant-pupil to Grocyn. Brixius was servant-pupil to Lascaris. Lupset was boy attendant on Colet. John Smith was servant-pupil to Erasmus. John Clement and Harris were boys in More's household.

of flattery, but he could not be a courtier any more than he could be a monk—he hated servitude.

On the long journey from Italy he meditated on *Moria*, and wrote his *Encomium*[1] in seven days after arriving at Sir Thomas More's house. At least, so he said; but it was two years before he took the MS. to Paris, and then he left Croke to see it through the press, so that he might disavow all responsibility for its publication if it became advisable to do so. All sorts and conditions of men are pilloried in this little book; but the cruellest criticism is reserved for bishops and monks.[2] The Abbot of St. Bertin, one of his best patrons, had subsequently to be propitiated; and Dorpius wrote from Louvain a friendly expostulation,[3] only to receive a long but disingenuous reply. Sir Thomas More leapt to the defence of the book which had been dedicated to him, for Erasmus in his eyes could do no wrong. Erasmus was "More's darling", as Tyndale remarked;[4] and More approved in Erasmus what he reprobated in Tyndale, because he understood Erasmus and could not understand Tyndale.

Both Erasmus and More desired the reformation of the Church and the conversion of sinners, and neither could see that books like the *Encomium Moriae* were ill-designed for their purpose. They both believed that sin was folly and that the sinner was ridiculous. They thought that, by making this clear, the world would be purified by honest laughter. Now, it is true, you can laugh a silly custom out of fashion, you can temper a despotism by epigrams, and you can destroy all reverence for an institution by caricaturing it; but you cannot convert a sinner from the error of his ways by telling him that he is a funny man—it makes him angry. A bad man may be made to acknowledge that he is a sinner, he will never acknowledge that he is a bad joke.

Ridicule, if it be effective, may destroy but it cannot reform. The barbed shafts of Erasmus' wit wounded the Church and brought all her practices into discredit. Until the end of his life he went on protesting that he had never laughed at ecclesiastical ceremonies, at fasts, votive offerings, the invocation of saints or pilgrimages, but only at superstitious worshippers.[5] The ridicule,

[1] Froude, *Life and Letters of Erasmus*, 136, is altogether wrong about the genesis of the *Encomium*, as may be seen from the first paragraph of the dedication to More, the letter to Dorpius (*Ep.* 337) and the *Lucubrationes* in Allen, i. 19.

[2] *Ep.* 739. [3] *Epp.* 304, 307. [4] Tyndale, *Works*, iii. 16. [5] *Ep.* 2263.

however, was in general terms—he was proud of the fact that he had abstained from personalities—and there was no indication of the limits to which the ridicule extended. The ordinary reader was never asked to consider the difference between use and abuse; and might, in consequence, be excused for believing there was none. Colet probably disapproved of the *Encomium* [1] when it was read aloud in More's house. At any rate, when Erasmus asked him to support Croke " while studying in Paris", he met with a flat refusal.[2] Colet probably knew why Croke was in Paris and disapproved of his errand. He was not going to supply money that the *Encomium* might be published to all Europe.

Erasmus when he wrote to Servatius,[3] his prior at Steyn, boasted of his position in England. He told him of his friendship with the King; of the liberality of the Archbishop of Canterbury; of Fisher, Mountjoy and Colet; of the honour with which he was everywhere received. He wanted to make it quite clear that so great a man as himself could not possibly return to Steyn and be a humble monk; and yet all the time he was a disappointed man. When he wrote to his friend Ammonius, a foreigner like himself, he speaks of the English as " Cyprian bulls, dung-eaters, who imagine that they alone feed on ambrosia and Jupiter's brain "—and he prudently writes his abuse in Greek for fear that Ammonius might leave his letter about for anyone to read.

Erasmus was irritable and a man of moods who could be spiteful when he was disappointed. Perhaps the letter to Bombasius in 1518 represents more truly the English court as he saw it in retrospect, though we must remember that he was replying to a letter in which Bombasius had boasted of the court at Rome and his reception there.

The King, the most sensible monarch of our age, is delighted with good books, and the Queen is well instructed—not merely in comparison with her own sex, and no less is to be respected for her piety than her

[1] My belief is not affected by *Ep.* 423, when Colet states the opposition to Erasmus' *Novum Testamentum* comes from those theologians which " you in your *Moria* truly and wittily describe ". It was a polite way of saying " I told you so ".

[2] *Epp.* 225, 227, 237.

[3] *Ep.* 296. An article by A. Kay, Edinburgh Bibliographical Soc. xiv., throws fresh light on the authenticity of this epistle.

[4] *Ep.* 245.

erudition. With such sovereigns, those persons have the greatest influence who excel in learning and prudence. (Here follows a list of scholars and their court appointments.) A palace filled with such men may be called a temple of the Muses rather than a court. What Athens, what Porch, what Lyceum would you prefer to a court like that? [1]

Between the autumn of 1509 and 1511 there are no materials for the life of Erasmus. He evidently spent some time in More's house at Bucklersbury, but we know that More's wife tired of him.[2] This is not surprising, as Erasmus spoke no English, and the good lady can hardly have appreciated a guest who continually set the table in a roar with jokes that she could not understand. He may have shared a lodging with Ammonius or have been entertained by Grocyn, but the latter must have been often at Maidstone, where he was warden of the college. Grocyn was not a rich man, and it is to the credit of Erasmus that he did not like sponging on him: Grocyn was always ready to welcome him but refused to have him as a paying guest.[3]

It was during this time that he definitely devoted himself to sacred literature, and Colet probably allowed him the use of the large library belonging to the chapter of St. Paul's.[4] After his brief visit to Paris in 1511 he went to Cambridge and made it his headquarters for the next three years. Fisher, who was chancellor of the University, induced him to go there to teach Greek, and he was lodged in Queens', of which Fisher had been master. Erasmus disliked the place. His pupils were few and did not pay the fees he expected of them. Few of them advanced beyond the

[1] *Ep.* 855 (Allen). Trans. in Nichols, iii. 421.

[2] *Ep.* 451.

[3] *Ep.* 241.

[4] There were a great many books belonging to St. Paul's and Peter Meghen—"the one-eyed Peter" of Erasmus was constantly employed in copying MSS. for Colet (Allen, *Age of Erasmus*, 141-143). In the reign of Henry VI, Sherington, Chancellor of the Duchy of Lancaster, had built a new library and a catalogue of its contents fills six and a half large pages of Dugdale (*St. Paul's*, 392-399). It chiefly consisted of the Fathers, of commentaries on the Scriptures, and of books on canon law. It also contained a Vergil, a Cicero and a Seneca. The treasurer had other books in his charge, chiefly liturgical. There was also a library in the chapter-house called the Bibliotheca Paulina. Leland mentions 21 codices. The Duke of Somerset pulled down the cloister and chapter-house of St. Paul's to obtain building materials for his palace in the Strand. The books were dispersed. When Alexander Nowell became dean of the Cathedral he found only a few minute-books and copies of the statutes. The only books now known to have belonged to St. Paul's are a MS. bequeathed by Henry de Cornhill in 1254, which remains in St. Paul's Library (Ellis ed. of Dugdale's *St. Paul's*, 183), and the *Chronicles of Ralph de Diceto*, now at Lambeth.

grammars of Gaza and Chrysoloras. It is true that he boasted he had taught his servant-pupil, John Smith, more Latin than he could have learned in St. Paul's school in spite of the fact that he had not flogged the boy. It is true also that the young Lupset attached himself to him, threw away the sophistical books required for the schools, and bought Greek books instead. He was to be the first professor of Greek at Oxford.[1]

Erasmus was discontented, but he was doing more than he knew. In those years at Cambridge he was fostering that love of Bible study which was to have such startling results a few years later. It was in this quiet time that the work was done on the New Testament and St. Jerome ; and it was Warham who made the publication of these works possible. In 1514 he started for Basle to see to their publication.

The same Erasmus who wrote *The Praise of Folly* in More's house, and competed with his host in translating Lucian, also discussed with Fisher and Colet the theology of St. Paul and prepared the text of the New Testament. The biting satirist was also the brilliant critic, and both by satire and criticism paved the way for a Reformation of which he ultimately disapproved.

[1] *Ep.* 271.

Chapter VI

THE CATHOLIC REFORMERS

I. *The So-called Oxford Reformers*

It is usual to speak of Colet, Erasmus and More as the " Oxford Reformers ", but the title is misleading. If they advocated reforms, they did not undertake any. Although they had all three been in Oxford, London was the real centre of their influence. They were all in touch with the court of Henry VIII ; and the young king, aggressive in his catholicity, cannot be left out of account. At no period of his life was Henry VIII a negligible quantity.

It is usual to regard these Oxford Reformers as ineffectual liberals who shrank from the means that were necessary to carry out the reforms which they advocated ; but the means ultimately adopted in no way furthered the reforms that they had at heart. At any rate, it is urged, they were not in the main stream of English religious life, and are only interesting as well-meaning failures so often are. This view overlooks their permanent significance. It is possible to argue that the Reformation was like a cloud-burst ; and that as the resulting flood subsided, the stream flowed in its old channels and carried on the religious ideals held by Colet, More, Erasmus and the youthful Henry VIII.

Owing to politics, the Reformers were able to capture and control the Church for a season, but they signally failed to convert the nation. The religion they taught was of alien origin, and was not in accord with national sentiment. From the beginning of the XVII century the Church of England may claim to represent the views of Colet, More, Erasmus and Henry VIII in everything except their acceptance of the papal claims.

Colet was a typical Evangelical ; More we should now call a Liberal Catholic ; Erasmus was a Broad Churchman insisting on conduct ; and the young king was a High Churchman insisting on tradition. They were very different in temperament, but for the time they were united and did not in consequence press their individual views to the falsehood of extremes. In their friendship we see the future comprehensiveness of the Church of England. They were all zealous for the New Learning, and the Church of England has ever since boasted of being the Church of sound learning. They were all prepared to accept the Bible, Creed, Sacraments and Ministry of the Church without change. If they desired freedom for development, they started on the ancient ways and believed in historical continuity. They none of them desired to be a separated Church, and of the four Henry VIII was at this time most concerned for the unity of Christendom.

II. *Colet the Puritan*

Colet [1] went to Italy a gay young scholar and came home a converted man burning to save souls, and horrified by the wickedness of the world about him. His faith was a matter of personal experience and he had no doubts. He accepted all the articles of the Creed and had no desire to prove them.[2] He knew his Bible very well and it never occurred to him to question any of its contents. He was well read in the Fathers, especially in St. Augustine, and derived from them much illustrative matter for his sermons. He read heretical books, and claimed that he often did so with profit to himself. He had also read the schoolmen, and detested them so much that he lost his temper when Erasmus commended Aquinas.[3] In some ways he was a narrow-minded man, but he was really learned and it was lack of sympathy that limited his understanding. While in Italy he had read many Italian authors, including Petrarch and Dante, but he had little interest in poetry ; and though a good grammarian and an accomplished rhetorician, he was out of touch with humanism because he was so convinced " that friendship with the world was enmity to God ". He disliked elaborate ceremonial, and branded

[1] Nearly every fact about Colet in this section is to be found in Erasmus' letter to *Jodocus Jonas* (Allen, *Ep.* 1211). I am also indebted to Lupton's *Life of Colet* and to Seebohm's *Oxford Reformers*, although neither of them would probably agree with my estimate of their hero.

[2] In Erasmus' colloquy, *Pietas Puerilis*, Gaspar remarks, " I believe firmly what I read in the Holy Scriptures and the Creed called the Apostles', and I don't trouble my head any further ". When asked who taught him, he replies, " Colet ".

[3] Notwithstanding Colet's disapproval, Erasmus continued to speak well of Aquinas. Vide *Methodus Verae Theologiae*, B, b. 2 (1521 ed.).

as childishness, superstition and lies much that entered into the popular religion. He waged war incessantly with the abuses and corruptions of his age, and in his passion for righteousness he tended to be censorious. Having sternly disciplined himself, he was not always tolerant of the weaker brothers, and it was a certain lack of sympathy with ordinary men that made him tactless when dealing with his Chapter. To his friends he was considerate and charming, and he could be blind to the faults of those whom he loved. Sometimes he was inconsistent, for he was after all very human, but no one ever doubted his sincerity.[1]

It was the reality of his religion that impressed men. The critical Erasmus listened to him as to one inspired. The laughter-loving More made him his confessor and allowed him to direct his life. Cornelius Agrippa came to England on a mission from Maximilian and lodged with Dame Colet, the dean's mother, at Stepney. Having met Colet, he not only neglected the court but for a time forsook the *cabbala*[2] that he might study St. Paul's epistles. Henry VIII declared, " Let every man have his own doctor, and everyone follow his own liking, but this is the doctor for me ".[3]

He made his reputation at Oxford by biblical lectures which he delivered gratuitously. In them he deserted the well-known method of isolating each text and treating it literally, allegorically, morally and anagogically according to the well-known distich :

> Littera gesta docet, quid credas allegoria,
> Moralis quid agas, quo tendis anagogia.[4]

There was much to be said for a preacher keeping these words in mind while preparing a sermon. He was first to explain the meaning of the words, and then to show how they might be treated as an allegory and applied to the circumstances of his audience. Next he was to show their practical value, and lastly their significance for God and eternity. Preachers, however, prided themselves on far-fetched allegorical interpretation, assigning to words such meanings as they chose without any reference to the context. In vain Nicholas of Lyra had

[1] *Vide supra*, 35.
[2] Allen, *Age of Erasmus*, 143 ; Lupton, *Life of Colet*, 199.
[3] Erasmus, *Ep.* 1211.
[4] Quoted Jourdan, *Movements towards Catholic Reform*, 26.

maintained "that the mystical explanation which departs from the literal sense ought to be deemed of no value".[1] The Bible is, after all, much more than a collection of sermon headings or an arsenal of proof texts. Dionysius the Carthusian had pointed out the right way when he published the Pauline epistles with a running commentary, brief and to the point.[2] Colet went still further, for in his lectures on 1 Corinthians he made his hearers understand what manner of man St. Paul was, and what was the situation with which he had to deal. The epistle was no longer a collection of texts but an historical document, all the more interesting because there were so many parallels between the primitive Church and the Church of his own day. It was from Colet that Erasmus learnt to approach the Bible as literature apart from dogmatics; and it is due to Colet and Erasmus that the Bible and the Fathers became books that the plain man could read for himself without the disturbing allegories which had destroyed the connexion between one verse and the next. Not only young men, but doctors and masters, thronged the lecture-room of Colet, amazed to find that the Bible was a living book dealing with a world not so very unlike the world they knew. Colet had found in the Scriptures the fount of inspiration; and having no intellectual difficulties, saw no need for the problems discussed by scientific and systematic theologians.

Colet came to St. Paul's, probably through the influence of Warham, at the end of 1503: but he was not installed as dean until May 1505, some eighteen months later. Sherborne, his predecessor, had been continually on diplomatic errands and had never resided in the deanery.[3] He was to be a bishop on his

[1] Quoted *ibid.* Nicholas of Lyra, the Franciscan, was a converted Jew born at Lyre in Normandy, died 1340. He wrote commentaries which were read at meal-times in Sir Thomas More's household, Margaret Gigs intoning them in the monastic fashion. Chambers, *Sir Thomas More*, 179.

[2] Dionysius the Carthusian lived in the XV century. He is known as *Doctor Ecstaticus.* He was a mystic, who wrote, however, on many subjects. His works fill 45 quarto volumes, and of him it was said, *Qui legit Dionysium nihil non legit*: Huizinga, *Waning of the Middle Ages*, 171. My edition of *In Omnes beati Pauli Epistolas Commentaria* is dated 1551 (Paris). They contain a running commentary on the epistles, concise, sensible and rather dull.

[3] If Colet entered on the duties of dean before the deanery was void, his successor Pace acted as dean in the last year of Colet's life and succeeded him. When Pace's mind became deranged in 1532, he was removed to Sion and Sampson was appointed coadjutor. He, though Bishop of Chichester, succeeded in 1536 on Pace's death, holding the deanery *in commendam*. Le Neve, *Fasti*, 184, is wrong in the date of Pace's death. See *D.N.B.*

return from Rome, and so Colet was allowed to enter on his office before it was legally void. Had Warham not been translated to Canterbury and had Barnes not died within a year of his appointment to London, Colet might have had a happy life. As it was from 1506 to his death in 1519 he was compelled to work with Richard FitzJames, a bishop who was consistently hostile to him.

Justice has not always been done to FitzJames,[1] because historians have relied entirely on the correspondence of Colet and Erasmus. He was anything but an obscurantist dunce, and was certainly not a negligent prelate. He had been a great warden of Merton, had enlarged the buildings and reorganised the college. He had been a vigorous vice-chancellor of Oxford and restored the University church. He had been a successful diplomatist and bishop, first of Rochester and then of Chichester. He was well known as a frequent preacher. On coming to London he rebuilt his manor-house at Fulham and did much for the restoration and adornment of St. Paul's. He looked into abuses and compelled the chancellor, Dr. Lichfield, to fulfil his duties as a theological lecturer. He was the friend of Richard Kidderminster, the learned and pious Abbot of Winchcombe. It was his one link with Colet. He hated Colet's school,[2] but he was zealous for education and founded a school of his own at Bruton. He belonged to the Old Learning, but he was by no means illiterate, and he left many of his books to Merton—among them were the works of Origen. He had a sense of *esprit de corps*, and fought stoutly, if not wisely, for his chancellor, Dr. Horsey,[3] and for the simple bell-ringer of St. Paul's when they were accused of murdering Hunne. He was not a good-tempered man, and when angry gave way to exaggerated utterances, but I do not suppose he could equal Colet in rhetorical denunciation.

Why, then, did he hate Colet? and why do old reformers generally hate young reformers? FitzJames was perhaps thirty years older than Colet and had had much wider and more varied experience. He had been concerned all his life in ordering people about and setting things to rights, and he was naturally annoyed

[1] FitzJames has been called "a superstitious and impracticable Scotist". See, however, Godwin, *Catalogue of Bishops*, 203 (1615 ed.); Fuller, *Worthies*, *Somersetshire*, 23; Wood, *Athenae*, ii. 720; Allen, *Epp. Erasmi* iv. 518.

[2] Erasmus, *Ep.* 258.

[3] *Vide supra*, pp. 29, 31, 32.

with a young man who said that what had hitherto been done was not worth doing, and that everything was as bad as it could be. Colet, as Erasmus tells us, did not disguise his contempt for bishops as a class, and within cathedral precincts the sayings of a dean are likely to be repeated. Colet was represented to have made fun of those who preached written sermons, and in his old age FitzJames could not preach without a manuscript. Perhaps FitzJames was jealous because crowds came to hear Colet, and he certainly did not approve of his sermons. He thought they were sometimes heretical. They at any rate had a revolutionary tone, and were always of a popular character. FitzJames as an old man was a stout conservative, and as a man of academic tradition he despised rhetoric or anything in the nature of an emotional appeal. So it came to pass that an admirable administrator met a prophet and did not like him ; and the prophet who was only concerned with the salvation of souls saw no merit in administrative efficiency.

Colet must have been a very great preacher, and it was well known that he practised what he preached. After he came to London he expounded the narratives in the Gospels rather than the arguments of St. Paul. Erasmus tells us that " he would start with some connected subject and pursue it right to the end in a course of sermons : for example, St. Matthew's Gospel, the Creed or the Lord's Prayer ". Crowds came to hear him, courtiers as well as citizens ; simple and illiterate Lollards as well as scholars like Sir Thomas More and Erasmus.[1] The Lollards found one who in simple language proclaimed a gospel they could understand, and understood his fearless exposure of abuses and vehement denunciations of formalism as the justification of their own attitude to the Church. Sir Thomas More also approved of the sermons, but he heard them in the context of his own faith. FitzJames disapproved of them, because he understood them in the same sense as the Lollards and wished in consequence to persecute the preacher. More and FitzJames were both right. The one saw the truth, and the other the danger of uttering it to a mixed congregation, certain to draw illegitimate inferences. The reformation, however, was bound to come, Colet or no Colet ; and it is the positive content of his teaching which is, after all, most important. He was calling men to repentance, to

[1] Foxe, *A. & M.* iv. 230, 246.

a personal devotion to our Lord, and to a spiritual life. Barclay expresses his complete justification when he writes :

> I tell thee, Codrus, this man hath won some souls.[1]

He appointed a steward to manage his household, and assigned to him his ecclesiastical revenues. They came to £217 a year, or £4340 of our money, but this leaves out of account what he received from offerings at the various shrines. He was always dressed with simplicity, and was content with one meal a day—he never ate supper ; but he liked his frugal meals to be well served and his house to be well ordered. Everything about him had to be neat and he abominated waste. He gave away money with discretion, and could refuse a beggar, even when the beggar was the beloved Erasmus.[2] He had a horror of display and all that he considered worldly. He did not entertain indiscriminately but liked to have learned and pious men at his table to dinner, when he proved himself a great conversationalist. When dinner began, his boy scholar read a passage from Scriptures, often from the Book of Proverbs, and then the guests were enlisted in a discussion on its meaning and application. He had apparently the art of drawing men out and delivering his own thoughts without becoming didactic. Erasmus says :

> When the requirements of nature, if not of pleasure, had been satisfied, he would start some other topic, and then bade farewell to his guests, refreshed in mind as well as in body, and better men at leaving than they came, though with stomachs not over-loaded.[3]

We may be sure that Erasmus went back to Ammonius with a healthy appetite for supper, and drank no small beer but Chian wine.

Colet's austere life was anything but pleasing to the chapter, who expected from the dean a lavish hospitality which they did not receive, and objected to his acting as if he were an abbot and they were monks. The chapter of St. Paul's was a very difficult body, for the dean did not preside over it by right—in fact there was a legal decision that the dean as dean was not a member of the chapter.[4] Colet sat in it as holding the prebend of Mora, and

[1] Barclay, *Eclogues*, iv.
[2] *Epp.* 230, 270.
[3] *Ep.* 1211.
[4] Lupton, *Life of Colet*, 129.

the bishop sat in it also as holding another prebend. The dignitaries had many rights and privileges and very few duties ; the vicars-choral formed a college of their own and were suspicious of any interference ; the chantry priests had nothing to do after saying their daily Mass and were often a cause of scandal ; the vergers and sacristans were for the most part married men who spent more time at home than in the cathedral ; the citizens not only used the church as a right-of-way,[1] but regarded it as a place for doing business, or a place to promenade. Only a man of consummate tact could have persuaded the chapter to co-operate with him in a thorough reformation ; and Colet, eager for reform, was devoid of tact. He looked on his canons as worldlings in need of correction, and not as men who might be persuaded to better things. Perhaps he was right, but they could only be disciplined by their own consent. Colet thought otherwise. He drafted new statutes by himself, which condemned many abuses, using in places passionate invective, out of place in what was intended for a legal document. The canons probably regarded them as an indictment of themselves ; and they were quite clear that no dean could revise the statutes except with their consent and in consultation with themselves. Needless to say their assent was not given, and so Colet went to Wolsey and asked him to impose the new statutes on the chapter by his legatine authority. The cardinal signified his approval and signed the statutes ; but for some reason he did not affix his seal, and the chapter maintained that his signature did not give them authority, and they never obtained it.

This man who shrank from the wickedness of the world about him was naturally attracted by the innocence of little children, and he constantly reminded his friends how our Lord held them up as examples. He was sure that if the world was to be reformed it must be by the proper education of the rising generation. So he determined to devote a large part of the fortune he had inherited from his father to the founding of a school.[2] The school was opened in 1510 in a building to the east of the cathedral, and on its front it bore the inscription :

[1] For condition of Cathedral, *vide supra*, 108.

[2] Colet did not devote the whole of his private fortune to founding the school, as stated by some historians. His will shows this. Lupton, *Life of Colet*, 231. He must have bestowed on the school some £3000 or £60,000 of our money. See Seebohm, *Oxford Reformers*, 206-210.

Schola catechizationis puerorum in Christi Opt. Max. fide et bonis litteris.

and in its statutes the founder stated : [1]

My intent is by this school especially to increase knowledge and of worshipping of God and Our Lord Jesus Christ, and good Christian life and manners in the children.

But would his intent be carried out ? That was the question that rendered him anxious. He saw the existing Cathedral schools [2] under Dr. Lichfield, the negligent Chancellor and Magister Scholarum. He had no wish to benefit him by his endowment—" Chancellors ", he told Erasmus, " consider themselves appointed to receive the fees rather than to look after the school, and think they have played their part to perfection, if they refrain from tithing the schoolmasters ". Bishops, he thought, would consider a school not worthy of much attention, and the civic authorities were either devoid of judgment or swayed by private interests. It did not apparently occur to him that he might found a college like Eton and Winchester, but probably the cost of doing so was prohibitive. So he gave his school in trust to the Mercers' Company, which has honourably administered the endowments and helped to make St. Paul's school a great educational institution, though the religious intent of Colet has been somewhat overlooked.

Colet built a great school-room which could be divided by curtains into three divisions, taught respectively by the high-master, sur-master and chaplain. Each division had three forms, and each form seated sixteen boys—the head of the class having a raised seat and desk for himself. The school opened at 7 A.M. and continued without a break until 11. It met again at 2 and closed at 5. There was no school on Sundays or Holy Days, and Colet reckons Sundays and Holy Days as 153 days in all ; but there were no vacations, and there was to be no Remedy [3] or extra holiday, and the High Master was to be fined 40s. if he granted one unless asked to do so by the king or bishop. There were to be no such games as cock-fighting or riding about of

[1] The Statutes and the Catechizon are to be found in Lupton's Appendices.

[2] There were three schools in connexion with St. Paul's, a song school, a grammar school, and a school for students in theology.

[3] Remedy. " At various schools (as still at St. Paul's and Winchester) : a time especially granted for recreation ; a half-holiday " (*N.E.D.*).

victory,[1] and the Paulines were not to take part in the yearly school disputations at St. Bartholomew's, " which is but foolish babbling and loss of time ".[2] No food or drink was to be brought into the school or tallow dips. When light was required every boy had to be provided with a wax candle at his own cost. Every Saturday the school was to be swept out by " a pore child ".

Above the high-master's desk was an image of the boy Jesus seated as in the act of teaching, with the words above, " Hear Him ". Every boy was to salute the image on entering school. The chaplain said Mass each morning for the school in the adjoining chapel, but the boys did not assist. When, however, the sacring bell rang they knelt in school until it rang again. Three times a day prayers were said, and when the boys went in procession to the Cathedral they were to walk two and two, repeating the seven penitential psalms.

Apart from religion, grammar in its wider significance was the one subject taught. At first there was some difficulty in procuring suitable school books. Linacre wrote a Latin Grammar for St. Paul's which had to be rejected as far too difficult.[3] Erasmus dedicated his *Copia* to Colet, and Lily produced his famous Grammar, from which all subsequent grammars for English boys have been derived.

[1] Riding about of Victory. In Strutt's *Sports and Pastimes*, Plate XL, is shown a boy riding upon a pole carried by two others with a cock in his hand. He is followed by a boy with a banner emblazoned with a bludgeon.

[2] Stow, *Survey of London*, 74 (1603 edition). At first and perhaps in Colet's time there were contests in logic, " but the arguing of the schoolboys about the principles of grammar hath been continued even to our time : for I myself in my youth have yearly seen on the Eve of Saint Bartholomew the Apostle, the Scholars of divers Grammar Schools repair unto the Churchyard of St. Bartholomew, the Priory in Smithfield, where upon a bank boarded about under a tree, some one scholar hath stepped up, and there hath apposed and answered, till he were by some better scholar overcome and put down ; and then the overcomer taking his place, did like as the first : and in the end the last apposers and answerers had rewards, which I observed not, but it made good schoolmasters and good scholars diligently against such times to prepare themselves for the obtaining of this garland. I remember there repaired to these exercises amongst others the masters and scholars of the Free schools of St. Paul's in London, of St. Peter at Westminster, of St. Thomas Acon's Hospital, and of St. Anthony's Hospital : where the last named commonly presented the best scholar and had the prize in those days." Stow, it may be noted, was one of " the pigs of St. Anthony ". He was at school probably from 1532 onwards, but his memory must have played him false about St. Paul's school (unless he intended the Cathedral school), for it is unlikely that a high-master would have broken Colet's statutes only a dozen years after his death.

[3] Linacre subsequently wrote the *Rudimenta Grammatica* for the use of the Princess Mary, which was translated into Latin by George Buchanan and became a standard book on the Continent. Mallet, *Oxford*, i. 426.

Colet would not allow logic to enter into his curriculum. He had an angry contempt for disputatious sophists. He believed that the study of a language was the best means of mental culture. Rhetoric was to take the place of logic. Logic was concerned with proof, rhetoric with persuasion. Logic appealed exclusively to the reason, but rhetoric to the whole man ; and Colet hardly grasped that it might appeal to man's prejudices and passions. As a preacher he knew that it was his business to persuade men to act rightly, and not necessarily to prove to them the principles of right action. He would have agreed with Aeneas Sylvius in his letter to Adam Molyneux—

Great is eloquence. Nothing is more powerful : political action is the result of persuasion : his opinion prevails best with the people who best knows how to persuade them.[1]

He abominated Low Latin—the Latin of the chronicles and schoolmen—" adulterate " Latin, as he called it. He wanted his boys " to speak and write clean Latin ", and very sensibly deferred the study of syntax until they were familiar with the language. He wrote :

In the beginning men spake not latin because such rules were made, but contrary-wise because men spoke such latin, upon that such rules were made. That is to say, latin speech was before the rules, not the rules before the latin speech.[2]

He knew " the very Roman eloquence " was to be found in Tully and Sallust and Vergil and Terence, but he did not intend that his scholars should read them. They were to read Prudentius, Lactantius, Mantuanus and " the holy doctors learned in their time ", Jerome, Ambrose and Augustine. His attitude towards pagan authors is expressed in one of his sermons on I Corinthians :

Now if anyone should say, as is often said, that to read heathen authors is of assistance for the right understanding of Holy Writ, let them reflect whether the very fact of such reliance being placed upon them does not make them a chief obstacle to such understanding. For in so doing you distrust your power of understanding the Scriptures by grace alone and prayer, and by the help of Christ and of faith ; but think you can do so through the means and assistance of heathens . . .

[1] Quoted by Creighton, *Hist. Lects.* etc. 197.
[2] Lupton, *Life of Colet*, 291.

Those books alone ought to be read, in which there is a salutary flavour of Christ—in which Christ is set forth for us to feast upon. Those books in which Christ is not found are but as tables of devils.[1]

He loathed the obscenities in classical authors and in their humanist imitators: "Blotterature" rather than literature,[2] is how he described them. He did not wish his boys to be immersed in heathen mythology, in fictions and fables. As a true Puritan he would have rejected all fairy stories as lies because they were not factually true.

Colet's principal interest was the teaching of religion. St. Paul's, like Eton and Winchester, was founded with a religious intent, but even clerical head-masters were apt to forget it, conscious that parents were only anxious that children should learn such things as would enable them to get on in this world. In most of the grammar schools there was no religious instruction, and none at the universities except for theologians.[3] Sir Thomas Elyot in his *Governour*, after describing in detail what a child should learn, pictures a boy of seventeen entering on philosophy and finding "the incomparable sweetness" to be derived from Plato and Cicero. It is then that he is advised to read Proverbs, Ecclesiastes and Ecclesiasticus. He is told, "All the historical parts of the Bible be most necessary for to be read of a noble man, after that he is of mature age". The New Testament is to be "reverently touched as a celestial jewel or relic", and those who presume to read it must beware of the fate of Uzza who touched the ark.[4] It was just when the upper classes were calling out for education that the Church missed its opportunity, and its teachers did not, like Colet, put the first things first.

Colet for his little children produced a *Catechyzon* which the chaplain was to teach. He was also to instruct them in the Articles of the Creed and in the Ten Commandments in English. The *Catechyzon* [5] is very simple. It begins with the Apostles' Creed and the Seven Sacraments. It then deals with charity under three heads: the Love of God, the Love of thine own Self, the Love of thy Neighbour. Then there are brief sentences on penance, houseling, in sickness and in death, and 49 Precepts

[1] Quoted Lupton, 76.
[2] *Ibid.* 280.
[3] Rashdall, *Universities*, ii. 700.
[4] Elyot, *Governour*, 48.
[5] *Catechyzon* in Lupton, 285-291.

for Living. A few may be noted : Fear God—Forgive gladly—Chastise thy body—Flee foul language—Obey thy superiors—Be fellow to thine equals—Be benign to thine inferiors—Believe and trust in Christ Jesus—Worship Him and His mother Mary—Use ofttime confession—Wash clean—Learn diligently—Teach that thou hast learned lovingly.

Then follows the Apostles' Creed, Lord's Prayer, and Hail Mary, in Latin, and two Latin prayers presumably composed by Colet. The first is addressed to Our Lady and the second to the boy Jesus. The second prayer is still used in the school. The *Catechyzon* concludes :

> Wherefore I pray you, all little babies, all little children, learn diligently this little treatise, and commend it diligently unto your memories. Trusting of this beginning ye shall proceed and grow to perfect literature, and come at the last to be great clerks. And lift up your little white hands for me, which prayeth for you to God, to Whom be all honour and imperial majesty and glory. Amen.

This stern preacher of righteousness had, like Savonarola, a love for little children and longed to claim them for God.

III. *More, the Christian Humanist*

No two people were more unlike than Dean Colet and Sir Thomas More. Colet, the senior by ten years, had loved More when he was a boy ; and More had always reverenced Colet and found him to be a refuge and a rock in the days of his own instability. More regarded himself as Colet's disciple ; but his attitude towards life was radically different. More was a true humanist ; while Colet, notwithstanding his New Learning, was a Puritan. Colet felt no necessity to reconcile his religion with a world which he condemned : More, with wider sympathies and more varied interests, had to harmonise his love of this world with his love for God.

Biographers have been amazed at More's versatility. He seems to have been fitted by nature to enjoy the fullness of life. He was the humanists' ideal of the complete man, and in everything that he undertook he was successful. He was a brilliant scholar, a sound lawyer, a skilful diplomatist, an accomplished courtier, a trenchant controversialist. He was a wit who finally achieved the greatest of all successes—he became a saint ; but he had not attained to sanctity in the period covered by this volume, and so the title is not used.

When only twenty-two years of age he lectured at Grocyn's request in St. Lawrence Jewry on the *De Civitate Dei* of St. Augustine. Like his author he was living in a corrupt age ; and he speculated on how a world-state might be reorganised in accord with the laws of nature. Like his author he believed also in a supernatural state—in a Church existing in the world but not of it—a Church with an inalienable right to freedom. Later his speculations on the world-state led him to write his *Utopia* ; and later still for the freedom of the Church he gave his life.[1] It may be said that at the beginning of the XVI century the Church of Rome was as unlike the Church for which he died as *Utopia* was unlike Tudor England ;[2] but More could distinguish between ideas and their temporary embodiment. He was loyal to his Church as he was loyal to his England, because he could see the soul of good in things evil, and pierce to fundamental principles which were for the moment obscured.

When twenty-six he was returned as a burgess to Parliament, and opposed an extortionate grant-in-aid demanded by Henry VII. It was an act of courage, for the king was not wont to be thwarted, still less to be bearded by " a beardless boy ".

> Whereupon, writes Roper, the King, conceiving great indignation towards him, could not be satisfied until he had someway revenged it. And forasmuch he nothing having nothing could lose, His Grace devised a causeless quarrel against his father ; keeping him in the Tower until he made him to pay to him a hundred pounds fine.[3]

What the father thought of the matter we are not told ; but his son lived a somewhat retired life until the end of the reign and

[1] Pickthorn, *Henry VIII*, 265-270, is puzzled because More was ready to swear to the succession, but not to acknowledge the supremacy ; but surely the paragraph he quotes on p. 26 makes More's position clear. More did not believe in the Divine Right of Kings, but thought that Parliament was competent to settle the succession to the throne even if they settled it on a bastard. The claim of Henry VII had been based on the very doubtful legitimacy of the Beauforts. On the other hand he did not believe that either Parliament or King could abrogate the spiritual rights of the Pope, which were based on what was believed to be a divine institution.

[2] Dom Bede Jarrett, *The Fame of Blessed Thomas More*, 113 : " He died for a Papacy, that, as far as men could see, was little more than a little Italian princedom, ruled by some of the least reputable of the renaissance princes ".

[3] Roper, *Life of More*, 155.

amused himself by translating Lucian and writing Latin epigrams on tyrants, which were not to be published while his tyrant was alive.

Before entering Parliament from 1501 to 1504, More and his friend William Lily were guests at the Charterhouse ; and both seriously contemplated entering into the silence and isolation of the Carthusian order. Both, however, left the cloister to be married, because they had come to the conclusion that marriage was their true vocation. More's youth had not been entirely blameless,[1] which is hardly surprising if we remember his emotional temperament, his ready affections and his abounding vitality ; but he longed to subdue the lusts of the flesh. Monastic life seemed a refuge, but many have entered upon it in the hope of escaping from temptation, only to find that they had no call to a contemplative life. More found that his very difficulties pointed the way to his real vocation. In the words of Erasmus, " he resolved to be a chaste husband for fear that he might be a lascivious priest ".[2]

Having decided that it was his duty to take a wife, he married Jane Colt, aged seventeen, the daughter of an Essex squire. It was not a love match, because he had been more attracted by her younger sister ; and the marriage did not lead to immediate happiness, for the bride, who had been brought up in the country with hawks and hounds, hated to be mewed up in London lanes, and was bewildered by scholars and their books. More, however, was very patient and his bride was very young. Love came at length and children came. After six happy years she died and More never forgot his dear little wife—*chara uxorcula*.

A few months later More married again for the sake of his motherless children. This time he chose Alice Middleton, a well-to-do widow much older than himself. Jane had been teachable, Alice was not ; and More was amused by her stubborn pose of stupidity. He loved to banter his " shrewd wife ", but she could protect herself. If he attacked her with a rapier-like wit, she

[1] Allen, *Age of Erasmus*, 205. See *Ep.* 999 : " Cum aetas ferret, non abhorruit a puellarum amoribus, sed citra infamiam, et sicut oblatis magis frueretur quam captatis, et animo mutuo caperetur potius quam coitu ". There is no doubt a studied ambiguity about the sentence, but I cannot think that Froude provides an adequate rendering of it. *Letters of Erasmus*, etc. 112: "He had his love affairs when young, but none that compromised him; he was entertained by the girls running after him".

[2] *Ep.* 999.

wielded a bludgeon called common sense and was not ineffective with her blunt weapon. She never came nearer to acknowledging defeat than by saying, " Tilly-vally, Master More ", pretending that she had no patience with such nonsense ; but as she often provoked the encounters, it may be presumed that she enjoyed them. So did More ; and when he came to write his epitaph for his monument in Chelsea church he did not know which was dearer, " the wife who bore his children, or the wife who brought them up ".[1]

Mistress Alice was a notable housewife and a kind step-mother. She insisted on everyone being employed, and the large household at Bucklersbury and Chelsea owed much to her practical common sense. She was proud of her home, proud of the children and proud of her husband, but dreadfully puzzled by his lack of ambition. She could not understand a man who preferred his home to a court, who when he might associate with a king, played with his children by the fireside, " drawing goslings in the ashes with a stick ".[2]

More was an ideal father and happy in his children. If Dame Alice looked after their physical well-being, More superintended their education and administered encouragement and reproof. The three elder children were girls, and they were to rival the sisters of Pirckheimer [3] in their attainments. Their lessons were made a pleasure to them, and they learnt the Greek alphabet by shooting at a target on which the letters were painted. They were taught the names and nature of plants, helping in the garden ; and they were allowed to keep pets, both rabbits and weasels, not to speak of the monkey [4] painted by Holbein, who provided Erasmus with a story and More with a moral. He found excellent teachers, Gunnel,[5] Clement,[6] Nichols [7] and

[1] The quotation is from the verses following the epitaph proper.

[2] Harpsfield, *Life of More*, 95.

[3] For the five daughters of Pirckheimer see Allen, *Epp. Erasmi*, ii. 40. 239.

[4] Erasmus, *Ep.* 999 ; Chambers, *Thomas More*, 188, 189, tells the story of the monkey. Cp. Roper, 167.

[5] William Gunnel or Gonell was a friend of Erasmus when at Cambridge. Erasmus recommended him to More as a tutor for his children. He was subsequently Rector of Conington: *D.N.B.* More wrote him a long letter on education: Stapleton, 101 ff.

[6] Clement. *Vide infra*, p. 473.

[7] Nichols. Nicholas Krutzer was a native of Munich, an astronomer and a wit. When Henry VIII complained of his English, he replied, " Pardon, your Grace, but how can a man learn English in thirty years " (Chambers, 182).

Harris,[1] who all lived in the house and belonged to the family circle. They formed, as Erasmus says, not merely a platonic academy but a Christian home.[2] There were many lessons and a round of religious devotions ; and, though cards and dice were forbidden, there were games, singing and jollity, besides Pattenson the professional fool, who was the licensed critic of everyone.

When More was away he wrote his children charming letters. When they told him that they had learnt the names of the principal constellations, he teased them by enquiring if they could distinguish the sun from the moon.[3] He expected long letters from them, and would not accept excuses such as " lack of time ", " the letter carrier is waiting ", or " there is no news and nothing to say ". " Girls ", he replied, " are born chatterboxes, and have a world to say about Nothing." He commends little John, " who puts out his matter prettily . . . and turns my jokes against myself. . . . He writes merrily with due moderation, showing that he does not forget that he is joking with his father."[4]

The family tie was very strong. The old judge and his fourth wife lived with his son, and the children as they grew up and married did not fly away from the parental nest. In fact they married their father's wards already domiciled with them. Margaret married William Roper ; Elizabeth, William Dancy ; Cecily, Giles Heron, and John, Anne Cresacre : and in a few years there were eleven grandchildren to enliven the house. Alice Middleton, the stepdaughter, married Sir Giles Alington ; Margaret Gigs, the adopted daughter, married John Clement ; and John Harris married Margaret Roper's maid, Dorothy Colly. These had in time work elsewhere, but continued to regard the Great House at Chelsea as home, while enterprising Rastells and merry John Heywood came and went as they pleased.

Erasmus in his letter to Ulrich von Hutten concerning More writes :

He seems to be born and made for friendship of which he is the sincerest and most persistent devotee. Neither is he afraid of that

[1] John Harris was More's secretary. To him we owe the preservation of More's letters. He married Dorothy Colley, Margaret Roper's maid, who as an old woman at Douai supplied Stapleton with many details to illustrate More's life (Stapleton, Preface, xvi).

[2] *Epp.* 999 and 1233.

[3] " I hear that you have so far advanced in astronomy that you cannot only point out the polar star or the dog-star, or any of the constellations, but also—and this requires a skilful and profound astronomer—you can even distinguish the sun from the moon " (Stapleton, 105).

[4] Stapleton, 106.

multiplicity of friends, of which Hesiod disapproves. Accessible to every tender feeling of intimacy, he is by no means fastidious in choosing his acquaintance, while he is most accommodating in keeping it on foot, and constant in retaining it.[1]

He had many friends and all men spoke well of him, but he remained unspoilt. He received many honours, but he esteemed them all at their very transitory value. When Henry VIII dined with him and afterwards walked for an hour in his garden with his arm about his neck, he told his son-in-law, Roper : "I have no cause to be proud thereof, for if my head could win him a castle in France, it should not fail to go ". When the Duke of Norfolk came to dine with him, he found him in a surplice singing in the choir of his parish church. " God's body ", cried the Duke, " My Lord Chancellor a parish clerk ! You dishonour the King and his office." "Nay", quoth Sir Thomas, " the King is your master and mine, but he cannot be offended at my serving God Who is his Master." [2]

Blessed in his family, admired by the world and successful in all he undertook, More might have looked forward to an old age, crowned " with honour, love, obedience, troops of friends " [3] but More looked beyond old age, and told his children—

> We may not look at our own pleasure to go to heaven in feather beds ; that is not the way. For Our Lord Himself went thither in great pain and by many tribulations : which was the path where He walked thither, and the servant may not look to be in better case than his Master.[4]

It was a vivid sense of the danger that beset him of being absorbed in the pleasures of life, innocent though they were, that accounts for his secret austerities—the hair shirt and the scourge. By stern self-discipline he was keeping himself fit to endure whatever fate had in store for him. Erasmus hinted that he was somewhat inclined to superstition ; [5] but Erasmus had never had a glimpse of the heavenly vision. When the time came More was prepared to sacrifice the world he loved so well. He

[1] Erasmus, *Ep.* 999.
[2] Harpsfield, 64. Cp. Roper, 180.
[3] *Macbeth*, Act V. Sc. 3.
[4] Roper, 166. Cp. 182.
[5] In 1533 Erasmus wrote to Faber about More, " Erat enim mentes tam religiosae ut proprior esset superstitionis quam impietate ". The statement of course implies a criticism, but Nisard, *La Renaissance*, 186, 187, emphasises it too much by reading it in a wrong context. He also emphasises the superstition of Erasmus, p. 103.

loved his family and his home; he had so many interests in life, and a little compliance would have saved him. He did not die scorning the world and its delights; but he sacrificed them all for his duty to his God. His claim to sanctity is so much the greater because it involved so great a sacrifice. The temptation had been terrible before he could " give the devil a foul fall "; [1] and his last words were his justification: " I die the king's servant, but God's first ".

In his youth he had been attracted by the life of Pico della Mirandola,[2] that " Phoenix among wits ". Pico like himself had been made to study law when his heart was devoted to the Muses. Pico, like himself, had served other ladies than the Muses, and had heard the call to repentance. Pico, like himself, was a knight-errant of the New Learning, and like himself, desired to reconcile his learning with his religion. Pico also had meditated entering a religious order, but remained in the world, an ornament in the court of Lorenzo the Magnificent, while he practised secret austerities and was profuse in unadvertised almsgiving. He had died at the age of thirty-four, worn out by the severity of his studies and the ardour of his religious life.

The works of Pico had been published at Bologna in 1496 after his death, and republished at Venice in 1498; [3] but it was the man rather than his works who fascinated More. More was no doubt impressed by an author who was said to have mastered Hebrew, Chaldee and Arabic besides Latin and Greek; but he cannot have agreed with his letter to Hermolao Barbaro in defence of the schoolmen, though perhaps he read it, like the scholars of Padua, as an essay in irony.[4] He would certainly have assented to the condemnation of the thirteen theses by the Roman Church if his mind had not been confused by the sophistical ingenuity with which Pico explained them away.[5] He was never

[1] Roper, 190.

[2] *The Life of John Picus, Erle of Mirandola* has been reprinted by Campbell and Reed in their edition of More's *Works*. It has also been reprinted by J. M. Rigg, 1890. Compare Rigg's introduction with the appreciation in Pater's *Renaissance*.

[3] Reed in Campbell and Reed's ed. i. 26. Rigg apparently did not know of the earlier edition.

[4] Hermolao Barbaro (1454–1494 ?) was educated under Pomponius Laetus at Rome and at Padua. In the latter place he was professor of philosophy. Venice employed him as their orator to Frederick III, Maximilian, Ludovico Sforza and Innocent VIII. He became Patriarch of Aquileia. His principal work was *Castigationes Plinianae*. Allen, *Epistolae Erasmi*, i. 293. Pico addressed to him at Padua a defence of the schoolmen: Rigg, p. vi.

[5] Rigg, Introd. vii-xii.

tempted like Pico to dabble in magic, and had no wish to be initiated into the mysteries of the cabbala. It is true that Pico's philosophy could not be reconciled with any form of Christianity, but Pico did not know this:[1] he believed himself to be orthodox, desired to be orthodox, and hoped that his overplus of misapplied learning would be serviceable to the Church. After all, Pico recognised the limitations of the human intellect when he wrote to Politian, "Love God (while we are in the body) we rather may, than either know Him or by speech utter Him".[2] It was this love of God so manifest in Pico's prayers and devotions that attracted More. He wanted others to share his admiration. He wanted even his friend, Joyce Lee,[3] who had recently become a Poor Clare, to know about him. It was for her that he translated as much of Pico's life as illustrated his religious character. He also translated for her three of his letters of good advice, a short commentary on the 15th Psalm, and his twelve rules for a devout life.

In the Florence of Pico the New Learning had long been dominant. Education had been secularised, and pious men like Pico had to plead that religion and learning should not be divorced. North of the Alps, scholastic theologians were entrenched in the universities; and at Paris, Louvain, Cologne and Oxford the clerical party was paramount. In England More was called on to fight for the toleration of learning and to persuade men that it might be a handmaid to theology. He engaged in controversies with Dorpius and Lee, he wrote his immensely long letter to a young monk whom he regarded as impertinent, and another letter, not so long, but even more sarcastic, to the Heads of the University of Oxford.[4]

[1] Rigg, xxvii, writes: "No exercise of ingenuity would ever succeed in harmonising his theology with the Catholic or any form of Christian faith; and it is equally impossible to dispute the sincerity of his piety".

[2] Rigg's ed. p. 20. Fairbairn, *Cam. Mod. Hist.* ii. 695, quotes from Pico, "Philosophy seeks truth, theology finds it, but religion possesses it; and the truth which religion possesses is God's".

[3] Chambers 19 and 95 has established the fact that Joyce Leigh or Lee was the sister of Edward Lee, Archbishop of York. The Lees were old friends of the Mores living in the same parish, St. Stephen's, Wallbrook. Joyce became a Poor Clare. Her mother was allowed to live with her in the convent at Aldgate. Miss Routh, *Sir Thomas More*, 30.

[4] More's Letters to Lee, to a monk, to Oxford and to Dorpius are all to be found in Jortin, *Erasmus*, ii. 646 onwards. There are long extracts in Bridgett's *Sir T. More*.

That this last letter was necessary in 1518 may surprise those who remember the remarks of Erasmus on Oxford in 1499. We can explain the change by a more modern parallel. If a French Abbé had visited Oxford in 1835 with letters of introduction given him by Keble, he would have been surprised by the theological enthusiasm and patristic learning of his new acquaintance, and noted the crowds that flocked to hear Newman preach at St. Mary's. Had he repeated his visit in 1851 he would have found that most of his old friends had been driven from Oxford, and that the spirit of persecution was active against those who remained. The lethargic clergy, who counted for so little in 1835, had been so disturbed by the noise made by the Oxford Movement, that they had woken up to violent denunciation and resolute opposition to anything that was contrary to their inherited prejudices.

Much the same had happened at Oxford in the early years of the XVI century. Somnolent teachers, content with the well-worn scholastic course, had become aware that their privileged and endowed position was being challenged by men professing knowledge with which they were unacquainted; and they resented it. There was considerable disorder at Oxford in 1506, but this was probably due to the recurrent rowdyism of mediaeval students. In 1508 Brasenose College was founded by Smythe, Bishop of Lincoln, and Sir Richard Sutton for the express purpose of safeguarding the scholastic theology and philosophy. Soon afterwards Fox, Bishop of Winchester, founded Corpus Christi College with a contrary intent. There was a note of defiance in his statutes.[1] His college was to be a beehive humming with industry; his lecturers were to be gardeners who were "to root out barbarism from the garden, and cast it forth should it at any time germinate there". The classical authors, both Greek and Latin, were to be read; and the Reader in Divinity was "to follow the ancient doctors", and not the schoolmen, who were "both in time and learning far below them". Brasenose took up the challenge; a Brasenose undergraduate named Hastings was imprisoned, and the bursar, Formby, was bound over to keep the peace with the freemasons and masters of the works employed on the Bishop of Winchester's new college.[2]

[1] Creighton, *Hist. Lects.* 209. Cp. Fowler in Clark's *Oxford Colleges*, 273 ff.

[2] Churton, *Lives of Smythe and Sutton*, 289.

The ordinary conservative said " *Timeo Danaos et dona ferentes*. The Greeks are schismatics, their language is the language of heresy, and their books must be regarded with suspicion." There were many such conservatives in Oxford, and they banded themselves together as Trojans—a don, with more years than wisdom, assuming the name of Priam, while another was known as Hector and a third as Paris. They bullied the small minority whom they called Greeks, when they met them in the streets, jeered at them in the schools, and applauded a Lent preacher, who denounced the study of Greek, the reading of pagan authors, and all that tended to a liberal education.

It chanced that the Court had come to Abingdon for the Lent of 1518 because of the sweating sickness elsewhere, and More had come with the King. He heard of the disturbances at Oxford, and wrote to the authorities in condemnation of this popular preacher :

> What right has he to denounce Latin of which he knows little : Science of which he knows less ; and Greek of which he knows nothing ? He had better have confined himself to the Seven Deadly Sins, with which perhaps he is better acquainted.[1]

No doubt the preacher was a fool ; but there is a tone of intellectual arrogance about More's letter which helps us to understand how elderly men, really learned in their own subject, resented the contempt of those who had been taught something else. More pointed out that the object of a university is not merely to produce theologians, but men trained for law and secular pursuits. Unlike Colet he believed that classical poets, orators and historians should be used by preachers, " if their congregations are not to think them fools ". He dignifies theology as " the august Queen of Heaven ", but maintains that none can serve her who does not know Hebrew, Greek and Latin. He calls on men to read the Fathers and expresses his contempt for the scholastic conundrums propounded at a later date. In fact More believed in the slogan, " Back to the primitive Church ", and did not foresee that those who echoed his cry would seek to destroy the existing Church which he loved so well.

The heads of the University were certainly not converted by More's eloquence or convinced by his commendations of

[1] Jortin, *Erasmus*, ii. 662.

Cambridge where Greek studies progressed; but they understood his threat that their chancellor, Warham, was displeased, that the dread Cardinal of York might interfere, and that the king, more learned than any king before him, would take action. Anyhow, Clement,[1] Lupset[2] and the "mellifluous" Vives[3] were received with many civilities and lectured to large audiences. Wolsey imported many Cambridge men to encourage the New Learning, and they came infected with Lutheranism. A few years later, many students were arrested for heresy. Six senior students of Cardinal College,[4] with several others, carried faggots from St. Mary's to St. Frideswide and burnt their books at Carfax. One of them, Clarke, died of the sweating sickness in prison. Dalaber[5] was set in the stocks; and Garret, who was not a Cambridge man but a Fellow of Magdalen, after repeated escapes and a recantation, was burnt at the same time as Barnes and Jerome. The "Trojans", reproved by Thomas More, no doubt went about saying, "We told you so". This was not what More had expected, and we can imagine his tart rejoinder, "Because the orthodox so stupidly rejected learning, many scholars have sought alliance with the heterodox". But this was not the only reason, because those who were delighted with novelties were naturally attracted to novelties in religion.

More was quite right when he believed that men's outlook

[1] John Clement, *d.* 1572. He was born in Yorkshire, educated at St. Paul's School, and taken into More's house as boy attendant. He went with More to Flanders and figures in the *Utopia*. Wolsey made him reader in Greek at Oxford. He married Margaret Gigs, More's adopted daughter. He studied medicine and became the court physician. He was in exile during the reigns of Edward VI and Elizabeth. He died at Malines.

[2] For Lupset in Oxford see Gee, *Life and Works of Lupset*, 94-102.

[3] Vives (1492–1541) was regarded as the equal of Erasmus and Budaeus. He was born in Valencia, studied in Paris, succeeded Lupset in Oxford, and was tutor to the Princess Mary. He spoke and wrote against Henry's divorce, was imprisoned, and retired to Brussels. Maxwell-Lyte, *Oxford*, 438, 439, etc.

[4] Warham in a letter to Wolsey on the heresy at Oxford points out that "Cambridge is thought to be the original occasion and cause of the fall of Oxford". No less than five Cambridge men of Cardinal College, John Clarke, John Fryth, William Bates, Richard Coxe and Henry Sumner were incriminated. Maxwell-Lyte, *Oxford*, 457-459. Dr. London, the Warden of New College, wrote, "It was a gracious deed, if they were tried and purged, and restored unto their mother from whom they came, if they be worthy to come thither again" (*ibid.* 466).

[5] Dalaber's narrative may be read in Foxe, *A. & M.* v. 421. By his own confession he was not a truthful man; and in his account he omits to mention that he betrayed twenty-two of his associates. Maxwell-Lyte, 465

might be broadened by the study of Greek authors. He had himself studied Plato, and recognised the fact that the *theories* of the philosopher unaided by revealed religion were in many respects in advance of the *practice* of his own age. As a Christian who was also a humanist, he wanted religion to dominate the whole of life and to be applied to the social, economic and political conditions of the world. Men had too often confined their religious activities to the cloister, and cultivated their souls in isolation from their fellows. More, in accepting his vocation as a layman, busy with law and politics, wished to show how the virtues of the cloister were just as necessary in the world outside. He was, however, tentative in his approach to practical problems when he wrote his *Utopia*, which half reveals and half conceals his thought.

The story is given an historical setting. In 1516 England sent an embassy to Bruges to discuss the revision of the *Intercursus Magnus*. Tunstall was the ambassador of the king, supported by Sampson : More represented the interests of the London merchants, and Clifford the merchants resident in the Netherlands. The conference dragged on for months and there had to be adjournments so that the Flemish negotiators might consult with the regents for Charles V. It was then that More and his boy attendant, John Clement, visited Antwerp, the richest city in Northern Europe, and the most frequented port. There they met with Peter Giles,[1] a most attractive humanist, who was town clerk of Antwerp ; and with Busleiden,[2] who was accountant-general of Brabant. The latter took them over to Mechlin, and showed them his beautiful home, his large library and collection of medals. These friends introduced them to men who had sailed the southern seas, and visited the newly discovered continent. More no doubt listened eagerly to many travellers' tales and tried to verify their truth in *Quatuor Americi Vesputii Navigationes*, which had been published in 1507, and itself contained

[1] Peter Giles (1486–1533) was not only chief secretary to the town of Antwerp, but the curator for Marten's press and the editor of many classical works. Not only the 1516 edition of More's *Utopia* was dedicated to him, but also two collections of Erasmus' Letters. Allen, *Epp. Erasmi*, i. 413.

[2] Gilles Busleiden (*c.* 1465–1536) was the brother of Francis Busleiden, Archbishop of Besançon, who founded by his will the College of the Three Languages at Louvain. Gilles carried out his brother's intentions and superintended the affairs of the college. Like his brother he was a humanist of renown, and he wrote the preface to the first edition of the *Utopia*. Allen, *Epp. Erasmi*, iii. 108.

some pretty tall stories. So far all is according to facts : fiction begins when More writes :

> Upon a certain day when I had heard the divine service in Our Lady's Church . . . and was ready to go home to my lodgings, I chanced to espy Peter (Giles) talking with a certain stranger, a man well stricken in age, with a black sun-burnt face, a long beard, and a cloke cast homely about his shoulders, whom by his favour and approach forthwith I judged to be a mariner.[1]

Peter introduced the stranger as Ralph Hythloday, a native of Portugal, who " was not a mariner as Palinure but as expert and prudent as Ulysses, yea, rather as the ancient and sage philosopher, Plato ". He had seen many men and many cities, voyaged with Vespucci, and left him to explore on his own account with only five companions. With them he had discovered Utopia and come home by way of Taprobane[2] and Calicut.

More and Clement repair with the stranger to Giles' garden, and have many questions to ask about the laws and customs of strange countries, but More adds, " as for monsters, because they be no news, we were nothing inquisitive ".[3] The dialogue in the first book is a damning indictment of Christian Europe and Hythloday is convinced that it compares unfavourably with Utopia, where the inhabitants had only the light of nature to guide them. In the second book it is after dinner that Hythloday describes Utopia—its communism, laws, discipline, education, sanitation and marriage customs ; its wars, diplomacy and religion. In the last paragraph More speaks for himself. There are many things with which he disagreed and more that he would have liked to discuss, but

> because I knew that he was weary of talking, and was not sure that he could abide that anything should be said against his mind. . . . I praising their institutions and his communications, took him by the hand and led him into supper. . . . As I cannot agree and consent to all things that he said . . . so I must needs confess and grant that many things be in the Utopian weal public, which in our cities I may rather wish than hope after.[4]

Ralph Robynson, who translated the *Utopia* in 1551, considered it " a faithful and profitable book . . . setting forth the

[1] *Utopia*, 25.
[2] Taprobane = Ceylon.
[3] *Utopia*, 33.
[4] *Utopia*, 308 ff.

best state and form of public weal ".[1] Sir Thomas More wrote to Peter Giles of " one virtuous and godly man, and a professor of divinity, who is exceedingly desirous to go into Utopia ", that he may convert the peoples ; and tradition says that he was none other than the famous preacher, Rowland Phillips, Vicar of Croydon.[2] Harpsfield thought that Budaeus and Paludanus took it for a true story, but this is not borne out by their letters.[3] Subsequent writers have described it either as the best of More's " merry tales ",[4] or as the ideal of a visionary,[5] while communists have adopted it as a text-book.[6] Unfriendly critics have striven to show that the author of *Utopia* was a brilliant if timid liberal, who became a reactionary, frightened by peasant revolts and Lutheran violence.[7] Other critics regard him as a conservative who was dramatising the teaching of Aquinas and anticipating the encyclicals of Leo XIII.[8]

No one would have been more pleased than More if he could have read those diverse interpretations, for he had a great gift for Socratic irony, and his object, as it seems to me, was to make men think for themselves. In consequence he mingles jest with earnest, and states both with equal gravity. Cresacre More tells us that he was wont to utter jests with such a solemn face that even the members of his family were doubtful about his meaning.[9] It amused him ; and in his *Dialogue* he makes the Messenger say, " Ye use, my Master saith, to look so sadly when ye mean merrily, that men doubt often whether ye speak in sport when ye mean in earnest ".[10]

More, being a practical man of affairs, did not expect that his Utopian Commonwealth would ever be established, and twice in the course of his book he denied that he believed in the possibility of communism ;[11] but that did not perhaps prevent his

[1] Robynson's dedication to Cecil : Lupton's ed. *Utopia*, 17. It is in this way that Sir Philip Sidney regarded it, for he spelt it " Eutopia ". *Works* (Feuillerat's ed.), iii. 157.

[2] More's dedication to Giles, 7.

[3] Harpsfield, 103. *Vide* Budaeus' letter to Lupset in Lupton's edition. Paludamus was a professor of Louvain and a friend of Erasmus and Dorpius. He wrote verses in More's honour.

[4] Dean Hook, *Archbishops of Canterbury*, v. 482, thought it was a skit on Lollard opinions.

[5] Karl Kautsky, *Thomas More* (1890).

[6] Nizard, *La Renaissance*, 184, 185.

[7] Creighton, *Persecution and Tolerance*, 104-109.

[8] Campbell, *More's Utopia and His Social Teaching*.

[9] Cresacre More, 179.

[10] *Dialogue*, Bk. I. ch. vi.

[11] *Utopia*, 109 and 308.

wishing that it might be. At any rate his speculations interested him, and he had thought out how they would work in life. His details, like those of Swift and Defoe, are so convincing that Harpsfield was right when he wrote, " This jolly invention of Sir Thomas More seemed to bear a good countenance of truth ".[1]

He was particularly successful in creating Hythloday, and we must not look on him as More in masquerade. Hythloday was a doctrinaire philosopher, learned, self-opinionated and self-satisfied, with a great contempt for inferior mortals, and a cynic's scorn for the evil of his time. More and Giles both think that so wise a man should be in a king's court ; but he has a detestation for courts and a contempt for kings. He might have said, " My mind to me a kingdom is ", and he could leave other kingdoms to the unintelligent : what was the good of his bothering ? " I prefer ", he said, " to live at liberty after mine own mind and pleasure." More did not agree, though he knew only too well that in the courts of kings " evil opinions and naughty persuasions cannot be utterly and quite plucked out ". That did not justify a man for standing aloof, for " a witty man may still be useful and what he cannot turn to good may be so ordered that it is not so very bad ". " For ", he concludes, " it is not possible for all things to be well, unless all men were good, which I think will not be for these good many years." [2]

Hythloday, it is true, does nearly all the talking, and in making him talk at large, his author enjoyed a sense of irresponsibility. If Hythloday talked nonsense, it was Hythloday's nonsense ; if he criticised kings and institutions in too truculent a fashion, were not Giles and More there to put in a moderating word ? Hythloday could be allowed to say things which More had not thought out, and might subsequently repudiate. He could express fugitive thoughts and indulge in speculations which More might entertain but not defend. All that More, as an artist, had to see was that Hythloday remained true to his character of a somewhat up-to-date Diogenes, who had read the *Critias* and *Republic* of Plato, Plutarch's Lives of Solon and Lycurgus, the *Germania* of Tacitus and St. Augustine's *City of God*.

Screening himself behind Hythloday, was More a progressive thinker planning for a remote future, or was he a reactionary

[1] Harpsfield, 103. [2] *Utopia*, 99, 100.

escaping from realities by cherishing dreams? Some think one and some the other, but all must confess that he was opposed to the tendencies of his age.[1]

We may assume that he was acquainted with the works of Sir John Fortescue, who had died only two years before he was born and must have been known to his father. Sir John Fortescue at the end of his long life was a *laudator temporis acti*. From him More would have learned the constitutional theories of Lancastrian parliaments and of the freedom and prosperity enjoyed by yeomen and labourers. He would not have learnt from him how badly the constitutional theories had worked, of the tyranny of manorial courts, of serfdom, and how unjust were the Statutes of Labourers. In consequence, we may imagine how he sighed for the good old days of which he knew so little, because he was conscious of the evil of his own time, of which he knew so much.

In the heyday of the New Monarchy, when the people all over Europe were surrendering themselves to autocrats and reverencing their divine right to do as they pleased, More maintained that a king existed for the good of his people, and was only great when his people were prosperous. He denounced wars of conquest, and saw that in dynastic quarrels the people of two countries were sacrificed to the ambitions of two kings. He feared the new commercialism, and saw that though England was increasing rapidly in wealth, the wealth was getting into fewer and fewer hands. He deplored the degradation of the peasantry, who were losing their rights in the soil, and he sympathised with the vast number of unemployed vagrants, who were driven to steal in order to live, and deprived of life because of their stealing. At the other end of the social scale he noted the senseless prodigality of the king and his courtiers, how they vied with one another in the splendour of their apparel and the liveries of their servants, how the passion for display had taken hold of all classes, how all alike were greedy for gold in order that they might go on spending. It seemed to him that avarice

[1] William Morris in his preface to the Kelmscott edition writes, " The value of *Utopia* as a book for the study of sociology is rather historic than prophetic ". Another socialist, Karl Kautsky, *Thomas More*, 340, says: " It needed more than 300 years before the conditions have come about which shew us that the aims which More set before himself are not the fancies of an idle hour, but the result of a deep insight into the actual economic tendencies of his age. . . . His ideals are not defeated, still they lie before struggling mankind."

and covetousness were the sins to beware of, and he came to doubt whether a state which tolerated all forms of competition could be reconciled with Christianity.

Believing that the love of money was the root of all evil, he pictured to himself a happy land where money was only kept for foreign commerce, where precious stones were only valued as the playthings of little children,[1] where everyone was dressed alike in a serviceable frock guaranteed to last for seven years,[2] where gambling was impossible[3] because all things were in common, and where field sports were despised, hunting being regarded as "the meanest form of butchery"[4]—which reminds us that More was city-bred.

If not a communist himself, he allowed Hythloday to assert that Christ held all things common, and that the truest societies of Christians, meaning the monasteries, had stood for the ideal; but he does not go on to say how far they had fallen short of it.[5] At the same time he is aware that communism could only be maintained by a Spartan discipline. All were to be educated alike, all were to feed in the common halls, all were to work their allotted six hours, and no one was to criticise the state in private under the severest penalties.[6] He tried indeed to preserve some individual freedom. Adults were not compelled to attend the lectures provided for them, though they mostly did so;[7] they might if they chose feed at home, though it was thought disgraceful;[8] and those who liked country pursuits might obtain permission to remain on farms longer than the compulsory two years.[9]

The family was the unit of the Utopian State; and, though it would seem that family life would prove fatal to communism, More believed in all that the Romans meant by the *Patria Potestas*. A man was to chastise his wife and children, unless their offences were so public that the State had to intervene.[10] Besides, before the festivals,[11] wife and children had to lie prostrate before the head of the house, to confess their faults and implore pardon. Perhaps More found it difficult to imagine Dame Alice submitting to this salutary discipline.

[1] *Utopia*, 176, 177. [2] 150, 151. [3] 144.
[4] 200. [5] 268, 269.
[6] 137: "It is death to have any consultation for the commonwealth out of the council or place of the common election". [7] 143. [8] 161.
[9] 122. [10] 230. [11] 291.

The Utopians were in theory pacifists, though they were ready to defend their own country if it were invaded. They abominated war and thought it better to pay for the assassination of a hostile ruler,[1] or to subsidise factions in his country,[2] or in the last resort to hire mercenaries to fight him.[3] The Utopian communists were not international, neither were they imperial, for they refused to rule other races and preferred to be self-contained and follow a policy of isolation.[4] In writing of their views More managed to express indirectly a great deal of criticism on international affairs ; and if people condemned the dishonourable diplomacy of the Utopians, he could with ironic gravity reply—they were not Christians.

Nevertheless the Utopians had many religions and all were tolerated by the State, because they were persuaded that " it is in no man's power to believe what he list ".[5] They excepted, however, those who were atheists or did not believe in the immortality of man, and deprived them of all civil rights.[6] Neither would they allow anyone to abuse the religion of others, so that when a convert of Hythloday, against his advice, began to preach Christianity, telling the Utopians that they were " the children of everlasting damnation ",[7] he was quite rightly exiled, for King Utopus had decreed that anyone " might do the best he could to bring others to his opinion ; so that he did it peaceably, gently, quietly and soberly without hasty and contentious rebuking and inveighing against others ".[8] If he did not abstain from " displeasant and seditious words ", he was banished or reduced to bondage.

On many points Sir Thomas More was far in advance of his age. He believed in town-planning, in public gardens and sanitation. He believed that the world's work could be done if every

[1] *Utopia*, 245. [2] 251. [3] 231.

[4] They, however, sent forth a surplus population to be colonists.

[5] 275. Nisard, *La Renaissance*, 185, argues from this text when More wrote *Utopia* he was nearer to philosophic doubt than to the creed of Rome. More, however, would have answered that where no revelation had been made men could only be guided by their own reason, and that where no divinely instituted church existed there could be no authoritative tradition. Nisard misses the point—Hythloday was insisting that the Utopians having only the light of nature to guide them put to shame the peoples of Europe blessed with a revelation.

[6] P. 274. It is interesting to note that More considered that the immortality of the soul could be proved by the light of natural religion, because Pomponazzo had recently published a book to prove that the doctrine was irrational and could only be accepted on the authority of the Church. [7] P. 270. [8] 271.

one was compelled to do six hours' labour every day. He believed in hospitals for the sick and in old-age pensions. He believed in free education for all—for girls as well as boys—and in facilities being offered to adults that they might pursue their studies. He advocated a stern discipline for law-breakers, with penalties including exile, slavery and death ; but he would have done away with the barbarous punishments which brutalised his own countrymen.

In Book I he shows us society as it was ; in Book II society as it might be. It was impossible to defend the one ; it was easy to criticise the other, but at any rate *Utopia* was free from the injustice which was rampant in Tudor England. More, in his comfortable house in Bucklersbury, was not easy in his conscience when he thought of the poor living under degrading conditions almost at his door. He had a passion for social righteousness and compassion for the unrighteous. He wanted to better men's condition ; but he was a statesman and no revolutionary. He had no wish to destroy such civilisation as existed in the hope of building a better in its place, so he planted Utopia very far away. No one could go there, but everyone could understand his description. He wanted men to realise that the evils about them were not inevitable ; he wanted to shake men out of the complacency due to twin errors—" It has always been so and always will be " ; and " Whatever is, is right ". He wanted men to work for a better England even if they could accomplish very little, and not like Hythloday to stand apart, regarding the world with cynical disdain.

It is usual to compare the More who wrote the *Utopia* and was the apostle of toleration, with the More who, as Lord Chancellor, persecuted heretics ; but the inconsistency cannot be proved. More remained the man who believed in toleration within the limits imposed in Utopia ; but as Lord Chancellor he had to act in accordance with the laws of England. He was ready to receive Grynaeus,[1] the Lutheran scholar, as a guest, and he was very forbearing with his son-in-law Roper, who was for a time infected with Lutheranism.[2] On the other hand, when one of his boy servants, who had been with Joye,[3] began to corrupt

[1] Chambers, *Sir Thomas More*, 282. [2] Harpsfield, 84-88.

[3] Jay also Joye and Gee was a fellow of Peterhouse who fled to Antwerp in 1527, when summoned to appear before Wolsey on a charge of heresy. He began

another by being profane about the Blessed Sacrament, he had him " striped like a child ".[1] He also admits that he had a man flogged, not for his heresies but for his indecent conduct to women in church. " Else ", he concludes, " had never any of them any stripe or stroke given them, so much as a fillip on the forehead." [2] We accept his word rather than the accusations of Tyndale, who was abroad at the time, or of Foxe, who accumulated gossip some thirty years later, though both probably wrote in good faith.[3]

Secondly, we must remember that Tyndale and his friends were not men who " peaceably, gently, quietly and soberly " tried to convert others to a purer faith. They denounced prelates and priests as Elijah denounced the priests of Baal ; they could not enter a sanctuary without wishing " to break down all the carved work thereof with axes and hammers ". They were convinced that the Mass was idolatry and they could not tolerate idolatry—the penalty for idolatry was death. More never for a moment thought that his opponents were apostles of toleration. He told his son-in-law,

> Son Roper, I pray God that some of us, as high as we seem to sit upon the mountains treading heretics under our feet like ants, live not the day that we gladly would be at league and composition with them to let them have their churches quietly to themselves, so that they would be concerned to let us have ours quietly to ourselves.[4]

The time came when, as a prisoner in the Tower, he wrote that *Dialogue of Comfort against Tribulation*,[5] and, under the transparent fiction of two Hungarians discussing the terrors of the Turkish invasion, tried to encourage his friends to face the persecution, in which he was himself to suffer.

Thirdly, he foresaw the break-up of Europe through the teaching of the Reformers who were preaching non-resistance to the Turks, and it is hard for us to understand to-day how real was the menace, and how horrible the sufferings caused by the

translating books of the Old Testament. In 1532 he was at Bergen-op-Zoom and in 1534 again at Antwerp. He quarrelled with Tyndale and was accused, probably falsely, of betraying him. More's boy had apparently been an attendant on Jay.

[1] *Apologye*, 182.

[2] *Ibid.* 133.

[3] Since the researches of Chambers and Taft it is unnecessary further to refute the calumnies on More.

[4] Roper, 178.

[5] It has been edited and reprinted by Monsignor Hallett, 1937. There is another reprint in *Everyman's Library* edited by Judge O'Hagan.

Mahommedan invasion.[1] Still more, because nearer at home, he feared the dissolution of society if the new doctrines spread :

> Then shall unthrifts flock together and swarm about, and each bear him bold of other, then shall all laws be laughed to scorn, then shall the servants set naught by their masters, and unruly people rebel against their rulers ; then shall rise up rifling and robbery, murder and mischief and plain insurrection, whereof what would be the end, and when ye shall see it, only God knoweth.[2]

We stare amazed at More's anticipation. It was not in that way that we were taught to regard the Reformation ; but we must remember that More was writing in 1529 when the peasants' war in Germany (1524) and the sack of Rome (1526) were regarded as results of the new teaching. People went to Germany to see for themselves, as people have gone recently to Russia, and most of them saw what they went to see, and came back enthusiastic or horrified. One, however, Barlow, afterwards bishop, went expecting to bless and came back to curse ; but his *Dialogue on Lutheran Factions*[3] was published two years after the *Supplication for Souls.*

Church and State in England were so intimately related that More feared that the ruin of the one would revolutionise the other, and in consequence he was prepared to justify the burning of heretic agitators, not because of religious bigotry but because he held *Salus reipublicae, suprema lex.*

We may think he was wrong, but we must not in consequence argue that he had changed the opinions he expressed in *Utopia*, for after all, in *Utopia*, no one was allowed to insult the religion of others without incurring penalties. King Utopus indeed had thought,

> Though there be one religion which alone is true, and all others vain and superstitions, yet did he well foresee (so that the matter was handled with reason and sober modesty) that the Truth of her own power would at the last issue out and come to light.[4]

But matters were not being handled with reason and modesty, and it is difficult in a confused situation to apportion the blame. More's *Dialogue*, though it contains much special pleading, is a good-tempered book that it is a pleasure to read ; the same

[1] *Dialogue*, Bk. IV. ch. xiv.

[2] *Supplication for Souls*, quoted Harpsfield, 172.

[3] Barlow, *Lutheran Factions*, reprinted and edited by J. R. Lunn, 1897.

[4] *Utopia*, 272.

cannot be said for Tyndale's reply, though we are bound to admire his style, his skilful dialectics and his utter sincerity. There were so many abuses in the Church that indignation was justified, and indignant people are apt to say more than they mean and more than they can prove. On the other hand the attack made by the Lutherans on the Church—her faith, order and sacraments—was so violent that we must allow for the temper roused in those who loved her. A man may be tolerant of other people's opinions, and yet resist those who would inhibit the expression of his own convictions, and who would destroy the Church to which he belongs.

The defects of More as a controversialist are due to his practice in the law courts. He wrote like one with an eye on a jury, not too intelligent, who had to be kept amused. He could never allow his adversary to score a single point, and he could not allow any argument, good or bad, to go unanswered. His sentences are often far too long: they are sometimes very involved and he is always too verbose; but if they are read aloud by someone who has mastered their content it will be seen how effective they are for retaining the attention of a listener. Tyndale required no lessons from More on how to write English, for his own style was superior; but Tyndale would probably have profited if More had taught him how to address a mixed audience. The two arts are distinct.

Men will never agree on the merits of More as a controversialist. He himself regretted that he had felt it necessary to write, and told the bishops who had wished to reward him—

> Yet wish would I . . . upon condition that all heresies were suppressed, that all my books were buried and all my labours lost.[1]

It is best to remember him as a man whose religion dominated the whole of his life, who proved that a layman concerned with the affairs of this world might yet be graduating in sanctity. He was a man of infinite charm, a loving father and a chivalrous friend. He was an enthusiast for learning, and an enthusiast for justice. He was a friend to the poor and a champion for the oppressed. He loved this world and all that was in it, but he gladly died for something of more value, for what he believed to be the cause of God and truth.

[1] Roper, 171.

IV. *Erasmus the Latitudinarian*

Erasmus, though Dutch by birth, was a real cosmopolitan, and spoke no language perfectly but the international Latin.[1] He was off and on in England for some sixteen years, and he found in England his best friends and his most liberal patrons. His works were early translated into English ; schoolboys were taught out of his *Copia* and struggled to translate his *Colloquies* ; and every parish church was bound by law to possess a copy of his *Paraphrases*. If, during the XVII century, his fame seemed to suffer somewhat of an eclipse, there were many writers unconsciously teaching what originated in him. To-day there are many members of the Church of England who are proud to dub themselves Erasmians and desire to initiate a new reformation on his lines.[2] They abhor metaphysics and are indifferent to dogmatic definitions, but they are interested in biblical criticism, in science and in historical research. They are tolerant of all opinions but those of traditionalists whose existence is a challenge to their freedom of thought. In their teaching they insist on the supreme importance of conduct, and they look forward to an age of sweetness and light—the light being mediated through a golden haze.

In the last chapter we dealt with Erasmus in England. In this chapter we must think further of his work as a would-be-reformer, and try to estimate the nature of his religion. Many have praised his wisdom and moderation ; many have doubted his sincerity and his courage. He has been extravagantly praised by his admirers and unjustly condemned by his detractors, while friend and foe have been able to justify themselves with the aid of apposite quotations. Erasmus wrote much about himself ; he was often compelled to defend himself against attacks ; besides, he liked to dramatise his past life, and was not always truthful about the details—he naturally wished to see himself in the very best light.

He was not born in wedlock. He was sent to school when he

[1] In his famous interview at Cologne with the Elector Frederick, he was asked to speak in his native language which the Elector understood, but he refused to do so although his refusal necessitated an interpreter : Mangan, *Erasmus*, ii. 159. He was particularly angry with Egmundanus for writing against him in Dutch, for the quarrels of scholars were with scholars and not with common people : *ibid.* ii. 235.

[2] *Vide* Elliott-Binns' very interesting Hulsean Lectures.

was five years old and he lost his mother when he was thirteen. All through his life he suffered because he had no roots anywhere, but was a vagabond on the face of the earth. With social gifts that would have made him an ideal club-man he was never at ease by a domestic hearth. Women played no part in his life, and in an age of reckless accusations no one impugned his chastity. Women probably did not like him—he failed to retain the favour of the Lady of Veer, and More's wife tired of him. Perhaps he had more feminine traits than women approve of in the other sex. He was as delicate and nice in his habits as a cat, as a cat he loved comfort, and as a cat he possessed the power of scratching.

At the age of twenty-one [1] he became a monk in the Augustinian monastery at Steyn.[2] There he became familiar with most of the Latin classics and wrote affectionate letters to young monks—Servatius, Cornelius, Herman and Francis—who shared to some degree his enthusiasm for the humanities. Having left the cloister for temporary service with the Bishop of Cambrai, he resolved that he would never return ; and for the rest of his life he felt compelled to justify to himself and to others his disregard of his vows. From the works of Erasmus we get three impressions of monks : [3] first, that they were always looking out for schoolboys of exceptional literary ability, and using undue pressure to obtain such recruits for their order ; secondly, that they cared nothing for learning, but were illiterate, idle, gluttonous and luxurious ; thirdly, that they were the superstitious adherents to an out-of-date Rule, who spent long vigils in a cold church,[4] and ate stinking fish when they were not altogether fasting. There is no need to reconcile these statements—the life of a community is seldom of one piece—Erasmus thought in pictures, and so for him any remembered incident was likely

[1] Allen, *Epistolae Erasmi*, i. App. 2, has pretty conclusively established the age at which Erasmus entered Steyn. Erasmus at times represents himself as sixteen, but that was to maintain the fiction that he was thrust into a monastery before he was able to know his own mind. Allen concludes that Erasmus was born in 1466, went to school at Gouda 1470, to Deventer in 1475, to Bois le Duc in 1484, and to Steyn in 1487.

[2] Steyn was famous for its very fine library. Mangin, i. 41.

[3] Here are two sentences from the epistle to Gunnius, *Ep.* 447 : (1) " Where is the boy of notable talent or position or wealth, whom they have not insidiously allured " ; (2) " The greater number became monks on account of stupidity, ignorance, despair, or desire of ease or the hope of being fed ".

[4] *Ep.* 447. cp. Ἰχθυοφαγία (*Coll.* ii. 43).

to be regarded as typical and made the ground of a sweeping generalisation. It is probable that he was not nearly so unhappy at Steyn as he afterwards believed; but he was certainly unfitted for the religious life.[1] In consequence, he was quite justified in seeking for a dispensation from his vows; but he was not justified in the indiscriminate abuse which he lavished on the life he had forsaken.[2] In the course of his life several monks were very kind to him.[3] Servatius treated him with great forbearance, and the Abbot of St. Bertin was his liberal patron. In England Charnock,[4] Kidderminster and Bere had been his friends; abroad Vitrier[5] and Volzius;[6] and Kuno the Dominican,[7] who helped him with his edition of St. Jerome. It is true that the monastic orders became his bitterest enemies, but this is not surprising considering the animosity he had shown to them. Erasmus the Augustinian canon and Luther the Augustinian friar were both shadowed through their lives because when young they had mistaken their vocation. Erasmus and Luther belonged to the new age; and the monks of the XVI century, good and bad alike, belonged to the age that was rapidly passing away.

In the Montaigu College[8] at Paris he found the food was worse than it was at Steyn, while the discipline was more brutal.

[1] *Ep.* 296, to Servatius. He speaks of how at Steyn he was regarded "with envy by many and with contempt by all"; though as a rule few would envy one whom everyone despised. He also complains of the silly and inept conversation of his associates. Erasmus was evidently unpopular. He was feeble, with a quick temper, a biting tongue, and an overweening sense of his transcendent attainments. Other novices, some of them robust boys of sixteen, no doubt took pleasure in ragging him.

[2] Servatius Rogerus had been the great friend of Erasmus at Steyn. He subsequently became prior and was very anxious that Erasmus should return to the monastery.

[3] Anthony Bergen, Abbot of St. Bertin by St. Omer, was the brother of Erasmus' first patron, the Bishop of Cambray. He was instrumental in negotiating the Treaty of Cambray. Allen, i. 134.

[4] Charnock was Prior of St. Mary's, Oxford (*vide supra*, 441-442); Kidderminster was Abbot of Winchcombe (*vide supra*, 86); Bere was Abbot of Glastonbury (*vide supra*, 44).

[5] Vitrier was a Franciscan of Tournay and St. Ouen. He was always in trouble with the theological faculty at Paris. Erasmus (*Ep.* 1211) expresses almost as much admiration for him as for Colet.

[6] Volzius (1480–1544) was Abbot of Hügshofen. In 1526 he became a Lutheran. In 1536 he renounced Lutheranism. In 1539 he was reconverted to Protestantism by Calvin.

[7] Joannis Kuno (1463–1513) was a learned Dominican who had worked with Aldus at Venice and translated St. Basil. Erasmus suggests that he died for want of means to support himself.

[8] Montaigu College. *Colloquia*, i. 7 and ii. 45.

He also found that he was quite as much bored in listening to the lectures of Scotist divines as he had been listening to the long-drawn-out chants of the monks. He found that he was no more fitted for the academic routine than he had been for a cloistered existence. He claimed the freedom of " a poet " and the patronage of those who would pay for his praise. For a time he had to earn money by teaching, but he found the occupation irksome. Erasmus has been called " the schoolmaster of all Europe " ; but he early determined that he would not spend his time teaching classes of boys the rudiments of Latin. Colet once hinted that he would like to secure his services at St. Paul's School,[1] but Erasmus was not taking service with anyone. He was always careful and resolute to maintain his freedom.

One accusation against Steyn and the College of Montaigu is certainly true—they ruined the digestion of Erasmus. Ever afterwards he was dyspeptic, which explains his irritability and fastidiousness. He became a confirmed grumbler. In reading his letters it seems that nothing ever went well with him. If he travelled, the sea was always rough and the roads were dangerous—inn-keepers were rude, their food was disgusting and their wine undrinkable. So his friends were never sufficiently appreciative, their gifts were never sufficiently large: and no one ever looked a gift horse in the mouth with more attention than Erasmus, as may be seen in his acknowledgment of one from Warham. On the other hand, if he was always grumbling he was never sour. The salt of wit purifies his complaints, and he is never more amusing than when describing his mishaps. His correspondents probably did not take him too seriously ; perhaps they did not take him seriously enough, for there can be little doubt about his ill-health. Besides there were friends of whom he always spoke well, like Colet, More, Warham and Fisher in England, and abroad like Vitrier, Beatus Rhenanus and, above all, Fröben.[2] In his last book, *Ecclesiastes*,[3] he pays a noble tribute to Warham, who had died without leaving him the expected legacy--the reason being that Warham had died so poor that he had very little to leave to anyone.

It is amazing that this man, starting with so many handicaps, always in feeble health, and having no settled habitation, should

[1] *Ep.* 230. [2] *Ep.* 1900. His eulogy on Fröben.
[3] *Ecclesiastes*, f. 30. (1535 ed.).

have written so many works of his own and edited so many ancient authors. He became the literary Dictator of Europe in spite of the academic world, who could not contend with his learning and so accused him of heresy. His success was due to the fact that he was not only a fine scholar and an acute critic but a keen student of men. He had travelled much, was an accurate observer with a most capacious memory. In that memory was stored a multitude of vivid impressions of things he had seen in many places, and of men he had known in all classes of society. No one was more fitted than he was to interpret the common mind and to reflect on the current issues of the world about him. In deft phrases and with consummate literary skill, he told men what they already knew and what they had always wished to express. The first half of the XVI century has been rightly called the Age of Erasmus, because though he was not an original or constructive thinker, and certainly not a great personality, he was much more representative of his time than Martin Luther, Leo X or Henry VIII. He began his career when men were interested in the New Learning which he did so much himself to popularise ; and he lived to see men much more interested in religion and perplexed about whither they were tending—Erasmus fully shared their perplexity. He had always been too detached from the movements, which he observed so intelligently, to do more than criticise them ; and he lived to see the things that he cared for most—sound learning, the peace of Europe and Christian conduct endangered by the zealots. *Ne Nimis* had ever been his own motto, and it was probably the motto of the inert multitudes ; but it is enthusiastic minorities who change the world.

Save for a brief experience of boyish fervour before entering the monastery, Erasmus does not seem to have been much interested in religion until he came to England in 1499. He had not been attracted by monkish piety at Steyn, nor impressed by the arguments of Scotist theologians. He had suspected a certain unreality in the devotions of the monks and in the dexterous distinctions drawn by the schoolmen. He had become flippant about the professional exponents of Christianity. Then he met with Colet and observed the consistency of his life—a life lived in the world but dominated by gospel precepts. He was impressed ; and, when he returned to the Continent, he wrote the

Enchiridion Militis Christiani. In England he had also been attracted by the charm of More, and on his subsequent visits he had seen much of him and come to sympathise with his zeal for social justice. After leaving him in 1516, he wrote his *Institutio Principis Christiani* in order that the young Charles V might rule his many kingdoms in the spirit of the Gospel.

The *Enchiridion Militis Christiani*[1] was written by Erasmus in 1501 at the request of the Lady of Veer for the instruction of her husband, a soldier of irregular life who had none the less an admiration for the scholar. In this little book Erasmus never misses an opportunity of sneering at monks and theologians ; and, though himself a priest, he writes as a layman to a layman, as one who would say, " there is no professional humbug about me ". The argument of the book is very simple—a man cannot be saved by forms and ceremonies, but only if he leads a good life : a good life cannot be lived without the grace of God, but God helps those who help themselves : life is a warfare and the *Enchiridion*[2] is offered as a " little dagger " which a soldier may carry in his pocket : it is a little manual on morals for a soldier who cannot be expected to have the *Secunda Secundae* of Aquinas in his knapsack.[3]

Erasmus would have agreed with Matthew Arnold that " conduct was nine-tenths of religion " ; but he would not have agreed with Matthew Arnold that " Religion was morality touched with emotion ", for Erasmus prided himself on being rational and despised emotion. It is said that St. Ignatius Loyola read the book, but put it away because it interfered with his devotions.[4] This is likely, because St. Ignatius belonged to the next generation, when men had other aspirations [5]—he was a Spaniard and not a Dutchman—and he felt chilled by a morality advocated on rational grounds. But the book itself is by no means frigid, though some critics have said so. Erasmus is often

[1] *Enchiridion.* See Methuen's reprint of translation published by Wynkin de Worde.

[2] *Enchiridion*. 73.

[3] Ep. to Volzius prefixed to later edition, 5.

[4] Froude, *Erasmus*, 130, writes : " Ignatius Loyola once looked into Erasmus' New Testament, read a little, and could not go on—He said it checked his devotional emotions. Very likely it did." But it was the *Enchiridion* and not the New Testament from which St. Ignatius turned away.

[5] The *Enchiridion* was translated into Spanish and became popular. See the letter of Fernandez, Archdeacon of Alcor, *Ep.* 1904.

eloquent, always interesting, always humane, and in this book he is very much in earnest.

The morality that he taught was definitely Christian. He could not understand why men should worry themselves with Aristotle's *Ethics* when Christ was a better moralist and more easily understood.[1] He felt no need for any systematic scheme, he relied on his intuitive perceptions into what was reasonable and right. He found in the Gospels self-evident truths, and he had a genuine devotion to our Blessed Lord. He found Him the great example and the perfect teacher. He wrote :

> Think thou not that Christ to be a voice or sound without signification, but think of Him to be nothing else but charity, simplicity or innocency, patience, cleanness, and shortly whatsoever Christ taught.[2]

He frequently calls Him the Saviour and quotes texts concerning the Cross, but in so doing he is using conventional language which he had not made his own ; but when he expounds the moral precepts of our Lord or moralises the Scripture stories, he is on his own ground. His friends were surprised by the piety of his book and he tells Volzius how one of them remarked, " there is more holiness seen in the little book than in the whole author and maker thereof ". [3]

The book shows a remarkable knowledge of the Bible, and some fondness for allegorical interpretations which Colet would not have approved, but Erasmus had been reading Origen since he said farewell to Colet.[4] Colet had tried to persuade him to stay in Oxford and interpret the Scriptures ; but in 1500 he was unwilling to give up his career as a humanist ; and he was also conscious that he did not yet know enough Greek.[5] Colet had taught him the historical method of interpreting the Epistles of

[1] In his *Paraclesis* Erasmus writes : " Platonists, Pythagoreans and the disciples of all other philosophers, are well instructed and ready to fight for their sect. Why do not Christians with yet more abundant zeal espouse the cause of their Master and Prince ? . . . Shall Christ be put in comparison with Zeno and Aristotle—His doctrines with their insignificant precepts ? . . . The philosophy of Christ, moreover, is to be learned from its few books with far less labour than the Aristotelian philosophy which has to be extracted from its multitude of ponderous and conflicting commentaries. Nor is anxious preparatory learning needful to the Christian. Its viaticum is simple and at hand to all." See translation in Seebohm's *Oxford Reformers*, 326, 327.

[2] *Enchiridion*, 99.

[3] Letter to Volzius, 2.

[4] Seebohm, *Oxford Reformers*, 173, is correct and the instance quoted is only one of many. The criticism of Mangan, i. 173, is here unnecessary.

[5] Nichols, *Letters of Erasmus*, i. 220.

St. Paul, and when he had freed himself from the influence of Origen he was to make that method his own ; but first of all he saw that it was necessary to secure a good text. Later in life he was to maintain that no one could be a theologian unless he were acquainted with Hebrew, Greek and Latin—for to Erasmus theology had come to mean textual criticism of the Bible, and exegesis based on a wide knowledge of grammatical forms.

The current texts of the Vulgate were very corrupt. Roger Bacon in the XIII century had complained of the *Exemplar Parisiense*, and a century later Pierre D'Ailly had re-echoed his complaints. The invention of printing had led to further deterioration. Over ninety editions of the Latin Bible had been issued before 1500. The demand for the sacred volume was great, and the printers were in a hurry to supply it. They did not, however, set up their type from expensive manuscripts, but bought the cheapest they could find for the rough work in their chapels ; [1] and cheap copies had as a rule been carelessly written. It was quite time that an effort should be made to restore the purity of the text. In 1499 Grocyn wrote to Aldus :

> Our Linacre tells me you are contemplating . . . the printing of the Old Testament in Latin, Greek and Hebrew, and the New in Greek and Latin—a most arduous work, and one most worthy of a Christian man. In this, if you are permitted to proceed, you will surprise not only those who have already dealt with it, but with a great stride distance also yourself.[2]

Aldus, however, never made that great stride. Three years later he must have heard that Cardinal Ximenez and his scholars at Alcala (Complutum) were engaged on the work.[3] The cardinal is said to have spent 50,000 ducats on the purchase of manuscripts, the payment of scholars and the printing of the book, while Aldus never had 50,000 ducats to spend. The New Testament, largely the work of Stunica (Lopez de Zuñiga), was complete and printed by 1514, but the cardinal waited for a papal licence before publishing, which enabled Erasmus to forestall him with his *Novum Instrumentum*, containing a Greek text and a new Latin translation.

Erasmus had been long contemplating the work. In 1505 he had republished the *Annotations on the New Testament* of

[1] H. J. White, " Vulgate " in Murray's *Dictionary of the Bible*.

[2] *O.H.S. Collectanea*, ii. 352.

[3] Hefele, *Ximenez*, 142.

Lorenzo Valla with a letter to his friend Christopher Fisher in which he bade defiance to the theologians.[1] First he defended the reputation of Valla, next he vindicated the right of a grammarian to concern himself with the sacred text, and lastly he maintained the necessity of similar work being done. Just as St. Jerome, because the old Latin texts were corrupt, had produced the Vulgate, so for the same reason it was now necessary to restore the text of Jerome. But Erasmus, greatly daring, made a new Latin version of the New Testament of his own; and one-eyed Peter made a copy of it for Colet in 1509, and that copy still exists.[2] At Paris he had also begun to study the New Testament in Greek, and at Cambridge he had worked on what is now known as *Codex Leicestrensis*,[3] while at Basle he was able to collate five other manuscripts. He did not in consequence do the work in five months—that was the time it took him to see his work through the press; and he did not make his Latin version in three weeks to oblige Fröben[4] that is probably the time it took him to prepare a copy of his version for the printers. He had also the help of Oecolampadius and others in correcting his proofs. The labours of Erasmus are sufficiently surprising without exaggerations, and it should be remembered that at the same time he was concerned in producing his edition of St. Jerome's works.

Omitting Valla, we may say that Le Fevre in France, Stunica in Spain and Erasmus in England were the pioneers of biblical criticism, and of these Erasmus was the greatest. We have said *Erasmus in England*, because Colet inspired him to undertake the task of editing the New Testament; because he did the greater part of the work in London and at Cambridge; because the work would not have been published but for the munificence of Warham; and because when published Sir Thomas More was the most notable champion in its defence.

The *Novum Instrumentum* was no sooner published than all the learned people in Europe were talking of it; and the unlearned heard the author praised and blamed. Leo X was graciously pleased to accept a copy and signified his approval;[5] the progressive people hailed it with delight, but it was denounced in more than one university and opponents were exceedingly bitter. A few had personal reasons for attacking it. Edward

[1] *Ep.* 182.
[2] Allen, *Age of Erasmus*, 142.
[3] *Ibid.* 144. Cp. Allen, *Epp.* ii. 165.
[4] *Ibid. Epp.* ii. 182.
[5] *Ep.* 864.

Lee, for instance, later Archbishop of York, had supplied Erasmus with a number of notes. Erasmus had made no use of most of them, and Lee was vexed ; he had appropriated some of them without acknowledging his indebtedness, and Lee was furious. In vain More wrote him three friendly letters of great length, defending Erasmus and asking him to desist from his attacks.[1] In vain, after his attacks were published, Bishop Fisher tried to persuade Erasmus to forgive.[2] The two scholars were not reconciled. Stunica had no ground for complaint, but he was a disappointed man. For twelve long years he had toiled at producing a correct Greek text to find himself forestalled when the work was finished. Naturally he preferred his own edition. He and Erasmus had used different manuscripts and both he and Erasmus thought their own codices of the first importance. Ximenez, no doubt, was also disappointed ; but he was a Spanish gentleman and he told Stunica—

> God grant that all writers may do their work as well as Erasmus has done his. You are bound either to give us something better, or not to blame the labours of others.[3]

Stunica for a time restrained himself, but the cardinal died the next year ; and then he attacked Erasmus in the most virulent fashion. The controversy went on for ten years ; but the spirit of Ximenez finally conquered, and before his death Stunica ordered that his further criticisms of the *Novum Instrumentum* should not be published but sent to Erasmus with the hope that they might be useful to him.[4]

Most of Erasmus' opponents, knowing no Greek, were unable to criticise his text, but they had a general dislike of the language, and argued that as the Greeks were heretics and schismatics it was probable that they had tampered with the Scriptures : while St. Jerome, an orthodox doctor of the Church, was certain in his version to have preserved the original meaning.

It was not so much the Greek text, but the Latin translation which raised an uproar. If few could read Greek, many could read Latin, and they scented heresy in the version of Erasmus. He had omitted the doxology in the Lord's Prayer (St. Matt. vi.

[1] Jortin, *Erasmus*, ii. 646-662.
[2] *Ep.* 936.
[3] Hefele, *Ximenez*, 159.
[4] *Ibid.* 158, 159.

13)[1] because it was an interpolation, and also the text concerning the Three Heavenly Witnesses (1 St. John v. 7)[2] which was so convenient for proving the doctrine of the Trinity. In both cases he was almost certainly right: but he re-inserted 1 St. John v. 7 in a later edition, having promised to do so if any manuscripts' authority could be found, and this Lee supplied; he was ill-advised and wrong when he translated Λόγος by *sermo* instead of *verbum*;[3] he was perhaps ill-advised but certainly right when he translated ταπείνωσις, *vilitas* and not *humilitas* in the Magnificat.[4] That perhaps occasioned most indignation, so that it became a proverb in describing a presumptuous man to say, "he would correct the Magnificat". He translated *ἐκκλησία congregatio* and *πρεσβύτερος senior* in accordance with etymology; and this caused no protest from Sir Thomas More, although he was furious when Tyndale substituted *congregation* for *church* and *elder* for *presbyter*.[5] Erasmus also added notes, and some of them were certainly irrelevant in a work of pure scholarship, and as certainly provocative.

Martin Dorpius,[6] the professor at Louvain, who was a pious man and a friend of Erasmus, put the conservative position quite clearly and without abuse. St. Jerome knew Latin and Greek quite as well as Erasmus, and he had probably many more and better codices to work from. His version was accepted by the Church, and was consecrated by the use of a thousand years. It might contain errors, but were they of any vital importance? If not, was anyone justified in disturbing men's faith in the

[1] See Westcott and Hort, *Introd. to N.T.*, App. p. 8.

[2] *Ibid.* App. p. 103. The authority discovered by Lee was *Codex Montfortianus*, now in the library of Trinity College, Dublin. Allen, *Epp.* ii. 165.

[3] For the translation *sermo* see More's defence in his letter to a young monk: Jortin, ii. 680.

[4] Erasmus defends his translation in *Colloquia*, ii. 156-157 (Merdardus). Maldonatus in his commentary on St. Luke, p. 62, strongly supports the interpretation of Erasmus without naming him, but would retain the Vulgate text.

[5] *Dialogue*, Bk. III. ch. viii. In his first edition Tyndale wrote *seniors*. More suggested it would be confused with *seigneurs*. Tyndale altered it to *elders*: Demaus, *Tyndale*, 260. When Tyndale quite correctly brought to More's notice that "your darling Erasmus" agreed with him, More replied, "If my darling Erasmus hath translated these passages with the like wicked intent that Tyndale hath done, he shall be no more my darling but the devil's darling". Quoted Jortin, *Erasmus*, i. 176.

[6] More defended Erasmus in a friendly controversy with Dorpius. He had a rare fortune for a controversialist—he converted his opponent: Chambers, 253. His last letter is in Jortin, ii. 668.

Scriptures? There were plenty of fundamentalists in the XVI century who believed every word in the Bible inspired. Erasmus met them on their own ground, saying, "Quite so, it is therefore the more necessary that we should have the exact words, or we may be crediting the Holy Spirit with the mistakes of a careless copyist".[1]

There were plenty of mistakes, mostly slips and printers' errors,[2] in his own first edition, but he was diligent in the work of revision, and apart from them the verdict of the learned was in its favour. Sir Thomas More wrote to the young monk:

> I consider Erasmus (as a good Greek scholar) to have given a better rendering of passages in the New Testament than I find in the received translation.[3]

Fisher wrote:

> In the New Testament translated by you for the common good, no one of any judgment can take offence. . . . I am exercising myself in the reading of St. Paul (in Greek) according to your directions. I owe it to you that I can now discover where the Latin differs from the Greek.[4]

And Warham having read the book and consulted with his fellow bishops, wrote to Erasmus:

> By these labours you will earn an immortality of fame amongst men, a divine reward among the saints above, and from myself whatever I can properly and conveniently bestow.[5]

It is not, however, the merit of the book that concerns us so much as the fact that its publication turned the attention of scholars and humanists from the classics to the Bible. It turned the streams of the Renaissance into religious channels. Cranmer, for instance, had been a disciple of Erasmus, and had abandoned the Old Learning for the New when Erasmus came to Cambridge in 1511: and it is on record that he abandoned the study of the law and the classics and took to theology in 1516 when the *Novum Instrumentum* appeared.[6] Little Bilney, in the pathetic letter he wrote to Tunstall in 1531 about his past life, says:

> At last I heard speak of Jesus; even then when the New Testament was first set forth by Erasmus; which when I understood to be elo-

[1] *Ep.* 182. [2] Drummond, *Erasmus*. [3] In Jortin, ii. 670.
[4] *Ep.* 592. [5] *Ep.* 425. [6] A. C. Deane, *Cranmer*, 19.

quently done by him, being allured rather by the Latin than by the Word of God (for at that time I knew not what it meant) I bought it even by the providence of God as I do now well understand and perceive : and at the first reading (as I well remember) I chanced upon this sentence of St. Paul (oh, most sweet and comfortable sentence to my soul) in 1 Tim. i. " It is a true saying, and worthy of all men to be embraced, that Christ Jesus came into the world to save sinners, of whom I am the chief and principal." This one sentence, through God's instruction and inward working, which I did not then perceive, did so exhilarate my heart, being wounded with the guilt of my sins, and being almost in despair, that immediately I felt a marvellous comfort and quietness, insomuch " that my bruised bones leaped for joy ".[1]

It was not only at Cambridge, but throughout Europe, that scholars were eager to read the New Testament for no better reason than that Erasmus had edited it, and that it was supposed to have confounded the theologians. The Vulgate had so long been a professional volume of the priesthood, or a book of meditations for the specially devout, that " the poets " had not deigned to read it ; but when a grammarian like themselves, though a doctor of Turin, brought out a new text in Greek and Latin, they were compelled to read it for the excellence of the Latin and for the improvement of their Greek. So it happened almost by chance that " Greece had risen from the dead with the New Testament in her hand " : [2] but many who bought the book from no better motive than Bilney, were, like Bilney, converted. Such people were perhaps unduly puffed up with their new knowledge and thought that they had made a great discovery. They were unaware that the devout people whom they had hitherto despised had always been aware of most of what they knew. In More's household, for instance, the Scriptures and the Commentaries of Nicholas of Lyra were read day by day ; [3] the little books of devotion were full of Biblical quotations, and the Breviary provided for most of the Bible being read every year.

A little group of young men began to meet together at Cambridge to read and discuss the New Testament by themselves. They were inclined to despise old expositions, and were ready to welcome any teaching provided that it was new. So when Luther arose, his books were brought by merchants to the eastern ports and found a ready sale at Cambridge where they

[1] Foxe, *A. & M.* iv. 605.
[2] Quoted Westcott, *English Bible*, 24.
[3] Chambers, 179.

were eagerly read.[1] The place where the group met was the White Horse Inn, which came to be called Little Germany. The group included Cranmer, Stephen Gardiner, Tyndale, Barnes, Joye, Bilney and Latimer. Cambridge was the seed-plot of the English Reformation, and it was Erasmus who had planted the seed.

The *Novum Instrumentum* having established his reputation as a biblical critic, Erasmus proceeded to write his *Paraphrases* and proved himself the most popular of commentators for his own generation, because he had a gift for recalling the dead past to life by interpreting it in the terms of present experience. He had already shown this gift by his comments in the *Adages* derived from classical authors. He now exercised it on the Gospels. He saw in it a mirror reflecting and condemning the age in which he lived. It enabled him to speak of tyrannous and lascivious kings, of unjust taxation, of corrupt judges, and of priests who sold the grace of God and were shameless in their traffic. He found there the ecclesiastical lawyers insisting that tithes must be paid on mint and anise ; and the quibbling scribes, like the schoolmen, making distinctions in matters of no moment. He saw the gorgeous Temple with its splendid ritual—like a Cathedral church—its sacrifices being daily offered with clouds of incense ; and he saw Jesus standing in the midst talking of that truth and righteousness for which nobody cared. He thought it was His very simplicity that caused Him to be despised and rejected by the people, and especially hated by those who wore long clothes like the monks, who decked themselves with religious symbols which did not symbolise their lives.

Erasmus was no Protestant, but he sympathised with Protestants in many of their negations ; and Protestant propagandists found his *Paraphrases* useful. Erasmus had a real hatred for the abuses in the Church, and was scathing in his condemnation of them. He had a distaste for the devotions of the people, thinking them puerile if not superstitious ; and he sometimes made fun of

[1] Nix wrote to Warham complaining of erroneous books, " Wherefore, I beseach your good Lordship . . . that a remedy may be had, for now it may be well done in my diocese, for the gentlemen and commonalty be not greatly infect, but merchants and such that hath their abiding not far from the sea. . . . There is a college at Cambridge, called Gonville Hall of the foundation of a Bishop of Norwich. I hear of no clerk that hath come out lately of that college but savoureth of the frying pan though he speak never so holy." (Strype, *Cranmer*, i. 695.)

them in a cruel fashion. He had a conviction that ceremonial had been so elaborated that the simple gospel of Jesus was obscured; and he was never tired of reiterating his warning that the correct performance of rites did not ensure salvation. But he had no sympathy with the way in which Luther had stressed the doctrine of justification by faith, no desire to penetrate the mysteries of reprobation, predestination and election; no belief that grace was either irresistible or indefectible; and he had never felt that comfortable assurance of salvation which Luther believed to be the experience of every true Christian.

Theologically, then, he and Luther were poles apart, and politically Erasmus thought that Lutheranism was heading for confusion and disaster. Erasmus loved peace though his biting phrases often led to strife: he reverenced charity although his critical temper made him unduly censorious; and he really believed that Luther loved warfare and did not know what charity meant. Besides, Erasmus was a thorough-going internationalist who believed in Christendom; and he had no wish to displace the one Pope and substitute many "Godly Princes", defending their own national churches and propagating their doctrines with the sword.

Before Lutheranism developed and schism became inevitable, Erasmus had encouraged the Reformer in his campaign against indulgences. In 1519 he had written, "You have in England those who sympathise entirely with your writings and great men are among them".[1] He had, and continued to have, friends among Luther's warmest supporters. These friends could not understand why he did not support them; but he explained to Zwingli: "though it is glorious to die for Christ, I do not intend to die for the paradoxes of Luther which I do not understand".[2] He continued to hold himself aloof, though he was denounced by the Catholics of Louvain and sneered at by the Reformers of Wittenberg. Luther wrote taunting him with cowardice and the betrayal of the Gospel.[3] He told Luther that he had been longer a worker for the Evangelical Faith than most of those who called themselves Gospellers; that he saw the disasters and seditions which resulted from Luther's teaching; that he saw the cause of learning being sacrificed and the friendships of scholars broken, and that he feared the bloody tumults

[1] *Ep.* 980. [2] *Ep.* 1384. [3] *Ep.* 1433.

which were likely to arise.[1] At length he yielded to the Pope, kings and princes, and consented to write against Luther ; but he was going to choose for himself the ground of his attack. He was not going to defend the existing order, but to strike at the very heart of Lutheran theology, and so he produced *De Libero Arbitrio*—his book on Free Will.

He took great pains in its composition, and was not to be hurried even by Duke George of Saxony.[2] He examined the relevant texts of Scripture, and maintained as a canon of interpretation that Scripture cannot contradict itself. He reviewed the teaching of the Fathers and schoolmen, and minimised the views of St. Augustine and Aquinas ; and at the end proclaimed that Scripture and the Church of fifteen centuries were on his side. But Erasmus was not primarily interested in either theology or philosophy ; he was a man who had reached his own conclusions not by comparing authorities but by the light of common sense. He believed wholeheartedly that God was good and that man was responsible for his actions. He could not believe that God was good if He first compelled men to sin and then punished them for sinning. He could not believe that any morality could exist except on the supposition that men were responsible. He was by no means a Pelagian. He starts from the fact that God created man, so that if man has a free will he derives it from God ; and he fails to see if God is almighty why He could not endow men with freedom. He acknowledges that neither the wits nor the will of man can create the standard of what is a good life —that is something that is revealed to him—his freedom lies in acceptance or rejection of it ; neither can man determine his end —that is in the hands of God. He admits that while man has freedom to will, he has only a very limited power of accomplishment. If he aspires after goodness he will soon discover his weakness, that he " cannot do the thing that he would ". He will always need grace, and only by grace can he succeed ; but he must co-operate with the grace given. He explains his argument by a parable. A father points out to his toddling son a desirable apple at the end of the room—the child would not have seen it if the father had not pointed it out, but immediately starts towards it and falls. The father picks him up and helps him to cross the room. He reaches the place, but the apple is out of

[1] *Ep.* 1435.

[2] *Ep.* 1448.

his reach, and the father gives it to him. The obvious conclusion is that the child exercised his free will, but he would never have got the apple but for his father's help. It will be seen that the real opinions of Erasmus are derived not from the authorities he quotes, but from his observation of life. He is always a humanist.[1]

When Luther replied to him in his *De Servo Arbitrio*, he approached the subject from his own experience of an instantaneous conversion, when it seemed to him that his life was entirely changed by the overmastering flood of God's grace. It filled him with a sense that man was nothing and God was all, that man could do nothing of himself, and that God did everything by the exercise of His arbitrary will. The grace he received was irresistible, therefore there was no need for human co-operation. It filled him with an assurance of salvation; therefore the grace was indefectible—he was saved, and saved in spite of himself.

To such a man the idea of free will was mischievous because it led men to try to work out their own salvation and trust in their own merits. Luther taught " the good deeds of the saints were sins which needed pardon by the mercy of God ", which sounds a paradox, but may be translated into a truism—" The best deeds of men are imperfect, and therefore unworthy of God's favour ". Luther had indeed a great truth to teach—that men cannot merit salvation and can only be saved by the blood of Christ; but he taught it badly because he did not realise that Christ died to save what was good in us.

Such an idea was abhorrent to him because he believed in the total depravity of man; and therefore he was compelled to regard our Lord's act as entirely arbitrary, and to maintain in as arbitrary a fashion that men were predestinated for heaven or hell. Having reached so far he was able to conclude that men had no free will of any kind, but were mere puppets. So in answer to Erasmus he writes:

Accordingly this doctrine is most chiefly needed and salutary for the Christian to know that God foresees nothing contingently, but He both foresees, determines and actually does all things, by His unchangeable, eternal and infallible will. By this thunderbolt the whole idea of

[1] I have only read analyses of this book by different authors. The parable at the end is condensed from a long quotation given in Nisard, *La Renaissance*, 92.

free will is smitten down and ground to powder. [And again] All things that we do, even though they may seem to us to be done mutably and contingently . . . in reality are done under immutable necessity if regard be had to the will of God.[1]

Melanchthon illustrated this teaching by writing that the treachery of Judas was just as much an act of God as the conversion of St. Paul.

Luther in argument had become a pantheist ; and in pantheism moral distinctions disappear. Erasmus, the cool-headed critic, knew this ; Luther, the hot-headed prophet with his passionate convictions, did not ; and when the Antinomians, his only too logical disciples arose, he discharged the vials of his wrath upon them. They at least had been freed from any sense of the law and could complacently regard their worst sins as acts of God.

Erasmus had written his diatribe with great moderation, and Melanchthon, who did not agree with him, acknowledged the fact and besought Luther to be as moderate in his reply. Luther promised, but did not keep his word. His *De Servo Arbitrio* opens indeed on the note of moderation, but Luther could not control his pen and he is soon calling Erasmus a Lucian, an epicurean, an infidel and an atheist, and describing his book as excrement on a dish of gold. Erasmus was indignant ; he complained to the Elector Frederick and then wrote his *Hyperapistes* in which he paid back Luther in his own coin. Luther was indignant at this rejoinder, and was convinced that Erasmus was no Christian. About his own book he said :

I am certain and sure that what I wrote therein touching the servile will is the unchangeable truth of God. And if God liveth in heaven, then Erasmus one day shall know and feel what he hath done :

Of Erasmus he said :

I truly advise all those who earnestly do affect the honour of Christ, that they would be enemies to Erasmus Roterodamus, for he is a devastator of religion.

As Luther really believed that in writing against Erasmus he was the mouthpiece of God, it was natural for him to believe that the

[1] Quoted by N. P. Williams, *The Ideas of the Fall*, etc. 433, 434. For More's horror of the doctrine see *Dialogue*, Bk. IV. chs. x.-xii.

rejoinder of Erasmus was blasphemy against the Holy Ghost.

Others besides Luther have doubted the sincerity of Erasmus. They have accused him of being a deist and have concluded that he only rendered lip service to the Catholic Church because he was a coward. A good case can be made out for such a view, although I believe that it is not only unfair but radically wrong. When men say that Erasmus was a coward it is natural to ask what is meant by courage. Nothing but a high spirit and great resolution could have sustained Erasmus for seventy years without means of his own, and could have kept him continually at work in spite of his bad health, his physical feebleness and the perpetual attacks from his enemies. At any time he might have retired to the safe seclusion of his monastery to be welcomed with all the kindness due on the return of a prodigal son. The monks at Steyn were only too anxious to house such a celebrity. On several occasions he might have entered the service of Pope or king and been loaded with honours as the eloquent mouthpiece of an autocrat. He preferred to maintain his independence and speak his own mind whether what he said was popular or not. He consistently refused to be a party man, and was in consequence disliked by all parties. It is true that, in order to maintain his position, he had to walk warily ; he showed great skill in explaining away his indiscretions and great dexterity in escaping from awkward situations. For years he was in an ambiguous position as a monk living apart from his community, and it was only after much underhand diplomacy that his position was regularised by the dispensation of Leo X. Erasmus never gave up hope and never surrendered to his enemies. He succeeded because there was nothing he did not know in the way of self-preservation, and but for that highly developed faculty he would not have survived. If an instinct for self-preservation is the same thing as cowardice, Erasmus was a coward ; but because of this highly developed instinct for self-preservation, Erasmus was enabled to live his own life and to do the work to which, rightly or wrongly, he felt called.

Erasmus had a sincere belief in God and His goodness, an intense admiration for our Lord's example and teaching, and a real desire for the betterment of this world in which he lived. He accepted the mystery of the Incarnation and Redemption and the sacramental system on the authority of the Church, but they meant but little to him. Luther was probably right in saying that he had no personal experience of the faith that justifies. Had he lived in the XVIII century he would probably have been a deist ; had he lived in the XIX century he would probably have been a literary agnostic, zealous for social amelioration and interested in religious problems ; but he lived in the XVI century and professed his allegiance to the Catholic Church, and there is no reason for thinking him insincere.

He was by nature extremely sceptical and critical, and he was inclined to write what first came into his head. He wished that the Apostles' Creed was the only profession of faith. He did not believe that the doctrine of the Trinity could be proved by Holy Scripture. He regretted that the word *homoousios* had been inserted in the Nicene Creed. He thought that the Arians had been badly treated and misrepresented. He confessed that he did not understand the doctrine of Transubstantiation ; but for all that he accepted the decisions of the Church ; [1] and when a correspondent wrote and asked him to send him a Rule of Faith, he replied : " I know of no Rule of Faith but that of the Catholic Church ".[2] His freedom of thought and respect for authority are both shown in the report he made to the Senate at Basle on Œcolampadius' book *De Coena*, to which Bishop Fisher wrote such a voluminous reply :

> I have read the book of John Œcolampadius concerning the words of the Lord's Supper, and in my opinion it is learned, well expressed and well thought out. I should add that it is pious, if anything can be pious which is in conflict with the opinion and consent of that Church from which I consider it is perilous to dissent.[3]

As a professor he gives the book full marks, as a scholar he considers the author has made out a good case, but as a churchman he is not prepared to adopt his conclusions. He wrote to Pirckheimer in 1526 :

> The opinion of Œcolampadius would not displease me, if the consent of the Church was not an obstacle to receiving it. For I do not see what good a body not discernible to the senses does, or that it would accomplish any good if it could be discovered, provided spiritual grace

[1] *Colloquia Mensalia* (trans. by Bett, 1652), 431, 433.
[2] Jortin, i. 609, 610 ; ii. 256-260. See also *Ep.* 2136.
[3] Jortin, ii. 273 and *Ep.* 1636.

be present in the symbols. And yet I cannot depart and never have departed from the consent of the Church.[1]

In these days when everyone considers that he has a right to his private opinions, and men form casual associations and call them churches, it is natural to consider Erasmus a dishonest man who assented to a creed in which he did not really believe ; but Erasmus did believe in the authority of a Holy Catholic Church, and could believe that the Church was wiser than himself. He no doubt wished that the Church had been more liberal-minded, and he took the fullest extent of any latitude she allowed ; but he also conscientiously believed that she offered more real freedom than the Lutherans, busy with their new scholasticism. To sum up, Erasmus acknowledged the Church as his mother and was a very troublesome child. He was always asking why ; he was always grumbling that he was not allowed greater liberty ; he was often disrespectful and sometimes rebellious ; but he never doubted that she was his mother and that she had the right to the final word.

It is true that his works, and especially his New Testament, had much to do with the success of the Reformation ; it is true that his works gave a great impetus to free thinking ; it is true that his misplaced and mistimed wit led his readers to be irreverent ; but it is also true that Erasmus was fundamentally an honest and sincere man, who believed in sound learning, in virtuous conduct and the authority of the Catholic Church. If, however, he lived to-day, only in one Church in Christendom could he find a home, and that Church is the Church of England. To-day also many would wish to cast him out, but they would find it difficult to do so, while he took full advantage of her " glorious comprehensiveness ".

V. *Henry VIII the Traditionalist*

We naturally think of Henry VIII as the protagonist in the English Reformation ; but, in Pre-Reformation England, Colet was his doctor and More was his friend. He attracted to his court scholars like Pace, Linacre, Erasmus and Vives, and was

[1] *Ep.* 1717. Fairbairn, *Cam. Mod. Hist.* ii. 699, most unfairly quotes the second sentence without the first and third. For Erasmus' final views see his letter to Louis Ber, 2136.

renowned for his punctual observance of religious duties. He was proud to be known as the champion of the Papacy, and delighted with his papal title—the Defender of the Faith.

He had been carefully educated, first, that he might be an archbishop; and then, after the death of his brother, that he might be King of England. He was an apt pupil and was early impressed with a sense of the value of authority, which remained with him until the end of his life. In his later life he saw that his most arbitrary acts were confirmed by authority of Parliament: he vindicated his most revolutionary measures by appeals to ancient and sure chronicles; his murders were always judicial acts; and his conscience had to be set at rest by casuists and canonists. So, in writing against Luther, who admitted the possibility of divorce, he stated quite clearly the Christian view of the indissolubility of marriage, though he allowed for the Matthaean exception.[1] He never varied from that belief, although he found it convenient that Thomas Cranmer, a learned canonist, should always be ready to discover an *impedimentum dirimens* which justified a decree of nullity, and saved him from his matrimonial mistakes. Henry was a stickler for legal authority and the due observance of legal forms; and when he acted in defiance of the moral law, he consulted casuists who discovered that he was justified by circumstances in acting as he did.

He was not interested, as Pole was, in discovering how much was true in Luther's exposition of St. Paul's argument concerning the works of the law and the freedom of grace; but he was shrewd enough to detect the antinomian tendencies in Luther's writings, which Luther himself was unaware of. In the *Assertio Septem Sacramentorum* he wrote:

He robs princes and prelates of all power and authority; for what shall a king or prelate do, if he cannot appoint any law, or execute the law which is appointed, but even like a ship without a rudder suffer his people to float from the land? Where is that saying of the Apostle, "Let every creature be subject to the higher powers? 'tis not without reason he carries the sword"? Where is that other, "Be obedient to your governors, to the king as excelling", and what follows? Why then doth St. Paul say, "the law is good", and in another place, "the law is the bound of perfection"?[2]

[1] *Luther's Primary Works* (trans. and edited by Wace and Buckheim), 226, 227, and the *Assertio* (trans. by T. W., 1688), 85.

[2] *Assertio*, 53.

Luther would reply to the king as he afterwards replied to the peasants that he had been misunderstood ; but the peasants of Germany had found in his teaching a stimulus to insurrection, and the king was sensitive to anything which might lead to disorder or menace the security of his throne.

Henry's opposition to Lutheranism was not merely due to his fears of revolutionary theories, for he had a genuine interest in theological questions. Lord Herbert of Cherbury says, " His more serious entertainments were the study of history and school divinity ". He was much addicted to the reading of St. Thomas Aquinas ; and so was his chancellor Wolsey, who was nicknamed " Thomisticus " by Polydore Vergil, so that " with the subtleties of the Thomists the king and the cardinal did more often weary than satisfy one another ".[1] Lord Herbert was repeating the evidence of Polydore Vergil, who was papal collector and much about the court. His evidence is corroborated by Erasmus in a letter to Cochlaeus on April 1st, 1529 :

> The King has never given up his studies, and as often as the business of his realm permits, he either reads or discusses, and does so with such friendliness and calm, that you forget he is not your equal but a king. He prepares himself for these little disputations by reading scholastic authors, such as Thomas, Scotus or Gabriel [Biel].[2]

Such a king was certain to be interested in a new heresiarch ; and as certain to point out the errors to his court—while the courtiers of course declared the king's criticisms to be unanswerable. Henry was vain. He had shown his skill in arms and diplomacy, in music and in sport. He had always been ready to descend from his throne in order to show his superiority as a man, and he did not consider it beneath his dignity to enter into controversy with a friar. He had yet laurels to win as a crowned theologian.

Henry had already written in 1518 a treatise in vocal prayer, and according to Pace been much gratified by the praise of Wolsey.[3] That treatise has been lost ; but perhaps it was never

[1] Herbert of Cherbury, *Henry VIII*, 15, 33, 94, 342. In the *Assertio*, 11, Henry speaks of " that learned and holy man Thomas Aquinas, which I the more willingly name here, because the wickedness of Luther cannot endure the sanctity of this man, but reviles with his foul lips him whom all Christians honour ".

[2] *Ep.* 2143. Cp. *Ep.* 1313, written to Duke George of Saxony.

[3] *L. & P.* ii. 4257, 4266.

printed. Early in 1521 Pace found Henry reading Luther's *De Captivitate Babylonica*,[1] and in July 1521 the *Assertio Septem Sacramentorum* was published, printed by Pynson. Two years later a German translation was published at Leipzig, and according to Cochlaeus[2] thousands were reading the little book.

Was Henry really the author ? Luther thought it had been written by Lee, who was a scholar of European celebrity though far inferior to Erasmus.[3] Others attributed it to Fisher or More, though this must seem impossible to anyone who has read Fisher's[4] sermon against Lutheranism or any of More's controversial writings. Cochlaeus thought it was beyond the capacity of any king ; and Erasmus confessed that he had had his suspicions until he was convinced by Mountjoy producing drafts of Henry's letters with the corrections and interlineations written in his own hand. He concludes :

> I will not say that the King had no help, for the most learned are at times helped by their friends ; but I have no doubt in asserting that he is the father and author of the book.[5]

Granting the conclusion and recognising how natural were the doubts, it is remarkable that the book which contemporaries thought worthy of the most distinguished scholars should be viewed by modern historians with unmitigated contempt.[6] They speak of his arguments as mere commonplaces, of his threadbare quotations gathered from some little manual, and of his barren orthodoxy. They assert that he could not understand the *De Captivitate*, but this is hardly complimentary to the Reformer. When Luther wrote a book *ad populum*, he meant to be understood, and hammered in his points as if with a sledge-hammer.

No one book of Luther is hard to understand, unless you

[1] *L. & P.* iii. 1220, April 10th ; and 1233, April 16th.

[2] Cochlaeus = John Dobneck (1479–1552), was born at Wendelstein near Nuremberg, and was educated at Cologne and Bologna. He was violently anti-Lutheran ; and his patrons were Albert of Mainz and Duke George of Saxony. He corresponded with More, Fisher and Tunstall, and dedicated books to them : Allen, *Epistolae Erasmi*, vii. 145.

[3] Luther says of Henry, " He was a fool for allowing his name to be abused by a parcel of empty-headed sophists, and for stuffing his book with lies and virulence, reminding the world of nothing more than of Lee or his shadow, and of such fat swine as are mewed in the sty of St. Thomas ". Quoted Brewer, *Henry VIII*, i. 606.

[4] Fisher's *Sermons*, E.E.T.S. This sermon was translated by Pace into Latin : *L. & P.* iii. 1273.

[5] *Ep.* 2143.

[6] Brewer, *Henry VIII*, i. 607 ; H. A. L. Fisher, *Pol. Hist. of Eng.* 235, 236.

wish to reconcile it with another. Henry was only dealing with one book, and had no doubt about its meaning. His answer is not distinguished by original thought ; but originality is not to be expected from one who writes in defence of tradition. It is true that Henry had not the learning of a specialist, though his critics have not pointed out the manual from which he derived his quotations. It is not true that his work is clumsy—his book is well arranged and clearly expressed ; he writes with commendable brevity, and he sticks to the main issues of his controversy. He was a layman who wrote from a layman's point of view ; and he knew enough to give a reason for the faith that was in him. He did not understand the depths that were in Luther or of the power that was behind his teaching, but he knew that it was likely to destroy the religion in which he had been educated, and he shows critical acumen in fastening on weak points. His arguments may be called " commonplaces ", because they have been repeated *ad nauseam* for the last four centuries. They were not commonplaces when Henry wrote them, but exactly what the defenders of the old faith wanted, and which nobody else had supplied.

We are no longer amused by the picture of " The Little Friar " (*Fraterculus*) in opposition to all the powers of Church and State, because we have come to regard it as Luther's claim to glory. We are more impressed by Henry's appeal to the Fathers, doctors and saints of the Church and his contentions have since been adequately sustained ; but we have to remember that Luther was much better acquainted with the Fathers than Henry was, and could quote them with effect. Henry asked if the Pope's Church was not the Church, where was it ?

> He separates . . . from Christ's Church not only Rome, but also Italy, Germany, Spain, France, Britain and all other nations which obey the See of Rome. . . . Which people being by him taken from the Church of Christ, it consequently follows, that he must either confess Christ's Church to be in no place at all, or else, like the Donatists, he must reduce the Catholic Church to two or three heretics whispering in a corner.[1]

To this, at the time, only one answer was possible—the Church was an invisible body composed of those who had been justified by faith ; but Luther, uninterested as he was in institutional

[1] *Assertio*, 90.

religion, was driven to see that religion must have some outward embodiment, but he was ready to entrust the organizing of a Church to the "Godly Prince"; while Henry, in controversy with Luther, had not yet thought of assuming that responsibility himself.

In his *De Captivitate* Luther denied that confirmation, marriage, orders and unction, were sacraments, and if we accept his definition of the word, which was a new one, he was right. Henry, however, had no difficulty in producing scriptural authority for confirmation,[1] and argued lucidly for the sacramental character of marriage, maintaining that the Vulgate version of St. Paul's words—*sacramentum hoc magnum est*—truly represented the Greek.[2] He vindicated the historic ministry and the "character" imposed by orders; [3] and in dealing with unction twitted Luther with not being true to his own canon of biblical infallibility, because, when it suited him, he threw over the Scriptures, as he threw over the epistle of St. James.[4] On all these points no modern theologian has anything to learn from Henry's book, for his arguments have been restated and better stated again and again during the last four hundred years. The merit of Henry is that he first stated them in a popular form—that he wrote as a layman for laymen when the scholastic opponents of Luther were incomprehensible in their ponderosity.

To the historian the contrast between the views of Luther and Henry on the Blessed Sacrament have an abiding importance, because Catholics and Protestants are agreed that "It is the Mass that matters". For Catholics it is the focus for worship, and the outward and visible sign of Christian unity; for Protestants it is an idolatrous ceremony in which no Christian can take part.

Luther had attacked Indulgences because of the practical abuses that resulted from Tetzel's sermons; and he attacked the received doctrines concerning the Mass because of the superstitions to which it had given rise. People had come to think of the Mass as productive of a quantitative measure of grace which the priest could assign at pleasure to anybody's credit. Masses were paid for, and the more anyone bought the greater was his store of grace; so that the rich could ensure an easy passage for themselves and their friends through purgatory.

[1] *Assertio*, 70-74. [2] *Ibid.* 78-80. [3] *Ibid.* 98. [4] *Ibid.* 104, 105.

This mechanical system of salvation by paid deputies was revolting, and Luther revolted violently. He struck at the very root of the system when he denied that there was any sacrifice in the Mass or offering made to God.[1] The Sacrament he argued was God's gift to men, and not an offering made by men to God.[2] The gift was according to the promise and testament of our Lord in the upper chamber, and was independent of the sacrifice made upon the Cross. He insisted on the literal meaning of the words *hoc est corpus meum* ; but, as he believed in the ubiquity of our Lord's humanity, all bread and wine were equally consubstantial with our Lord's body and blood, and there was no real need for a priest or for consecration.[3] In order to receive the benefits promised by God only one thing was necessary—the faith of the recipient.[4] That normally there should be a minister and a congregation Luther took for granted ; but, as a priest was offering nothing, there was no reason for a congregation to come to church to see a priest communicating himself. That people receiving the gift should give thanks was natural, but the Mass itself was not a good work : man did nothing, God everything.[5] Men might, of course, say their prayers for others, but such prayers were outside the scope of the sacrament, which was only available to the communicant.[6] He saw no harm in the elevation of the Host, and commended eucharistic adoration,[7] although he refused to condemn as heretics those who refused to adore, because there was no command to do so in Scripture.[8] He had no love of ceremonial which he thought tended to obscure the nature of the service ; but he recognised that ceremonies might be helpful to the illiterate, and did not condemn them.[9] Luther was very far removed from being a puritan.

[1] *De Captivitate* in *Primary Works*, 176. [2] *Ibid.* 177.

[3] *Ibid.* 179. Luther's views on the ubiquity of Our Lord's manhood are not expressed in the *De Captivitate*. For them see Darwell Stone, *Hist. of the Eucharist*, ii. 22 ff. Tyndale saw, if Luther did not, that granting the ubiquity there was no need for his controversy with Zwingli concerning the Real Presence. He wrote to Frith, " For as to believe that God is everywhere hurteth no man that worshippeth Him nowhere but within, in his heart in spirit and verity : even so to believe that the body of the Lord is everywhere, though it cannot be proved, hurteth no man that worshippeth Him nowhere, save in the faith of His gospel ". Foxe, *A. & M.* v. 133.

[4] *Primary Works*, 166, 174, 181, etc.

[5] *Ibid.* 161. [6] *Ibid.* 175, 176. [7] *Ibid.* 178, 179.

[8] *On the Adoration of the Sacrament* (1523). See Darwell Stone, *op. cit.* ii. 18.

[9] *On Christian Liberty*, 135, 136. Published the same year as the *De Captivitate*.

No one can do justice in a single paragraph to one of the few great books which has changed the course of history, but enough has been noted for the reader to see the contrast between Luther and Henry. It is unnecessary to follow Henry's criticism, but the following passage will sufficiently indicate his own standpoint :

Christ in His most Holy Supper, in which He instituted this Sacrament, made of bread and wine His own Body and Blood, and gave to His disciples to be eaten and drunk. A few hours afterwards He offered the same Body and Blood on the altar of the Cross, a sacrifice to His Father for the sins of the people, which sacrifice being finished, the Testament was consummated. Being now near His death, He did (as some dying persons are wont to do), declare His will concerning what He desired should be done afterwards in commemoration of Him. Wherefore, instituting the Sacrament, when He gave His Body and Blood to His disciples, He said, *Do this in commemoration of Me*. He who diligently examines this, will find Christ to be the Eternal Priest, Who, in place of all the Sacrifices which were offered by the temporary priesthood of Moses' Law, whereof many were but types and figures of this Holy Sacrifice, has instituted One Sacrifice, the greatest of all, the plenitude of all, as the sum of all others, that it might be offered to God, and given for food to the people : in which thing as Christ was the priest, so His disciples did for that time represent the people, who themselves did not consecrate, but received from the hands of their priest the consecrated sacrament. But God did shortly after elect and institute these priests, that they might consecrate the same sacrament in commemoration of Him. And what else is this but that they should consecrate, and not only receive it themselves, but likewise give it to the people, and offer it so to God : for if Luther should argue that the priest cannot offer, because Christ did not offer in His supper, let him remember his own words, *That a testament involves in it the death of the testator* ; therefore it has no force or power, nor is in its full perfection, till the testator be dead. Wherefore, not only those things which Christ did first at His supper do belong to the testament, but also His oblation on the Cross: for on the Cross He consummated the sacrifice which He began in the supper : and therefore the commemoration of the whole thing, to wit, of the consecration in the supper and the oblation on the Cross is celebrated and represented together in the sacrament of the Mass, and therefore the death is more truly represented than the supper. And therefore the Apostle when writing to the Corinthians in these words, *As often as ye shall eat this bread and drink this cup* adds not the supper of the Lord, but *ye shall declare the Lord's death*.[1]

Luther acknowledged the sacrifice on the Cross and the eternal

[1] *Assertio*, 32, 33.

priesthood of our Lord, and he would have been driven to acknowledge the sacrifice of the Mass if he had admitted the connexion between our Lord's ritual acts in the upper chamber and the offering made to His Father on the Cross, both being made with one object—for the remission of sins.

The doctrine of Henry VIII was reiterated by Fisher, More and Cardinal Pole ; but it requires some dexterity to show that it is the doctrine of the Council of Trent.[1] It remains the official doctrine of the Church of England, as may be seen from the Liturgy and from the reply of the English archbishops to Pope Leo XIII.[2]

Luther had written his *De Captivitate* with great power and intensity, but his language, for him, had been moderate and his statements sustained by reasons. Henry in his reply, unfortunately, had too often adopted the style of an irate schoolmaster correcting an impudent and rebellious boy. He speaks of Luther in contemptuous diminutives as *fraterculus*, *doctorculus*, *sanctulus* and *eruditulus* ; and Luther, who was not humble, furiously resented his tone. If Henry had written his reply like a schoolmaster, Luther rejoined like a bargee full of beer. Father Bridgett has collected the adjectives he applied to Henry and the names that he called him ; and some of them must ever remain in the decent obscurity of a dead language.[3] When Luther lost his temper he reverted to the sort of abuse which he may have heard as a boy in a mining village, and was so indiscriminate in his bad language that he nullified its effect. Henry laughed when he read it, and said the author was only fit to be a fool at a Lord Mayor's banquet.[4] Fisher, however, wrote a learned and laboured reply to Luther's arguments, and More, under the name of Rossaeus, competed with Luther in scurrility. Dr. Brewer writes :

I should be glad to believe that More was not the author of this work. That a nature so pure and gentle, so adverse to coarse abuse, and hitherto not unfavourable to the cause of religious reform, should soil

[1] *Canones et decreta Concilii Tridentini*, Sess. xxil. c. 1. Père de la Taille, *The Mystery of Faith and Human Opinion*, 301, 302, is persuasive but has not converted his fellow Roman Catholics. Speaking of Henry VIII views on p. 292, he writes : " The rite of the Supper contained a kind of Triology—a testament, a sacrifice and a sacrament. A testament sealed by a sacrifice that yielded a sacrament ".

[2] *Responsio Archiepiscoporum*, 17, 18.

[3] Bridgett, *Blessed Thomas More*, 211, 212 footnote.

[4] Quoted Brewer, *Henry VIII*, i. 608. The story comes from the opening letter of Gulielmus Rossaeus, *i.e.* More.

its better self with vulgar and offensive raillery, destitute of all wit, and humour, shocks and pains like the misconduct of a dear friend.[1]

More had certainly for once forgotten his manners, and Luther never had any. We excuse Luther because of the provocation he had received, and we must excuse More for the same reason. Nearly all the controversies of the XVI century are in many respects deplorable. More's book, however, is certainly not deficient in reasoning or humour. He wrote in his best forensic style, and much of his raillery is inspired by wit.

Naturally Henry's book received a very different reception at Rome and in diplomatic circles. Campeggio wrote to Wolsey that he was " overcome with joy in reading the King's golden book ", which he felt must have been inspired " by an angelic and celestial rather than a human spirit ".[2] Faber, who was to be Bishop of Vienna,[3] was equally enthusiastic. He became lyrical in writing about it and burst into poetry. Aleander wrote, " If Kings are of this strength, farewell to us philosophers ; for if we were little thought of before, now our credit will be still less ".[4]

We may read these diplomatic encomiums with some reserve. So we need not believe that Leo X was really as interested in the book as he appeared to be when Clerk gave him a presentation copy, subscribed by the king's own hand and bound in cloth of gold. His Holiness liked the " trim decking " and read some five leaves without interruption. The book was next presented formally at a private consistory, where Clerk made an oration on his knees to his own great discomfort—he thought he would have spoken better standing up. The following day in full consistory Henry received his coveted title—Defender of the Faith.[5] It is a sad commentary on all this enthusiasm that a year later Clerk wrote to Wolsey that the twenty-eight copies splendidly bound, which had been sent to the Pope for distribution, were lying about neglected and forgotten.[6] It is true that in the interval

[1] Brewer, i. 608. Lengthy extracts will be found in Bridgett, 212-220.

[2] Campeggio to Wolsey, *L. & P.* iii. 1592.

[3] Faber=John Heigerlin (1478–1541) was a son of a smith. He was in sympathy with the humanists and at first inclined to reform, but he reacted from Luther. He became the minister of Ferdinand of Austria and Bishop of Vienna. He was a man of immense activity : Allen, *Epistolae Erasmi*, ii. 189. Extracts from his letter on Henry's book will be found in de la Taille, *op. cit.* 282.

[4] Quoted by Creighton, *Papacy*, v. 163.

[5] Brewer, *Henry VIII*, i. 603.

[6] Ellis, *Orig. Letters*, III. Series, cxii.

Leo had died, and his court had not been famed for its interest in theology.

Henry was delighted with his new title, and when he quarrelled with the Pope he had it ratified by Parliament. He could claim that his skill in theology had been acknowledged in the highest quarters, and that he had in consequence a right to meddle in all spiritual affairs. The time came when he defied the Pope and robbed the Church, but he never ceased to be Defender of the Faith. As king he might hang and disembowel those who denied his supremacy, but at the same time, as Defender of the Faith he burnt those who departed from his standard of orthodoxy. He became more and more odious as he grew older, but he never lost his interest in theology, and it was the interest of a man with brains. The continuity of the Church was preserved with its creeds, orders, sacraments and discipline, because a wicked king knew something about the faith and was proud of his knowledge. The Reformation was to come and pass, but the Church was to remain—not a sect devoted to any man's opinions, but a body wide enough to include those who sympathised with Colet or with More or with Erasmus, a body suffering violence, but not destroyed ; and this was so because Henry VIII was in all things a traditionalist, and because he had no wish to impair the prestige of the Church, believing himself to be its head and its defender.

Chapter VII

SUMMARY

I. *The Causes of the Reformation*

It is easy to assume that the Reformation in England was due to the desire of Henry VIII for a divorce. That desire no doubt prompted the king to act and so may be accounted the proximate cause ; but a personality, however dominant, is restricted by his environment. Henry II and Frederick II, both greater men than Henry VIII, had entered into conflict with the Church and been defeated, so we are bound to conclude that the circumstances were different and that there was a world ripe for change. In this book an attempt has been made to provide the materials for understanding how a reformation came about, which contemporaries did not expect and found bewildering. It was not the result of one cause, but of many—they combined, and the result was almost inevitable.

The Popes had ceased for the time to be the spiritual leaders of Christendom and become Italian princes who did not even merit respect, so that claims to supremacy which had some justification in the days of Gregory VII and Innocent III seemed to be impertinent when Julius II or Clement VII asserted them. The bishops in England were nominated by the king to be great officers of state, and not to be fathers to their flocks. They were at the king's mercy, and no longer able to vindicate the independence of the Church. The clergy were in many places unpopular because of their immunities and monetary exactions, so that anti-clericalism was rampant in London, Bristol and other towns. This anti-clericalism did not indicate any desire for a change in religion, for the anti-clericals did not understand that the financial ruin of the clergy would result in the ruin of the Church.

The people as a whole were devout and zealous in the performance of their religious duties ; and if they had little conception of the Church as a whole, they were full of parochial enthusiasm. Their religion, moreover, interpenetrated every department of life until what was spiritual and what was material became so confused that there were a multitude of superstitions. These superstitions were a contributory cause of the Reformation, for they provided the Reformers with their most effective texts.

Politics were being secularised, and the kingdoms of this world were being organised without any reference to the Kingdom of God. The ideal of a united Christendom was dead, and men had grown accustomed to accept a world of conflicting units. Their own unit and its survival alone concerned them, and nationalism is hardly consistent with an international Church. Englishmen had almost made a religion of patriotism and a god of the king, who was the embodiment of the national spirit. It was easy in consequence to represent papal claims as a challenge to national independence, and to concentrate on the Pope the hatred which Englishmen felt for foreigners.

Social life was also being secularised and men were thinking more of this life than of another to come. The ideal of renouncing the world was dying and the duty of working in the world was being emphasised. The active life was esteemed more than the life of prayer and contemplation. There were fewer and fewer vocations to be monks and many of the monasteries were half empty. Yet the monasteries remained great land-owning corporations, and it is not surprising that some believed that the estates would be better developed if freed from the dead hand of the Church.

Through the rise of a middle-class of busy townsmen, a new insistence was put on the virtues of thrift and industry. The advantages of capital were beginning to be understood, and success in business was regarded as a mark of divine approval. The economic teaching about *gain*, the *just price* and *usury* were out of date, although churchmen did not recognise the fact. Merchant adventurers were not going to be fettered by ecclesiastical restrictions upon trade, and the Reformers found their stoutest supporters among the commercial class.

There had ceased to be a conflict between the cloister and the hearth, for the hearth has conquered. The church was ceasing to be the centre of social life, and the home was becoming more important. Family life was being exalted instead of celibacy, and the ideal of a good man was not one who practised asceticism, but one who made life more comfortable for himself and others. Such being the tendency of the age, it is not surprising that the Reformers who denounced celibacy and sneered at the ascetic met with a hearty response.

But above all, the discovery of a New World and the rediscovery of an Old Civilisation were unsettling men's minds. New books were coming from the printing press, new luxuries were imported by the merchants, and new careers were open to the laity. The young were very unwilling to walk in the old ways, and were without any reverence for what their fathers had told them. They thought that they lived in an age of enlightenment ; and they were even quite ready to listen to religious teaching, provided that it was new.

But if we would understand the causes of the Reformation it is not sufficient to survey the ecclesiastical and social conditions of England on the eve of the great change. It is necessary also to take into account the intellectual movements of the XV century.

Lollardy had begun as an attack on the temporal power and wealth of the Church. It prospered until it was suspected of being an attack on the structure of society and all vested interests. Then Church and State entered into an alliance to suppress it, but only succeeded in driving it underground. Lollardy was by no means extinct when Henry VIII came to the throne. Lollard literature survived hidden in the homes of the poor ; and many men were infected with the spirit of Lollardy who would have repudiated the Lollard name.

The schoolmen of the XIII century had aimed at a synthesis of all knowledge—human and divine. The schoolmen of the XVI century so reverenced their work that they were unwilling to receive the New Learning, or to interpret the Old in more modern terms. They all possessed one method, but were divided into disputatious sects, with the result that each school was discredited by the criticism of another. They were all agreed on the fundamental articles of the Faith ; but, taking them for granted, they waged continuous war over distinctions which the ordinary man could not perceive. Theology became ever more and more academic, and less and less in touch with the religion of the people. When dogma and devotion were divorced, the dogmatist went on repeating his shibboleth and the devotee declined into superstition. Then the humanists arose to cover both with ridicule, and the way was open for the Reformers with new doctrines and a revised system of worship.

The English mystics of the XIV century were the most popular authors from the time they wrote until the outbreak of the Reformation. They were all of them orthodox, although some of their books were largely interpolated by Lollards. They wrote on the spiritual life and personal religion, and relied upon intuitions rather than on reason. They attacked nobody, but unconsciously they prepared the way for the Reformation. They had little to say about institutional religion, the sacraments and corporate worship ; and so their readers were apt to become indifferent to a Church with sacerdotal claims.

A new literature in the vernacular had come into circulation dealing with mundane matters. It was not antagonistic to religion, but as it spread, men were no longer restricted for information to what the pulpit and cloister supplied. The lay mind had found expression and a lay public opinion was being formed. Ballads were sung as well as hymns, and men listened to tales of Robin Hood quite as eagerly as they listened to stories about the saints. Thanks to the invention of printing, the lay moralist found his opportunity ; and so did the lay satirist, who, with no ill intention, found it easiest to be funny at the expense of the clergy.

Among the more educated the New Learning was raising new questions and creating doubts. Historical enquiries into the Donation of Constantine, the Isidorean decretals, and the authenticity of the works of Dionysius the Areopagite—textual criticism of the Scriptures and the Fathers—the restoration of classical Latin and contempt for the Latin of the schoolmen—and above all the knowledge of Greek, were bewildering the minds of men. The New Learning in England was not, as in Italy, pagan ; but it was all the more disturbing because it was religious. Theologians, instead of welcoming the new knowledge as Aquinas had welcomed the discovery of Aristotle, were obscurantists. They were proud to dub themselves *Trojans*, and assault those whom they called *Greeks*, with the result that many advocates of the New Learning became apostles of a Protestant revolution ; and at any rate when the Reformation came, the ranks of churchmen were hopelessly disordered.

Colet, Erasmus and More prepared for the Reformation, and set in motion forces which they could not control. Colet denounced the scandals in the Church that he loved and longed to purify, and his denunciations were repeated by those who did not love the Church but longed to destroy it. More and Erasmus thought that they could explode superstitions by laughing at them ; and the next generation treated with irreverence everything that had hallowed associations. Colet, Erasmus and More believed that the New Learning would not only enlighten men's minds, but would diffuse a spirit of sweet reasonableness, forgetting that no one may be more narrow-minded than a good scholar with a passion for exactitude, and that no one can be more ruthless than the pedant turned fanatic.

Narrow-minded people, however, often accomplish great things. They see so clearly that something ought to be done, and they do not see the reasons for not doing it. The Reformers saw the abuses of the Church and they could see nothing else. The abuses for the most part were of such long standing that men had become acquiescent about them. The Reformers were not acquiescent, and they found that violent stimulants were necessary to stir inert consciences. Their energy led them to exaggerate the evils about them, but the evils were very real. In this book it has been suggested that the scandals and superstitions of the Middle Ages have been somewhat exaggerated by some modern historians ; and there is not the least doubt that they were exaggerated by the hot-heads of the Reformation. They did not, however, have it all their own way. The people resented change, and the king only allowed just as much iconoclasm as suited his purpose. Thanks to the imperious will of Henry VIII, the Church was not altogether overthrown.

Henry had received an education to fit him for a churchman ; and he had a mind that revelled in theological distinctions, and a memory stored with ecclesiastical precedents. He could always draw a distinction which permitted him to do what was forbidden ; and he could generally find a precedent which justified his act. We may hate the casuist who robbed the Church, bullied the clergy and acted as a lay Pope, whose supremacy was the more terrible because he was on the spot and not in distant Rome. But Henry was also a theologian who understood what the Church was, and did nothing to destroy the continuity of her existence or to change her faith, orders and sacraments. His vindication of the independence of national Churches may or may not be accepted ; but it also had a long history behind it, and is even now to some extent recognised by the Roman Church. Henry VIII was a bad man but he was a well-instructed theologian ; and during the confusion of the early Reformation, England owes much to the fact that the king, unlike the princes in Germany, knew what was fundamental and what was a matter of opinion.

II. *The Changes the Reformation brought about*

Everyone will acknowledge that a reformation was necessary, however much they may dislike the Reformation which took place. Mediaevalism flowered in the XIII century ; but its fruit in the XIV century hardly fulfilled the earlier promise, while in the XV century the whole system was manifestly running to seed. The time had come for encouraging new growths and grubbing up much that was old ; but the work was done very rashly and there was much loss as well as gain. England lost much : the rest of Christendom lost more, so that it is possible to compare XVI century protestantism unfavourably with mediaeval catholicism ; but it is well to consider the gains as well as the losses—and in some ways both those who seceded and those who remained in the Roman obedience were better for the Reformation.

There had been plenty of life in the Church ; but it was undisciplined and not always directed to the highest ends. Popular religion had lost much by being divorced from theology, and theology had lost much by pursuing its speculations apart from social life. Popular religion had been degraded because the authorities had regarded superstitious extravagances with a good-humoured tolerance, and were far too complacent with regard to ignorant enthusiasm. The time came when common sense asserted itself, and a return to common sense had been long overdue ; but common sense does not appeal to the emotions and has but little sympathy with the poetry of life.

In the early Middle Ages men and women had fled from a world lying in wickedness, and sought for salvation in lives of prayer, labour and austerity. The admiration they excited enabled the Church to conquer the world. She then endeavoured to leaven it with her own spirit : but was ultimately leavened by it and became saturated with worldliness. Then at the Reformation the world conquered the Church, carefully limited her sphere of action and told her in future to mind her own business.

The rigorist saints, like St. Bernard, had shut their eyes to the beauty of nature, and avoided all that might satisfy the lust of the eyes ; but the later Middle Ages were fully convinced that " the earth is the Lord's and the fullness thereof ". So in all nature they discovered symbols by which God might be better understood. Art flourished in consequence of this belief, and ceremonial became ever more complicated. All the mysteries were clothed in material garments, and came to be interpreted in a material sense. The system became in time almost ridiculous; and then a long-suppressed but undying puritanism triumphed. The world, however, refused to be deprived of the arts, and only insisted that in future artists should minister to luxury and pleasure, leaving religion strictly alone.

Symbolism had run riot in the interpretation of Scripture. The literal sense had counted for nothing ; preachers were only concerned with discovering allegorical and anagogical meanings. The method, when applied by a theologian like St. Bernard or a poet like Dante, bore spiritual fruit ; it was the ignorant and stupid who rendered it absurd. Then the humanists arose, who were primarily interested in the exact definition of words, in grammatical constructions and the sequence of thought. They read the Bible like any other book, and their labours enabled the plain man to understand its literal message. It contained songs which Erasmus thought the ploughman and the weaver might sing, and stories that might beguile travellers on their journey. He did not think that wayfaring men, though fools, could err therein.[1] The result did not altogether answer to his expectations. The plain man who read his Bible began to exercise his private judgment, and then came to believe that, armed with a misunderstood text, he was an infallible teacher of other people. He accepted oriental imagery as scientific statements of fact, and he believed that the bloody deeds of Old Testament heroes were intended for his imitation. In consequence sects multiplied indefinitely, the quarrel between science and the faith began,

[1] *Paraclesis*, M. m. 4 (ed. 1621).

and the horrible Wars of Religion lasted a hundred years. The open Bible was the greatest gift that men received through the Reformation, but, like all great gifts, it might be and was misused.

In the Middle Ages the popular religion expressed itself in external acts. They brought home to man the social and corporate nature of the Faith, and emphasised worship as the first duty of man. There was, however, always a danger that men would be satisfied with ceremonial observances, or would suppose that the Church could guarantee salvation to those who bought indulgences or made the right offerings. It was quite time that the doctrine of justification by faith should be preached as it had been taught by St. Thomas Aquinas, and as it was going to be taught by the Oratory of Divine Love in Italy. But Luther in preaching justification by faith alone shattered the mediaeval system. This doctrine is logically inconsistent with any external standard of creed, conduct or worship. It renders a Church and ordinances alike unnecessary. It teaches men to seek for an internal assurance of salvation, and finally centres religion in self. Luther himself never admitted the logical conclusion of this theory, for he continued to believe in the sacraments as conveying the gifts of God. When he insisted on infant baptism, he could only escape from an *opus operatum* view of the sacrament by assuming that the faith of the community into which the child was baptized was availing, and so approximated to a Catholic view of the Church.[1]

In the Middle Ages men believed devoutly in the Incarnation : that the God from everlasting had become Man for evermore. It was the perfect humanity of our Lord that appealed to men ; it was the humanity of Our Lady and the saints that made approach to them so easy. Men liked to hear Gospel stories and the lives of the saints ; they liked to think of heaven as not very far away ; and they liked to think that the inhabitants of heaven were interested in their everyday pursuits and not so very unlike themselves. This familiarity with the other world

[1] Jacques Maritain, *Trois reformateurs*, has with great lucidity drawn out the implications in Luther's doctrine of justification. Troeltsch, *Social Hist. of the Christian Churches*, vol. ii. 483 and *passim*, has shown how Luther's views on the Church approximated to those of the Middle Ages. Heiler, *On Worship*, and Stählin, *Mystery of God*, have shown that convinced Lutherans may hold very High Church views.

led to a loss of awe and reverence, and there was a tendency to forget that God is not as we are. The Reformation was a violent reaction. Sermons were no longer preached on Gospel stories but on the more obscure passages in the writings of St. Paul. It was not the winning Jesus, the Good Shepherd appealing to the poor, who was set forth, but the Divine Saviour, fulfilling His high and awful office in a plan of salvation that would accord with the legal requirements of justice.

In the Middle Ages men had thought of the whole material world as interpenetrated with spiritual power. They thought of spiritual beings, good and evil, constantly acting through material objects. Their eyes were open to perceive miracles, and they believed quite naturally in sacred places, holy wells and wonder-working relics. This belief in spiritual immanence may, and did, degenerate into silly superstitions. The Reformers approached the supernatural in quite another way. They believed in a God wholly other to ourselves, Who ruled by inscrutable decrees. They drew a sharp distinction between the material and the spiritual, and believed that they had nothing in common. Forms and ceremonies were in consequence alien to true religion, which had very little to do with this world. A dread Being was over all, and a new era dawned for religion when Calvin with logical precision drew out the implications in the doctrine of a transcendent God.

Mediaeval friars had preached terrifying sermons on the pains of purgatory, with the result that men had built churches and endowed altars in order that Masses might be offered for the welfare of their souls, while poor people who could not afford such gifts bought indulgences issued by the Popes out of the treasury of merit accumulated by the saints. Then Protestants, indignant at this shameless traffic, proclaimed that nobody had any merits, that there was no intermediate state, and that purgatory was " a fond thing vainly invented ". Protestant preachers, however, went beyond the friars in preaching about hell-fire. Calvin taught that the God of loving kindness had created the great majority of mankind for eternal torments. No prayers could aid them, no good works would avail them ; they had been damned before the creation of the world. A hell without hope became for many people a maddening thought ; but it is charitable to doubt if many in their hearts really believed in the doctrine of predestination as set forth by Calvin and defined at the Synod of Dort.

The contrasts stated above are at best only broadly true, and are more true of the continental Reformation than of our own. In Germany, Switzerland and France there were great leaders with the people behind them insisting on reforms. In England there were statesmen pursuing political, economic and personal objects who made use of the Reformation for their own ends. The Reformers in England had a following in London and other centres, but the great mass of the people had no desire for change. Englishmen have a hatred of revolution, but are always ready to make the best of accomplished facts. When the Reformation occurred, they bowed their heads to the storm and acquiesced in the havoc it occasioned. When the storm was past, they adapted themselves to the new conditions, retaining as far as possible old ideas, traditional customs and prejudices rooted in the past.

The storm in England had done good. It had destroyed a multitude of superstitions, or at least condemned them. It had removed some, but not nearly all, the abuses that existed in the Church. It had cleared the air and swept away the cobwebs spun by decadent schoolmen, and this had allowed the Church to enter into an alliance with sound learning. The storm had shaken the structure of the Church but not destroyed it, so that, when it had blown over, the Catholic creeds, orders and sacraments were intact. The Reformers had loudly asserted the rights of individual consciences, and though they generally denied those rights to others, they had opened the way to religious toleration. Many things that had been ordered were left to the individual's discretion, and this led to reality in religion as well as to individual independence. In principle, at any rate, freedom of thought was conceded within the wide limits imposed by the creed, and gradually this principle has established itself, so that men of very varied opinions can find a home in the Church. This comprehensiveness has been her weakness and her strength. A more disciplined Church may be sometimes more effective in action, but it is less catholic. Both before and after the Reformation the Church of England has claimed to be the Catholic Church in this land.

A LIST OF THE BOOKS

Referred to in the Notes

Ad Fratres de Monte Dei, trans. by Shewring (Sheed & Ward, 1930).
Abraham and Isaac (De la More Press, 1905).
Adam of Usk.—Chronicle, ed. by Maunde Thompson (Frowde, 1904).
Ælred.—Institutio Inclusarum.
Allingham, W.—Ballad Book (Macmillan, 1864).
Ancren Riwle (The Nun's Rule).—Mediaeval Library (Chatto & Windus, 1926).
Andrewes, Bishop.—Sermons, 5 vols. (Parker, 1850).
Anselm, St.—Proslogion, ed. by C. C. J. Webb (Methuen, 1903).
Aquinas, St. Thomas.—Summa Theologica, recogn. Billuart, 8 vols. (Paris, 1858).
  Contra Gentiles, trans. by English Dominicans, 5 vols. (Burns, Oates & Washbourne, 1924).
  Thomas Aquinas, by M. C. D'Arcy (Benn, 1930).
  Thomas Aquinas. Manchester Lectures (Blackwell, 1925).
Archæologia.
Archæologia Cantiana.
Ascham, Roger.—Works, ed. by Giles, 4 vols. (Library of Old Authors, 1865).
Ashley, W. J.—Economic History, 2 vols. (Rivingtons, 1888).
Assertio Septem Sacramentorum, trans. by T. W. (1688).
Astle, T.—Will of Henry VII (London, 1775).
Aubrey, J.—Brief Lives, ed. by A. Clark, 2 vols. (Clarendon Press, 1898).
Audelay, J.—Poems, ed. by Ella Whiting (E.E.T.S., 1931).
Bacon, Francis.—Henry VII, ed. by Lumby (C.U.P., 1889).
  Advancement of Learning, ed. by Aldis Wright (Clarendon Press, 1920).
Bacon, John.—Liber Regis (1786).
Bale, Bishop.—Index Britanniae Scriptorum, ed. by Lane-Poole (Clarendon Press, 1902).
  Majoris Britanniae Scriptorum Summarium, 1559.
  Enterlude of John Baptist in Pollard's Miracle Plays.
Barclay, Alexander.—Eclogues, ed. by Miss White (E.E.T.S., 1927).
  The Shyp of Folys, ed. by Jamieson, 2 vols. (Edinburgh, 1874).
Barlow, Bishop.—Lutheran Factions, ed. by Lunn (Ellis & Keene, 1897).
Barnard, F. P.—Companion to the Middle Ages (Clarendon Press, 1902).
Barraclough, G.—Papal Provisions (Blackwell, 1935).
Bartholomeus Anglicus.—Mediaeval Lore, selected by Steele (Chatto & Windus, 1924).
Baskerville, G.—English Monks and the Suppression of the Monasteries (Cape, 1937).
Batiffol, Pierre.—Eucharistie (Lecoffre, 1920).
Beard, C.—Hibbert Lectures, 1583 (Williams & Norgate).

Becon, T.—Works, ed. by Ayre, 2 vols. (Parker Society, 1843, 1844).
Besticci, Vespasiano da.—Memoirs, trans. by W. G. and E. Waters.
Bigg, Charles.—Wayside Sketches in Ecclesiastical History (Longmans, 1906).
Blackstone, Sir W.—Commentaries on the Laws of England, 4 vols. (Murray, 1862).
Blakiston, H. E. D.—Trinity College, Oxford (Robinson, 1898).
Blunt, J. H.—Tewkesbury Abbey (Simpkins Marshall, 1898).
Boas, F. S.—Shakespeare and his Predecessors (Murray, 1896).
Five Pre-Shakespearean Comedies (O.U.P., 1934).
Boehmer, H.—Luther, trans. by Potter (Bell, 1930).
Bonaventura, St.—Breviloquium et Itinerarium mentis in Deum.
Bond, F.—Screens and Galleries (Frowde, 1908).
Booklet of the Mass, ed. by Dearmer (Alcuin Club, 1903).
Boorde, A.—A Dietary of Helth, ed. by Furnivall (E.E.T.S., 1870).
Bossuet.—Lettres sur l'adoration de la Croix.
Brand, John.—Popular Antiquities (Chatto & Windus, 1877).
Brentano.—Origin and Development of English Gilds (*vide* Toulmin-Smith).
Brewer, J. S.—Reign of Henry VIII, 2 vols. (Murray, 1884).
Bridgett, T. E.—Blessed Thomas More (Burns & Oates, 1891).
Blessed John Fisher (Burns & Oates, 1888).
Brightman, F. E.—The English Rite, 2 vols. (Rivingtons, 1905).
Browning, R.—Poems.
Bruce, H.—The Age of Schism (Rivingtons, 1907).
Bryce, J.—The Holy Roman Empire (Macmillan, 1887).
Bull, Bishop G.—Works, ed. by Burton, 8 vols. (Clarendon Press, 1827).
Burnet, Bishop G.—History of the Reformation, ed. by Pocock, 7 vols. (Clarendon Press, 1865).
Bury, J. B.—History of Freedom of Thought (Butterworth, N.D.).
Bury, Richard de.—Philobiblion (Routledge).
Bury Wills and Inventories (Camden Society).
Busch, W.—England under the Tudors (Innes, 1895).
Butler, Alban.—Lives of the Saints, 12 vols. (Dublin, 1845).
Butler, Bishop Joseph.—Analogy of Religion.
Calendar of Papal Letters, ed. by Twemlow.
Calendar of State Papers, Milan, ed. by Hinds.
Calendar of State Papers, Spanish, ed. by Bergenroth.
Calendar of State Papers, Venetian, ed. by Rawdon Brown.
Calvin, J.—Treatise on Relics (Edinburgh, 1854).
Cambridge History of English Literature.
Cambridge Mediaeval History.
Cambridge Modern History.
Camden Society Miscellany, vol. ii.
Canons, 1604.
Capes, W. W.—A History of the English Church in the XIV and XV Centuries (Macmillan, 1900).
Capgrave, John.—Ye Solace of Pilgrimes, ed. by Mills (Frowde, 1911).
Cardwell, E.—Documentary Annals, 2 vols. (Oxford, 1839).
Carlyle, A. J.—Mediaeval Political Theory, 5 vols. (Blackwood).

Carlyle, Thomas.—Miscellaneous Essays, 3 vols. (Chapman and Hall, 1887).
Castiglione, Baldesare.—Il Cortegiano.
Catherine of Genoa, St.—Treatise on Purgatory, ed. by Cardinal Manning.
Catholic Encyclopaedia (Caxton Publishing Company, 1907–1914).
Cavendish, George.—Life of Cardinal Wolsey, ed. by Singer (London, 1827).
Caxton, W.—Prologues and Epilogues, ed. by Crotch (E.E.T.S., 1927).
Reynard the Fox (Arber's Reprints, 1878).
The Golden Legend of Jean Voragine, ed. by Ellis, 7 vols. (Dent, N.D.).
Cellini, Benvenuto.—Memoirs (Everyman).
Chambers, E. K.—Mediaeval Stage, 2 vols. (O.U.P., 1903).
Chambers, R. W.—Thomas More (Cape, 1935).
Continuity of English Prose (*vide* Harpsfield).
Chaucer, Geoffrey.—Works, ed. by W. Skeat, 7 vols. (Clarendon Press, 1894–1897).
Child, F. J.—English and Scotch Ballads, 5 vols. (Riverside Press, U.S.A.).
Christ Church (Canterbury) Letters (Camden Society).
Church, R. W.—Dante and other Essays (Macmillan, 1897).
Church Quarterly Review.
Churton, R.—Lives of William Smyth, Bishop of Lincoln, and Sir Richard Sutton (Oxford, 1800).
Clark, Andrew.—The Colleges of Oxford (Methuen, 1891).
Clay, Miss.—Hermits and Anchorites (Methuen).
Cloud of the Unknowing, ed. by Dom McCann (Orchard Books, 1924).
Collier, Jeremy.—The Ecclesiastical History of Great Britain, 2 vols. (London, 1708).
Contarini, Cardinal.—De Potestate Pontificis in Compositionibus.
Cooper, C. H.—Memorials of Cambridge, 3 vols. (Cambridge, 1860).
Margaret Beaufort.
Coulton, G. G.—Five Centuries of Religion, 3 vols. (C.U.P., 1923–1936).
Ten Mediaeval Studies (C.U.P., 1930).
Life in the Middle Ages, 4 vols. (C.U.P., 1928–1930).
Art and the Reformation (Blackwell, 1928).
Cox, J. C.—Churchwardens' Accounts (Methuen, 1913).
Cranmer, T.—Works, ed. by J. E. Cox, 4 vols. (Parker Society, 1844–1846).
Remains, ed. by Jenkyns, 4 vols. (Oxford, 1833).
Creighton, Mandell.—History of the Papacy, 5 vols. (Longmans, 1882–1894).
Historical Essays and Reviews (Longmans, 1902).
Historical Lectures and Addresses (Longmans, 1903).
Persecution and Tolerance (Longmans, 1895).
Cunningham, W.—English Industry and Commerce, 3 vols. (C.U.P.).
Cursor Mundi.
Cust, Mrs.—Gentlemen Errant (1909).
Cutts, E. L.—Parish Priests and their People (S.P.C.K., 1898).
Dalgairns, J. B.—Holy Communion (Dublin, 1868).
Dante.—La Divina Commedia.
D'Arcy, M. C.—Thomas Aquinas (Benn, 1930).
Darwin, F. D. S.—Louis d'Orléans (Murray, 1936).
Dawson, Christopher.—Mediaeval Religion (Sheed & Ward, 1934).

Deane, A. C.—Thomas Cranmer (Macmillan, 1927).
Malvern Priory (Bell, 1914).
Decretals.
Decretum.
Delehaye, H.—Sanctus, Subsidia Hagiographica, 17 (Brussels, 1927).
Demaus, R.—William Tyndale (R.T.S., 1886).
Denton, England in the Fifteenth Century (1888).
De Quincey.—Works, ed. by Masson (A. & C. Black, 1889).
Dictionary of Church History, ed. by Ollard and Crosse (Mowbray, 1912).
Dictionary of National Biography.
Digby, Kenelm.—Broadstone of Honour—Godefridus (London, 1829).
D'Israeli, Isaac.—Curiosities of Literature, 3 vols. (Routledge, 1859).
Dives et Pauper.
Dixon, R. W.—Church History, 6 vols. (O.U.P., 1895–1902).
Dublin Review.
DuCange.—Glossarium, ed. 1884.
Dugdale, W.—History of St. Paul's Cathedral, ed. by Ellis (London, 1818).
Duncan, E.—Story of the Carol (Scott, 1911).
Durandus, W.—Rationale Divinorum Officiorum, trans. and ed. by Neale and Webb (Gibbings, 1893).
Durham Diocese, Ecclesiastical Proceedings (Surtees Society).
Durham Rites, ed. by Raine in 1844, and by Fowler in 1903 (Surtees Society).
Ecton, John.—Thesaurus Rerum Ecclesiasticarum 1763.
Einstein, L. D.—Italian Renaissance in England (O.U.P.).
Ellis, Sir H.—Original Letters, 11 vols. (1825–1846).
Elyot, Sir Thomas.—The Governour (Everyman).
Emden, A. B.—An Oxford Hall in Mediaeval Times (Clarendon Press, 1927).
Encyclopaedia Britannica, viii and ix editions.
Encyclopaedia of Religion and Ethics, ed. by Hastings, 11 vols. (T. & T. Clark, 1925).
English Historical Review.
Episcopacy Ancient and Modern, ed. by Claude Jenkyns and E. D. Mackenzie (S.P.C.K., 1930).
Epistolae Obscurorum Virorum, ed. by Stokes (Chatto & Windus, 1919).
Erasmus.—Colloquia Familiaria et Encomium Moriae, 2 vols. (Holzer, Leipsig, 1893).
The Whole Familiar Colloquies, trans. by N. Bailey (Hamilton Evans, 1877).
In Praise of Folly (Sesame Library: George Allen, N.D.).
Enchiridion Militis Christiani: Bellum, etc. (Halle, 1724).
Enchiridion in English (Methuen, 1925).
Methodus verae Theologiae et Paraclesia (Basle, 1522).
Ecclesiastes (Basle, 1535).
Opus Epistolarum Des. Erasmi Roterodami, recogn. P. S. and H. E. Allen, 9 vols. (Clarendon Press, 1906–1938).
The Epistles, trans. by F. M. Nichols, 3 vols. (Longmans, 1901–1918).
Froude, J. A., Life and Letters of Erasmus (Longmans, 1904).
Allen, P. S.—Age of Erasmus (Clarendon Press, 1914).
Drummond, R. B.—Erasmus, his Life and Character, 2 vols. (1892).

Elliott-Binns.—Erasmus the Reformer (Methuen, 1928).
Jortin, J.—Life of Erasmus, 2 vols. (1758, 1760).
Mangan, J. J.—Desiderius Erasmus of Rotterdam, 2 vols. (Burns, Oates & Washbourne, 1928).
Everyman, ed. by Quiller Couch.
Fabyan's Chronicle, ed. 1811.
Feasey, H. J.—Ancient Holy Week Ceremonial (Baker, 1897).
Field, Mrs.—The Child and his Book (Wells, Gardner, Darter, 1891).
Fife, R. H.—Young Luther (Macmillan, U.S.A., 1928).
Figgis, J. N.—From Gerson to Grotius (C.U.P., 1907).
Divine Right of Kings (C.U.P., 1914).
Fioretti.—The Little Flowers of St. Francis (Kegan Paul & Trench, 1899).
Fish, Simon.—Supplication for Beggars (Arber's Reprint, 1878).
Fisher, H. A. L.—Political History of England, 1485–1547 (Longmans, 1906).
Fisher, Bishop John.—English Works, ed. by J. E. B. Mayor (E.E.T.S., 1876).
Mourning's Remembrance, ed. by Baker (1708).
Flick, A. C.—Decline of the Mediaeval Church, 2 vols. (Kegan Paul, Trench, 1930).
Floyer, J. K.—English Church Endowments (Macmillan, 1917).
Fortescue, Sir John.—De Laudibus Legum Angliae (Cambridge, 1825).
Governance of England, ed. by Plummer (Oxford, 1885).
Foster.—Alumni Oxonienses.
Fox, Bishop.—Letters, ed. by P. S. Allen (Clarendon Press, 1929).
Foxe, John.—Acts and Monuments, ed. by Townsend and Catley, 8 vols. (Seeley, 1841).
Froude, J. A.—History of England, 12 vols. (1858–1870).
Fuller, Thomas.—Church History of Britain (1655).
A History of the Worthies of England (1662).
Gabell, Miss.—Benefit of Clergy in England in the later Middle Ages (Northampton, Mass., U.S.A., 1929).
Gairdner, James.—Memorials of Henry VII (Rolls Series, 1858).
Henry VII (Twelve English Statesmen : Macmillan, 1889).
A History of the English Church from 1509 to 1558 (Macmillan, 1902).
Lollardy and the Reformation, 4 vols. (Macmillan, 1908–1913).
Gardiner, Bishop Stephen.—De Vera Obedientia, ed. Janelle (C.U.P., 1930).
Gardner, E.—Cell of Self Knowledge (Seven Mystical Treatises printed by Pepwell, 1521) (Chatto & Windus, 1925).
Dukes and Poets of Ferrara (Constable, 1904).
Gascoigne, Thomas.—Loci e Libro Veritatum, ed. by Thorold Rogers (Clarendon Press, 1881).
Gaspari, Cardinal.—Codex Juris Canonici (Rome, 1921).
Gasquet, Cardinal.—Eve of the Reformation (Bell, 1927).
Old English Bible (Bell, 1908).
Gee and Hardy.—Documents illustrative of English Church History (Macmillan, 1896).
Gentlemen's Magazine Library.—Manners and Customs, ed. by Gomme (Elliott Stock, 1883).

Gibbon, E.—Decline and Fall of the Roman Empire, 12 vols. (London, 1820).
Gibbs and Lang.—Bishops and Reforms (O.H.S.).
Gibson, Bishop Edmund.—Codex Juris Ecclesiastici Anglicani, 2 vols. (London, 1713).
Gibson, Bishop E. C. S.—The XXXIX Articles (Methuen, 1912).
Gilson, E.—Le Philosophie au moyen âge (Payot, 1930).
Études de philosophie médiévale.
Godwin, F.—Catalogue of the Bishops of England (1615).
Gordon-Duff.—Fifteenth Century Books (Quaritch).
Green, J. R.—History of the English People, 4 vols. (Macmillan, 1885).
Green, Leighton.—The Early English Carols (Clarendon Press, 1935).
Green, Mrs.—Town Life in the Fifteenth Century (Macmillan, 1894).
Gregorovius, F.—Rome in the Middle Ages, trans. by Hamilton, 13 vols. (Bell, 1894–1902).
Gregory, John.—Posthuma (1649).
Gregory's Chronicle.—Collections of a London Citizen (Camden Society, 1876).
Grossetête, Bishop.—Epistolae (Rolls Series).
Gurney-Salter.—Tudor England through Venetian Eyes (Williams & Norgate, 1930).
Hakluyt.—Principal Voyages, 8 vols. (Everyman).
Hale, Archdeacon.—Precedents in Causes of Office against Churchwardens (1841).
Hall, Edward.—Chronicle (1809).
Hallam, Henry.—History of the Middle Ages, 3 vols. (Murray, 1872).
Constitutional History of England, 3 vols. (Murray, 1884).
Literature of Europe, 4 vols. (Murray, 1872).
Hardwick, Archdeacon.—History of the Articles of Religion (Bell, 1890).
Harleian Miscellany, ed. by Park, 10 vols. (London, 1808).
Harnack, A. von.—History of Dogma, 7 vols. (T. & T. Clark).
Harpsfield, N.—Life of More, ed. by Hitchcock and Chambers (E.E.T.S., 1932).
Harris, C. R. S.—Duns Scotus, 2 vols. (Clarendon Press, 1927).
Harris, Miss Dormer.—Coventry (Mediaeval Towns : Dent, 1911).
Harrison, W.—Description of England, ed. by F. J. Furnivall, 3 vols. (New Shakespeare Society, 1877, 1878, 1909).
Hartridge, R. A. R.—A History of Vicarages in the Middle Ages (C.U.P., 1930).
Haureau.—Philosophie scholastique, 2 vols. (Paris, 1850).
Hawes, Stephen.—Pastime of Pleasure in Southey's Specimens of English Poets (1831).
Headlam, Bishop.—Christian Theology (Clarendon Press, 1934).
Heath.—Pilgrim Life in the Middle Ages.
Hefele, von.—Life of Cardinal Ximenez, trans. by Dalton (Baker, 1885).
Heine, H.—Gods in Exile (The Works of Heine, trans. by Leland, vol. vi, Heineman, 1892).
Hentzner, P.—Travels (London, 1797).
Herbert of Cherbury, Lord.—Life and Reign of Henry VIII (1622).
Herman, Mrs.—Meaning and Value of Mysticism.

Hilton, Walter.—The Scale of Perfection, ed. by Dom Noetinger (Orchard Books, 1927).
Minor Works, ed. by Dorothy Jones (Orchard Books, 1929).
Hobhouse, Bishop.—Churchwardens' Accounts (Somerset Record Society).
Register of Drockensford (Somerset Record Society).
Hoccleve, Thomas.—De Regimine Principum, ed. by Wright (1860).
Hodgson, Miss.—Sanity of Mysticism (Faith Press).
Holdsworth, Sir W.—History of Law in England, 12 vols. (Methuen).
Hook, Dean.—Lives of the Archbishops of Canterbury, 11 vols. (1860–1877).
Hooper, Bishop.—Remains, ed. by Carr, 2 vols. (Parker Society, 1843 and 1852).
Hort, F. J.—Hulsean Lectures (Macmillan, 1894).
Hügel, Baron von.—The Mystical Element in Religion, 2 vols. (Dent, 1909).
Hugo of St. Victor.—De Sacramentis.
Huizinga, J.—The Waning of the Middle Ages (Arnold, 1927).
Hunt, W.—Bristol (Historic Towns : Longmans, 1889).
Hutton, W. H.—English Saints (Wells, Gardner & Darton, 1903).
Inge, R. W.—Christian Mysticism (Methuen, 1912).
Outspoken Essays (Longmans, 1919).
Italian Relation of England, ed. by Miss Sneyd (Camden Society, 1847).
Jacob, E. F., *vide* Bulletin of the John Ryland's Library, vol. xiv.
James, W.—Varieties of Religious Experience (Longmans, 1904).
Janelle, P.—Angleterre catholique à la veille du schisme (Paris, 1935).
Jebb, R. C.—Romanes Lectures (Macmillan, 1899).
Jessopp, A.—Visitations of the Diocese of Norwich (Camden Society).
Jourdan, G. V.—Movements towards Catholic Reform (Murray, 1914).
The Stress of Change (Scott, N.D.).
Jusserand, J.—Wayfaring Life in the Middle Ages.
A Literary History of the English People, 3 vols. (Fisher Unwin, 1895–1909).
Kempis, Thomas à.—Imitatio Christi, ed. Hirsche (Berlin, 1874).
Trans. and Introd. by C. Bigg (Methuen, 1898).
Kidd, B. J.—Later Mediaeval Doctrine of the Sacrifice of the Mass (S.P.C.K., 1898).
Kingsford, C. L.—Prejudice and Promise in the Fifteenth Century (Clarendon Press, 1925).
Chronicles of London (1905).
Kirk, Kenneth.—The Vision of God (Longmans, 1931).
Kitchin, G. W.—History of France, 3 vols. (Clarendon Press, 1881).
Winchester (Historic Towns : Longmans).
Knighton.—Chronicle, ed. by Lumby, 2 vols. (Rolls Series, 1889, 1895).
Knox and Leslie.—Miracles of Henry VI (C.U.P., 1923).
Lacey, T. A.—Wayfarers' Essays (C.U.P., 1934).
Lamb, C.—Works, ed. by E. V. Lucas, 7 vols.
Lane-Poole, R.—Illustrations of Mediaeval Thought (Williams & Norgate, 1854).
Le Neve, J.—Fasti Ecclesiae Anglicanae (London, 1716).
Langland, W.—Vision of Piers Plowman, ed. by W. Skeat, 2 vols. (O.U.P., 1924).

Latimer, Bishop Hugh.—Works, ed. by Corrie, 2 vols. (Parker Society, 1844–1845).
La Tour Landry, The Book of, ed. by Miss Rawlings (Newnes, 1902).
Lay Folks' Catechism, ed. by Simmons and Nolloth (E.E.T.S., 1901).
Lay Folks' Mass Book, ed. by Simmons (E.E.T.S., 1879).
Lea, H. C.—Studies in Church History (Philadelphia, 1869).
Leach, A. F.—The Schools of Mediaeval England (Methuen, 1916).
Le Brun.—Explication de la messe (Liége, 1777).
Lechler, G. V.—John Wicklif and his English Precursors, trans. by Lorrimer, 2 vols. (1878).
Lecky, W. E.—European Morals, 2 vols. (Longmans, 1897).
History of Rationalism, 2 vols. (Longmans, 1897).
Legacy of the Middle Ages, ed. by Crump and Jacob (Clarendon Press, 1927).
Leland, J.—Collectanea, ed. by Hearn, 6 vols. (Oxford, 1744).
Itinerary, ed. by Miss Toulmin-Smith, 5 vols. (Bell, 1907–1910).
Lethaby, W. R.—Westminster Abbey re-examined (Duckworth, 1925).
Letters and Papers of the Reign of Henry VIII, ed. by Brewer and Gairdner, 1867–1910. Vol. i reissued by Brodie, 1920.
Lewis and Short.—Latin Dictionary (1886).
Lightfoot, Bishop J. B.—Apostolic Fathers, Pt. II, vol. i, (Macmillan, 1889).
Lilley, A. L.—Sacraments (S.C.M., 1928).
Lilley, H. T.—History of Standish (1932).
Little, A. G.—Roger Bacon (Hertz Lecture, 1928).
Lobel, Miss.—Bury St. Edmunds (O.U.P., 1935).
Loftie, W. J.—Westminster Abbey (Seeley, 1890).
Love, Nicholas.—Mirror of the Blessed Jesus (Orchard Books, 1926).
Ludus Coventriae, ed. by Miss Block (E.E.T.S., 1917).
Lunt, W. E.—Papal Revenues in the Middle Ages, 2 vols. (New York, 1934).
Lupset, Thomas.—Life and Works, ed. by J. A. Gee (O.U.P., 1929).
Lupton, J. H.—Life of Dean Colet (Bell, 1909).
Luther, Martin.—Primary Works, trans. and ed. by Wace and Buckheim (Murray, 1883).
Colloquia Mensalia, trans. by Bell (London, 1652).
Lydgate, John.—Dance of Death, ed. by Miss Warren (E.E.T.S., 1929).
Fall of Princes, ed. by H. Bergen, 4 vols. (E.E.T.S., 1917–1919).
Troy Book, ed. by H. Bergen, 4 vols. (E.E.T.S., 1906–1910).
Temple of Glass.
Lyndwood, W.—Provinciale (Oxford, 1679).
Macaulay, T. B.—Essays.
Machiavelli.—The Works of Nicholas Machiavel, trans. into English 1675.
Machyn, Henry.—Diary ed. by J. G. Nichols (Camden Society, 1848).
Macleane, Douglas.—History of Pembroke College, Oxford (O.H.S., 1897).
Maine, Sir Henry.—Ancient Law (Murray, 1888).
Maitland, F. W.—Roman Canon Law in the Church of England (Methuen, 1898.
Constitutional History of England.
Maitland, S. R.—Reformation in England (Rivington, 1849).
Mallett, F.—History of the University of Oxford, 3 vols. (Methuen).

Malory, Sir Thomas.—Le Morte d'Arthur, ed. by A. W. Pollard, 2 vols. (Macmillan, 1900).
Mandeville, Travels of Sir John, ed. by A. W. Pollard (Macmillan, 1900).
Mangan, J. J.—Desiderius Erasmus of Rotterdam, 2 vols. (Burns, Oates & Washbourne, 1928).
Manners and Meals, ed. by Furnivall (E.E.T.S., 1868).
Maritain, Jacques.—An Introduction to Philosophy (Sheed & Ward, 1934).
Maskell, W.—Monumenta Ritualia, 3 vols. (Oxford, 1882).
Maxwell-Lyte, H. C.—A History of Eton College (Macmillan, 1877).
A History of the University of Oxford (Macmillan, 1886).
Memoirs of Martinus Scriblerus.
Micklethwaite, J. T.—The Ornaments Rubric (Alcuin Club, 1898).
Mill, J. S.—Three Essays on Religion, etc. (1874).
Dissertations and Discussions, 4 vols. (1859–1875).
Milman, Dean.—History of Latin Christianity, 9 vols. (Murray, 1883).
Mirabilia Urbis Romanae.
Mirror of Simple Souls, ed. by Miss Kirchberger (Orchard Books, 1897).
Montalembert.—Monks of the West, with an Introd. by Cardinal Gasquet, 6 vols. (Nimmo, 1896).
More, Sir Thomas.—Utopia in Latin and English, ed. by J. H. Lupton (Clarendon Press, 1895).
—— with Roper's Life and some letters (Chiswick Press, 1903).
—— trans. into modern English by G. C. Richards (Blackwell, 1923).
The English Works, ed. by Campbell, Reed and Chambers, vol. i containing Poems, Richard III, Life of Pico, Novissima (Eyre & Spottiswoode, 1931).
The Dialogue, ed. by Campbell and Reed (Eyre & Spottiswoode, 1927).
Life of Richard III, ed. by Lumby (C.U.P., 1883).
Life of Pico della Mirandola, ed. by Rigg (Nutt, 1893).
The Apologye, ed. by Taft (E.E.T.S., 1930).
Dialogue of Comfort against Tribulation, ed. by Monsignor Hallett (Burns, Oates & Washbourne, 1930).
The Utopia and Dialogue of Comfort, ed. by Judge O'Hagan (Everyman).
Selections, ed. by P. S. and H. E. Allen (Clarendon Press, 1924).
Harpsfield's Life of More, ed. by Hitchcock and Chambers (E.E.T.S., 1932).
Stapleton's Life, trans. and ed. by Monsignor Hallett (Burns, Oates & Washbourne, 1938).
Thomas [Cresacre] More.—Life of Sir Thomas (1726).
Bridgett, T. E.—Blessed Thomas More (Burns & Oates, 1891).
Routh (Miss).—Thomas More and his Friends (O.U.P., 1934).
Chambers, R. W.—Thomas More (Cape, 1935).
Campbell, W. E.—More's Utopia and Social Teaching (Eyre & Spottiswood, 1930).
The Fame of Blessed Thomas More (Sheed & Ward, 1929).
Morley, Henry.—English Writers, A History of English Literature, 6 vols.
Mullinger, J. B.—The University of Cambridge, 3 vols. (C.U.P., 1873).
Mundy, Peter.—Travels (New Hakluyt Society, vol. iii).

Myrc, John.—Instructions for Parish Priests, ed. by Peacock (E.E.T.S., 1868).
Festyval.
Myrour of Our Lady.
New English Dictionary, ed. by Murray and Bradley (Clarendon Press).
Nisard, D.—La Renaissance (Paris, 1855).
Noetinger, Dom.—Le Feu d'amour (Paris, 1928).
Northumberland Household Book, ed. by Bishop Percy (1827).
Nova Legenda Anglie, ed. by Horstman, 2 vols. (Clarendon Press, 1901).
Offer, C. J.—The Bishop's Register (S.P.C.K., 1929).
Ogle, A.—Canon Law in the Church of England (Murray, 1912).
Original Letters (Parker Society).
Owst, R. G.—Preaching in Mediaeval England (C.U.P., 1926).
Literature and Pulpit in Mediaeval Life (C.U.P., 1933).
Oxford Historical Society, Collectanea, vol. ii.
Pace, Richard.—De Fructu, qui ex Doctrina Percipitur (Basle, 1517).
Richard Pace, a Tudor Diplomatist, by J. Wegg (Methuen, 1932).
Palmer, H. P.—The Bad Abbot of Evesham, and other Essays (Blackwell, 1932).
Pantin, W. A.—Chapters of the English Black Monks, 3 vols. (Camden Society, 1933, 1937).
Parsons, Robert.—Three Conversions of England.
Paston Letters, ed. by James Gairdner, 3 vols. (Constable, 1896 ; Introduction, 1901).
Pastor, L.—Lives of the Popes, trans. by Antrobus and others, vol. ii (Kegan, Paul).
Pater, Walter.—The Renaissance (Macmillan, 1888).
Peacock, E.—Church Furniture at the Period of the Reformation (Hotten, 1866).
Pearce, Bishop Ernest.—Hartlebury Castle (S.P.C.K., 1926).
Thomas de Cobham (S.P.C.K., 1923).
Monks of Westminster (C.U.P., 1916).
Pecock, Reginald.—The Repressor, ed. by C. Babington, 2 vols. (Rolls Series, 1860).
The Book of Faith, ed. by Morison.
The Donet, ed. by Hitchcock (E.E.T.S., 1918).
The Folewer of the Donet, ed. by Hitchcock (E.E.T.S., 1920).
The Rewle of Christen Religion, ed. by Greet (E.E.T.S., 1926).
Peers, Alison.—Ramon Lull (S.P.C.K., 1929).
Percy, Bishop.—Reliques of Ancient Poetry, 3 vols. (1775).
Phillimore, R.—Ecclesiastical Law, 2 vols. (Sweet & Maxwell, 1895).
Pickthorn, K.—Early Tudor Government, Henry VII, Henry VIII, 2 vols. (C.U.P., 1934).
Pits, John.—De Rebus Anglicis.
Platina, B.—Lives of the Popes, ed. by Benham, 2 vols. (Griffith & Farren, N.D.).
Plot, Robert.—History of Staffordshire (Oxford, 1686).
Pollard, A. F.—Henry VIII (Goupil, 1902).
Wolsey (Longmans, 1929).

Pollard, A. W.—Miracle Plays (O.U.P., 1927).
Pollock and Maitland.—History of English Law, 2 vols. (C.U.P., 1928).
Polydore Vergil.—Angliae Historiae (1651).
Portland Papers (Historical MSS. Commission).
Porwicke, F. M.—Christian Life in the Middle Ages (Clarendon Press, 1935).
Pourrat.—La Spiritualité chrétienne, 3 vols.
Power, Dr. Eileen.—Mediaeval English Nunneries (C.U.P., 1922).
Prick of Conscience.
Prymer, ed. by H. Littlehales, 2 vols. (E.E.T.S., 1895, 1897).
Pugin, A. W.—Contrasts (Dolman, 1841).
Pullan, L.—History of the Book of Common Prayer (Longmans, 1900).
Puller, F. W.—Orders and Jurisdiction (Longmans, 1925).
Pusey, E. B.—Truth and Office of the Church of England (Parker, 1865).
Puttenham.—Art of English Poesie (Arber's Reprints).
Rabelais, F., trans. by W. F. Smith, 2 vols. (Watt, 1893).
Raine, J.—York (Historic Towns : Longmans, 1893).
Rand, E. K.—Founders of the Middle Ages (Harvard Univ. Press, 1928).
Rashdall, H.—Universities of Europe in the Middle Ages (Clarendon Press, 1895).
Rastell, John.—Pastime of the People (reprint London, 1811).
The Four Elements (Percy Society, 1848).
Rationale of Ceremonial, 1540, ed. by Cobb (Alcuin Club, 1910).
Reed, A. W.—Early Tudor Drama (Methuen, 1926).
Religious Pieces in Prose and Verse, ed. by Perry (E.E.T.S., 1867).
Rimbault, E. F.—Ancient Poetical Tracts (Percy Society, 1842).
Ripon Act Book (Surtees Society, 1875).
Ritson, J.—Ancient Songs and Ballads (Reeves & Turner, 1877).
Robin Hood, 2 vols. (1795).
Robinson, Miss.—In a Mediaeval Library (Sands, 1918).
Rock, D.—The Church of Our Fathers, ed. by Hart and Frere, 4 vols. (Murray, 1905).
Rogers, Thorold.—Agriculture and Prices, 7 vols. (Clarendon Press, 1876–1902).
Rolle, Richard, Writings ascribed to, by Miss Emily Hope Allen (O.U.P., 1927).
Incendium Amoris and Emendatio Vitae, ed. by Miss Comper.
The Fire of Love, trans. by Misyn, ed. by Harvey (E.E.T.S., 1896).
Le Feu d'amour, trans. and ed. by Dom Noetinger (Mane et Fils, N.D.).
Selected Works, by E. C. Heseltine (Longmans, 1930).
The Amending of Life, Misyn's trans. (Orchard Books, 1927).
Our Daily Work, ed. by Miss Hodgson (Faith Press, 1929).
The Penitential Poems, ed. by Miss Hodgson (Faith Poems, 1928).
The Sanity of Mysticism, by Miss Hodgson (Faith Press).
English Prose Treatises, ed. by Perry (E.E.T.S., 1921).
Rushforth, G. McN.—Mediaeval Christian Imagery (Clarendon Press, 1936).
Ryves, Bruno.—Mercurius Rusticus (Cambridge, 1685).
Sabatier, P.—S. François d'Assise (Paris, N.D.).
Saint German, Christopher.—Division, printed by Taft, with More's Apologye (E.E.T.S., 1930).
Doctor and Student (London, 1721).

Saintyves.—Les Saints, successeurs des dieux.
Sanday and Headlam.—Commentary on the Epistle to the Romans (T. & T. Clark, 1907).
Sandys, Sir J.—Classical Scholarship, 3 vols. (C.U.P.).
Sarpi, Paolo.—History of the Council of Trent.
Sarum Missal, trans. by Warren, 2 vols. (De la More Press, 1911).
Scot, R.—Discovery of Witchcraft (Rodker, 1930).
Scott, Sir Walter.—Minstrelsy of the Scottish Border (Henderson's edition).
Scudamore, W. E.—Notitia Eucharistica (Rivingtons, 1876).
Searle.—History of Queens' College, Cambridge.
Seebohm, F.—Oxford Reformers (Longmans, 1896).
Selborne, Earl of.—Ancient Facts and Fictions concerning Tithes (Macmillan, 1888).
Shakespeare.
Sharp.—Pageants of Coventry (Coventry, 1825).
Shillingford Papers, ed. by Moore (Camden Society, 1871).
Skelton, John.—Poetical Works, ed. by Alexander Dyce, 2 vols. (1843).
Smith and Onslow.—Worcester (Diocesan Histories : S.P.C.K., 1883).
Sparrow-Simpson.—Old St. Paul's (Elliott Stock, 1881).
Spenser, Edmund.—Faery Queen.
Stacyons of Rome and Pilgrim Ship, ed. by Furnivall (E.E.T.S., 1867).
Stanley, A. P.—Memorials of Westminster Abbey (Murray, 1868).
Starkey, Thomas.—England in the Reign of Henry VIII (E.E.T.S., 1871, 1878).
Staveley.—Roman Horseleech.
Stephens, W. R. W.—Chichester (Diocesan Histories : S.P.C.K.).
Stone, Darwell.—History of the Eucharist, 2 vols. (Longmans, 1909).
Stonor Letters, ed. by Kingsford (Camden Society, 1919).
Stow, J.—Survey of London (1603).
Strype's ed. of Stow's Survey, 2 vols. (London, 1720).
Annales (London, 1631).
Streeter, B. H.—The Chained Library (Macmillan, 1931).
Strutt, J.—Sports and Pastimes of the People of London, ed. by C. J. Box (Methuen, N.D.).
Strype, John.—Ecclesiastical Memorials, 6 vols. (Clarendon Press, 1822).
Life of Cranmer, 2 vols. (Clarendon Press, 1840).
Life of Whitgift, 3 vols. (Clarendon Press, 1822).
Stubbs, Bishop W.—Constitutional History of England, 3 vols. (Clarendon Press, 1880).
Lectures on Mediaeval and Modern History (Clarendon Press, 1886).
Registrum Sacrum Anglicanum (Clarendon Press, 1897).
Suarez.—De Legibus.
Summers, M.—History of Witchcraft and Demonology (Kegan Paul, 1926).
Symonds, A. J.—Revival of Learning (Smith & Elder, 1904).
Symonds, H. E.—Council of Trent and Anglican Formulaires (O.U.P., 1933).
Tawnay, R. H.—Religion and the Rise of Capitalism (Murray, 1929).
Taylor, A. E.—Philosophical Studies (Macmillan).

Thompson, Hamilton.—Growth of the Parish Church (C.U.P., 1913).
York Historical Tracts (S.P.C.K., 1927).
Three Fifteenth-Century Chronicles, ed. by Gairdner (Camden Society, 1880).
Thureau-Dàngin, Life of St. Bernardino, trans. by the Baronin von Hügel (Medici Society).
Toulmin-Smith, Miss.—English Guilds (E.E.T.S., 1870).
York Plays.
Tout, T. F.—Political History of England, 1216–1357 (Longmans, 1905).
Townley Mysteries.—Surtees Society, 1836.
Trail, H. D.—Social England, 6 vols. (Cassell, 1894).
Trent. Camones et Decreta.
Catechismus.
Trevelyan, E. M.—Age of Wyclif.
Trevelyan Papers, ed. by Collier, vol. i (Camden Society, 1857).
Tudor Studies, ed. by Seton Watson (Longmans, 1924).
Tyndale, W.—Works, ed. by Wallis, 3 vols. (Parker Society, 1848–1850).
Life, by Demaus (R.T.S., 1886).
Life, by J. F. Mozley (S.P.C.K., 1937).
Tyrer, J. W.—Historical Survey of Holy Week (Alcuin Club, 19[illegible]).
Underhill, Evelyn.—Mysticism (Methuen, 1930).
Vacant.—Histoire de la conception du sacrifice de la messe.
Victoria County Histories : Buckinghamshire, Essex, Hertfordshire, Kent, London, Norfolk, Sussex.
Villari, L.—Life and Times of Savonarola (Fisher Unwin, N.D.).
Waddell, Helen.—Wandering Scholars (Constable, 1927).
Wall, J.—Durham Cathedral (Dent, N.D.).
Walsingham, ed. by H. T. Riley, 2 vols. (Rolls Series, 1863, 1864).
Warre-Cornish, F.—Chivalry (Swan Sonnenschein, 1901).
Warton, T.—History of English Poetry, 3 vols. (Tegg, 1840).
Westcott, Bishop B. F.—Religious Thought in the West (Macmillan, 1901).
The English Bible (Macmillan, 1895).
Westlake, H. F.—Parish Gilds of Mediaeval England (S.P.C.K., 1919).
The Story of Westminster Abbey (Philip Allan, 1934).
Wey, W.—Itineraries (Roxburgh Club).
Whitehead, A. N.—Science and the Modern World (C.U.P., 1926).
Adventures of Ideas (C.U.P., 1933).
Whitford, R.—Werk for Householders.
Wilkin, D.—Concilia Magnae Britanniae, 4 vols. (London, 1737).
Williams, C. H.—England under the Tudors (Longmans).
Williams, N. P.—The Fall and Original Sin (Longmans, 1927).
Willis-Bund.—Sede Vacante Register (Worcester Historical Society).
Wood, Anthony à.—Athenae Oxonienses, ed. by Bliss, 4 vols. (London, 1813).
Wordsworth, Christopher.—Mediaeval Services (Baker, 1898).
Wordsworth, Bishop John.—Ministry of Grace (Longmans, 1901).
Wordsworth and Littlehales.—Old English Service Books (Methuen, 1904).
Workman, H. B.—John Wyclif, 2 vols. (O.U.P., 1926).
Wright, T.—Chester Plays, 2 vols. (Shakespeare Society, 1843).
Political Poems and Songs, 2 vols. (Rolls Series, 1859, 1861).

Wright, T.—(*continued*)
Suppression of the Monasteries (Camden Society, 1843).
Womankind in Western Europe (Groombridge, 1869).
Wriothesley Chronicle (Camden Society, 1875).
de Wulf, Maurice.—History of Mediaeval Philosophy, trans. by Messenger, 2 vols. (Longmans, 1926).
Wyclif, John.—The English Works, ed. by F. D. Matthews (E.E.T.S., 1880).
Select English Writings, ed. by Winn (O.U.P., 1929).
Fasciculi Zizaniorum, ed. by Shirley (Rolls Series, 1858).
Life, by H. B. Workman, 2 vols.
Life, by G. V. Lechler, 2 vols. (1878).
Age of Wyclif, by G. M. Trevelyan.
Wylie.—History of Henry IV, 4 vols. (Longmans, 1884–1898).
York Fabric Rolls, ed. by Raine (Surtees Society).
York Historical Tracts (S.P.C.K., 1927).

INDEX

THE END

Printed in Great Britain by R. & R. Clark, Limited, *Edinburgh.*